D1831837

HISTORY, CULTURE AND CUSTOMS OF SIKKIM

HISTORY, CULTURE AND CUSTOMS OF SIKKIM

J.R. Subba

GYAN PUBLISHING HOUSE
NEW DELHI-110002

History, Culture and Customs of Sikkim

Rs. 1350

© Jash Raj Subba

ISBN : 9788121209649

All rights reserved. No part of this book may be reproduced
in any manner without written permission

First Published 2008, reprint 2016 in India by
Gyan Publishing House
5, Main Ansari Road, Daryaganj,
New Delhi - 110002

E-mail: books@gyanbooks.com
website: gyanbooks.com

To
My family
Budha Maya (wife),
Babita, Sarita, Bindiya
and Khusboo (daughters)

Contents

LIST OF ILLUSTRATIONS

Foreword

A bureaucrat of the Sikkim Government by profession Mr. J.R. Subba has carved a niche for himself in the field of serious research. With a deep interest in the socio-historical studies of far eastern Nepal and Sikkim, particularly the Limbu (Tsong/Chong) community to which he belongs. Mr Subba has penned a number of books and bulletins on Limbu society and culture.

The Limbus were the dominant population of far eastern Nepal hills and also inhabited Sikkim since distant past. The eastern part of Nepal and the dominant ethnic groups of that region are indigenously called Kirat. The land was sub-divided by the people into three regions, namely, the Wallo, Majh and Pallo or the near, the middle and the far Kirat. The first two regions were predominated by Rai Kirats and the last one had Limbu Kirat preponderance, hence it was also referred to as Limbuwan. The far Kirat was one of the last regions to be annexed to Nepal, the kingdom being formed as a consequence of the conquests and annexations by the rulers of a small and comparatively poor principality of Gorkha lying about a hundred kilometers to the west of the Kathmandu valley. The spree of forays by Gorkha against its neighbours continued for almost a century since the middle of the eighteenth century.

That, the Limbus and other tribes, more particularly the Magars, that were to be constituent elements in the emergence of the Nepali (also called Gorkha by some) community lived also in Sikkim find ample references in the old annals of Sikkim and oral traditions of those tribes. Some Limbu Chiefs are recorded to have played very significant role in the polity of Sikkim. A part of far Kirat land is also said to have been belonged to Sikkim once. Though such a claim is often disputed by others in view of the probable population figure and the overall condition of Sikkim, there are yet references cf some Limbu Kirat Chieftains paying tributes to the Sikkim rulers even after Pallo Kirat or Limbuwan was annexed by Nepal.

The role of the Limbus in the polity of Sikkim is also highlighted by a singular event of the past. Mr. J. R. Subba has ably shown in his works how the erstwhile kingdom of Sikkim came into being in the fourth decade of the seventeenth century as a result of an agreement then made by the Bhutiuas, the Lepchas and the Limbus or Tsongs. This tripartite agreement was known as "*Lho-Mon-Tsong-Sum*".

Mr. Subba has very diligently collected his data and presented very informative outlines of the history of Sikkim. Old annals of the land claim Sikkim to be an extensive kingdom which besides a large tract of the North Bengal Terai also included parts of eastern Nepal. Mr. Subba has given the name **"The Greater Sikkim"** to that kingdom of the past Sikkim was shrunk to its present shape and size as a result of annexations of its territories by Bhutan, Nepal and the British at different periods of time.

The Limbus, whether they lived in some parts of Nepal or Sikkim, followed and still follow, to a great extent, their own customs. They have their own systems of religious beliefs and practise their own rites and rituals. They spoke their own language. At present they are found mostly to be bilingual, adopt in both their own and the Nepali language. In Nepal, the Limbus owned their land collectively. This communal ownership of land or the *Kipat* system was retained by them till much after their homeland was annexed by Nepal. They also enjoyed autonomy till much later. However, the gradual erosion of their *Kipat* system and autonomy under the State pressure of Nepal was bound largely to change their society.

Many scholars, including those from the West, have made this society a subject of their study. A number of books on the Limbu scripture, *Mundhum*, its religious teachings and Limbu culture have appeared in Nepal.

In India, Mr. J. R. Subba is definitely in the forefront as far as research and writings on the Limbu lores are concerned. He has also brought out books on agri-horticulture of Sikkim. His "The Limboos of the Eastern Himalayas, with special reference to Sikkim" (1999) is almost of an encyclopaedic nature on the subject.

The present work, *"History, Culture and Customs of Sikkim"* is very informative and quite exhaustive in its survey. This work should provide a useful background in understanding the socio-political dynamics of the Sikkim society.

The demographic picture of Sikkim presents the picture of a melange of diverse ethnic as well as linguistic elements. The three main groups of the Sikkim people are the Lepchas, the Bhutias and the Nepalis. The Lepchas are generally regarded as the aboriginal inhabitants of Sikkim.

The land witnessed immigrations of the Bhutias or people of the Tibetan origins from early seventeenth century and also their rise as the ruling group. The Nepalis are composed of many ethnic elements and that some of them like the Limbus and the Magars lived in Sikkim even before the immigration of the Bhutias find mentions in the old accounts of Sikkim. After a very informative survey of history of Sikkim from the remote past to the present times Mr. Subba has dealt separately on some of the ethnolinguistic groups that compose the predominant Nepali community. Apart from the Rai and Limbu Kirats, Khasas and Newars Mr. Subba has described the history and culture of many other groups, like Magars, Gurungs, Tamangs, Sunuwars, Thamis etc. in a chapter captioned "Communities Analogous to the Kiratas".

Other scholars may hold different opinions because the name Kirata is taken generally to mean all people of the Mongoloid origins. The Newars are also believed to have sizable Kirat elements. However, such matters remain open for further researches and discussions. This informative and comprehensive account of the history and people of Sikkim undoubtedly presents a valuable background for the analysis of the currents and cross-currents that work in the making of a pluralistic society like that of Sikkim.

Lastly, perhaps this book would have appeared months before but for the delay caused by my physical problems in reading Mr. Subba's valuable works. I feel deeply sorry.

June 10th, 2007

Dr. Kumar Pradhan,
Ex-Principal of
Kurseong College,
Darjeeling District,
West Bengal

Acknowledgements

Sikkim came in existence, as **"The Greater Sikkim"** in 1642 AD with distinct identity of its own as a Himalayan Kingdom after signing the tripartite treaty of "*Lho-Mon-Tsong-Sum*". Since then, the Namgyal Dynasty ruled the country till 1975. Sikkim was much larger in the time of the first Chogyal than it is these days. The frontiers of the Kingdom was "Dibdala in the North, Shinsa Dag-pay, Walung, Yangmag Khangchen, Yarlung and Tamar Chorten in the West, down along the Arun and Dudh Kosi rivers, down to the Maha Nodi, Nuxulbari and Titalia in the south, on the east Tagong La, and Tang La on the North" (Namgyal and Dolma, 1908: 30; Risley 1894:1-2: Subba 1999: iv). These frontiers would include in the greater Sikkim of those days whole of Limbuwan, now in the eastern most part of Nepal, southern Tibet from Nathu La and the Jelep La to the Thang La, beyond Phari Jong, western Bhutan up to the watershed range between the Ammo Chu valley and Har Chu valley, and the northern plains of Bengal as far south as Titalia and Purnea of Bihar (Sprigg, 1999 in Subba's, book foreward, 1999: vi).

However, the Kingdom disintegrated part by part in eight phases when it finally lost its identity as the Himalayan Kingdom and finally integrated into a constituent state of Indian Union in 1975. The history of existence of the Himalayan Kingdom and its disintegration in various phases; and ethnic diversity with culture and customs of the people from antiquity to the present day are presented in this comprehensive overview.

I have tried to provide insight into the Sikkim's history, culture and customs of across-section of society in the various chapters in brief as:

- History and Culture
- Land, People and Livelihood
- Landscape, Agricultural Ecosystems and Sacred Places
- Shelter and Architecture
- Food and Dress Culture
- Religion and Social transformation

- Language and Literature
- Folk Culture
- Festivals and Leisure Activities
- Art and Culture
- Health and Culture
- Ethnic Diversity of – the Lepcha, the Bhutia and the Nepali.

The book narrates and incorporates the cultural development from antiquity to the present supported by numerous data and photographs.

I gratefully acknowledge my profound sense of gratitude to Dr. Kumar Pradhan, Ex-Principal, Kursong College and Editor, Sunchari at present for writing a befitting foreword. He is an eminent writer and critic in Nepali; Ph. D. from Kolkata University; author of "A History of Nepali Literature" (1984), "*Pahilo Pahar*" (1982); and "The Gorkha Conquests" (1991). In spite of his ill-health and his bussy schedule he accepted my request for writing this foreword.

I am extremely grateful to those who helped me on various aspects of study conducted for writing its various chepters for which I was not conversant with the subjects namely Mr. Gary on architecture, Mr. Bhaichung Bhutia on Bhutia culture and passage of rites, IPR Department, Government of Sikkim for photographs Dr. J.P. Tamang for food culture and many other friends.

I extend my grateful thanks to all the learned scholars, whose works I have consulted and referred in this book. This study could not have been possible without the works of numerous scholars from whose works, (as recorded in the reference), I have derived heavily, which enabled me to produce this comprehensive review on various topics

I acknowledge my thanks to Gyan Publishing House, New Delhi.

I also acknowledge my sincere thanks to Mr. Dependra Dewan for Lasser Type Setting. My thanks are also due to my family members specially my wife Budha and my daughters for their constant interest and cooperation enabled me to accomplish this assiduous task.

Jash Raj Subba

Acronyms

ABS	Akhil Bhujel Sangh
ACHP	Acid phosphatase
ADA	Adenosine Aminase
AKDS	Akhil Kirat Dewan Sangh
AKRS	Akhil Kirat Khambu-Rai Sangh
ASGBA	All Sikkim Gurung (Tamu) Buddhist Association
ASMA	All Sikkim Magar Association
ASTA	All Sikkim Thami Association
ATBS	Akhil Tamang Buddhist Sangh
BNSD	Bharatia Newar Sangathan
BW	Brother's wife
CHCP	Child Health Check Up
CSS	Centrally Sponsored Scheme
DGH	Darjeeling Gorkha Hill-Council
(e)BW	Wife's elder brother
FCI	Food Corporation of India
FS & ADD	Food Security and Agriculture Development Department
FYM	Farm Yard Manure
GIDS	Fishman's Graded Intergenerational Disruptive Scale Rating
GOI	Government of India
GOS	Government of Sikkim
GSDP	Gross State Domestic Product
H & CCDD	Horticulture and Cash Crop Development Department
H(y)B	Husband's younger brother
IAS	Indian Administrative Service
IFS	Indian Forest Service
INTACH	Indian National Trust for Art and for Cultural Heritage
IPS	Indian Police Service
LSR	Livestock Survey Report
MBC	Most Backward Class
MISA	Maintenance of Internal Security
MTA	Mid-term Appraisal

NSDP	Net State Domestic Product
NTS	Nepal Thami Samaj
OBC	Other Backward Class
PDS	Public Distribution System
SARD-M	Sustainable Agriculture and Rural Development in Mountainous Region
SDF	Sikkim Democratic Front
SREDA	Sikkim Renewable Energy Development Agency
SSK	Sikkim Sunuwar (Mukhia) Koinch
SSP	Sikkim Sangram Parisad
STBS	Sikkim Tamang Buddhist Sangh
SYSS	Sukhim Yakthung Sapsok Songjumbho
S(y)B	Sister-in-law of Younger Brother
W(e)B	Wife's elder Brother
W(e)S	Wife's elder Sister
W(y)B	Wife's younger Brother
W(y)S	Wife's younger Sister
W(y)B	Wife's younger Sister

Chronology

7-8th Century	Reign of Thekong Adek, the First Lepcha Panu in the present area of Sikkim
746	Padmasambhava came to Sikkim to study the Mun Bongthism
7th Century	Mow Rong Hang developed "Rong Chhyo" script and taught reading and writing to his subjects
9-10th Century	Reign of Thup Athak, the Second Lepcha Panu in the present area of Sikkim
9th Century	Sirijunga Hang developed and taught Sirijunga Script reading and writing
1275	Thekong Tek, Neukung Nal and Khe-Bumsa observed the treaty of brotherhood at Kabi Lungchok
13th Century	Reign of Thekong Tek, the Third Lepcha Panu in the present area of Sikkim
1353-1410	Reign of Rujo Panu;
1425-1454	Reign of Tarvey Panu
1454-1481	Reign of Tarsong Panu
1481-1520	Reign of Tar-eng Panu
1520-1564	Reign of Tarjyi Panu
1564-1595	Reign of Tar-eak Panu
1595-1642	Reign of Thekong Mun Solong Panu
1642	Installation of the first Bhutia King of Namgyal Dynasty in Sikkim
1642-1670	Reign of the First Chogyal Phuntso Namgyal
1642	Tripartite Treaty of "*Lho-Men-Tsong-Sum*" at Denzong Phuntso Khangsar;
1642	Emergence of "**The Greater Sikkim**" by integration of land resources of the Lepchas, Limboos and Bhutias in the Eastern Himalayas.
1643	Establishment of Palace at Tashi Tenka, Lhakhang Marpo and Kathog Monastery.
1670-1700	Reign of the Second Chogyal Tensung Namgyal

1670s	Capital of Sikkim shifted from Tashi Tenka to Rabdentse
1697	Sanga Choling Monastery was built
1700-1716	Reign of the Third Chogyal Chagdor Namgyal
1700	First Invasion of Bhutan King Dev Zidar.
1700-1708	Bhutanese occupation of Sikkim except Limbuwan and Chumbi valley for eight years.
1700	First Phase of disintegration of "**The Greater Sikkim**"; Annexation of the areas of Kalimpong, Damsang, Darlincote, Jonksa, Sangbe upto Taigon Pass known as "*Man-Loong-Kha-Bzi*" by Bhutan.
1715	Construction of Guru Lakhang at Tashiding
1717-1733	Reign of the Fourth Chogyal Gyurmed Namgyal
1718	Bhutan's Second Invasion; permanent loss of "*Man-Loong-Kha-Bzi*" area to Bhutan.
1725	Revolt of the Lepcha Chief Tasso Bidur
1725-1733	Second phase of disintegration of "**The Greater Sikkim**"; loss of Limbuwan area inclusive of Terai areas; as the Limboos threw allegiance with the Chogyal and started ruling themselves
1733-1780	Reign of the Fifth Chogyal Namgyal Phuntsog
1733-1737	Period of anarchy due to question of legitimacy of the young Chogyal
1738-1741	Rule of Tamding Gyalpo in Sikkim.
1734-1741	Propagation of Yuma religion, reading and writing of Sirijunga script by Teyongshi Sirijunga
1741	Assassination of Mahatma Teyongshi Sirijunga by *Ta-Tsang* Lamas
1741	Sikkim administration banned reading and writing of Sirijunga script in Sikkim
1741	First Yuma religion text "*Yahang Se-ma Mundhum*" by Teyongshi Sirijunga was written at Martam (manuscript)
1747	Rabden Sherpa introduced Taxation system for the first time in Sikkim
1752	Tsong upring; Grant of full autonomy conferring *Nagara Nisani* to the Limboos of Sikkim

1770 (1772)	Third Invasion of Bhutan; Sikkim gained some areas at Rhenock.
1773	Kazis were chosen for the first time in Sikkim
1774	First Gorkha Invasion;
1774	Third phase of disintegration of "**The Greater Sikkim**"; lose of Limbuwan, Eastern hills and Terai areas of Sikkim
1775	Sikkim tried to expel the Gorkhas from Limbuwan but was unsuccessful
1776	The Gorkhas harassed the Limboos at Limbuwan after the war of 1775, who fought for Sikkim; 32,000 Limboos migrated to Rangpo, Aho, Rhenock, and Mangshila villages of Sikkim; Kuching, Tendu and Jumsa villages of Bhutan; and Beni, Kalchini and Mech-Koch Villages of Assam
1780-1793	Reign of the Sixth Chogyal Tenzing Namgyal
1780	Regrouped and tried to expel the Gorkhas but was not successful
1782-83	The Gorkha provided arms and ammunitions to the Limboos to fight against the Bhutia forces of Sikkim
1788	Second Gorkha invasion of Sikkim, Rabdentse Palace was attacked by Johar Singh; Purna Ale, and Jung Khatri under the command of Damodar Pandey ransacked Sikkim forces.
1788	Fourth phase of disintegration of "**The Greater Sikkim**" - occupation of the entire area of Western Sikkim including Rabdentse Palace
1789	Damodar Pandey devasted Sikkimese army
1793-1864	Reign of the seventh Chogyal Tsugphud Namgyal
1791	Annexation of Piahte-Gong and Rerinchhen-Tse Jong of Tibet by Tibetans.
1814	Capital of Sikkim shifted from Rabdentse, West Sikkim to Tumlong, North Sikkim
1815	Treaty of Sugauli was signed between British India and Nepal
1816	Treaty of Titalia was signed between British India and the seventh Chogyal Tsugphud Namgyal
1817-1947	Sikkim was under British Protectorate

1826	Assassination of Bolek, the Lepcha Prime Minister of Sikkim at Tumlong; 800 houses of Lepchas of Chidam and Namthang fled to Ilam and settled with Dathup, Jerung and Kazi Gorok.
1834	Katopa resurrection: the fled Lepchas inroads upon Sikkim
1835	Fifth phase of disintegration of "**The Greater Sikkim**"; Darjeeling District was annexed by the British India for Health Sanitation
1841	Sikkim was granted Rs.3,000/= per annum as annual compensation for Darjeeling by the British India
1846	Annual compensation was raised to Rs.6,000/=
1849	Drs. Campbell and Hooker arrested and detained for six weeks by Sikkim
1851	Compensation of Rs.6,000/= was also stopped.
1857	The boundary of the present Sikkim and Nepal was demarcated by treaty of Titalia
1860	Captain Murray, Lt. Beaver and sergeant John were beaten back by Sikkimese Mokmi (Lepcha) at Rinchenpong.
1861	Sixth Phase of disintegration of "**The Greater Sikkim**"; all the land lying between Rammam in the North, Rangit and Teesta in the east and the Terai areas were annexed by the British India
1863-1874	Reign of the Eighth Chogyal Sridkyong Namgyal
1866	War between Lhopos lead by Lempen and Lepcha-Limboo force lead by Monaffimo at Chungthang was held.
1866	Assassination of Chianguepachen or Agenthing, the Limboo Shaman
1867	Lachimidas Pradhan and his uncle Kesap Narayan started settling in Sikkim
1868	Annual compensation of Darjeeling released and also it increased to Rs. 9,000/ =
1872-73	Rev. Macfarlane started few mission schools in various parts of Sikkim
1873	Annual compensation of Darjeeling raised to Rs. 12,000/
1874-1914	Reign of the Ninth Chogyal Thutub Namgyal

1875	Modern Education started in mission schools with History, English, Hindi, Science and Tibetan. Hindi was the medium of Instruction.
1876	The first Lepcha grammar was published.
1880	Tibetan force attacked the Nathula and Jalepla
1880	Finish missionaries started primary schools at Khamdong, Sang and Martam
1883	Lachmidas was permitted to mint cheptewy paise
1884	Scottish missionaries started schools at Rhenock, Pachekhani, Pakyong, Namthang, Chidam, Vok, Chakung, Soreng, Damthang and Turuk
1886	Colman Macauley Mission enter Sikkim
1886	Tibetans occupied Lungthu
1887	J.C.White arrieved in Sikkim
1887-88	Sikkim Capital Shifted from Tumlong to Gangtok
1888	Armed clash between British and Tibet took place at Gnatang, Rinchengong and Chumbi
1889	J.C. White was appointed as Assistant Political Officer in Sikkim
1890-1908	White encouraged Nepali settlement in Sikkim; introduced landlordism, Kazism, Zamindarism, Thekadarism and also diarchic taxation system and thus created differences between Bhutia-Lepcha and Nepali ethnic groups in Sikkim
1891	First Population Census conducted in Sikkim
1893	The Royal couple Thotup and Yeshe were arrested and detained for 2 years in Kalimpong and Kurseong Jail
1895	The Royal couple were removed to Darjeeling and detained for six months and then released
1888-89	Tibetans evacuated Lungthu by the British Force
1890	The Seventh phase of disintegration of "**The Greater Sikkim**"; Annexation of Chumbi valley by China due to the British and China convention of 1890 signed at Calcutta
1896-97	First Allopathic Government Dispensary started at Gangtok, Sikkim

1899	Establishment of the first Bank --Jetmull and Bojraj in Sikkim
1904	Younghusbands Military Expedition to Tibet
1908	J.C. White retired; replaced by W.F.O'Connor
1909	Department of Foıest was established
1912	Indian Capital moved to New Delhi from Calcutta
1913	Department of stationary was established
1914-1914	Reign of the Tenth Chogyal Sidkyong Tulku
1914-15	Lalshor Sendang re-propagated "Sirijunga script" at Thambong and also propagated Yuma Religion
1915-1963	Reign of the Eleventh Chogyal Sir Tashi Namgyal
1915	C.A. Bell introduces collection of land revenue in cash
1916	Chief Court of Sikkim (now High Court) was established
1917	First modern hospital Sir Thutob Namgyal Memorial Hospital (STNM) started
1917	Introduction of revenue No. 1 by C. A. Bell
1921	Public gambling was made illegal
1923	P.N. Girl's School was started
1924	Bhutia and Nepali boarding schools were amalgamated
1924	Use of unpaid labour was prohibited
1924	Sir Tashi Namgyal banned the Mandal and Karbari's attrocities
1925	First literary Organization "*Yakthung Hang Chumlung*" was established at Kalimpong
1925	The First motor vehicle "Beatle" was arrived in Gangtok
1928	First Primary book of Limboo Language "*Tum Yakthung Ningwaphu Sapla*" was published by I.S. Chemjong and Bajbir Tholong from Calcutta
1928	Sir Tashi Namgyal recognized Namsoong as official festival of Sikkim and renamed as Loosong
1932	J.C. White inaugurated the White Hall in Gangtok
1935	C.R. Cooke scale Mt. Kabur
1936	Gangtok Church was established
1937	Jhon Morris and Geoffrey Gorer visited Dzongu

1941	Death of crown prince Paljor Namgyal in Air Craft accident
1942	I.S. Chemjong was appointed as teacher at Gyazing School
1944	Department of SNT was established
1945	Jharlangi curtailed
1946	Jharlangi forbidden
1947	Kuruwa abolished
1947-1964	Jawaharlall Nehru, Prime Minister of India
1947	First meeting of joint political party was held
1947	Mahatma Gandhi assassinated
1948	I.S. Chemjong published "*Kirant Itihas*"
1948	Judicial and magisterial functions of the landlords abolished
1948	Agreement of standstill was signed and Sikkim National Party was formed
1949	Indian Constitution adopted
1949	No rent & No Tax movement
1949	Satyagraha agitation was launched in Sikkim
1949	A democratic government formed under the Chief Ministership of Tashi Tshering for the first time but lasted only for 29 days.
1949	I. S. Chemjong appointed Revenue Inspector and posted at Namchi
1949	Sri J. S. Lall was appointed as Dewan of Sikkim
1950	Harish Dayal was appointed as administrator
1950	Sri Harish Dayal, Political Officer, Government of India and Tashi Namgyal signed an agreement, and thus Sikkim became protectorate of India. The Govt. of India had to provide Rs.3,00,000/= annually.
1950-1974	Sikkim was under Indian Protectorate
1950	First Panchayat election was held
1951	"*Tum Yakthung Ningwaphu Sapla*" was re-published by I.S. Chemjong, M.B. Khamdhak, and P.S.Subba

1952	Indian Prime Minister Sri Jawaharlall Neheru visited Sikkim
1953	Tashi Namgyal introduced Diarchic electoral system for constitution of state council and thus created bitter feeling amongst Bhutia-Lepcha and Nepali ethnic groups.
1953	First general council election was held for the first time in Sikkim for 18 councilors; First Sikkim State Council was formed
1953	The Tsong Community requested the Chogyal for nomination of a councilor in the Ministry of Sikkim.
1954-60	First Five Year Plan implemented
1954	A separate Directorate of Agriculture was established
1957	Namgyal Institute of Tibetology was established.
1957	Government Institute of Cottage Industry was established
1958	Second general councilor election with 24 seats was held.
1958	Sangha seat was created by nomination
1958	The Tsong Community again requested the Chogyal for nomination of a councilor as no one was elected from the community.
1958	Indra Prasad Limboo (Sawaden) of Bandukey was nominated for the first time in the council of Ministers in the second council election of 1958 by Tashi Namgyal.
1958	Trigonomical Survey of all lands was made
1960	Sikkim National Congress was formed at Singtam
1960-65	Second Five Year Plan implemented
1961	I. S. Chemjong appointed as Specialist in the Department of Kiranti Language and Culture in Tribhuwan University, Kathmandu
1961	Sikkim Subject Certificate was provided to the Bhutia, Lepcha and Limboo communities
1961	Tashi Namgyal Academy and Tashi Namgyal Sr. Secondary Schools established
1962	Border war with China

1962	Sikkim Subject Certificate was provided to other Nepalese also
1962	Emergency declared in Sikkim for war between India and China
1963-1975	Reign of the Twelfth Chogyal Palden Thondup Namgyal
1963	P.T. Namgyal married to Hope Cooke
1963	Namchi District was created
1964-1966	Lal Bahadur Shastri, Prime Minister
1966-1977	Indira Gandhi, Prime Minister
1965- 1970	Third Five Year Plan
1966	Sikkim Independent front and Sikkim Janata Party was formed
1967	Sikkim National Congress Party own the third general election with eight seats.
1967	Harka Dhoj Subba of Samdong, West Sikkim was nominated as councilor
1968	The Chogyal approved Limboo language study as an optional subject in the schools of Sikkim up to Class II for the first time.
1968	Itcha Purna Das Subba of Samdong was appointed the first Limboo language teacher at Samdong primary school. By 1975 there were 8 Limboo language tachers in Sikkim.
1968	State Bank of India (SBI) was established
1968	Indira Gandhi visited Sikkim
1968	Name of Political Officer changed to India House Administrator
1968	Disastrous floods occured in Sikkim
1970	Fourth general election was held
1970-1975	Fourth Five Year Plan Period
1973	Fifth general election was held
1973	Sri B. S. Das was appointed the Chief Administrator of Sikkim
1973	Joint Action Council was formed
1973	Following rigging of general election of 1973 agitation of people started ending with a tripartite agreement

	known as May 8th agreement between Government of India's representative Shri Kewal Singh, Chogyal Palden Thondup Namgyal and the Political Parties of Sikkim.
1973	The Tsong Community lost its lone seat in the council
1973	The Tsongs (Limboos) lost their separate Identity and they were clubbed as one of the components of Nepali ethnic group
1974	Sikkim became the Associate State of India
1974	L.D. Kazi, the First and the last Chief Minister of Associate State of Sikkim
1974	Department of Power was established
1974	Department of Animal Husbandry was established
1975	The Eighth and the Final disintegration of "**The Greater Sikkim**"; Sikkim became the 22nd Constituent State of India
1975	Sikkim lost the identity of a Himalayan Kingdom
1975-1979	L.D. Kazi, the first Chief Minister of 22nd State (Sikkim) of India
1975	First Governer Bipin Bihari Lal of Sikkim was swomed
1975	Mrs Indira Gandhi visited Sikkim
1975-1977	Mrs. Indira Gandhi declares Emergency in India
1975	Violated Establishment Rule 4(4) of 1974 by adopting the Central Cadres IAS, IFS, and IPS
1975	Sikkim Government approved formal Limboo Language study in the Schools of Sikkim up to Class V.
1975	Sri B.B. Subba was appointed as Limboo Textbook Writer in the Education Department.
1975	Sikkim categorized under Special Category State of India
1976	Mother Teresa visited Sikkim
1976	Devastative fire gutted down 100 house in Singtam
1975- 1980	Fifth Five Year Plan Period
1977	Public Accounts Committee was formed
1977	Sikkim Government College, Tadong established
1977	Lepcha, Bhutia and Nepali languages have been provided Official language status

1978	Tibetan Herbal Dispensary started in STNM Hostipal
1978	All India Governors Gold Cup football tournament was initiated in Sikkim
1978	Estimate Committee was established
1979	First Democratic election was conducted in Sikkim
1979	Sikkim assembly constituted with one for Sangha, 12 for Scheduled Tribe and 2 for scheduled caste seats
1979	The Nepalese lost the entire seats reserved in the Legislative Assembly; Bhutia and Lepcha seats converted to Scheduled Tribe seats and also reduced to 12 Nos and one Sanga seat. Limboo lost the lone seat in the assembly
1979- 1984	N. B. Bhandari, the Chief Minister of Sikkim
1979	Mr. N. S. Reddy the president of India visited Sikkim
1980-1984	Indira Gandhi, Prime Minister
1980-1985	Sixth Five Year Plan
1981	Homi J. H. Taleyarkhan appointed as Second Governor
1981	Limboo language was provided Official Language Status
1981	Central Board of Secondary Education introduced Limboo language as core subject for class IX & X.
1981	His Holiness the 16th Gyalwa Karmapa passes away
1982	First Helicopter Service between Bagdogra and Gangtok started
1982	The 12th Chogyal Palden Thondup Namgyal passes away
1983	Central Board of Secondary Education examination held on Limboo Language as core subject for Class XI
1983	All India Radio, Gangtok started broadcasting Limboo songs and news
1983	Eighth Finance Commission headed by Sri Y.B. Chauhan visited Sikkim
1984	Central Board of Secondary Education examination held on Limboo Language as core subject for Class XII
1984	Enforcement of Cardamom Act, 1965 (42 of 1965)
1984	Sri B. B. Guroong, Chief Ministership of Sikkim lasted for 14 days

1984-1994	N. B. Bhandari, the Chief Minister of Sikkim, 2nd & 3rd Term
1984	President Rule imposed in Sikkim
1984	Clinical Research Unit of Homopathy was established in Sikkim
1984	Mrs. Indira Gandhi assassinated
1984-1989	Rajiv Gandhi, Prime Minister
1987	President R. Venkataraman inaugurated G.B. Pant Leprosy Hospital at Sajong, East Sikkim
1987	Maenam Wildlife Sanctuary established
1988	Centre of Computers and Communications Technology established
1988	The New Sikkim House inaugurated in New Delhi
1991	Rajiv Gandhi assassinated
1991	Sri Hukam Singh and Yoshio Ogata scaled Mount Kingchumdzonbu (Lepcha) / Kanchanzonga
1991-1996	P.V. Narasimha Rao, Prime Minister
1992	Inclusion of Nepali language in the 8th Schedule of Indian Constituency
1993	The SDF party was established
1993	Team from Sonam Gyatsho Mountaineering Institute scaled Mt. Pandim
1993	Revival of ancient Lepcha festival Tungdung Lho Rumfaat
1994	Sri N. B. Bhandari looses vote of confidence
1994	Six month Chief Ministership of S.M. Limboo
1994	Loyolo B. Ed. College inaugurated at Namchi
1994-1998	The Fifth Chief Minister of Sikkim Sri P.K. Chamling sworn
1995	Karun Thapa and his associates computerized Srijunga script fonts which was later on updated in 2000 on the basis of B.B. Subba's design
1996	A.B. Vaipayee, Prime Minister for 12 days
1997	Provided Official Status of Gurung, Magar, Tamang, Khambu-Rai, Newari, Sherpa and Sunuwar languages

1997	Initiation of G. B. Mainwaring literary award
1997	Regional Research Station of Ayurveda was established
1997	Sikkim Government College, Namchi was established
1997	Manipal Institute was established
1998-2002	A.B. Vajpayee, Prime Minister
1998	Nuclear test, Pokharan
1999-2004	Sri P.K. Chamling, as Chief Minister for the Second term
2000	Introduction of Lepcha, Limboo and Bhutia language at degree level under the NBU
2000	Establishment of Sikkim Academy
2000	The Lepcha Language is affiliated in ICSE syllabus
2002	Limboo and Tamang communities were included in the Tribal list
2003	Inauguration of Lepcha Traditional House at Namprikdang, Dzongu
2003	The New Ropeway at Deorali inaugurated
2003	Provided 33% Seat reservation for women in Zilla and Gram Panchayat
2003	Provided reservation for Government jobs, and higher strudies to ST, SC, MBC, OBC, and Women
2004	Dr. Manmohan Singh, Prime Minister
2004	138 ft. tall statue of Guru Padmasambhava inaugurated at Samduptche, South Sikkim
2004	SDF Party won the 31 out of 32 seats in Assembly election 3rd time
2004	Sri P.K. Chamling Chief Minister sworn for the third term

1
History and Culture

Available records do not reveal much about the ancient history, both the origin and the way of life of the ancient people of Sikkim; nor has any serious research been done on the ancient history and culture of Sikkim. Western scholars and their Indian counterparts maintain the view that Sikkim was not politically consolidated and it was not a single political unit till 1642, when Phuntsho Namgyal was consecrated as the Chogyal of Sikkim (with both Temporal and Spiritual powers) by the three Lamas at Yoksom Norbugang, West Sikkim. There were a number of autonomous Chieftains belonging to the Lepcha, Tsongs (Limboos) and Mangar community and they ruled this territory of "The Greater Sikkim" when many of these Lepcha and Tsong (Limboos) Chieftains (other than Mangar Chieftains) accepted the supremacy of Namgyal Dynasty in 1642, signed the Tripartite Treaty of "*Lho-Mon-Tsong-Sum*", integrated their land resources with the migrant Bhutias and emerged as a country known as "*Mayel*" and later on "*Renjong*" by the Lepchas, "*Yioksom*" (fort or a fortified place) by the Limboos and "*Deyjong*" by the Bhutia, which was later on named "*Song Khim*" (New Home or Palace) by the Limbooni Queen Thungwamukma of Tensung Namgyal, second Maharaja of Namgyal Dynasty and then corrupted to "Sukhim" and again to"Sikkim" (Namgyal & Dolma, 1908: 27; Risley, 1984: 1-38; Chemjong, 1967: 162-164).

In order to know the ancient history of Sikkim it is essential to know the prehistoric period of "The Greater Sikkim" and the inhabitants of these areas.

1. The Prehistoric Greater Sikkim

The legendary account of "The Prehistoric Greater Sikkim" reveals that there were no establishments of settled governments. A number of Petty Rulers or Chiefs or Kings were ruling over these areas in different period of time. By around 4,000 B.C. (Neolithic Age of 5,000 - 2,000 B.C.) the Neolithic humans developed the art of land cultivation due to scarcity of food available for hunting and gathering. Agriculture required people to stay in one spot and so fixed settlement emerged. According to the legend of the Kiratas (Mundhum - oral tradition of the Limboos), the black soybean was the first crop, domesticated and cultivated by the Kiratas (Limboos) in this part of the country. The lone cultivated crop was thus eaten in a variety of ways to avoid monotonousness of eating. Thus, they ate it as raw, boiled with pods, dry frying, crushing, fermenting inclusive of the famous "*Kinema*". The area was very rich in flora and faunal diversity. Later on a number of crops were added up through domestication of wild plants and through plant introduction. Thus, the people of the Greater Sikkim adopted eating of tender shoots, leaves, flowers, fruits, seeds, roots and tubers of a variety of plant and animal species available in the areas (Subba, 1999: 49-52, 159-160; Subba, 2002:48-187; Tamang, 2005).

The prehistoric areas of the Greater Sikkim and the people resided comprized of the followings:

1.1. The present area of Sikkim and the inhabitants:

The present area of Sikkim is 7096 sq. km. lying between 27° 04′ 46″ and 28° 07′ 48″ north latitude and 88° 00' 58" and 88° 55′ 25″ east longitude in the eastern Himalayas. It extends approximately 114 km from north to south and 64 km from east to west with altitude ranging from 250 m to 8,598 m. To its north lay the vast stretches of Tibetan plateau, with Nepal on the west, Bhutan and Chumbi Valley of China (Tibet) on the east and Darjeeling district of West Bengal in the south.

The Lepchas are the earliest aboriginal inhabitants of the present area of the Greater Sikkim. The next aboriginal inhabitant tribes are the Limboos. They are living in this part of Sikkim from time immemorial. After the Blood Brotherhood treaty between Khye-Bumsa and Thekong-Tek in 1275 AD the Bhutias also slowly migrated to the present area of Sikkim. (Note: many claim that the Treaty was written down in both Tibetan and Lepcha script but both have been lost now while others say that there was no script either of Tibetan or of Lepcha that time and hence there is no written evidence available of this treaty so far. No historical evidence is yet available so far of this event). The Maharaja's History (Namgyal and Dolma translated by Dawa Samdup in 1908) the only available source of the ancient people of present Sikkim, has described the ancient people of Sikkim as follows:

(*a*) The Lepchas (Monrees, Mon-pas or Rongs):

The Maharaja's book reveals that "..amongst the three above mentioned races of people inhabiting Sikkim, the origin and history of the Lepcha race as far as can be ascertained runs thus: The foremost tribe of Lepchas who are known to have existed in Sikkim, was called "***Nah-***

angs" who were a race of barbarians who dwelt in a place called Lunghem near Dallam, but this tribe soon died out and there are none of them now in Sikkim. There appear to be in reality about 12 different castes among Lepchas. They are: (1) The Sengdeng-mo, (2) Lingsim-mo, (3) Hee-mo (which comprises) (4) Karthok-mo, (5) and the descendants of Thekong Salung. The rest are named after the places they inhabit,..." (ibid pp 19).

The Lepchas believe themselves to be of common stock, descended from Fodong Thing and Nazong Nyu. K.P.Tamsang's entry for "fa-grongthing" in his "The Lepcha-English Encyclopedic Dictionary" (1980) reads: "name of the first man and the husband of Nazong Nyu, whom God had created from the untrodden snows of Mt. Kanchanjunga and later became the progenitor of Lepcha race" (Sprigg, 2005: 83):

Mon-pa refers to non-Tibetan dwellers south of the Himalayas and around the border of Tibet or people that resided (and continue to reside) in the Greater Sikkim prior to migration of the Tibetans, namely the Lepchas, Tsongs/Limboos and Magars. While, Rong-pa refers to dwellers in the steep country is used occasionally to describe the Lepcha inhabitants (Risley, 1894: 39; Mullard, 2005: 39).

According to Halfdan Sieger (1967) the Lepcha chieftainship of Mayel Lyang (present Sikkim) were as follows:

Name of the Chieftains/ Panu (Petty Kings)	*Years of their Rule*
Thekong Adek	7-8th Century
Thup Athak	9-10th Century
Thekong Tek	13th Century
Rujo Panu/Athing	1353-1410 AD
Tarvey Panu	1425-1454 AD
Tarsong Panu	1454-1481 AD
Tar-eng Panu	1481-1520 AD
Tarjyi Panu	1520-1564 AD
Tar-eak Panu	1564-1595 AD

Thekong Mun Solong Panu (the last Panu who witness the consecration of the First Chogyal of Namgyal Dynasty) 1595-1642 AD.

Source: Halfdan Sieger (1967)

(*b*) The Bhutias (Lhorees or Lhopos or Lhopas):

"From a long time ago, Sikkim has been occupied by Bhutia (Lhorees), Lepchas (Monrees) and Limbus (Tsongrees). The Bhutias, according to one authority, are said to have descended from the followers which are said to have consisted of 12 tribes known as *Tong-du-ruzhis* (four tribes, the close descendants of Khe-Bumsa), and *Beb-tsan-Gyat* (the eight tribes of the great other ancestors of Khye-Bumsa), a prince or chief from ldong clan migrated to Kham Minyag of Tibet, and then who further migrated to Sikkim while others say that it was from Khye-Bumsa's three sons that they have descended and multiplied......." (ibid pp.10). The details of this have been described in ethnology of Bhutias.

(c) The Limboos or Tsongs (Tsongrees):

The Maharaja's book says about the Limboos "As stated in detail in the Sikkim Gazetteer the most authentic account we can have of them is only through the annals and traditions related by old men. According to their own traditions, which they call *Mundhum* it is said, that when the pioneer Lamas of Tibet, visited Sikkim, for the first time, a tribe who revered the Katog Lama as their Guru, followed him from Tsang, and settled with him in Sikkim. The word "Tsong" has been derived from Tsong Province of Tibet (China). But the Gorkhas call them Limbus. They first settled down in the banks of the Arun River, right down to Kangkai. Their headman used to be called Subahs. And they have 10 sub-divisions, called Thars, and they call themselves the 10 Limbus. Again mode of differentiating is by grouping themselves into local blocks called "*Thums*". Of this too there are ten, called the 10 *Thums*, and another group of 17 *Thums*. These have all been absorbed under the Gorkhas. They are: (1) Yangrup, (2) Mewa, (3) Mahikhola, (4) Phedap, (5) Tamborkhola etc. Sikkim contains almost 50 per cent of settlers both old (U-Tsong) and new (Khar-Tsong), from those places. Amongst themselves again half would be descendants of old settlers, while half would be new."(ibid pp. 30)

Contrary to the above, the oral tradition "*Mundhum*" explains that the Limboos were created by the creator god "*Sigera Yabhundin Mang Porokmi Wamphami Mang*" guided by the Almighty Goddess "*Tagera Ningwaphuma*" at the base of *Phoktanglungma Pembenlunga* (Kumbhakarna) mountains through the *law of Biogenesis*. Because of this, the souls of the living Limboos are carried over there to the "*Chotlung*" for fortification while the souls of the dead are accompanied and reached to this place and handed over to one of the ancestors. Thus, the views of Vansittart, (1896) that "the *Bhuiphutta* tribes of Limboos originated from Phedap" support this tradition of the Limboos (Subba, 1995; Subba, 1999: 453-508; 2005: 79-88; 105-109; 119-129).

(d) The Mangars or Magars or Mong-pas:

The Mangars were also there in prehistoric period of the present Sikkim, ruling some of the areas in Sikkim. They were there at Mangsari

Magarjong area of West Sikkim. The Mangar King Santusati Sen (or Santu Pati Sen) fought with the Bhutia force that opposed the Bhutia supremacy and was killed in the battle. His wife also invited the Bhutia force in last rite of her husband and many Bhutias were killed with poisoned alcoholic drink. The incidence is also indirectly mentioned in the last para of the Tripartite Treaty of "*Lho-Mon-Tsong Sum*" (Subba, 1999: 126-128). Sufficient evidence is available as mentioned in the Maharaja's History (1908: 28) while Phuntsho Namgyal was being taken to Yoksom Norbugang for consecration as the first Chogyal of Sikkim as follows:

"The next day they crossed over the Rag-dong bridge, and proceed through Yangang. While passing through Yangang, where there were Lepchas and Mangars, as the party happened to be riding on ponies and some of the retainers had matchlock guns, when they went firing along the road, the simple natives who had never seen ponies nor firearms, said to others the entire parties rode on huge hogs, and some of them bore sticks which when pointed towards you produced great sounds."

It is imaginable how innocent the people of Sikkim were there at that time. It was because of this there was no resistance put forward to the consecration and establishment of the Namgyal Dynasty in Sikkim.

Further, Santosh Alle (2003: 44-69) in his book claims the presence of Mangars in the various Jongs of Sikkim. In the absence of historical evidence to support this fact it may not be possible to believe that the Mangars were in such a great proportion in Sikkim that time as described in the book. The Jongs (forts) are common for the entire Sikkim Administration during Namgyal dynasty (Bhutia, Lepcha and others) and the entire Nepalese too, and not only for the Mangars.

1.2. The Chumbi Valley of "The Greater Sikkim" and the inhabitants:

The Chumbi Valley lies towards the Northeastern part of Sikkim. The original inhabitants of Chumbi valley were also the Lepchas. Heybum Panu or Dungpemsar was the Chieftain and his capital was at Chumbi. Meanwhile the struggle and conflicts among the followers of the "Yellow Hats" and the "Red Hats" of Buddhism in Tibet forced the later to seek refuge in Sikkim and other places. These Tibetan migrants were the followers of the Red Hats sects. Of these Tibetans Khye-Bumsa left Phari and proceeded slowly southwards living some time in Tromo-khang-chung and Chumo-shong and then down to Chumbi. He spent six years in Chumbi. During his stay at Chumbi he was trusted and faithful friend of the Lepcha Chieftain. He was even given the permission of conducting public meeting and was also the key person of the chieftain. Later on some conspiracy began and that led to assassination of the chieftain. Thus the Chumbi Valley was captured by Khe-Bumsa and became the chief of Chumbi Valley overnight (Halfdan Sieger, 1967). This was the Summer Capital of the Chogyals of Sikkim till 1890 (Before British China treaty of 1890 held at Calcatta (photo enclosed). He built a monastery house and lived there. Then hearing about Thekong-Tek he came down to Sikkim where he was conferred the boon of progeny by Thekong Tek. Later on he was blessed with three sons. He came down to Ringchom to perform thanks giving worship of the deities of Sikkim. He met Thekong-Tek and established blood brotherhood relations between the Bhutias and the Lepchas before returning Chumbi. Thus the Lepchas were the original inhabitants of Chumbi Valley also (Halfdan Seiger, 1967: 29; Maharaja's History, 1908: 17-23).

1.3. The Hah Chu Valley and The Ammo-Chu Valley of "The Greater Sikkim" and the inhabitants:

Prior to migration of Tibetans, the Mon-pas (Lepchas, photo enclosed) inhabited both the Hah Chu Valley and the Ammo-Chu Valley. The Ammo-Chu comes through Phari, and passes close under the Sikkim Raja's Chumbi Palace, and runs through Bhutan into Brahamputra. The important inhabiting places were Darlingcote, Moinagoore, Kattam, Jonkso, Nieboo, Sangbe, Har-Timpoo, etc. The Mon-pas are there in Bhutan (4 villages of present Bhutan) even today namely, Jangbi, Wangling, Phumbzor and Oolay with a total of 48 houses (283 persons) as forest dwellers mostly depending on shifting cultivation and hunting. The Tibetan migrants namely Lachungpas and some of Lachenpas of present Sikkim were migrated from Har-Timpoo area of Hah Chu Valley (Namgyal & Dolma, 1908:10; Chand Raghubir, 2007; Eden Ashley, 1863-64: 55-113).

1.4. The Limbuwan Area of "The Greater Sikkim" and the inhabitants:

The landmass lying between the Arun River and the Teesta River was known as "Limbuwan" (Pallo Kirat) by the Nepali natives of this area (Chemjong, 1976; Sanyal, 1979; Shrestha, 1985; Subba, 2003; Risley, 1894; Pradhan, 1991). The aboriginal people, who have resided there from time immemorial, were known as Limbus or Limboos. Their tradition reveals that they were known as *Sawa Yethang-sa* from the time immemorial, derived from their legendry eight brothers (*Sawa Yethang*) who were left by their father Sutsuru Suhangpheba with their mother Tetlara Lahadongna at *Sangarek Nugarek Tembhe* of this part of the Himalayas. The father Sutsuru Suhangpheba had to leave for *Muringla Kharingla Tembhe* with his nine sons known as *Phanghangs* due to his incestuous relation with his own sister. Later on he changed his name and also known as the Ďemigod *Sodhung Lepmuhang. Sawa Yethangs,* eight brothers multiplied and increased in numbers and after they came in contact with the Aryans, the Aryans knew them as Kiratas. After many years or centuries when they multiplied in large numbers and established their homeland by fighting with the eight kings of the inhabited areas; they divided their homeland into *Thibong* (Ten) *Yioks* (Regions) and 17 *Thums* (Sub-regions) to be ruled by the *Thibong* (Ten) Chiefs. Thereafter, they were known themselves as "*Susuwa Lilim Yakthumba*" (means the brave fighter-descendents of Sutsuru Suhangpheba), (Note: Yakthungba is the corrupt word of Yakthumba; some writers relate this word with drinkers or Yak herders but it is not true. Yak is known as *Phungbit* in Limboo language not Yak). When they came in contact with the Gorkhas during 1774 AD the Gorkhas named them as Limbus or Limboos (short form of *Susuwa Lilim Yakthumba*), though they call themselves by the name of *Yakthumba*. They started using Limboo surname post-fixed only in 1806 AD (Subba, 1999; Shrestha, 1985; Khamthak, 2007:212-216). The Bhutias of Nepal and Sikkim call the Limboos by the name Tsang or Tsong or Chang, which is probably given to them on account of their having migrated to Limbuwan from Tsang province in Tibet. The Limboos are said to be composed of three sources:

(*a*) Temporarily migrated to Tibet and again migrated back from Tsang in Tibet known as *Lasa keyuba* Clans; or re-migrated from Unan Province of South China (Chemjong 1967: 7),

(*b*) Temporarily migrated to Kashi (Benares) and again migrated back known as *Kashi thangba* Clans and

(*c*) From those who remained in Phedap area (Indigenous Clans) (Vansittart, 1896: 133), or originated at Kumbhakarna (Jannu) Himalaya and remained in the mountains of this areas (Subba, 2005:85-87).

According to Chemjong (1967), Vansittart (1896), Subba (1995), Subba (1999) the Limboo tradition says that they are descendants from ten brothers whose names are as follows:

1. Thosoying Kanglaying Hang.
2. Thindang Sawaro Hang.
3. Thosoding Hamlewa Sawaro Hang.
4. Thoding Tangsak Sawaro Hang.
5. Yokooding Sawaro Hang.
6. Moguplungma Khambek Sawaro Hang.

7. Moguplungma Langsoding Sawaro Hang.
8. Yokphoding Sawaro Hang.
9. Yokpooding Laingbo Hang.
10. Totoli Toingbo Hang.

With these ten brothers there were three spiritual advisers, namely Phejiri Phedangma, Sambahang Eblyhang Samba and Samundum Yepmundum. These priests did not know how to read and write, but they knew Mundhums (oral traditions). The first five brothers and their descendants temporarily migrated to Benares and came back again from Benares to Limbuwan and were called *Kashi thangba* clans (not *Kanshigotra*); and the second five brothers and their descendants who temporarily migrated with Mawrong Hang to Tibet and again migrated back to Limbuwan were called *Lasa keyuba* clans (not *lasagotra*), because they respectively journey to Benares and Tibet, and from there to Limbuwan. Now these ten brothers again mixed with the Indigenous clans (*Khambongba Lungbongba* clans) and settled in a place called Ambepojoma Kamketlangma, Sumhatlungma. The Petty Kings of the country were the ten brothers lived were called:

(1) Honden Hang, (2) Yeketet Hang, (3) Chasbi Hang, (4) Laraso Pangbo Hang, (5) Khesiwa Hang, (6) Ekangso Hang, (7) Khadi Hang, and (8) Ime Hang.

The ten brothers had many children, and their descendants multiplied very quickly, till they became a nation and were called Limboos. The Limboos were, however, subject to the kings of the country and they were very much oppressed. The kings ruled them with such a hard rule, and oppressed them so greatly, that eventually the Limboos having joined together in the place called Ambepojoma Kamketlangma Sumhatlungma, consulted together, and determined to fight the kings of the country, and drive them out of the country.

So every Limboo swore upon the holy place (Ambepojoma etc.), that he would conquer in the fight or die, and every man swore that he would not return from the war until the kings had been driven from the country, and that he would die sooner than run away in battle.

So there was a great war between the Limboos and the kings, and the former won many victories and drove out the kings from the land, and the Limboos seized the country as their own and fixed its boundaries on the north by Tibet; on the south up to the Mades (plains); on the west up to the Arun River; and to the east up to the Mechi River.

Then the Limboos assembled again together and consulted, and they determined to elect unto themselves ten chiefs (Hangs), one from each tribe, and so the following ten chiefs were elected, and each chief built himself a fort and called it by a name, and each chief marked the boundaries of his country and called it by some name as follows:

1. Samlupley Samba Hang ruled Tamber Khola and his fort was at Tamber Yiok;
2. Sesekkum Satrenu Hang ruled Phedap and his fort was at Poklabung Yiok;
3. Akluk Hang ruled Atrai and his fort was at Pemajong Yiok;
4. Thindolung Koya Hand ruled Yangrup and his fort was at Hastapur Yiok;
5. Sesiang Sereng Hang ruled Mewa Khola and his fort was at Meringden Yiok;
6. Niyaso Papo Hang ruled Panchthar and his fort was at Pheden Yiok;
7. Emibhu Khewa Hang ruled Chathar and his fort was at Takluk Yiok;
8. Soyak Hang ruled Chaubise and his fort was at Kurley Yiok;
9. Ing Hang ruled Das Majhiya Panch Khapan (Sankhusobha) and his fort was at Chenlung Yiok.; and
10. Ime Hang ruled Ilam and his fort was at Angdang Yiok;

With the establishment of *Thibong* (Ten) *Yioks* they designated themselves as "*Susuwa Lilim Yakthumba*" (the brave fighter-descendents of Sutsuru Suhangpheba) or in short "*Yakthumba*" (Brave fighters). In due course of time the Indigenous tribes (*Bhuiphuta* or *Khambongba-Lungbongba*) multiplied and became the most powerful and numerous. Their chief *Bhuiphuta* Hang (actual name is not known) ruled over eastern Nepal for many years; after its decline the Kashi tribe became powerful, and its chief massacred all the members of the Hang royal family. After the fall of *Bhuiphuta* Hang's dynasty there was anarchy all over Eastern Nepal, there being no supreme ruler to keep all the clans of the Limboos in peace and unity. In this way they continued for several years, when at length there sprang from among the Srisobha tribe a powerful man called Maw Rong Hang (7th century A. D.), from *Lasa keyuba* clan, who succeeded in reconciling the different tribes to each other.

The Srisobha claims to be of second batch of Shan Mokwan people under the leadership of Maw Rong Hang who came to East Nepal from Unan Province of South China via North Burma, then fled to Khampa Jong due to the attack of the Ten Limboos. Hangsu Deva the King of Kirat of Kathmandu Valley died on 640 A.D. He had no sons and his son-in-law King Srong-Tsen Gampo of Tibet occupied the throne of Kathmandu, Nepal. King Srong-Tsen Gampo, then ordered his Vassal Maw Rong Hang of Khampa Jong to invade India through Limbuwan. He defeated the Ten Limboos and became a revered and celebrated ruler of the area from Khampajong of Tibet to Mithila province of Northern India.

After the successful conquest of all the Kirat land of the Eastern Himalayan region, Maw Rong Hang divided his country into four major provinces namely the Khambuwan, Limbuwan, Lapchan and Morong and ruled this state in accordance with the feudal system of the times. The land between the Kathmandu valley and river Dudh Koshi was called Khombuwan. The Limbuwan state extended from the river Dudh Koshi in the west to river Mechi in the east. The district of Khampajong was situated in the Limbuwan state then and became the capital. The Lapchan province laid between river Mechi and river Teesta in the east. Mawrong was the name assigned to identify all the plain lands that he had invaded and subjugated. After a prosperous reign of many years, Maw Rang Hang died, and among his successors in the chieftainship founded by him, Mokani Hang became distinguished (Chenjong, 1967: 92-93).

Tradition says that Maw Rang Hang was the first man who introduced writing among them (Rong or Lepcha script), which however, owing to the long prevailing anarchy, fell into disuse. After Mokani's death the Limboos again fell into anarchy, there being none able to persuade all the tribes to live peacefully together, which state of things lasted more than a century. At last, probably in the ninth century, appeared the famous Sirijunga Hang, the defied hero of the Limboos. The Limboos believe that Sirijunga Hang found the Limboo script of the Soumer Kiraras of 4,000 B.C.and further developed which is now known as Sirijunga script in his honour. He taught the Limboos the art of reading and writing the Limboo language.

The ten Limboo chieftainsmentioned above, together with the names of the ten principalities as first marked out, and their respective forts (capitals), after this division of the country the Limboos remained rulers of their country until the Gorkhas waged war against them. For twelve years did the Das (ten) Limboos fought with the Gorkhas, after which they accepted the Gorkha's sovereignty. The Limbuwan is now divided into six districts in Nepal, namely, Dhankuta, Tehrathum, Sankhuwa Sobha, Tapleyjung, Panchthar and Ilam (Vansittart, 1896: 134-135; 139-141; Chemjong, 1967: 7; Subba, 1995; Subba, 1999: 74-77).

1.5. Ilam Area of "The Greater Sikkim" and the inhabitants:

The above Kirant tradition says that the Ime or the Lepchas or the Rongs are one of the ten Limboo Kiratas who occupied the Eastern corner of Limbuwan called Ilam or the Lepchan province of Maw Rong Hang in antiquity. However, the Lepchas or the Rongs neither believe in *Rong Chhyo* nor agree as one of the Kiratas of the Himalayas. This may be because of their closer relation with the Bhutias after the blood brotherhood treaty of Kabi Lungchok held during 13th century AD.

However, the Lepcha are one of many tribal groups of Nepal. They live in Ilam, one of the Eastern hilliest districts of Nepal. Ilam lies sandwiched between the Mahabharat and the Singalila Ranges. Surrounding it is Panchthar in the North, Darjeeling in the East, Jhapa in the South and Dhankuta and Morang in the West. Its major rivers from east to west are: Mechi, Mai, Jog Mai, Pua Mai (also called Kanki), and Dew Mai. The region between the four Mai rivers is called Char Khola since ancient times. The area was claimed by Limbuwan as well as by Sikkim in 1774 (Jeffrey, et al, 2000: 7).

1.6. Migration of forefathers of The Namgyal Dynasty to "The Greater Sikkim":

According to the Maharaja's History (1908), the race of the Namgyal rulers were spoken of as belonging to the Nyans race, but there is no genealogical record on the subject. Some people again ascribe the origin to the Mi-nyag Sehu-yi Gyalpo. But, in a history compiled by one Ye-sges Paljor, it is mentioned that Gyal-God's descendants was the Dar-seng family who lived in the northern portion of the Tsang province. These married with the Sakya family, and for some generations were known as the Sakya Pan-Chen. So, in the absence of all authentic records relating clearly and authoritatively the origin of the family of the rulers of Sikkim, brief allusions found in the introduction or preface to the Law book ascribed to the foremost Maharaja of Sikkim must be given credit to, as they are more over supported by the oral narratives of the oldest people living, who again ascribe their narrative to the annals of their parents whom they had heard relating so. The race of the Rulers of Sikkim was sprung from the former and pure stock of the ruling family of the kings of Tibet, the Khri-srong Deu-Tsan (ibid: 14-23).

The 25th King of Kham Mi-nyak started forth with his sons. He came to Lhasa and then to Sakya to the residence of his own Guru. He visited all the reputed places of pilgrimage throughout Tibet and came to Sakya where the monastery was being built. The eldest prince of the emigrant, having risen up the pillars of the monastery, obtained the name of Khye-

Bumsa (equaling a lakh of men, in strength). He dwelt in Sakya for sometime and married the lady named Jomo Guruma of the Hierarch family. Shortly after this he left Sakya and came towards Sikkim. Arriving at a place called Pakshi (north of Khampajong) he built a monastery called Pakshi Gumpa, where he established some 400 priests. One of the brothers became a priest and lived there as the Abbot of the same monastery. Then coming down, he sojourned for some time in Phari, where he built another monastery called Samdup Lhakhang. There the father died. At Khangbu the son Khye-Bumsa meets with Shabdung Lhari and had him to perform the funeral rites and then all other periodical Pujahs etc. for the living. Some of the brothers named Seshing, Tsan-tong and Kar-tsog separated and proceeded southwards to Hah in Paro. Some ascribe the origin of the eight chief Bhutia clans of Sikkim to these brothers (ibid: 14-23).

Khye-Bumsa himself also proceeded slowly southwards living for some time in Tromo-khang-chung and Chumo-shong and thence down to Chumbi where he built a monastry house and lived for some time. Khe-Bumsa had no issue. Hearing about Thekong-Tek, who could confer the boon of progeny, he paid a visit to Thekong-Tek. Thekong-Tek performed worship for the Khye-Bumsa's progeny. After returning to Chumbi he was blessed with three sons (ibid: 14-23).

Khye-Bumsa came down to Ringchom for offering worship of the gods and goddesses of Sikkim as he was blessed with three sons. He met Thekong Tek and they established blood brotherhood relationship at Kabi Lungchok. This friendship was cemented by a ceremony at which several animals, both domestic and wild were sacrificed and all the local deities involved to bear witness to this solemn contact of friendship, binding the Lepchas and Bhutias in a inseparable bond. They sat together on the raw hides of the animals, entwined the entrails around the persons, and put the blood troth to each other. Thekong invoking all the Sikkim local spirits, asked them to stand witness to this solemn contact, invoking blessings on those who observed these faithfully, and curses on those who broke this eternal hereditary and national contact between the two races. This was in the 13th century. The Government of Sikkim is protecting the place where the Blood brotherhood treaty was held at Kabi Lungchok, which is now a sacred place (ibid:14-23).

The folk history is certainly interesting but there still remains a number of historical uncertainities which need to be clarified. There is still no historical evidence at present to confirm the existence of Khe-Bumsa and Thekong Tek (Mullard, 2005:72).

Thenceforth the Lepchas gradually came under the influence of the Tibetans, the descendants of Khe-Bumsa, who migrated slowly with other Tibetans. Of the three sons Khya-Mo rab, Lang-Mo-rab and Mi-Pon-rab, the youngest Mi-Pon-rab married a lady from the Sakya Heirarch's family. She soon conceived and gave four sons namely Sang-po-dar, Tse-chu-dar, Nyima Gyalpo and Guru Tashi. All of these sons – called ***Tongduruzi*** along with Khye-Bumsa family were settled together in Gangtok (Gang-tog Zil gnon rtse ?). Of these above Guru Tashi's family became pre-eminent and inherited the princely dignity and name. Guru Tashi's son was Jowo Nagpo, his son was Jowo Aphag, Jowo Aphag's son was Guru Tenzing and Guru Tenzing's son was Phuntsho Namgyal, the first Maharaja of Sikkim. He was born in the year 1604 A.D. i.e. the Shing Dug (wood dragon) year of the 10th Tibetan Era. He married a lady of the Beb-tsan-gyad clan residing in Sikkim. The Guru Tashi family became very influential and prosperous. The Lepchas came under his influence and power in a very short time. Gradually the Lepchas of Gangtok (Gang-tog Zil gnon rtse ?), Tashi-teng-kha and Seng-deng came under the direct influence and control of the chief- Sambar (Nang-Zan), they were called ministerial Lepchas (Mon-pas) (ibid: 14-23).

1.7. The Migration of Three Lamas to "The Greater Sikkim":

According to Maharaja's History (1908: 23-27), and Mullard (2005:31-48; 2005: 56-85), the three Lamas played a significant role in the establishment of Namgyal Dynasty in Sikkim.

(*a*) Lha-tsun Nam-kha Jig-med (1595-1650): He is the founder of the Zog-chen sect of Mahayana Buddhism in Sikkim. He was born in 1597 in sByar yul southern province of Tibet in a family from the nobility of that area. His father was Chokyong Gonpo and his mother was Yid'ong bu dga and received instructions from Grub thob sod rnam dbang po, Ringzing Jatsonnyingpo and Pemalegsgrub. He repaired Samyes monastery six times. He started from Kong po and came to Sikkim at the request of one of his principal teachers, Jatshon snying po gradually with about 15 followers, proclaimed that it was time for serious people to enter the sacred hidden land. Lha-tsun Chempo remained in Kong po during the most turbulent time of the Tibetan civil war practicing and revealing treasure texts until the mid 1640s; leaving Tibet atleast three years after the establishment of the Central Tibet State under the Dalai Lama in 1642. Indeed it was not until the 13th day of the fifth month of the Fire Dog, or Me Khyi, year 1646 that Lha-tsun Chempo, left Kong po for Sikkim. He passes through Sam yas and by the seventh month of the same year he reaches a point where he makes the necessary offerings to the deities of Sikkim. After the ninth month of the same year he meets with Nga-Dag before he finally arrives in Sikkim via Phu Chu dkar lha. He arrieved Yoksom, Sikkim in the ninth month of 1646 and began discovering prophesies, ritual treatises and gnas yig which reinforced the definition of Sikkim. Thus, he is credited with the formation of Sikkimese State in traditional histories (Namgyal & Dolma, 1908; Mullard, 2005).

(*b*) Kathog Kuntu Zangpo (? - 1694): The second pioneer Lama saint was the high priest of the Nyingma monastery of Kathog Dorjeden, and having obtained celebrity as being a perfectly accomplished Lama of the Vajrayana sect, and perfectly capable of upholding and spreading of the doctrines of his sect. He came through U and Tsang and explored the northern and eastern passes leading into Sikkim, contending with great difficulties, dangers and hardships. Then he turned round and came by the western pass, viz: the Singalila pass into the interior of Sikkim and reached Yoksom Norbugang in 1642 A.D.

(*c*) Nga-Dag Sempa Phunsog Ringzing (1592 -1656): He was born in the palace of Sag Khri mkhar in Western Tibet in 1592, after which he and his father left Western Tibet for dBus gtsang. He was born in a privileged family that ruled a portion of Western Tibet, bordering on Mang Yul Gung thang and the family had an important connection with the kings of Mustang as the king of Mustang was married to the second daughter of Phu tshogs rig 'dzin. He spent most of his early years in training with his father, before he embarked upon a period of meditation and seclusion, which lasted for twelve years. His entry to Sikkim is marked, as it is with Lha-tsun Chempo, by the prophetical tradition of the Nyingmapa school. On the 25th day of the third month of the Water Horse year (1642 AD), Phuntshogs rig 'dzin leaves from Zhigatse, the capital of the Tsang province, with his son in search of sBas Yul Bras mo ljongs. He arrieved Yoksom on the third day of the eighth Tibetan month (four months and eight days after he left Zhigatse). Phun tshogs rig 'dzin and his son began the construction of the dMar po lha khang in Yoksom during the 11th month of the Water Sheep year (1643). He with his son also constructed the monastery of Zil gnon (Sinon), which they began in 1649 and completed in 1651. It was also around this time that the Byams pa lha khang was constructed in bKra Shis lding (Tashiding). He was also involved in the coronation of Sikkim's first King Phuntsho Namgyal at some point of time between 1642 - 1647 (Mullard, 2005: 31-48; 55-85).

2. The Modern History of Sikkim:

The modern History of Sikkim (i.e., The Greater Sikkim) starts from the installation of Namgyal Dynasty in Sikkim in 1642 A.D. In the absence of literacy as well as script for writing system amongst the indigenous people of the Greater Sikkim areas that time, no authentic historical evidence is available except that of the Maharaja's History of Sikkim 1908 (Translated by Dawa Samdup) and foreign writers who collected the information from the elite people of Sikkim. Such folk informations with some historical evidences available on the history and culture of the Greater Sikkim, needs further investigation. The Gazetteer of Sikkim, and many such earlier old and new documents available with us were drawn freely under this text, and tried to churn it together to streamline the history and culture of Sikkim in this chapter. My intention is not to hurt the sentiments of any community or person if any in this text.

According to Mullard (2005:55-85; 2005: 31-48) the orthodox approach to Sikkimese history contends that Phuntsho Namgyal was brought from Gangtok (the current state capital) and enthroned in Yoksom -Norbugang in the year 1642 AD. He pointed out that the year 1642 for coronation/cosecration of the first king Phuntsho Namgyal is problematic due to a number of reasons. Among the various reasons he mentioned are (a) arrival of Lha-tsun Chempo to Yoksom-Norbugang only in 1646 AD; (b) settlement of Gangtok (the present capital) only in 1888 AD onwards; (c) Nga-dag's chronicle of Gang-tog Zil gnon rtse where Sikkimese royal family resided in Western Sikkim etc.

He suggested three possibilities for consideration on the installation/ consecration/coronation of Phuntsho Namgyal as follows:

(*a*) Phuntsho Namgyal was already King by the time Lha-tsun arrieved in Sikkim;

(*b*) The date of 1642 was fixed retrospectively to associate the formation of Sikkim with the establishment of the dGa-ldan pho brang in Lhasa; and

(*c*) Phuntsho Namgyal did indeed obtain political power over an area of West Sikkim in 1642, but only in 1646 or 1647 AD was he involved in an event which inaugurated him as the Chogyal of Sikkim.

However, the "*Lho-Mon-Tsong-Sum*" tripartite agreement of Bhutias (Lhopos), Lepchas (Monrees) and Tsongs (Limboos), the oldest historical document of Sikkim available with us confirms that the first king Phuntsho Namgyal was already a king of the Greater Sikkim in 1642 AD (Report of OBC, Government of Sikkim, 1998; Subba, 1999: 13-20; 126 128).

The document reveals that Phuntsho Namgyal was already king when the tripartite agreement was signed in 1642 AD. The actual coronation might have taken place only in 1646 or 1647 AD as suggested by Mullard (2005: 76-77), as in the case of Sir Tashi Namgyal (Sir Tashi Namgyal was enthroned on 19th February 1915 as the eleventh Chogyal of Sikkim, but the event of coronation was held only on 15th May 1916).

2.1. The Coronation or Installation of the First Chogyal of Sikkim - Phuntsho Namgyal (1642-1670):

The three learned Lamas (saints) namely Lha-tsun Nam-kha Jig-med, Kathog Kuntu Zangpo and Nga-Dag Sempa Phuntsog Ringzing acting from perfect knowledge and acquaintance with all the prophecies contained in the Apocalyptical books of the sacred Guru of Urgyen, regarding the rulers of Sikkim, performed all the necessary rites and ceremonies as prescribed in the installation of a Royal dynasty, and coronation of the first king in that line, in the most impressive style. He was given the power, conferring rites of the eight auspicious objects and the eight auspicious or Royal emblems. Next that came the rite of the seven objects, which constituted a Chakravartic emperor. He married a lady from Bep-Tshan-gye family and had bore a son, Tensung Namgyal (Namgyal and Dolma, 1908: 29).

Phuntsho Namgyal was installed on the throne of Sikkim with the title of Chogyal (Dharmaraja, king of righteousness), having two fold powers (Spiritual and temporal). He ruled for about 28 years and died in 1670 (ibid: 29) (photo of Norbugang enclosed).

During the ceremony the Lamas gave a present of a coral rosary to the Maharaja. The Ka-thog Lama attached the tassels and pendants; and the top bead (button) was added by Lha-Tsun Chempo. From this also the omens turned that Lha-tsun's creed and followers would thenceforth be the most honoured in Sikkim. The Lamas presented this garland to the Raja with a great many benedictions and prayers. Then they gathered earth and stones from all the parts of Sikkim and built a Chorten with it at Yoksom called the Trashi-Wod-hBar Chorten (photo enclosed); the relics and other internal deposits were contributed by Lha-tsun, and the three Lamas then spent 21 days in prayer for the benediction and consecration ceremonies. After that the Lamas by turn wished blessings on the Raja with the proper ceremonies. Next all the priests and the Raja combined in entreating Lha-tsun to found a monastery on the spot. So the Dubdi monastery was built by Lha-tsun (photo enclosed) (Ibid: 29-30).

2.2. The Consolidation and Emergence of "The Greater Sikkim":

There was no resistance put forward to the installation and establishment of the Namgyal Dynasty in Sikkim as Bhutias, Lepchas and

Tsongs (Limboos) agreed and signed the tripartite treaty of "*Lho-Mon-Tsong-Sum*".

(*a*) The resistance or Challenge to the Installation and Supremacy of Namgyal Dynasty in Sikkim: Dharnidhar Dahal (1984: 24) has stated in his History book "The Lepchas and the Limboos offended the installation of Namgyal Dynasty while the Phuntsho Namgyal party was preceding for coronation towards Yoksom in 1642. They fought with the Bhutia force who were well equipped with guns, swords, arrows and spears at Gyezing, West Sikkim but were defeated and killed or fled away from there. The Bhutias were also killed. The corpse of the Bhutias were buried at Geyzing and later they erected Mendang on it, which is still there. They declare that place Geyzing which means a "Victory Place". However, in the absence of evidence and also in the absence of mention of this incidence in any of the historical writings so far makes it difficult to believe it.

There is no doubt that the Mangar's Petty King Santusati Sen of Mangarjong of Mangsari, West Sikkim offered resistance to installation and supremacy of Namgyal dynasty in Sikkim. He fought with the Bhutia force. When he was defeated, he fled away to Lungchok, West Sikkim. He sought the help of Nahang Mabohang petty Limboo King of Lungchok, West Sikkim and fought jointly with the Bhutia force. However, Santusati Sen was killed (some say fled away from Sikkim. The queen committed suicide at Ranikhola. Most of the Magars fled away towards Western Nepal). Thereafter the Limboo petty Kings also accepted the supremacy of Namgyal Dynasty. After the Tripartite agreement of "*Lho-Mon-Tsong Sum*" the Mangars were finally driven away by the Bhutia, the Lepcha and Limboo forces from the entire areas of the Greater Sikkim. However, many Mangar *royiats* accepted the supremacy of Namgyal dynasty and settled as a common man (Alle, 2003: 44-53; Vansittart, 1896: 118; Chemjong, 1976:138-150).

The second paragraph of "*Lho-Mon-Tsong Sum*" Tripartite Treaty of the Bhutias, Lepchas and Limboos also reveals that the Mangars did not accept the Installation and Supremacy of the Namgyal dynasty. As a result they were driven away from the areas of Greater Sikkim. The paragraph translated by Prof. Ringu Tulku in 1984 is as follows:

"During the last Mongpa war (Magars were known as Mongpas) (Chemjong, 1967: 138-150) some people's action were noted and let them be beware of now from this year of water horse (1642) onwards we will abide by the commands of the King, his Guru and his sons and will never let arise a bad thought against Sikkim".

Risley (1894: 10) writes that "very little is known of the First Chogyal's reign; but in all probably he was chiefly engaged in subduing or winning over the chiefs of the petty clans inhabiting the country east of the Arun. It is said that with the aid of Lha-tsun Lama he overcomes one Shintu Satichen, or Mangal Gyelpa; ... this tribe occupied the valleys to the south of the Kanchenjingna-Everest range. The chief disappeared leaving no trace, after vowing he would petition the sun and moon for the injuries done to him."

According to Chemjong (1967: 162-167) the Mangar chief and Limboo chief made war against Phuntsho Namgyal for which he had to bring Tibetan soldiers and through their help he won the victories over the Mangar and Limboo chiefs. As a result of this, he became the King of the Greater Sikkim including the Northern part of Limbuwan State where lies Tambar, Yangwarok, Northern Panchthar, Ilam, Phakphok and Darjeeling. The Kirat chiefs of the above mentioned districts also agreed to regard Phuntsho Namgyal of Sikkim as their King and paid him a nominal tribute. The Tsong Subhas or Limboo chiefs were given full autonomy for their districts and remained himself their nominal King. However, the historical evidence is yet to be seen to support the Chemjong's views.

(*b*) Integration of Land Resources of the Bhutias, the Lepchas and the Limboos and Emergence of "THE GREATER SIKKIM": After the installation or coronation of the First Chogyal (Spiritual and Temporal King) of Sikkim, the task ahead was to consolidate or to integrate all the land resources of the Communities inhabited in the entire nearby areas and to establish supremacy of the Namgyal Dynasty in Sikkim. With the advice of the three learned Lamas, Phuntsho Namgyal successfully accomplished this task. He forcibly settled the resistance of Mangars.

(*c*) Signing of Tripartite Treaty of "Lho-Men-Tsong Sum": The Chogyal Phuntsho Namgyal invited all the Leaders of the Bhutias, the Lepchas and the Limboos and signed a Tripartite Treaty of "*Lho-Mon-Tsong Sum*" in Tibetan Script which has been translated by Prof. Ringu Tulku in 1984 (Report of OBC Commission, Government of Sikkim, 1998; Subba, 1999: 13-20; 126-128) as follows:

"Hi! Please observe, please behold, please listen, Name. From the Kumtu Zangpo the Foremost Buddha, to the root Guru of our time and their occasion like guardian deities of Dharma may please appear in their wrathful form and behold (at this occasion) without your body, speech and mind distracted elsewhere. All the ocean like guardian deities; the male Dharma Palas, Female protectors of the Chogyal of this country and the Dharma, may also appear in their fiercely wrathful forms and behold at this occasion without distractions of their body, speech and mind. Pal Yeshe-Kyl Gompo Mahakala Manning Nangpo, Gompos of body, speech, mind, quality and action Za-Yi Gehen Ra-hula and light division of Gods and Demi-Gods may please listen without being distracted. Chogyal Chempo, his all consorts, Ministers and followers to whom the Guru Rimpoche gave his commands, his followers, Demons, Nagas and Tsen (Dud, Tsen, Lu), Baishramana, Dorjee shugden, Dorjee, Dadul, Pehar Gyalpo and Gualpos of recent and ancient with eight divisions of wrathful spirits may also appear in their wrathful form and behold this occasion not having their body, speech and mind distracted elsewhere. Moreover, Zad-nga Taktse the great treasure holder of this Valley, Thang Lhe, Gabur Gangtsan, Twelve Tonmas, Ya-dud Cham-dral the gardian deities of the lower valley. Sride Rongtsen Ekazati and all the female guardians, the guardians of middle Valley Pawa hunger and hundred thousand of millions of armies of Lha Tsen, Dud and Lu-may also appear in their wrathful form and behold at this occasion not having their body, speech and mind distracted elsewhere. In this hidden valley of Guru Rimpoche, the guardian deities of the retreat centres holding the lineage of Zongpo Chempo; the armies of Dud, Tsen, Lu and treasure holders residing in mountains, valleys, srees, rocks and lands and lawns, the guardian deities of Thek-Chek Yangtse, Pema Yangntse, Radenatse, Tashiding and other places may appear in their wrathful form and behold at this occasion. All the deities and guardians worshipped by us the people of four parts of Ti-Ting Hkapa Barpung, Linguam, Dangs Zongs, Tsongs and Mongpos may please behold undistracted.

We the leaders and ministers have met here according to the wishes of the Lord of Men and we hereby pledge and put our seals to the agreement that the people "*Lho-Mon-Tsong-Sum*" will hereafter integrate our wishes and will not have our separate self government of Lho (Bhutia), Mon (Lepcha), and Tsong (Limboo) but will abide by one order only. During the last Mongpa war some people's action were noted and let them be beware of now from this year of water horse onwards we will abide by the commands of the King, his Guru and his sons and will never let arise a bad thought against Sikkim.

We the ministers and leaders of Sikkim including these of the eight communities of Lhopas hereby pledge that "*Lho-Mon-Tsong-Sum*" will have one destiny and one government. They will fight together with their foes and they will feast together with their friends. They will bring in

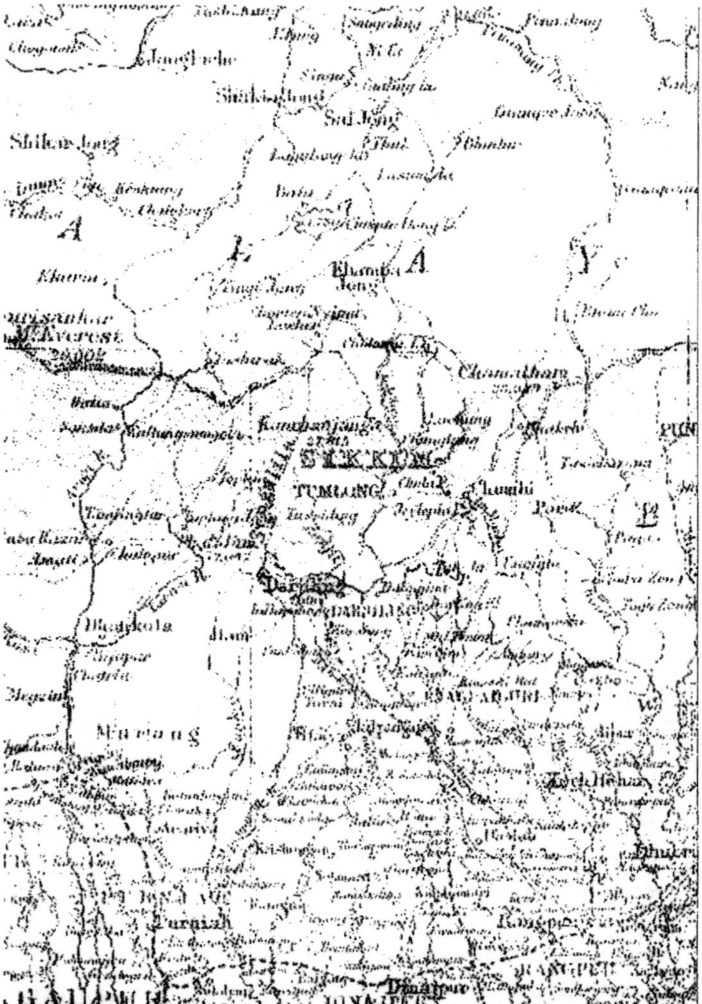

MAP with areas of The Greater Sikkim; Source: NET

the intelligence of others but they will never take out the secret of inside. If there be any not abiding by this pledge and mischief and disturb the peace and harmony of "*Lho-Mon-Tsong-Sum*", whoever he may be. The above mentioned guardian deities will see the truth. In such a case the afore mentioned deities are beseeched to appear in their wrathful forms and with their forceful sound of Hung! Phat! and they are beseeched to make the criminals go mad and devour their flesh, blood and heart without delaying for years, months, days and even for a moment. Kharam Kha Hi! Those who abide by this pledge, respect the above mentioned deities abide by the agreement signed by us, the ministers and leaders, wish only good for the Chogyal, his Gurus and his sons, and serve the nation both physically and peace (Mak, Lag, Jung, Sum), may they be seen by the afore said guardian deities and may their life, fortune glory and wealth be made to increase like the waxing moon. If any among "*Lho-Mon-Tsong-Sum*", would not abode by the pledge will be made to pay three ounces of gold as pledge breach fee and there after he will be punished according to the degree of crime he has committed from slight physical punishment to the extreme of death penalty. No hesitation will be made in execution of this punishment so that all may keep this in their minds.

The seal of following were put.

1. The Minister of Sikkim – Dag Shar;
2. Dechen Namgyal of Tritong Khampa (Tshongkor Lak-Kor);
3. Thar Thim of Barpung;
4. Tamchin Dorleg;
5. Twencho of Lingdam;
6. Chpe Drop;
7. Gu-Ju of Drang Tod;
8. Nangpo of Bodrongpa;
9. Tsong Subba of Namphang;
10. Tsong Yug Shug;
11. Mo Zang (or Morang) Mig Tshep;
12. Tsa Tai;
13. Poshing;
14. Matsi To;
15. Labung Thopa Kui;
16. Deshe Hang;
17. Mig Yom Ajamta;
18. Modenpa;

19. Peghapa;
20. Bolobir;
21. Tapa Agod of Rathang Chung Gupa;
22. Tapa Shuphang of Ringbi Chinggupa;
23. Tapa Gea Kyab of Galed Chung Gupa;
24. Pelo

Thus, this agreement was signed on Water Horse Year (1642 A.D.) at Denzong Phuntso Khangsar which was translated by: Prof. Ringu Tulku in 1984 (a photocopy of the treaty enclosed).

The treaty was signed by 24 persons out of which 8 were Bhutia Ministers, 12 were Tsong leaders and 4 were the Lepcha leaders. This also reveals overwhileming presence of the Limboos in the Greater Sikkim during 1642 AD. Thus, integrating the entire land resources in their possession during that point of time by the Bhutias (Chumbi Valley of present Tibet-China), the Lepchas (Most of the areas of present Sikkim, Hah Chu and Ammo-Chu Valleys of present Bhutan, Ilam of present Nepal) and the Tsongs (present area of West Sikkim and Limbuwan), and with this treaty of "*Lho-Mon-Tsong-Sum*" the First Chogyal Phuntsho Namgyal of Sikkim established a country "**The Greater Sikkim**" in 1642 A.D. (Subba, 1999: 13-20; 126-128).

The Greater Sikkim is the result of the Tripartite Treaty of "*Lo-Mon-Tsong Sum*", which identifies the Bhutias, Lepchas, and Limboos as the three original races of the Kingdom of Sikkim at the time of the First Chogyal, signed on the "Water Horse Year' in (1642) at Denzong Phuntsong Khangsar between the Ministers of Chogyal Chempo, on one side and leaders of Lepchas and Tsongs on the other side (Subba, 1999: v-vi; 125-128). The Buddhist Lunar Calendar follows 60 year's cycle and the Chu Ta (Water Horse) year falls on 1642, 1702, 1762, 1822, 1882, 1942, 2002, 2062 and so on. This confirms the year of signing the tripartite treaty in 1642.

The Maharaja's History (1908) has mentioned the boundaries of The Greater Sikkim as follows:

"Dibdala in the North, Shingsa Dag-pay, Walung, Yangmag Khangchen Yarlung and Timar Chorten in the West, down along the Arun and Dud Kosi rivers, down to the Maha Nadi Nuxalbari, Titaliya in the South. On the East Tagong La and Tang La on the North. These constituted the boundaries of the Greater Sikkim, with which the Raja reigned in righteousness, making the land enjoy such peace and happiness as was enjoyed during the Sat-yug periods of the world"(Ibid: 30-31) (a Map reconstructed as per the above is enclosed).

MAP with areas of The Greater Sikkim; Source: Political map of India

MAP of Sikkim and Tibet (China); Source: Buffetrille Katia (2004: 40-1:38)

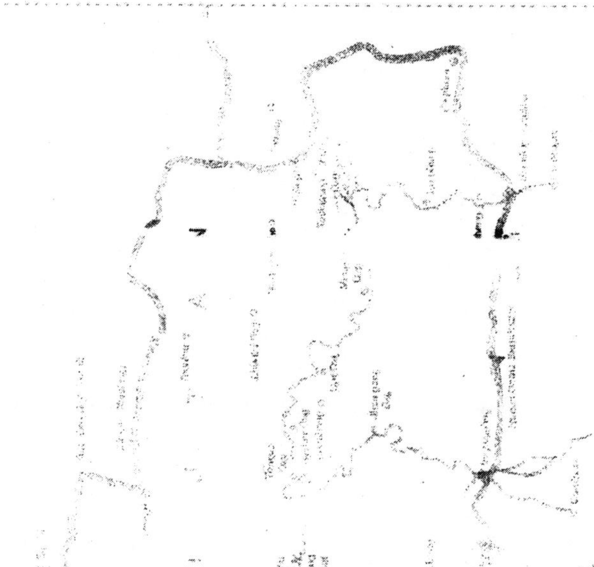

MAP OF BHUTAN WITH HAR & AMMO VALLEYS

Source: Nest & Wings

Lho-Mon-Tsong-Sum Tripartite Agreement. Source:OBC Report 1998

In the reigns of the earlier Sikkim Rajas their realms extended from the Arun river on the west to the Tegon La range on the east, and thus included the Tamber and Mochu valleys. In a Sikkim paper, which recites various old works, it is thus described "This sacred country is bounded on the north by the "*Mon-Thangla*" mountain, which is guarded by the spirit "*Kiting*". On the east lies the "*lTas-hGons*" mountain. Its southern gate is "*Nagsharbhati*", which is guarded by "*Ma-mGon-lCham-Bral-yab-lDud*". It's western gate, "*lTimar mChhod-rTen*", is guarded by the terrible female spirit -"*Mamos*". The '*mDsod-lNga*' mountains and the spirit "*Phra-Man-dGe-Man*" of Zar guard it on the north" (Risley 1894: 1-2).

On the 3rd day of the 11th month of Chu-lug (Water Sheep) year 1643 A.D. the Nga-Dag Lama built the Lhakhang marpo (red temple, photo enclosed) and the Kathog Lama built the Kathog monastery (photo enclosed), while the Maharaja built a Palace at Tashi Tenkha (photo enclosed). Having brought all the Lepchas and Bhutias under his direct power, he selected twelve Kazis from amongst the tweleve Chief Bhutia clans then existing and likewise he selected twelve chief Lepcha Jongpons from amongst the superior families of Lepchas of Sikkim. Proclamations were made promising due recognition and emoluments to those who distinguished themselves by loyal and faithful services, saying that the posts of ministers and Prime Ministers (Chag-mzod) would be conferred on them. On the other hand those who did not serve well would be classed amongst the common people, and required to contribute such services as were required by the Maharaja, and that thencefourth they would not be allowed to remain masterless as before (Namgyal & Dolma, 1908: 30).

From the Maharaja's history, it reveals that the Limboos were not given any official posts and were treated merely as common people since the beginning of the Namgyal Dynasty. They integrated their land resources and signed the Tripartite Treaty of "*Lho-Mon-Tsong-Sum*" and participated in the formation of "**The Greater Sikkim**" but were not given their due share either in the administration or in other matters and were treated merely as a common people since the beginning of the Namgyal Dynasty not abiding the pledge of the Tripartite Treaty of "*Lho-Mon-Tsong-Sum*" (Subba, 1999:129-140; Kutturen, 1983).

The Lamas also fixed upon Tashiding as being the central key of Sikkim, and agreed that it was a most sacred spot (Namgyal & Dolma 1908: 31).

2.3. The Second Chogyal Maharaja Tensung Namgyal (1644-1700):

Tensung Namgyal born in 1644, succeeded his father Phuntsho in 1670. During his reign Sangacholling monastery started by Lha-Tsun was completed and Pemayongtse monastery was constructed. Tensung married three times; the first a lady from Tibet – Nambi Ongmu who gave birth to a daughter named Pande Wangmo; the second from Tinkejong, Deba Zam Sar, who gave birth to a son, the next Maharaja, Chagdor Namgyal; and the third a Princes Limbooni, Thungwamukma, daughter of a Limboo Raja Yong-ya Hang from Arun, who gave birth to a son, named Guru, who resided at Dingrong in Pathing, whose line is now extinct. She also gave birth to a daughter called Pande-Tshering Gyenu who married a man of the Nam-Lsang-korpa tribe residing in Yangang, and died there. With this lady queen came seven Limboo ladies with her, were taken as wives by the highest Kazis and ministers of Sikkim (Namgyal and Dolma, 1908).

King Tensung Namgyal built a new palace near the famous Pemayongtse monastery in the name of his Tsong queen Thungwa Mukma and asked her to name it according to her own choice. She also named it "*Song Khim*", which later on became *Sukhim* and then *Sikkim*. In Limboo language "*Song*" means new and "*Khim*" means a home or palace; so "*Song Khim*" meant New Home or Palace. It is from the name of this palace, originated the name of the country, that is "Sookhim (Kirkpatrick, 1793) and "*Sikkim*" (Hamilton, 1819). The original name of Sikkim was "*Mayel*" in Lepcha, "*Yioksom*" (one of the fort or fortified place) in Limboo and "*Deyijong*" in Lhopo or Bhutia language. The Rabdentse site was identified by Lha-tsun in 1649. The Chogyal Tensung shifted his capital to Rabdentse in 1670s (Chemjong, 1967:164; Risley, 1894:40; Namgyal & Dolma, 1908: 108).

The Princess Pande Wangmo became the concort of the Nga-Dag Lama, Rinchengon. About this time there was a Lepcha Tumyang (headman), called Tasa Aphong, who was descendant of the former Lepcha Chief Thekong-Tek, serving under Raja Tensung Namgyal, who was residing at Barphag. Once while he was away on in Tibet on Palace work, his wife Nambong was seduced by the Raja, and the offspring of this illicit intercourse was called Yukthing Arup. He was appointed head of the Lepchas, and subsequently became the Chagzod. Tensung died in 1700 (ibid: 36-37).

2.4. The Third Chogyal Maharaja Chagdor Namgyal (1786-1716):

The Chagdor Namgyal born in 1786 and was put on the throne in 1700 A.D. The Raja was very young. Pende Wangmo being the eldest sister and wanted to usurping the throne, which set a feeling of enmity between the brother and sister, from his very childhood. Pende Wangmo along with a few other persons, whose minds had been disturbed by the evil spirit, conspired together and seeking aid from Bhutan invited external enemies to come inside.

While the King was very young, a Bhutanese King, Dev Zidar invaded and took possession of Eastern Sikkim. The date of this Bhutanese invasion is variously given from 1700 to 1708. King Chagdor Namgyal fled away to Lhasa via Ilam and Walungsum after handing over Sikkim Darbar to his Chief Minister Yukthing Arup. As the Sikkim force was not well prepared to encounter the external enemy, they captured the Sikkim Palace and took the king's regent Yuk Thing Arup as a captive to the Bhutan Palace where his son Joom Tashi was born. The Bhutan Government ruled Sikkim for eight years but did not bother to learn about the boundaries of Sikkim and so the territory of Limboo Chiefs remained unknown to them. When the Sikkimese King then grew up to be a young man, he presented the case before the then Dalai Lama and pleaded him for his assistance. As a result of it, the Dalai Lama wrote a letter to the Bhutanese King requesting him to withdraw his Bhutanese force from Sikkim because Tibet, Bhutan and Sikkim being the lands of same nationality, there should be a friendly feeling among them. Tibet should be like father, Bhutan the mother; and both, as their own child should love Sikkim. As soon as the letter reached the Bhutan Palace, the King sent an immediate order to his military officers to withdraw the Bhutanese soldiers from Sikkim. When all of them withdrew from Sikkim, King Chagdor Namgyal returned to his native land and took charge of his Kingdom (Namgyal & Dolma, 1908:18).

Raja Chagdor married a lady of U in Tibet, who is known as the Lhogyelma. By her he had a son, afterwards Raja Gyurmed Namgyal. Chagdor came to Sikkim via Khangpachen pass and reoccupied the Palace of Rabdentse. The date of his arrival to Sikkim in not known. Upon the return of the Bhutanese forces which were in the west of Teesta to Bhutan, it was found that those forces which had occupied the East-Teesta portion of Sikkim, such as Kalimpong, Damsong, Dalling, Jongsa and all the places this side of the Tagong La hill, had settled down and it was found impossible to remove them. So the reason of the cessation of the above places to Bhutan were mainly as they are mentioned in the Sikkim Gazetteer.

As soon as Chagdor came back from Tibet, he expelled the remainder of the Bhutanese forces that still loitered in Sikkim East of Teesta river. But subsequently, another Bhutanese force under the leaders named Magpon Agyal, Rampa and Rupa again invaded Sikkim, and took formal possession of the lands lying between the Teesta and Rongpa. They were encouraged to come by one Shal-ngo Achhok, who was not in good terms with the Raja. So Achhok sought refuge under the Bhutanese and it was thus that the Bhutanese forces were sent to invade Sikkim again. But subsequently he was betrayed by the Bhutanese king and was killed at Ambiyok near Daling fort and the Bhutanese thenceforth took possession of all the lands and inhabitations there of, between Teesta and Tagong La in 1718 A.D.

Chagdor remained several years in Lhasa, studing hard, and gradually rose in scholastic eminence, until he became Chi-Tung-yig to the Dalai Lama. His long sojourn amongst the learned priests at Lhasa had exercised a great influence towards monasticism in the Raja, and he accordingly on his return devoted himself to the cause of religion and learning. Aided and encouraged by Lama Jig-med Paw, he founded the present monastery of Pemiongchi for Ta-Tsongs (Pure Lamas), and richly endowed it. The establishment was to consist of 108 monks, and the Raja himself shaved his head and became number one. He also appointed 108 lay officials to serve with the Lamas and assist them in secular business. He made a rule to depute second son of every Bhutia family for Buddhist learning – Lama in the nearby Monastery. Among other works he wrote a book on monastic discipline, called *Chags-Yig*, composed a religious dance – *Rong-Chham*, in honour of *Takpoo* or warlike demons, and design an alphabet for the use of his Lepcha subjects. During his reign Kargyu sect (Mahayana) of Lamaism was established. He died in 1733 (Sikkim Coronation 1965: 2). (Note: it is not known whether he developed out of the Maw Rong Hang's Lepcha script "*Rong Chhyo*" or devised independently).

For his services in the Dalai Lama's household, Chagdor was given the fiefs of Piahte-gong (Pendi-gong) near Lake Yam-dok-tsho and of Re-Rin-Chhen-Tse-Jong near Shigatzi in Tibet. These were enjoyed by his successors up to the beginning of the nineteenth century; when the Tibetan Government resumed them in Tsugphud Namgyal's minority, in the confusion resulting from the Nepalese Tibetan war in 1791 A.D.

But he was not allowed to rule his country peacefully as his own stepsister; Pende Wangmo conspired against him, assassinated him and tried to usurp his property in 1716 A.D. But she also could not enjoy her stepbrother's property for the king's men also murdered her soon after the king's assassination (Gazetteer of Sikkim: 11-14; Chemjong, 1967: 165-167; Namgyal & Dolma, 1908: 37-50; Dahal, 1984: 28-29).

2.5. The Fourth Chogyal Gyurmed Namgyal (1707-1733 A.D.):

Chogyal Gyurmed Namgyal was born in 1707 and was the son of Chagdor Namgyal by his Rani whom he married in Lhasa, the daughter of the Lowo Raja. He ascended the throne in 1717. He married a lady from Mindoling Tibet known as Mingyur Paldon in 1721. The marriage could not be a happy one owing to the ill luck of the Sikkimese in general. The Raja took a dislike to the lady on account of her homely appearance; and the coldness of their feelings towards each other; accordingly he removed himself to the Di-chhenling monastery. Worn out by these dissentions and in disgust, the Raja disguised himself as a fakir and went on a pilgrimage to Tibet. The 9th Karmapa Lama recognized him. Shortly after, the Raja returned to Sikkim, but his behaviour was still inconsistent with his position. The Rani returns to Mindol-Ling. In 1734 the Raja was taken dangerously ill, and being on his deathbed was asked to name his heir. In reply he pointed out a daughter of Neer Gahden of the Tak-chhungtar family, of Sing-Jyang and has a son by him. The son was called Namgyal Phuntshog. The Raja shortly afterwards died (Namgyal & Dolma, 1908: 50-59; Risley, 1894:14-15).

He ruled for 17 years. During his reign, in 1725 a Lepcha chief Tasso Bidur, of the Chyakung estate conspired against the king with a Magar Chief and tried to stop the revenue of Siliguri district. He collected many Lepcha and Mangar soldiers to revolt against the King. But he was timely checked and put to death by the king at a place called Garat below Badamtam of the Darjeeling district. From that time, the Lepcha subjects of Sikkim were not too loyal to the Bhutia King of Sikkim (Chemjong, 1967:166).

2.6. The Fifth Chogyal Namgyal Phuntsog (1733-1780):

Chogyal Namgyal Phuntsog was born in 1733. The Changzod Tamding of the Tsechudar family refused to acknowledge the legitimacy of Namgyal Phuntsog, and assumed the reign of government. For three years (1738 to 1741 A. D.) or so Tamding declared himself as "Gyalpo" and sat on the throne of Rabdentse, but finally the Lepcha or national party in favour of Namgyal Phuntsog gained strength, and Tamding was forced to flee to Lhassa and lay his cause before the Tibetans. During the quarrel there were several fights, and bloodshed on either side (Namgyal & Dolma, 1908: 59-68; Risley, 1984:16).

To settle this dispute and the succession, the Tibetans sent a commission under one Rabden Sherpa Gyalpo to make a full enquiry and report. Having once obtained a footing in Sikkim he actually reigned for five years. He returns to Tibet only after the Raja Namgyal Phuntsog placed on the throne. He introduced annual taxation in Sikkim; a fixed system of revenue such as *Bahpa, Zolung*, a tax on forest produce, and *Tshong-skyed*, a custom or income tax. Namgyal Phuntsog married

Rabden's granddaughter as his first wife but died without any issue. Later on he married a daughter of Deba-Shamsher-Khiti-Phukpa as second wife, who bore him a son known as Tenzing Namgyal the 6th Chogyal of Sikkim. During this time Changzod Karwang was very powerful. His son Chothup became famous as *Satrajeet* from his victories over the Gorkhas (Risley, 1894:16-17).

In 1741 A.D., a learned Limboo man of the Yangwarok district of North Limbuwan known as Srijunga Teyongsi revived the Kirat literature and taught the *Yuma Mundhum* to all the Kirat people of Limbuwan as well as those of Martam, Hee, Bermiok, West Sikkim. The Tibetan Lamas or "*Ta-Tsangs*" of the Pemayongtse monastery stood against this activity of the Limboo learned man. They put him under arrest, bounded him on a tree and shot him to death. At the cruel action of the *Ta-Tsang* Lamas, all the Limboos of Northern Limbuwan rose against the Sikkimese ruler and prepared to fight them to the last. The Lepcha minister, Changzod Karwang Barphong also raised the Lepcha soldiers who very willingly joined him for the action against the Bhutia Gyalpo. He built a small fort at Singchel in Darjeeling district and kept the infant king in that fort called Fara Dee (Namgyal & Dolma, 1908: 59-68; Chemjong, 1967:166-167).

The Lepcha chief and the Limboo chief consulted one another and declared war against the Bhutia force of Tamding Gyalpo. The Bhutia force fought very bravely but could not stand before the combined force of the Lepcha and Limboo Kirat people. They were defeated in every battle and therefore, Tamding Gyalpo left the Rabdentse palace and fled away towards Tibet. The Lepcha Minister, Changzod Karwang placed the infant King Namgyal Phuntsog on the throne of Rabdentse palace in 1741 A.D. and acted as his regent till the infant matured. From that time onwards, all the Lepchas began to regard Changzod Karwang of the Barphungmu family of the Bermek Estate as their tribal chief with the title of Denshobu in Lepcha and Densapa in Bhutia language. He was famous by the name of Bermek Athing (Namgyal & Dolma, 1908: 59-68; Chemjong, 1967:167-168).

Again in 1752, a Tsong uprising took place but it was timely suppressed by giving full autonomy with the following Royal Proclamation;

"The Tsongs or Subba or Limboo Chiefs are hereby authorized to rule their districts under the title of "Subhas" with all the facilities of enjoying their tribal rites in social and religious functions by beating the royal band called Nagara (Perlge) or cattle-drum." By order of the King of Sikkim from Yarsa Palace Dated Earth and Sheep years (Sa Luk Dawa Dum Chhe 27 Yarsa) (Subba, 1999: 128).

The reign of Namgyal Phuntsog saw the threat of the expanding Bhutan in the West and the Gorkhas in the East of Sikkim. Sikkim was sandwiched between the two mighty forces and the war waged continuously either from the East or from the West. The people suffered due to frequent war and there was no watertight compartment between these three countries. The people sometimes were the subjects of Bhutan, sometimes the subjects of Chogyal of Sikkim and some times the subjects of Gorkha rulers. The common *royatis* (common dwellers) migrated from one place to another in small groups and settled at their convenience (Namgyal & Dolma, 1908: 59-68).

In the year 1770 A.D. (1772 as per Chemjong, 1967: 212), a vast invading force from Bhutan instigated by a Mangar Chief of Sikkim border area came up as far as the eastern bank of river Teesta and their main body took possession of those portions of Sikkim, while the scouts, advanced patrols and skirmishing parties came up as far as Mangbrue and Barphong in Sikkim. One platoon of the Bhutanese force penetrated as far as Ralang and Samdong. But these enemies were, however, entirely surrounded by the Sikkimese force and totally cut off from their main body. They tried their best to save themselves while trying to do so, they were entrapped at a place called Tama Byag at the foot of the Maphila hills where the Sikkimese force had driven sharp bamboo stakes at the foot of the precipice, below which they had hung ropes made up of twisted reeds called the Payum bamboos. Thus, most of them were perished in that trap and the rest who escaped from that catastrophe joined their main body and soon after that they sued for peace. The negotiation was carried out between Sikkim and Bhutan at Pob Chhyu, near the Rhenock hill spur in 1772 A.D. as the result of which the Sikkim obtained the possession of a plot of big land of Bhutan territory situated near Rhenock (Chemjong, 1967: 212; Chogyal & Dolma, 1908: 68-69).

The Gorkhas defeated upper half of Majh Kirat in January 1773; and they defeated Bijayapur on 17th July 1774. Hearing these defeats, the Sikkim Raja had signed a treaty with the Gorkhali commanders, which marked out boundaries between the two states to the mutual satisfaction of both parties. By 1774 the Gorkhas had gained the whole of the eastern hills, including all the territory west of the Singalila watershed. In the tarai the Gorkhas controlled the entire territory as far east as the Teesta River (Acharya, 1968: 612; Stiller, 1968: 110).

After 1774 A.D. there were a number of wars between Sikkim and Gorkhas, but most of the Sikkim land West of Teesta River was under Gorkhas but not formally occupied by the rulers of those areas east of

Singalila range. The Chogyal of Sikkim was not happy with the Gorkhas who had taken away the entire western areas of Teesta River. In 1775, the Sikkim organized two battalions and kept them under Dep Chhang Rinzing of Yangthang and Athing Chhyok .Thup of the Rhenock and invaded the Gorkha occupied areas through Chainpur and the Morong plains. Dep Chhang Rinzing or Dev Thakarpa led his army to the Chainpur Sidhipur fort. They defeated Sidhipur but suddenly a reinforcement of the Gorkha force arrived and drove away to Sikkim again via Tamber and Ilam. The Limboo chief of Ilam during that time was Hangsu Phuba of Lingdom Family, who surrendered to the Gorkha Raja conditionally. The Gorkha Raja also gave him full autonomy of Ilam with Royal Order (Namgyal & Dolma, 1908: 59-68; Chemjong, 1967:213-214).

However, the Lepcha and the Limboo forces under the command of Chhyok Thup and the Limboo chiefs Sunu Hang, Yong Ya Hang, kept on fighting in the plains of Morong. They defeated the Gorkhas in seventeen battlefields. So, the Sikkimese Lepcha General Chhyok Thup Barphongpa was called "*Satrajeet*" by the Gorkhas; and "*Athing*" by the Lepchas. A big battle took place near the Rangeli town between the Gorkhas and Sikkimese. In this battle also, the Gorkhas were very badly defeated and therefore, the Gorkha officers sued for peace. Accordingly, a treaty was conclu' 'd at Bijaypur in 1775 A.D. By this time the Gorkha Raja Prithivi Narayan Shah was dead and his son Pratap Singh Shah had succeeded him on the throne. The representatives of Gorkha and Sikkim with the mediator Tibetan Government representatives fixed the boundary from river Shango Chhyu in the higher hills, Shangdi Jong and river Kankai in the Terai lands. Each of these boundaries was fixed and settled as Sikkim Territory. Any breach of the above treaty would entail the party who broke it, and would have to give an indemnity fine of one hundred *dharnis* of gold. Sikkim also paid Rs.4,000/- in cash to the Gorkhas as money for the slaughter of the four Brahmins upon which the Gorkhas were annoyed. But the same year the Gorkhas broke the treaty and invaded Sikkim through Tapling Jong and Ilam. They took possession of Tapling Jong and Ilam and through these two passes; the Gorkhas entered Sikkim under the leadership of Purna Ale Magar. They concurred the Ralling, Karmi and Chyakung estates. The Sikkimese force under Dechhang Rinzing encountered them at Namchi, (South Sikkim) and repulsed them by killing one hundred Gorkha soldiers. Another Gorkha force of 500 soldiers under a Subedar had crossed river Rangeet and had penetrated as far as Chungthung near Darjeeling. But they were driven back by the Lepcha force of Chhyok Thup (Namgyal & Dolma, 1908: 59-68; Chemjong, 1967:215-216).

The Sikkimese asked help from Tibetan and Chinese governments against the Gorkhas. The Tibetan officials Nalungding Kharwa and Tashi Khangsarwa studied the situation and went back to Tibet. After that, the two Sikkimese generals Bepchhang Rinzing and Chhangzod Chhyok Thup jointly drove away all the Gorkha soldiers from West Sikkim and expelled all the other soldiers who had been stationed at Tapling Jong, Kota Jong and reached as far as Arun. They kept on fighting for many days in Chainpur. When the Gorkha Limboos saw the Sikkimese Limboos fighting for Sikkim, they challenged them at the Nigrum battlefield, so a big battle took place between Limboos themselves. After other Magar Gorkhas reinforced the Gorkha Limboos, the Sikkimese Limboos were defeated in the battle and so they fled away. Those Gorkhas who were fighting towards the Yangwarok, Limbuwan were encountered by the force of Singli Makpen and Yuk Ada and fought near Hastapur fort, defeated them. The Sikkimese force under Chhyok Thup then pursued the Gorkha soldiers as far as the Morong Terai again. A big battle took place at Phu and there too, the Gorkhas were defeated. Mean while, the Bhutia soldiers under Depchhang Rinzing crossed river Arun and attacked the Dingla fort and the Phali fort of Majhkirat and occupied them. After that, the Gorkha Raja again sent a big battalion of reinforcement who attacked the Sikkimese force stationed at the Phali and Dingla forts of Majhkirat. The Sikkimese force was defeated and withdrew from Phali and Dingla forts of Majhkirat and retreated back to Chainpur, Sidhipur fort of Limbuwan. The Gorkhas again pursued the enemies there. In the battle of Sowa near Chainpur, the Sikkimese commander Depchhang Rinzing Thakarpa was hit by a bullet and he died instantly. Seeing this, the Sikkimese force withdrew from the battle and returned to their country. Thus, from 1776 A.D., Chainpur fell into the hand of Gorkhas. The Lepcha General Chhangzat Chhyok Thup was also hit by a bullet on his hand, so he left the battlefield and went to Kalimpong which was under Bhutan and stayed there for his safety. Then the Lepcha soldiers were all scattered everywhere and they returned to Sikkim. The war then stopped abruptly (Namgyal & Dolma, 1908: 59-68; Chemjong, 1967: 217-218).

The policy laid down by Prithivi Narayan was to recruit only the Khasas, Thakurs, Magars and Gurungs. The regular army was officered by Chhetris. The Kirats fought during 1791 on the side of the Gorkhas but they were not regulars. This was also the case when Nepal forced a great crisis in 1814. The Kirats then enlisted were also not reguilars, but were allowed to keep all they might obtain, specie excepted by plunder (Pemble, 1971: 28)

When the Sikkim-Gorkha war stopped at Limbuwan in 1776 A.D., some of the backbiters gave an ill report of some of the Limboos who had sided with the Sikkimese force during the war. The Gorkha officers began to trace out the people who had really sided with the Sikkimese party and began to give them death punishment. Seeing this, all the Limboos who fought against the Gorkhas by siding the Sikkimese King, assembled at a place called Ambe Pojoma, consulted one another and decided to quit Limbuwan forever and migrate to other countries. They were altogether 32,000 in number and migrated in three groups. The first group migrated to Sikkim and settled in the Rangpo, Aho, Rhenock and Mangshila villages. The second group migrated to Bhutan and settled in the Kuching, Tendu and Jumsa villages. The third batch migrated to Assam and settled in Beni, Kalchini and other Mech and Koch villages (Chemjong, 1967: 218-219).

2.7. The Sixth Chogyal Tenzing Namgyal (1769-1793):

Born in 1769 from the third Queen, Tenzing Namgyal ascended the throne of Sikkim in 1780. In 1780, he regrouped the Sikkimese to expel the Gorkhas and achieved many victories and captured many forts but there was no decisive victory. The Gorkha Raja Pratap Singh died in 1778 A.D. His son Ran Bahadur Shah succeeded him. With a view to invade Sikkim he collected a big number of soldiers and also wrote to the Kirat Subbas to make war with Sikkim Raja in 1782 A.D. and 1783 A.D. He provided arms and ammunitions and requested them to join the Gorkha forces.

According to Pradhan (1991) "there is no evidence of a Gorkha invasion of Sikkim between 1775 and 1788. The invasion of 1788 was not an event isolated in itself, but closely connected with Nepal's Tibetan Policy. The dispute was with the problem of debased coinage on the one hand and opening of Trade Route to Tibet through Chumbi Valley leading to Sikkim in 1784. The Nepal-Tibet Trade Policy was violated by this trade route. The logical conclusion of Nepal's Tibet policy was to stop this circumvention by conquering Sikkim itself" (Ibid, pp 131).

In 1788 A.D. the Gorkha force under the command of Jahar Singh who again invaded Sikkim from the Chiwa Bhanjyang and Purna Ale attacked Sikkim from the Maney Bhanjyang and occupied the Laring, Karmi and Chakung estates. Jung Khatri's forces attacked the fort of Nagri near Darjeeling and occupied it. Damodar Pandey was the commander of the Gorkha reinforcement at Kathmandu then. The Gorkha soldiers searched for the Sikkimese soldiers and fought with them. Jahar Singh (Tiurar Singh by Hamilton) entered Sikkim by the Singalila range, crossed the Kalej River and proceeded upwards quickly by the bank and surprised and captured the Sikkim palace of Rabdentse on 28th October 1788 (Hamilton, 1819: 120). The Raja Tenzing Namgyal, Rani and their son had scarcely any time to dress, when they had to take flight. They plundered the Sangacholing monastery. All the Lamas fled from there and hid in the forest. The Gorkhas took out all the Buddhist books from inside the monastery and burned them.

With the help of Bhutan, Sikkim forced the Gorkhas to lift the siege. However, the Bhutanese retired soon because they were allowed no pay, and the country was poor to admit of plunder. On the return of the Bhutanese on 29th March 1789, the greater part of the people of Sikkim submitted to the Gorkhas (Hamilton, 1819: 120-121). Another Gorkha force, more numerous and more powerful subsequently reinforced the Gorkhas which took possession of all the country beyond river Teesta. They sent out parties to pry and prowl about all the valleys of river Teesta and its tributaries. Settling down in the Southern and Western sides of river Teesta, they proceeded to take possession of every Jong or Fort and monastery. They stripped off the properties and administrative powers of every fort and monastery. Thus, the Gorkhas remained masters of Sikkim, beyond the Teesta, while the Raja took to flight and all the Sikkimese were compelled to take refuge in the valleys of the rivers, hills and caves suffering great privations and hardships (Namgyal & Dolma, 1908:76-79; Chemjong, 1967:221-223).

In 1791, the Tibetan Government deputed the Phari Shar Jong to Sikkim, who along with layman and Lamas convened a meeting. They summoned the Gorkha leader Johar Singh from Rabdentse, and told him that as long as they did not get a communication from Nepal, he must vacate Rabdentse and retire at Bijapur, and he did so for a time (Namgyal & Dolma, 1908:76-79; Chemjong, 1967:221-223).

The boundary of Nepal in the east remained extended upto the Teesta both in the hills and the plains. For some years, Risley says, Pemiongchi and all the south Testa tract paid rent to Nepal, until in 1815 (Risley, 1894: 19). Thus, in the first decade of the nineteenth century, the area, often referred to as **"Greater Nepal"**, extended for 1300 miles from the Satlaj in the west to the Teesta in the east (Pradhan, 1991: 138).

At that time, Kalimpong was under a Bhutan Raja and the Lepcha General Chhangzod Chhyok Thup was also hiding there. A party of the

Gorkha force under Subedar Birey Pun, crossed river Teesta and attacked a Lepcha village at Parvung. After a fierce combat, the Lepcha fighters were defeated and they fled away and hid in the dense forest. The Gorkhas built a fort at Rangkenpong and after placing some soldiers to guard, Birey Pun returned to join his main party. However, the soldiers returned after a few days to their main party. Thus, the Gorkha Raja remained the ruler of Sikkim beyond river Teesta or of Western Sikkim including Pemiongchi Estate, Darjeeling, Kurseong and Siliguri for nearly 25 years i.e.1789 to1814 (Namgyal & Dolma, 1908:76-79; Chemjong, 1967: 221-223).

The Sikkim Raja was harassed by the frequent attacks of the Gorkhas so he shifted his capital from Rabdentse to Tumlong in 1814 and kept on writing to the Tibetan Government and the China government for help against the Gorkhas. Mean while, the Sikkim Raja's Bhardar wrote an official letter to the Gorkha Raja through a Kirati Subha Yudimma Rai of Limbuwan, to send a Royal order or Lal Mohor for the land of Western Sikkim or the land between river Teesta and the Singalila mountain ranges. The letter states that "the land situated between the Singalila range in the west and river Teesta in the east has already been ceded to Gorkha Kingdom and even at present it has been given to them so kindly request the Gorkha Raja Sri Panch to confer upon us with a Royal Order or Lal Mohor for the same. The day the Lal Mohor reaches here we shall send a tribute of horse for the same. Dated Chait 11th from Sikkim." The above letter is an official letter sealed with the red seal of the Sikkim Raja and proves the fact that Western Sikkim including Darjeeling, Kurseong and Siliguri were under the Gurkha Raja upto 1814 A.D. (Namgyal & Dolma, 1908:76-79; Chemjong, 1967: 224-226).

Although the Gorkhas were engaged in resisting the Chinese invasion in Nepal in 1792, the Gorkha officers did not hesitated to administer Western Sikkim. However, a Sikkimese force under Jomgyal and Yuk Namchha tried to expel the Gorkha force under Jung Khatri from the Nagri Jong situated to the south of Darleeling. They attacked the Nagri Jong one night and a terrible fight started. The Gorkha soldiers fought so ferociously against the Sikkimese force, which had combined, with the Kirat force of Khambu Rai and Yakha Rai soldiers that they could not be dislodged the fort of Nagri (Namgyal & Dolma, 1908: 76-79; Chemjong, 1967: 227-228).

The Arbitration Treaty of Gorkha, Bhot and China 1792 A.D. were signed. There was no representation from Sikkim and was assumed that "they were conquered and powerless". However, during the discussion the King Thang Thai Tsung said that the Royal family and Sikkim people

of a Political Officer who so prominently represented the economic and military power of the British Empire, and until his retirement in 1908, White effectively ruled Sikkim through a Durbar that he appointed and controlled. When White took up his position, Sikkim had no police, no law courts, no public works, no secular education system, and no public health system. White was expected to develop his domain, but imperial government funding for this was limited to a subsidy of Rs.12,000 per annum. This was originally paid directly to the Sikkimese ruler, but with White determined to stamp his authority over the state, the Chogyal was effectively exiled from Gangtok until 1895, and after his banishment the subsidy from "towards the expense of management of the State by a British Officer" suggesting that the Political Officer used this money for his own expenses (White, 1992: 3).

In order to obtain the finance necessary to create and develop the State structures seen by the British as essential to modern government, White initiated a series of revenue-raising measures in Sikkim. A land revenue settlement was made, forest excise measures were introduced, and acting through the council that he dominated, White was able to introduce the popular measure of increasing immigration from Nepal in order to enlarge the tax base and raise agricultural production. White introduced **diarchy taxation system** in 1889 for the two ethnic the Bhutia-Lepcha and Nepali groups; and thus sown the seed of discontentment and dissatisfaction amongst the Bhutia-Lepcha and Nepali inclusive of the Tsong community of Sikkim. White further revised this diarchy taxation system in 1898. For the first time White, clubbed the Tsongs with the migrant other Nepalese for taxation. Within a decade the revenue of the Sikkim state which in 1891 was home to just Rs.30,458/=, had increased to over Rs.22,00,000/= per annum (White, 1992: 27). This income enabled White to begin financing modernization initiatives such as the education of Sikkimese youths in British India and the introduction of allopathic, or what is popularly known as "Western" medicine (Risley, 1894).

2.11. The Tenth Chogyal Sidkyong Tulku (1879-1914):

In 1879, the first wife of the 9th Maharajah of Sikkim, Thutob Namgyal, gave birth to their second son, Sidkeong Namgyal (Tulku), following the birth of a daughter in 1876 and their first son, Tsodag Namgyal, in 1878. The Maharani died during childbirth in 1880, and the years that followed were difficult ones for the Maharajah, as the interests of Sikkim clashed with those of the British Indian empire. Following the conflict of 1888, a British Political Officer was appointed to oversee the administration of Sikkim. The officer selected, John Claude White (1853-1918), was a mean, petty and domineering individual who, during the following two decades in which he dominated the state of Sikkim, carried on a long vendatta against both the Maharajah and his son Tsodag Namgyal. J.C.White's successors in Gangtok Residency included some of the outstanding frontier officers of the British empire, men such as Lieutenant-Colonel F.M. Bailey (1882-1967) and Lieutenant-Colonel Sir W.F. O'Connor (1870-1943), as well as forward-thinking and culturally sensitive diplomats such as Sir Charles Bell (1870-1945) and Sir Basil Gould (1883-1956) (Alex McKay, 2003: 27).

In February 1899, the British Government of India recognized Sidkeong Tulku as the heir to the throne of Sikkim, passing over Tsodag Namgyal, who had sided with his father in various disputes with J.C.White, and who remained in exile in Tibet while his father managed an uneasy reconciliation with the British. In so doing, White apparently hoped to make a clean break with the past, and to install as Sikkim Maharajah a more compliant ruler (Namgyal and Dolma, 1908: 98-142). The Maharajah Kumar had learned Hindi and Tibetan in 1893-95 from the Rajah Tendook at Bhutia Basti near Darjeeling, and as early as 1895, the British had sought to educate him in the English language. In 1899 he was sent to St. Paul's School at Darjeeling. In 1906 he was sent to Pembroke College Oxford, where Mr Bernard Blackiston was to be his tutor. He was given education on forestry and agriculture, political economy, especially tax, and Indian law. After his study he was given a study tour to America, Japan, China, Hong Kong, and many other countries. He wanted to marry a Japanese but could not find a suitable girl. He also wanted to marry Ma Lat daughter of Limbin Mintha of Rangoon, but finally married Cheoni Wangmo, a lady from the Tibetan aristocracy. A few months later the Kumar succeeded his father in February 1914, but the young man himself died on 5th December of that year, apparently from the effects of a fever while suffering from jaundice (OIOC, V/10/1977). Cheoni Wangmo travelled to Bodh Gaya and Benares to burn butter lamps in his memory. The Chogyal Sidkeong Tulku, succeeded his father Thutob Namgyal, as the tenth consecrated Chogyal of Sikkim on April 29th 1914. During the last two years of Chogyal Thutob's rule Sidkeong Tulku was at the helm and it was during this time, in 1913, the abolition of imprisonment as a penalty for non-payment of debts and the ban on settlement of plainsmen were introduced (Alex McKay, 2003: 27-49).

On becoming the Chogyal of Sikkim, Sidkeong Tulku made no secret of his desire to remove vested interests, and his proposal to liquidate the system of landlords created staunch enemies among a large number of landlords. In addition his spirit of independence and his assertive nature stained relations with the Political Officer, Charles Bell. The Chogyal ruled only for about 10 months and died without a heir on 5th December1914 (Sikkim coronation, 1965).

2.12. The Eleventh Chogyal Tashi Namgyal (1893-1963):

Born on 26th October 1893 when his parents were at Kurseong Jail. Sir Tashi Namgyal was the son of Chogyal Thutob Namgyal and Maharani Yeshe Dolma who succeeded his half-brother Sidkeong Tulku and was enthroned on 19th February 1915 as the eleventh Chogyal of Sikkim, but the actual coronation was held on 15th May 1916. His actual name was Tashi Wangyal. He married Kunzang Dechen Tshomo Namgyal (1904-1987) on 8th October 1918. Sir Tashi Namgyal had three sons Kunzang Palzor Namgyal born 26th November 1921, who was killed in air accident, Palden Thondup Namgyal, and Jigdal Tsewang Namgyal born on 26th August 1928; and three daughters Pema Tsedeun Yapsi born on 6th September 1942, Pema Choki Yapshi born on 25th December 1925, Sonam Padeum Trateng born on 27th May 1927.

His long and enlightened rule of fifty years saw many social and economic reforms and all round development of the country, some of which are as follows:

Chief Court was set up and a full time judge appointed in 1916 thereby bringing the judicial functions of the landlords under the supervision of a superior court. He established High Court in 1955 and a separation of higher judiciary from executive was completed. The judicial and magisterial functions of the landlords were completely abolished by 1948. In 1918 complete restoration of Governmen... authority was obtained and the Chogyal was invested with full ruling authority. Measures to eradicate social evils and inequity followed. Public gambling was made illegal in 1921 and in 1924 the use of unpaid labour was prohibited. The use of *Jharlangi,* a form of paid conscripted labour for Government work, was curtailed in 1945 and in 1946 the landlords were forbidden the use of *Jharlangi* from the peasants. Another form of obliged labour known as *Kuruwa* was abolished in 1947. He started Sikkim Nationalized Transport. A Trigonomical survey of all lands was made in 1958 and the land assessed on the basis of this survey did away with the previous system of assessing rent based on the approximation of the quantity of seeds required for a piece of land.

The all round development of the country was uppermost in the mind of the Chogyal and a development Plan was drawn up in 1945, which was however, could not be put into effect for lack of funds. During Jawaharlal Nehru's visit to Sikkim in 1952, the Indian Prime Minister agreed to provide necessary loans, which were later given as aid. Thus, followed Five Year Plans since 1954-60 and 1961-65. The Indo-Sikkim Treaty, for which negotiations were started in 1949, was signed in December 1950 and governed the relationship between Sikkim and India.

Steps were taken to bring popular elements into the administration and all party agreement was reached in 1951 for an elected council with seventeen members, reserving six seats for Bhutia-Lepchas and six seats for Nepalese, and five seats to be nominated by the Chogyal at his discretion. A council was elected and an Executive Council formed, to govern Sikkim in 1951.

The Namgyal Institute of Tibetology for study of Buddhism was established in 1957. The Government Institute of Cottage Industry was also established in 1957. In 1961 he provided citizenship (Status of *addibashi haak*) through the Sikkim Subject certificates to the persons of Sikkim domicile – the Bhutias, the Lepchas and the Tsong (Limboos) origin (Govt. of Sikkim, Notification No.S/277/61 dated 3rd July 1961). This was further amended in 1962 and provided citizenship to the remaining Nepalese domicile on the basis that the Limboos and other sects of Nepali community were considered as one community. Thus, Tashi Namgyal provided citizenship to Bhutias, Lepchas and Nepalese to protect the aboriginal status of these people in Sikkim (Govt. of Sikkim Notification No.S/277/62 dated 16th January 1962, Gangtok Sikkim). This regulation has greatly safeguarded the interests of Sikkimese of all communities. In the rural areas it is only with the Sikkim Subjects who can purchase land and with this regulation this has been firmly assured. He founded Tashi Namgyal Academy, and Tashi Namgyal Senior Secondary School. He was patron of Thundup Namgyal Memorial Hospital during 1917-63.

The Chogyal Tashi Namgyal's benevolent reign of fifty years will go down as the brightest period in the history of Sikkim. The last ten years of his reign saw an all round advancement in all fields, economic, social, political and cultural. Himself a painter of no mean distinction, the Chogyal's rule witnessed a great cultivation of arts and culture. A devout follower of the Mahayana Nyingma tradition, the Chogyal never suffered from bigotry or intolerance in administrative and academic fields. The fruitful reign of Chogyal Tashi Namgyal came to an end at his passing away on the 2nd December 1962 (Sikkim Coronation, 1965).

2.13. The Twelfth Chogyal Palden Thondup Namgyal (1923-1982):

The Chogyal Palden Thondup Namgyal was born on 22nd May 1923 as the second son of Sir Tashi Namgyal, succeeded his father as the twelfth Chogyal on December 1963. He started his schooling at Saint Joseph's Convent, Kalimpong, at the age of six but had to discontinue his studies because of severe attack of malaria. He studied for the monkhood from 1931-34 under his uncle, Lhatun Rimpoche, at which time he was recognized as the spiritual leader of Phodong and Rumtek Monasteries in succession to Chogyal Sidkeong. In 1935 he continued his studies at Saint Joseph's College, Darjeeling, and completed his studies at Bishop Cotton School, Simla in 1941. His elder brother Paljor Namgyal, the heir apparent, who was then serving as an officer in the Royal Indian Air Force, was killed in an Air Craft accident at Rawalpindi, Pakistan on 20th December 1941.

In 1942, Palden Thondup underwent the Indian Civil Service training course at Dehra Dun and after his return he took on the task of administration and subsequently became the principal adviser of the Chogyal in matters of judicial and executive. He was selected as the President of Sikkim's State Council in 1944, an office he held until 1949. He was his father's adviser on External Affairs and led the Sikkim team, which negotiated the treaty with India in 1949-1950. He has been the President of the Mahabodhi Society of India since 1953. The Five Year Plan development 1965-70 and 1971-75 was also implemented during his reign. During his reign three hospitals and 12 dispensaries, two high schools, a junior high school and 91 primary schools were established in Sikkim. For seed multiplication and distribution to the farmers, Hilley seed potato farm was established, scientific cultivation of apple at Lachung and Lachen were started, Tea garden at Temi was started, Livestock farms for sheep, cross-bred bull rearing, pig breeding was started. Rangpo distillery and Singtam Fruit Preservation Factory were established. He was patron of National Institute of Tibetology (1963-82), Tashi Namgyal Academy (1969-82), Tashi Namgyal Higher Secondary School (1963-75), Palzor Namgyal Girl's School (1963-75), and Sir Thondup Namgyal Memorial Hospital (1963-75). He received Order of the British Empire in 1947 and Padma Vibhushan in 1954 (Sikkim Coronation, 1965).

In August 1950, P.T. Namgyal married Sangey Deki (1929-1957), daughter of Theiji Tsewang Rinzing Namgyal of Yapshi Samdup Phodrang family of Lhassa, Tibet. Sangey Deki died in June 1957. She bore two sons, Tenzing and Wangchuk Sisum and one daughter,

Yangchen. In March 1963 he married Miss Hope Cooke, granddaughter and ward of Mr and Mrs Winchester Noyes of the United States of America. She bore one son – Palden Gyurmed in 20th February 1964 at Calcutta, and one daughter – Hope Leezum in 12th February 1968 at Calcutta. On 4th April 1965 a grand marriage of Paden Thondup and Hope Cooke was celebrated. Gyalmo Hope Cooke was deeply interested in Education and in handicraft industry. She introduced new and better textbooks about Sikkimese culture and history in Sikkim. She helped to train boys and girls in the traditional arts and crafts such as carpet weaving and *thanka* paintings (Sikkim Coronation, 1965).

A dispute aroused between the people and the Chogyal administration on Council's election of 1973. The people were demanding "One man one vote". The Chogyal administration sought the help of the Indian Government to settle the issue. While settling the dispute, the Government of India first provided an "Associate Status" to Sikkim through the Constitutional Amendment in 1974; and finally merged the country - Sikkim into the Indian Union as the 22nd State of India through the Constitutional Amendment in 1975. Thus, unfortunately he was also the last Chogyal of Namgyal Dynasty in Sikkim. He died in 1982 due to throat cancer (Sikkim Coronation, 1965; Subba, 1999: 47).

3. The Disintegration of "The Greater Sikkim":

The emergence of "The Greater Sikkim" was held in 1642, started disintegration during the Third Chogyal Chagdor Namgyal with the invasion of Bhutanese in 1700; and the process continued till it finally disintegrated into a constituent State of India in 1975.

3.1. The First Phase of Disintegration of "The Greater Sikkim" Annexation of *Mon-Loong-Kha-bzi* area by Bhutan:

The first Bhutanese invasion of early 1700 A.D. occupied the entire area of Sikkim except Chumbi, Ilam and Limbuwan area of the Greater Sikkim. The Bhutan Government ruled Sikkim for eight years but did not bother to learn about the boundaries of Sikkim and so the territory of Limboo Chiefs remained unknown to them. On the Raja Chagdor Namgyal's return to Sikkim, the Bhutanese retired and evacuated all Sikkim west of the Teesta, but they still maintained their position at Fort Dumsang and retained what is now the Kalimpong district and up to Tegongla. Thus, Sikkim lost the bulk of the *Mon-loong-kha-bzi* area of Greater Sikkim (Gazetteer of Sikkim: 12-13). This area was inhabited by the Mon-pas (Lepchas) during those period. The Maharaja's history says that the lands and inhabitants between Teesta and Tagong La were annexed by Bhutan during the second invasion of Bhutan in 1718 A.D. (Ibid: 41).

While the Ashley Eden (1864: 112-113), has a different story to tell on this as follows:

> "Deb, Raja Jeedhah of Bhutan, aided by Pende Wangmo, the Sister of the Sikkim Raja Chagdor Namgyal, invaded Sikkim, and held possession of it for six or seven years, during which time it was administered by a Bhutan Governor, Tabajung Tinlay, and his Dewan, Phenlay. During the war the Bhutias had seized and confined at Poonakh a Sikkim Chief named Yukthing Aroop – the ancestor of the Gangtoke Kazee, who confined Drs. Hooker and Campbell, and again fought with the British in 1861. The Sikkim Raja on his return procured his release, and the Bhutias on setting him free bribed him to remain a tied to their Government. He had been well treated during confinement, and his son Dzoom Tashi, born during his captivity, turned out a thorough Bhutia; he eventually became the most powerful man in Sikkim, and kept up continual correspondence with the Bhutanese; and some year later, when there was a dispute between Bhutan and Sikkim regarding the boundaries of the two countries, he treacherously gave up to Bhutan all the tract between the present Sikkim border and the Taigon Pass, including Darlincote, Jonksa, and Sangbe, which in those days were richly cultivated tracts. Sikkim, though a very petty State then, was formerly a fair-sized country, reaching from the River Arun on the West to the Taigon Pass on the East, from Thibet on the North to Kissengunge in Purneah on the South".

Risley's view was that the "Joom Tashi is looked up to as the ancestor of the present leading families in Sikkim, and was the father and grandfather of two of their famous men, Chanzod Karwang and Kazi *Satrageet*. it is much more probable that Joom Tashi found himself unable to expel the Bhutanese from their position at Dumsong, and so had to accept the situation and the Teesta boundary (Risley, 1894: 14; Subba, 1999: 14).

3.2. The Second Phase of Disintegration of "The Greater Sikkim" – loss of Limbuwan Area:

During the reign of the Chogyal Gyurmed Namgyal various building and fortification works were done, in which the Tsong (Limboo) subjects were harassed so much by calling them out unnecessarily to fight and again to built forts and walls. In spite of signing a Tripartite Treaty of "*Lho-Mon-Tsong-Sum*", the Tsongs was not given their due share neither in aministration nor in other benefits, and thus were as a common people. The Chogyal harassed them by calling them *Mu-thepa* (*Neptey*). Thus in frustration they finally threw off their allegiance and started ruling their own country by themselves in Limbuwan country. Thus, Sikkim began to loose Limbuwan area – the land of the Limboos of the Greater Sikkim (Risley, 1894: 14; Chogyal & Dolma, 1908: 54).

During Gyurmed's reign, a boundary question arose again between the Bhutanese and Sikkim States. (No date is mentioned for this.) The Tibet Government deputed the Tsang Depon as mediator. Gyal-Tsering represented Bhutan, and the Dagkar Changzod Karmatargay represented Sikkim. The two parties plead their own cases but the meeting ended without any result. In the next year Depon Changlo came from Phari and summoned the two representatives from Bhutan and Sikkim. This time Don-nyer Tenpa Chhopel represented Bhutan, and Sikkim by Butsao Pontsang Dahlo. At the discussion which ensued the Sikkimese representative lacking the boldness of his predecessor, and being unable to present a bold front to the overbearing bullish of the Bhutanese representative, the boundary was fixed at Rongchu, and an almost compulsory agreement drawn up to that effect. Thus, Sikkim lost the area east of Rongchu or Teesta River including the present Kalimpong and the Tarai areas to Bhutan forever (Note: this may be the case referred by Ashley Eden 1864: 112-113 but name of representatives differs) (Chogyal & Dolma, 1908:57; Risley, 1894: 14-15; Subba, 1999: 14-15).

3.3. The Third Phase of Disintegration of "The Greater Sikkim":

(*a*) The Permanent Loss of Limbuwan: The Chogyal Gurmed Namgyal harassed them by calling the Tsongs *Mu-thepa* (*Neptey*). Thus in frustration they finally threw off their allegiance and started ruling their own country by themselves in Limbuwan country. Thus, Sikkim began to loose Limbuwan area – the land of the Limboos of the Greater Sikkim. Further, after the uprising of the Lepchas under the leadership of the Minister, Changzod Karwang Barphong and the Limboo Chiefs in 1941, and the Limboo uprising of 1752 A.D. the Limboo chiefs of Northern Limbuwan ceased to regard the Sikkim King as their overlord and stopped paying tribute to him and declared themselves independent Kirat States from 1741 A.D. Thus, Sikkim lost the areas of Limbuwan (Risley, 1894: 14; Namgyal & Dolma, 1908: 54; Chemjong, 1967:167-178; Subba, 1999: 14-15).

(*b*) Annexation of Eastern Hills & Tarai areas by the Gorkhas: In the Gorkha invasion of 1774 A.D., Sikkim lost the whole of the eastern hills, including all the territory west of the Singalila watershed. In the terai the Gorkhas controlled the entire territory as far east as the Teesta River (Acharya, 1968: 612; Stiller, L.F. 1968: 110; Subba, 1999: 14-15).

According to Dr. Kumar Pradhan (1991) a historian of repute of this region, has precisely demarketed the boundary of the Terai Region of Limbuwan annexed by the Gorkhas in 1774 AD. "...Vijayapur was taken in Gorkha's possession in June-July 1774. ... The land between the Kankai and the Teesta in the plains known as Morang, belonged to Vijayapur. The course of the river helps to dispel the confusion. The Kankai flows in a south-easterly direction from the Singhalila Range, which divides Limbuan from Darjeeling, before it takes a sharp bend towards the east and flows somewhat constantly southward to the plains. The references made by Sikkim were to the upper reaches of the river, that is, it lay claim upon the northern part of Ilam, parts of Pachthar and Taplejung. Till much later date Sikkim kept claiming Kankai as its western boundary. .... The extension of the Gorkha conquest to the east by September, 1774 can be precisely demarketed. Of the different zones into which Nepal is now divided for administrative purposes, the hill districts of Taplejung, Pachthar and Ilam in the Mechi Zone touching the boundaries of Sikkim and Darjeeling lay outside it. The eastern part of the Jhapa district in Morang or the land to the east of the Kankai in the flat land which touches the Mechi in the Siliguri Sub-division of Darjeeling and the Purnea district of Bihar was also not a part of it. The Kiratas, who had accepted the Gorkha rule, had been asked to do away with other chiefs and were told that the terms offered to them did not apply to the Nine Lakh Kiratas of the other side, the otherside being Limbuwan" (Pradhan, 1991: 121-122).

Similarly, the boundary of the Gorkha annexed area of the eastern hills has also been precisely demarketed by Dr. Pradhan. "...The lofty denuded peak Falut, of the Lepchas, on the north-western tip of Darjeeling, is where its border meets with those of Sikkim and Nepal. From these the Singalila range runs northwards forming the boundary between Nepal and Sikkim and southwards between Nepal and Darjeeling. A little above Falut, over the same range, there is a pass called Islimba in Pachthar on the Nepal side; a little further up joining Sikkim and Nepal is the Chiyabhanjyang pass, to the west of which is a place called Chyangthapu" (Pradhan, 1991: 123).

By the end of 1774 the Gorkhas crossed not only the Kankai but also the Mechi in their drive towards the Teesta. Ilam surrendered without a fight. After the promise given to Sikkim in 1775 the eastern border remain peaceful for 13 years. Pradhan also pointed out that the Gorkhas were driven out from Ilam and that of the Sikkimese penetrated as far as Chainpur in 1787 does not appear to be correct (Pradhan, 1991: 123-129).

3.4. The Fourth Phase of Disintegration of "The Greater Sikkim"— The occupation of Western Sikkim by the Gorkhas for 34/25 years (1780/1889-1814):

The official letter of Sikkim Raja's Bhardar to the Gorkha Raja through a Kirati Subha Yudimma Rai of Limbuwan requesting to send a Royal order or Lal Mohor for the land of Western Sikkim or the land between river Teesta and the Singalila mountain ranges clearly indicates that the Gorkhas occupied Western Sikkim from 1780 A.D. to 1814 A.D. (34 years). The letter states that: "..the land situated between the Singalila range in the west and river Teesta in the east has already been ceded to Gorkha Kingdom and even at present it has been given to them so kindly request the Gorkha Raja Sri 5 to confer upon us with a Royal Order or Lal Mohor for the same. The day the Lal Mohor reaches here we shall send a tribute of horse for the same. Dated Chait 11th from Sikkim".

The above letter is an official letter sealed with the red seal of the Sikkim Raja and proves the fact that Western Sikkim including Darjeeling, Kurseong and Siliguri were under the Gurkha Raja upto 1814 A.D. (Namgyal & Dolma, 1908:76-79; Chemjong, 1967: 224-226).

However, many other historians including Hamilton (1819: 120), Pradhan (1991) and Kharel (2002) do not agree with Chemjong. The Gorkha invasion of 1788 to Sikkim was sieged with the help of Bhutan force. However, the Bhutanese retired soon because they were allowed no pay, and the country was poor to admit of plunder. On the return of the Bhutanese on 29th March 1789, the greater part of the people of Sikkim submitted to the Gorkhas.

Further, most of the secondary literature seems divided on the actual geographical distinctions between Nepalese controlled Sikkim and the areas under the authority of the Sikkimese Chogyals. F.I.S. Tucker (1957: 57), for example, states that the six thousand troops that were dispatched Sikkim in 1788 overran most of the Sikkimese territory in the Terai and the hills but was unable to penetrate and obtain a substantial gain in area. B.J.Hasrat (1971: 268), however, seems confused in regard to the limits of Nepalese conquest as he states that the Gorkhas possessed most of Sikkim but the area of Nag po ri (presumably this refers to Nag ri – which equates roughly with the modern Indian administrative district of Darjeeling) (Regmi, 1999: 55) was held jointly by Sikkim and Nepal. This seems to be mistaken as this particular region remained under direct Nepalese control until the end of the Anglo-Gorkha war and the signing of the treaty of Sugauli in 1815. L. F. Stiller (1973) on the other hand shows the eastern border of Nepal as following the Ramam river until its confluence with the Teesta (the territory to the east of Teesta was under the administration of Bhutan). The map in Bajracharya's book entitled "Bahadur Shah: the Regent of Nepal (1992:1), shows that Nepal had possession of all of Sikkim's territory in the Terai south of the Ramam river, west of the Teesta and east of the Mechi river. While it has been established that the Nepalese had control of the Sikkimese capitol of Rabdentse in 1789, what is not known is for how long they occupied this territory to the west of the Teesta and in the hills (Mullard, 2005: 61).

However, from the histroy it reveals that the Gorkhas vacated the Rabdentse Palace and the Gorkha leader Johar Singh retired at Bijapur for the time being in 1791 AD. It appears that the West Sikkim was under the direct or indirect control of the Gorkha Administration from 1889 to 1914 that is for 25 years (Namgyal & Dolma, 1908:76-79; Chemjong, 1967: 224-226; Subba, 1999).

3.5. The Fifth Phase of Disintegration of "The Greater Sikkim":

(*a*) Annexation of Piahte-Gong and Rerinchhen-Tse Jong of Tibet: For his services in the Dalai Lama's household, Raja Chagdor Namgyal was given the fiefs of Piate-gong (Pedi-gong) near lake Yam-dok-tsho and of Rerinchhen-Tse Jong near Shigatzi in Tibet. These were enjoyed by his successors till 1791 A.D. The Tibetan Government annexed these lands after the Nepalese-Tibetan war of 1791 (Risley, 1894: 13; Subba, 1999:14).

(*b*) Annexation of Darjeeling area of "The Greater Sikkim" by the British: O'Malley (1907), in his compilation "Gazetteer of Darjeeling District" has described the process of annexation of Darjeeling as follows:

Darjeeling district contains a total of 1,164 square miles, and a population of 2,49,117 souls (1901). The Sikkim area occupied by the Gorkha ruler was obtained by the British India through the Treaty of Sugouli in 1814 A.D. and reinstated to Sikkim through the Treaty of Titalia in 1817 A.D. under which the whole of the country between the Mechi and the Teesta, a tract extending over 4,000 square miles, was restored to Sikkim, and the sovereignty being guaranteed by the British India. Under this treaty, the British India assumed the position of the paramount power in Sikkim. Ten years after it was signed, disputes arose due to Kotapa's insurrection on the Nepal and Sikkim frontier. Accordingly, as per the Treaty of Titalia, the matter was referred to the Governor General of British India. In 1828, General Lloyd was deputed to effect a settlement. The company with Mr. J.W. Grant, penetrated the hills, which were still a *terra incognita* to the British, as far as Rinchenpong, and during this journey was attracted by the position of

Darjeeling. On 18th June 1829 he strongly urged the importance of securing possession of the place for the purpose of sanitation. After a few years of negotiations a deed of grant on the 1st February 1835 was signed. This was an unconditional cession of what was then a worthless uninhabited mountain; but in 1841, the government granted the Raja an allowance of Rs.3,000/= as annual compensation, and raised the grant to Rs.6,000/= in 1846, and to Rs.9,000/= and Rs.12,000/= in 1868 and 1873 respectively. Thus, the British Company annexed Darjeeling area of Sikkim in 1835 A.D. forever (Risley, 1894: 19-21; O'Malley, 1907: 14-34; Subba, 1999:15-16)

3.6. Sixth phase of disintegration of "The Greater Sikkim"— Annexation of the Terai Region and Hill areas of Sikkim by the British:

As pointed out by O'Malley (1907), the relations of East India Company and Sikkim had been far from satisfactory. The climax was reached in November 1849, when Sir Joshep Hooker and Dr. Campbell were suddenly seized and made prisoners by the Pagla Diwan of Sikkim, while traveling in Sikkim. Doctor Campbell and Hooker visited Sikkim, and were touring towards the Tsola side. The Tibetan Government had issued stringent orders forbidding foreigners to be allowed beyond the boundaries after the Sikkim Raja leased out Darjeeling. The Raja was too aged and infirm and the Tokhang Donyer Namgyal and other Ministers of Sikkim asked the two gentlemen not to go beyond the Tsola range but as they did not mind, they were arrested and retained for about six weeks. Annoyed by this action, in 1860, the British government sent up a force under the Darjeeling Superintendent and annexed all the Terai areas of Sikkim inclusive of Morang area and all the land lying below Rammam in the north, and the Rangeet and Teesta in the east, and the Nepal Sikkim frontier in the west, the areas which were recovered from Gorkhas and returned to Sikkim through treaty of Titaliya in 1817 to Darjeeling. The British Government also stopped annual rent of Rs.6,000/= from Darjeeling. The lands thus attached at one swoop by the British government meant a loss of six Jong-khags, or Kazis' elakhas in the hills, and *Roiyats* in the plains estimated at Rs.40,000/= annual income in cash and kind (Risley, 1894: 19-21; O'Malley, 1907: 14-34; Subba, 1999:16-17).

3.7. The Seventh Phase of Disintegration of "The Greater Sikkim"— Anneation of Chumbi Valley by China (Tibet):

The Macauley Mission was in progress in 1886. In the same year, after the stoppage of the Macauley Mission, the Tibetans advanced in to

Sikkim and built a fort at Lingtu, which they persistently refused to evacuate. In March 1888 the Sikkim Expeditionary Force was sent against Lingtu, which the Tibetans were compelled to evacuate, and in September the campaign ended with the complete expulsion of the Tibetans across the Jelep. In December 1888 the Chinese Resident, His Excellency Sheng Tai arrived at Gnatong, and negotiations were opened with a view to a settlement of the Sikkim-Tibetan dispute, but were unsuccessful, and so were formally broken off on the 11th January 1889. On the arrival in Darjeeling of Mr. James H. Hart, of the Chinese Imperial Customs Service, fresh attempts at the solution of the difficulties were made, and after long interchange of views, negotiations were re-opened towards the close of 1889, and resulted in the convention signed in Calcutta on the 17th March 1890. The convention between Great Britain and China relating to Sikkim and and Tibet was signed which includes I to VIII articles. According to this the boundary of Sikkim and Tibet shall be the mountain range separating the waters flowing into Sikkim Teesta and its affluent from the waters flowing into the Tibetan Monchu and northwards into the rivers of Tibet. The line commences at Mount Gipmochi on the Bhutan frontier and follows the above-mentioned water parting to the point where it meets Nepal Territory. Thus, Sikkim lost Chumbi Valley through this convention to Tibet on March 17, 1890 (Risley, 1894: 26; Namgyal & Dolma, 1908: 105-216; Subba, 1999: 17).

3.8. The Eighth and the Final Phase Disintegration of "The Greater Sikkim" and Integration into the Indian Union in 1975:

The Fifth Council Election held in 1973 served as a turning point in the political history of Sikkim. The agitation that started in Gangtok on the issue of rigging of the election soon engulfed the State. The political parties and the people wanted "One man one Vote" system of electoral practice. The political turmoil that rocked the State ultimately led to the signing of the tripartite agreement on the 8th May, 1973, between the Government of India, Political Parties of Sikkim and the Chogyal Palden Thondup Namgyal the 12th Maharaja of Sikkim. It was agreed to establish a fully responsible democratic Government under the over-all supervision of the Chief Executive to be nominated by the Government of India. The agreement also provided for an executive Council, which was to consist of the elected members of the assembly and to be appointed by the Chogyal on the advice of the Chief Executive. The Chief Executive was further empowered to preside over the meetings of the Executive Council. Any difference of opinion between the Chogyal and the Chief Executive was to be referred to the Indian Political Officer in Sikkim who had to obtain the advice of the Government of India, which was to be binding. This agreement made it clear that the people had more faith in India than in the Chogyal (Bhadra, 1992: 88).

The Chogyal issued the proclamation of Representation of Sikkim Subjects Act, 1974, in the month of February 1974. According to this Act, the Assembly was to be composed of 32 members and Sikkim was divided into thirty-one territorial constituencies and one Sangha Constituency. The Sangha constituency was to comprise the Sangha belonging to Monasteries recognized by the Chogyal. Out of the 32 seats, 15 seats were reserved for the Bhutia-Lepcha and 15 seats reserved for the Nepali Community. One seat was reserved for Sangha and other for Scheduled Caste people. The reserved seat of Tsong (Limboo) community was abolished by this proclamation. Election to the 31 territorial constituencies of the Assembly would be held on the basis of adult suffrage for the first time in Sikkim. Thus, the election of the Assembly was held and results declared. On 10th May 1974, Chogyal inaugurated the newly constituted Sikkim Assembly. A four member Council of Ministers led by L.D. Kazi as the Chief Minister of Sikkim was appointed in July 1974. But the Ministry, in no time, came into conflict of power with the Chogyal. The conflict of ideal, mingled with the conflict of power assumed such a dimension that by May 1975, the tiny Country lost its identity as a Protectorate, first by being an Associate State, and later by completely merging with and becoming a constituent State of India. The Sikkim Assembly, formed through the elections of 1974 with 32 members, became the Legislative Assembly of the State of Sikkim duly elected under the Constitution. Sikkim was allotted one seat in the Lok Sabha and the whole of Sikkim formed one parliamentary constituency (ibid: 134-137).

Thus, the complicated electoral practice denying the democratic right of the majority of the people was another important factor for the end of 333 years of Namgyal Dynasty of Sikkim.

4. Political, administration and Socio-economic Condition of the people during Namgyal Dynasty (1642-1975):

The political, administrative and socio-economic condition of Sikkim during the reign of Namgyal Dynasty was very miserable. Throughout this period the common people were exploited by the Administration-Kazis, Landlords, Thekadars, Mandals and Karbaries. The people were harrassed more during the period of British protectorate period of 1917 to 1949. This could be described briefly as under:

4.1. Politics and Administration:

The Bhutias (Lhorees) according to one authority, are said to have descended from the followers which are said to have consisted of 4 + 8 = 12 (twelve) tribes (4 *Tong-du-ruzhis* plus 8 *Beb-tsan-Gyat*) of the great ancestor of Khe-Bumsa, a prince or chief from Dome in the Kham province of Tibet, while others say that it was from Khe-Bumsa's 3 (three) sons that they descended and multiplied. And when they migrated to Sikkim, the native chief of the Mon or Lepcha Mon Thekong Tek and Thekong Salong, who received them as a prophesized ruler peacefully lived under them. Next when the three Buddhist Lamas assembled at Yoksom and after their failure to control and exploit the people through spiritual authority alone, decided to do so through a temporal institution – monarchy, Phuntsho Namgyal as Raja in 1642 (Namgyal & Dolma, 1908:1, Part III; Bhadra, 1992:76). The Namgyal dynasty adopted the system of "*Lugs gnyis*" and its associated concepts of Tibet for Politacal and Administration. *Lugs gnyis* is probably best understood to be a religio-political theory of state and society, in which the united territories of the political and religious worlds play a complementary, although not always equal, role in the formation and direction of policy. Thus, certain guarantees and concessions are set in place, theoretically atleast, to maintain the balance and stability of both social orders (Mullard, 2005: 77). He selected 12 Bhutias out of the 12 Bhutia heads as *Kahlons* (Ministers) and 12 Lepcha heads as heads of *Jongs* or castles. The Officers of the country appointed were:

(*i*) Changzot (d) : Prime Minister,

(*ii*) Donyer : Dewan,

(*iii*) Trung-Yig : Secretary,

(*iv*) Nyer-chen : Controller (Grand Steward),

(*v*) Ding-Pon : Chief officer over the guards and orderlies in attendance a fort of Jamadar or Subedar,

(*vi*) Chupon : Something like a Havildar or Naik; chief over ten men as the words mean.

The country was divided into 12 *dzongs* (districts). The Raja selected 12 Lepchas from among the superior families of Lepchas of Sikkim "to serve as *Jongpens*" (district administrative officers). A *Koshag* (council) composed of 12 Bhutia chiefs representing their 12 clans in Sikkim was set up to assist the King in administering the country. The local administration was under the landlords (known as Kazi or Thikadars) who were responsible for maintaining law and order in their respective jurisdictions. They were further responsible to collect revenues from the tenants and deposit the required portion of the collection to the country's treasury. In spite of "*Lho-Men-Tsong-Sum*" agreement the Limboos were not given any administrative responsibility. They were as a common *royiats* and exploited for 333 years (1642-1975 AD) by the administration.

Since its inception the Bhutia monarchical system was both exploitative and callous. The king being an appointee of the Lamas and dependent on the Bhutia chieftains was not a superior person but just one among them. The king had to satisfy the Bhutia nobility and thus strong landlordism grew in Sikkim. The landlords could even flout the orders of the king and rule over the area under them most autocratically. The King and his family thus, had the largest and most fertile lands as their personal estates in the country. The Kazis and Thikadars exploited the common, Bhutias, common Lepchas and the Tsongs (Limboos) for 333 years (1642-1975). After the Gorkha conquest of 1774 AD, and especially after the Gorkha's occupation of West Sikkim, the migrant Nepalese (inclusive of migrant Limboos) occupied most of the areas in the Western part of Sikkim. It was after Titalia Treaty of 1817 AD, Sikkim came under the protectorate of British India. During this time, the British Government of India much to the consternation of the Bhutias and the Lepchas of Sikkim openly patronized the Nepali migration. The Namgyal Dynasty continued exploitation of the Limboos along with the Nepalese imposing diarchic taxation policy. Due to this long period of exploitation, even after 31 years of democracy as the 22nd state of the Indian Union, 72% of land holdings are owned by 30% of these elite persons, while the small and marginal farmers constituting 70% farmers own and operate their own land of only 28% of the total operated land (Subba, 2006; Bhadra, 1992:74-80).

India got independence on 15th August 1947. This inspired people of Sikkim also. On 7th December 1947, all the three political parties namely, (*i*) Praja Sudharak Samaj of Temi Tarku lead by Shri Gobardhan Pradhan and Shri Dhan Bahadur Tiwari; (*ii*) Praja Sammelan of Chakung lead by Shri Lhendup Dorjee; and (*iii*) Praja Mandal of Gangtok lead by Shri Tashi Tshering, Shri Sonam Tshering and Shri Kejang Tshering; of Sikkim assembled at Polo ground, Gangtok and merged to form a new party known as "Sikkim State Congress" with the President Shri Tashi Tshering. The newly formed party prepared a seven-point memorandum and submitted to the Chogyal Sir Tashi Namgyal. The Chogyal paid no attention to this memorandum.

Frostated with the situation, Shri Tashi Tshering and C. D. Rai went to Delhi and met the Prime Minister of India Jawaharlall Nehru. After their return the "Sikkim State Congress" continued to press their demand. Consequently, following these demands on 9th May 1949, a democratic government was formed under the Chief Ministership of Tashi Tshering for the first time in Sikkim. This was a historic event for Sikkim. However, on 2nd June 1949, Indian Government sent a troop of army and dismissed the democratic government on 6th June 1949 only after 29 days and the administration was handed over again to the Chogyal Tashi Namgyal. On 11th August 1949 Shri J.S. Lall was appointed as Dewan of Sikkim. He became the actual ruler of Sikkim and immediately accepted various demands of reformation suggested by Sikkim State Congress which were as follows:

(*i*) Household Tax of Rs.6.75 each was reduced to Rs.2/= per household;

(*ii*) The forest Tax was simplified and made reasonable;

(*iii*) The landlords were also made to pay land tax;

(*iv*) Abolished the Private State courts; and

(*v*) Constituted a Government advisory committee.

Thus, the actiual power of Sikkim was shifted from the Chogyal to the Dewan and the Dewan was actually the ruler of Sikkim.

An agreement was signed on 5th December, 1950 between Shri Harish Dayal, Political Officer, on behalf of Indian Government and Sir Tashi Namgyal, the Maharaja of Sikkim and confirmed Sikkim as on Indian Protectorate. The treaty provided the powers of defence, Foreign policy, Exise and Communication to the Indian Government. According to that agreement the Government of India had to provide Rs.3,00,000/ = annually. Thus, Sikkim became the protectorate of Indian Government after the British left India.

In 1952, Indian Prime Minister Shri Jawaharlall Nehru visited Sikkim. Following this Five Year Plan was initiated in Sikkim (Subba, 1999:147-151).

4.2. Socio-economic condition during Namgyal Dynasty (1642-1975):

The Namgyal Dynasty when established in 1642 AD, they aligned themselves with the leading families of the Lepchas but the common Lepchas and Limboos were left to be exploited and subjugated, their fertile lands were annexed, their religion was destroyed or not allowed to practice, and although the Lepchas were converted to Buddhism, they were never accorded high position in the Lamaistic order. They did not allow practicing Yuma religion of the Limboos. They were reduced to the status of serfs at the mercy of the influential Bhutias. They had let to continuous strife between these four communities. The Limboos or Tsongs had a separate status till 1973 due to tripartite treaty of Lho-Men-Tsong-Sum. They had a separate councilor seat reserved in the State Council. This was done away by the May 8th agreement, and the Limboos were clubbed with the Nepali ethnic group.

With Mr. J. C. White's Nepali settlement policy the existence of existing Bhutia, Lepcha and Limboos were threatened. The socio-economic condition of the Lepchas and the Limboos had already gone beyond repair. The administration exploited the poor Limboos and Nepalese through diarchic taxation policy (Subba, 1999: 149; Stiller 65-88; Bhadra, 1992: 74-80).

The socio-economic condition of the common Lepchas, Limboos, and all other Nepali community was extremely poor. Thus, deep-seated hatred and antagonism came to prevail among the majority of the Nepalese inclusive of Limboos and common Lepchas against the minority of ruling Bhutias combined in uneasy alliance with the high class Kazis or Lepchas (Bhadra, 1992: 74-80).

5. Taxation Policy during Namgyal Dynasty (1642-1975):

Unequal treatment of Taxation Policy of the Namgyal Dynasty (Diarchy taxation system introduced by J.C. White in 1891/1898) to the Bhutia-Lepcha group and Nepali Community (inclusive of Limboos) group was one of the greatest causes of discontentment and dissatisfaction amongst the two ethnic groups (Bhutia-Lepcha group and Nepali inclusive of Limboo group). The Government of India took advantage of this bitter feeling of each other's group at the time of annexation of Sikkim into the Indian Union in 1975.

5.1. Rabden Sherpa Gyalpo's Taxation Policy of 1740s:

The Tibetan regent deputed by the Tibet Government was the first man to introduced annual taxation in Sikkim, after he took over the entire administration in 1747 A.D. To every subject who came to pay him respects, he gave a present of a plateful of salt. As salt was a very rare thing, it induced every one to come to him, so that they might secure the *Bakshis* of the plateful of salt. Thus, it was a means to obtain a pretty correct census. He had all the names of the recipients of the salt *Bakshis*, noted down in a roll, and next year the first assessment of taxes was made according to the above roll. This was the beginning of the collection of annual rents from the people of Sikkim. He introduced a fixed system of revenue such as *h Bah-pa, b Zolung*- a tax on forest produce, and *Tshong-skyed,* a custom or income tax. The exact amount or in kind of Tax revenue is not known in detail.

5.2. Taxation Policy during the British Protectorate of Sikkim (1917-1949):

The Anglo-Chinese Treaty of 1980 gave the British government exclusive control over the internal administration and foreign relations of the Kingdom. For almost twenty years, the British (Mr J. C. White) directly administered Sikkim. The Chogyal Thutob Namgyal was effectively exiled from Gangtok until late 1895. Only in 1908 (after Mr White left Sikkim) Sikkim restored the internal administration to its ruler.

J.C. White encouraged Nepali immigration from Nepal, settled them and a series of revenue raising measures were introduced after his appointment as Assistant Political Officer in Sikkim in June 1889. He also introduced Landlordism, Kazism and Zamindarism, Thekadarism and used all unfair means for raising the revenue mainly from the Nepali Ethnic group inclusive of indigenous Tsongs (Limboos). White worked through a coterie of wily Kazis who were the members of the Royal parisad and also the Zamindars. Using their proximity to power, they often claimed that they were the members of the royal family, and that they have the right to exploit, to tax, and to adjudicate the cases of the king's subjects. In short they exploited the masses. These exploitations took various forms (Edited by Gaunley, 2002: 13-27; Kashyap, 1996; Subba, 1999: 43-51). They are briefly described as under:

(*a*) Zamindari System: In the beginning, J.C. White's wily Zamindars (Kazis) and Thekadars used middlemen to allure people in areas, which they wanted to be inhabited. Then from those settlers, the Zamindars collected Re.1/- as tax per house. Out of this the Zamindar kept 10 annas for himself and 6 anna was transferred to the government as land rent. Finally, from every house, the Zamindars collected Rs.6.75, out of which Rs. 5.75, was kept by them and Rs.1/- was transferred to the Government. Later, the Zamindars collected taxes similarly from all subjects of the king.

In addition to this, in the council meeting of 5th September 1898, it was decided that in those lands where the Lepchas, the Bhutias and the Nepalese were settled together; unequal rate of taxation was imposed:

(*i*) A preference rate of 8 annas (half a rupee) per *pathi* of seed swon be charged to the Lepchas and the Bhutias while the Nepalese inclusive of the aboriginal Limboos would be charged 14 annas (87.5% of rupees), and

(*ii*) All the Lepchas and Bhutias should be allowed to graze three cows free of charge while the Nepalese inclusive of the aboriginal Limboos be taxed at the rate of 8 annas (half a rupee) per cattle head.

Thus, the unequal rent to be paid by the farmers was fixed irrespective of the productive capacity of the land. In spite of "*Lho-Mon-Tsong-Sum*" treaty the Limboos were not given any type of concession, and were clubbed with the newly settled other Nepali communities. This was the greatest point of discontentment and dissatisfaction amongst the Nepali Community inclusive of the Tsongs of Sikkim. The unequal rate of taxation impacted the Nepali community inclusive of Tsongs (Limboos) both economically and health-wise. The Kazis, Zamindars, Thekadars etc. grabbed away the land of the Nepalese who failed to pay such a heavy Tax. The Kazis and Thekadars enjoyed the sweat of the common people.

The Kazis and Thekadars used the system of Kalobhari, Kuruwa, Theki-bethi and rents to amass a lot of wealth. As Zamindars, they monopolized control over the agricultural land, where the people simply worked. Unable to bear the suppression of the Kazis, Thekadars, Mandals and Karbaris many Sikkimese families left Sikkim and took refuge in Nepal, Assam, Darjeeling and Siliguri.

During those days, every peasant was made to pay Rs.6.75 as the rent for their dwelling space (*Dhurikhazana*) and this amount was equal to the price of a set of oxen – dream cherished by every peasant. Besides such exorbitant rate of taxation, the formers had to carry the Kalobhari or Black bag on the order of the Kazis. If they failed to do so, even on account of their health, the Kazis put them behind bars, which they maintained in their houses. In Sikkim, the total number of Kazis alone then were just 52. In addition to this there were many Thikadars acting same as that of Kazis e.g. Baburam Pradhan of Namthang, Dhan Bahadur Gurung of Dentam etc.

***(b)* Kalobhari:** The British sold arms and ammunitions to Tibet. The terrain and the inclement weather condition made the trading difficult. The commodities, to save them from rain and snow, were wrapped in cardboards and put inside gunny bags bedaubed with tar. The black colour gave the load its name *Kalobhari* or black load. These loads were 40 kg weight. Besides using these as a means to transporting arms and ammunitions, they were also used to transport viands necessary for British staying at Yatung of the Chumbi valley. On their way back they were loaded with gold dust, which came to Sikkim.

To carry this transport, porters were fixed by the British depending on the Kazi-Thekadar- contractors. For the transport of each bag paid Rs. 2, per labour per day was to be paid but the Kazi and Thekadar contractors kept the whole amount themselves or Rs.1/- and 10 annas and used to pass 6 annas per day to the labourer. The contractors usually

Kazis, Thekadars, Mandals and Karbaris hardly used to pay any amount to the labourers. They did not pay the porters; rather they forced them to carry the load through the difficult Tibetan terrain daring the lashes of rain, thunder, sleet and snow. This system of carrying on the trade and transport was called *Kalobhari.*

(*c*) Jharlangi: The British were supposed to maintain the pathways or trade routes along with the necessary security. But here too they depended upon the Kazis, Thekadars, Mandals and Karbari contractors. They paid them, but the contractors used their peasants to work for them without paying their wages. This system of labour without wage was called Jharlangi system. There was no fixed time or place for carrying on such tasks. The Kazi contractors could order any of their peasants to offer their unpaid labour according to their convenience. Once ordered, the labourer had no choice, but to obey. Disobedience invited punishment. Besides these, the Kazi contractors demanded Jharlangi even to carry the beddings of government officials on transfer.

(*d*) Theki-Bethi: In Sikkim, below the Zamindars (Kazis), and Thekadars, there was a class of people called Mandals and Karbaris. The function of these people was to collect the rents of the Zamindars (Kazis) and Thekadars. But they too, as middlemen, exploited the masses. On festive occasion they were supposed to be welcomed by gifts. These gifts were packed in special receptacle called the *Theki.* It contained meat, curd, bananas and other items. Along with Theki, the peasants also offered, the mandals and the Zamindars (Kazis), their wageless labour. This wageless labour was called *Bethi.* Sometimes, the Zamindars or mandals fed them, but that was all. There was no limit to the amount of time or labour that was to be given, nor was there any specified place for doing it.

(*e*) Kuruwa: Literally Kuruwa means a long wait. Sometimes, on account of the road condition and other factors, people sent to transport the *Kalobhari* wiated for several days for the arrival of the commodities. During such wait, they survived on their own supplies. This process of waiting for a long time on ones own resources was called *Kuruwa.*

The process of exploitation especially of the Nepali ethnic group inclusive of aboriginal Tsongs started during the reign of Chogyal Thutop Namgyal introduced by J.C. White, continued even during the reign of Chogyal Tashi Namgyal who was enthroned on December 5, 1914. A five-member team of "Sikkim State Congress" met the Maharaja Tashi Namgyal of Sikkim on 9th December 1947 and submitted the seven-point memorandum, which included abolition of Zamindari system, equal treatment of the three ethnic group Lepcha, Bhutia and Nepali, and uniform rate of land taxation. However, the Maharaja Tashi Namgyal paid no attention on the request of the people.

Thus, after 1949 when J.S. Lall came to Sikkim, the actual power of Sikkim was shifted from the Chogyal to the Dewan and the Dewan was actually started to rule Sikkim, because of the adamant nature of the Maharaja Tashi Namgyal on the advice of the Kazi landlords. Unequal and exorbitantly higher taxation policy of the Maharajas of Namgyal Dynasty leading to discontentment amongst the people was one of the major causes of down fall of Namgyal Dynasty in Sikkim.

5.3 British Policy in Sikkim as a Protectorate State

According to Dr. M. P. Kharel, Head of History Department, Government College, Tadong Sikkim, "British played a dominating role after it entered into Sikkim through the Treaty of Titaliya in 1817. From 1817 to 1861 they remained outside the internal affairs of Sikkim. However, it remain busy to acquire a place from where it could serve trading interest. The cession of Darjeeling in 1835 could fulfill colonial objective of establishing a suitable place through which it could enhance trade prosperity. Between 1861 and 1888 the policy rested on wooing the Sikkim Maharaja on the one hand and to follow divide and rule policy on the other. They became successful to create pro-British Lepcha faction in the State. By the end of 1888 when the British learnt that the Maharaja in spite of their efforts could not be amiable king they decided to keep him aside and bring Sikkim under British administrative control. This arrangement was effected by 1889 and thereafter Sikkim was fully utilized according to their needs and requirements in spite of the Maharaja's denial in many cases. After 1918 when the next Maharaja Sridkyong Namgyal was moulded under the British line of thinking, administrative power was restored to him. However, political, military and commercial powers were still rested in the hands of the British" (Ibid, pp. 103-104, 260).

"Between 1889 and 1947 about half a dozen Political Officers administered the State. During J.C. White's stay in Sikkim between 1889 and 1908 he had to deal with the Maharaja and establish a new system of administration in the State. White was succeeded by Charles Bell and remained in the office till 1918. F.M. Bailey succeeded Bell in 1918 and continued in his office till 1928. J.L.R. Weir succeeded Bailey in 1928 and continued in his office till 1933. Weir was succeeded by Derrick in 1933 and continued his office till 1935. Sir Basil Gould succeeded Derrick in 1935 and continued his office till 1946. Hopkinson was the last

Political Officer and remained in office between 1946-47. With the achievement of Indian independence the office of the Political Officer was handed over to the Government of free India. Harishwar Dayal was appointed to the post of Political Officer on 1st April 1948" (Ibid, pp. 260).

"A new economic class consisting of Kazis and Newar Thikadars (Mimic) were created and empowered to implement the British policies in the State. Thus, the colonial administrative control through the local elite were incorporated in the British project of Socio-economic transformation of the state. With the help of these "mimic" the British realized their objectives of cultural transformation. They became successful (to some extent) to de-Tibetanize (***de- Lugs gnyis system)*** the Sikkimese traditional administrative structure into a proto-type British Colony different from the classical colony. The reformative measures created an aristocratic class in hierarchical order with judicial and executive powers in the rural areas called the Thikadars, Mukthiyas, Mandals and Karbaris. They exercised powers in favour of the British. After 1918 a three tier judicial system was established" (Ibid, pp. 261).

6. Electoral Practices of Namgyal Dynasty and Empowerment to the People between 1953 and 1975

Electoral Policy of the Namgyal Dynasty was another important factor of discontentment and dissatisfaction amongst the Bhutia-Lepcha and Nepali ethnic groups. The Government of India took advantage of this bitter feeling of each other's group during annexation of Sikkim.

The Maharaja Sir Tashi Namgyal issued in 1953, a proclamation proposing the institution of the State Council and the Executive Council. With a view to instituting the State Council, at first "a complicated system of voting was introduced: the Bhutia-Lepcha candidates were first to be elected on the votes of the Bhutia-Lepcha electorate and later to be re-elected by all the communities. The Nepalese candidates were to be elected on the joint electorate system". The constitution of 1953 was based on the "Parity Formula" whereby it was decided that the seats in the State Council would be divided equally among the Bhutia-Lepchas and the Nepalese communities. The constitution reduced the 75% of the Nepalese majority to make them equal to 25% of Bhutia-Lepcha community. The Maharaja reserved the right to nominate five members to the council. This further reduced the importance of elected members; he introduced diarchic electoral system in Sikkim (Bhadra, 1992: 85).

This complicated voting system was substituted by a more intricate counting system in 1958. In 1967, the strength of the State Council was raised from the initial 18 to 24 with six seats to be nominated by the Chogyal; and voting remained on the party basis and the rest 6 seats to be nominated by the Chogyal (out of the 6 seats, one for Tsong, one for Sangha, and one seat for Scheduled caste were reserved). The term of the State Council was for three years, but during the last 19 years only four general elections were held in Sikkim. Under this electoral practice the Nepali ethnic group were always marginalized. This was another important point of discontentment and dissatisfaction amongst the Nepali Community (Subba, 1999:48-51).

7. After integration of Sikkim into the Indian Union:

After integration of Sikkim into the Indian union the state achieved trenendously in terms of infrastructure development, socio-economic development, literacy development etc. The people's high expectation however, could not be satisfacotory which could be describes as under:

7.1. The First Chief Minister of Sikkim Sri L.D.Kazi (1975-1979):

Kazi Lhendup Dorji was born in Pakyong, East Sikkim in a Khangsarpa family in the year 1904 and died in August 2007. He entered the Rumtek monastery at the age of 6. Sidkyong Namgyal (Tulku), the then Maharaja of Sikkim, took him to Gangtok, where he studied in a Tibetan School. At the age of 16 Kazi returned to Rumtek monastery and underwent strict training of Lamaism for two years. He succeeded as the Head Lama of Rumtek monastery and served for 8 years. He left the Monastery to work with his brother Phag Tshering, who founded the Young Men's Buddhist Association at Darjeeling. The two brothers founded a large number of schools in West Sikkim and were instrumental in bringing about a number of social and other reforms.

In 1945, L.D. Kazi started the Sikkim Praja Mandal and was elected its first President. In 1953, he became President of Sikkim State Congress and held the post till 1958. In the 4th general elections held in 1970, Kazi was appointed an Executive Councillor and was allotted the portfolio of Agriculture and Animal Husbandry and Transport Authority. Under his presidentship in 1973, the united party secured 31 out of 32 seats of State Assembly and became the first and last Chief Minister of Associate State of Sikkim in 1974, and the first Chief Minister of 22nd State of the Indian Union in 1975.

During L.D.Kazi's Chief Ministership, the people experienced both positive as well as negative aspects of life in the State of Sikkim.

The Positive Aspects are:

(*a*) The people obtained the Democratic right in Sikkim;

(*b*) With the integration of Sikkim into the Indian Union in 1975, Sikkim was categorized as a Special Category State of India, which has a provision to provide 90% of Plan funds as Grant and 10% as loan. Thus, the Plan funds for over all development of the State started flowing enormously, and thus laid the foundation of Infrastructural Development in Sikkim.

(*c*) The Lepcha, the Bhutia and the Nepali languages have been recognized as the official languages of Sikkim in 1977. During Namgyal Dynasty (1642-1975) the Tibetan was the official language of the country.

The negative impacts of L.D.Kazi's Chief Ministership are many as follows:

(*a*) Sikkim lost its identity as a tiny Himalayan Kingdom;

(*b*) During 1979, 15 Nos. out of 32 Assembly Seats reserved for Nepali Community was done away with, and thus violated the old laws of parity system established during 1953 in Sikkim. The 15 Nos. of Bhutia-Lepcha reserve seats has been reduced to 12 Nos. retaining one seat for Sangha and Two seats for Scheduled Caste. Thus the parity system prevailed since 1953 was done away with during Kazi's Chief Ministership in 1979;

(*c*) Under Kazi's leadership, the Tsong (Limboo) reserved Assembly seat was done away with by May 8th agreement in 1974, and thus the community lost its separate identity in Sikkim. Thenceforth, the community was included in the Nepali ethnic group once for all.

(*d*) The Central Service Cadre such as Indian Administrative Service (IAS), Indian Forest Service (IFS), Indian Police Service (IPS) etc. were introduced in Sikkim, which has violated Establishment Rule 4(4) of 1974. This will have a long term negative impact to the people of Sikkim in the days to come. The administrative power of Sikkim will be handed over to the plainsman (IAS/IFS/IPS) for ever.

(*e*) Sikkim integrated into the Indian Union without any constitutional protection of its limited area and the people.

7.2. Nar Bahadur Bhandari's Chief Ministership (1979-84 & 1985-1994):

Born on 5th October 1940 at Malbasey, West Sikkim N.B. Bhandari is the son of Balaram Bhandari. He has two sons from his first wife. He married Dil Kumari Bhandari and has three daughters and a son from his second wife. He had his early education at Soreng and Namchi School and graduated from Government College, Darjeeling. He joined Sikkim Government service as a teacher in Soreng School and later served few other schools. In 1974 he formed United Independent Front and contested Assembly Election of 1974. He was arrested under Maintenance of Internal Security Act (MISA) during L.D. Kazi's Government and was kept in Behrampur Jail from 1976-1977. After his release, he formed the Sikkim Janta Parisad in October 1977. Under his leadership, the party own 16 seats in the general election 1979 and became the 2nd Chief Minister of Sikkim in 1979. In May 1984 his government was dismissed allegedly on ground of corruption charges though he had majority support in the Assembly. Later he founded Sikkim Sangram Parisad and successfully fought the Lok Sabha elections in December 1984. In March 1985, his party fought the Assembly Elections and own 30 out of 32 seats and became the Chief Minister of Sikkim again. His wife Dil Kumari Bhandari was elected uncontested for the Lok Sabha seat vacated by him. His party once again returned to power in 1989 for the third time. He lost a vote of confidence in May 1994 in Sikkim Assembly and resigned from the Government. His reign has also seen both success and failure impacting the life of the people of Sikkim.

The positive aspects are:

(*a*) Sikkim saw a tremendous achievement on infrastructural development of roads and bridges, building and housing, culture, ecclesiastical affairs, education, finance, food and civil supplies, forest, health and family welfare, home, power development, public health engineering, social welfare, urban development and tourism.

(*b*) The Limboo language has been recognized as one of the official language of Sikkim in 1983.

(*c*) The Nepali Language has been included in the 8th Schedule of the Indian Constitution in1992.

The negative aspects of his reign are:

(*a*) Liberal flow of Plan Funds and Industrial policy lapses of the State resulted a rampant corruption in the higher political circle and higher bureaucracy.

(*b*) Over dominance of certain section of people on the masses.

(*c*) Developed upper hand by the Business community, which were the means of minting wealth to the high level politicians and higher bureaucracy.

(*d*) Inter-state migration to Sikkim and migration of Nepalese Nationals from Nepal accelerated (as there is no pasport system to check);

(*e*) Denouncement of Other Backward Class (OBC) policy of the country (1984).

7.3. Chief Ministership of B.B.Gurung (May 11, 1984 t- 24 May, 1984):

Born on 11th October 1929 at Chakung, West Sikkim, graduated from Calcutta University; he served as teacher but left for journalism. He married and has three sons and a daughter. Gurung worked under the leadership of L.D.Kazi led by Sikkim National Congress in 1972. Gurung was elected in 1974 Assambly and also in October 1979 and was appointed Speaker on the demise of C.S. Roy the then Speaker of the Assembly. B.B. Gurung was appointed the Chief Minister of Sikkim on 11th May 1984 as the then Chief Minister N. B. Bhandari was removed on corruption charges. But his ministry lasted only for 14 days. The Government of India imposed President's Rule in the State on 25th May 1984.

7.4 Chief Ministership of Sanchaman Limboo (May 18, 1994-December 11, 1994):

Born on 15th January 1949 at Hee Yangthang, West Sikkim, son of Man Sing Subba, Mandal of Hee Yangthang, married to Nirmala Subba and has one daughter and two sons. A graduate from North Bengal University served as teacher, Assistant Education Officer, and joined politics in 1979. Fought election in 1979, elected and served as Minister, Education, Health and Industry under the Chief Ministership of N.B.Bhandari. He became the Chief Minister of Sikkim on 18th May 1994. His Ministry lasted only for about five months when the general election 1994 was declared but remained a caretaker Chief Minister from September 1994 to December 11, 1994. During his period the central act, of OBC was enforced in Sikkim.

7.5 Chief Ministership of Pawan Kumar Chamling (1994-1999, 1999-2004, 2004..):

Born on September 22, 1950 at Yangang, South Sikkim to Ash bahadur and Ashrani Chamling, weaves his poem of idealism primary level in the school and later served in the Police Department during Chogyal's time for some years. He worked as Government contractor before joining the politics at the age of 22. He was elected as the President of Yangang Gram Panchayat Unit in 1982. He slowly joined the mainstream politics and in 1985 he finally got elected to the Sikkim Legislative Assembly. He served as Minister for Industries, Printing and Information and Public Relations under the Leadership of N.B. Bhandari of Sikkim Sangram Parisad (SSP).

In 1993, he defected from SSP and formed Sikkim Democratic Front (SDF) and came to power in 1994 Assembly election. Since then, he is in power as the Chief Minister of Sikkim for the last three Assembly terms.

He has many positive contributions for Sikkim; a few are as follows:

(*a*) Provided social justice to the poor and downtrodden;

(*b*) Allowed to foster the identity and development of the other Hill Tribes of Sikkim (Limboo, Khambu Rai, Yakha, Gurung, Tamang, Sunuwar, Newar, Sherpa, Magar, Bhujel, Thami, Majhi, etc.) by recognizing their festivals, languages, culture and traditions.

(*c*) Provided official language status of Gurung, Sunuwar, Newar, Sherpa, Tamang, Khambu Rai, and Mangar; and started primary education of these languages developing the text books.

d) Recommended, pursued and provided Tribal status for the Limboos and Tamangs.

(*e*) Tourism development accelerated.

(*f*) Improved Financial status of the State.

(*g*) Achieved high level of Infrastructural Development of the State.

(*h*) Seat reservation of 33% for Woman in the Zilla and Gram Panchayat Level was provided in 2003.

(*i*) Decentralization of all 3Fs (Finance, Functionaries and Functions) to the Gram Panchayat Level was provided in 2003. Bottom up Planning process has now started.

(*j*) Reservation for higher studies and Government jobs for all categories such as ST, SC, MBC, OBC, Woman, sports personnels, disables etc. has been provided in 2003.

(*k*) Sikkim included in the North Eastern Council.

(*l*) Rural Village connectivity has improved during the Xth Plan period.

The negative impacts of his reign are as follows:

(*a*) Due to liberal flow of development funds, corruption, which was only upto the Higher Politicians and Bureaucrats during N.B. Bhandari's time has now been percolated down even to the Zilla, Gram Panchayat Units, Youths and Women organizations also.

(*b*) Decentralization of powers has widened the base of curroption and the public funds meant for pro-poor people are being misused due to party system introduced in Zilla and Gram Panchayat Units election.

(*c*) Development is not percolating below the substrata of Gram Panchayat level as desired.

(*d*) The Social Fabric which was brought about by Nepal Unification process of Prithivi Narayan Shah during the later half of eighteenth century (Nepalese people) has now been torn apart into different communities.

(*f*) Considering the huge flow of central fund for socio-economic development. The greatest constraint at present being politicalization of Zilla and Gram Panchayats, and decentralization of 3Fs which enabled the state for widening the base of corruption. Earlier, the corruption was limited to higher Politicians and higher Bureaucrats; but now expanded upto Zilla and Gram Panchayat level. The development does not percolate down to the common people as desired and limited upto the Gram Panchayat level only. In recent years the State Taxation has increased beyond the reach of the common people. The socio-economic gap of have and have nots is widening day by day inspite of huge funds being pumped from the Central Government.

(*g*) He provided undue favour in promotion and preferential posting to the plainsman (IAS/IFS/IPS) at the cost of the local officers of Sikkim, even replacing Head of the Departments (HODs) of Technical Departments. HODs of Technical Departments were reserved for the Sikkimese Officers so far in the previous Governments.

Post-Script:

Sikkim has come a long way from antiquity to Monarchy for 333 years (1642 – 1975), and now to more than 31 years of Democracy as the 22nd state of Indian Union (1975-2006). Sikkim emerged as a country with a vast Hill and Plain areas in 1642, but disintegrated to a tiny country "Sikkim" with limited area by several phases of disintegration, and finally lost its identity as a Himalayan Kingdom in 1975. The country, then integrated into the Indian Union as a constituent state of Indian Union in 1975 with much expectation by the common people of Sikkim but the aspiration could not be achieved as expected due to the following factors:

(*i*) The Indian Constitution adopted for Sikkim, as 371F is just another version of Proclamation of Electoral System of Sir Tashi Namgyal in 1953. It provides 41% of seat reservation in the Sikkim Assembly to 25% of Bhutia-Lepcha (inclusive of Sherpa and other allied) population, equaling 25% Bhutia-Lepcha with

75% Nepali ethnic group, and thus it has deprived the political right of 75% of the common people. The Bhutia-Lepchas especially Kazis were the rulers of Sikkim for 333 years in Sikkim are enjoying the Scheduled Tribe facility of the Government now besides undue advantage of excess seat reservation enjoyed by them.

(*ii*) Due to the above No. (*i*) the eleted representatives or the Government in power always connivence with the 25% Bhutia-Lepcha (who were the ruling class during Namgyal Dynasty) for their political interest, and thus the democratic right of the common people (75%) are ignored.

(*iii*) The land resource distribution is skewed. The ruling class and landlords comprising 30% who ruled Sikkim for 333 years has 72% of land resources in their possession while the common people comprising 70% have only 28% of their own land for cultivation. For equity distribution of land resources the Land Reformation Act, 1977 was enacted immediately after integration of Sikkim into the Indian Union. But the Five Chief Ministers till now have never bothered to enforce the Land Reformation Act, 1977 passed in 1977 so far because of undemocratic constitution 371F holds for the State of Sikkim..

(*iv*) The tremendous influx of population after 1975 to Sikkim from the one billion population of the vast country (India) and Nepalese Nationals (as there is no pasport system) has blown away the aspirations and development of the State. Sikkim's population was only 209,843 in 1971. It has increased to 540,851 in 2001 (increase of 158% in 30 years).

(*v*) The widening base of corruption has percolated upto Zilla and Gram Panchayat Level as the Zilla and Gram Panchayats are also in the formation of political party system. Rampent corruption from top to bottom on both politicians and bureaucrates has nullified the process of development. The development does not percolate down to the grassroot level. The common people feel that they are deprived of all their rights.

In spite of all these problems, the common people of the small state hopes to see a light one day and prosper and develop as one of the developed and beautiful state with a befiting Gross State Happiness (not 9% or 10% annual economic growth) and full-fledged democracy provided by the Indian Constitution of India.

2
Land, People and Livelihood

Sikkim is a small State in the eastern Himalayas, lying between 27° 04′ 46″ and 28° 07′ 48″ north latitude and 88° 00′ 58″ and 88° 55′ 25″ east longitude covering an area of 7096 sq km. Mount Kanchendjunga, the third highest mountain system in the world is located in Sikkim. Sikkim constitutes 0.22 percent of the total geographical area of India. Completely landlocked and criss-crossed by mountains, high peaks, rippling rivers, decorated by array of the flora and fauna, Sikkim is one of the most beautiful States of the country. It extends approximately 114 km from north to south and 64 km from east to west with altitude ranging from 250 to 8598 m. Sikkim came into existence as a country with the integration of the landmasses of the three communities of Sikkim, the Bhutia, the Lepchas, and the Limboos as "The Greater Sikkim", and the boundary of the country extended from Chumbi Valley of present Tibet (China), Harchu Valley and Amochu Velley of the present Bhutan to the East of Arun River (present Nepal) in 1942 A.D. The name of the country was derived from the Limboo word "Su-khim" (happy palace or home) (Risley, H.H. 1894; Subba, J.R. 1999). The country was integrated into Indian Union in 1975. To its north lay the vast stretches of Tibetan plateau, with Nepal on the west, Bhutan and Chumbi valley of Tibet (China) on the east and, Darjeeling district of West Bengal in the south. Being a part of inner ranges of the Himalayas, Sikkim is entirely a hilly state.

1.1. Physiography

The topography of Sikkim is characterized by great variation in elevation, ranging from 250 m to 8,598 m. Almost half of Sikkim is the North District and falls in Greater Himalayan zone. The southern slope of the State is under East, South and West District and falls in the Lesser Himalayan zone. To the north the convex arc of the Greater Himalayas separates the state from the Tibetan highlands. A number of peaks built up of crystalline rocks accentuate the demarcation between Tibet (China) and Sikkim. The high-serrated snow capped spurs and peaks crowned by Kanchanjunga or *Sey-Sey Lungma* (8,586 m), from an attractive feature in scenery of Sikkim. On the left of Kanchanjunga are the peaks known as Kumbha Karna or *Phoktanglungma* (7,710 m), Narsing (5,825 m), Pandim

(6,705 m), and on the right are the Simvo (6,827 m), Nepal (7,162 m), Tent peak (7,315 m), the Pyramid (7,132 m), Fluted peak (6,827 m), and the Siniolchu (3,657 m). A magnificent panorama of snows is always visible on those peaks from almost anywhere in Sikkim (Subba, J.R.1997).

1.2. Glaciers:

Glaciers are the perennial sources of fresh water that is discharged in the two major rivers, namely Teesta and Rangit. A substantial area of Sikkim lies above the snowline which is around 5,000 m. An extensive area remains snowbound throughout the year, especially in the northern, eastern and western parts. The snowfields of Sikkim give rise to several medium and small-sized glaciers. They include Teesta Khangsa glacier, Lhonak North and Lhonak South glaciers, Langbu glacier, Chungsang glacier, Tent Peak glacier, Nepal gap glacier, Hidden glacier, Talung glacier, Zumthul Phuk glacier, and Rathong glacier (Choudhury, 1998).

1.3. River Systems:

There is only one major river system in the State, that is the river Teesta. The Chola range in the east and the Singalila range in the west determine the boundary of the Teesta. The Teesta, its numerous tributaries and innumerable sub-tributaries, drains the entire State. The master stream Teesta originates from a glacial lake Chho Lhamo located at the northeastern corner of the State. While it flows down to the plains, it has scores of tributaries on side of its course. The Rangit River, a right-bank tributary of the Teesta originates from a comparatively low altitude area in the south district of Sikkim. However, its chief feeder, the Rathong River originates from the Rathong glacier in the west district of Sikkim. The Rangit receives quite a large number of tributaries on its way to the Teesta. The Zemu River, another right-bank tributary of the Teesta, originates from the snout of the Zemu glacier.

1.4. Lakes:

Sikkim consists of more than 150 lakes located at different altitudes and all these are considered sacred and holy (Ray and Thapa, 1996). These water bodies are natural and mostly a product of glaciations.

1.5. Climate:

The climate of a locality is the synthesis of day-to-day values of the meteorological parameters like precipitation, temperature, humidity, sunshine, and wind velocity. It is now well established that climate and weather variability play an overriding role in different fields ranging from the development of water resources to the eradication of diseases. It is, therefore, highly essential to make full use of all available meteorological information and services in their planning and at the operational level.

In respect of time, weather is the state of atmosphere at an instant of time while climate may be considered as quassi-steady statistical weather ensemble of earth atmosphere-ocean system for the period of a few decades. The climate of a locality is the synthesis of the meteorological elements that affect the locality. The main climatic elements are precipitation, temperature, humidity, sunshine, wind velocity and such phenomenon as fog, hailstorm, frost, thunder, gale, soil temperature, potential, evapo-transpiration, evaporation, cold waves and heat waves. The climate of a place is mainly governed by the following factors: (*a*) latitude, (*b*) longitude, (*c*) position relative to large-scale atmospheric circulation pattern like monsoon, (*d*) local geographical features like forest vegetation and (*e*) position relative to continents and oceans (Bandyopadhyaya and Singh, 1998).

Sikkim has its own climatic peculiarities caused by its geographical location, relief and altitudinal variation. As such, temperature conditions vary from sub-tropical in the southern lower parts to cold deserts in the snowy north. It is the most humid region in the whole range of the Himalayas, because of its proximity to the Bay of Bengal and direct exposure to Southwest monsoon. The State is the catchments of the Teesta river and its tributaries which carries most of the water into the Brahmaputra. The climate of the state depending upon elevations varies from sub-tropical humid at lower hills and valley to alpine cold at higher altitude. The state as a whole receives 80-90% of the annual rainfall during monsoon season from May to September. Rainfall varies from 4500 mm (Pangthang, East) to 841 mm (Thangu, North), intensity varying from dazzling showers to torrential rains and snowfall at higher altitude. Relative humidity ranges from 77% in the month of December to 92% in July, the mean annual humidity being around 82% and humidity of 95% during rainy season is not uncommon. The mean velocity of wind varies from 2.3 km/hr. in August to 5.4 km/hr. in April. The maximum and minimum temperature depending upon season and elevations varies from 31.1°C to 4.2°C.

1.6. Agro-Ecosystems:

Sikkim is a land of great climatic contrasts within very short distances. Latitudinally, the basin is located within the subtropical climatic regime. But due to the presence of high mountains, here one can experience climates as varied as temperate, alpine and even arctic type. Elevation plays the prime role in fashioning the climatic types of the state. The differences in climatic types are due not only to the differences in altitude but also to the configuration of the neighbouring mountain ranges which largely affects air movement, rainfall and temperature.

An agro-ecosystem is a man-made ecosystem which is geared to meet basic human needs of food, fodder, fuel, manure, fiber, timber, medicine and commodity crops with some economic returns from the available resources under a particular set of growing conditions. There are three major components of agro-ecosystems, landscape (physiography and soils), bio-climate (rainfall, temperature, vegetation, potential evapo-transpiration) and length of growing period. These components of ecosystems have resulted in different type of land use, cropping patterns, livestock production and productivity in distinguished zones of Sikkim as follows:

Agro-Ecosystem Zonations of Sikkim:

Area	*Climate (Altitude m.)*	*Ecological adaptation*	*Agricultural, horti-cultural crops and livestock*
Lower hills	Tropical (300-900 m)	Wet and rainfed agriculture, sedentary farming, horticulture, livestock.	Rice, maize, millet, wheat, pulses, oilseeds, vegetables, potato, guava, lime, lemon, mandarin orange, ginger;
Mid hills	Sub-tropical (900-1800 m)	Wet and rainfed agriculture, livestock, horticulture and minor forest produce.	Rice, maize, millet, wheat, pulses, oilseeds, vegetables, potato, mandarin orange, large cardamom.
High hills	Temperate (1800-2700 m)	Rainfed agriculture, trans-humane livestock.	Maize, barley, vegetables, potato, plum, peach, pear, peas.
Higher Hills	Sub-alpine (2700-4000 m)	Yak herding, horticulture pastoral economy (wool, cheese, butter, hides) and potato.	Mainly used for pasturage, seed potato and vegetables.
Very High hills	Alpine (4000-5000 m)	Trans-humane groups visit the area.	Mainly used for pasturage, seed potato and vegetables.
	Alpine (>5000 m)	....ditto..	....ditto...

Source: Patiram, Subba & Verma, N.D (2001)

2.1. Sikkim: Land Resources

In Sikkim, like any other mountainous areas of the world, land is a scarce commodity. Out of the total geographical area of 709,600 hectares, only 13.67% of the land is available for cultivation, including current and other fallow land. The statistics on land utilization provide insights to understanding the constraints and potential available for agricultural development in any region. The availability of these statistics thus helps to formulate plans in order to harness natural resources, e.g., forests, to maximize production and at the same time preserve the environment and ecology. The area under forests accounts for 42% of the total and this has tended to increase over time. This is mainly in response to the measures taken by the government and also large tracts of agricultural lands having been converted into cardamom plantations, which require almost 80% of tree cover. Land utilization under old classification is divided into six classes as follows:

Land Utilization (1976-77 to 2004-05):

(A) Land Utilization (Old land classification):

	1976-77	*1980-81*	*1990-91*	*2000-01*	*2004-05*	*+/(–) % 1976 to 2005*
Net area sown	54, 927	78,321	63,254	63,250 (8.91%)	63,250	15.15
Current fallow	501	4,428	3,906	3,910	3,910 (0.55%)	680.44
Other cultivated land excluding fallow	4, 925	4,500	10,830	10,830	10,830 (1.53%)	119.90
Fallow other than current fallow	944	9,474	9,204	9,200	9,200 (1.30%)	874.58
Culturable wasteland	1,153	681	9,807	9,800	9,810 (1.38%)	750.82
Land not available for cultivation	6,613	11,604	14,300	14,300	14,300 (2.01%)	116.24
Total operated	79,062 (11.14%)	109,068 (15.37%)	111,301 (15.69%)	111,290 (15.68%)	111,300 (15.68%)	40.78

Land utilization under new land classification could be of nine types as follow:

(B) New land classification in hectares (2004-05):

Irrigated Area	11,310 (1.59%)
Un-irrigated	49,310 (6.95%)

Non-agricultural Use	6,220 (0.88%)
Barren land	8,980 (1.27%)
Forest/Jungles/Bushes	17,340 (2.44%)
Grasses	4,120 (0.58%)
Uncultivated fallow	8,540 (1.20%)
Cardamom	21,220 (2.99%)
Operational area	127,050 (17.90%)

Source: Bureau of Eco. & Statistics, G.O.S.; Food Security & Agriculture Development Department, G.O.S.

2.2. Per Capita Availability:

The per capita availability of different types of land utilization has declined rapidly over time as a consequence of the mounting population pressure. Per capita availability of net cultivated area has recorded a sharp decline from 0.31 hectare in 1976-77, to 0.27 in 1981, to 0.17 in 1991, to 0.12 hectare in 2001, thus declining 61.29% in a period of 25 years. Similarly, the per capita availability of operational area declined from 0.38 ha. to 0.21 ha.; and forest area from 1.26 ha. to 0.6 ha. at 44.73% and 53.38% within a period of 25 years (1976-77 – 2000-01) respectively. Total operated land was only 15.69 per cent in 2001. The extent of fragmentation and partition of land can be assessed from the phenomenal increase in the number of land holdings from 31,061 in 1976-77 to 56,198 in 1980-81 to 111,302 in 1990-91.

Per capita land availability and Operational Landholdings (1976-77 to 2000-01):

Type of land in hectare:

	1976-77	*1980-81*	*1990-91*	*2000-01*	*+/(-) % 1976 to 2005*
Net cultivated area	0.31	0.27	0.17	0.12	(-) 61.29
Operated area	0.38	0.36	0.28	0.21	(-) 44.73
Land for non-agricultural use	0.33	0.38	0.21	0.03	(-) 90.91
Forest area	1.26	0.83	0.65	0.60	(-) 52.38
Total No. of operational holdings	31,091	56,198	52,697		(+) 64.60
Area of operational holdings	79,540	109,068	111,302		
Average size of holdings	2.56	1.94	2.11		(-) 17.25

Source: Food Security & Agri. Dev Depart. G.O.S.; Agriculture Census 1976-77, 1080-81, 1990-91, 2000-01 (provisional).

2.3 Distribution of Landholdings:

The extent of fragmentation and partition of land can be assessed from the phenomenal increase in the number of land holdings from 31,091 in 1976-77 to 56,198 in 1980-81, to 52,697 in 1990-91. In 1990-91 the lowest strata of landholders, the marginal holders, representing about 50% of the population, held 10.3% of the total operational land area. The east district had the highest concentration of landholdings by marginal farmers both in terms of number of holdings (56%) and area (12.8%). In contrast, farmers with large holdings (more than 10 hectares) accounted for 2.3% of the landholdings, but owned 20.2% of the operational area. The north district had the highest number of large farmers who, with 5% of the operational holdings, owned over 30% of the operable land within the district. However, except in the east district, landholdings and operable area are well distributed at least among the small and semi-medium farmers.

Distribution of landholdings and area (in %) by size classes (1976-91):

Category	*1976-77*				*1980-81*				*1990-91*			
	No.(%)	*%*	*Area (%)*	*%*	*No.(%)*	*%*	*Area*	*% (%)*	*No.(%)*	*%*	*Area*	*% (%)*
Marginal	34.30	59.53	6.84	21.00	45.43	68.71	10.97	28.20	49.56	70.76	10.30	28.00
Small	25.23		14.17		23.27		17.23		21.19		17.70	
Semi-medium	23.92	40.47	26.44	79.00	19.44	31.29	27.97	71.80	17.19	29.24	23.68	72.00
Medium	13.79		31.66		10.30		30.77		9.68		28.11	
Large	2.75		20.90		1.55		13.06		2.37		20.20	

Source: Agri. Census 1976-77, 1980-81, 1990-91.

The small and marginal farmers were 59.53% during 1976-77 had increased to 68.71% in 1980-81, and 70.76% in 1990-91. The categories were holding 21% of operational area in 1976-77, increased to 28.20% in 1980-81, and again decreased to 28.00% in 1990-91 of the total operational area.

The Semi-medium, medium and large category farmers were 40.47% in 1976-77, declined to 31.29% in 1980-81, and 29.24% in 1990-91. They were holding 79% in 1776-77, declined to 71.80% in 1980-81 and 72% in 1990-91 of the total operational area.

2.4 Economic Activities and Livelihood in Mountainous Sikkim:

About 89% of the population of Sikkim is living in the rural areas (72% in the country) (Census of India 2001) and the economic activity of mountainous Sikkim is primarily a mix-farming – agriculture, horticulture and livestock rearing, in a limited cultivable land resources.

2.5 Cropping Pattern:

The cropping pattern of a region is determined by a variety of factors, most notably, elevation, topography, precipitation and so on. All kinds of seasonal, off-season and perennial crops can be grown in Sikkim due to climatic variations caused by altitudes. The mixed farming system of agriculture, horticulture and livestock rearing practices are common in Sikkim. The climate of Sikkim is conducive for growing a large number of high-value cash crops such as cardamom, seed potato, ginger, variety of fruits, off-season vegetables and numerous other horticultural crops along with agricultural crops and livestock. In general, maize - ginger inter-cropping or maize-urd are common practices in low and mid elevation dry-fields; paddy–maize/wheat/tori/potato crop rotation at lower elevation; orange-legumes/ginger at mid elevation, cardamom at mid and higher elevation, seed-potato-maize or maize-soybean or seed potato-pea/soybean/temperate fruits at high elevation are common crop rotations. The cropping patterns of the State have undergone metamorphic changes since the merger with India in 1975. These changes are significant indicators of the ongoing process of agricultural transformation from cereal-dominated subsistence agriculture to high-value, cash-crop dominated commercial horticulture.

2.6. Horticulture Transformation:

Sikkim's diverse ecological conditions ranging from tropical to alpine support the cultivation of a variety of fruits, vegetables, in and out of season, and are also excellent for commercial crops like cardamom, ginger, orange, etc. The present trends towards rapid expansion of horticultural crops will have positive implications for improving food and economic security of the farmers of Sikkim. However, perusal of yield data and other parameters like net income per ha, market demand, peak season of arrivals and price trend in major markets should be kept in mind to regulate the production-marketing chain. Ginger, Vegetable farming, seed potato farming in horticulture and also livestock rearing especially dairying has particularly helped small and marginal farmers of Sikkim to come out of poverty trap. The concern of such small and marginal farmers today is sustainability of the option and not the alternative.

2.7. Changes in Area of Major Crops cultivated in Sikkim:

The precise changes in cropping patterns in terms of area under different agricultural and horticultural crops from 1975-76 to 2004-05, indicates a definite shift in cultivation towards horticultural crops.

Temporal changes in area ('000 ha) of major crops cultivated in Sikkim 1975-76 to 2004-05:

Crops	*1975-76*	*1985-86*	*1995-96*	*2000-01*	*2004-05*	*Gain/Loss in 3 decades (%)*
Agricultural Crops:						
Paddy	11.40	15.90	15.94	15.21	14.74	29
Wheat	0.15	10.10	8.42	7.21	5.74	—
Maize	28.50	8.10	39.94	39.90	36.70	29
Other cereals	7.20	9.00	8.27	7.69	7.39	3
Total Cereals	47.25	73.10	72.57	70.01	71.96	52
Pulses	1.70	9.50	6.73	6.03	6.71	295
Oilseeds	2.00	10.75	9.73	9.99	9.95	398
Total Agri. Crops	50.95	93.35	89.03	86.03	88.62	74
Hosticultural Crops:						
Fruits	2.90	9.05	9.20	9.43	8.24	184
Vegetables	1.00	3.80	5.80	6.89	9.01	801
Potato	2.40	5.00	5.50	6.20	7.50	213
Other root & tuber crops	0.10	0.20	0.50	0.40	0.41	310
Large cardamom	10.00	20.90	23.55	23.48	24.80	148
Ginger	0.50	2.30	4.50	5.00	6.52	1204
Turmeric	—	—	0.20	0.40	0.52	—
Floriculture	—	—	0.02	0.04	0.08	—
Total Horti. crops	16.90	41.25	49.27	51.84	57.08	238
Total Cropped Area	67.85	134.60	138.30	137.87	145.70	115
Area under Agri. Crops (%)	75.09	69.35	64.37	62.40	60.82	
Area under Horti. Crops (%)	24.90	30.65	35.63	37.60	39.18	

Source: F S & ADD; Horticulture &CCD, GOS

The figure mentioned above highlights that; although the gross cropped area under agricultural crops during 1975-76 to 2004-05 increased from 50,950 ha to 88,620 ha (74%), the proportion of cultivated area of total cultivated crops has declined markedly from 75.09% in 1975-76 to 60.82% in 2004-05. All cereal crops have witnessed a decline, to varying degrees, with maize constituting 41% of total cereals being recorded at the lowest (42% in 1975-76 to 25% in 2004-05), followed by rice (17% to 10%) and other cereals (11% to 5%). Wheat, almost non-existent in 1975-76, was introduced in the early 1980s and now occupies nearly 4% of the total cultivated area.

The area under pulses and oilseeds increased by 295% and 398% respectively with the increase of proportion to the total cultivated area of 2.5% to 4.6% on pulses and 2.9% to 6.8% on oilseeds during the last 29 years ending 2004-05.

On the other hand, conforming to the ongoing process of horticultural-led transformation, the proportion of gross cropped area under horticultural crops has increased markedly from 25% in 1975-76 to 40% in 2004-05. The overall increase in area under horticultural crops was 16,900 ha in 1975-76 to 57,080 ha in 2004-05 (238%) as compared to area under agricultural crops during the same period (74%).

The overall low level of cropping intensity is attributed to various factors:

(*a*) Extensive cultivation of Large cardamom exits on 30 –50% or even upto 75-100% hill-slopes as perennial mono-crop occupying about 39.2% of the total "Net area sown". If the cardamom area is excluded from the "Net area sown", the remaining "Net area sown" will be only about, 57,421 ha., 39,704 ha., 39,770 ha., and 38,450 ha. during 1975-76, 1985-86, 1995-96, 2000-01, and 2004-05 for the remaining agricultural and horticultural crops respectively. If the cardamom area is excluded from the "Net area sown" the cropping intensity for the rest of the agricultural and horticultural crops, will be very high for a mountainous State like Sikkim. In that case the cropping intensity works out to be about 129% in 1975-76, 198% in 1985-86, 298% in 1995-96, 288% in 2000-01 and 314% in 2004-05.

(*b*) Limited availability of area having less than 30% slope about (6%), and about 34% with 30 – 50% slope, thereby limiting area for intensive cultivation;

(*c*) Considerable area falls under temperate and alpine climate where crop duration extends from 6 to 8 months;

(*d*) High rainfall area and extended post-monsoon period making difficult in field preparation for Rabi crops specially in paddy fields. Despite all these factors, the cropping intensity has increased from 129% in 1975-76 to 314% in 2004-05, which is at a higher side for a mountainous Sikkim.

2.8. Return from major crops:

The return from horticultural crops is more remunerative than the agricultural crops, which has been worked out in the table as follows:

Economics of Major Crops cultivated in Sikkim (2004-05):

Major Crops	*Triennium area ending 2004-05 ('000 ha)*	*Triennium production ending 2004-05*	*Triennium prices ending 2004-05 (Rs./tonnes) ('000 tonnes)*	*Triennium value ending 2004-05 (Rs. in lac)*	*Cost of cultivation (Rs. per ha)*	*Net triennium Income ending (Rs. in lac)*
Agricultural Crops :						
Paddy	14.75	21.34	14,470	3087.89	19,195	256.63
Wheat	5.93	8.40	8,780	737.52	12,000	25.92
Maize	36.70	56.15	8,700	4885.05	12,000	481.05
Finger millet	4.21	3.64	7,640	278.10	6,000	25.50
Barley	1.23	1.51	10,210	154.17	12,000	6.57
Buckwheat	2.00	1.55	14,020	217.31	7,000	77.31
Total Cereals	64.82	92.59	—	9,360.04	—	872.98
Pulses: Urd	3.78	2.81	36,275	1,019.33	13,460	510.54
Other pulses	2.92	3.55	23,365	829.46	14,700	400.22
Oilseeds:						
Rape & Mustard	5.60	3.95	25,000	987.50	13,085	254.74
Soybean	3.89	3.12	24,800	773.76	17,820	80.56
Other Oilseeds	0.06	0.03	15,000	4.50	6,000	0.90
Total Agri. Crops	78.07	106.05	—	12,974.59	—	2,119.94
Horticultural Crops :						
Mandarin Orange	4.94	6.62	27,020	1788.72	20,055	798.00
Other fruits	2.79	3.15	15,270	481.00	8,493	244.05
Total fruits	7.73	9.77	—	2269.72	—	1042.05
Kharif Vegetables	2.73	12.40	16,448	2039.55	27,460	1289.89
Rabi Vegetables	3.38	14.72	17,286	2544.50	33,245	1283.75
Off-season Vegetables	2.69	12.60	17,286	2178.04	33,245	1283.75
Total Vegetables	8.80	39.72	—	6762.09	—	3994.46
Seed Potato	3.47	13.83	15,000	2074.50	52,700	245.60
Table potato	3.43	16.01	7,770	1243.97	26,025	351.31
Other root & tubers	0.42	1.90	14,792	281.05	26,025	171.74
Large cardamom	18.80	3.90	114,600	4,469.40	9,250	2730.00
Ginger	5.98	27.94	22,660	6,331.20	74,825	1856.66
Turmeric	0.48	1.55	11,849	183.66	37,050	5.82
Cut flowers	0.04	17.67 lac	2	35.34	57375	12.39
Bulbs/plants	0.04	22.90 lac	2	45.80	57,375	22.85
Total Horti. crops	49.20	114.62	—	23,696.73	—	10,433.28
Per cent Agri. Crop to total	61.34	—	—	35.38	16.89	
Per cent Horti. Crop to total	38.66	—	—		64.62	83.11

Note: triennium = average of three years ending 2004-05.

Source: FS & ADD; Horticulture & CCD; Bureau of Economics & Statistics; Agriculture Census; Saving farmers & Saving farming by National Commission on Farmers, GOI.

The above analysis of data reveals the following:

(*a*) Agricultural crops occupying an area of 61.34% accounts for 35.38% of total combined value of agricultural and horticultural produce whereas, the horticultural crops occupying area of 38.66% only accounts 64.62% of total combined value of the produce at triennium ending 2004-05 in Sikkim.

(*b*) Agricultural produce contributed only 16.89% of combined total profit of agricultural and horticultural produce; whereas, horticulture share of profit was recorded 83.11% of combined profit at triennium ending 2004-05. In other words, horticultural crops are more profitable in the marginal lands than the agricultural crops in the mountainous State of Sikkim.

(*c*) The most important reason of less profitability of foodgrains in the sloppy marginal lands of the state is due to the inherent marginality of production of foodgrains of the sloppy hills. The sloppy marginal lands are three to four times less efficient in meeting the food needs of calorie and protein because it can hardly sustain three to four persons per ha per annum against the sustainability of nine to ten persons in a plain land. Further, intensive cropping on sloppy marginal lands cannot be done more than three to four years (Awasthi and Prasad, 1987).

(*d*) The triennium prices computed above reveals that the market prices of foodgrains (cereals and pulses) and oilseeds are tremendously affected by the price fixation and procurement policy of the Central Government. Minimum Support Price fixed for these crops annually and their distribution through Public Distribution System (PDS) network in the State as well as in the country under various centrally sponsored programmes (CSS) of the Central Government (about 46,000 tonnes of foodgrain inflows in Sikkim annually) has stabilized the market prices of these commodities at the minimum level.

(*e*) Horticultural crops cultivated in sloppy marginal lands of Sikkim e.g. large cardamom in the agro-forestry system, ginger-maize intercropping in Agri-horti system, orange plantation in agro-forestry system, maize-pulses relay cropping system, maize-soybean inter-cropping, vegetable crops intercropping, broom-grass/ fodder tree plantation on shallow-barren lands, mixed farming-dairy with cross-breed cows/goat/pig rearing and recycling of byproducts (both agri-horti and livestock manure) make the horticultural crops most profitable.

(*f*) Location specific comparative advantage crop adoption both for specific production and marketing e.g., Seed potato of Hilley area of West Sikkim; Montulal bean of Mikkhola-Shyampani area of South District; Pea seed of Dentam and Rinchenpong of West District; Off-season crops of Lachung, Hilley, Chuba-Parbing of North, West, and South District; Large cardamom of North, East, South and West District; Ginger of Central Pandam of East District; South District, Jeel Hathìdunga of WestDistrict; Cherry pepper of Khamdong and Namphok; Gladilus flower of Turuk-Sumbukof South District; rearing of livestock with horticultural crops for byproduct mutual utiliation of the two systems in East District; make the horticultural crops most ec onomically viable and environmentally sustainable in the State.

2.9. Agriculture, Horticulture and livestock as livelihood options:

The primary livelihood options of the hill people in mountainous Sikkim are mixed farming. The development measures of the **"green revolution"** implemented in other Indian States were not successful in mountainous Sikkim because, fertilizer responsive crop varieties for the hills were not available; adequate fertilizers were never available in time; irrigation could not be developed, and the hill-slope soils are very fragile and not suitable for intensive cultivation. Top priority of the State Government on non-agricultural sectors of development during previous plan period, rapid population growth and consequent fragmentation of farmland in the State has caused reduction in per capita holdings. The state being hilly has limited scope of industrial growth, and hence has not adequately succeeded in decreasing the pressure on agriculture/ horticulture as the agrarian population has increased rather than decrease. Thus, the farmers were forced to cultivate more and more horticultural cash crops such as potato, ginger, off-season vegetables, and orange all of which have caused rapid nutrient depletion of the soil. Instead, cultivation of another perennial cash crop, large cardamom, grown beneath the forest cover on marginal lands has been a boon to the people of the area (Sharma et al, 2000a).

Although, Sikkim like any other mountainous area is a food-deficit State, and foodgrain produced in the state can feed its population only for three and half months; while foodgrain has to be brought from other states for feeding its population for seven and half months every year. Yet about 89 per cent of the people living in the rural areas are directly or indirectly depend on agriculture, horticulture and livestock, as they have no other options for their livelihood. Food is the very foundation of life and food and nutritional security in the mountainous Sikkim is a difficult proposition and one has to depend on multiple sources of agriculture, horticulture and animal husbandry. In the mountainous Sikkim, mixed farming is the only means of livelihood for food and nutritional security of the people which depends on agriculture production, diversification of the food basket, availability of low cost and environmentally safe food products, and equitable distribution and management. It involves efforts to generate purchasing power for physical and economical access to food by all people at all times.

2.10. Reduced Fuel, Fodder and Timber:

The various impact of human and livestock population on forest resources is enormous. Households in an upland farming system depend on a number of resources, which are linked to forest, agroforestry, agriculture, and livestock, and also to the market.

As per the estimate of Sikkim Renewable Energy Development Agency (SREDA) a household requires about 16 to 32 kg of firewood for cooking per day. Taking average consumption of 24 kg of firewood per day a household requirement of a family comes to about 8,760 kg per annum. Considering only rural households of Sikkim 1,01,225 Nos., the requirement of the State works out to 8,86,731 tonnes per annum. A considerable quantity of firewood is also used for space heating during winter months. Biomass has been a vital part of the State energy scenario. Environmental degradation arising out of persistent over dependence on the biomass and adverse health effects of biomass combustion, particularly in confined spaces in the rural Sikkim, are now reaching alarming levels. Since, most biomass fuel is used in domestic cooking, the highly inefficient traditional cooking methods make the energy wastage from biomass conversion very high (Sikkim Human Development Report 2001).

3.1. Sikkim: Human Resources

The population of India has increased to 1.027 billion in 2001 (Census of India 2001). The decadal growth rate decreased from 23.86 during 1981-1991 to 21.34 in 1991-2001. Sex ratio for females per 1000 males has increased slightly from 927 in 1991 to 933 in 2001. The population density has increased alarmingly from 267 persons per sq. km to 324 persons per sq km from 1991 to 2001. The overall literacy rate of the country is 65.38%. The literacy rates for males and females are 75.83% and 54.16% respectively.

The population of Sikkim was 5,40,851 in 2001 as against 4,06,457 in 1991. The State has around 0.22% of the total area of India and its population constitutes 0.05% of the national total. This clearly indicates that the state is still sparsely populated compared to other parts of the country. This is the general trend for all the eleven mountainous states of India. However, the annual growth rate of Sikkim was 3.31%, which was higher as compared to 2.13% of the national average during 1991-2001. The geographical, climatic characteristics, unprecedented growth of population after integration of the State into Indian Union in 1975 that has exerted tremendous pressure on land and other resources of the State have deeply influenced its economic and social development. It is a matter of concern in the context of the fragile mountain environment. Sex ratio of Sikkim was much lower (875 females) than the national average (933 females) in 2001. The overall literacy rate of the state is higher by more than 4% compared to the national average which is mainly contributed by greater literacy rate amongst women in Sikkim (more than 7% of the national average).

3.2. Temporal Changes in Population 1891-2001:

The population changes from 1891 to 2001 shows a growth of 17.76 times in Sikkim. The growth has been phenomenal during the past three decades. The sex ratio increased from 709 to 970 during 1901 –1921, and then started declining to the lowest value of 835 in 1981. There has been increase to 878 in 1991, compared to 1981, then again deceased to 875 in 2001. The density of the population per sq km was around 4 in 1891, which has increased to 76 in 2001. There has been substantial increase from 57 persons per sq km in 1991 to 76 persons per sq km in 2001.

Sex Ratio has also decreased with the increase of population and literacy in the State. Sex Ratio in 1000 persons was 916 in 1901, 951 in 1911, 970 in 1921, 967 in 1931, 920 in 1941, 907 in 1951, 904 in 1961 was slowly decreasing to 863 in 1971, to 835 in 1981, to 878 in 1991, to 875 in 2001 against the country of 931 in 1971, 934 in 1981, 927 in 1991 and 933 in 2001 respectively.

According to the 1981, 1991 and 2001 Census of India, the population of Sikkim during 1891 was 30,458 which was increased to 59,014 in 1901, to 87,920 in 1911, to 81,721 in 1921, to 1,09,808 in 1931, to 121,520 in 1941, to 1,37,725 in 1951, to 1,62,189 in 1961, to 2,09,843 in 1971, to 3,16,385 in 1981, 4,06,457 in 1091 and to 540,851, 480,981 (88.90%) rural and 59,870 (11.07%) urban in 2001. Decadal population growth rates have been fluctuating in the case of Sikkim, which showed negative growth in population during 1911-1921. This decline has been partly attributed to deaths resulting from the great plague epidemic of 1917 and partly to the death of soldiers from Sikkim in World War I.

Temporal Changes in Population 1891-2001:

Year	*Male*	*Female*	*Total (Children)*	*Sex ratio (females/ 1000 males*	*Decadal % variations*	*Density of population sq km.*
1891	11,589	10,563	22,152	912	93.75	4
			+(8,306)	709	48.98	8
1901	39,795	28,219	39,458	951	(–) 7.05	12
1911	45,059	42,861	59,014	970	34.75	12
1921	41,492	40,229	87,920	967	10.66	15
1931	55,825	53,983	81,721	920	13.34	17
1941	63,289	58,231	1,09,808	907	17.76	19
1951	72,210	65,515	1,21,520	904	29.38	23
1961	85,193	76,996	1,37,725	863	50.77	30
1971	1,12,662	97,181	1,62,189	835	28.47	35
1981	2,16,427	1,90,030	3,16,385	875		76
1991	2,16,427	1,90,030	4,06,457			
2001	2,88,217	2,52,276	5,40,851			

Source: Census of India, 1981, 1991, and 2001; Subba, J.R. 1999.

Since then, for half a century (from 1921 to 1971), population growth was steady but low. Between 1971–1981, there was a substantial increase (at a rate of 5.07% per annum), especially in the urban areas. This could be attributed to the merger of Sikkim with the Indian Union and the subsequent in-migration triggered off by large-scale development activities in the state. In the following decade (1981-1991), population grew at a much lower rate of 2.85% per annum, whereas in 1991-2001, the rate of growth was higher at 3.30% per annum. This is again due to in-migration to cope with various developmental activities like road constructions and hydropower projects.

3.3. Decennial Growth

The decennial growth before integration of the State into Indian Union, that is during 1931 to 1941 was 10.67, during 1941 to 1951 was 13.34, during 1951 to 1961 was 17.76, during 1961 to 1971 was 17.76, which was increased to unprecedented growth rate of 50.77% during 1971 to 1981 after the merger of the State into Indian Union due to in-migration to cope with the development activities. The present decennial growth is still at a higher side of 33.06% during 1991 to 2001 against the country's 24.66%. As a result, the population density per sq. km increased from 4 in 1891, to 19 in 1951, to 23 in 1961, to 29 in 1971 (before merger into Indian Union) to 45 in 1981, to 57 in 1991, to 76 in 2001. The literacy rate has increased from 17.74% in 1971 to 34.05% in 1981, to 56.94%

in 1991, to 69.68% in 2001 against the national literacy of 34.45, 43.56, 52.21 and 65.38 per cent respectively.

Districtwise comparison of the population profile shows that the east, where the state capital lies, is the most populated which accounts almost 50% of the state population. The north district has the lowest population. The decadal growth rate of north district increased substantially to 31.32% during 1991-2001 compared to 18.09% during 1981-1991. The annual growth rate between 1991-2001 has been highest in the east district, which is 3.7%.

Population distribution, Percentage decadal growth rate, Sex ratio and Density of population:

State/ District	*Population in 2001*			*Percentage decadal growth rate*		*Sex Ratio (female per 1000 males*		*Density of population per sq. km*	
	Total	*Male*	*Female*	*1981-91*	*1991-01*	*1991*	*2001*	*1991*	*2001*
Sikkim	5,40,851	2,88,484	2,52,367	28.47	33.06	878	874	57	76
North Dist.	41,030	23,414	17,616	18.09	31.34	828	752	7	10
West Dist.	1,23,256	63,912	59,344	30.55	25.57	915	929	84	106
South Dist.	1,31,525	68,241	63,284	29.78	33.39	892	927	131	175
East Dist.	2,45,040	1,32,917	1,12,123	28.60	37.31	859	844	187	257

Source: Census of India 1981, 1991, 2001.

3.4. Scheduled Tribe and Scheduled Caste Population

Scheduled Tribe population was 20.6% as the two Communities Limboo and Tamang were recognized as Scheduled Tribe only in 2002 (22% in 1991), and were not enumerated as Scheduled Tribes in 2001 Census against the country of 8.2%. The Scheduled Caste population was 5% in 2001 (5.93% in 1991) against the country of 16.2%. The Limboo and Tamang tribes were included in the list of Scheduled Tribe only in 2002.

3.5. Sex Ratio

Composition of sex ratio shows that the north district has the lowest sex ratio, 725 females per 1000 males. The ratio was above 900 in the west and south districts. The density of population in the different districts have increased from 1991 to 2001, substantially in the cases of west district (from 84 to 106 persons per sq km), south district (from 131 to 175 persons per sq km) and highest in the east district (from 187 to 257 persons per sq km). The north district comprises 60% of the total geographical area accounted for hardly 7.6% of the total population in 2001. The density was 10 persons per sq km, which is insignificant.

3.6. Rural and Urban Population:

In 2001, total households were distributed in 411 revenue blocks, 447 villages and 8 towns in the state, comprising of 4,80,981 people in rural areas and remaining 59,870 in the urban areas. Of the total population in 2001, 89% came from the rural areas and remaining 11% from the urban areas, thereby making Sikkim predominantly a rural economy.

Comparison of urban population in different districts between 1991-2001 shows that there is higher percentage residing in the north, south and east districts in 2001 as compared to the west district whereas urban population has decreased from 1.79 in 1991 to 1.48 in 2001.

District's Administrative Share in Area and Rural/Urban population during 1991 and 2001

Districts	*Area in sq. km.*	*Percentage population*			
		Rural		*Urban*	
	4226	1991	2001	1991	2001
North	1166	97.43	96.95	2.57	3.05
West	750	98.21	98.52	1.79	1.48
South	954	97.39	96.99	2.61	3.01
East	7096	82.14	78.35	17.86	21.65
Total		90.89	88.89	9.10	11.07

Source: Census of India 1991, 2001.

3.7. Literacy

Total literacy rate in Sikkim increased in the pre-merger period from 6.59% in 1951 to 17.74% in 1971; while the female literacy increased from 1.2% in 1951 to 8.90 in 1971. After the merger of Sikkim into Indian Union the literacy rate increased from 34.74% in 1981 to 69.68% in 2001. The female literacy rate increased tremendously from 22.20% in 1981 to 61.46% reducing the gap between male and female literacy.

Literacy Rate of Sikkim and India:

Year	*Sikkim (%)*			*India (%)*		
	Male	*Female*	*Total*	*Male*	*Female*	*Total*
1951	11.19	1.20	6.59	27.16	8.86	18.33
1961	19.50	4.20	12.30	40.40	15.34	28.31
1971	25.37	8.90	17.74	45.95	21.97	34.45
1981	43.85	22.20	34.05	56.50	24.97	43.67
1991	65.70	46.76	56.94	64.13	39.29	52.21
2001	76.73	61.46	69.68	64.8	53.70	64.80

Source: Census of India 1981, 1991, 2001

3.8. Birth Rate and Death Rates

An analysis of birth and death rates of Sikkim with that of India as a whole showed an interesting trend. During 1981-1985 birth rate of Sikkim increased but decreased to the national birth rate. The national death rate has been decreasing since 1981 until recorded value of 1997. In the case of Sikkim, death rate increased in 1985 compared to 1981 and thereafter it is on the decline. The death rates were always lower in Sikkim compared to the national average.

Estimated Birth and Death Rates

Year	*Birth Rate*		*Death Rate*		*Natural Growth Rate*	
	Sikkim	*India*	*Sikkim*	*India*	*Sikkim*	*India*
1981	31.0	33.9	8.9	12.5	22.1	21.4
1985	33.1	32.9	0.7	11.8	22.4	21.1
1990	26.3	30.2	7.3	9.7	19.0	20.5
1995	22.5	28.3	6.9	9.0	15.6	19.3
2000	21.8	25.8	5.70	8.5	16.2	17.3
2001	21.6	25.4	5.1	8.9		
2002	21.9	25.0	4.9	8.1		
2003	21.9	25.8	5.0	8.0		

Source: Sample Registration Scheme, Office of the Registrar General.

3.9. In-migration

In-migration to Sikkim became more conspicuous after 1975, when Sikkim became a constituent state of India and large quantum of resources was allocated for developmental purposes. According to the census data on migration, which primarily covers migration by place of birth and last residence, between 1971 and 1981, Sikkim recorded a very high level of in-migration (35%). By 1991, the percentage of migrants to the state decreased in both categories, 19 to 13% by place of birth, and from 16 to 9% by place of last residence. The proportion of male in-migrants has always been higher than that of women, although between 1981 and 1991 a decline was recorded (moving from 61% in 1981 to 57% in 1991)) (Lama, 2001). An analysis of the origin of migrants in the "by birth" category reveals that while there was a steady decline in the proportion of in-migrants from neighbouring countries (moving from over 46% in 1971 to 43% in 1981 and 35% in 1991), there was an increase in the proportion of in-migration from within the country (moving from 54% to 65% between 1971 and 1991). Thus, by 1991, the percentage of in-migration within India was higher than that of in-migrants from neighbouring countries.

3.10. Workforce Profile:

Work is always related to productivity, profitability as well as economic efficiency of the workers themselves or the various sectors, which they represent. a workforce profile would serve to provide sufficient indication of the economic development of a State, as it is essentially the ground level workers who contribute to the production of goods and services and help sustain a satisfactory life standard for one and all. On the basis of what one is doing or not doing, the population of a place may be distinguished as workers and non-workers, the workers being further grouped as the main workers and the marginal workers. A person who has worked for a period of six months or more is treated as a main worker and the one who has worked for less than six months is a marginal worker. A non-worker is one who has not worked for any of the above two periods. The whole range of cultivators, agricultural labourers, industrial workers and all others engaged in regular form of activities comprise the main worker while the non-workers include students, household dependents, pensioners and casual workers. The person who did not work at all during the reference period is treated as a non-worker. The main workers are categorized into cultivators, agricultural labourer, worker in the household industry and other workers. Categories of the non-working population include students, household dependents, prisoners and casual workers.

Percentage Distribution of Workers in Sikkim 1991 & 2001

	Total Workers		*Main Workers*		*Marginal Workers*		*Non-Workers*	
Persons	1991	2001	1991	2001	1991	2001	1991	2001
Males	41.51	48.72	40.72	39.31	1.06	9.41	58.49	51.28
Females	51.25	57.58	57.58	50.89	0.43	6.69	48.75	42.42
	30.41	39.59	28.63	26.09	1.78	12.50	69.59	61.41

Source: Census of India 1991, 2001

The percentage of Main Workers to total population has decreased with the increase of population and literacy, which was 53.18 in 1971, to 46.60 in 1981, to 40.45 in 1991 to 39.31 in 2001 against the country's average of 33.06, 33.45, 34.19 and 30.54 respectively. The Marginal workers during 1991 were 1.06 per cent has increased to 9.41 per cent in 2001. The State has a big chunk of Non-Workers constituting 58.49 per cent during 1991 and 51.28 per cent in 2001. The decrease of Main Worker Percentage and a big chunk of Non-Worker population in Sikkim has been the worrying factor for the State at present

3.11. Temporal Changes in Occupational Structure by Sex (1971-2001)

Of the 48.72 per cent workforce, 49.9 per cent are cultivators, 6.4 per cent agricultural labourers, 1.2 per cent engaged in household industries and the remaining 42.4 per cent belonging to other kinds of vocations. There is a steady decline in the number of cultivators during the period 1971 to 2001 from 81 per cent to 49 per cent. The number of agriculture labourers came down from 3.8 per cent in 1971 to 3.31 percent in 1981 but again ascended to 7.81 per cent in 1991. a similar trend is noticeable in respect of the main workers in relation to the total population of the state: it was 53.17 per cent in 1971, 46.6 per cent in 1981, 40.45 per cent in 1991, the number of main workers again improving to 48.72 per cent in 2001. Employment in other services has substantially increased from 6.23 per cent in 1971 to 17.93 percent in 1981, which, however again decreased to 13.43 per cent in 1991.

Temporal Changes in occupational structure by Sex (1971 to 2001)

Sector	*1971*			*1981*			*1991*			*2001**		
	Male	*Female*	*Total*	*Male*	*Female*	*Total*	*Male*	*Female*	*Total*	*Male*	*Female*	*Total*
Cultivators	74.53	92.28	81.00	50.16	79.52	60.10	50.96	71.74	57.84	42.3	49.9	66.8
Agriculture Labourers	4.12	3.16	3.77	3.45	3.06	3.31	8.04	7.37	7.81	5.3	4.3	6.5
Livestock, forestry, hunting, fishing, plantation and allied	0.60	0.48	0.55	1.93	0.92	1.59	2.99	1.58	2.53			
Mining & quarrying	0.09	0.00	0.05	0.17	0.00	0.11	0.30	0.05	0.22			
Manufacturing, processing, servicing and repairing												
(*a*) Household industry	0.50	0.04	0.34	1.25	0.74	1.08	0.99	0.33	0.77	1.7	1.6	1.1
(*b*) Other than household indusrtries	1.31	0.26	0.93	3.14	1.29	2.51	3.94	1.88	3.26			
Construction	4.85	0.87	3.40	10.47	4.98	8.62	8.84	3.54	7.09			
Trade & commerce	3.09	0.48	2.14	5.08	1.00	3.70	6.79	2.08	5.23			
Transport, storage and communication	2.27	0.42	1.59	1.55	0.07	1.05	2.62	0.24	1.82			
Other services	8.64	2.01	6.23	22.80	8.42	17.93	14.53	11.19	13.43	53.4	46.7	31.0
Total workers % of main workers to total	100.00	100.00	100.00	100.00	100.00	100.00	100.00	100.00	100.00			
Population	62.97	41.82	53.17	56.55	34.69	46.60	50.82	28.63	40.45			

Source: Census of India 1971,1981,1991,2001* (provisional)

3.12. Labour and Employment

Both the State and the Central Government's failure to generate employment in line with the growth of the labour force and the rising expectation of high quality jobs is a major weakness in economic performance. The Central Government's effort on establishing a Food for Work Programme in the mountainous Sikkim as an interim measure and Employment Guarantee Bill in the Parliament passed recently will provide a measure of support at the low end of the employment spectrum i.e., casual manual labour in the rural areas, but it cannot address the problems of the educated unemployed who are typically looking for employment of a higher quality. This type of employment can come from robust growth of the economy especially in labour using sectors. Accelerating the rate of growth of the economy, while ensuring acceleration in agricultural (horticultural, animal husbandry, dairying, fisheries etc.) growth, must be an integral part of any sustainable employment strategy and the various policy initiatives emerging from the MTA (Tenth Plan Mid-term appraisal) will all help to achieve this objective.

3.13. Poverty:

Poverty is not about money but is about access to the basic rights of food, clothes and shelter, education, proper health care, clean water, rights which most of us takes for granted. In the past 50 years there has been greater poverty reduction than in the previous 500, with more and more people across the world gaining access to these rights. Yet over one billion people still live in severe poverty today and the clock is turning backwards, with poverty on the increase once again. Acute levels of poverty characterize mountain regions. Nepal, Ethiopia, Bolivia and others mountainous/landlocked countries are often among the poorest in the world. The less-developed areas or countries such as Uttaranchal of India, Yunnan and Xizang in China, North Pakistan are generally among the poorest regions in these countries. Even the mountainous regions in developed economies, such as Australia and Switzerland, are comparatively less affluent than the lowland areas of these countries.

The persistence of poverty in Sikkim is in stark contrast to its relatively high achievement in the social sectors as compared to the national average. However, this could be explained by considering that Sikkim remained marginalized from the development activities that characterized mainstream India. Prior to its merger with India, its very political economy and limited resources did not, in fact, permit Sikkim with development interventions of a democratic variety. Only in the last 25 years, the philosophy of growth with equity and self-reliance in the planned development of the State has become important (Lama, 2001). The other explanation of poverty persistence in Sikkim in spite of 30 years of plan investment is due to its inherent problem of mountain specificities (Limited accessibility, Fragility, Marginality, Niche and Human adaptations). In absence of its' own mountain policy to reduce the impacts of mountain specificities in the mountainous Sikkim and extremely high cost investment requirement, the plan investments made so far could not make any impact on poverty reduction in the State.

Percentage of Population below Poverty Line:

Districts	*All India*	*Rural*	*Sikkim* *Urban*	*Combined*	*State* *Ranking*
	4226	1991	2001	1991	2001
North	1166	97.43	96.95	2.57	3.05
West	750	98.21	98.52	1.79	1.48
South	954	97.39	96.99	2.61	3.01
East	7096	82.14	78.35	17.86	21.65
Total		90.89	88.89	9.10	11.07

Source: Planning Commission Government of India.

1.13 State Domestic Product

Sikkim's steady economic growth at a macro level is reflected both in its GDP and per capita income. Both of them at current prices and constant prices recorded a steady increase between 1993-94 and 2001-02.

Per Capita Gross State Domestic Product (GSDP):

Districts	*India GSDP at current prices (Rs. in crores)*	*India GSDP at constantprices (Rs. in crores)*	*Sikkim GSDP at currentprices (Rs. in crores)*	*Sikkim GSDP at constantprices (Rs. in crores)*
1993-94	781,345	781,345	377.43	377.43
1994-95	917,058	838,031	402.77	371.83
1995-96	1073,271	899,563	481.30	411.22
1996-97	1243,546	970,083	552.62	456.30
1997-98	1390,148	1016,594	651.06	520.02
1998-99	1598,127	1082,748	781.84	579.83
1999-00	1761,838	1148,369	840.03	595.83
1999-01	1902,998	1198,592	976.34	642.13
2001-02	2090,957	1267,833	1139.25	696.13
2002-03 (P)	2249,493		1251.35	
2003-04 (Q)			1358.18	

Source: CSO, GOI & ESSME, GOS

According to the Planning Commission estimates, based on the Expert Group Recommendations, except in 1993-04 the percentage of people below the poverty line in Sikkim has continued to be lower than the national average. Though, Sikkim recorded a decline in the incidence of poverty in the decade 1977-87, it suddenly increased in 1993-04 moving from 36% in 1987-08 to 41.43% in 1993-04. While the decrease in urban poverty has been constant, rural poverty decreases have alternated with increase. In 1993-04, 45.01% of the rural population was below the poverty line, while in urban areas only 7.73% of the population was below the poverty line (Lama, 2001).

Sikkim Net State Domestic Product (NSDP):

Districts	*India NSDP att current prices (Rs.)*	*India NSDP at current prices (Rs.)*	*India NSDP at current prices (Rs.)*	*Sikkim NSDP at constant prices (Rs.)*
1993-94	7,690.00	7,690.00	7,690.00	7,550.00
1994-95	8,857.00	8,857.00	8,857.00	7,113.00
1995-96	10,149.00	10,149.00	10,149.00	7,633.00
1996-97	11,564.00	11,564.00	11,564.00	8,236.00
1997-98	12,707.00	12,707.00	12,707.00	9,125.00
1998-99	14,396.00	14,396.00	14,396.00	9,666.00
1999-00	15,625.00	16,563.00	16,563.00	10,250.00
1999-01	16,563.00	16,563.00	16,563.00	10,703.00
2001-02	17,947.00	17,947.00	17,947.00	11.232.00
2002-03 (P)	18,912.00	18,912.00	18,912.00	
2003-04 (Q)				

Source: CSO, GOI & ESSME, GOS

The per capita income during 1993-94 was Rs.7,550/= has increased to Rs.16,658/= in 2001; and further increased Rs.21,586/= by 2003-04.

3

Landscape, Agricultural Ecosystems and Sacred Places

Sikkim is a part of globally significant biodiversity hot spots of the world within the greater quadri-national junction of Kanchendzonga landscape in the Eastern Himalayas. The region is an assemblage of sacred landscapes called ***Deyjong*** (the valley of rice) or the ***Shangrila*** (the hidden paradise on earth). This cultural-landscape is endowed with rich agrobiodiversity adopted and managed through traditional ecological knowledge of the culturally diverse ethnic communities (Lepcha, Limboo, Bhutia, Sherpa, Thakuri, Bahun, Chettri, Kami, Damai, Sarki, Majhi, Rai, Yakha, Gurung, Tamang, Sunuwar, Magar, Thami, Bhujel, Jogi, Newar, etc. besides plainsman ethnic groups). It comprises of trans-Himalayan agro-pastoral system of the ***Dokpas*** (grazers) in the alpine plateaus, traditional forestry such as alder-cardamom and farm-based systems in the temperate zones, and terraced/valley rice systems in the lower sub-tropical zones. It is paradoxical to see that culturally and biologically diverse landscapes are marginalized. The development opportunities are enormous but persistent problems of poverty, access to markets, economic and ecological fragility are prevalent.

1. Landscape and the Agricultural Ecosystems

The range of landscape and ecosystem diversity extending from the rice cultivation systems along the valleys of glacier fed river Teesta and Rangit in the subtropical zones (above 300 m), traditional agroforestry such as alder-cardamom and farm-based systems in the subtropical and warmer temperate zones (600 – 2200 m), extreme subsistence farming in the cool temperate zones (2300 – 4000 m), to the trans-Himalayan nomadic Tibetan agro-pastoral landscape and ecosystems in the alpine plateaus (4000 – 6000 m) of the Kanchandzonga in the Eastern Himalayas.

The characteristics and functioning of the agricultural ecosystems can be categorized into three broad systems:

(*i*) Agro-pastoralism of the Nomadic Tibetan Herders;

(*ii*) Traditional Agricultural Systems; and

(*iii*) Valley Rice Cultivation Systems

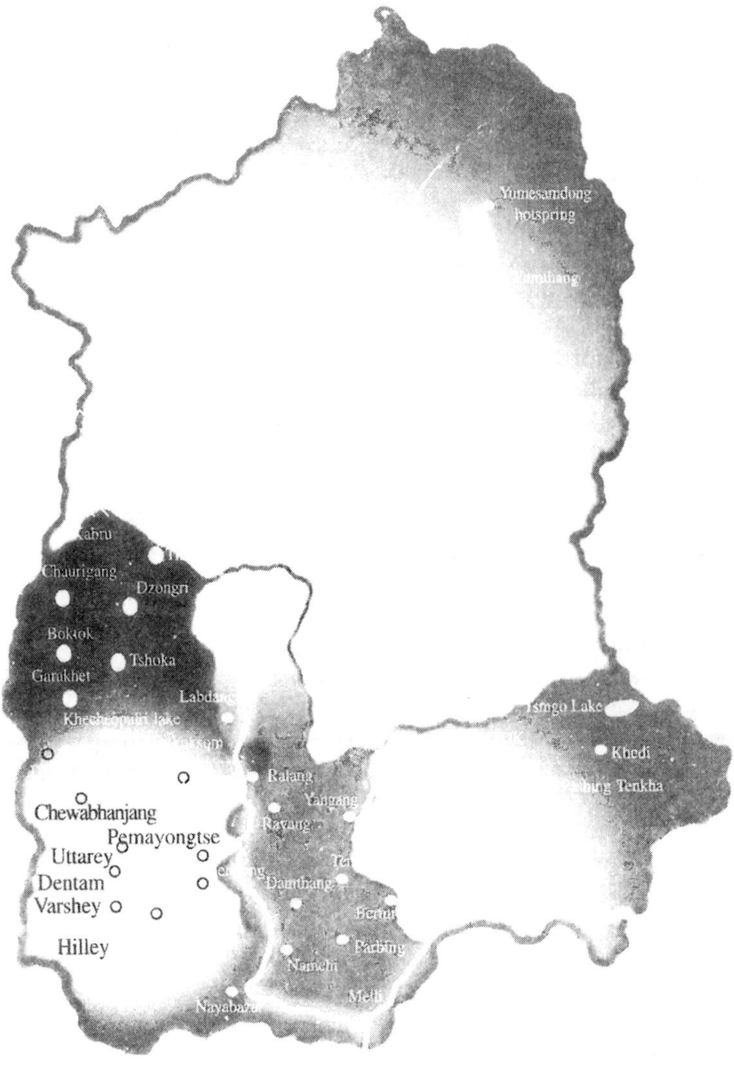

Map of Sikkim showing Important places and lakes of Sikkim

Sikkim surrounded by Natural Biodiversity Conservation Areas

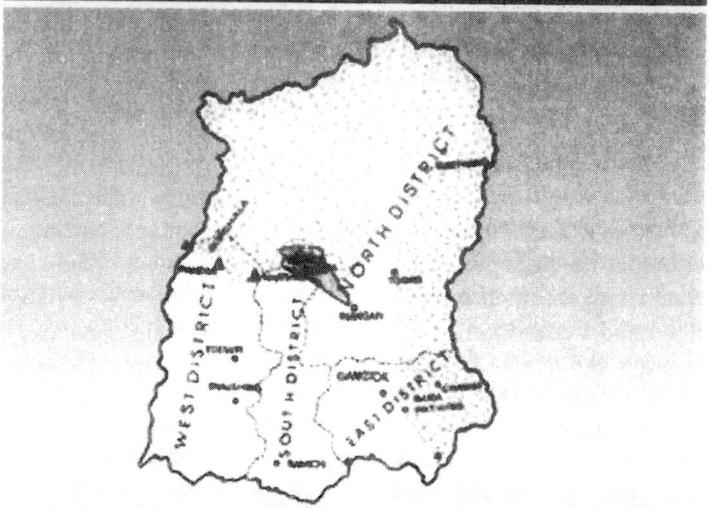

Protected Areas of Sikkim

1.1. Agro-Pastoralism of the Nomadic Tibetan Herders:

Agro-pastoralism in the alpine cold deserts of Lhonak valley, Chho Lhamo and Lashar valley above 4000 m asl in North Sikkim has been a part of human life support systems over several centuries. The trans-Himalayan nomadic Tibetans the Dokpas (grazers) herd yaks, dzos (cow-yak hybrid), sheep and goats (*pasmina* types) in the high altitude Tibetan plateaus and meadows adopted to sustain the harsh climatic conditions. The dry grasslands of these unique valleys of the world have been traditionally managed and inhabited by the Tibetan nomads, a unique example of how people survived in such drought-stricken landscapes in the history of mankind through mobile livestock production systems tolerating all environmental fragility, marginality and poverty.

Presently there are only 32 families of the **Dokpas** managing about 90% of yak population of the state. Yaks and dzos are important pack animals. The wool, meat, cheese, fat (*tsilu*) of yak and sheep, and other various products are rare items. In recent years, through intriguing challenges and pressures, the Dokpas are restricted to a limited patch of the vast Chho Lhamo, Lhonak and Lashar plateaus, **the Roof of the World.** In the olden times, herders had open movements from Chho Lhamo, or from the Lhonak valley into Tibet and back through *Nyima La* or *Naku La* pass during the time when the border was open. The cross border grazing had advantages for yak crossbreeding and social-cultural relationships in the form of marriages, trade and religion. Once the boarder was closed, apparently after 1975, there emerged the challenges into their socio-economic lifestyles, the herd reproductive rates intricately decreased with consequent reduction of their population. While in the present times, enormously rich medicinal plant wealth of high altitudes, wildlife and livestock are threatened from downstream population by pressuring and using un-sustainable harvesting practices. However, a recent development of opening of the Nathu La pass between Tibetan Autonomous Region of China and Sikkim of India in 2006 has raised the hopes of resuming the traditional practices.

1.2. Traditional Agricultural Systems

The agro-ecosystems are innovated, adapted, managed and evolved over 600 years by traditional communities in antiquity initially by aboriginal Lepchas and Limboos (now under ethnic group Nepali), followed by Bhutias after 1275 AD and later on by the other Nepalese (Rai, Yakha, Gurung, Mangar, Tamang, Sunuwar, Thakuri, Bahun, Chettri, Kami, Damai, Sarki, Majhi, Newar, Sherpa, Thami, Bhujel, Jogi) after 1774 onwards through the generations to the present state. Mass clearing of forest area for agricultural use was accelerated during the British protectorate period (1817-1947 AD) mainly after the policy of Nepali settlement in Sikkim for revenue rising by Mr. J.C. White (1889 to 1908 AD), while the terrace cultivation system was accelerated after the Maharaja of Sikkim Sedkeong Tulku's time of 1914 AD on wards. The traditional shifting agriculture system and practice over centuries gradually conversed into sedentary system which is still continuing. The mixed system is a combination of compartments such as agroforestry, forestry, livestock, and parcel of agricultural land forming together a unit mountain garden-based farming system. In the recent times, remains of shifting cultivation are rarely observed in the form of *Khoriya* in Dzongu North Sikkim (Lepcha reserved area) and elsewhere.

The microcosms of traditional agriculture are typically organic in Sikkim, the people and their knowledge of steep slope conversion to agroforestry and terraced productive zones (traditionally called *pakho-khet, pakho-bari, bhiraulo, sim-kholyan*), ridges of operational fields, and management of very steep slopes as *bhasmey* and *khoriya*. The agricultural tools, farm implements and techniques, cultivation methodology, farm raised animals, local crops, irrigation systems etc. are traditional. The Bhutias and Nepalese are composed of a number of ethnic communities with different languages/dialects, and social and cultural background. The cultural diversity attributes to a rich agrobiodiversity and traditional ecological knowledge.

Below the trans-Himalayan agro-ecosystem between 3000-4000 m, the communities mostly ***Bhutia*** and ***Sherpas*** in Phadamchen-Kupuk, Lachen, Lachung, Thangu, Thegu, Okharey, Ribdi, Bhareng, upper Uttarey, Upper Sankhu and Ravangla area practice subsistence farming by cultivating a variety of crops and fruits such as barley, wheat, maize, peas, beans, potato, apple, peach, plum, cabbage, medicinal plants etc. Grazing of cattle is a part of their life and livelihood. The communities are very enterprising; their traditional homestead products such as blankets, carpets, rugs, and other handicrafts made from the wools of high altitude sheep are rare marketable products apart from other products such as meat, cheese, butter etc. Communities collect medicinal plants, mushrooms, tubers and many edible products from the wild for household consumption and often sell them in small quantities in the nearby markets.

The lower agro-ecological zone consists of a wide range of traditional production systems, that includes the terraced and valley rice cultivation, locally called the *Khet* system, agroforestry systems such as alder-cardamom (*alainchi-bari*) or farm-trees-mandarin (*suntola-bari*) agroforestry, *Sukha-bari, Pakha-bari* system, and forest-based agroforestry system. Livestock are mostly stall-fed as grazing land is very limited. This system has traditional irrigation systems, management regimes, several cropping systems, crops diversity including medicinal plants, wild edibles, a large number of under-utilized or lesser-known crops, semi-domesticated crops and their wild relatives. Land parcels are classified under traditional system for resource allocation and utilization. Farmers have developed systematic management and conservation alternatives of mixtures of crops and farm animals with multipurpose agroforestry tree species that create appropriate environment to some high value crops and intercropping of many other local varieties.

1.2.1. The Ghar-Ghuryan (Homestead)

The mountain homestead in a marginal farm consists of intensive livestock raising, multiple crop production systems such as cereals and pseudo-cereals, legumes, vegetables, spices, fruits and nuts, medicinal and aromatic plants, roots and tubers, and farm-trees.

Home gardens are traditional sources of food and nutrition and are important contributors of food security and differ between the ethnic communities. Diversification of crops in the homestead is a traditional practice, as different communities require a large number of local crops and wild plants for performing their cultural and customary rituals. Mixed fruit trees, vegetables and crop varieties in home gardens provide subsistence and cash income to ingenious farmers. Home gardens are the basic units of agrobiodiversity and are custodians of seed bank of large number of agricultural and horticultural crops and provide significant economic benefits.

1.2.2. Agroforestry Systems

The traditional agroforestry systems are rich in agricultural biodiversity. They are the centre of in *situ* conservation of high species and genetic diversity, of both managed and wild crops, and associated trees. These agroforests can be categorized into the farm-based, forest-based and the traditional high-value crop-based types.

1.2.3. Farm-based and Forest-based Agroforestry

In the farm-based agroforestry, farmers manage multipurpose tree species for sustained provision of fodder, fuel and timber and for multiple benefits, both direct and indirect. Trees are grown in and around the cultivable land and in the terrace risers for soil stabilization. Livestock is an integral component and management of fodder species is critical. Intercropping is a traditional practice under farm-raised trees, but the tree canopies cause shade effects resulting into fairly less productivity and agronomic yield of understorey crops. To achieve a balance between generating high quality resources and crop production, farmers manage N_2-fixing trees with the cultivable land and other multipurpose species on the terraces or at the edges.

The forest-based practice of agroforestry is developed for supporting cultivated systems. This system comprises of bamboo groves, good timber, fuel-wood and often fodder species and supplies litter, nutrients and organic matter to the farm. Farmers collect minor forest products such as wild edible fruits, mushrooms, leafy vegetables, medicinal plants, and tubers. This agroforestry is an efficient land-use scheme for resource utilization, protection of traditional slope-land of agricultural technology, biomass, biogeochemical cycling of nutrients and improvement of agro-ecosystem performances and services. For seasonal water regime management, control of excessive flooding and erosion, and for stabilization of the slopes, these agroforests are developed along the ridges and furrows through the slopes vertically and between the slopes, horizontally. The terraced cultivated slopes are then necessarily protected from four sides by the agroforests. Such intersection of agroforests both on horizontal and vertical zones in upland-terraces play a strong protection mechanism to the system.

1.2.4. Alder-cardamom and *Albizzia*-mixed trees-mandarin Agroforestry

Large cardamom (*Amommum subulatum*) is a high value cash crop grown in about 30,000 ha in the Sikkim Himalaya. The cultivation is cost-effective compared to other farming systems and has high international market potential. It is an understorey crop, which was believed to be domesticated first by Lepchas that was later on adopted by others. Cardamom is grown both under N_2-fixing trees and mixed forest trees. It has large genetic diversity and wild relatives (Table I). Himalayan alder (*Alnus nepalensis*) is an excellent tree associate to cardamom for its appropriate shade, N_2-fixation ability (100-155 kg ha^{-1} $year^{-1}$) and nutrient rich litter. In the lower altitudes, between 600-1200 m, *Albizzia* and alder are together as shade trees. The annual cash return from cardamom is about USD 15 million. The system has strong social acceptance for its greater economic viability and ecological sustainability. This is an intensive self reliant system and an example of harnessing mountain niche that also provides basic support services of resources. Soil and nutrient loss are negligible; the system maintains live fence of trees and other associate biodiversity. It is a comparatively advantageous crop for the region.

In the *Albizzia*-mix trees-mandarin agroforestry, mandarin orange is a major tree crop while intercropping of maize, pulses, ginger, buckwheat, fingermillet, oilseeds, taro, sweet potato, potato and yam are also practiced. Mandarin orange and ginger are potential cash drops in Sikkim after cardamom. *Albizzia* is widely grown with other agroforestry trees in mandarin-based farming. Mandarin orange is a high value, comparatively less labour intensive cash crop. Diversity of crops and other associate tree species are maintained in the system for other subsistence requirements and benefits.

The on-farm agroforestry species such as *Erythrina indica, Ficus spp. Alnus nepalensis, Albizzia spp., Atrocarppus lacoocha, Thysanolema maxima, Dendrocalamus spp.* etc. are agro-ecologically adapted and socially accepted keystone species for their role in conserving and enhancing biodiversity in the mountain watersheds. *Alnus* and *Albizzia* have been a boon to the region for their role in nitrogen fixation, ecological adaptability, natural regeneration and restoration of degraded landslide areas, and accelerated nutrient cycling in the cultivated systems.

1.3. Valley Rice Cultivation Systems

The ancient ***Demazong*** *vis-a-vis* Sikkim is characterized by *Ghyya-dhan* (dryland paddy), which is followed by the valley rice cultivation along the river banks on flat lands traditionally called *Thang* (sometimes examples are *Tarey-thang-byansi, Pi-thang-byansi*) and along the typically terraced slopes in the lower hills. A large number of landraces of rice are cultivated. Some of the dryland paddy varieties were *Ghyya-dhan, Takmari, Bhuindhan, Marshi* etc. while the irrigated rice varieties now are *Attey, Timmurey, Krishnabhog, Bachhi, Nuniya, Mansaro, Baghey-tulashi, Kataka, Champasari, Sikrey, Taprey,* etc. adapted to agro-ecological zones between 300-1800 m. Krishnabhog, Nuniya and Kataka are famous for their aroma, medicinal importance and fine quality grain as good as Indian basmati rice. Almost all the dryland paddy landraces have now disappeared from the state while many traditional irrigated landraces have now disappeared already and others are on the verge of disappearance. The household mothers are generally the custodians of gene-banks of crop diversity; they keep the record of varieties/yields and preserve germplasm by growing them at different parcels of home garden allotted for growing heterogeneity of landraces. Farmers allow a variety of pulses and beans to grow along the raised bunds with terrace rice and allow maize, wheat, buckwheat, rape-mustard etc. after rice is harvested. Legumes are the source of protein, household earning and enrich fertility to the soil through the roots. Between the terraced open rice fields, along the slopes, are the traditional landscape systems, mostly cardamom-based and forest-based agroforests. Such traditional landscape designing of multifunctional agroforestry and protection to the terraced open rice cultivation system is characteristic of unique agro-ecosystem management in the mountains. The system in addition supports with water conservation and flood control, nutrient and biomass to the rice field and farm.

1.4. Biodiversity and Functioning of Agro-ecosystem

Sikkim Himalaya is a part of the 34 globally significant biodiversity hot-spots and endemism with rich agrobiodiversity as one of its principle components for livelihood security of the mountain people. It forms a part of the meeting ground of Indo-Malayan and Indo-Chinese biogeographical realms as well as Himalayan and Peninsular Indian elements that has given rise to a very rich biodiversity both wild and in cultivated landraces. Sikkim is phytogeographically rich and houses about 4500 species of plants (about 26% total plant wealth of Indian sub-continent), 60% of which are endemic. In Sikkim, 36 species of Rhododendrons, 450 species of Trees, 515 species of orchids, 424 species of medicinal plants, and 363 species ferns and allies are found. While it also houses a great number of wild animals consisting of 150 species of mammals, 552 species of birds, 690 species of butterflies, 48 species of fishes, 33 species of reptiles and 16 species of amphibians reported till date. About 80% of the total geographical area of the state is under the administrative control of the Forest Department, Government of Sikkim, the major land use is forestry (44%) with about 39% under protected area network.

Wild biodiversity and agrobiodiversity, in the context of Sikkim Himalaya, can be considered integrated agro-ecosystem and holistic which is characterized by the proximate interaction between natural systems and human dimensions. The high crop diversity and agro-ecosystem diversity is due to heterogeneity of landraces adopted by different traditional societies. Rich agrobiodiversity is a part of indigenous culture attributed to advancing agro-ecological variations within short distances, offering a unique example to the world. The prevalence of diversity of crops and local livestock breeds is the result of centuries long human breeding efforts depending on the locally differentiated resources in this part of the world.

1.5. Landscape and Land and Water Resource Management Characteristics

The unique mountainous landscape consists of varied physiographic factors and topography giving rise to microclimatic variations and a range of ecosystem, species and genetic diversity. As stated above, Sikkim consists of diverse natural-cultural landscapes and ecosystems that has brought together a network of ingenious cultural societies and management systems into a single regular natural continuum. Here, the biophysical features of landscapes at a shorter distance are conducive for genetic variations and landraces with sustained natural resource management.

Sikkim Himalayan glaciers e.g. the Zemu glacier are the water tanks, a key limiting factor for any land use in the downstream. The traditional ways of conservation of water such as local water seepage (***pani-pandhero***) is linked to cultural antiquity of the communities. Natural springs, streams and seepages, cliffs and peaks are all considered sacred and are conserved. The ***Devisthan*** (place of mother god), ***Dewrali*** (hill-tops, abode of deity), ***Teesta mai, Rangit mai*** and their tributaries (mother goddess in rivers), sacred groves and agroforests are the existing examples how people conserve land and water resources through social-cultural and traditional systems. The forests and mountains, valleys and plateaus are reservoirs of clean water. Indigenous communities have strong belief that the Maharani-Thakurani (mother goddess who keeps the vigil on them) would punish upon disturbing these sacred places. Slight pressure would result into calamities, diseases and illness, and also an extreme situation (*aapat-bipat*) is their cultural belief.

2.1. Sacred Places

Supernatural phenomena are immanent in the material world of Sikkimese people. The qualities of sacredness attach to space – Mountain peaks, Hills, Rivers, Lakes, Caves, Rocks etc., whether domestic architecture or the subcontinent itself. An enormous range of geographical features possesses sacred properties. Some are inherent and some are acquired through association with a holy individual or deity. The most sacred places are the places of worship of different faith and belief. For Hindus the Hindu temples, for Christians the Churches, for Limboos the Mangkhims, for Buddhists the Monasteries, for Muslims the Masjids etc scattered throughout the state of Sikkim are the sacred places of worship.

The state Government of Sikkim had constituted a Committee vide Notification No. 52/Home/98 dated 24th September 1998, to examine the background of all the monasteries, religious places of worship including important historical monuments and sacred lakes in Sikkim, and documented places of worship and Institutions in Sikkim which are 100 (hundred) years old and above. On the recommendation of the Committee submitted to the Government on 24th April 2001, the Government has declared all sacred peaks, caves, rocks, lakes, chhoedten and hot-springs as the most sacred Buddhist places of worship in Sikkim and protect them under the provisions of the places of worship (Special Provisions) Act, 1991 vide Government Notification No.355 dated 29th September, 2001. The state Government has banned the scaling of the sacred peaks and also defilement of the sacred caves, sacred rocks, sacred lakes, chhoedtens and sacred hot-springs. These are namely as follows:

2.2. Sacred Peaks

(*i*)	Ghangchhen-m Zod-Nga (Khangchendzonga)	(Kanchanjunga –Main 28,208 ft.) (Kanchenjunga- South 27,803 ft.) (Kanchenjunga –West 27,625 ft.)
(*ii*)	Mt. Narsing,	19,111 ft.
(*iii*)	Gabur Gangtsen:	(Kabru North, 24,075 ft.) (Kabru South, 24,005 ft.) (Kabru Dome, 21,600 ft.)

(*iv*) Pandim Peak, 21,658 ft.

(*v*) Mt. Simvo, 22,346 ft.

(*vi*) Goecha Peak, 20,100 ft.

(*vii*) Fork Peak, 20,382 ft.

(*viii*) Pao Hungri (Pauhungri), 23,180 ft.

(*ix*) Mt. Siniolchu, 22,609 ft.

2.3. Sacred Caves

(*i*) Sharchhogbayphug at Sangmo, South Sikkim.

(*ii*) Khadosangphug at Sanganath, South Sikkim.

(*iii*) Dechenphug above Nampung, West Sikkim.

(*iv*) Lharinyingphug via Kongri-Labdang, West Sikkim.

(*v*) Phagmorong, West Sikkim.

(*vi*) Tragtungrong, West Sikkim.

2.4. Sacred Rocks (Naydo)

(*i*) Yongzokdrak, West Sikkim.

(*ii*) Tragkar rock at Tashiding, West Sikkim.

(*iii*) Gyalwa Lhatsun Chhenpo's Footprint at Yuksam,

(*iv*) Coronation throne at Yuksom, West Sikkim,

(*v*) Thegchhok Yangtse Khadoi Drora rock, West Sikkim,

(*vi*) Guru Rimpoche's Footprint Naydo at Tsunthang (Chungthang), North Sikkim,

(*vii*) Kabilongtsok stone Naydo at Kabi, North Sikkim.

2.5. Sacred Lakes (Tsho)

(*i*) Omechho (Omai-tsho), West Sikkim,
(*ii*) Sungmteng Chho (Tsho), West Sikkim,
(*iii*) Lamchho (Lham-tsho), West Sikkim,
(*iv*) Tolechho (Dhole-tsho), West Sikkim,
(*v*) Kabur Lamchho (Gabur Lah-tsho), West Sikkim,
(*vi*) Khachoedpalri Pemachen Tsho (Khachoedpalri lake), West Sikkim,
(*vii*) Kathogtsho at Yuksam, West Sikkim,
(*viii*) Tsho-mGo lake, East Sikkim,
(*ix*) Guru Dongmar lake, North Sikkim,
(*x*) Tsho-lhamo, North Sikkim,
(*xi*) Mulathingkhai-tsho (Green lake) at Zema Glacier, North Sikkim.

2.6. Shhoedtens (Chorten/Stupa)

(*i*) Norbugang Chhoedten Tashi Hodber at Yukam built by Naljor Chi dshi,
(*ii*) Chhoedten Thongwa Rangdrol at Tashiding built by Gyalwa Lhatsun Chhenpo and its surrounding Chhoedten built more than 100 years ago;
(*iii*) Khachoedpalri Bheyul Chhoedten built in 19th century, a replica of Nepal's Boudhanath Stupa,
(*iv*) Dhud-Tsen-Lu-Sum Chhoedten at Rabdentse, West Sikkim,
(*v*) Gyalshing Mendang built by Kyabgon Jigme Pao to avert famine, West Sikkim,
(*vi*) Merimdang at Singnek, Tashiding, West Sikkim.

2.7. Hotsprings (Tshachhu)

(*i*) Phurtshachhu at Khadosangphug, South/West Sikkim,
(*ii*) Ranglop tshachhu Borong, South Sikkim,
(*iii*) Gangyab chhutshen, West Sikkim,
(*iv*) Takrumtshachhu, North Sikkim,
(*v*) Yumasamdongtshachhu, North Sikkim,
(*vi*) Yumthangtshachhu, North Sikkim,
(*vii*) Zee tshachhu, North Sikkim,
(*viii*) Shagyong phedok tshachhu, North Sikkim,
(*ix*) Tholung Kangtshachhu, North Sikkim.

2.8. Post-script

The members of the Committee constituted vide Notification No.52/Home/98 dated 24.09.1998 selected sacred places only from the Buddhist point of view. They completely neglected the sacred peaks, caves, rocks, lakes, etc of the ancient people of the Lepchas (Menrees), Tsongs (Tsongrees or Limboos) and other communities. The ancient tradition of the Lepcha says that the progenitor Lepchas "*Fodong-Theeng*" and "*Na-Jong-Nue*" were created by the their God *Rum* out of the snows of the untrodden peak of the *King-tzum-Song-bu* mountain. Their leader Thekong-Tek signed the blood brotherhood treaty with Khe-Bumsa at Kabi-Lungchok. Similarly, Sirijunga cave where the Mahatma Sirijunga of the Limboo community of Sikkim was hiding; and the Stone where he started his preaching of Yuma religion at Martam during 1734-1741 AD, are also missing from the list. The Limboo tradition believes that the Creator God created the Limboos at Kumbhakarna mountain (*Phoktanglungma Pembemlungma*), and considered the most sacred mountain by the community. The priest for fortification carry the souls of the living over there; and the souls of the dead are reached and hand over to the ancestors on the mountain in the Limboo tradition. All such sacred places are missing from the list. Thus, there is a need of revising the sacred list of Sikkim for inclusion of the remaining sacred places, rocks, and caves etc., which are more than 100 years of all other communities of Sikkim.

4

Shelter and Architecture

Sikkim bears a sensitive ecology. Nestled in the middle Himalayas in the lap of the majestic Kanchenjunga, the third highest mountain in the world, the landscape is perpetually blessed with wild fruits, medicinal plants, great climatic spectrum and unique customs and lifestyles. A delicate balance of Man and Nature relationship governs the existence of life here. The people have modified the environment, used available materials to create structures for shelter and work, and expressed their cultural values through architecture and landscape. Landscape, the physical imprint of culture on the environment, is important in looking at architecture for it links individual structures to both settlement pattern and sacred geography. The Indian National Trust for Art and for Cultural Heritage (INTACH) is also working in Sikkim to save endangered sites for future generations.

1. Settlement Pattern and Architecture

The basis of shelter and settlement involves climate, materials, and technology. Sikkim has extremely cold climate at higher mountains, seasonal cold climate at the mid and humid hot summer at lower hills. This extremity of the climate where the elevation rises from a little over 300 ft to 10,000 ft in a matter of few km distances, and this peculiar feature is variable through the entire state. Due to this factor major climatic zones can be categorized in the state with areas as unique as low, mid and high mountains, diverse topography, vegetation, soil types, recipient of heavy rainfalls, areas of extreme climate, area of high winds, areas of snow and blizzards, humid and wet, and material variables influence the land use pattern, what can be built, and the forms it takes. This often intertwines with sacred concepts. As unique as the climatic variation may sound, the architectural vocabulary of the state is also as unique as the state itself.

The settlement pattern in Sikkim is a farmhouse type in general. Most of the people in rural area (79%) are basically mixed farmers; and depend on forest for fodder, fuel and timber. The early settlement pattern of the ethnic groups followed by their economic interests: the Bhutia's preferred the higher altitudes for pasturing of their cattle and trade, the Lepcha's preferred the middle valleys between 5000-7000 ft being ideal for hunting and the Nepalese the lower river valleys for their fertile soil and the farmlands for terrace cultivation.

Mountain terraces create fields where rice, wheat, maize, barley, buckwheat, finger millet, pulses, oilseeds and other crops can be grown. Large cardamom and orange fruit Agro-forestry is common on sloppy humid and sunny areas respectively. Villages are generally situated on the slopes of hills known as *Bustee*. Villages subdivide their lands by use: compact settlements and dispersed residences, croplands, watersheds, forest on the higher mountains, and pastures.

2. Dwelling houses of antiquity

2.1. The Lepcha House - Dukenculee

The dwelling houses of Lepchas, the earliest settlers of Sikkim are known as "*Dukenculee*" in their language, which has generally a rectangular ground plan with a circular roof made of straw (*Siru* -thatch grass). A few huts with a rectangular roof of bamboo mat are also constructed for their livestock. The floor of the house is generally made with wooden planks (*Anto*) and the walls with bamboo matting plastered with a thin layer of clay. The roof is supported by a number of good-sized undressed timbers known as *Dampu,* which is inserted in the ground. They do not use nails or screws. The big wooden beams meant for supporting the roof are generally inserted through one another in a criss-cross way. The wooden floor of the house is generally constructed 3'-4' above the ground, keeping a continuous space beneath it which is used for keeping domesticated animals such as pigs, poultry birds etc. The dwelling house of the Lepchas generally consists of two bedrooms, one kitchen-cum-store room and in each of these rooms at least one window can be found. The houses are quite well ventilated having sufficient light. Both in front and back portion of the house there are small verandahs, which can be used as sitting or drawing rooms (Photo enclosed).

2.2. The Limboo House

Their traditional house is made of stone and mud. The house-roof are generally four-sided and made of thatch grass. However, the corrugated metal sheets have replaced the thatch grasses now. The upper parts of the house are plastered with white colour mud or slack lime while the lower parts are plastered with red or black-colour mud. In the middle of the house inside is a little raised or sunken fireplace for cooking food. Just above the fireplace (*Sumhatlung*), a little raised bench-like area is used for keeping cooked foods. Above the fireplace hang a mat-like bamboo work used for drying the meat and other items. The ground floor is rectangular and there is a worship place known as *Mangdhan* at one corner. On the four walls of the house are the windows. The doors are locked with wooden "*agloo*" from inner side and an iron chain (*Sangli*) from outside. In front of the house is a sitting space known as *Sikuwa*. A few huts with a rectangular roof of bamboo mat are also constructed for their livestock (Photo enclosed).

At places where the society is predominantly agricultural the design and layout of the dwelling units are governed by their usage and social status. The house of the common Limboo peasant is generally subtle, rectangular single story raised about six feet off the ground so that the lower portion of the house can be used as a space for sheltering the cattle from rain and cold. The space is also used for the storage of wood and other household items. The wooden members form the structural framework and the load bearing walls with infill panels of woven bamboo called "ikra" rendered with a paste made of cow dung, local red soil, straw and pieces of wood. The dwelling units are laid along the slope usually detached from the neighboring house.

Another typology is of a slightly richer peasant where the storage space and cattle shed is separate from the residential area is either single stored or double stored with kitchen and living space at the ground floor. These are individual detached dwelling units with load bearing stone masonry walls rendered with mud plaster.

3. Architecture after Later Half of 17th Century

Sikkimese Architecture has been developed over a period of 400 years and has strong elements influenced by her neighbours. One can see Tibetan, Chinese, Bhutanese, Nepali and Indo influence in its architecture and because of this complexity, Sikkimese architecture becomes all the more interesting to study. According to Architect Mr. Gary of Building and Housing Department, Government of Sikkim, the architecture development took place in Sikkim from the later half of 17th century as follows (Gary Chopel, 2007 unpublished manuscript):

The recorded history of Sikkimese architecture starts from the time when the *Dubdi Gumpa* (the oldest gumpa in Sikkim, reconstructed in 1701 AD) at Yuksom was commissioned under the patronage of the first Chogyal Phuntsho Namgyal in the later half of the seventeenth century right around the time when the mighty Shah Jahan was overseeing the construction work of the famous Taj Mahal at Agra (photo enclosed).

The earliest record of architecture in Sikkim was in the form of the monasteries, which were setup as institutions to promote Buddhism and to also have them perform as power centers and places of importance.

Among these the gumpa's at *Sangha Choeling* and *Pemayangtse* above present day Pelling town, *Kechopalri gumpa* in west Sikkim together with *Dubdi* formed the power corridor in the state around the mid 18th Century AD. (sketch-photo enclosed)

This region was the centre of *Demajong/Sukhim* (old name for Sikkim) till the mid 18th century AD when the capital was shifted to Tumlong in north Sikkim after the invasion of Sikkim by the Nepalese army of Prithvi Narayan Shah leaving the then palace at Rabdantse in ruins in 1814 A.D.(photo enclosed).

It may be mentioned here that though the first royal palace was at Tashi Tenka (Photo of the ruin enclosed), near the coronation throne at Norbugang in Yuksom, Rabdantse, the second capital of Sikkim (photo enclosed) could be deemed as the first planned complex with its palace, temples, houses, granary stores, courtyards and other amenities showing signs of rural planning and architecture.

During this time other centres of importance also sprung up and places like Drakar Tashiding, Ralang Rabdenling and the Tholung gumpa were also emerging as centres of importance. In Drakar Tashiding one type of archetypal form were particularly getting prominent. These were the group of *Chortens* in the complex and *Mendangs* on the way to the monastery complex.

The late 18th Century saw the chortens develop into newer and larger forms and these can be particularly seen in the later chortens at Tashiding and the most fascinating being the one at Kechopalri next to the gumpa. This one was commissioned by the 4th Chogyal Gyurmed Namgyal and is made in the shape of a mandala and on the lines of the Boudhanath stupa in Kathmandu though much less in scale and magnitude.

After the invasion of Sikkim by the Nepalese (1774 AD onwards) army the architectural history of Sikkim remains slow in progress with very few structures being commissioned in the scale of previous centers of importance. But it is during this phase that the shelter of the common man which had been so far not in the foreground gains importance and magnificent houses in form of *Thashas, Kothis, Kacheris* and *Garo ghars* gains momentum and are seen built all over the state with some amount of regional touch and social necessity.

Together these formed the majority of samples of architecture in this area are the best clubbed under local vernacular houses that are unique as the region itself.

According to Mr. Gary of Building and Housing Department, Government of Sikkim, the vernacular houses of these times can be put into four broad categories:

First type is the WOOD HOUSE or IGRA- GHAR or SINGKHIM or the '*TSHE-KHIM*', which means the house made of wood or the wooden house. Wood historically was suppose to be cheaper and was easily available as compare to the dressed stone, which was expensive and was only used by some. Houses made of wattle panels and wooden framework fall under such category (photo enclosed).

Second category is WOOD-STONE HOUSE or the "DOW-KHIM" or TALEY GHAR, which is a combination of wood and dressed stone masonry. The stone used was slate which is soft and brittle. The '*Kothi*' are the house of Landlord's, Thasha's (monks dwellings) at Ralang, Pemayangtse are some of the examples, which fall under this category (photo enclosed).

The third category is RUBBLE-EARTH HOUSE or the "GARO-GHAR" which is a combination of rubble earth structural walls with timber members as supporting grid and structural members and laid in mud mortar. The '*Garo ghar*' are the house of Nepali families and are found with different window and bracket design depending on the community that owns one. The houses at Central Pendam, Duga ('*Druka*' is the original name), Tharup and Hee gaon are some of the best examples of houses of this category.

The Fourth category is COMMON MAN's HOUSE or the "CHIRTA KO GHAR" which is a combination of bamboo framework with mud walls and full bamboo as supporting grid and structural members. The '*Chitra ghar*' are the house of rural low-income houses of common man and are found in abundance dotting the village landscape mostly in the middle and the lower areas (photo enclosed).

Historically, depending on the region, thatch, bamboo mats, wooden boats and flat stones tied on wooden frame was used to cover the top was replaced with GCI sheets later.

The "*Kothi*" or the house of a landlord is generally more elaborate, spread over a large area with extensive carving and ornamentation that distinguishes its typology with the house of a common peasant. The form or styles of these vary with region and generally acquire their features and form from the religious structures like Gompas or British Colonial buildings. For example, the Kazi Kothi at Rishum and Ralang has a cross plan with dressed stone masonry at the ground floor and decorative wooden members on the upper floors were highly influenced by the historic religious structures (photo enclosed).

The Mathilo Kothi at Duga village is more influenced by the Colonial architecture and layout. It is again use of indigenous materials with rich craftsmanship, which make them stand out among the other houses of the settlement (photo enclosed).

Another category is the "*Thasha*" or the residence of a Lama (priest). These *Thashas* share similar architectural styles, materials that are available and prevalent locally. But sometimes lama's residences do have decorative features acquired from the Gompa building with carved lattice and window panels. Thashas generally have their storage space at the lower level and living area on the upper level (photo enclosed).

The houses are raised about 4ft to 6ft off the ground so that the lower part of the house can be used as basement for sheltering the cattle from rain and cold. It is also used for storage of wood and other household items. Also the older construction was very local material based and was a great state of art and a piece of craftsmanship.The corner joints were a craft of carpentry using mortise and tenon joints which were excellent under seismic conditions and this old method of construction is also very eco-friendly. A bamboo mat wall called 'ikra' is woven and a paste made of cow dung, wood pieces, local red soil and pieces of straws are splashed over the bamboo mat wall. This wall acts as a great insulator as it provides warmth in the winters and keeps the house cool during the summer seasons and is also very cheap to construct.

Since Sikkim is an earthquake prone area, the heritage houses were made of groves and nail work was minimized so that the structure stands during the time of the earthquake. The houses were mostly of timber. Old method of construction was eco-friendly and was a great structure during earthquake and especially in winter. The houses had few bamboo nails or no nails at all and were great works in terms of craftsmanship and the details. The corner joints were a craft of carpentry and the foundations were of wood. These houses can stand the test of time and houses 150 – 200 year old can also be seen at a few remote places like Lachung and Lachen in the North of Sikkim. The walls were made of a paste of cow dung, local red soil and bamboo leaves which would act as insulation and they were laid over a skeleton of bamboo. These houses were warm to live in and had a very different charm about it.

After a lot of experimentation with the materials and construction techniques, different structures had been created in history corresponding to the climatic and geographical conditions and needs, which have lasted many years since inception. These structures are an integral part of Sikkim's architectural heritage. Physical, cultural and trade links between the neighboring areas like China, Nepal, Bhutan and Tibet have unconsciously imported architectural elements that have made Sikkimese vernacular architecture more complex and irregular.

During the 19th Century already established monasteries like Pemayangtse and Tashiding grew in importance and a small settlement began to grow at the foothills of these centers and gave rise business and other social activity. It was during this time that the famous Enchey monastery in Gangtok was built and is one of the most beautiful examples of architecture in the state. Other centers like Phodong and Phensang were setup and along with it grew settlements, which have today emerged into towns of today.

After the *treaty of Titalia* in 1817AD Sikkim parted with the most of the Gorkha hills and the Darjeeling hill station region (1835) which became the summer retreat of the British. This important phase brought with it expeditions by the British, Finnish and other European missions to Sikkim and along with it brought their culture and lifestyles. The earlier Finnish missionaries set churches and centers for Christianity in the state and centres like *SamarTek* in Mangan and the Roman Catholic Church were established in times to follow.

This was also an era where rest houses or Dak Bungalow were setup. The British were explorers and penetrated deep into areas unexplored by other for their academic and strategic interest thus these Dak Bungalows were setup all over the state along the major trails (mostly Dr. Hooker's trail) and had a style and statement of its own to make. These single and double storey residences were strategically located on vantage points and are amongst some of the earliest British architectural contribution to the state.

With the interest of the British East India ever growing in the state, many new constructions were made which were done with cement and RCC though made in the traditional style. It was during this time that major architectural landmarks like the White Memorial Hall, the present State Archives Building (old assembly), the Health secretariat and the present *Raj Bhawan* (old India House) were commissioned and brought with it other institutional prototypes. The houses of this era had British influences in the form of arches, bay- windows and fire place and can be seen in houses like the present Palace in Gangtok, *Kazi Kothis*, and *Mathilo kothi at Duga*. These were houses of the more influential people and were made lavishly for those times.

4. Landscape and Architecture after 1975

With the 20th century coming to the end, it brought democracy to the state of Sikkim with the erstwhile Kingdom of Sikkim merging with the Indian mainland becoming the 22nd state of India. The architectural activity in the state is now dictated by major government projects and some private players with the establishment of buildings like the State Legislative Assembly, the Tashiling Secretariat and numerous official buildings etc.The present day construction activity has been on an all time high with cement and RCC and the major ingredients for construction defacing the landscape and the built heritage of the state.

Religious institutions always formed a major part of constructions activity in the state historically and even today. Today one can see religious centres like mandir, maang-hims, mosques, gumpa's, gurudwaras all over the state sharing the landscape in harmony and leading a way to the future of new architectural landmarks in Sikkim.

The status symbol for anyone who aspires to become middle class is a Pakka house. Those who can afford it use concrete, stone, and brick to build homes with chunky exteriors, iron grills, and colorful trim. The Kaccha homes of the poor use local materials, and they often combine wattle-and-daub and straw thatch with diverse manufactured elements.

5
Food and Dress Culture

Food and Dress links the State of Sikkim to history, culture, and identity to the country. They also link people to cosmological theories of inner substance and its transformations, to concepts of ritual purity and pollution, to modernity and to tradition. The great stories of food and dress in the State in the later half of twentieth century are movements to improve indigenous farming, and creation of a distribution system that aims to ensure that every individual will have access to an adequate basic diet and clothing. It examines food cosmology, the theories of food and diet that underline cuisine and food-related etiquette in the State. Cosmology links food, medical perspectives, and concepts of purity and pollution. Shift in dress signal status changes of the people of the State or a country.

1. Food Culture:

Food culture of Sikkim is directly related to the pattern of food production in the State. It has evolved as a result of traditional wisdom and experiences of generations over a period of time. It has been based on agro-climatic conditions suitable for cultivation of different crop species such as cereals, pulses, oilseeds, fruits, vegetables, spices and availability of wild edible plants, ethnic belief systems and preferences, socio-economic development status, regional and cultural practices. Traditional foods have an important bearing in the dietary habits of the people of Sikkim (Tamang, 2005: 1-2).

Stone Age (Paleolithic Age Antiquity to 5,000 B.C.) nomadic hunter-gatherers were roaming across the world at least 70,000 years ago and some researchers believe the primitive humans may have lived in Sardinia (Italy) as long as 400,000 years ago. By around 4,000 B.C. (Neolithic Age of 5,000-2,000 B.C.) the Neolithic humans developed the art of land cultivation due to scarcity of food available for hunting and gathering. Agriculture required people to stay in one spot and so fixed settlement emerged. According to the legend of the Kiratas (Mundhum–oral tradition of the Limboos), the Black Soybean was the first crop, domesticated and cultivated by the Kiratas (Limboos). The lone cultivated crop was thus eaten in a variety of ways to avoid monotonousness of eating. Thus they ate it and still eating it as raw, boiled with pods, dry frying, crushing, boiling the beans, as fermented product etc. and thus developed a variety of products including famous "*Kinema*". Later on a number of crops were added up for cultivation through improvement of wild crop plants and through plant introduction. Sikkim is very rich in flora and faunal diversity. Thus, the people of Sikkim adopted eating of tender shoots, leaves, flowers, fruits, seeds, root and tubers of a variety of plant and animal species available in Sikkim. This practice has ultimately evolved a number of traditional food culture in Sikkim Himalayas (Subba, 1999: 49-52, 159-160; Subba, 2002: 48-187).

1.1 Food Production:

About 89% of the population of Sikkim are living in the rural areas (72% in the country) (Census of India 2001) and the economic activity of mountainous Sikkim is primarily a mixed farming – agriculture, horticulture and livestock rearing, in a limited cultivable land resources. The various crops produced and the changing levels of production of different agricultural and diversified horticultural crops from 1975-76 to 2004-05 are as follows:

The State is deficit in food production and thus the State Government obtains foodgrain such as rice 45,849 tonnes and wheat 636 tonnes annually under different Centrally Sponsored and State programmes from FCI and distributes to the consumers through PDS (Subba, J.R. 2005: SARD-M Report, FAO/ICIMOD: pp 37-38).

1.2. Livestock Production:

Livestock wealth of Sikkim is modest, but is rich with diverse species. The most popular and so preponderant among all species is cattle and milk production is the major livestock related economic activity. Livestock holding in Sikkim is equitable: over 85 per cent of all species including crossbred cows are owned by the marginal and small holders, individual holdings are small though and the usual mix is cow/calf 2, goat 2, and poultry flocks of over 10 including a cock or two. Pigs are not so common; barely 25 per cent of households; and sheep are localized in the high altitudes of North and West districts. Less than 30 per cent of the households own bullocks. Hiring of work bullocks, both in and out is an established system among Sikkim farmers.

Over the last 26 years, the highest increase of livestock species was recorded in pigs (103.86%), followed by crossbreed cattle (85.64%) yaks (63.23%) and poultry (45.75%). Drastic reduction on population of sheep (64.00%) and buffaloes (61.05%) was recorded followed by indigenous cattle (49.76%).

Temporal Changes in Production ('000 tonnes) of Major Crops Cultivated in Sikkim (1975-76 to 2004-05):

Major Crops	*1975-76*	*1985-86*	*1995-96*	*2000-01*	*2004-05*	*Gain/loss in about three decades (%)*
Agricultural Crops:						
Paddy	10.00	16.50	21.87	21.35	21.61	31
Wheat	0.15	16.20	15.30	10.10	8.25	—
Maize	16.50	47.60	56.56	59.61	58.19	253
Other cereals	4.50	7.70	8.00	6.97	6.68	48
Total cereals	31.15	88.00	101.79	98.03	94.73	204
Pulses	0.70	8.45	5.91	5.16	6.44	820
Oilseeds	0.70	10.25	7.64	7.38	7.56	980
Total Agri. Crops	32.55	106.70	115.34	110.57	108.73	234
Horticultural crops:						
Mandarin Orange	3.60	5.00	7.00	7.50	8.35	132
Other Fruits	1.10	3.50	3.30	2.45	3.86	251
Total Fruits	4.70	8.50	10.30	9.95	12.21	160
Seasonal Vegetables	5.00	11.86	18.40	22.80	29.65	493
Off-season Vegetables	—	0.04	7.60	9.55	12.02	—
Total Vegetables	5.00	11.90	26.00	32.35	41.67	733
Seed Potato	2.00	13.50	12.00	13.00	14.78	639
Table Potato	3.00	12.90	12.00	12.50	17.83	494
Total Potato	5.00	26.40	24.00	25.50	32.61	552
Other root & tubers	0.10	0.40	1.00	1.80	22.24	—
Large Cardamom	2.30	3.90	3.60	4.67	3.74	63
Ginger	2.00	10.90	24.00	24.00	34.71	1636
Turmeric	—	—	0.60	1.29	1.74	—
Floriculture						
Cut flowers (lac Nos.)	—	—	5.00	10.00	14.00	—
Bulbs/Plants (lac Nos.)	—	—	10.00	20.00	13.70	—
Total Horti. Production	19.10	62.00	89.50	99.47	128.92	575

Source: F S & ADD; Horticulture &CCD, GOS

The major livestock products in 2001 were: milk 37,000 mt; meat 35,000 mt; poultry meat 500 mt; eggs 10.03 million; and Farm Yard Manure (FYM) 112,939 tonnes for crop agriculture and horticulture production. The total output value of the livestock sector in Sikkim in 2002 was Rs.797.79 million and the livestock sector contribution to the GSDP was about 8.16 per cent (LSR Estimates 2004).

The State is deficit in Livestock products also. The State's production is supplemented through import of livestock products from other states as follows:

Sikkim Livestock Census:

Species	*1977*	*1988*	*1997*	*2003*	*Change from 1977 to 2003 in (%)*
Indigenous cattle	157,784	140,399	90,721	79,263	(–) 49,76
Cross-breed cattle	—	42986	52,303	79,799	85.64
Buffalo	5,438	3,088	1,970	2,118	(–) 61.05
Sheep	16,104	10,933	5,023	5,796	(–) 64.00
Goat	88,986	98,210	82,980	123,841	39.17
Pig	18,595	31,402	26,975	37,907	103.86
Yak	3,995	5,354	4,731	6,521	63.23
Horses/mules/donkeys	—	—	1,960	—	
Poultry	2,20,927	209,255	221,406	321,995	45.75

Source: Sikkim Livestock Census 1977,1988, 1997, 2003.

Inflow of Livestock and Livestock Products during 2003-04 & 2004-05:

Year	*Information*	*Cattle*	*Buffalo*	*Goat*	*Pig*	*Poultry*	*Fish*	*Total meat (in tons)*
2003-04	No. of livestock	2,821	1,150	5.668	2,880	1,01.519	no record	
	Carcass Yield %/kg	50-55/100	50-55/110	50-55/10	60-70/80	70-75/1		
	Meat in tons	282.10	126.50	56.68	230.40	101.52	no record	797.20
2004-05	No. of livestock	2.880	1,164	5,784	2928	1,03,588	no record	
	Meat in tons	288.00	128.04	57.84	234.24	103.59	do	811.71

Source: Check-post Records of AH & VS, Govt. of Sikkim.

2. Food Mealtime:

The people of Sikkim are basically rural, and generally take two heavy meals and two light refreshments. Unlike in the other parts of the country, people of Sikkim in the rural area prefer to eat four meals a day: Morning meal (*Bihan ko Khaza*) before going to morning field-work; mid-day meal or lunch (*Din ko Bhat*) before going for the day's field-work; afternoon refreshment (*Deunso ko Khaza*) and evening dinner (*Beluka ko Bhat*). The urban people also follow the same pattern with some difference.

2.1. Morning Light Meals:

In the rural village of Sikkim the morning starts with tea or alcoholic beverage (*Chang/Jaanr/Bhati ko Jaanr*) with dry-fried whole maize or soybean or beaten rice/maize or boiled potato or colocasia or *ghar tarul,* or any seasonal foods, and proceed for morning work of fodder/fuel-wood collection or agricultural works such as ploughing, field preparation, manuring, sowing, transplanting, weeding, harvesting, storing etc. Tea is taken with sugar or salt, with or without milk, or with a pinch of black pepper or ginger paste.

2.2. Mid-Day Meals (Lunch):

After finishing the morning work the rural people may come for lunch at home or the lunch is served to the field depending on the nature of work. *Bhat-dal-tarkari-achar* (rice-legume soup-curry-pickle) is the basic of the Sikkimese meal corresponding to cooked rice, *dal* or vegetable mixed with potato curry, meat or milk product –*mohi* and various kinds of *achar* with hot chilly (Tamang, J.P. 2005: 2-3). The rice is very often substituted by *Makai ko Bhat-Dhenro, Hariyo Makai, Kodo ko Roti, Phapar ko roti, Gahun ko roti* etc. The legume soup-curry is often substituted with seasonal vegetable curry or meat curry or *mohi.*

2.3. Afternoon Refreshment:

In the late afternoon, the rural people may take light refreshment with tea or alcoholic beverages (*Chang/Jaanr/Bhati ko Jaanr*). The refreshments may be of seasonal root or tuber crops (boiled cassava, potato, colocasia, greater yams, sweet potato, Iskus-chayote root or fruit etc.), dry-fried maize or soybean, *phapar ko roti, kodoko roti, gahun ko roti, chewra* (beaten rice), *murai, champa* (roasted and powdered maize, wheat, barley, gram etc.).

2.4. Evening Meals (Dinner):

In the evening the rural people take tea or alcoholic beverages (*tongba* –fermented millet beer put in bamboo or wooden cans / *Chang/ Jaanr/Bhati ko Jaanr*) before dinner. The dinner is also composed of the basic *Bhal-dal-tarkari-achar* as mentioned above. The Bhutia and Lepcha tribes usually eat thug-pa, noodles in soup. The rural people mostly eat cooked maize as staple food such as *Dheroh,* boiled maize rice, and continues to be a staple food in villages. The rice is slowly being replaced by *roti* or *chapati* (wheat-based baked bread), even in the rural areas today. In high altitudes mainly in North Sikkim, people drink *pheuja,* butter tea prepared from yak milk (Tamang, J.P. 2005: 2-3).

The urban people generally take morning tea, breakfast or early lunch in the morning, lunch or afternoon refreshment in the mid-day meal, and dinner. They may take non-alcoholic or alcoholic beverages before dinner. The food items may vary depending on their ethnic traditional choice of food items available in the cosmopolitan areas.

Most of the people in Sikkim are non-vegetarians but some members of Bahuns and Chettris are vegetarians. Sikkimese food is less spicy and prepared in *gheu* or butter, or mustard or rape oil or animal fat in the rural areas. The non-vegetarians take beef, pork, mutton, chicken, fish, buffalo, sheep etc. depending on the community preferences and social taboos. The average intake of nutrients is still below the minimum required, which is as follows:

Average Intake of Nutrients in Sikkim (consumption per capita per day):

Nutrient	*Rural*	*Urban*
Energy (K. cal)	2197	2157
Protein (g)	64.5	70.2
Fat (g)	25	31.3
Calcium (mg)	566.2	560.8
Phosphorous (mg)	1343	1413.7
Iron (mg)	21	22.5
Vitamin A (mg)	376.1	322
Vitamin B_1 (mg)	1.5	1.7
Vitamin B_2 (mg)	1.3	1.3
Niacin (mg)	23.6	22.9
Vitamin C (mg)	64.8	75.4

Source: Department of women and child Development, GOI (1997)

3. Food Culture and Ethnic Tourism:

According to Tamang J.P. (2005: 104-108), **"Rice-soybean-fish-alcoholic beverage"** diet is the characteristic food culture of the Far-East and South East Asia, whereas **"Wheat-milk and milk products-meat-wine"** is the basic diet in the Western part of the world. The food culture of Sikkim Himalayas shows an amalgamation of both Eastern and Western food cultures. In East Asia rice is the staple food whereas in West Asia wheat or barley is staple food. Milk products similar to west and alcoholic beverages similar to East are encountered in the food culture of Sikkim. Most of the traditional fermented foods are prepared by processes of solid substrate fermentation in which the substrate is allowed to ferment either naturally or by adding starters. In East and South-East Asia, moulds are predominant microorganisms in the fermentation processes, whereas in Africa, Europe and America, fermented products are prepared exclusively using bacteria or combination of bacteria-yeasts. Moulds seem to be seldom or never used. However, in Eatern Himalayas, all three major groups of microorganism (moulds-yeasts-bacteria) are associated with traditional fermented foods and beverages showing the transition of food culture (Tamang 1998a). Food culture of Sikkim presents a kaleidoscopic panorama. Every item prepared in Sikkim by different ethnic groups is unique and unparallel.

4. Traditional Foods of Sikkim:

Traditional foods are generally categorized into fermented foods and alcoholic beverages, produced by microorganism(s), and non-fermented foods. These inexpensive, culturally accepted traditional foods provide the basic diet. Pickle, confectionery, condiments and alcoholic beverages supplement to enhance the level of nutrition with palatability, wholesomeness, flavour and texture. *Kinema* and *Maseura* are the two most important fermented legumes; *Gundruk, Sinki*, and *Mesu* are the important fermented vegetables; *Dahi, Mohi, Gheu, Chhurpi* (Hard), *Chhurpi* (soft), *Chhu, Somar*, and *Philu* are fermented milk-products; *Sukako Maacha, Gnuchi, Sidra*, and *Sukuti* are fermented fish products; *Marcha, Kodo ko Jaanr* or *Chyang, Bhaati Jaanr*, and *Raksi* are the alcoholic beverages; and *Dheroh, Phulaurah, Momo, Thukpa or Gya-thuk, Pakku, Kodo ko Roti, Phapar ko Roti, Chambrey, Achar, Su Zom, Po Ngu Zom, Khu Zom, Wachipa, Alum, Foldong, Falki, Chhwelaa, Kwanti, Chatamari*, edible ferns, etc. are some of the traditional Non-fermented foods of Sikkim (Tamang 2005: 8-93)

4.1. Traditional Fermented Foods:

Fermented foods are prepared by the action of microorganism (s), either spontaneously or by adding starter culture(s), which modify the substrates biochemically and organoleptically into edible products. These are thus generally palatable, safe and nutritious. Tamang, (2005: 6-7) has identified more than 30 varieties of ethnic fermented foods in the Sikkim Himalayas. Some of these are commonly prepared and consumed for centuries. Few products are lesser known and confined to particular communities and places. About 20 per cent of the total food consumed daily constitutes fermented foods (Yonzon and Tamang, 1998). Women play an important role with their indigenous knowledge of food fermentation. Their participation spans from cultivation to harvesting, fermentation to culinary skills and production to marketing.

4.2. Traditional Alcoholic Beverages:

Traditional alcoholic beverages constitute an integral part of dietary culture in Sikkim. These beverages have strong ritualistic importance among the ethnic people in the Sikkim Himalayas where social activities require provision and consumption of appreciable qualities of alcohol (Tamang et, al, 1996; Subba, J.R. 1999). Making and use of fermented beverages are of widespread interest among various Sikkimese communities. Home made alcoholic beverages have high religious and cultural significance. Alcoholic beverages are exclusively prepared from locally grown cereal-grains using traditionally prepared mixed *inocula* or starter called *marcha*. These alcoholic beverages are also nutritious. Traditional alcohol brewing is a home-based industry mostly taken care of by rural women using their indigenous knowledge of alcohol fermentation. The followings are the popular alcoholic beverages in Sikkim:

The followings are some of the better-known fermented foods of Sikkim

Product	*Major Ingredient(s)*	*Nature and Use*	*Major Consumer*
Kinema	Soybean	sticky soybean; curry	Non-Bahun
Maseura	Black Mung	Dry, ball-like; condiment	Newar
Gundruk	Leafy vegetables	Dried, sour; soup/pickle	All
Goyang	Green vegetables	Curry	Sherpa
Sinki	Radish tap root	Dried sour; soup/pickle	All
Khalpi	Cucumber	Sour; pickle	Bahun-Chettri
Mesu	Bamboo shoots	Sour; pickle	All
Selroti	Rice-flour	Round, deep fried; bread	Nepalis
Phalgi	Corn	Boiled; staple	Sherpa
Chhurpi (soft)	Cow/Yak milk	Soft, cheese-like,	All
Chhurpi (hard)		curry/pickle	All
Chhu/Sheden	Cow/Yak milk	Hard-mass; masticator	Bhutias, Lepchas,
	Cow/Yak milk	Soft; strong-flavored, dish	Sherpas
Philu/Shyowshin	Cow/Yak milk	Cream; fried curry with butter	Bhutias, Sherpas
Samar	Cow/Yak milk	Paste; flavored;	Sherpas
Dahi/Shyow	Cow/Yak milk	condiment	All
Mohi	Cow milk	Curd; savory	All
Gheu	Cow milk	Butter-milk	All
Maa	Yak milk	Butter	Bhutias
Chur	Cow milk	Butter	Bhutias
		Wet cheese-like; curry	Non-Bahuns Nepalis
Sidra	Fish	Dried fish; curry	Non-Bahuns Nepalis
Sukuti	Fish	Dried, salted	Non-Bashuns
Sukako maacha	River fish	Dried/ Smoked	Nep[alis
Gnuchi	River fish	Smoked fish; curry	Lepchas
Shakampo	Beef/Yak/Pork	Smoked meat; curry	Bhutias, Lepchas
Kanrgong	Beef/Yak/Pork	Sausages; curry	Bhutias, Lepchas
Kheuri	Beef/Yak/Pork	Sausages; curry	Bhutias, Lepchas
Satchu	Yak/Beef	Dried smoked; curry	Bhutias
Sukula	Buffalo meat	Dried meat; curry	Newar
Sukakomasu	Mutton/Pork	Smoked meat; curry	Non-Vegetarian
Mohi Sumbak	Mohi, oil, spices	Oil-fried mohi with spices; staple	Limboos
Sura Sumbak	Cheese (soft), oil, spices	Oil-fried cheese with spices	Limboos
Sura-Keek Sumbak	Cheese (soft), further fermented, moldy	Oil-fried moldy Cheese with spices.	Limboos
Chembikeek Sumbak	Kinema, oil, spices	Oil-fried kinema with spices; staple	Limboos
Phanook keek sumbak	Fermented bamboo shoots	Oil-fried fermented; curry	Limboo

Source: Food culture, Tamang 2005: 6-7; Subba, 1999: 159; Kirat Yakthung Chumlung; 2002

4.3 Traditional Non-Fermented Foods:

Every community living in Sikkim has its own native dishes. According to Tamang (2005: 82-93) there are more than 150 different varieties of non-fermented traditional food products including edible wild plants in Sikkim. The people to develop a variety of traditional foods have utilized the rich floral and faunal diversity of Sikkim in a various ways. The faunas and floras being used by the people of Sikkim has been listed by Subba (2002) in his book "Biodiversity of the Sikkim Himalayas". However, some of these popular ethnic foods of Sikkim could be listed as follows:

Products	*Ingredient*	*Nature and Use*	*Major Consumer*
Marcha/Khesung/ Phab/Buth	Rice, wild herbs, spices	Starter culture to ferment alcoholic beverages	Limboo, Khambu Rais and Lepcha women are major producers
Kodo ko Jaanr/ Chyang/Chee	Finger millet	Mildly-alcoholic, slightly sweet-acidic; beverage	Non-Bahun Nepalis, Bhutias, Lepchas
Bhaati jaanr	Rice	Mildly-alcoholic, sweet-sour,food beverage; paste	"
Makai ko jaanr	Maize	Mildly-alcoholic, sweet-sour, food beverages; paste	"
Gahoon ko jaanr	Wheat	Mildly-alcoholic, slightly acidic, beverage	"
Simal tarul ko jaanr	Cassava roots	Mildly-alcoholic, sweet-sour, food beverage; paste	"
Jao ko jaanr	Barley	Mildly-alcoholic, slightly acidic, beverage	"
Faapar ko jaanr	Buckwheat (*Fagopyrum tartaricum*)	Mildly-alcoholic, slightly acidic, beverage	"
Raksi/Arak/ Sejongwa	Any Cereals	Clear distilled liquor; high alcohol content drink.	"
Phung khey Sejonwa	*Cana sp*, finger millet/maize Pear, finger millet/	Fermented tubers clear distilled liquor; high alcohol content Fermented, clear distilled	Limboos

Food culture not only depends on different communities living in Sikkim but also on economic status of the people and availability of food crops especially seasonal vegetables (Kharif and Rabi season) and fruits in different season in a year. It also changes with the people, space and time.

Products	*Ingredient*	*Nature and Use*	*Major Consumer*
Dheroh	Corn/millet	Cooke dcorn/millet; porridge; staple	Nepalis
Phulaurah	Buckwheat	Deep-fried, snack	"
Kalo dal	Black Mung	Thick dal mixed with jimmu	"
Kodo ko roti	Finger millet	Baked millet flour; staple food	"
Faaper ko roti	Buckwheat (both Fagopyrum tartaricum & F. esculentum)	Baked buckwheat flour; staple	"
Chamrey	Rice	Soaked, fried rice; staple	"
Chiura	Rice	Beaten rice; snack	All
Khir	Rice-milk-butter-sugar	Rice pudding	Nepalis
Rayo Sag	Mustard leaves	Fried vegetable; side-dish; curry	All
Ban Tarul	Wild Yam (Dioscorea hemiltoni)	Boiled/roasted; staple	All
Ghar tarul	Greater yam (D. alata)	Boiled; staple	All
Simal Tarul	Cassava	Boiled; staple	All
Piranlu	Colocasia	Boiled; staple	All
Shimrayo	Water cress	Cooked young leaves; curry	All
Ghario Sishnu	Nettle (Urtica dioica)	Boiled young shoots /flowers; curry	All
Patle sishnu	Neetle (Laportea terminalis)	Boiled young shoots /flowers; curry	All
Bhangrey Sishnu	Neetle (Girardinia palmata)	Boiled young shoots/ flowers; curry	All
Sauney ningro	Fern (Diplazium esculentum)	Vegetable; curry	All
Tite Ningalo	Bamboo (Arundinaria intermedia)	Vegetable curry	All
Tama	Young bamboo shoots	Boiled, fry; curry, pickle	All
Kalungey cheu	Mushroom (Agaricus sp.)	Curry	Non-Bahun Nepalis, Bhutias, Lepchas
Kanney cheu	Mushroom (Pleurotus sp)	Curry	"
Siitimbur	Szechwan pepper (Litsea cubeba)	Fruits; pickle	Nepalis
Laharay Timbur	Bokey Timbur (Xenthoxylum armatum)	Fruits, seeds; pickle	Nepalis
Chinday	Pentapanax leschnaultii	Young shoots; pickle	Nepalis
Lapsi	Hog plum (Choerospondias axillaris)	Fruits; pickle	Nepalis

Products	*Ingredient*	*Nature and Use*	*Major Consumer*
Dalley khorsani	Cherry pepper	Pickle	All
Thotne	Aconogonum molle	Young shoots; pickle	Nepalis
Koirala	Bauhinia vareigata	Pickle	"
Chimphing	Sikkim herb (Heracleum wallichii)	Dried fruits; pickle	"
Kabra	Ficus infectoria	Un-opened leaf-buds; pickle	"
Kukurdaine	Greebriet (Smilex spp.)	Tender shoot; pickle	"
Nakima	Tupistra nutans	Flower, vegetable; pickle	All
Halhaley	Yellow dock (Rumex nepalensis)	Vegetable	All
Silam	Perilla frutecens	Seeds; pickle	Nepalis
Bhatmas ko achar	Soybean	Pickle	"
Phillingey	Niger (Guizotia sp.)	Seeds; pickle	"
Momo	Wheat flour with meat/vegetable	steamed dumpling; staple	"
Thukpa	Wheat noodle	Boiled, mixed with minced meat; stew/soup; staple	Bhutias Lepchas
Gyathuk	Wheat noodle	Noodles in soup; staple	Bhutias Lepchas
Shya phaley	Wheat flour-meat	Stiff, fried, mixed with meat	Bhutias
Chempo	Pork/beef	Liver cooked in souce	Bhutias
Phituk	Rice/barley flour	Porridge with meat; staple	Bhutias
Fing	Vermicelli	Cooked with mushroom, meat; soup	Bhutias
Khuri	Millet/buckwheat flour	Roll with meat and vegetable; snack	Bhutias
Phaktoo	Macaroni	Macaroni, cooked with meat; soup	Bhutias
Nya phachung	Fish	Fish grilled in bamboo; side dish	Bhutias Lepchas
Khanakpa	Evodia fraxinifolia	Dried fruits; pickle	All
Zhero	Wheat	Deep fried; snack	Bhutias & Tamangs
Chadung	Wheat	Snack	Bhutias
Khapjey	Wheat flour/rice	Deep fried; snack	Bhutias & Tamangs
Phoshya gyari	Pork	Cooked pork; curry	Bhutias
Nya cham	Barley flour	Roasted; snack	Bhutias
Gyuma	Meat, rice	Stuffed sausage; side dish	Bhutias
Ken-tsong	Maize flakes	Roasted; snack	Bhutias
Tsampa	Barley	Roasted barley grains; snacks	Bhutias
Cha (ja)	Tea, butter	Tea in boiled water with salt and butter; beverage	Bhutias

Products	*Ingredient*	*Nature and Use*	*Major Consumer*
Moongarbuk	Sweet potato	Boiled; staple	Lepcha
Kasalok	Sweet potato/yam	Boiled; staple	Lepcha
Sarongbee tuluk	Rice and nettle	Cooked as porridge; staple	Lepcha
Cho-nyok	Rice, butter, vegetable	Cooked as porridge; staple	Lepcha
Po Nguzom	Rice, fish, vegetable	Grilled in bamboo; staple	Lepcha
Khu zom	Wheat, millet, maize	Baked on hot stone; staple	Lepcha
Kwanti or Kokti	Nine types of legumes (beans, mung, soybean, horsegram, peas, ricebean, rajmah, cowpea, and lentil), mixed, kept for 3 days or 5 days for germination.	Cleaned and cooked sprouted legumes and prepared soup; special food of the community, prepared during Rwanti Purnima	Newar
Chhwelaa	Buffalo meat	Boiled, cooke meat curry	Newar
Lakhamari	Wheat flour, sugar	Deep fried cookies	Newar
Kegu	Peas	Pickle	Newar
Chatamari	Rice flour	Rice pancake; snack	Newar
Yamari	Rice, spices	Steamed rice dumpling	Newar
Wa	Pulses, soybean	Roasted; snack	Newar
Takha	Buff meat	Cooked; pudding	Newar
Kachila	Meat, spices, ginger, oil	Raw minced meat, mixed with spices and mustard oil; side-dish	Newar
Wachipa	Feathers of hen; flowers of damlapa plants with rice	Fried with boiled rice; side dish	Kirant Khambu Rais
Chakho	Rice, millet	Cooked; staple	do
Bauwa	Rice	Boil rice flour in more water; stew; staple	do
Lauwa	Rice, vegetable	Cooked rice with vegetable; staple	do
Alum	Finger millet/buckwheat	Rolls, boil; staple	Tamangs
Foldong	Rice, cardamom, dry fruits, butter	Rice ball; staple	Tamangs
Falki	Maize, legs/head of lamb	Cooked with preferably more bones, gravy; staple	Gurungs
Rigi choboo	Potato	Boil and cooked well; staple	Sherpas
Aree	Wheat, potato, meat, salt	Cooked wheat, meat, potato; staple	Sherpas
Phando	Soybean	Whole soybean fried, grounded and cooked as dal	Limboos
Khoreng	Wheat/millet/buckwheat/ maize/rice flour	Baked bread roti; staple	Limboos
Nambong muchhi	Silam	Fry, grinded, mixed with chilly, dry pickle	Limboos

Products	*Ingredient*	*Nature and Use*	*Major Consumer*
Zebre	Rice, gheu, milk, molasses	Sweetened rice rings	Nepalis
Malpua	Wheat flour, molasses dahi, spice, gheu	Fried sweet pancake	Nepalis
Poponda	Finger millet flour	Baked, wrapped in fresh leaves and cooked under the fire; staple	Limboos
Lunghakcha	Maize Flour	Baked, rolled in Maize khoselas and cooked	Limboos
Sigolya and Penagolya	Millet or barley flour	Baked, rolled and cooked; staple	Limboos
Pena Manda	Millet flour	Cooked in more water	Limboos
Khareng	Maize, millet, wheat roti	Baked and cooked; staple	Limboos
Sargyangma	Yangben Moss, Phul Kharani, pork blood, Pork intestine	Boil Yangben, mixed pork blood, put in sausages and cook, side dish	Limboos
Yangben Sumbak	Yangben, pork, blood, liver, spices	Mixed and cooked as dry fried; side dish	Limboos
Sagee Sumbak	Neetle tender shoots, flowers/fruits	Boil and cooked as curry; staple	Limboos
Wamyuk	Hen's inner feathers, liver, head, wings, intestine etc and spices	Oil cooked as gravy curry; special dish	Limboos
Yakhoo Kusee Muchhi	Seeds of Pumpkin, chilly	Dry-fried, powdered and mixed with power chilly	Limboos
Yanglukma chaa	Himalayan Giant frog, spices	Cooked with spices; seasonal curry	Limboos
Sirukma chaa	Sawaney Paha, spices	"	Limboos
Piringtukma chaa	Pirey paha	"	Limboos
Khekkrokma chaa	Tadpoles of frogs, maize/rice flour	"	Limboos

Source: Tamang (2005: 82-87); Kirant Yakthung Chumlung (2002): Subba (1999: 159).

5.1. Food culture before 1642 A.D.:

Food culture of antiquity was gathering and hunting of wild plants and animals. Once the Neolithic men started cultivation of crops around 4,000 B.C. settle agriculture commenced out of their necessity. Before 1642, mainly Lepchas, Limboos, early migrants of Magars and Bhutias inhabited Sikkim. Their food culture was rough cereals such as maize, dryland paddy (Ghaiya), millet (Pandurey), barley (Jau, Wa), buckwheat (Titey and Mithey Phapar), pulses (soybean, rice bean, mung, cowpea), oilseeds (rape and mustard), a few domesticated vegetables, mostly wild vegetables and wild fruits. Their non-vegetarian food items may be pig, chicken, mutton (goat), beef, water buffalo, and wild birds and animals. Their food was roughly boiled or cooked on animal fat or rarely cooked in rape and mustard oil.

5.2. Between 1642 to 1774 A.D.:

This is the period when the Tibetans were migrated to Sikkim in large numbers. During this period more of food crops with improved varieties of wetland paddy, wheat, barley, oilseeds, seasonal vegetables such as iskus, potato in vegetables and avocado banana, orange, apple, pear, plum, peach etc. in fruits were introduced for cultivation. Domestic animals such as sheep, yak, chengra (high altitude goat), domestic animals, ducks, were introduced for non-vegetarians. However, the general food items were comparatively rough- boiled, cooked in pig-fat and rarely oil cooked. However, the food items of the royal family and rich people (mostly rich Bhutias and Kazis) could afford better food, and in varieties. These communities commonly took the traditional foods of the Lepchas, the Limboos, and the Bhutias as mentioned in their ethnography during those days.

5.3. Between 1774 to 1975 A.D.:

This is the period when most of the area of Sikkim was under Gorkha rulers and the Nepali community spread through out the length and breadth of Sikkim even after Titalia Treaty of 1817. The Nepali community included Bahuns, Chetris, Kamis, Damais, Sarkis, Majhis, Limboos, Rais, Yakhas, Magar, Newars, Tamangs, Sherpas, Thamis, Thakuris, Bhujels, Sunuwars, Lepchas, and many other minor communities. Thus, they brought a variety of ethnic food culture as mentioned in their ethnology to Sikkim. The present ethnic food culture mentioned above are the outcome of all the ethnic food culture of these communities in Sikkim.

5.4. After 1975 A.D. onwards:

This is the period when improved varieties of all types of cereals, pulses, oilseeds, vegetables, fruits, spices, flowers etc were introduced for cultivation in Sikkim. Also, all kinds of food materials were in access to the people, and thus the modern food culture was made available to the people of Sikkim for those who could afford to it. Development of tourism also improved modernization of food culture in Sikkim. However, the food culture in the rural areas remained almost ethnic due to their preference and cheaper. The economic condition of rural people was changing faster after 1975 onwards due to planned economic development. This resulted changing of their food habits towards urban food culture to some extent. Development of Village tourism and faster economic upliftment of the rural poor has tremendously affecting the food habits of the younger rural people in Sikkim.

6. The Blood Type Diet:

According to Benny and Antony (2006: 16-21) the modern concept of right type of diet depends on the type of blood, as the blood is the most essential part in our body. To be healthy and livelong is more important than an unhealthy long life. Right type of balance diet plays an important role to have a healthy life. Blood is the connecting link between the cells. It is the fundamental source of nourishment to the body and the change in this, changes the health of a person.

6.1. Blood Groups:

Different groups characterize the blood type. There are four types of blood groups depending on the presence of Antigents ABO system of classification. Each of these group is again divided as positive or negative based on the presence or absence of Rh factor, and O group is considered as the universal donor group.

Their Characteristics and behavioural pattern are as follows:

	Group "O"	*Group "A"*	*Group "B"*	*Group "AB"*
General Characters	"O" is for old. Originated 50,000–40,000 BC in Africa (Cro-Magnon ancestors). They were skillful and formidable hunters, protein-meat was their fuel.	"A" is for Agrarian. By 30,000 – 20,000 BC the "O" group types hunter ancestors migrated in search of meat to Europe and Asia. "A" group appeared in Asia of the Middle East between 25,000 – 15,000 BC in response to new environment of settled agriculture during the Neolithic period.	B" is for balance, originated between 15,000 –10,000 BC in the area of the Himalayan highlands of Pakistan and India (Ural region of Asia) from the migration of "A" group ncestors.	"AB" is for the modern. Originated in Europe between 500 BC to 900 AD, prone to allergies other anti-immune diseases such as arthritis, inflammation etc.

	Group "O"	Group "A"	Group "B"	Group "AB"
Behavioural pattern	The hunter, acidic stomach, protein meat lover or act as a fuel, extreme exercise style, hardy digestive tract, diary products and grains are not user friendly, hypothyroidism	The first vegetarian, sensitive digestive tract, tolerant immune system, responds best to stress with calming action, requires agrarian diet to stay lean and productive, meals depend on agriculture, grains, vegetables, and leaves.	Strong immune system, tolerant digestive system, diary products eater.	Modern merging of "A" and "B", sensitive digestive tract, only 1000 years old, rare, two-five per cent of total populations, biologically complex.

Source: Benny and Antony (2006: 16-21)

6.2. Common Food Types:

The food we take is digested in the stomach and absorbed directly into the blood from the small intestine. The food ingredients can directly influence the quality of blood. The common food items can be divided into:

Meats and poultry	Grains
Sea food	Vegetables
Dairy and eggs	Fruits
Oils and fats	Juices and fluids
Nuts and seeds	Spieces
Beans and legumes	Condiments
Cereals	Herbal teas
Breads and muffins	Miscellaneous beverages

Each of these diet groups are divided into three categories:

1. Highly beneficial: Food that act like a medicine;
2. Neutral: Food that act like a food;
3. Avoid: Food that act like a poison.

Based on this classification, the food items highly beneficial, Neutral and avoid for each blood group, has been summarized by Benny and Antony (2006: 16-21) as follows:

	Group "O"	*Group "A"*	*Group "B"*	*Group "AB"*
Food – Highly beneficial	Beef, lamb, liver, mutton, buffalo, all types of fish like sardine, mackerel, salmon, olive oil, garlic, broccoli, horse radish, sweet potato, pineapple juice, plums, turmeric, ginger, fenugreek, pepper mint, brown/white wild basmati rice, barley	Fish, all types of fish like sardine, mackerel, soymilk and cheese, olive oil, peanuts, peanut butter, wheat bread, rive cakes, rice flour, pasta, noodles, carrot. garlic, horse radish, onion, sprouts, lemon, pineapple, plums, cherries, water melon, ginger, fenugreek, green tea, coffee, red wine.	Lamb, mutton, rabbit, sardine fish, mackerel, cod, goat milk, yogurt, milk, cheese, olive oil, kidney beans, oat bran, brown rice, bread, rice cakes, rice flour, oat flour, cabbage, carrot, cauliflower, mushroom, mustrad, pepper, chilly, potato, bananas, grapes, papaya, pineapples, plums, ginger, horse radish, green tea.	Lamb, mutton, rabbit, sardine, mackerel, tuna, kingfish, goat milk, yogurt, cheese, olive oil, beans, rice bran, oatmeal, bread, rice cakes, rice basmati, brown, white, cauliflower, broccoli, cucumber, garlic, mushrooms, mustard, sweet potato, cherry, gooseberry, grapes, lemon, plums, pineapples, cabbage, carrot, celery, papaya, brown rice syrup, green tea, coffee.

Source: Benny and Antony (2006: 16-21)

Type of food	*Group "O"*	*Group "A"*	*Group "B"*	*Group "AB"*
Food – Neutral	Chicken, duck, rabbit and anchovy, lobster, chrimp, crab, soymilk, butter, sesame oil and seed, green peas, beans, barley, oat meal, black beans, beer, wine, and green tea	Chicken, turkey, shark, tuna, goat milk, yogurt, canola oil, nuts, green peas, barley, corn flakes, rice bran, cream of rice, oat bran, rice brown, white and basmati, celery, cauliflower, cucumber, coriander, lettuce, mushroom, mustard, apple, dates, grapes, guava, melon, strawberries, vegetable juices, nutmeg, rosemary, cumin, cloves, cardamom, low fat salad dressing, fruit jam.	Beef, liver, shark, white-flesh, squid, buttermilk, butter, soymilk, whole milk, coconut oil, nuts, green peas, all type of beans, cream of rice, soya flour breed, pasta, basmati rice, garlic, cucumber, celery, fennel, onion, apple, guava, melon, gooseberry, orange, vegetable juice, water melon, fruit jams, pickles.	Liver, catfish, shark, squid, white-fish, mussels, milk, soymilk, peanut oil, mustard oil, nuts, green peas, cream of rice, barley, onion, potato, tomato, melon, vinegar, turmeric, tamarind, sugar, paprika, fruit jam, salad dressing, bear, club soda, wine.

Type of food	*Group "O"*	*Group "A"*	*Group "B"*	*Group "AB"*
Food – to be avoided	Pork, butter milk, cheese, ice cream, yogurt, cotton seed oil, peanut oil, cashew, peanuts, kidney beans, lentils, cornflakes, wheat, brand, high protein bread, pasta, cabbage, cauliflower, mushroom, potato, orange, coconuts, black berries, apple, nutmeg, pepper, vinegar, ketchup, coffee, soda, cola, and tea.	Pork, beef, duck, lamb, liver, mutton, rabbit, anchovy, shrimp, lobster, squid, frog, butter, butter milk, cheese, ice creams, whole milk, cotton seed oil, sesame oil, peanut oil, corn oil, cashews, pasta, cabbage, tomatoes, potatoes, banana, coconut, mangoes, orange, papayas, pepper, vinegar, pickles.	Anchovy, frog, lobster, crab, shrimp, mussels, oysters, cheese, ice creams, cotton seed oil, peanut oil, sesame oil, sunflower oil, cashew nut, peanuts, sesame seeds, corn flakes, barley, wheat, tomato, coconuts, tapioca, ketchup, soda and cola.	Pork, beef, chicken, duck, heart, anchovy, crab, lobster, frog, shrimp, butter, butter milk, ice creams, whole milk, cotton seed oil, sesame oil, sunflower oil, corn flakes, pasta, bananas, orange, mangoes, coconuts, chilly, tapioca, pepper, pickles, ketchup, fenugreek, tea, liquor, cola.

Now a days, people are very conscious about their life style and food habits. But they are not so much aware about the type of food their body needs. This makes the men ill in early middle age. Changing the food pattern and modifying the types and forms of food we take can avoid the early attack of diseases. Adopting the blood type food is an easy way of changing the food habit that makes the man healthy and long live (Benny and Antony, 2006: 16-21).

II. Dress Culture:

As in the case of Food Culture, the Dress Culture of the people of Sikkim has a tremendous diversity, divided into the various communities living in Sikkim. With its most colourful diversity and pattern also links Sikkim to the history, culture, and identity of its own in the country. Different communities of Sikkim have their own traditional dresses, colour, pattern etc. distinctly identifying themselves like a variety of flowers in a beautiful garden in this part of the Himalayas. Defining and wearing traditional dress symbolizes their commitment to their distinct community, identity and culture. The effect of globalization has caused a shift in dress towards western culture, which also provide signal of status changes. New materials and designs signal commitments to modernity. The youth show that they are trendy by following Western fashions. Wives prefer the wrapped, draped garments, the sari, often in easy-care polyester.

Their husbands' dress of choice is usually Western business grab. Farmers and other rural folk often prefer less Western fashions. Synthetic fabrics have a big following here, too, as women appreciate their durability, resistance to fading, and especially, that they are wash and wear.

Since the State do not produce dress materials of their own except a few traditional dress materials, the dress culture of Sikkim is largely influenced by the availability of dress materials in the market. The Nepali ethnic group prefer to natural fibers like cotton, silk, and wool materials for traditional dresses available in the market from Nepal, as it matches the traditional dress design and colour of their choice. Similarly, the Bhutia ethnic groups prefer to the materials available from Tibet (China) for the same region. The Lepcha ethnic community prefers to use their own hand-weave material and silk for their traditional dress. However, for general dress materials, availability of dress material guides the choice of the person.

In both public and private schools of Sikkim, the school uniforms adapted are of Western school dress. The boy's uniform comprises of shirt, pant, half-pant, suitor, coat, tie, leather belt, under-wear, vest, shoes, canvas shoes, leather shoes, socks etc. Similarly, the girl's uniform comprises of shirt, frock, suitor, foam-belt, under-wear, vest, coat, socks, leather shoes and canvas-shoes. The choice of fabric varies from terry-cotton, terry-wool, and polyester to cotton. Colour varies from school to school and ranges from white, gray, brown, and yellow, blue, green to red. The shoes are mostly black. However, during their cultural shows in the stages, the school children adopt the traditional dresses depending on the song or dance being shown as per the different communities mentioned in their ethnographic description.

Generally, the Nepali ethnic group has adapted the traditional dresses of *Khasas* (*Bahun, Chetri, Kami, Damai, Sarki*) in the rural areas of Sikkim. Hence, most of the rural folk dress adopted by the men are *Dawra, Suruwal, Patuka, Thutey-suruwal, Dhaka-topi, waist-coat, coat, Golfan, moja* and *laber ko jutta.* They may also wear *Sirupatey Khukuri, Sunako Aunthi, Sunako-chain* and *Sunako Kundal.* Most of the rural women are dressed in *Fariya, Chaubandi-cholo, Hembari, Mujetro, Patuka, moja and Labarkojutta.* They may also wear *Chaptey-sun, Dhungri, Bulaki, Kalli, Reji, Potey-mala, Aunthi* etc. The traditional dresses of the other communities of Nepali ethnic group of Sikkim such as Limboos, Gurungs, Khambu Rais, Sunuwar, Yakhas, Tamang, Bhijel, Thami, Mangar, etc. are mostly used only in their special festivals, *Utsavas* and their stage performing arts. They do not dress their traditional dresses regularly in day-to-day life in the rural areas of Sikkim.

Globalization has tremendously affected the rural folk in Sikkim since 1975-76, after the integration of Sikkim into the Indian Union. Thus, most of the rural folk of Sikkim, especially from the Nepali Ethnic group generally prefer to dress in Western fashion. The men usually wear under-wear, vest, half-pant, pant, shirt, waistcoat, coat, turban, cap, hat, socks, leather shoes, leather belt etc. The women folk prefer to dress on sari, blouse, vest, under-wear, shawl, or the Punjabi dress *Salwar-Kamij, chunni* etc. They may also wear gold rings, gold-chain, gold earring etc. The materials and colour vary depending on the availability in the rural market. Small markets are scattered even in the nock and corner of the State. Hence, the rural folk are access to every modern materials, colour and shades of the fabrics.

The retention of their traditional dress is higher amongst the Lepcha community of Sikkim. Most of them are found to dress their own traditional dresses in the rural areas. However, the quality of fabrics has changed but still retain the design, colour and pattern matching to their traditional dresses. The Lepcha men wear *Dum-Praa* which as three designs *Tagaap, Khemchu* and *Tamblyoak*. Other dresses of the Lepcha men are *Tago* (shirt-type), *Tomoo* (trouser), *Tanggyip* (bag), *Thyaak Tok* (hat), *Papri* (cane hat), *Samoak* (hat), and *Yaanglo* (shawl). The Lepcha women wear *Dum Bun* or *Dum-Den, Jyoordong Tago, Tago* (blouse), and *Taroa* (scarf) (For details see ethnic description).

However, the young Lepchas prefer to wear Western fashion, and a considerable percentage of rural Lepcha folk are dressed in western fashion.

Like Lepchas, the Bhutia ethnic group has also retained their traditional dresses as mentioned in their ethnic description in the rural areas of Sikkim. Globalization has also affected the young Bhutia people. Like Lepcha community the Youth Bhutias also prefer to dress in Western fashion. A considerable percentage wears all western dresses even in rural areas of Sikkim.

In the Urban areas of Sikkim, the formal dress code is western fashion. The men prefer to dress suit- pant, shirt, waistcoat, coat, necktie, leather belt, suitor, muffler, under-wear, vest, socks, leather shoes etc. while the women prefer to dress sari, blouse, shawl, under-wear, brazier, or Punjabi dress *Salwar-Kamij, Chunni*, highly raised leather shoes or sandal etc. They occasionally prefer to dress their community traditional dresses especially in their New Year Day or special Community functions like *Bhanu Jayanti, Panglapsol, Tendong Lho Rum-Faat*, New Year Days of the Limboos, Gurungs, Tamangs etc.

7.1. Dresses of Antiquity and before 1642 A.D.:

The dress materials available before 1642 A.D. was of fibres of wild plant known as *Bhangrey Sisnu* (*Girardinia palmata*) and cotton. The

Lepchas and the Limboos used to colour these fibres with various plant extracts and used to weave their own traditional clothes. Weaving clothes were the responsibility of the women folk and they were very skilled in this matter. They also used to weave materials required for bedding and other purposes (photos enclosed).

7.2. Between 1642 to 1774 A.D.:

This is the period when the Tibetans migrated in large numbers from Tibet. They introduce Sheep, Chengra, and Yak to Sikkim, and thus they introduced Sheep-wool, Chengra-wool, Yak-hair. Now, both the cotton and wool were available for making the traditional dresses of the Lepchas, the Limboos and the Bhutias. The wool and hair materials constituted the warmer dress materials for the mid and high hill-people of Sikkim. Thus, a variety of carpet weaving, cloth weaving industries was started both as household industry and community level industry in the early years 1700s in Sikkim (photos enclosed).

7.3. Between 1774 to 1975 A.D.:

This is the period when the Nepalese spread through out the length and breadth of Sikkim. They are responsible for emergence and promotion of Nepali dress culture in Sikkim. Now the entire Nepali ethnic communities wear the ethnic Nepali dresses and they wear their community dress as mentioned in the ethnic description only in certain occasion even today. With Sikkim coming under the British protectorate in 1817, the people started modern education initiated by the missionaries in Sikkim. With the association of missionary people as most of the schools they started aided schools, the people started adoption of western dresses. By 1975, all the school uniforms or dresses are of western style with shirt, pant, half-pant, coat etc. that attracted the entire young generation to the western dresses (photos enclosed).

7.4. After 1975 onwards:

With the integration of Sikkim into the Indian Union, a number of Indian ethnic groups such as Biharis, Marwaris, Punjabis, Bengalis, Keralites, and others migrated to Sikkim for better opportunities made available due to various works and business by the Plan Economic development in the State. These people brought their dress culture along with them and made popular in Sikkim. Now, the urban women prefer to wear Sari, blouse, shawl, sandal etc. rather than their ethnic dresses. Similarly, urban women, young girls and children even in rural areas of Sikkim prefer to wear *Kurta Paijama, chunni* etc. of Punjabi dress. The urban as well as the young men in the rural areas prefer to wear western suit, coat, pant, shirt, pea-cap, leather shoes, socks belt, long Hindustani coat, *Kamij*, etc. The dress culture of Sikkim is changing faster with the increase in literacy rate of Sikkim.

6

Religion and Social Transformation

The history of religion and socio-religious transformation in Sikkim moved with the time in the past, as the land and the people kept on changing since antiquity. The changes in religion, faith and belief systems in different point of time subjected the different ethnic people of Sikkim differently, and changed the new ways to understand the meaning of life. The temporal changes thus brought about by the migrants in Sikkim and also by the globalization may be described in various stages in brief as under:

1. Religions of Antiquity and Social Transformation:

As is natural with all primitive tribes of antiquity, the Mon-pas– the non-Tibetan dwellers south of the Himalayas and around the borders of Tibet or the people that resided (and continue to reside) in "The Greater Sikkim" area prior to migration of the Tibetans, namely the Lepchas, the Tsongs (Limboos) and the Magars (Mongpas) were basically animists. The Lepchas are also known as Rongpas - the dwellers in the steep country (Risley, 1894: 39; Mullard, 2005: 39; Foning, 2003:237).

In antiquity the Mon-pas- Lepchas (Rong-pas) resided the areas of "The Greater Sikkim", namely Ilam area of present Nepal (and continue to reside), present area of Sikkim (and continue to reside), Chumbi Valley of present Tibet Autonomous Region of China, the *Mon-loong-kha-bzi* area inclusive of the present Kalirnpong Sub-division (and continue to reside) of West Bengal, and Hah Chu Valley and Amo Chu Valley (and continue to reside) of present Bhutan. The Animist Lepchas consider themselves as the children of the Himalayas. They believe that the first man and woman were created by *Rum* (God) out of the snows of the untrodden peak of Kanchenjunga. Religious specialists are called shamans. The highest class is called *Tung li Mun*. Lower ranks are *Yeba, Mun*, and *Bongthing*. The right term to refer this type of religion is Shamanism. The Lepchas of Sikkim believe in two types of spirits, the good, which bring, good things to the people and the bad, which do harm to them. They perform religious ceremonies to ward off evil spirits from doing harm to them. They believe in the powers of *Bongthing* and the *Mun* the priest and the priestess. They perform all the ceremonies from birth to death for the Lepcha society as a whole. They have powers to stop evil spirits from doing harm. They acquire these super natural powers by constant prayer and deep meditation (Jeffrey et al, 2000:35; Foning, 2003:236-246; Das & Banerjee, 1962: 105-119).

The Limboos (Tsongs) in antiquity resided (and continue to reside) in the areas of "The Greater Sikkim", namely the Limbuwan area (East of Arun River to the West of Teesta River) inclusive of Koshi and Mechi Anchal areas of present Nepal, the present Darjeeling and Jalpaiguri District areas of West Bengal, some parts of Northern Bihar, and West, South and Chungthang-Bob areas of present North Districts of Sikkim. The Limboos believe on Yumaism or Yuma Samyo (Yuma religion) and on the myth of *Mundhum* of creation of the Limboos with the theory of biogenesis by the creator God at Phoktanglungma Pembenlungma (Kumbhakarn or Jannu mountain, 7710 m) (Subba, 1999: 31-37). The Limboos believe that their souls have to be fortified there in the Kumbhakarna mountain (Phoktanglungma Pembenlungma, *Chotlung*) while living, and also have to be carried accompanying the souls of the dead to the mountains known as Phoktangma Pembenlungma, to Sey-seylungma (the third highest mountain (Kanchenjunga, 8586 m), to Mooralungma (the second highest mountain Koramkurum or K_2 8591 m), to Choombhutlungma (the highest mountain of the world, Mount Everest, 8848 m) and then to the first atmospheric layer above the earth known as *Samyuknaden* (ancestor's village) to hand over to their ancestors after their death. They have nine types of shamanic priests known as *Muhikkum Ongshi, Phegiri Phedangma, Samboko Samba, Yeboko Yeba, Yeboko Yema, Yuma, Sammundhum, Yepmundhum* and *Sida Samba*. They performed (and continue to perform) all types of life rituals of the Limboo community. Yumaism was promoted and spread by the Kings of Limbuwan, such as Ubahang (849-865 A.D.), Mabohang (865-882 A.D.), and Sirijungahang (882-925 A.D.). In Sikkim Sirijonga Teyongshi propagated Yumaism (Yuma Samyo) during 1934 to 1941 at Martam, Hee, Pacrek area of West Sikkim; and Lalsor Sendang (1840-1926) in 1914-24 A.D.at Daramdin, Thambong, Lungchok, Tharpu and Tikpur areas. The religion had influenced immensely on the culture, tradition, faith and lifestyle of the Limboo community since then (Subba, 1999: 31-37; 2003: 75; 2005: 79-88; 105-109; 119-129).

In antiquity, the Mongpa -Magars resided (and continue to reside) in some parts of "The Greater Sikkim" and ruled for some time, namely, Tamber Valley of present Nepal, Mangarjung areas of Mangsari and many other Magarjungs of present Sikkim, and the Khangpachen Valley of present Tibet Autonomous Region of China. Mangars were essentially animists. They worshipped a host of spirits through their own shamans. Worship of ancestors was another critical religious element among them. They sacrificed animals for their gods and goddesses (Alle 2003: 91-92).

2. Introduction of Buddhism in Sikkim during the 8th Century:

According to Sikkimese cultural and religious history as related in old anecdotal accounts, Buddhism was introduced in Sikkim in the eighth century AD. The land was then, blessed by Padmasambhava (Guru Rimpoche). He personally consecrated many of Sikkim's sacred landmarks, and blessed Drakar Tashiding as the land's spiritual centre. During the first dissemination of Buddhism in Tibet in the eighth century, Guru Rimpoche and his twenty-five disciples (rje 'bngas nyer lnga) are said to have visited and blessed this land known as Beyul Demojong (sbas yul 'bras mo ljongs) or 'the hidden fruitful valley'. Thereafter, they tamed all malevolent beings and evil forces which infested the country, selected and blessed the sites of some of Sikkim's future monasteries and erected a number of stupas. He subdued all the hostile spirits of the land and converted them into Sikkim's guardian deities, dZonga, who resides on Khanchenjunga mountain was appointed the supreme Guardian Deity. Sikkim was designated the Hidden Land, to be discovered when the Dharma was under threat in Tibet. It was here that Padmasambhava is believed to have scripted his nine texts of "unerring prophesies". Guru Rimpoche, on his return journey to Urgyen, also hid religious texts, known as *Ters*, at various places around Sikkim, and locked the doors to this Hidden Land. These *Ters* were to be discovered later by *Tertons* during different times, each discovery reinforcing Sikkim's status as the most sacred of all hidden lands and celebrating Khangchenjunga as the most supreme of all Guardian Deities (Dokhampa, 2003, 39-1: 25-30; Pema & Zulca, 2007: 83-85).

3. Buddhism During 13th and 14th Century AD:

After the blood brotherhood treaty of Khe-Bumsa, the Lhopo (Bhutia) leader and Thekong-Tek, the Lepcha leader during 13th century AD, the migration of Tibetans to Sikkim increased. Later, in the fourteenth century, the great *terton* (*gter ston* = revealer of hidden treasures) Rigzin Godemchen (Rig 'dzin rgod ldem chen 1337-1408) came to Sikkim and established monasteries and meditation centres at Sinon or Zilnon, near Tashiding and nearby Pawo Hungri. Following this, the reincarnation of Rigzin Godemchen, *terton* Ngari Rigzin Chempo Lagden Dorje (mNga' ris rig 'dzin legs ldan rdo rje 1512-1625), a master of the Nyingmapa tradition of *guhyamantra,* discovered the sublime mKHa' 'gro'i mkha' lang ma'i rgyud tantra or the *Sadhana* (sgrub thabs, method of accomplishment) of *Amitayus* in the northern cave of Lhari rinchen nying phuk in 1568 (Dokhampa, 2003, 39-1:25-30).

During that time, the Bhutias of Sikkim had basically two faiths: the first lot – some of the early migrant Bhutias were followers of Bon religious belief system (*Bonpas*), and were not much influenced by the Mahayana Buddhism as yet, while the second lot of people were the followers of Ningmapa sect (Red Hat sect) of Mahayana Buddhism.

Although, Buddhism was introduced in Sikkim as far back as in the eighth century AD, Sikkim experienced the emergence and rooting of Mahayana Buddhism (Ningmapa sect) only after 13th century A.D. However, the influence of newly brought religion and philosophy of life from Tibet on the existing society of Mon-pas - Lepchas, Limboos and Magars was at minimal. The Bhutias were minority and Buddhism was establishing its roots in the Greater Sikkim slowly. The religious Lamas were confined only to their own community and thus avoiding any type of conflict. They thought that the time is not yet ripe for the new pressure to bear on other communities. As such, *Animism* of the Lepchas and Magars, *Yumaism* of the Limboos and Buddhism-Bonism of the Bhutias were the religion or faith that prevailed over the respective communities in Sikkim till the mid-seventeenth century. The influence of the existing religions on social transformation was enormous within the respective tribes but interference on each other's community in respect of religion was minimal during that period.

4. Buddhism in the 17th Century AD:

The seventeenth century was a turning point in the history of Sikkim. Khe-Bumsa's four grandsons Shangpodar, Tsechudar, Nima Gyalpo and Guru Tashi, collectively known as ***Tongduruzi*** settled together in the present areas of Sikkim during the last quarter of 13th century A.D. multiplied and increased with other Lhopo migrants from Tibet. Of these above *Tongduruzi* four brothers, Guru Tashi's family became pre-eminent and inherited the princely dignity and name. Guru Tashi's son was Jowo Nagpo, his son was Jowo Aphag, Jowo Aphag's son was Guru Tenzing and Guru Tenzing's son was Phuntso Namgyal, the first Maharaja of Sikkim, born in the year 1604 A.D. i.e., the Shing-Dug (wood dragon) year (Namgyal & Dolma 1908: 22).

The kingdom was founded when the first Chogyal Phuntsho Namgyal was enthroned at Yoksom in 1642 by three great lamas of Tibet: Lhatun Namkha Jigmed (1597-1650), Ngadag Sempa Phuntsog Rinzing (1592 –1656) and Kathog Kuntu-bzangpo Chenpo (?- 1694). Under the patronage of the Chogyal, the monasteries, hermitages and stupas were built and Buddhism was proclaimed the state religion. Following the revealation of the *Rig 'dzin srog sgrud* text to Lhatsun Namkha Jigmed at Tashiding, Sikkim became the main centre of Dzogchen (*rdzogs chen*) teaching and meditation practice in the Tibetan world. Its followers came to be known as Denjong Dzogchenpa (Namgyal & Dolma, 1908:22).

Ngadag Sempa Chenpo, one of three lamas who had consecrated the first Chogyal, was a great scholar from Central Tibet. Together with his grandson Ngadag Rinchen Gon, he established the monastery at Drakar Tashiding and consecrated it as the main seat of the followers of the Nyingma northern treasure (*Byang gter*) tradition, which was brought to Sikkim from the Tibetan monastery of Dorje Drak (rdo rje brag) by Ngari Rigzin Godemchen.

Once the installation of Phuntsho Namgyal, the first king was accomplished in Chu-Ta (Water horse) the year corresponding to the year 1642 A.D. (Phuntsho Namgyal was already a King in 1642 as per the historical evidence available with us known as Tripartite Treaty of "*Lho-Men-Tsong-Sum*" recorded in the OBC report of 1998 of the State Government, and also by the Maharaja's History 1908: 29; contrary to Mullard's 2005: 41,1: 76 view of installation only in 1646-47). The newly introduced religion and philosophy of Mahayana Buddhism exerted pressure on the Lepcha and Limboo communities of Sikkim. The Magars did not accept the sovereignty of the Chogyal and most of the tribes might have left the Greater Sikkim (as it is evident from the *Lho-Men-Tsong-Sum* treaty). Full emergence and spread of the new religion weakened their old religion and faith of the Limboos and the Lepchas and they started seeking new ways to understand the meaning of life. The Sangacholing Monastery was first established by Lha-tsun Chempo was constructed for religious teaching of Buddhism especially for the Lepcha and Limboo subjects in 1697. Similarly, the Dubde monastery, established by Lha-tsun Chempo was constructed in 1701; and the Pemayongtse monastery, the site for which was located by Lha-tsun was constructed in 1705 for *Ta-Tshang* Lamas (Bhutia Lamas) to spread Buddhist religious instructions. Later on about 36 numbers of Gumpas were constructed, scattered throughout Sikkim by 1884 for spread of Nyingmapa, Sakyapa and Kagyukpa sects of Mahayana Buddhism. By 2006, there were 81 monasteries established and recognized by the Government of Sikkim for Nyingmapa, Sakyapa and Kagyukpa sets (Red Hat sect) of Buddhist worship and learning centres in Sikkim, some of which are as follows:

The important Monasteries built by the Namgyal Dynasty of Sikkim are as follows:

Name	*Translation of Vernacular title*	*Date of Construction*	*No. of Monks*
Sangacholing	Secret place of religious instructions	1967	28
Dubdi (Dubde)	Happy place for meditation	1701	30
Pamayongtse	The sublime perfect lotus	1705	108
Enchey	The Tsen's house	1716	55
Tashiding	The elevated Central glory	1716	38
Sinon	The suppressor of intense fear	1716	12
Rinchenpong	The precious knoll	1730	12
Ralang		1730	106
Meli		1740	23
Rumtek	God left	1740	126
Phodang	The Chapel royal	1740	125
Chungthang	Monk's meadow	1788	13
Katsupari	The noble heaven reaching	1850	23
Lachung	The large plain	1788	3
Takung (Tolung)	The stony valley	1789	26
Phensang	The excellent banner or Godbliss	1840	121
Kartok	The founder of Schism	1840	121
Doling	The stony place	1840	35
Yangang	The cliff or lucky ridge	1841	19
Labrang	The lama's dwelling	1844	40
Lachung	The Bonpo's ridge	1788	23
Lhuntse	The lofty summit	1850	13
Simik		1850	38
Ringon	Hermit's hill	1852	25
Linghthen		1855	36
Hungri	The Big pass	1852	26
Lachen	Plain	1860	15
Gyathang		1860	42
Lingkeo	The sublime victor	1862	15
Phag-gyal	The western place	1875	8
Nubling	The sky top	1836	34
Namchi	—	1875	25
Pa-phyug	The sky top	1884	8
Singtam			8
Change			15
Tumum	King's minister	—	—

Source: Subba, 1999 : 130-31.

Buddhism was founded by Siddhartha Gautama (566-586 B.C.), who taught the "four noble truths": Viz: (*a*) Existence was embedded in Sorrow. (*b*) This resulted from human desires. (*c*) Humans could never fulfill all their desires. (*d*) Hence, the way to end sorrow was to end desire. Buddhist teachings emphasized social equality, for every individual could seek to attain salvation. The Buddhist of Sikkim believes in Nyingmapa sect, Kargyupa sect, and Sakyapa sect (Red Hat Sects) of Mahayana Buddhism. However, the latter entrants from Tibet (China) to Sikkim are believers of Gelukpa sect (Yellow Hat Sect) of Mahayana Buddhism (Risley, 1894: 241-384; Subba, 2005: 130-131).

According to the concept of Budhism, man is merely a coming together of certain properties or qualities categorised by Buddhists under five heads termed ***Skandhas:*** (*i*) ***Rupa,*** organized body, (*ii*) ***Vedana,*** sensation, (*iii*) ***Samjna,*** perception, (*iv*) ***Samskara,*** discrimination, and (*v*) ***Vignana,*** consciousness. When physical dissolution takes place these components disperse leaving no residue. And since there is no residue there can be no soul. However, when a man dies there will be left over from his life's activities, so to speak, a certain balance of unrequited action. It may be good action or it may be bad action; but in accordance with doctrine of karma reward or retribution must follow automatically. And it is that fundamental necessity which causes a fresh assemblage of ***Skandhas*** for the working out of the unexhausted karma. Rebirth, then is a mere manifestation of the effects of certain causes. The link between death and re-birth is impersonal and imponderable. By treading the **Noble Eight-fold Path** a man so lives that his karma works itself out, leaving over no balance of unrequited action at the moment of death; then he leaves behind him nothing capable of causing a reassemblage of the five ***Skandhas.*** The **Noble Eight-fold Path** laid down by Gautama Buddha, has been transformed into a single narrow track of the mystic incantation "***Om mani padme hum***!". Its literal meaning is a salutation to the patron deity of Tibet, **Cheresi,** and also a mystic meaning of profound significance for the repetition of the syllables of which bars the doors of the various worlds of existence, Viz: ***Om*** of the heavenly world, ***ma*** of the world of spirits, ***ni*** of the human world, ***pad*** of the animal world, ***me*** of the world of tantalised ghosts, and ***hum*** of the spaces of hell (Ranaldshay, 1923: 59-78).

The new religion affected the existing faith of *Animism* and *Yumaism* of the respective Lepcha and Limboo communities. Most of the Lepchas abandoned their existing faith and adopted Buddhism. Some of the Limboos also adopted Buddhism and started attending Buddhist learning with the Lepchas at Sangacholing monasteries during the later half of seventeenth century, and continued upto1741. The social transformation on the Lepchas and Limboos was tremendous during this period (Subba, 2003: 75-76).

5. Awakening of the Limboos by Teyongsi Sirijunga Singthebe (1704-1741):

Knowing the declining faith of the Limboo community of Sikkim, Teyongsi Sirijunga Singthebe, with his eight disciples entered West Sikkim from Sinam Yangwarok, Nepal in 1734 and started awakening, strengthening and reaffirming the faith on Yuma Samyo of the Limboos at Martam, Hee and Bermiok of West Sikkim by teaching the Limboo script reading-writing and Yumaism Mundhum Khahuns. The Limboos who were going to Sangacholing monasteries during that point of time for Buddhist teachings stopped going there, as they knew that they had their own religion and script. The process redefined the meaning of life and brought about social transformation tremendously in the community. However, this irritated the *Ta-Tshang* Lamas of Pemayongtse monastery. They assassinated Teyongsi Sirijonga and some of his disciples in 1741. One disciple of Pegha clan was caught at Omchung village, west Sikkim, tortured for seven days by pricking and cutting his body and putting salt and chilly on the cut-wounds at Gyalshing where a long Mendang has been built by the Lamas at present. He breathed his last on the seventh day of his torture. Many of the disciples fled away from Sikkim to Limbuwan area of present Nepal. The Bhutia administration put a ban on reading and writing of Limboo script; teaching and learning of Yumaism Mundhum. The Teyongsi Sirijonga and his disciple's sacrifice bore the fruit today. Their sacrifice created a great awakening in the Limboo community, affirmed the Yumaism faith, and thus, the community was not much affected by Buddhism afterwards. However, Buddhism tremendously affected the Lepcha community during that period (Chemjong, 1967; Subba, 2003: 75; 2004: 1-36).

6. Yumaism:

Yumaism is a Henotheist or Kathenotheist religion and believes in a Single Almighty Goddess "*Tagera Ningwaphuma*", which is popularly known as "*Yuma*" while still recognizing other gods and goddesses. *Tagera Ningwaphuma* is the Ultimate Goddess, Omniscient (all knowing), Omnipresent (in all places at all time), Omnipotent (all powerful), Infinite (without beginning or end), and Eternal force or Power of Existence which has none of the attributes. She is the Creator, the Preserver, the Sustainer, and should be prayed every morning and evening to establish a close relationship with Her by the believers.

Yumaism believes on "**Biogenesis theory of life**". In other words, it believes that life is created only through life or life products with the blessing of Almighty Goddess *Tagera Ningwaphuma* (*Yuma*). Creator god tried to create immortal life with elements like gold, silver, copper, bronze etc. but failed. Ultimately, the creator god could create only a mortal life with easily degradable bio-products with the blessing of Goddess *Tagera Ningwaphuma*. The mortal human beings have to survive with the judicious use of all living and non-living objects that were created for his survival. There comes the role of Karma in one's life. It is because of this, the afterlife of the followers of Yumaism depends on his Karma as well as the individual's attachment to the Almighty Goddess *Tagera Ningwaphuma* or *Yuma*. They believe that, depending on their attachment with the Almighty Goddess as well as their Karma, their afterlife take the course to *Sangram Pedang Den* (Ancestor's Village on the land of Goddess on the top of the atmospheric layer) or to "*Khema Yongsong Den*" (the innermost core of the Earth) to burn away the negative Karma earned by Man during his existence with physical body on earth. Once, the negative karma gets burnt completely, the individual takes rebirth again on the earth to repeat the Karmic Cycle and get a chance to improve his/her Karma as well as to improve the attachment with the Goddess. Contrary to the Hinduism or Buddhism's belief the individual is never reborn as a lower form of life in Yumaism. It is because; the creator god has created the lower forms of life for the Man's survival through its judicious use. The creator god neither could create immortal life with elements nor self-sustaining mortal life. Yumaism believes that, Man has to sustain himself through judicious use of both living and non-living resources around him. Man's afterlife can go to "*Sangram Pedang Den*" and "*Khema Yongsong Den*"and stay there depending on the Man's Karma account and attachment with the Goddess *Tagera Ningwaphuma* (*Yuma*). Once the account of Karma is exhausted, they have to take rebirth with physical body on earth to earn "Karma" and develop attachment with the Almighty Goddess. The realm of existence other than on earth is without the physical body and hence "Karma" as well as attachment to Goddess cannot be earned for the afterlife in other two realms. Man's afterlife is guided by the Man's Karma and attachment to Almighty Goddess *Tagera Ningwaphuma* (*Yuma*).

Other gods and goddesses are classified into (*a*) *Mangs* (Deities); (*b*) *Sammangs* (Divinities) and (*c*) *Sammang chyangs* (retinue of divinities). The *Mangs* are prayed for better afterlife but never worshipped with any kind of sacrifices or offerings; while the *Sammangs* are the spirit or soul gods or goddesses. They are worshipped with offerings and even with blood sacrifices for want of worldly comforts, and thus, the act is liable to result one's negative Karma. *Sammangs* are further divided into *Him Sammangs* (Household divinities), *Tap Sammangs* (Nature divinities), *Thokley Sammangs* (clan divinities), and *Sam Sire* (*Auvtars*). The *Sammang Chyangs* are attendants around divinities and known as malicious, obnoxious, detrimental and wicked. They have to be propitiated before initiating the invocation rite of the main divinities. There are a number of gods and goddesses in each category of the above.

The community worship place is known as "*Mangkhim*". In Sikkim, the Limboos have started to construct *Mangkhims* since 1983 when they constructed *Mangkhim* for the first time in 1983 at Mangshila. It is a three-storied house with a five-cone star on the top, thus representing total of eight Dens (atmospheric layers). With the living layer of the earth it represents nine Dens, as they believe nine Dens with Earth above and nine Dens below the earthen layer. They believe that different gods and goddesses govern all these eighteen Dens mentioned above. Till now 11 Mangkhims have been constructed in Sikkim and nearby West Bengal area, each at Mangshila, Martam, Timburbung, Thambong, Darap, Assamlinzey, Aho, Rabitar, Yongthong, Mahakal Danra Darjeeling, and Looksan Duars (Subba, 2005: 1-21).

7. Emergence and Spread of Hinduism 1774 onwards:

The Gorkha invasion and the Gorkha rule over Sikkim territory for many years West of Singalila range and plains of Teesta river and also occupation of West Sikkim for many years (25 years), brought about a tremendous socio-cultural transformation to the existing people especially inhabiting these areas i.e., the Limboos, the Lepchas and the Mangars (*royiats*). Most of the Bhutias were in the present East and part of North Sikkim, and hence the Gorkha influence was minimal. The Lepchas of Ilam area of present Nepal; and West and South Sikkim were affected. A number of Nepali ethnic people such as Khasas (Bahuns, Chhetris, Kami, Damai, Sarki), Kirats (more of Limboos, Khombu-Rais, Yakhas), others Gurung, Tamang, Mangar, Sunuwars, Majhis, Bhujels, Thamis, Sherpas, Newar etc. came to occupy the Gorkha occupied areas of Sikkim during that period. Along with these people came Hinduism and also other faiths highly influenced by the Hinduism. The Gorkha rulers imposed "***Char Jat Chattish Varna***" Hindu caste classification (Brahaman, Kshatriya, Vaishya, and Shudra), to the entire Hill tribal communities also. They placed all the Hill tribe communities (Limboo, Gurung, Tamang, Masngar, Khambu-Rais, Yakhas, Sunuwars, Majhis, Bhujels, Thamis, Sherpas, Newar etc.) in the lowest category under ***Sudras*** and thus lowered the social status of these communities, which however, they never accepted. The entire Nepal Unification process described by Stiller (1968: 65-84) has affected the different communities living in "The Greater Sikkim".

They also banned reading and writing of their language and literature and imposed to adopt Sanskrit or *Khas Kura* (Nepali), which continued upto 1930 AD.in Nepal. They promoted Sanskritisation by imposing celebration of Durga Puja with animal blood sacrifice and *Malsiri* (Sanskrit text) reading. The village heads were imposed to celebrate Durga Puja compulsorily, and were verified by the rulers through stamping of sacrificed blood on the main door, which was made compulsory for the Puja. Thus, the Nepal Unification process promoted and imposed one language (*Khas Kura*), one religion (Hinduism), one administration (Gorkha rule), and suppressed the overall development of language and literature, religion and faith, culture and tradition etc. of the entire Hill tribe communities mentioned above of Nepal and Sikkim during this period. The Gorkha rulers of Sikkim and Nepal effectively monitored the process of unification in such a way that the process continues even today as these Hill-tribe communities have forgotten what is their own.

8. Hinduism:

Hinduism refers to a vast array of religious movements and believes on "**Abiogenesis theory of creation**". It believes that life is made of five elements viz. the Water, the Air, the Sun, the Earth, and the Sky and out of these the earlier four elements are sent back to nature by the process of cremation of the dead body. The Sky or the Ether is the soul, which takes its own course to take rebirth to repeat the karmic cycle on the earth, or to be assimilated to *Parmatma* (Almighty God) depending on the individual's Karma and the individual's attachment to the Almighty God. They claim a special connection with texts such as the Vedas, the Dharma Shastras, and the Puranas, the earliest written forms of which date to the Gupta era (300 –500 B.C.). In the time of Emperor Ashoka Maurya (272-235 B.C.), Vedic religion began to face challenges from Jainism and Buddhism, and from local belief systems associated with agrarian states. In this, Brahamans advanced caste's model of the four categories of humanity (Brahaman, Kshatriya, Vaishya, and Shudra), and placed themselves on top as most ritually pure. Buddhism and Jainism contradicted this perspective. They appealed to many with their three key ideas: nonviolence; teachings that all could attain salvation; and *karma*, the idea of gaining merit in one's life through appropriate thoughts and deeds.

In the early Gupta Empire (300-400 B.C.), the result of these movements produced a combination of elements called the *Sanatana Dharma* (the eternal righteous duty). The law books such as *Manusmriti* elaborated the duties of the different broad categories of castes. Typical practices include prayer, worship, fasting, hymn-singing sessions, and festivals. Sometimes deities possess their believers in a trance, or altered states of consciousness.

The second characteristic of Hinduism is its subdivision into three strands: worship of the god Vishnu in one of his many forms (Vaishnavism), worship of Shiva (Shaivism), and worship of the Devi (the Goddess). The three most important male deities are Brahma, the creator; Vishnu, the preserver; and Shiva, the destroyer.

Vishnu preserves the universe and maintains the social order. Vishnu's consort is Lakshmi, goddess of wealth. Vishnu has returned to earth many times, and has taken ten forms: the great Fish, the Tortoise, the Boar, the Man-lion, the Dwarf, and as Ram, Krishna, Buddha, Kalkin, and Parasurama.

Shiva, the Great God, unties excesses of being and of power. Shiva is both creator and destroyer, ascetic and renouncer. Shiva's wife is Parvati.She also appears in other guises: Kali is the most dreadful, born from Durga's bow in order to destroy two demons (*Mahisasur* and *Raktabeej*) that threatened the earth. To kill the second demon whose drops of blood sprang to life as new demons, she swallowed him and licked up his blood. Durga is powerful yet maternal. Shiva's mount is the bull.

Four-headed Brahma creates the world. His mount is Hamsa, the Central Asian wild goose. Brahma has only one temple dedicated to him at Ajmer in Rajesthan. His consert Saraswati, goddess of learning and music, receives more attention than he (Henderson, 2004:27-37)

The socio-religious transformation of the existing Limboo community of "the Greater Sikkim (Sikkim and Nepal) was affected the most (as most of their people inhabited in Nepal and in West Sikkim) followed by the Lepcha community while the Bhutia community remained unaffected because of effective networking of religious institutionalization through monastery System (Subba, 2003: 76).

9. Emergence and Spread of Christianity 1817 Onwards:

The Gorkha rulers returned some part of the occupied areas of the Greater Sikkim to the British Rulers through the Treaty of Sugauli in 1815. But the British rulers retained most of the plain areas themselves and return some of the hill areas of Sikkim, and thus Sikkim recovered some of its lost areas occupied by the Gorkhas through the Treaty of Titalia in 1817 A.D. However, Sikkim came under British protectorate through this treaty over and above the 23 clause of "British –Sikkim Tumlong Treaty" of 1861. They also annexed Darjeeling areas of Sikkim in 1835 in the pretext of Health Sanitation unconditionally. The British rulers established Political Office in Sikkim in 1887-88 and started interference in the Sikkim administration and in other aspects.

Church of Scotland missionaries from Kalimpong made several visits to Sikkim in the 1880s, but were unable to obtain permission for a missionary to reside there. So the Reverend MacFarlane used the Lepchas, who had proved so amenable to conversion in Kalimpong district, to spread the Gospel among their fellow tribesmen in Sikkim. His efforts enjoyed some success; by 1886, there were 26 Christians in Sikkim, and by 1888 their numbers had doubled (Fader, 2004: 8-10). The Chogyal continued to resist missionaries establishing a permanent presence until, in the changed political conditions after 1888-89 he was forced to allow them to establish a base in Sikkim. Gangtok itself remained out-of-bounds, but a site was selected in Chidam, in southern Sikkim, just a day's journey from Darjeeling, and a mission house was completed there in 1890, the same year that White moved into the newly built Residency in Gangtok (McKay, 2004: 40:2: 25-48).

The missionaries were much less successful in attracting converts. After its initial florescence among the Lepchas, Christianity seems to have made little impact in Sikkim, with the number of Christians declining from 368 in 1913 to 343 by 1922. The missions responded with a new emphasis on medical activities. In 1901, in describing the missionary's main activities in Sikkim as evangelistic, educational, and vocational training, the Reverend Mackean made no mention of medicine. But in January 1921, when he left Sikkim after spending a total of 14 years there, he recommended that his successor should be a medical missionary, highlighting the one area where the missions had succeeded. In 1897, the Scottish missionaries had opened a dispensary at Chidam staffed by a compounder, Elatji Matiyas, a Lepcha convert to Christianity. By 1906 further dispensaries staffed by local Christian compounders had been opened at Rhenock, Seriyong, and Dentam. In 1923-24, there were 11 mission dispensaries in Sikkim (McKay, 2004: 40:2: 25-48).

After Mackean's departure, another missionary willing to serve in Sikkim was eventually found. This was the Honourable Mary Scott, and just as the Reverend Graham took on the David Livingston role in Kalimpong, so does she fill the 'heroic' role in histories of the Sikkim

Church, where her arrival is described as 'the most important watershed in the history of Christianity in Sikkim'. Born in Scotland in 1877, a daughter of the 8th Lord Polwarth, Miss Scott travelled to Kalimpong in 1905. She remained there 18 years, with the Church of Scotland Mission, and received the Kaisar-i-Hind medal for her medical services to villagers during epidemics such as the influenza outbreak of 1918-19. Miss Scott agreed to fill the vacancy in Sikkim, and although her medical skills seem to have been self-taught, her aristocratic background and established reputation for good works stood her in good stead when she arrived there in April 1923. She was permitted to live in Gangtok, a great concession by the Sikkim Maharajah, that was apparently a personal tribute to her character and reputation rather than a result of any initiative by the Political Officer. With her effort she established Palzor Namgyal Girl's High School in 1924. Marry Scott remained in Sikkim for 16 years, where she was responsible for all missionary and church activities. Despite her lack of qualifications, she devoted much of her time to medical matters, supervising the mission dispensaries, organizing medical camps, nursing and relief programmes during kala-azar epidemics, and even caring for the sick in her own home (McKay, 2004: 40:2: 25-48).

Marry Scott became a friend of the Maharani, accompanied Sikkimese royalty on a tour of India, and even acted as a hostess to the palace. Her efforts were rewarded when the Chogyal allowed the opening of a Christian Church in Gangtok in 1936. She left Sikkim on her health ground and was replaced by Reverend Gavin Fairservice and his wife Ruth but were not permitted to reside in Gangtok as missionaries, and a 1938 regulation requiring Sikkimese to obtain permission from the Darbar to convert to Christianity suggests Christianity's gains in Sikkim owed more to Mary Scott's personal influence than to any great enthusiasm for the new faith by the Sikkimese rulers (McKay, 2004: 40:2: 25-48).

The Christianity has affected the Lepcha community the most, and more than 80% of Lepcha population adopted Christianity. Numerous Churches were constructed then onwards and Christianity spread like a wild fire in Sikkim. The other communities were also affected but to the lesser extent. However, in the last quarter of nineteenth century Christianity tremendously affected the Khambu-Rai community. Now, more than 70% Khambu Rais are Christians in Sikkim today.

10. Secularism in the 22nd State of India 1975 onwards:

Sikkim integrated as the 22nd State of the Indian Union in 1975. The people of the vast country with diverse religion and faith started visiting Sikkim. Many of them settled here while many religious teachers and Gurus found a virgin land for religious practices. Many of them started religious institutions such as Hindu temples, Sikh Gurudwaras, Churches, Islam Musjids etc. Thus, the Hindu religion was enormously strengthened. New emergence and spread of Bahai society, Sa-ain Baba societies, Islam, Sikh, Jain and various sects of Christianity are practicing and vigorously impacting the existing religions and faiths in the State. Fresh encounter of these religion and faith has brought about a tremendous socio-religious transformation in the State.

Religious Composition of Sikkim and the World:

Religion	*Population of Sikkim in 1981*	*Per Cent of total population*	*Population of the World in 1991*	*Per cent of otal Population of the World*
Christianity	7,015	2.23	1,900,174,000	33.56
Muslims	3,241	1.03	1,033,453,000	18.26
Hindus	167,780	53.04	764,000,000	13.50
Buddhists	90,848	28.72	338,621,000	5.99
Chinese folk	—	—	149,336,000	2.65
New Religions	—	—	128,975,000	2.28
Tribal religions	—	—	99,150,000	1.76
Sikhs	322	0.10	20,204,000	0.37
Jews	—	—	13,451,000	0.06
Shamanists	—	—	11,010,000	0.19
Confucians	—	—	6,334,000	0.11
Bahal's	—	—	5,835,000	0.10
Jains	108	0.03	3,987,000	0.07
Shintoists	—	—	3,387,000	0.06
Yumaism	45,000	14.22	400,000	0.01
Other religions	1,987	0.63	20,419,000	0.36
Non-religions	—	—	924,078,000	16.32
Atheists	—	—	239,111,000	4.22
Total	316,385	100	5,661,525,000	100

Source: Sikkim Census 1981; Nunes, Antonio B. (1996) Statics on Religion internet; Subba, J.R. (2005: 210).

In Sikkim, individual religiosity varies as much as it does in any State or country, ranging from atheism to deep belief. People think about religion and their role in it, as they grow older and older. According to 1981 census the believers of Hinduism were more than 53%, Buddhism about 29%, Yumaism about 14% and 2% Christians in Sikkim. In the world, the believers of Christianity rank the first with about 34%, followed by Islam (18%), Hindus (14%) and Buddhist (6%). There are about 16% people who do not believe in any religion (Nunes, 1996; Subba, 2005: 210).

7
Language and Literature

The Sub-Himalayan races of Nepal, Sikkim and Bhutan are all closely affiliated, and are one and all of northern origin, which seem to result from sufficient evidence from the comparative vocabularies. In Sikkim, the State Government has provided the status of State Language to eleven languages so far, namely, the Lepcha, Bhutia, Limboo, Nepali (*Khas Kura*), Mangar, Gurung, Sunuwar, Tamang (Murmi), Newari, Khambu Rai (Bantawa), and Sherpa, There are many other spoken dialects also namely, Thami, Bhujel, Yakhas, Kulungey, Khalingey, Sotangey, Thulungey, Waingey, Umbuley etc. in the state. With the exception of the first i.e. Nepali (*Khus Kura*), the above languages and dialects are all of Trans-Himalayan stock and are closely affiliated. Many of these are extremely rude, owing to the people who speak them having crossed the snowy mountains before coming downed upon Tibet (Hodgson, 1874). In addition to the lingual evidence, other evidences deducible from the physical attributes, and from the creeds, customs, and legends of these races which have been described in their respective ethnography. The aboriginal stock of Sikkim is most undoubtedly Mongolian. This fact is inscribed in very plain characters in their faces, forms, and languages (Vansittart, 1896: 56-57). Amongst the ancient people of Sikkim must be counted the Lepchas, the Limboos and the Bhutias (Namgyal and Dolma, 1908).

The Lepchas are supposed to be the original inhabitants of Sikkim. The Yakthumbas (called Limbu by Nepalis and Tsongs by Tibetans) are the oldest inhabitants of Sikkim having settled there before the Tibetans (17th century) and the Nepalese (18th century) came to settle in the land (Hermanns, Fr. M., 1954:107-109).

1. Language and Literature before Emergence of "The Greater Sikkim" 1642 A. D:

The ancient Monree (Lepcha) and Tsongree (Limboo) dialects, oral traditions of the *Bongthing* and the *Muns* of the Lepchas, and oral Mundhums of the *Phedangmas* of the Limboos prevailed during this period of antiquity of Sikkim. After the Blood Brotherhood Treaty of Khe-Bumsa and Thekong-Tek during the 13th Century A.D. the Bhutias slowly started migration to the present areas of Sikkim. Since than, the Tibetan dialects and oral tradition of Lhorees (Bhutias) as well as the written texts of Buddhism were also started emerging in the present area of Sikkim. Further, the dialects and oral traditions of Mangars (Mongpas) were also there in the Mangar occupied areas at Mangarjongs in Sikkim.

Prof. R. K. Sprigg (1999: v) while writing foreword of my book entitled "The Limboos of the Eastern Himalayas with special reference to Sikkim" remarks that the Limboos were living in Sikkim before there was a Sikkim for them to live in! The same remark is applicable also for the Lepchas, and the Bhutias of the Greater Sikkim. By his remarks he meant that the Limboos, the Lepchas, and the Bhutias were inhabiting the different part of "The Greater Sikkim" of that time; but Sikkim came in existence only since 1642 A.D., a Water Horse Year, and the year in which Phuntsho Namgyal ascended the throne as First Chogyal at Yoksom Norbugang, in what is now West Sikkim".

Sprigg (1999) also writes that Sikkim was much larger at the time of the First Chogyal (1642-1970) than it is these days. The Maharaja of Sikkim's "History" (1908) translated by Dawa Samdup gives the frontiers of his ancestor's new Kingdom as --"Dibdala in the North, Shingsa Dagpay, Walung, Yangmag Khangchen, Yarlung and Timar Chorten in the west, down along the Arun and Dudh Kosi rivers, down to the Maha Nodi, Nuxulbari and Titalia in the south, on the east Tagong La, and Tang La on the north". These frontiers would include in the Greater Sikkim of those days the whole of Limbuwan, now in the eastern part of Nepal, southern Tibet from the Natu La and the Jelep La to the Thang La, beyond Phari Jong, western Bhutan up to the watershed range between the Amo Chu valley and the Har Chu valley, and the Northern plain of Bengal as far south at Titalia. **"The Greater Sikkim"** came into existence as a result of integration of the entire land resources of the Bhutias (Chumbi Velley), the Lepchas (present areas of East, North, South, and West district of Sikkim, Ilam area of Present Nepal, Hah Chu Valley and Amo Chu Valley of present Bhutan) and the Limboos (present area of Sikkim and the entire Limbuwan area extending west of Teesta river to east of Arun River of Nepal inclusive of Darjeeling, and Kalimpong areas of West Bengal) of that point of time after the "*Lho-Men Tsong Sum*" Tripartite Treaty signed by the leaders of these communities at Denzong Phuntso Khangsar on Water Horse Year corresponding to 1642 (Subba, 1999: vi; 126-128).

Although the Lepchas, the Limboos and the Bhutias had their own script prior to formation of the country "The Greater Sikkim" but the languages were not so popular during that time. This appears that the

Lepchas, the Limboos and the Bhutias of "The Greater Sikkim" had the ancient oral literatures and dialects popular among their communities. The Lepchas were having oral literature used by the Lepcha shamanic priests *Bongthings* and *Muns*, and used while performing life rituals, worship ceremonies etc. for the society. Similarly, the Limboos had oral literature of Mundhum used by the Limboo shamanic priests *Phedangmas* (a collective term of nine types of priests) while performing life rituals and worship ceremonies for the society. Most of the Bhutia communities were also the followers of Bon religion and had their oral literature of Bon religion used by the Bon priests the *pawo* (*dpa' bo*) and the *nejum* (*rnal 'byor ma*). The Bhutias might be having the Tibetan script brought from Tibet or oral Buddhist literature during that time but appears not to be so popular as it was limited to Lamas and Buddhist Gumpas. The Mangers might also be having their own dialects and oral literature.

2. Language and Literature after Emergence of "The Greater Sikkim" in 1642 ADS:

This period (1642 to 1774) was marked by emergence, spread and consolidation of Buddhism in Tibetan text. A number of Gompas were constructed for spread and consolidation of Buddhism. The Bhutia Language in Tibetan text was the official language both for administrative and monastery affairs. Buddhism was the religion of the country and both the Lepcha and the Limboo subjects were compelled to adopt it. This is the period when most of the Lepchas adopted Buddhism. Some of the Limboos also adopted Buddhism in the early half of the 17th century but after assassination of Teyongshi Sirijunga in 1741 A.D. the Limboos denounce Buddhism and reconsolidated their faith on Yumaism. This is the period when the Limboos of Sikkim started learning Sirijunga script reading and writing. They started propagation of Yumaism amongst the Limboos of Sikkim and Burma (Mayamar) in their language and script. The Limboos of Sikkim knew that they have their own language and literature; and also have their own Yuma religion.

2.1. The Tibetan Language, Script and Literature:

After the coronation or installation of Phuntsho Namgyal by the learned Lamas - Lha-Tsun-Namkha Jigmed (1597-1650), Ka-thog Kuntu Zangpo (? -1694), and Nag-Dak Sempa Phun-tsog Rinzing (1591-1656) as the Chogyal of Sikkim (Dharmaraja, king of righteousness), having two fold powers (spiritual and temporal) on the throne at Norbugang, Yoksom (Maharaja's History 1908: 29), the Bhutia ruler with the advice of Lha-Tsun-Chen-po, constructed a number of monasteries scattered through out Sikkim and spread Buddhism with monastic texts written in

Tibetan script to not only to his Bhutia subjects but also to the Lepcha and the Limboo subjects. The Tibetan language was declared as the official language of the country and the Tibetan script was the official script used both in Monastery and Administrative affairs (Ibid: 30-32).

Lotsawa Thonmi Sambhota devised the Tibetan script during the first half of seventh century in Tibet. Taking the Sanskrit *Lantsa* letters as copy, he formed, the Tibetan *Uchen* (headed or capital) character, and taking the *Wartu* (Urdu) letters as copy, he formed the *Umed* (headless or nuns) character of the Tibetan. Thus, he was the foremost man to introduce the art of writing in Tibet and introduce the Tibetan dialect to a written language (Maharaja's book, 1908: 6). The Tibetan language and Tibetan script was in use as the official language and script in Sikkim during the entire period of Namgyal Dynasty in Sikkim that is in 1642 to1975.

2.2. Lepcha Language and Literature:

According to the royal chronicles of the kings of Sikkim, Chagdor Namgyal (1686-1717), the third consecrated ruler of Sikkim (1700-1717) was the one who designed the alphabets of the Lepcha language (script) during the early period of 18th century (Rishley 1894:13). However, K.P.Tamsang (1983:28) claims that the Lepcha script had existed and was widely spread among the Lepchas long before the coming of the first Tibetans into Sikkim in the 13th century. The oath of blood treaty was not only sworn between Khe-Bumsa, and The-kong-Tek, the Lepcha divine priest, at Kabi Lungchok, in the 13th century, but the blood treaty was then written and signed both in Lepcha and Tibetan, which clearly proves that the Lepcha script was existing during that period of time in Sikkim. However, there is no historical evidence to prove the claim as yet. Neither, the Treaty of Kabi Lungchok in Lepcha language and script nor in Tibetan language and script has been seen so far (Foning, 1987: 154-156).

Some claim that Thekong Mensalong, a legandary figure among the tribesmen, invented it. He lived towards the beginning of the 17th century. Others say and believe that it was given along with the mountains, rivers and lakes by *Itbu-moo*, the Mother-Creator herself. The latter of course, may be viewed and dismissed as a fairy tale like the theory itself. A Tibetan scholar Tsepon Shakabpa claims that it was Lama Lhatsun Nangkha Jigmed (1597-1650), who gave the script of the language to the Lepchas. According to Chemjong (1948: 94) the King Maw Rong Hang had invented the Lepcha script in the 7th century, known as "*Rong Chhyo*" and taught reading and writing to his subjects. Till all these theories are to be proved true, the generally accepted Chagdor Namgyal version will stand (Foning: 1987:154-156).

Further, the Tibetan language being the official as well as the monastic affairs language in Tibetan script, there is no evidence to prove any Lepcha language and literature development in Sikkim during the entire period of Namgyal Dynasty (1642-1975). Once the Sangacholing Monastery was built in 1697, the Lepchas and the Limboos were being taught Buddhist texts in Tibetan script during the first half of 18th century (Chemjong, 1948: 166-167).

2.3. Limboo Language and Literature:

According to Sir John Hammerton (1966) "the Kiratas are one of the Mongolian races. Their original home was "*Sinar*" which was also known as "*Sumeru*" located in the northern plain of Persia. They were civilized. Cultivation was being done with *Nahar* irrigation. They had their script. Every Village had their own King and used to fight every now and then for their boundary line. They used to write their agreement on the stones and rocks and used to place on their boundary line. One of the groups went to the east in about 3000 B.C. and established a kingdom in China. From the same group some went to Kabul, Punjab, and then to the Gangetic plain and started inhabiting there. From there they went to the Himalayas. They might have brought the civilization of Babylon. As such there is a great similarity on the folktales of Kiratas with the creation history of Babylon, water disaster, language ruin etc."

The above remark is extremely important from the two points, Viz: (*i*) the Limboo Script and (*ii*) the belief system. The existing multiple soul "*Yetchham Thim*" (eight soul system excluding the physical body) belief system of the Limboos is similar to that of ancient Egyptian belief system (nine soul system including the physical body) (Subba, 2005:22-32; 138-148), and this provides a linkage and support for those who believe in the theory of migration of the Kiratas like Hammerton (1966), I.S. Chemjong (1948/1967) and others. The other point is of Kiranta script. It provides linkage that the Kiratas had their own script even before 3000 B. C. and used to read and write on stones and rocks. The 7th century King of Limbuwan Maw Rang Hang was the first man who introduced writing and reading system "*Rong Chhyo*" among the Kiratas (Lepchas), which however, owing to the long prevailing anarchy, fell into disuse (Vansittart, 1896: 135). Another King of Limbuwan (Eastern Nepal) of the 9th century Sirijunga Hang (880-915 A.D.) said to have found the Limboo script in the caves of Himalayas, further developed the script and used for educating their subjects (Vansittart, 1896: 135). Whether the present "*Rong Chhyo*" and "Limboo script" were found and developed from the existing Kirata script of 3000 B. C. or codified and developed independently by Maw Rang Hang of 7th century, and Sirijunga Hang of 9th century respectively, are the subjects of research. There is no historical evidence to prove this fact as yet.

After the formation of "The Greater Sikkim" by signing tripartite treaty of "*Lho-Men-Tsong Sum*" the Bhutia kings thought that the agreement would bring peaceful administration. But once the administration was strengthened the Bhutia administration constructed a monastery at Sangacholing initially established by Lha-tsun in 1697 and compelled to study Buddhism in Tibetan script to the Lepcha and the Limboo subjects. Many Lepcha subjects gave up Animism (or *Bongthism* and *Munism*) and adopted Buddhism during that time. Many Limboo subjects were also going to Sangacholing monastery for Buddhist study. Having come to know these developments in Sikkim, Teyongshi Sirijunga (1704-1741), the incarnate of the Sirijunga Hang of 9th century, was prompted to enter into Sikkim in 1734 A.D. He first came to Martam, West Sikkim and started creating awareness about the Limboo script and Yumaism (Yuma Religion), and started teaching reading and writing of Limboo language in Limboo script to the Limboos of Sikkim. He continued his work of awareness till 1741 hiding him as the Bhutias were against him of his activities. The *Ta-Tashang* Lamas of Pemyangtse monastery were annoid by his activity and they assassinated him at the confluence of Kalej Khola and Reshi Khola in 1741. He compiled the Mundhum book namely " *Yakthung Mundhum Sapla*" when he was at Martam Sikkim, and is the first book written in Limboo script in Sikkim. After the assassination of Teyongshi Sirijunga the Bhutia administration banned reading and writing of Limboo language in Limboo script till 1968 (Subba, 1999). Thus, further development of Limboo language and literature was completely stopped after Sirijunga's assasination in 1741 (Chemjong 1967:166-167; Subba, 1999; Yakthungchum 1998; Subba, 2004: 10-38).

2.4. Mangar Language and Literature:

The Mangars or Mongpas were also there in Sikkim during 1642 A.D. In the Tripartite Treaty of "*Lho-Men-Tsong Sum*" translated by Prof. Ringu Tulku in 1984, there is a mention of one para, which runs as follows:

"During the last Mongpa war some people's action were noted and let them be beware of now from this year of Water Horse onwards we will abide by the commands of the King, his Guru and his sons and will never let arise a bad thought against Sikkim."

From the text of the Treaty it appears that the Mongpas (Mangers) were ruling some areas of "The Greater Sikkim" as petty rulers who opposed the supremacy of King Phuntsho Namgyal of Namgyal Dynasty in Sikkim. They opposed the supremacy of Bhutia King and revolted against the King Phuntsho Namgyal. Consequently, the Mangar rulers were driven away by the Administration of The Bhutias, Lepchas and finally the Limboos towards the Western Himalayas. As such there was no Language and literature development even if some common Mangar subjects were there in Sikkim. Hence, the Mangar language and literature development could not take place during that period.

3. From Gorkha Invasion (1774) to Treaty of Titalia (1817):

This period is recognized as the emergence of Nepali language and literature development in Sikkim. The landmark contribution of this period is to bring the socio-cultural transformation of the entire gamut of hill-tribes and castes of the Himalayas into a single community known in the world today as Nepali through the process of Nepal Unification as described by Stiller (1968) in his book by the greatest visionary King Prithivi Narayan Shah of Nepal. The Nepal Unification not only introduced Nepali language (*Khus Kura*) in Sikkim but also introduced a number of dialects of the Hill tribes. The entire people of the areas of Sikkim occupied by the Gorkhas were compelled to adopt *Khas Kura* as a *lingua franca* of the region/country, Hindu religion, *Khas* culture and adopt the entire Nepal Unification process described by Stiller (1968) as a whole. A tremendous social transformation process happened during this period (Stiller, 1968:65-68).

The unification of Nepal by Prithivi Narayan Shaha, the father of modern Nepal and the leader of Gorkha conquest, started his conquest in 1744-45 from the Western end of the present Nepal rocked Sikkim in 1774. By January 1773 the Gorkhalis controlled the upper half of Majh Kirat (Khambuwan), and by the end of February their control extended to the southern half as well. Bijayapur (Limbuwan) fell into Gorkhali hands on 17th July 1774. Sikkim Raja signed a treaty with the Gorkhali commanders, which marked out boundaries between the two states to the mutual satisfaction of both parties. By 1774 Nepal had gained the whole of the Eastern Hills, including all the territory west of the Singali La watershed. In the Tarai the Gorkhalis controlled the entire territory as far east as the Teesta River. West Sikkim was occupied and ruled since 1889 to 1814 including Rabdentse Palace by the Gorkhas (Stiller, 1968:109-110; Chemjong, III Edition, 1967:221-230).

During the Nepal's rule of West Sikkim(1889-1914) and other areas of the Greater Sikkim a number of Nepali ethnic communities came to the Ghorkha occupied areas of Sikkim and settled there. The hill tribes mostly entered in Sikkim included the Kiratas (Khambu Rais, Yakhas, and more and more of Limboos were also added up), Khasas (higher *Khasas* such as Bahun, Chhetris; lower *Khasas* such as Kami, Damai, Sarki), Thakuris, Majhis, Bhujels, Thami, Sunuwar, Newar, Mangars, Gurungs, Tamangs, Sherpas, Yelmos, and more and more of Lepchas from Illam. Along with the people, a number of culture, dialect and language, ancient oral literature, religion and belief systems, etc. also came to the Gorkha occupied areas of Sikkim. However, all the tribes and castes of the ethnic groups were highly hinduized in all respect of culture, language and literature, religion etc. Even if they were having their own dialect, language and literature, religion, culture etc. the Nepal administration had banned the promotion of their identity till 1930 AD. The Nepal unification promoted only one culture i.e. *Khas* Culture, only one language and literature i.e. *Khas Kura* now known as Nepali; only one religion, i.e. *Hinduism*; and only one administration, i.e. Gorkha administration. Thus, although the different hill tribes may be having different language, culture and religion, but could promote only the one specified as above amalgamated into one culture known as Nepali/Gorkha.

During this period Hinduism in religion, *Khas Kura* in language and literature and *Khas* culture in culture was introduced in the Gorkha occupied areas of Sikkim also. However, not much of development of Khas language and literature, culture and tradition etc. could take place, may be due to threat of frequent Gorkha-Sikkim war taking place during this period in Sikkim.

4. From Titalia Treaty (1817) to Sikkim Integration into Indian Union (1975):

This period is marked as a movement away from Tibetan to Hindi to Nepali and English language and literature development. The medium of instruction in the schools was also changed from Hindi to Nepali and English. This period is also marks the beginning of the modern education system in Sikkim.

Although the rulers and administrator has changed from the Gorkha and Chogyal to a single Chogyal now in the Gorkha occupied areas of Sikkim, the process of Nepal unification—socio-cultural transformation continued within the society in the entire areas of Sikkim as the people–the Gorkha or Nepalese in the Gorkha occupied areas spread through out the length and breath of Sikkim during this period due to Nepali settlement policy of the British Political Officer J.C.White. It is because of the British India promoted settlement of Nepalese through Kazis and Nepali Thekadars (Landlords) throughout Sikkim despite opposition of the Chogyal and the Lepchas.

During 1814-16, Nepal was defeated and compelled to signed a treaty at Sugauli in 1815. This took away much territory of Nepal area by the British India from both the west and eastern border. By the treaty of Titalia in 1817, the British returned much of the area of Sikkim occupied by Nepal in 1774 and 1789 to1814 upto the western border from Kankayi to the Phalut range and the Mechi river of Sikkim (Risley, 1894: 19). The British took away Darjeeling for health Sanitarium in 1835. With the Treaty of Titalia, Sikkim came under the protectorate of British India. In June 1889 Mr. J.C.White, Executive Engineer, was appointed as Assistant Political Officer at Gangtok to advise and assist the Maharaja in his administration of the country.

4.1. Beginning of Modern Education System in Sikkim:

Until late in the nineteenth century, education in Sikkim was confined to the study of scriptures and religious philosophy in the various monasteries. The beginning of the modern education can be traced back to 1880 when the Finnish missionaries entered Sikkim. In the year 1872-73, a missionary, Rev. Macfarlane, who was pioneering the cause of education in Darjeeling district, visited Sikkim and is said to have established a few mission schools in various parts. During the year 1875 some landlords are said to have started their own schools purely of their own resources and on their own premises. Later when missionaries moved from village to village, these schools are said to have run by them on the basis of grant-in-aid. Schools run by the missionaries were imparting instructions not only in the three 'Rs' but were also teaching subjects like Geography, History, English, Hindi, Science and Tibetan. The medium of instruction was Hindi (Veda Prakasha, 1976: 100).

Finnish missionaries started three primary schools in Khamdong, Song and Mangan in 1880. In 1884, Scottish missionaries started primary schools at Rhenock, Pachekhani, Pakyong, Namthang, Chidam, Vak, Chakyong, Soreng, Sombaria, Damthang and Turuk. Bhutia boarding school and Nepali boarding school at Gangtok were started in 1889 and 1906 respectively. While Sidkeong Tulku founded Enchey School in 1909, P.N.Girls School was founded in 1923. In 1924, Bhutia and Nepali boarding schools were amalgamated into Tashi Namgyal High School. It was only in 1966 that Tashi Namgyal High School split into Tashi Namgyal Secondary School and Tashi Namgyal Academy (Mathur, 1976: 99).

Nepali education was started in Sikkim during 1920, when Rashmi Prasad Alley (1892-1974) was appointed by the Chogyal Sir Tashi Namgyal as Headmaster of the Nepali Boarding School, Gangtok.on 26th April 1920. Thus, the foundation of education through Nepali language was laid from 1921 in Sikkim.

The role played by Kazi Lhendup Dorjee Khangsarpa and his brother the Kazi Phag Tshering in the late 1920s is worth mentioning. Phag Tshering founded the Young Men's Buddhist Association at Darjeeling and established large number of schools in Western Sikkim and was instrumental in bringing about very many social and other reforms. Sikkim had only one Teacher's Training Institute at Temi.

4.2. Planning and Development in Education Sector:

The idea of planned economic and social development in Sikkim goes back to the year 1952 when the matter was for the first time taken up for discussion between the late Prime Minister Pandit Nehru and late Sir Tashi Namgyal, the then Chogyal of Sikkim. With the inauguration of the First Five Year Plan (1954-61), planning was formally initiated in 1954. The First Plan was followed by three Five year Plans; the year 1975-76 was the last year of the Fourth Five Year Plan. By 1971 census, the literacy rate in Sikkim was 17.7%. In 1966 English was made the medium of instruction in all the schools and colleges. By 1970, there were 226 Primary Schools, 31 Junior High Schools, and 6 Higher Secondary Schools besides a Public School and an evening College. The children enrolled in these institutions number 17,657 in primary Schools, 3,291 in Junior High Schools and 683 in Higher Secondary Schools giving a total enrollment of 21,631. The evening College has a small enrolment of about 60 students (Mathur 1976: 9). Thus, this period marks the beginning of modern education system in Sikkim.

4.3. Nepali Language and Literature:

During this period, a good start of Nepali language and literature development took place in Sikkim. An Italian, Cassiano Beligatti, who published his Alphabetum from Rome in 1771, had mentioned Nepali in it as a major language. J.A. Ayton an assistant professor in Fort Wlliam College in Kolkata, published the first grammar of this language as a "Grammar of the Nepalese Language" in 1820. Till 1927, the Bengal Government termed the language as "Nepalese Pahariaya or *Khaskura*". The Nepali Sahitya Sammelan, founded in Darjeeling in 1924. Number of Newspapers were started such as "Sikkim Herald (1959), Kanchanjungha (1957), Tintara (1958), and Sikkim (1966) in Sikkim. Maharaja Sidkeong Tulku established a printing press in 1913 initially for printing Tibetan books but Nepali and English books were also printed latter. The influence of independent movement of India and of great literary personalities like Lekhnath Poudyal (1884-1965), Lakshimi Prasad Deokota (1909-1965) and Balkrishna Sama (1902-1981) is very much evident on the poets associated with "Apatan Sahitya Parisad" in

Sikkim. This was the time when Parasmani Pradhan, Surya Bikram Gewali and their worthy associates had already had their influence on the young poets. During the early twentieth century Dharanidhar Koirala's "Naibedya" (1920), Mahananda Sapkota's "Mana Lahari" (1920) marked a break with fradition and ushered a new age in the history of Nepali literature (Subhas Deepak 2004: 99-142).

Agam Giri from Gangtok written the poems "Samasyapurti" and "Chandrika Patrika yo", "Preeti Lahari" (1919), "Ghar Mero Ganduk" by Prasad Singh Nechali Rai, "Viswa Brahman Varnan" (1925) containing two poems "Anubhaav" and "Nivendan" by Manbir Sing Rasaily. Before the establishment of Apatan Sahitya Parisad, Late Santabir Limboo of Sikkim had been writing poems in various journals published from Darjeeling, Nepal and Benares. A large number of his poems were published in Indrakil Pushpanjali (1950), Sharda, Gorkha, Udai, Bharati, Hamro Katha etc., the leading literary journals of the 1940s. The themes of his poems were patriotism and ethnic pride. He was opposed to social evils and dogmas prevalent in the Nepali society in those days and showed intense love for his culture and tradition. He was the first to put Sikkim in the literary map of Nepali literature.

The establishment of "Apatan Sahitya Parisad" in 1947 was a historic event in the literary history of Sikkim, which spearheaded the Nepali literary movement. Indrakeel Puspanjali an anthology of poems published in 1950 by Padam Singh Subba, Secretary of the Apatan Sahitya Parisad, Gangtok, contains poems of Agam Singh Tamang, Tulsi Bahadur Chettri, Padam Singh Subba, Nima Tshering Lepcha, Chandra Das Rai, Ram Dutta Lal Thakur, Bhupal Lamichaney, Shivanath Mishra, Santabir Limboo and Man Bahadur Subba. A number of literary works published and by 1975, Nepali language and literature was fully developed, and had become a *lingua franca* of the country Sikkim.

4.4. Limboo Language and Literature:

By 1914-15, the Sirijunga script had almost disappeared, when late Lalshor Sendang (1840-1926) came to Thambong and Daramdin and started teaching Srijunga script reading and writing, and Yumaism Mundhum to the Limboos of that area in Sikkim again. He went to Kalimpong 1924 and taught the same to the people of Kalimpong inclusive of late I.S. Chemjong. Under his inspiration a Literary society "Yakthung Hang Chumlung" was constituted in 1925. In 1938, the society established a Limboo language School known as "Jambok Memorial School" at Kalimpong for the first time in the world. Late I.S.Chemjong wrote a number of books on the Limboo history, language and literature and culture. Subedar Bajbir Tholong, Iman Singh Chemjong, M.B. Khamthak and P.S. Muringla published "*Tum Yakthung Ninwaphu Sapla*" the first Limboo language primary textbook from Gangtok also in 1951. The Chogyal Palden Thondup Namgyal approved Limboo language study as an optional subject in the schools of Sikkim upto class II in 1968. Accordingly eight Limboo language teachers were also appointed in the Government Schools of West Sikkim. Thus, the period marks the emergence and introduction of modern Limboo language study in Sikkim.

4.5. Education System During 1960s and 1970s:

Anderson (1990: 113-114) has pointed out that the education system of a nation is often used to promote a shared history, culture, and language among its youth. The quest for a national identity in Sikkim led to a review and transformation of primary education. Prior to 1967 no coherent program or policy for grades kindergarten existed in Sikkim. In 1960, 9,700 students were enrolled in 117 lower primary schools (grade I-3), 47 upper primary schools (grades 4-5), 13 middle schools (grades 6-8), and 5 high schools. By 1975, 20,959 students were enrolled in 52 lower primary, 176 upper primary, 29 junior high schools, and 7 higher or senior secondary schools (Datta, 1991: 41-50). Education hinged on write learning and memorization; textbooks, when available, came from India and did not contain any Sikkim-specific material. In 1967 a "textbook and curriculum committee" was established; its goals were to "define and develop educational goals and curriculum" for grades K-8 and to make education "more suitable to the special conditions and character of Sikkim". Over the next five years, in addition to extensive teacher training, textbooks were produced for social studies (including books on community studies, Sikkim history, geography, and nature studies 1-8), English (readers based on Sikkimese folks tales and literature 1-8), and the three mother tongue languages (primers 1-3 and readers 1-8) (Jackie Hiltz, 2003: 75-76).

In Sikkim the complicated issue of language posed challenges for the educational system. English was the official language in this small country where people spoke three distinct languages – Bhutia, Lepcha, and Nepali – but in fact, Nepali was the unofficial lingua franca. In grades 1-3, children were to be instructed in their mother tongue, with English taught as a second language, but in reality, this was rarely the case as most schools were understaffed. English was the medium of instruction in schools after third grade. Since English continued to be used for most of the grades even after the review, the committee amplified efforts to make the content of what the children studied "more relevant, more

Sikkimese". The committee developed an archive of Sikkimese material for the textbooks through the efforts of teams of high school students. Armed with tape recorders, the volunteers fanned out across the most remote reaches of the kingdom to collect Sikkimese myths, folk tales, and music from every possible ethno-linguistic group, which were then translated into the three national languages of Sikkim. In this way, "all the children, although studding different languages would absorb a shared frame of reference on their national culture (Jackie Hiltz, 2003: 75-76).

5. After Integration of Sikkim into the Indian Union (1975):

The education policy evolved during 1960s and 1970s is being continued in Sikkim even today. However, the policy of educating more and more about its own state and culture to the students could not be successful as desired, because of absence of its own Board of Education and University so far. From the linguistic point of view, this is a period of a movement away from Tibetan and Nepali to the regional vernacular languages, emerged from ancient oral literature to written forms, stimulated by the integration of Sikkim into the Indian Union as the 22nd State of India. The Government of Sikkim through the Sikkim Official Language Act, 1977 recognized the Nepali, the Bhutia and the Lepcha language as the official languages of Sikkim on the 17th October 1977. Development of regional languages namely Nepali, Bhutia, Lepcha, Limboo, Tamang, Khambu Rai, Newari, Mangar, Sunuwar, Sherpa and Gurung (11 Nos) language emerged, and intensified with the approval of State language status to seven more languages in 1997 . The Limboo Language which was an optional subject approved by the Chogyal Palden Thondup Namgyal vide Memo No. (32)62/990 Edn dated 11.03.1968 upto class II, was made a regular subject upto Primary level of ClassV in 1975. Sri B.B.Subba was appointed as a Limboo language Text Book Writer in 1975-76. The Limboo Language was recognized as an official language on 31st March 1981 through the Sikkim Official Language Act 1977 amendment passing the Sikkim Official Language (Amendment) Bill, 1981 and through Notification No. 6/LD/81 dated 31. 03. 1981. The Sikkim Official Language Act 1977 was further amended in 1997 and recognized Gurung, Khambu-Rai (Bantawa), Tamang, Newari, Sherpa, Mangar and Sunuwar (7 Nos.) as Official languages of Sikkim. Thus there are now 11 (eleven) official languages in Sikkim. Out of these languages the Bhutia, the Lepcha and the Limboo languages have been introduced in the North Bengal University from the academic session 2001. The Nepali language has already been introduced in several Universities.

5.1. The Bhutia Language and Literature:

The Bhutias speak in their own language – Bhutia, among themselves. This is one of the oldest language spoken in the ancient times by "*Bhompu*" or the "*Bon*" people. The dialect was one of the *Lingua Franca* in the Himalayan region. This dialect is different from the official Tibetan language and is simpler. Sikkimese Bhutia language had so far been a spoken dialect only and for all literary, cultural and educational pursuits, Tibetan was the language used by the Bhutia population of Sikkim. Therefore, , the need to render it into a written form was being felt during 1970s. Until 1975, Tibetan was the official language of Sikkim. After adoption of Sikkim Language Bill 1977, the Bhutia has been the official language of the Sikkimese Bhutias. The Bhutia language Textbooks were developed using Sambhota Tibetan Script by the Textbook Unit of the Department of Education, Government of Sikkim, and regular subjects were introduced in the schools and colleges now. Norden Tshering and R.P. Lama are among the pioneer textbook writers whose contributions in this difficult task have been immense. There are several teachers who have contributed in the preparation of textbooks in the language. Bhaichung Bhutia has written *Richi* a novel, *Lossong* Festival, and *Zigten Namtok* and a book of poems. There are many poems, essay, stories written by several writers of the language. The prominant writers are Pema Rinzing Bhutia, Palden Tshering Gyamtso, Norden Tshering, Yapchung Kazi, etc.(Subhas Deepak, 2004: 10-20; Bhutia, 2007).

5.2. The Lepcha Language and Literature:

The Sikkim Government through the Sikkim Official Language Act, 1977, accorded official language status to the Lepcha language in 1977. The Lepcha textbooks were developed in the Textbook unit of Education Department for the schools and colleges. College education on the Lepcha language was started in 2001. The Lepchas have their own Lepcha script. The first Lepcha grammar book was written in 1876 by General G. B. Mainwaring of Bengal Staff Corps, stationed at Lebong, Darjeeling. He also compiled the first Lepcha-English dictionary in 1898. D.C. Luksom wrote a Lepcha-Hindi-English Dictionary in 1983. The first Lepcha Reader, *Rong Arok Chhukalbo* was published in 1961. The first literary magazine, *Mayel Lyang* was published by Renjyong Mutanchi Ringmom Kurmom (Sikkim Lepcha Literary Organization) in 1978. *Kongchen Kung Cho* (1987-1989) by Norgain Sangdyang and *Mingama Lhamu, Lyangdok* (1995) by Ugen Lepcha are other Lepcha language publications. *Rong Dungit Vom* (Lapcha folk songs) published in 1977 by Sonam Tshering Lepcha and *Kayu Rong Vom Chhyo* (Lepcha song book) published in 1986 by Hildamit Lepcha are some of the important Lepcha publications. The prominent Lepcha writers are D.C. Luksom, D. K.Luksom, Sonam Tshering Lepcha, Lha Tshering Kunchudyangmoo, Topden Tongden Lepcha, Ugen Lepcha, Norgain Tshering Sangdyang, Nima Lhamu Lepcha, Dhendup Lepcha and Ongdi Tshering Lepcha (Subhas Deepak, 2004: 21-45).

5.3. The Limboo Language and Literature:

The Limboo language is a Tibeto-Burman language and is written in Sirijunga script. Textbooks were written in the Textbook Unit of Education Department since 1976 onwards. The textbooks were written by Sri B.B.Subba (Muringla), who was assisted by Chandra Mangyung (Limboo Language Teacher in the formative years of Development), Mohan Prasad Subba (Phurumbho), Assistant Limboo Textbook Writer, and numerous Limboo language Teachers working in the various Schools of Sikkim. They have contributed immensely for the textbook writing and publication for schools and colleges. Several other Limboo Language literates and experts such as P.S. Subba (Muringla), S.R. Khajum, Bal B. Subba, P.R. Khewa and others also contributed for the development of Limboo language and literature. Degree College study was introduced in 2001 session in the University of North Bengal. The Limboo language and literature is very rich. J.R. Subba has listed out 47 books other than textbooks and 34 journals published from 1951 to 2001 in his book " History and Development of Limboo Language"(2002). A number of Limboo language Dictionaries have been written by Campbell (1848), HWR Senior (1908), Limboo-Nepali- English by Iman Sing Chemjong (1960), B. B. Subba (1979), Hindi-Limboo dictionary by Padam Singh Subba, B.B.Subba, and Braj Behari Kumar (1981) and Nepali-English-Limboo edited by Bairagi Kainla (2002). Limboo Radio Broadcasting was started from Gangtok from 3rd April 1983. By the later half of the 1970s, the movement for education in Limboo language took a new turn. New textbooks were developed, the existing writing system was modified and codification in the Unicode and standardization of the language began (Subba, 2002:1-65; Subhasdeepak, 2004).

Limboo Literary Association (Sukhim Yakthung Sapsok Songjumbho) was registered in 1979. Numerous Limboo folklores, poems, essay, Novel, etc. have been published in Sikkim. The prominent Limboo writers are B.B. Subba, Padam Singh Subba, Suk Raj Subba, Jash Raj Subba, R.B.Limboo, Mohan Prasad Subba, Bal Muringla, Mohan Ijum, Chandra Mangyung and many school teachers of Sikkim.

Subhash Deepak has listed out 39 books published till 1991. Sirijunga script was computerized in 1995 (Subba, 2002; Subhas Deepak, 2004).

5.4. The Tamang Language and Literature:

Tamangs have their own dialect and script. It is a Tibeto-Burman language and it uses Sambhota Script for writing with little modification and known as *'Tamayek Lipi*''. The Government of Sikkim by an Official Gazette Notification dated 31st March 1995 has recognized the Tamang language as a Official State language. *Jikten Tamchhyoee* or Tamang Vanshavali written by Buddhiman Moktan (1957) is considered to be the first book in the history of Tamang publications. Another book titled *Tamba Kaeeten Rimthim* written by Santabir Lama published from Darjeeling in 1957. Nearly 99 titles pertaining to language, culture and tradition of the Tamangs have been published between 1957 to 1997. The magazines and Journals published are *Thweendel* (1975) from Nepal, *Phyapulla* (1982) from Darjeeling, *Tsargyam* from Sikkim.

In 1975, the Sikkim Tamang Buddhist Association published G.D.Lama's *Sherab-Gno-Syepo* (introduction of Alphabets). *Hyang Tamang Gyot Lokpe* (let us learn Tamang language) written by K.M.Tamang was published in 1977. Sikkim Herald in Tamang language published in 2001. There are six Tamang language schools presently being run by block committees of the Sikkim Tamang Buddhist Association. These schools were established at Passi on 25th November 1996, Namthang on 14th July 1997, Kateng on 12th February 1997, Padamchey Gompa on 8th June 1997, and Singling and soreng on 15th March 1998. Tamang teachers have been appointed from the 2002 academic session. A Tamang translator was appointed in the Legislative Assembly in 1976. The prominent Tamang writers are K.M.Tamang, Kumar Yonzon, Lama Lhakpa Bomzon, G.D.Lama and Pempa Tamang (Tamang, M.K.1998: 96-105).

5.5. Khambu Rai Language and literature:

The Government of Sikkim accorded Official status to Khambu-Rai (Bantawa) language along with six others 1995. The Khambu-Rais have their own dialect and script (used for the first time by Kripa Shaylan Rai when he wrote *Rai Aksharko Varnamala* in 1969). With the active co-operation and help rendered by the members of the Akhil Sikkim Khambu Rai Association, two pucca school buildings have been constructed at Parengaon in West Sikkim and Kopche busty in South Sikkim. Books published in Rai script so far are Rai Sabdakosh by Kripa Shalyan, *Kiraba Chhaplabob Lachhep* by B.B.Rai, Rai Text Books I, & II by B.B.Rai, S.B. Sukmaya Rai, S.B.Rai, Prabhat Siwahang Rai, Rai Dictionary by

B.B.Rai. The Rai language is in infancy but started education in two schools of Sikkim run by the Association at present. The writers are San Kumar Rai and Kripa Shalyan Rai (Subhas Deepak 2004:73-77).

5.6. The Newari Language and Literature:

The language of the Newars is called Newari, which is a Tibeto-Burman group of Sino-Tibetan family. The Newari language was amongst the seven languages recognized by the State Government as the State Languages in 1995. The Newari language is written in "*Ranjana Script*" developed from Brahmi script. The Sikkim Newar Guthi, which was established on 3rd October 1993, had appointed two Newar language teachers for Rhenock and Mellidara Primary Schools in the year 1997-98. Since 1996, Mrs Durga Kasaju, wife of Dharma Pratap Kasaju of Namthang Kothi has rendered her selfless service for the development of Newari language by imparting teaching of Newari language to the students of the surrounding areas.

Sikkim Newar Sangathan, headed by Khagendra Pradhan of Turung, South Sikkim, with the help of Dharma Pratap Kasaju, Purna Kumar Maskey and others established an institute of Newari Language and culture at the Namthang Kothi in 2000. The duration of the learning course is of 12 months and refresher course is three months. There were 26 students in the first batch and 24 students in the second batch up to July 2001. After successful completion of the course, the students are awarded with certificate. The prominent writers are Mrs Durga Kasaju, and Mrs Punam Gougali of Nemthang, Mrs Ranjana Shrestha of Rhenock, and Mrs Kalpana Shrestha of Sumbuk. The publications are Newa, a periodical magazine, Bhasha Varna Ra Lipi (Two editions) published by Rachana, Gangtok, owned by Karuna Devi Smarak Dharmarth Guthi and edited by Mrs Ranjana Shrestha and Rajiva S Shrestha (Karunadevi Smarak Dharmarth Guthi, 2001; Sikkim Newar Sangh 2006).

5.7. The Mangar Language and Literature:

The Mangar language falls under Tibeto-Burmese language of the Sino Tibetan family. Y.B.Thapa mentions that the Mangar Lipi is known as "*Akharika*" script and is as old as 500 B.C. to 2,500 B.C (Subhara Subba Dahal 1999: 119). Since 1995, the Sikkim Government has recognized Mangar language as an official language of Sikkim along with other languages. Since 2002, Sikkim Herald has been piublished in Mangar Language and a translator has been appointed in the Sikkim Assembly in 1999. All Sikkim Mangar Association established in 1993, is engaged in the development of Mangar language in Sikkim. Abimaya Thapa, D.M.Thapa, Tulsha Thapa and Bishnu Rana are collectively engaged in writing readers from Class I to IV under Sikkim Government Textbook Unit (Santosh Alle, 2003:170-183).

5.8. The Sunuwar Language and Literature:

The Sunuwar language and script belongs to the Tibeto-Burman group. The Sunuwar language is written in Sunuwar script and is known as *Koincha Brehs*. The Government has recognized Sunuwar language as the official language of Sikkim in 1995. Sikkim Sunuwar (Mukhia) Koinchbu was established in 1990. Kiratvanshi Sunuwar (Mukhia) Koinch is a historic book relating to the origin, culture, traditions, language, script and literature of the Sunuwars. This book was compiled by Raghubir Mukhia; was written by B.M.Pradhan and published by the Sikkim Sunuwar (Mukhia) Koinchbu, Gangtok, Sikkim in 1999. They have not been able to publish any textbook for education in Sunuwar language in Sunuwar script so far in Sikkim (Sunuwar, K.B., 1998:113-131).

5.9. The Sherpa Language and Literature:

The Sherpa language is written in Tibetan Sambhota script. It falls under Tibeto-Burman group of languages. The Government of Sikkim has granted Official status to Sherpa language in 1995. Efforts are being made for its development and promotion for which the Government has granted all possible assistance. Two teachers have been appointed at Perbing Senior Secondary School, South Sikkim and Okharey School, West Sikkim from the year 2002 for teaching Sherpa language in these schools. A translator has also been appointed for translation in the Sikkim Assembly in 1998. School textbooks for class I & II "*Sher-Pa-Lob-De Dep Dang-Po*" (Sherpa Alphabets) and "*Sher-Pai-Ket-Lob-Khyee*" (let's learn to speak Sherpa language) have been published by the Text Book Unit of Education Department in 1998. Sikkim herald was also published in Sherpa language in 2001. The Denzong Sherpa Association registered in 1984 is actively engaged in development and promotion of Sherpa Language (Sherpa, D.G., 1998: 90-95).

5.10. The Gurung Language and Literature:

The Gurungs call their language as "*Tamu*", which falls under Tibeto-Burman family. The language is written in "*Khema*" script. The Gurung language is called "*Tamu Khye*". All Sikkim Gurung (Tamu) Boudh Sangh is trying its best to develop textbooks for the schools and promotion of the language and culture. The State Government has recognized official status in 1995. A translator has been appointed in the Sikkim Assembly in 1998. Under the patronage of Akhil Sikkim Gurung (Tamu) Boudh Sangh, opened schools at Burthuk, East district, Dodok, West District, and

Chuba-Perbing, South district on private basis. The Government has appointed six teachers so far for teaching Gurung language in Sikkim. Meghraj Gurung is a Gurung writer who has written "*Tamu Khye Lule*" (let us learn Gurung language) 1997, textbook for Class I to III, "*Tamu Yhar Khye*" (Gurung Gramar) in 2001 and Gurung Dictionary in 1997. A magazine called "*Tungna*" has been brought out by the All Sikkim Gurung (Tamu) Buddhist Association in 1994 (Subhas Deepak, 2004: 93-95).

The First Chief Minister of Sikkim Shri L.D.Kazi provided Nepali, Bhutia and Lepcha languages the official status in 1977. Limboo language was formally introduced in schools of Sikkim during L.D.Kazi's Chief Ministership in 1976 onwards, and provided an official status in 1981 during Shri N.B Bhandari's Chief Ministership. All other remaining languages Viz, Gurung, Tamang, Sherpa, Sunuwar, Mangar, Newari, and Khambu Rai have been provided official status in 1997 by Shri P.K.Chamling, the present Chief Minister of Sikkim.

5.11. Inclusion of Nepali Language in the Eighth Schedule of the Indian Constitution:

Before the merger of Sikkim with the Indian Union in 1975, Nepali was the national language of Sikkim The Namgyal Dynasty of Sikkim had given due recognition to Nepali language. But after its merger with Indian Union, Sikkim had to join the struggle for the recognition of Nepali language in the Eighth Schedule of the Indian Constitution.

Nepali had been the *lingua franca* of Sikkim for more than one century. Since 1925, with the sincere efforts of noted literateur Rashmi Prasad Alley, Nepali was introduced as a medium of instruction in the schools of Sikkim (Alley, 1963). The West Bengal Legislative Assembly adopted a resolution and recommended to the Central Government the Constitutional recognition of Nepali language and its inclusion in the Eighth Schedule, so that the Nepali speaking people can participate more deeply in the national life of India on 2nd July 1977. Three months later, the Sikkim Legislative Assembly also unanimously adopted a resolution on 23rd September 1977 recommending the inclusion of Nepali language in the Eighth Schedule. The resolution read: "the Assembly therefore, resolves to recommend to the Central Government of taking necessary steps for the inclusion of the Nepali language in the Eighth Schedule of the Constitution". The tripura Legislative Assembly also adopted a resolution which read: "that the Tripura Assembly requests the Central Government to take immediate steps for inclusion of Nepali language in the Eighth Schedule of the Constitution" Himalayan Today, New Delhi, Vol. III Nos. 3&4, Dec. 91, May 92, p-20).

Finally, the Parliament on 20th August 1992 unanimously passed a Constitutional Amendment Bill according official status to Nepali, Konkani and Manipuri languages. The Lok Sabha approved the Bill, in 1992 with 343 votes in favour and none against. The Rajya Sabha passed the bill without debate with 130 in favour and none against. The Bill was moved in both of the houses by the Union Home Minister S.B. Chavan and passed unanimously (Himalayan Today, New Delhi, Vol. IV, No. 2 & 3, Sept. 1992, February 1993).

The above languages if viewed through Fishman's Graded Intergenerational Disruption Scale (GIDS) rating, none of the languages of Sikkim qualify for the first category. Nepali language is at the second GIDS scale while Limboo, Lepcha and Bhutia languages are at 4b GIDS scale. All other languages Viz, Gurung, Tamang, Mangar, Khambu Rai, Sunuwar, Sherpa and Newari are in between the 4th to 5th GIDS scale in Sikkim at present.

8
Folk Culture

Folk culture refers to the localized lifestyle of a subsistence or otherwise, inward looking culture. It is usually handed down through oral tradition and a strong sense of community, and values the "old ways" over novelty. Finally, folk culture is quite often imbued with a sense of place. If its elements are copied by, or removed to a foreign locale, they will still carry strong connotations of their original place of creation. This chapter of folk culture of Sikkim comprises of Folk Dances, Folk Musical Instruments, Folk Music, Folk Songs, and Folk Tales.

1. Folk Dances of Sikkim:

The performing arts of Sikkim combine folk song, folk music and folk dance. The range of performing arts, genres, and styles is enormous in Sikkim - yet globalization of mass media (TV channels, Cinemas, pop songs, classical songs and dances etc.), changing tastes of the young generations, excess to new technology, and new performing arts patrons are profoundly transforming the performing arts of Sikkim also as in the other parts of India. Political and economic changes have transformed social relationships between performing groups and their patrons. Many performing arts such as folk songs, folk music, folk dances and folk musical instruments associated with various communities of Sikkim are disappearing with the passage of time along with the older generation people day by day. Folk culture especially folk songs, folk music, and folk dances of Sikkim are under intense pressure from the mass media, whose aesthetics are dominated by Hindi and English pop standards.

Performance traditions provide space in which to give voice to these regional and local aspirations, set against those of national elites or the nation state. Folk music and folk dance provide a forum in which to protest subordination as well as a means of experiencing a few moments of release from the cares of life. This type of folk culture translates uneasily to tourism, today an important market both for folk artists and livelihood for the people of Sikkim. The State Government is trying its level best to promote eco-tourism, village tourism, adventure tourism etc. in which this type of performing arts has a major role to play. Regional festivals sponsored by the Indian Tourism Development Corporation, by the State Government, by corporate entities, and civic groups such as *Sukhim Yakthung Sakthim Phojumbho*, Tharpu, held annually on 23rd August, provide important performance venues. Folk culture find that these audiences, both domestic and international tourists, are largely ignorant of local aesthetics and are satisfied with stereo-typed, shortened displays that meet the call for entertainment.

Different communities (both tribal and non-tribal) living in Sikkim have their own folk dances to celebrate their life and also entertain the audience. The performing arts like folk dances of Sikkim combine all the components of folk culture, namely folk songs, folk music instruments, traditional dresses, make up and folk dance, and thus exists both in time and in space. The religions developed in the Western World from the Greek Philosophy believe in one life with the physical body of this world, while the religions developed in the Eastern World from the philosophy of "*Karma*" believe on a cycle of numerous lives. The Yuma religion based on "*Karma*" of the Eastern world believes that nature does not provide self-sustaining life on earth with its physical body. For his survival, he has to depend on judicious use of the living organisms and non-living materials surroundings him. He has to support his life by his effort that is by collecting and eating plants and animals. When the primitive man was successful in obtaining wild plant food or killing wild animals by hunting, his heartbeat throbbed faster with happiness. He started jumping and dancing with happiness, which ultimately evolved a kind of folk dance. He started producing some sound by beating or rubbing stone, wood or other non-living materials to match his dance, that created the folk musical instruments. He started producing some voice himself through his vocal cord to imitate the voices of wild animals or to match his dance, which resulted some kind of folk songs. Although, the shaman priests of various communities of Sikkim know the mortal life of man, - yet they sing ritual songs (Mundhums), dance with their shaman instruments, predict the cause of illness and try to cure illness of their community people through trance and worship rituals; and thus drive away the death temporarily (Subba, 2005: iii). His awakened thought could clearly see that Life manifests itself in rhythm. Heartbeat, breathing, walking, all these signs of a living body are basically rhythmic. The difference between a living and a dead is that while the former has rhythm within him, the latter has no rhythm. Therefore his faculty of reasoning suggested to him that if he engages himself in some kind of exalted rhythmic activity, Life will be celebrated giving him a sense of immortality, even though for a while. And what rhythmic activity else than dance and music could be more exalted for celebrating life? That is why man began dancing long before he learnt speaking some kind of dialect. Many scholars are therefore of the opinion that dance is the mother of all arts. Pursuing his earliest and the ultimate aspiration, man has been trying unceasingly to concuer or transcends death. He has not been successful, but he has found the way of having a secret sense of immortality in his mortal existence by immersing himself in dancing. This secret sense of immorality is experienced at the deepest depth of the body (Pani, 2000:1-2; Subba, 2005: 1-44).

Earlier, dance was being considered as the best of all arts, because arts, like music exists only in time, not in space; whereas arts like sculpture and painting exist only in space, not in time. It is only dance and theatre that exist both in time and in space. Again, the beauty of human body can be enhanced in two ways; by makeup, jewellery etc. and by dance; while the former is superficial, dance wells up from within. Further, artists engaged in creative activity can spontaneously experience the divine, with which the God can be worshipped. This is the reason why many tribal folk dances, classical Indian dances etc. have originated from religious rituals and temples (Pani, 2000: 1-2).

A group rather than a solo dancer mostly performs folk dances. While dancing in unison with several other dancers each experience that he or she has been multiplied and the individual has become universal. It is the pulsating togetherness that they wish to enjoy deeply. Most of the folk dances are performed as an essential aspect of the festival/*Utsava*. Hence, most of the folk dances are either ritualistic or simply celebrative. They may be those, which are performed basically for an audience, and those, which do not pre-suppose any audience. There are different kinds of festivals. While quite a few are associated with agricultural operations, others are celebrations of the birthdays of some gods/goddesses or mythological celebrations. Festivals are also held to celebrate the incoming or outgoing seasons. Many folk dances although can be performed at any time of the year or at any occasion, like the purely recreational dances, according to the tradition they are performed on particular occasions or festivals (Pani, 2000: 2-5). Some of the important folk dances of Sikkim could be briefly described under ten sub-divisions as follows:

1.1. Ritual Dances:

The social scientists define ritual as a symbolic enactment of a myth. Each of the ritual is steeped in metaphysical symbolism contained in the myth behind it. If the symbolism of the myth is rightly understood, the ritual will appear as a poetic enactment; not an empty religious act. Myths are stories or beliefs that attempt to express or explain a basic truth. Most of the Mythological literature is full of epic poems steeped in fascinating symbolism. Many folk dances have been inspired by the mythology or legends (Pani, 2000: 10).

(a) Khainjari Bhajan and Balun: The *Khainjari* and *Balun* dances of the Higher *Khasas* (Bahuns and Chettris) contain verses of the Ramayana and the Mahabharata. These dances are performed by 5 to 15 numbers of male members, during the religious and social festivals when the episodes of the epics are recited to the rhythmic beating of small hand drum called *Khainjari*. *Balun* is generally staged in an open space so is the *Khainjari*. Before the performances of these dances the names of the gods and goddesses are invoked. Long bamboo poles are fixed on the courtyard. Earthen lamps are lit on the sacred papaya fruits, which are hung on bamboo poles before the performance of the dance. Each man in pair move round the poles narrating the *Bhajan* to the rhythmic beats of the drum, comes forward and goes backward touching each others back. In the case of *Khainjari Bhajan* there is a leader of the group who narrates the verses of the Ramayana and asks others of the group whether it is true or not? (photos enclosed) (Gurung and Lama, 2004: 44-45).

(b) Sakyo Rum Faat: It is a ritual dance of the Lepcha tribes of Sikkim, is an example of dances inspired by local legends. It is performed during the month of November. The dance is performed as a food offering worship of the seven immortal couples of "*Mayel Kyong*". The Lepchas believe that seeds of all kind of agricultural and horticultural crops were brought from the seven immortal couples. They also believe that the birds were sent to them for guiding them for sowing of seeds. To express their gratefulness they offer all kinds of food to the immortal couple of "*Mayel-Kyong*" during this festival. They sing and dance to celebrate the festival (for details of legend see folk tales section) (Gurung and Lama, 2004: 73-76).

Both men and women participate in the dancing. They dance in rows moving around the terrace. The musical accompaniments are provided by *Palitkeng* (flute with four holes), *Pentong* (flute), *Pentong* (Bigger flute with four holes), *Nibryok Palit* (double barrel flute), *Satsang* (Sarangi), *Tanbuk* (Vina), *Tang Dar* (a small round drum), *Chakpurjang* (Longish drum), *Bom Pochuat* (a kind of whistle), Tangue (a small instrument made of bamboo and played by tongue) and *Sahnai* (a kind of Sahnai) (ibid: 124).

(c) Tendong Lho Rum Faat: It is a ritual dance of the Lepchas of Sikkim and is also inspired by local legends. It is performed on the 8th

August every year. Realizing its importance the Sikkim Democratic Front Government has declared state holiday since 1997. This festival dance is connected with a legend of deluge that nearly swallowed Sikkim, which was ultimately stopped by *Rum* (God) and saved Sikkim from drowning. The dance is performed as a worship of the Tendong hill. The local legend associated with this annual dance performance runs as follows:

Rongnue, which was later, called Teesta and Rangit were born at the sacred lap of the Himalayan Mountains. They grew up together happily and as their youth bloomed they began to love each other secretly. But some how people got to know about this and started talking all sorts of things about it. They then decided to leave the place of their birth and go far away down to the meeting place of the hill and the plains. This place was called "*Pazook*" by the Lepchas (*Peshok*), which means covered by dense forest near the Teesta Bazar. Both did not know the actual path leading to the place. So they decided to take guides with them separately. Rongnue (Teesta) the female caught hold of *Paril-Bu* a snake and Rungit the male caught hold of a bird called *Tut-Fu* (*Danfey*). He at first hesitated but then agreed to be a guide.

The snake lead Rongnue wriggling and running with all his strength and reached *Pazaok* in time and waited for her lover Rungit to appear. Rungit, which had been guided by the bird, *Tut-fo* (*Danphey*) had taken a longer and steeper road through the rocky and difficult terrain. Being hungry he had stopped on the way to collect insects for his food. So at last he arrived at their destination seeing the *Rongnue* waiting for him he was surprised. Rungit the male got very much ashamed to be defeated by a female. So he decided to go back to his usual home in the Himalayas. As he started returning the water of the river began to rise up swallowing up the dales and the hill by the deluge. There were two high mountain peaks at *Renjyong* where the water of the river was still to reach. One was called Maanom and the other was Tungrong popularly called Tendong.

The people of *Renjyong* had gathered at the peak of Tendong to save them from the deluge. They saw the water of the river slowly touching the hill of Maanom. They began to pray to the almighty to save them from the deluge. They offered "*Chi*" to "*Itbu-Debu-Rum-Daor*" the creator and destroyer. A hill partridge called "*Kohom Fo*" appeared on the hill and drank "*Chi*" offered by the people. The water then began to subside slowly and that was the end of the deluge. Peace and happiness once again prevailed at the land of the Rongs.

Both men and women participate in the dancing. They dance in rows moving around the terrace. The musical accompaniments are provided by *Palitkeng* (flute with four holes), *Pentong* (flute), *Pentong* (Bigger flute with four holes), *Nibryok Palit* (double barrel flute), *Satsang* (Sarangi), *Tanbuk* (Vina), *Tang Dar* (a small round drum), *Chakpurjang* (Longish drum), *Bom Pochuat* (a kind of whistle), Tangue (a small instrument made of bamboo and played by tongue) and *Sahnai* (a kind of Sahnai). (Gurung and Lamas, 2004: 120-123).

(*d*) Yagrangsing Lang: It is a ritual dance of the Limboo tribes. It is performed on the full moon day of *Mangsir Purnima*, which falls during *Mangsir* (December). The dance is performed as a worship of the gods and goddesses meanly the Almighty God *Tagera Ningwaphuma*, and Sam Sires – the incarnate Deities of the five incarnate priests (*Muhikkum Ongshis, Phejiri Phedangmas, Samboko Sambas, Yeboko Yebas,* and *Yeboko Yemas*). They offer newly harvested rice and other cereals, *Piuna* (*satabew-palabew*) (all kinds of cereals, pulses, oilseeds etc.), *Thi-sook* (freshly fermented millet bear out of the newly harvested millet, marigold flowers, bird-meat, chiken, pig etc. and express their gratefulness of sending them to this earth (*Iksa Khamber*) for protection of the society. The entire Limboo community come with the freshly harvested crops and fermented millet beer for offering.

The dance performance may take place for one night or three nights or seven nights or nine nights. However, they perform only for one night these days, as it is expensive or conduct a collective performance. They construct a *Yagrangsing* Pole in the middle of the house terrace and the all kinds of priests dance, wearing their respective gear around the pole. The musical instruments are *Yethala* (brass plate), *Sirpong* (brass bells), *Yehang pongey* (big brass bells) etc. The day also falls the birth anniversary of Teyongsi Sirijunga Singthebe (1704-1741), a social, educational and religious awakener of the Limboos. Realizing the importance of the day the state Government has declared State Holiday since 1997 (**Photo enclosed**) (Subba, 1999:303 –339; 453-509; Subba, 2005).

1.2. Trance Dances:

Trance or spirit dances are different from ritual dances, although superficially it may appear the same. In a trance dance the dancer becomes a temporary embodiment of either a spirit or a deity; whereas in a ritual dance the dancers are either worshippers or ritual objects. In a ritual, many kinds of inanimate materials like incense, joss stick, kush grass, burning lamps, etc. and inanimate objects like mask, ideal, icon, etc. are used. In a trance dance rituals are performed either by a priest or the dancer himself with the sole aim of invoking a spirit or a deity to possess the body of the dancer. Once possessed the dancer is transformed into the involved spirit or deity. He also behaves and talks that way. It is a kind of self-hypnosis under which the dancer goes into a deep trance (Pani, 2000: 19).

(*a*) Phedangma Dance: These are the trance dances performed by the Limboo shamanistic priests namely, *Muhikkum Ongshi, Phejiri Phedangma, Samboko Samba, Yeboko Yaba, and Yeboko Yema,* etc. for divination, cure of illness, warding away of evil spirits etc. in the community people. During these dances, the priests become possessed, shriek with excitement, beat the *Niyara Hongsing Ke* and brass plates in a frenzied state and dance vigorously. They become temporary embodiment of either a spirit or a deity (their own incarnate *Sam Sire*) to perform the job assigned to them. The recitation of Mundhums and utterances of spells at this moment are rather different than on other occasions. Usually, they perform such dances moving around the *Pengiri Pengkesing, Tongsing* or any other altar (*Lasso*). Such dances can be observed in *Phungsook Timma, Tongsing Tookma, Sitongsing Khema, Nehangma*, or any other occasion where such trance dance is required to perform the shamanistic functions for the people of the community (Subba,1999: 222).

(*b*) Lakhey Mask Dance: In the Newar pantheon, dances are numerous and these have been amply described in connection with the Newar festivals. These dances take the theme of the fight between the gods and the demons and idealize the triumph of virtues over evils. In the field of songs, music, dramatics and dances, the Newars are equally skilful. The Newars have their own "*Nasa-Khala*", an association to train the boys in singing, dancing and music. The Sikkim Newar Sangathan has established an Institute of Newar language and culture to train the Sikkimese Newar boys and girls for different aspects of Newar language and culture.

Out of many masked dances in the Newar pantheon, Lakhey Masked Dance is one of the traditional classified tantric dances of the Newars. It is a worship dance in the form of a mask. The mask is made of wood and painted to look fearful. The worship dance is performed specially during the Indrajatra festival. Lakhey literally means a demon living in the dense forest. It haunts animals as well as the human beings of different places. Whenever the Lakhey is worshipped and get good worshipping, the animals and the people are supposed to be protected from Lakhey's haunt. It gives a great joy and happiness to the people. The dancer gets spirits of the demon and seems to be in religious trance while he wears sacrosanct Lakhey mask. Other dancers accompany the main dancer. The dancers wear typical Newari clothes and make up. Live musical instruments like *Dhoa, Pachhima, Bhusya, Babhoocha* and *Taa* accompany this dance (photo enclosed) (*Nasa-Khala*, Namthang, South Sikkim, 2006).

1.3. Ceremonial dance:

There are two kinds of ceremonies: religious and social. The religious ceremonial dances have ritualistic overtones and are celebrative in character, while some of the dances have fascinating symbolism, others only celebrative important religious occasions (Pani, 2000: 28).

(*a*) Marooni Dance: Marooni dance is the most popular dance of the entire Nepali Ethnic communities of Sikkim. It is performed to celebrate Diwali (*Tihar*) festival from the evening of the *Laxmi puja* and lasts until the *Ekadasi* of the festival. This dance is not only confined to singing and dancing but dance dramas like the "*Vijaya Bharat*", "*Sorati*", and "*Ghantu*" fall within its ambit. *Marooni* dance includes songs, music and dance and relates to four different types of movement as explained in the *Natya Veda* of Bharata. These four movements are (*i*) sacred emotions and feelings, (*ii*) gestures (*angika*), (*iii*) songs (*bhasika*), and iv) clothes (*asarya*). The dance is full of emotions. *Karuna, Birani, Khiyali* and *Bivasa* are the main ragas, which express tender feeling of heart. The other ragas like *Garra, Tappa,* and *Chakara* depict the experiences of day-to-day life. The other ragas of *Samala, Saroti, Bivasa* are based on the ancient social or mythological stories. These are actually dance dramas. The dance drama called *Soroti* takes a whole night for its proper rendering.

These dance dramas contain singing, dancing and acting. Each item of clothes to be worn by the dancers (*Maroonies*) and the jester (*Dhatwaray*) should be according to the certain laid down ancient rules as mentioned in the Natya Sastra. Three types of musical instruments i.e. *Madal* (drum), flute and cymbals are used.

The main characters taking part in the dance undergo fasting before the performance of the dance. They all assemble at the house of the Guru and offer prayers to the *Ganapati (Madal)*. The guru start playing the *Madal* in a slow tempo and then the decoration of the *Maroonies* (dancers) start. The *Maroonies* are adorned with different items of ornaments and clothes according to the songs sung on the occasion. The *Madals* too are decorated with marigold flowers (photo enclosed).

The *Marooni* dance is performed on the courtyard of every house. *Sakhi* or *Sasi* songs are then sung to play obeisance to all the gods and goddesses of the earth, the sky, the under world and of all the four directions of the earth. The jester keeps alive the dance with his gestures and humor as the dancing goes on. When the dance comes to an end the family members of the house collect the scattered flowers to keep them in safe custody until next year. The dancers thus visit house after house. In simple solemn ceremony the spirit of various deities are invoked. They sing blessing songs for the household, long life and well being of the family, good health of the elders and prosperity. They say that they have come for this by the order of Bali Hang the Kirata King and not by their own. They ask forgiveness from the gods of heaven for them in errors and pay their last respect to the god of heaven (Gurung and Lama, 2004: 46-58).

(*e*) Kagyed Mask Dance: Before Losoong festival starts, monks in the monasteries perform a ceremony dance (*chham*) called "*Gutor*". "*Kagyed"* means the eight teachings of the Guru are depicted in the dance forms. These dance forms are the most important part of the "*Gutor* ceremony" and is held on the 28th Day of the 4th Month (December-January) at the monasteries at Enchey, Tsuklhakhang, Phodong, Rumtek and other old monasteries. The other religious dance or *Chhams* that are performed prior to Losoong are *Rolchham* (Cymbal Dance), *Tshamche* (Animal headed mask dances), *Shyak* (Dances of horned animals), *Namding* (Dances of winged birds/animals), *Thakshobalop* (Dances of the beasts), *Dhur Chhams* (Skeleton dances), *Shanag* (Black Hat Dances), etc. The dancers wear coloured wooden masks, other costumes and perform the dance with typical leg, head and body movements like the animals (photo enclosed) (Bhutia, 2007).

1.4. Harvest dances:

More than 70% of Sikkimese people are engaged in cultivation for centuries. Agricultural operations are associated with rituals and festivals (*Utsavas*). The Limboo community of Sikkim believes that soybean was the first crop given by their Almighty Goddess for their survival to the human beings for cultivation. There was no other crop, and hence they eat its pods row, after boiling in water, dry-frying (*Bhute ko Bhatmas*), by dry-frying and by crushing (*fando sumbak/curry or fando achar*), boiling in water (*Karih*), fermenting or in a variety of ways which led to a variety of food items including a fermented product now known as the *Kinnema*. Later on the Goddess also gave the Finger Millet and other crops to the people. Hence, they offer the newly harvested crops especially fermented finger millet to the Goddess during *Kok Phekla Lageng* (which coincides with *Mangsir Purnima*) every year. The soybean is offered as *Piuna* (*Satabew-Pallabew*) along with various crop seeds, without which the *Piuna* (*Satabew-Palabew*) is incomplete. This is also a very good example of conserving agro-biodiversity by the community. Dance is a part of the ritual or of the *Utsava*. Right from the time of preparing the field for sowing seeds to the end of harvesting, during each stage of agricultural operations, various kinds of dances are performed (Subba, 1999).

(*a*) Yialakma: *Yialakma* (*Dhan Nach* - Khas Version) is the most popular dance among Limboo community. It is a harvest dance in which teenagers to late adults of both sexes participate enthusiastically in this dance. The dance is usually organized at night during the paddy harvest season. Nowadays, it is organized in daytime in any festive occasion such as marriage, Maghey Mela, hat days, or as item of entertainment. The dance is followed in rhythm of songs known as *Pallam* and steps. Musical instruments are not used, as it is not possible in the real life situation. The dance also provides forum of courtship for the young boys and girls as they sing love songs and express their feeling through love songs one after the other. Number of dancers depends on the availability of space for dancing which varies from a male and female to even hundred in a raw. Usually, 10 to 20 persons of both sexes form a good *Yialang* dance (photo enclosed).

The myth says that *Yialang* or Dhan Nach has a Mundhum (oral tradition) origin, when the *Phedangma* priests collect the newly harvested paddy, dehusk around their altar of *Yagrangsing* inviting the young boys and girls to accompany. When the operation of paddy de-husking is complete, the birds known as *Muphik Phirikwa* (*Lonchura striata*) are attracted on the rice; the *Phedangmas* drive away the bird as well as the boys and girls saying *haa.. haa* ...Thereafter, the *Phedangmas* offer the newly harvested rice, fermented finger millet from the newly harvested crop, and other newly harvested items to the Gods and Goddess, and *Sam Sire* (deity) etc. at the time of *Phungsook Timma* ritual conducted during *Kok Phekla Tongnam (Mangsir Purnima)*. These young boys and girls being unsatisfied continue their dance at the nearby paddy threshing areas known *Takten* or *Khala* and thus the tradition was continued. Now, *Yialang* has become a source of entertainment and performed in all happy occasions in the state (Subba, 1999: 217-220).

1.5. Social Dances:

Extreme happiness calls for a celebration. Dance and celebration go hand in hand. Human beings are essentially social. There are some events in the social life that fill one with great happiness which enkindle the desire for celebration. Such occasions are marriage and birth of a child. It is not only the family but also the entire community living together in the village feel very happy. These are the events that ensure continuity of the community and of the tradition nurtured by it. Therefore marriage and childbirth are celebrated by all the societies. There is yet another kind of social dance in which unmarried boys and girls choose their partners. This kind of dances will also falls under this category (Pani, J. 2000: 62). Such dances are *Yialakma, Ke-langma, Sangini* etc. which have been described under different types of dances in this chapter.

1.6. Seasonal dances:

Seasons are closely connected with the agricultural operations. Since agriculture is the main stay of the people of Sikkim, especially those living in rural areas, seasonal changes are of great importance. Majority of folk dance forms can be said to be seasonal, because they are performed in particular seasons. For instance, all the harvest dances are seasonal. But under this sub-heading those dances will be discussed which are performed to celebrate or welcome the season. Their connection with the agricultural operations is secondary (Pani, 2000: 74).

Sikkim divide the year into six seasons, namely Pre-monsoon (*Grishma*), Monsoon (*Varsha*), Post-monsoon (*Autumn/Sharad*), Pre-winter (*Hemantas/Autumn*), and Spring (*Vasanta*). The year begins with the lunar month of *Vaisakh* and the solar month of *Mesha*, the beginning of the summer season. The year ends with the lunar month of *Chaita* and the solar month of *Meena*, the end of spring season. Most of the seasonal dances are performed either in Spring or in Autumn. The dances performed during the rains and in the winter are predominantly associated with agricultural operations or have ritualistic overtones.

(*a*) Sangini Nach: The word *Sangini* actually means friends. To trace the origin of this dance one has to go back to the mythological story of Shiva and Parvati. Parvati's heart was filled with anguish and pain to see many young widows who had lost their husband. She pleads to Shiva to save the young married girls from their curse. Shiva advises her to ask these young married girls to offer *puja* in his name. Hence, it is possibly believed that they would be saved from being untimely widow if they offer *pujas* to Shivji.

The women folk of the village perform *Sangini* dance at the courtyard of the house amid the green sylvan surroundings. The dancers themselves sing Songs. This dance belong to the high caste Khasas - Brahamans and Chettris, and performed on the day of "*Tij*" festival, which falls on the month of *Bhadow* every year. The dance is performed on other occasions also for entertainment but not in a big scale. The married away daughters come from afar and assemble in the house of their parents to take part in the dance. They meet their long forgotten friends there and take part in the dance with them.

The life cycle of *Tulsi* plants are compared to the life of human beings as they grow and bloom. It is said that to perform a Sangini dance in a grand scale there should be five virgin girls, five kind of musical instruments, five lights and five priests. On the day of "*Tij*" the married away daughters of the village come to their parents's house and assemble at the courtyard of the house where Sangini dance is to be performed. To these women, their homecoming is like mingling into the sea. They come to refresh their memories of their childhood where they used to be so happy and carefree. The Khasas had a tradition to give away girls of tender age in marriage to elderly persons. Some of them have already become widows even before their youth have bloomed. They have anguish and pain in their hearts due to the atrocities they have borne in the hands of their in-laws. Some of them are taken as second wives. They assemble here to forget their worries and to get peace of mind.

A day earlier, a special type of food is prepared which is known as *Dar*. After taking this food the womenfolk go on fast, except unmarried daughters and widows. *Sivalinga* is erected on the bed of the *Tulsi* plants. The walls of the houses are painted with mud and sketches are made of gods, goddesses, birds and animals, which is called *Jimtha*. Now the Puja begins with the chanting of three chapters on Shiva and Parvati from the holy book. The village women and girls begin to gather and stand in pair and move forward and backward and turn rhythmically moving their hands and feet singing in a slow tempo. The themes of their songs are generally sad telling of their pain and sorrows. The dance continues until the early hour of the dawn (photo enclosed) (Gurung and Lama, : 2004:39-43).

(*b*) Tamkey Ookma: It is a seasonal dance of the Limboo community, which is performed at the time of maize first earthing up operation during pre-monsoon season of *Chait-Baisak. Tamke Ookma* is performed same as that of Yialangma but in this case earthing up of maize crop is done in the field side by side while dancing and singing. The tune of *Pallam* is slow and is different from *Yialang*. The digging (*Ookma*) is done three times and once the dancer stand up holding the spade on the right hand for a moment and again bends for digging three times. The number varies from 30 to 40 and the dance continues whole the day. The young boys and girls take part in the dance with love songs. The live performance could be seen during the season at Hee, West Sikkim. The number of dancers vary from 10 – 15 depending on the space available for dancing in this case. The dance is also popular in the stages during various cultural festivals (Subba, 1999: 220-221).

1.7. Game and Martial Dances:

War and dance now appear antithetical, but it was not so in ancient days when there were no aeroplanes, no bombs, no ballistic missiles and even no guns. The weapons like sword, club, spear, etc. were quite weighty and to wield them with consummate artistry required such pliability of the body as a dancer only could have. At the time of that antiquated past, men at arms used to parade the artistry of wielding the weapons to the beat of drums. Out of this practice originated several forms of dance, which are still surviving in many parts of this country. Every game has an inherent rhythm of its own. In most of the cases it is so covert that unless very carefully observed it is not perceptible.

(*a*) Nahangma Dance: The Limboos Shamanistic priests and the male family members take part in this dance. They dance with swords (*Laphiza*) on right hand or spear (*Tu*) on the left hand or arrow on the right hand and bow on the left hand together forming a group while performing *Nahangma* ritual. This is done to protect the altar (*Lasso*) of *Nahangma* (raising of moral) during the journey to *Tuttu Tumyang Yakla Suhangma Chotlung* of the family head while performing *Yahangsema Mundhum* from the evil spirits, *Nahen, Sogha* and *Sugut* etc. (Subba,1999: 221).

1.8. Drum Dances:

Most of the folk dances of Sikkim require drum accompaniment. Generally the drummer provides the percussion accompaniment with dances. There are many dances in which the dancer himself plays the drum while dancing. Such dances come under the category of drum dance (Pani, 2000: 99).

(*a*) Ke Lang or Chybrung Lang: *Ke Lang* is one of the most popular drum dances of Sikkim danced by the Limboo community. The dancers ranging from 5 to 20 number depending on the space available for dancing, sometimes accompanied by dancing females in between each of them, play the drum themselves while dancing. It is essentially a religious ritual drum dance of Shamanistic *Phedangma* priest of the Limboo community at the time of offering the new harvested festival of *Phungsok Timma* ritual, new house opening ceremony of *Thok Thamma* ritual, solemnizing marriage ritual of *Metkamma,* as gesture of welcome occasion *Lamthan* or any happy occasion. Usually the young boys slung the *Ke* or *Chabrung* in front of the body with leather cord and play on it while dancing. It is a dance with *Ke Lang Samlo* or without any song performed by the male dancers and in some occasions, the female dancers accompany them. The female dancers do not carry the *Ke* but stand in between the male dancers and follow the beating sounds by clapping their hands and perform dance through proper stepping and bodily movements. It is essentially a nature dance and the dancers imitate actions of animals, insects and other living creatures. They dance imitating movements of different kinds of animals such as deer, buffalo, goat, elephant, sheep, frog, pigeon, eagle, peacock, jungle fowl, butterfly etc. through variety of stepping and bodily movements (photo enclosed).

The myth says that the primitive man constructed his house but was destroyed by wood insects and termites known as *Mudhok Thoknam*, caused by the evil spirit (*Sogha*) of his sister *Mellonghangma* who was killed in accident during the house construction. Then the primitive man invited Lokpha Temba Hangpha Temba; the *Ke Lang* experts who played on the *Niyara Hongsing Ke* on the main pillar of the house and made fall the insects on the ground. Then they invited a bird known as *Temlana Lakherek Pu* (woodpecker) to eat away the fallen insects and thus they saved the house for man. The myth is followed then onwards in the community at the new construction of a house. Another myth says that the *Phedangma* priests of the Limboo community accompany and reach the soul of the deceased to the village of ancestors and hand over to the *Hangsam* (soul receiving ancestor) after the death. While returning, they imitate various creatures by *Ke Lang* dance stepping so as to confuse the evil spirits or the souls of the dead, and thereby the souls and evil spirits do not come down to the earth following them. The drum dance is also used to enhance concentration of the shamanistic priest while worshipping during harvest festival of *Phungsook Timma. Ke Lang* is also essential to introduce the new bride to the household deity *Akwanamma* during *Metkamma* (marriage) ritual. *Ke Lang* is also popular in other happy occasions for *Lamthan* and stage entertainments in Sikkim (Subba, 1999: 215-216).

1.9. Dances of Boys as Girls and vice versa:

In Sikkim there are not many folk dances in which boys perform dressed as girls or girls perform dressed as boys, but the tradition of female or male impersonation, especially in traditional theatre forms is custom. In almost all the theatrical forms boys play the female roles or girls play the boys roles even today. In fact the girls are better in dancing than the boys. In many theatrical dances the girls dress as boys and dace as the boys.

1.10. Recreational Dances:

There are many forms of recreational dances prevalent in Sikkim. The performance of these dances while giving recreational pleasures to the dancers, entertains the onlookers. Under this category of dances are included those forms of folk dances which have unmistakable elements of theatre. There is a very thin line between dance and theatre, and there are seasonal theatre forms in which dance is the most dominant dramatic expression. Many recreational dances are traditionally performed on a particular occasion or season, but they are being considered under this category because entertainment is the predominant objective of the performance. Most of them are associated with festivals and their performance imparts the desired festive atmosphere to the festivals (Pani, 2000: 110).

(*a*) Singhi Chham: Singhi Chham is a recreational dance of Bhutia Community of Sikkim, performed mainly for recreation especially during Panglapsool festival. It has also religious associations. Mount Khan-chen-Dzong-pa (Kanchenjunga) the third highest mountain in the world is sacred to the people of Sikkim as their guardian deity. As decreed by Guru Rimpoche (Guru Padmasambhava), this majestic mountain stands guard over the land, holding within its crevices the sacred five treasures. Its associate peaks look like the legendary Snow Lion, fierce and fiery with its gorgeous mane hued in turquoise. The Snow Lion is considered an important cultural symbol of the state and is elaborately depicted in the *Singhi Chham* or the Snow Lion dance. Usually two or four dummy lions perform the dance. Each dummy Snow Lion is made of white fur and the face is bluish. Actually, it is total mask made of cloth and fur. Two dancers get into each lion mask and position themselves inside the mask in such a way that the Snow Lion looks somewhat like a real lion. The legs of the dancer positioned on the front become the two forelegs of the lion and the two legs of the dancer positioned at the back form the hind legs. With amazing synchronization the two dancers move so that the movement of the Snow Lion appears realistic. Only a drum is used with the dance. A man dressed in Tibetan dress controls and directs the dance of the Snow Lions (photo enclosed) (Bhutia, 2007).

(*b*) Tungna Dance: It is the most beautiful and the simple dance of the Gurungs. One of the main occupations of the Gurungs is rearing herds of sheep in the Himalayan region. A legend has it, that a young Gurung shepherd was sitting by the side of a peaceful blue lagoon watching his sheep, which were grazing in the nearby hills. He was very sad and lonely as he was away from his home since long time. All of a sudden high in the sky a group of wild swans appeared. They were flying towards the Himalayas singing a sad tone. The song of the swans made him even more sad. All of a sudden he felt the wind bellowing and a dry branch of an old tree fell in the lake making waves in the water of the peaceful blue lagoon. An idea flashed in his mind. He took out his clothes swam into the lake and brought with him the big branches of the tree and made a *Tungna* with sheep skin and intestines. He began to play the strings made of sheep intestines with his fingers. The air was filled with the sounds of music of the *Tungna* which the young shepherd had created. He forgot all his sadness. He no more felt lonely as the *Tungna,* his own creation became his companion and with which he could share his joys and sorrows. In all recreational places and festivals the *Tungna* dance of Gurungs has become very popular in Sikkim (photo enclosed) (Gurung and Lama 2004: 178-181).

(c) Damphu Selo: This is a recreational dance of the Tamang Community of Sikkim. Both boys and girls take part in dancing and singing. The boys dance with *Damphu*, made of mountain goat skin (*Nemorhaedus goral*) one side wrapped and pegged around with 32 bamboo nails on a wooden circle known as *Ghero* made of *Ambusing* (*Bahuhinia variegata*). In practice goat skin is used in place of mountain goat skin. The songs are known as *Selo*. In the early period of nomadic life, a legend Tamang leader named Peng Dorjay went for hunting with some men with him. The whole day passed without a kill and as they were returning to their shelter disheartened Peng Dorjay's eyes fell on a mountain goat which was grazing on a high stony cliff. He moved forward cautiously and aimed his arrow at the goat and let it go from the bow, which flew at a great speed and struck the right place on the body of the goat. The goat came rolling down the cliff. It was dead. He carried it to his temporary place of halting. He skinned the animal and let the skin dry in the open ground. When the skin was dry completely he created the small roundish drum called *Damphu*. He offered his first prayer of thanks giving to god by playing the *Damphu* and singing *Selo* (song). This small drum *Damphu* still exists in the same form to this day without any change. The Tamang *Selos* are light with philosophical thoughts and express the day-to-day joys and sorrows of life. In all recreational places and festivals the *Damphu Selo* of Tamang has become very popular in Sikkim (photo enclosed) (Gurung and Lama, 2004).

The different communities of Sikkim have a number of folk dances of their own, but all these folk dances cannot be described in detail in this chapter. However, most of these important folk dances have been listed out in their respective ethnography.

2. Folk Musical Instruments:

Sikkim is very rich in Folk Musical Instruments but very difficult to trace the first musical instrument of the State, because all primitive people all over the world seem to have made music of some sort. Folk musical instruments exist only in space not in time. According to the myth of Mundhum of the Limboo community, the first musical instrument was a bamboo harp known as *Simikla Koom* (*Binayo* in *Khas* Language) made for their sister Tetlara Lahadongna, made by the sons of Sawa Yukphung Kemba, namely – Samdang Khewa and Lingdang Khewa for their sister Tetlara Lahadongna in antiquity. The myth says that the next instrument was the *Niyara Hongsing Ke* of Lokpha Temba and Hongpha Temba brothers who danced around the main pillar of the new house to protect the newly constructed house from the evil spirits. In another myth of Mundhum, it is also said that *Yeba* and *Yema* Limboo priest came to the village of Sawa Yethangs the primitive men with their gear *Yegeysing* pole tied with *Niyara Hongsing Ke* to drive away the evil spirits from the villages. Similarly, there are a number of myths about the origin of musical instruments amongst the different communities living in Sikkim in antiquity (Subba, 1999: 203-204).

The folk musical instruments of Sikkim could be classified into seven groups depending on *Sur, Tal*, make and ways of playing by the player on of the instruments as follows:

2.1.Tala :

(*a*) String instruments played with scratching on the strings: These instruments are triangular or round kettle with leather at the lower side, and the strings vary on thickness, length and one to eight number. The strings are made of intestines of sheep or goat, but steel or nylon strings are popular these days. The instruments are played scratching the strings with nails or *nakhi* made of wood or bamboo. The important folk musical instruments which fall under this type are namely, *Aktantri bina, Aktare, Ghuggumuggu, Jhumtar, Tungna, Tungma, Dongmen, Dhamken, Tamura, Tamang tungna, Tungeba, Premtal, Bhantey madal, Yalumber, Yakucha wavu, Bina, Hyanjing, Hyolmo tungna,* and *Tri-tantri bina.* Many of these folk instruments are disappearing and rarely played by the people in Sikkim (Kandel, 2004; Subba, 1999).

(*b*) String instruments played with a bow, rubbing on the strings: These instruments are made of one to twelve numbers of strings, made of intestine, nylon or steel wire and played by rubbing with a bow made of horsetail or nylon strings. A variety of music is produced by rubbing on the strings on one hand and playing with fingers on the other. These folk musical instruments are namely, *Kingruwa, Teentare sarangi, Dodra, Dhanusbaja, Dhanu sarangi, Nawnriya, Piwancha, Piwang, Mayura, Reuni, Sarangi,* and *Serenja.* Many of these folk musical instruments are not in use today and are rarely seen in Sikkim (Subba, 1999; Kandel, 2004).

2.2. Susira:

(*a*) Wind instruments played by blowing the air and tuning the node with fingers: These are known as *sur baja* played by blowing the air and the folk music indicates the type of various forms from different communities of Sikkim. The range of these folk musical instruments varies from Flute to Narsinga, having two to nine holes, and made of bamboo, metal or wood. The player blows the air from the mouth and plays with fingers. These instruments are namely, *Indreni baja, Kakubya, Gojey murali, Ghor bansuri, Teep bansuri, Teep sahaney, Dhungrey murali, Tamang ghyaling, Tariyo, Pongue, Piwra, Pudipu, Puli, Bonsi, Boyocha, Bosh, Bimbili, Bausi, Majhwal bansuri, Murali, Mohola, Rasa, Sherpa ghyaling, Sahana, Sipi bharuwa bansuri,* and *Sipi bharuwa murali.* Many of these folk instruments are disappearing with the older generations day by day (Subba, 1999; Kandel, 2004).

(*b*) Wind instruments played by blowing the air without tuning the node with fingers: The folk musical instruments are played by from the air deposited in the lungs of the player and blown with balance. Such instruments vary from *Sankha* to *Karnal Baja*, and vary from six inch (one *Kuret*) to 17 feet (11 *haat*) long. These are made of bones, horns, shells of mollusk, copper, brass, wood etc. These instruments are namely, *Karnal, Karnali baja, Kalash karnal, Kah, Kangling, Kahal, Kundong, Koom mikla, Koya, Kohili, Khaprang, Gonggop, Gauri gankar, Ghoral singi, Chyaling, Jor muchunga, Jor binayo, Jau nali, Tiglicha, Theyagi, Dalle sankha, Tamako Kangling, Tamesh, Tung, Turahi, Tetlaphekwa, Dahiney sankga, Narsingha, Nagfeni, Nagbeli, Nadi, Neku, Pat Kainyo, Paluwa, Pipari, Pifi, Pihung, Pung, Ponga, Pothi muchunga, Pyan pyan, Famuk, Fenjey, Bans sahaney, Bano, Bijuli bana, Binayo, Billuri, Bhaley muchunga, Bhatayo, Bhairi, Bhukkor, Mathuri, Muchunga, Megfama, Moti sankha, Lawa, Bisannad, Sikhar, Sanginad, Singa, Suseli, Dhwati,* and *Hitimong.* Many such instruments have not been lost from Sikkim (Subba, 1999; Kandel, 2004).

2.3. Ghana or Solids:

(*a*) Solid instruments like sticks and cymbals played by beating with sticks or metals: These are *tal bajas* and beaten with hand or any other materials; and made of brass or any other metal and played by beating or beating one another. These are namely, *Akharananda nad, Alanka, Rishital, Kanyapi, Kaptera, Kanchakancha, Kalwal khuruwa, Kasta kartal, Kani fu, Khachhar ghanta, Khanjari, Khandali, Khankar, Khincha kho gno, Khowalimali, Garur ghanta, Galumbey, Gopal dandi, Gow ghanta, Gyapung, Ghaghala mala, Ghorabaja, Ghori ghanta, Ghanti mala, Ghant, Ghanro, Ghori ganta, Ghau, Ghyabuk, Chanp, Chimta ghyali, Chethya, Chunri ghanta, Chhyanla, Chumchum, Jyan gun, Jhrri, Jhanjhar, Jhal, Jhillim, Jhurruma, Jhautal, Tuttumala, Taktukey, Dilbu, Dhonre kartal, Tah, Ta, Tainai, Tali, Tinimuni, Tinchhu, Thanauro, Thalia, Thali, Thatra, Dibya ghanti, Daurali ghanta, Dautara, Dharma ghanti, Ghwanipatra, Nupur, Newar, Taptapey, Paira, Pawju, Falamey jhyali, Fakwa, Phyatphyatey, Phey gon, Babhu, Bans tumba, Balun tal, Bupsel, Bokey ghanta, Bhatbhatey, Bhusyaha, Mangaley angaley gon, Macheta, Mak kathin, Minja, Resamchauki, Lakheypeti, Basnau ghanta, Sapoksa, Siling, Syang, Swankunla,* and *Trisul ghanta* (Subba, 1999; Kandel, 2004).

2.4. Avandya- Instruments of Percussion:

(*a*) Hollow wood or metal drums covered one side or both sides with animal skin with *Khari* pasted on the Skin: These are Tal bajas and made of wood, mud or other metals with skin and *Khari*. Most of these instruments are made of hollow wood with skin with a smaller *khari* on one side, and a bigger *khari* on the other side. The instruments are played with fingers. They are namely, *Yelopo dhimey, Kansi jaba, Kwata, Chaling, Jwa khin, Dakkari, Tatali, Danga khin, Damo khin, Dakchin baja khin, Dyo khin, Pokhawaj, Pachima, Pasta khin, Paita khin, Mag khin, Manra, Madal, Ma dhimey, Maner, Mridunga, Mridanga, Yak khin, Rani Madal, Lata khin, Lal khin,* and *Sorathi madal* (Subba, 1999; Kandel, 2004).

(*b*) Hollow wood or metal drums covered one side or both sides with animal skin but without *Khari* pasted on the Skin: These instruments are made of wood, mud or metals with skin on one or both side but without *khari*. The player plays with hand, wooden sticks or metal sticks. They are namely, *Awaj, Akpatey nah, Kapal damaru, Kaling, Kanta dabdab, Tuktukey, Ke (Chyabrung), Korbing, Khilupa, Khol, Nah, Na, Chhattish nagara, Chhyongna, Jarungey, Jor nagara, Jhankri dhyangro, Jhyali damphu, Teymki, Tyakko, Tyamkko, Dabdab, Dabdamfu, Damba, Dimki, Dugdugi, Dauri, Dak, Dhol, Dholaki, Tanamakacha, Tamring, Tassa, Tunjai, Twahutu, Thundar, Dah, Damaha, Dainu Damau, Dibya nagara, Durga damaru, Dibya damaru, Duparyya digari, Dhah, Dholak, Nagara, Nagara Nisan, Nirgun khaichardi,*

Nuwakot khainjardi, Negra, Puttungey, Bainu damau, Balun khainchardi, Bijuwa dhyangro, Bhajira, Majhaula dah, Mafna, Roila khainjardi, Laghu kah, Salyani sarangi, Salaijyo damfu, Sindung, and *Hudko* (Subba, 1999; Kandel, 2004).

The people of Sikkim believe that no musical instruments should be played during the month of *Srawan*. The old popular belief of the people is that the gods and goddesses descend down and go to the underground world to take rest during the month of *Srawan,* hence one should not disturb them by the sound of music.

Different communities of Sikkim have their own folk musical instruments which have been listed out in their ethnographic details.

The Panchai Baja and Nawmati Baja of Sikkim:

The *Panchai Baja* and *Nawmati Baja* played by the Lower Khasas (*Damai*) are the most popular musical instruments of the Nepali Ethnic Communities of Sikkim. In the *Panchai Baja* there are five musical instruments whereas there are nine or more musical instruments in *Nawmati Baja*. It is said that the *Panchai Baja* is the symbol of *Pancha Tatwa* (earth, water, fire, air, and sky) and *Pancha Dhatu* (gold, silver, copper, lead and tin). While forming these musical instruments the five forms of gods too has been imagined i.e. *Ganesh, Vishnu, Devi, Sun and Shiva*. The five musical instruments of *Panchai Baja* are *Teep Sahanai, Dholaki, Jhurumma, Domaha* and *Tiamko.*

Nawmati Baja is the comprehensive form of the *Panchai Baja*, with addition of four or more musical instruments. These additional musical instruments of *Nawmati Baja* are *Narsingha, Karnal, Dhodre Sahanai,* and *Bikul*. Some more musical instruments may also be added in *Nawmati Baja* such as *Tyakko, Turahi, Dahinu Damau, Bheyri, Rasa,* etc. (Subba, 1999; Kandel, 2004; Gurung and Lama, 2004).

3. Folk Music:

The basic elements of music is provided by the folk musical instruments such as *Tal bajas* - string instruments, percussion instruments and solid instruments provide *Tal* (rhythm) for the folk music, while the *Sur bajas* the wind instruments provide *Sur* (drone). Folk musicians favour the small barrel-shaped, two-headed drums to produce rhythm. The *Bol* or rhythm pattern, called *tihai*, consists of the repetition of a pattern three times in succession, for instance: "*taka dha, taka dha, taka dhja*" is not so popular in the folk music of Sikkim. The folk musicians also use the concept of *raga*, but they often subordinate this to melodic tunes. Nevertheless, the statement of a raga will guide the whole conception of the composition, its ascending tones and descending tones, plus microtonal intervals. These basic tones are *Sa, Re, Ga, Ma, Pa, Dha,* and *Ni.* Other terms denote microtonal intervals. These too must be defined. Sa is the most important: its pitch defines the rest. The next formal theory element is the beat (*bhaka*). Drummers know many different rhythm patterns with complex beat using different parts of the drumhead, struck by different parts of the hand or sticks. The fifth classical component use vocables such as "*aah, na, ta*" for improvisation is not popular so far in folk music in Sikkim (Gurung and Lama, 2004; Henderson, 2002).

Different communities of Sikkim have their own musical instruments and have evolved their own music patterns. The community-wise details in brief have been mentioned along with their ethnography.

4. Folk Songs:

Sikkim has a rich tradition of singing folk songs. The different communities of the State have different folk songs, which are gradually disappearing, or being replaced by Hindi cinema songs, Hindi pop songs, English pop songs, or other modern form of songs etc. The folk songs of Sikkim are under intense pressure from the mass media, whose aesthetics are dominated by Hindi pop standards. Most of the folk song of different communities has been listed under their ethnic culture. Some of the important folk songs could be mentioned as follows:

4.1. The Limboo community

is very rich in folk songs. Their folk songs has been divided into five groups namely:

(a) *Khyali* – dialog songs where the young boys and girls express their day to day romantic feelings, views on poetic language with tune.

(b) Love Songs:

(i) Shorokpa Pallam Samlo;

(ii) Pallam Samlo; and

(iii) Taamkey Ookma Palam Samlo;

In all the above love songs they sing love songs by the young girls and boys while dancing or working and provide a forum of courtship for marriage. The song may continue a few hours to several days and nights continuously.

(*c*) *Hakpare Samlo* – Gentlemen and Women song, which is, sung in special festive occasions by the elder people for entertainment.

(*d*) *Nisammang Sewa Samlo* – Ceremonial songs sung as inaugural song on festive occasions by the young boys and girls; and (*e*) *Ke Lang Samlo*- song sung while dancing Ke lang on special occasion or for entertainment (Subba, 1999: 208-213).

4.2. Folk Songs of *Khas* Community:

(*a*) The *Baramasay* song or the song for all twelve months is sung throughout the year by the entire Nepali communities of the village of Sikkim during their day to day works i.e. while tilling the soil, cutting fodder for the domestic animals or while collecting grasses and fuelwood in the forest. The song describes the significance of each month painting the natural scene and feelings of devotion.

(*b*) The *Juwari* Songs are an important part of the traditional culture of the Khasas community but has now been adopted by the entire Nepali community of Sikkim. It has its own importance among the folk songs, and is also called *Dohori.* It is a kind of question and answer song among people of the opposite sex. This type of songs is mainly related to love and romance among men and women. When the young boys and girls moved together in groups with a dream in their mind for a better future the emotion of love must have arisen in their young hearts. This emotion must have come in the form of songs (Gurung and Lama, 2004: 36).

Different communities of Sikkim have their own folk songs, which have been described in brief under their ethnography.

5. Folk Tales From Sikkim:

Anyone studding the culture of a state or a country needs to study not only its written classics but also its oral traditions, of which folktales or folklores are important part. Folktale provides childhoods, families, and communities as the symbolic language of the non-literate parts of the people and the culture. Sikkim with diversity of culture of large ethnic communities is very rich in folklore such as proverbs, lullabies, folk medicine, and folktales. Wherever people live, folklore grows; new jokes, proverbs, rhymes, tales, and songs circulate in the oral tradition.

Folktales could be i) Male centered tales, ii) Women centered tales, iii) Tales about families, iv) Tales about fate, gods, demons, and such, v) Humorous tales, vi) Animal tales, and vii) Stories about stories (Ramanujan, 1991).

Folk Tales from Sikkim are the cultural wealth of the State as these contain the knowledge of the ancient past and also throw light on the historical, social and religious background of the different communities of Sikkim. The folk tales show us the action, reaction, interaction, relationship, and judicious use of these resources that existed between men, beasts, birds and the vegetation kingdom of the earth. They lived side by side in peace and harmony understanding the need of one another. Modern civilization has brought this beautiful earth to the brink of destruction where man has become the greatest enemy of the beasts, birds and the vegetation of the earth. These folk tales still live to some extent in the forms of song and dance. The grandparents do narrate these tales and legends to grand children sitting by the fireside in the evening time.

Folktales of antiquity of Sikkim were based on the Lepcha and Limboo communities, such as the great deluge, *Sakya-Rum Faat, Tendong Lho Rum Faat* etc. More folktales were added on the above after the migration and settlement of Bhutia communities after the 17th century onwards such as *Pang Lapsol, Singi Chham* etc. With the Gorkha invasion and settlement after 1774 onwards a number of folktales like *Sunkesri Rani*, etc. were added on. Similarly, more and more folklores based on the cultures of Bengali, Punjabi, Bihari, etc. was added on after the integration of Sikkim into the Indian Union in 1975 onwards. Thus, the folklore is always dynamic, ever changing to suit the culture and tradition of the people of that point of time and space.

The different communities of Sikkim have their own folktales. For instance, a few important folktales could be described in brief as under:

(*d*) The Great Deluge: The Almighty Goddess *Tagera Ningwaphuma* found that the world was filled with sins. The human being whom She thought to be Her greatest creation were committing all kinds of sins for their selfish ends. There were only a couple named *Sodhung Lepmuhang* (Demi-God) and *Laoti Phungphahangma* (Demi-Goddess) who were trying to bring people to the path of virtue and goodness but they could not succeed. The Goddess knew this, so She decided to save these couple only by destroying all others.

The Almighty Goddess sent a messenger *Musekha Sekhanama* to *Sodhung Lepmuhang* in the form of a small fish of a stream. One day *Sodhung Lepmuhang* rose early and went to bathe in a nearby stream. There, he found a small fish that asked him to help by transferring him to a pond as a big fish was trying to swallow her. The fish also told him that he would save him from distress for this good act. *Sodhung Lepmuhang* picked her and put the fish into a pond. After sometime as he was passing by the pond he heard the voice of the same fish that requested him to take her to a river as he was growing fast and the pond would be too small for her, she was put into the river.

Days rolled by, *Sodhung Lepmuhang* had forgotten the fish and the work he did for her. One day as he was passing by the river, he heard the voice of the same fish that had grown very big. The fish again asked to put her into the sea as she was fast growing in size and the river would be too small for him. The fish further told him that she would come back to help him in a great deluge which is likely to come and destroy all men of the earth. She further instructed *Sodhung Lepmuhang* to build a big ship of many compartments where pair of animals, birds and other creatures should be kept. The food also should be collected and kept in the ship. The fish further told him that as all the earth would go down the water she should come near the ship along with his wife *Laoti Phungphahangma*. She would have a long horn where he should tie the top of the ship with a strong knot. The ship would not sink but would follow her. *Sodhung Lepmuhang* heard the words of the fish and believed each word uttered by the fish.

Sodhung Lepmuhang returned home and did everything as desired by the fish. A big ship was built having many compartments where pair of each animal, bird and other creatures were taken into the ship. The stock of food was also deposited inside the ship. He then along with his wife shut the door of the ship.

Soon after torrential rain started coming down from the sky. There was darkness everywhere. The deluge started enveloping on earth. Nothing could survive in the deluge. At that time a fish of huge size appeared near the ship and *Sodhung Lepmuhang* tied the ship to the horn of the huge fish. The ship went after the fish. After days and nights the rains stopped and there was silence everywhere. The sun appeared in the sky. The water started going down. The hills around started appearing. The ship stopped on a hillock. The fish told *Sodhung Lepmuhang* to go down to the earth with all the creatures of the ship to start a new life of peace and happiness and also guide the future generation, the path of sustainable peace and happiness. For this, the Limboo Kiratas invoke *Sodhung Lepmuhang* as Demi-God even today for all social and religious rituals.

The folk tale is based on the myth of Mundhum of the Limboo Kiratha tribe. The Aryans too have similar kind of legend of the deluge. The theme of the legend is the same. The Mundhum of the Kiratas has come down since generation from mouth to mouth. This legend of the Aryans is found written in the volume of Satpath Brahman which is supposed to be written five hundred years before the Christ. It may be assumed that the oral legend of the Kitara is older than that of the Aryans. It is also interesting to note that the legend of Noah's ark of the Bible has the same overarching theme. A deep study into the folk legends of Sikkim and its tribes would help relate all these legends (Subba, 1999; Gurung and Lama, 2004: 71-72).

(*e*) Sakyo-Rum-Faat: In ancient time the Lepchas cultivated ten kinds of paddy, nine kinds of millet, four kinds of wheat, nine kinds of maize and other cereals. They also grew many kinds of vegetables.

In days of antiquity the livelihood of the Lepchas in Sikkim was animal hunting and gathering of wild plants. One day a Lepcha hunter called Sheyraboo went on hunting expedition. He searched for an animal the whole day but found nothing. Tired and thirsty he sat to rest, after quenching his thirst in a nearby stream. Suddenly his eyes fell on a big boar grazing beyond the stream. He forgot his thirst and tiredness on seeing the animal. He moved forward cautiously towards the boar and let fly the arrow from his bow aiming at the animal. The boar was only injured and started fleeing from the place. The hunter Sheyraboo also went after the boar following the blood of the injured boar. As darkness set on he could not follow the animal any more. So he went towards a bamboo grove for the night-rest. He wake up in the early dawn and started following the animal. He could not find the animal anywhere. Still he did not stop following.

At last when the sun was about to disappear in the far away horizon he saw the boar moving forward slowly. He went after it and reached a village farmhouse. He was surprized to find the animal resting in the group of other pigs of the farmhouse. As the dog started barking, a very old man with gray hair came out of the house. This old man was also pleased to find the long lost pig resting with other pigs. He thanked the hunter for his help for finding out his lost pig. The hunter was taken inside the house and was offered food and strong *Chee*. He was really tired and fell into sound sleep in the bed made for him.

He waked up from his bed as the sun had already come up in the sky. He looked for his host and his wife but they were not seen anywhere. He saw a girl and a boy playing in the courtyard. He was surprised to see the children as he had not seen them anywhere yesterday night. He went out for a while and came back to the house but still could not find out the old man and his wife. He just waited for them closing his eyes. He was feeling sleepy as he was still very tired. As he opened up his eyes he saw that the two children had grown to become man and woman. He was filled with fear as he now thought that the place was the abode of evil spirits. At midday the two had again grown into a young man and a young woman. The young man told the hunter not to be afraid of them, assuring him that they were not evil spirits but immortal people who never die. The two people offered delicious food. The young man then took the hunter to a hillock just above the house and pointed at the valley down below the hillock told him that the valley is situated between the two Himalayan Mountains "*Paki* and *Mendong*". It is the most fertile valley of the land. The name of the valley is "*Mayel Kyong*" i.e., hidden village.

The valley was full of all kinds of fruits, flowers, and foodgrain crops. There were cascading waterfall and budding mountain streams which added fertility to the soil of the valley. It was certainly a paradise on earth. The heart of the hunter was filled with awe and happiness. The young man told the hunter that there are seven couples in this land of "*Mayel Kyong*" since the beginning of the earth. They are immortal beings that never die. They have no children. They have the power to be invisible anytime as they wish. In the early dawn they are small children at midday they become young persons and in the evening they become old couples. The agricultural crops, vegetables, fruits and flowers, and the beasts and birds of the world were first created in the land of "*Mayel Kyang*".

Hearing these words of the young man he knew that this young man too was the same person who was a child in the morning and an old person in the evening. He took him down in the valley and introduced him to the immortal old couples of "*Mayel Kyong*". The two wandered through the valley observing all the beautiful things there. As the evening came the young man had already turned into an old person. The old person returned home leaving behind the hunter to rest for the night there. The hunter slept in one of the house of the old couple for the night after heaving a hearty meal.

The next day at midday the seven couples of "*Mayel Kyong*" filled a basket with all kinds of seeds of foodgrain crops, fruits, vegetables and flowers and took him towards a very steep mountain ridge and told to sow and propagate all these in the land of *Renjyong*. He was also told that birds would be sent to tell the people of *Renjyong* when to sow these seeds at different seasons. After some time the basket touched the ground with a thud. As he took out the cloth from his eyes he found himself at the same place where he had hit the boar with the arrow.

It is believed that every year in each season the seven immortal couples send *Mayel –Fo,* the birds to tell the exact time for sowing seeds. The Lepchas do believe that various kinds of agricultural crops and horticultural crops are the gifts of the seven immortal couples of "*Mayel Kyong*". So to show their gratefulness to them they offer all kinds of foodgrains, fruits, vegetables spices etc. every year during the month of November. The Lepchas dance and sing to celebrate the occasion. It is called the festival of Sakyo-Rum-Faat (Gurung and Lama, 2004: 73-76).

(c) Sunkesri Rani: This is a popular folktale of the Nepali community in Sikkim. Once there was a princess with golden hair. She used to count her hair every night before going to sleep. One day she had gone to bathe in the nearby stream and on that night she started counting her hairs as usual, but she found that few of her hair were missing. She could not sleep the whole night due to sadness, at the loss of her precious golden hair. The king, her father heard about the loss and the sadness of the princess. He could not bear the pain of his daughter. So he made a proclamation that whoever finds the lost golden hairs of the princess, would offer his daughter to the person as his wife.

At the proclamation of the king many young men went to the stream in search of the missing golden hairs of the princess but none succeeded in the venture. Ultimately these lost hairs were found by one of the brothers of the princess. According to the promise made by the king in his proclamation her own brother now had to marry her. Princess could not think of such a bad situation. So the princess ran away from the place with her youngest brother and hid herself in a tree.

All person who went to bring back the princess died on accidental deaths. The princess then found a prince of another land and married him. This folktale must have traveled from one country to other where the girls have golden hair. Many folktales have traveled far and wide in this way. This folktale has also a mortal lesson beside entertainment, i.e., one should not make a promise without proper thought (Gurung and Lama, 2004: 80).

(*d*) The Sun and the Wind: Once there was a hot discussion between the sun and the wind. The sun thought that he was stronger than the wind. The wind did not like it. Then they decided to test their strength. At that very moment a man was passing through the forest wearing a shawl on his shoulder. The wind said with pride that he would take away the shawl of the man to prove his strengths. So it started blowing with great force. The traveler clasped the shawl with both hands as he was feeling cold due to blowing of the wind. The wind blew and blew but failed in his attempt to take away the shawl from the shoulder of the traveler.

The sun gave a smile. As the hours passed the sun came at the center of the sky. It was so hot that the traveler had to take off the shawl from his shoulder. The wind took this defeat in good spirit and both of them became friend again (Gurung and Lama, 2005: 83).

(*e*) The Secret of Happiness: Once upon a time there lived a king. He was not only very rich and ruled over a vast country but was blessed in other ways also. He had a beautiful wife, good friends and no enemies. His kingdom was free from miseries and people lived an easy life. Yet, the king was always unhappy. For him there was no joy in life.

He kept on asking people how to find happiness. One of his friends, who loved eating delicious food, suggested that the king should eat only the best food to lead a happy life. The king collected an army of good cooks and began to eat the best meals prepared by these cooks. But after some time, boredom and unhappiness again took over. After a few days he found that he had no desire to even eat. After this experiment failed another well wishers of the king suggested that wealth was certainly the source of great happiness. The king liked the idea. His treasure-house was opened and he began to purchase gold, gems and pearls in large quantities. Yet, the happiness he had been seeking for so long eluded him. Another friend suggested him that lies in the war front. The king found this to be a fine suggestion. He ordered his army to immediately prepare for war. In no time he defeated all the nearby kingdoms. Now no kingdom was left for him to conquer. Yet, he remained as unhappy as ever. To make himself happy he began organizing hunting trips where he hunted down the most fearsome of the beasts. He fought and killed tigers and lions. People looked at him awe and respect and admired him for his strength and courage. Only, he was still not happy.

When nothing could make him happy, his wife suggested he seek advice from Mahatma Buddha. The king along with his family and friends went to the place where the Mahatma was preaching those who went to him. The king touched his feet and told him all that he had done so far to be happy but all in vain. All that he heard amused Mahatma Buddha. He thought for a while and then replied. "My child, go and find a person who believes that he is happy. You will certainly find happiness if you borrow and wear the shoes of such a person. The king could not believe that the solution of his problem would be so simple. He once again touched the feet of the Mahatma and returned to his palace.

His friends and courtiers began searching for a person who declared himself to be happy. They talked to all – the rich, the wise, and the successful. Yet, not one of them believed he was happy. The king was disheartened beyond words to hear about their failure. Then he decided to make the search himself. After much time had passed, when he had given up the hope of finding a happy man, one day he heard the sound of someone singing blissfully. He immediately searched for that person, who happened to be a poor labourer. The king approached him and inquired, "Do you consider yourself a happy man?" "Not just happy, your highness" the labourer replied, "I think I am the happinest man on earth". "Oh, in that case, will you kindly lend me your shoes?", the king requested.

The labourer was now thoroughly embarrassed. With folded hands, he humbly submitted, "I am sorry your honour, but I am not in a position to fulfill even your simple request. I have no shoes, Sir! In fact I have never owned one!"

It was then the truth dawned upon the king, "What a fool I have been", he cried out aloud. Happiness flows inside me and like a stupid person I have been desperately searching for it outside. He thanked the poor labourer and returned to his palace and lived happy thereafter (Jha and Avasthe, 1999:6-9).

9
Festivals and Leisure Activities

Festivals or *Utsavas* means delivering one at a higher mental state. Most of the *utsavas* are therefore associated with some rituals. Modern thinkers define a ritual as a symbolic enactment of a myth. All rituals performed at the time of holding an *utsava* have symbolic myths behind them. *Utsava* is inappropriately translated into English as festival. Festivals are periods of intensified social and ritual interaction. These are times when people exit the routines of daily life into festival time. The *utsava* may be a great public event shared by thousands, a community festival or a private fast or a family festival.

Sikkim has a number of different *utsavas* or festivals that range from domestic events or ones focused on local shrines to great State holidays. Every community has at least one independent, voluntary committee that plans, raises funds for, and organizes its festivals. The State Government has declared public holidays for every big festival of every community. Women observe many festivals at home with fasting and prayer. These fasts, undertaken as a matter of private devotion and need, associated with public festivals. New festivals have emerged and older ones have vanished. Festival forms were adapted to new ends for political reasons in recent decades. For instance, the celebration of *Bhanu Jayanti*, New Year days of a number of communities, *Viswakarma puja*, etc. in Sikkim are the new festivals.

1. Festival Time and Structure:

In festival time, the boundaries of the human social world intertwine with sacred time, space, and beings. The suspension of normal time and relationships during this period is often marked by a key event or ritual that opens the festival or that begins the pilgrimages. Festivals draw attention to group boundaries, intensifying the sense of difference between participants and non-participants, and increasing the solidarity of participants. Some festivals emphasize a common identity. Other festivals divide social groups from one another, as they become badges of distinct identity.

In Sikkim, most of the Nepali ethnic group follows the lunar calendar, popularly known as the *Vikramaditya* calendar, that is fifty-seven or fifty-eight years ahead of the Gregorian calendar. The State Government uses the western calendar. New Year is a great holiday on January 1. Thus, many festivals vary on the date of Gregorian calendar. But then there is also the Hindu New Year, Buddhist New Year, Muslim New Year, Limboo New Year, Tamang New Year, Sherpa New Year, etc. celebrated at different times of the year. Full moon and new moon days have the greatest significance.

2. Seasonal Utsavas/Festivals

The festivals of Sikkim are scattered throughout the year. Most of the festivals cluster in the springtime and in the fall. Spring festivals correspond roughly with the conclusion of the winter agricultural season and the beginning of the hot season. Fall festivals mark the harvest and the beginning of the cold season. The cold season, less busy for farmers, is a time for weddings and fairs. This is when people can get free from work for events as these.

The important *Utsavas* or festivals of Sikkim, for which State Government has granted public holidays, are as under:

The date of traditional festivals celebrated on Gregorian calendar vary year after year as most of the traditional festivals are calculated using *Vikramaditya* calendar or Tibetan Calendar. The secular festivals such as State Day, Independence Day need no mention here in.

In the *Vikramaditya* calendar, months are divided into dark half or fortnight, *badi,* ending on new moon day and a bright half, *sudi*, ending on the full moon. This is the last day of the month. A lunar date is given in terms of the month, the fortnight, and the day. *Chait sudi* 1, the first day after the new moon of *Chait*, is the first day of the *Vikramadiyta* lunar New Year.

Some of the important festivals celebrated in Sikkim are as under:

2.1. Guru Rimpoche's Thrungkar Tshechu:

The birth anniversary of Maha Guru Padmasambhava, also known as Guru Rimpoche, *Thrungkar* means (Birth Anniversary) is celebrated with great pomp, and observed annually with great devotion and religious fervor all over Sikkim. The most auspicious Guru Rimpoche's *Thrungkar Tshechu* falls on 10th day of sixth month of Tibetan Lunar Calendar, coinciding July-August. On this day, Guru Rimpoche, was born at Dhanakosha, Udyan, a place in North India. Guru Rimpoche's visit to Sikkim is traced back to 8th century, when he personally visited Sikkim and sanctified the place from all negative forces and established Buddha dharma.

In the State capital, a weeklong worship ceremony is generally organised jointly by the Sikkim Buddhist Duechen Organisation and

Sikkim Buddhist Association at Tsuklakhang from the day *Drukpa Tsheshi* is observed. In the morning, a religious procession carrying the idol of Guru Rimpoche is taken out from the Deorali Chorten by a large number of devotees from all walks of life chanting the sacred mantra "*Om Ah Hung Vazra Guru Padma Siddhi Hung*". The procession is lead by Sherbhang lamas of the Deorali Chorten goes through the 31 National Highway and finally ends at Tsuklakhang Monastery covering a distance of two kilometres. Once the procession reach at Tsuklakhang monastery, the devotees offer prayer and offering before the statue of Guru Rimpoche. The High Officials of the Government of Sikkim also take part in the procession and prayer at the Statue of Guru Rimpoche

Month & Date (approximate)	*Festival/Event*	*Importance*
January 1st	New Year Day	First day of the year in Gregorian calendar
January 13th & 14th	Maghe Sankranti	13th &14th January is the *Udhauli* Nature divinity's (gods and goddesses of nature) worship days of all mongoloid hill tribes inclusive of Kiratas of Sikkim. The 14th January is the Limboo's New Year Day. The festival is celebrated by taking ***Ban Tarul*** and ***Makar Nuhaunu*** (holi deep in the Triveni).
January 26th	Republic Day	The day of adoption of Indian Constitution by the people of India
January	Sonam Lhochar	New Year day of Tamang Community of Sikkim.
February	Losar	New Year Day of Tibetan community
March	Holi	Marks the end of cold season and start of the hot season
April	Ram Navami / Chaite Dasain	Birth anniversary of god Ram Chandra
April 14th	Good Friday/ Dr. Ambedkar Jayanti	Festival of Christians, Birth day of Dr. Ambedker who wrote Indian Constitution
May 16th	State Day	State Day, Formal integration of Sikkim into the Indian Union
May	Sakewa (Chandi Purnima)	Festival of Khambu Rais, worship of Ubhauli, Paruhang and Sumnima
June	Sagadawa	Lord Buddha's Triple blessed festival; Birth, enlightenment and attaining *Nirvana*.

Month & Date (approximate)	*Festival/Event*	*Importance*
July 13th	Bhanu Jayanti	Birth Anniversary of Nepali Adi-Kavi Bhanu Bhakta Acharya
July	Drukpa Tsheshi	The day is the Buddha's first preaching of Four Noble Truths to his Five disciples.
August Falls on 10th day of sixth month of Tibetan Lunar calendar	Guru Rimpochi's Trungkar Teshechu	Guru Rimpoche's birthday, who visited Sikkim during 8th century. A.D. and sanctified the place from all negative forces.
August 8th	Tendong Lho Rum Faat	The Lepcha festival is for praying "*Itbu-Debu-Rum-Daor*" to save them from deluge; celebrated with befitting manner with worship of gods and goddesses.
August 15th	Independence Day	The day in which India obtained independence from the British Rule.
August	Janam Ashtami	Birth anniversary of god Krishna Festival is a worship of mountain gods of Lepchas and Bhutias, celebrated with dances.
September	Pang Lhapsol	The festival marks the blood brotherhood treaty of the Bhutias and the Lepchas.
September-October	Durga Puja (*Dasain*)	Worship of Goddess Durga; and blessing of children by the elders; the greatest festival of the Hindus
October 2nd	Gandhi Jayanti	Birth anniversary of Mahatma Mohan Das K. Gandhi, Father of the Nation.
October	Laxmi Puja (*Tihar*)	Festival of light and prayer to *Yama*raj - the God of death for long life and celebration with *Bhailoo-Dewsey, Bhaitika* and *Maruni* dance. Also a worship of Goddess of wealth Laxmi; marks the end of business year and start of new year for Hindus
October 25th	Id-ul-Fitr	The one month Ramzan fast of Muslims ends with the sighting of the new moon, at Id-ul-Fitr.
November	Lhabab Dhuechen	The day marks the descent of Lord Buddha from Ancestor's world to the Earth again after visiting his Mother.

Month & Date (approximate)	*Festival/Event*	*Importance*
December	Sirijunga Teyongsi Sawan Tongnam	Birth Anniversary of the great Socio-religious and educational awakener of the Limboos- Teyongsi Sirijunga (1704-1741)
December	Kagyed Dance	This is a Mask Dance festival of the Bhutias. The Lamas perform mask dance in the Monastery to signify the end of the Year and beginning of the new Year. This depicts the change of season.
December -January	Lossong	Losoong marks the end of the harvest season and also the end of the tenth month of the Tibetan year.
December 25th December	Christmas	The greatest festival of Christian community
August 23rd	Tamu Lochar	New year day of Tamu Gurung Community
July	Cultural festival of the Limboo community, Tharpu, West Sikkim	Foundation day of Sukhim Yakthung Phojumbho, Tharpu Limboo Cultural festival day, celebrated with great pomp and show
December 28th	Sawaney Sakranti	Worship of Yuma; marks the end of hunger and famine and visit of food giving goddess of the Limboo community
	Barahimjong	Worship of god and goddesses by the Magar Community

Source: Home Department, Govt. of Sikkim (2007).

As mark of tribute to the Guru, the Chamling Government in its first term in 1994, declared the Guru Rimpoche's *Thrungkar Tshechu* as a Government Holiday. Thereafter, his government also constructed a 135 ft. tall statue of Guru Rimpoche at Samdruptse. This is the tallest statue of Guru Rimpoche in the world today. Samdruptse has now become a pilgrimage centre as well as a hot tourist spot. Every day hundreds of people from all over the world pay visit to this place. The Guru Rimpoche's *Thrungkar Tshechu* is also observed in various places of Sikkim by the Buddhist Associations in a befitting manner. A large number of people participate in this religious ceremony (Sikkim Today, 2004; Bhutia, 2007).

2.2. Pang Lhasol:

Pang-Lhasol is a quite unique to Sikkim. The third Chogyal Chagdor

Namgyal of Sikkim popularized this festival in Sikkim. In this festivai the snowy range of Kanchan-Dzonga (Ganchen-Mjod-Nga) is worshipped by offering brewed millet (*Chyang*), local distilled liquors, fruits for its unifying powers and to praise the mountain gods and goddesses, and seeking blessings to grace timely rainfalls and bountiful harvests, and also pray for safety against natural misfortunes etc. This festival marks the signing of the treaty of brotherhood between the Lepchas and the Bhutias by Khe-Bumsa and Thekong-Tek around 13th century, when the local deities were invoked to witness the occasion. In fact *Pang* means witness, *Lhasol* means worship on this day. The guardian deity is portrayed by masked Lama Dances as a fiery Red-Faced Deity with a crown of fine skulls, riding on a snow lion. To lighten the mood of the spectators, jester called "*Atchar*" play antics during the *chaams*. This festival is held on the 15th day of the 7th month of the Bhutia calendar around the end of August. The worship ceremony of mountain deities is observed in Tsuklakhang (royal monastery), and all other monasteries of Sikkim. The daylong ceremony starts with worship of Guardian Deity – Kanchanjunga by the *Rimpoches*, Lamas and *Boongthings* (Bhutia, 2007).

The Lamas, dressed in their colourful and dazzling costumes and masks, come round and display their various dances. Smart young laymen, after undergoing rigorous training for at least a month, and with equal religious fervor, come whirling round to the delight and awe of the onlookers. Among other Lamaistic dances, the famous and inevitable "*Sha-nak*" or the Black Hat dance is performed. This dance depicts the victory of the Buddhist creed over the evil, destructive non-Buddhist forces. *Radong, gyalings* drums and cymbals accompany the lama dances. Nowadays, the various types of cultural shows, *Singhi Chham*, other cultural dances, songs, play etc are also organized to entertain the onlookers (Sikkim Today, 2004; Foning, 1987).

2.3. Tendong Lho-Rum Faat:

It is an indigenous festival based on the myth of the Lepchas of Sikkim, and is celebrated on 8th August of every year. In the festival the Lepchas pray through their priest *Boongthing* and *Mun* the Almighty Goddess "*Itbu-Debu-Room-Daor*" who is the creator as well as destroyer of the Lepchas of Sikkim. They pray and offer "*Chee*" (millet beer) to save them from the myth of deluge. The festival is celebrated with great pomp and show in the State where the people of all the community participate along with the high level officials. It is a ritual festival of the Lepchas of Sikkim and is also inspired by local legends. Realizing its importance the Sikkim Democratic Front Government has declared state holiday since 1977. This worship festival is connected with a legend of deluge that nearly swallowed Sikkim, which was ultimately stopped by *Rum* (God) and saved Sikkim from drowning. The *Boongthings* and the *Muns* perform the ritual dance as a worship of the Tendong hill. The local legend associated with this annual festival has been described under ritual dance (Gurung and Lama, 2004).

2.4. Tihar Festival:

Tihar is one of the greatest festivals of Nepali Community, which falls in October every year. According to centuries old Kirata Mythology, there lived a benevolent Kirat King known as Bali Hang (Hang means Raja in Limboo), well loved by his subjects. He was a great fortuneteller and knew his own death, taking place on the day of *Aunshi* (Badi, new moon day). The crows (*Kag* in Nepali or *Kakwa* in Limboo) carried the bad news of king's death to his subjects all around his country. The crows are believed to harbingers of bad or good news as well as messengers of God of death – *Yamaraj*. The dogs also new the bad news and informed the King's subjects by crying at night. It is also believed that the *Yamaraj* comes in the form of a dog known in the Kirat world as *Sandey*. The role of dogs has been elaborately described in Limboo Mundhum and is considered not only as faithful watchmen, but also bearer of bed news if they cry at night.

The king informed his courtiers about his death. The courtiers requested him to find out the solution of death. He told them that there is no solution of death; the mortal man has to die one day. But if all his subjects really want to prolong the life of their king they have to pray to god of death throughout the night lighting mustard oil lamp. The *Yamaraj* may prolong the king's life. Hearing this, his faithful courtiers of the king advised all the king's subjects to pray God for the long life of the king. To disseminate the message to the king's subjects, the young girls and boys went from house to house throughout the night and told them to pray God whole the night with light (*Laooti-Namooti* in Limboo language) for long life of their king, and thus help each other (*Pha-asiroo*, means let us help each other in Limboo language).

The Kirat people believe that the king Bali Hang died at 12.00 at night but after some time he came alive. They believe that the *Yamaraj*, King of Death, seeing so much of love and affection of his subjects, prolonged the king's life. The people were happy. The king thanked his subjects and ordered his subjects to enjoy happiness. Later on, the legend became the annual tradition of *Bhailoo-Bhaileyni* (*Pha-asiloo*). Again to disseminate the message of happiness the young boys were detailed to go to house to house of his subjects and spread the message of happiness that the death of the king has come and gone prolonging the live of the king (*tyye churey*, means the death came and gone in limboo language). The event has become the annual tradition of *tyye churey* and now corrupted to *dewsurey*. The women folk were detailed to prepare food and drinks to enjoy the happiness. After the boys returned from complete dissemination of the King's good massage to the king's subjects, the boys were garlanded by their sisters and feed them with *syalroti, dahi, swagun*, meat etc. Before that the sisters break the Okhar seed (*Juglans regia*) as a symbol of breaking the head of *Yamaraj* in the name of their brothers as *Phungwa changma* (victory over death). The legend has become an annual tradition of *Bhaiaduj* now. Thus, the annual tradition of *Bhailoo-Bhaileyni, dewsurey* and *Bhaitika* started in Tihar in the Nepali community. While playing *Bhailey-Bhaileyni* and *Dewsurey*, the girls and boys say that they have come to the houses by the order of Bali Raja, and not by themselves. The tradition is known as *Laringgaek-Namlingaek* in Limboo.

At the same time, a tradition of *Maruni Nach* of the Mangar Kirata of the Nepali community was also started to enjoy the happiness in this festival. The details of this dance has been described under *Maruni* dance in Folk Culture chapter.

Interestingly, the festival also coincides with the Hindu festival of *Dipawali*. Amongst the Nepali Community, the *Khasas* (Bahun, Chettri, Kami, Damai, and Sarki) are the Hindus. Besides many Nepali Communities have adopted Hindu religion. They worship and welcome the goddess of wealth, Luxmi by lighting of Deep (light), decorating the house with marigold and light. They also worship cows as the symbol of Luxmi and bullocks as the symbol of mythological Ram and Luxuman. The festival is also celebrated as a symbol of victory over evil.

The first day of *Tihar* is the festival of Crows or *Kag tihar*. The crows are fed with *siyalroties* and other foods as they serve as the messengers of bad news and also as scavengers, so that they may not bring any bad news like that of the death of Bali Raja. The second day is the *Kukkur Tihar* (festival of dogs). They are garlanded with marigold flowers and fed with good food and meat as they are faithful and also bearers of bad news, so that they may not bring bad news like the death of Bali Raja. The third day is the day of prayer for *Yamaraj* with light. The Kiratas believe that their humble prayer may be accepted by the *Yamaraj* and prolong their life as in the case of Bali Raja. For the Hundus, it is also known as "*Gai Tihar*" festival of cows and thus a prayer or *puja* of goddess of wealth Luxmi and Cows are performed on *Dipawali.* In the morning the cows are worshipped with oil, garland of marigold and fed with *naibed* or *Siyalroti.* The day is celebrated as the day of victory over evil. At evening the Goddess of Wealth Luxmi is welcomed with light. The next day is the festival of bullocks known as "*Goru Tihar*". Oxen are worshiped this day as a thanksgiving for tilling the land and making it fertile for agricultural purposes. The bullocks are also considered as the Mythological brothers Ram and Luxuman. *Bhai Tika* falls on the fifth day is a special day for brothers who are honoured by their sisters. The brothers (*maity*) are garlanded with marigold flowers by their sister with marigold flowers after breaking Okhar, symbolizing the head of *Yamaraj,* and *Tika* is put on their forehead and fed with *siyalroti* and *dahi* etc. They are honoured for their long life and prosperity, and supposed to protect the sisters from the evil eyes.

To mark the importance of the legendry festival, annually on the night of *Badi*, new moon day (*Aunshi)* the young girls go from house to house whole night as *Bhaileni* (*Pha-asiloo*) singing the songs of *bhaileni/ Phaisiniroo* without accompaniment of any musical instrument. Similarly, the young boys also go from house to house whole night for *Bhailoo* singing the songs of *Bhailoo (Pha-asiloo)* often accompanied with *Chyabrung, Madal* or other instruments like Harmonium, Gitar, *Sayong/ Jhampta* etc. these days. The visitors are generally provided cash on rice kept on brass plate with *Diyo* (*Laoti-Namoti*) and *Kalash* (*Lashari*). From the next morning to next day upto 12.00 noon (30 hours) the young boys again go house to house day and night as *Deosurey* singing the songs of *Dewsurey* (*Tyye-Churey*) and then they retire for *Bhaitika* the next morning. But many may continue upto 12.00 noon. This completes the celebration of *Tihar*. *Maruni* dance is the most popular dance performed during this festival (Subba, 1999).

2.5. Dasai

Dasai is one of the greatest festivals of Nepali Community especially of Khasas who are Hindus by religion. The festival is celebrated as the arrival day of Mythological Heroes Ram and Luxhuman with Sita to home after 14 years of exile (*Banbas*). As welcome and blessed them by the elders in Ayodha, the children or other younger members of the family rush to home for blessing of the elders during this day annually. This is the festival when the dwelling houses are washed with White soil (*Kamero*) and Red soil (*Ratomato*) atleast one or two days before the start of the festival; the house is decorated with flowers, food materials are arranged for the visiting guests and cash is also arranged for *Tika.*

The elder members specially parents and grandparents bless the younger members putting rice and *abir Tika* on their forehead and blessing them for long life, success, and prosperity. This is the time to pay respect to the elder by paying visit. The household members take good food and meat and depart for work again (Subba, 1999).

2.6. Sonam Lochar

This is a new year day of the Tamang community, falls on the *Basanta Panchami* of Manjushri Lunar Calendar based on the Nature worship, celebrated throughout the State. The festival starts in the morning with worship of gods and goddesses of Buddhist pantheon and offering freshly collected water. The Tamangs wear new clothes. Relatives and family members come to visit the elders. They go house to house and spread the message of goodwill and friendship among the neighbours. They organize celebration in the Tamang Gumpas where the Government high officials also take part in prayer to gods and goddesses of Buddhist pantheon. The cultural programmes are also arranged for entertainment of the onlookers (Muktan, 1999: 36-37).

2.7. Bumchu Festival

The Buddhist community of Sikkim celebrates this festival with great religious festivity at Tashiding Monastery in the month of January-February. In fact "*Bum*" means "pot or vase" and "*chu*" means water. *Bumchu* celebration is one of the most important and holiest events in Sikkim and thousands of devotees from all over the state and its neighbouring countries come on pilgrimage and participate in the holy occasion. The Vase, containing holy water, is kept in a miniature mansion (*Chosham*) under lock and seal of the high officials of the Government of Sikkim. Every year special recitation is conducted and the high officials and Lama check the seal before the Vase is taken out of the mansion. The Vase is opened on the night of the 14th day of the first month of the Tibetan Almanac. From the Vase three cups of the water is first taken out and is distributed among the lamas and devotees on the full moon day. Fresh water is brought from Rathong Chuk, which is also considered as a blessed river, as replacement.

In some years the Holy Water in the Vase increases by 21 cups and other times it decreases. In some cases the water of the Vase remains at the same level but other time it is found dusty. These are believed to be the predictions of auspicious and inauspicious occurrences in the state/country. When the water level increases it is a sign of prosperity and when it decreases it is an indication of bad year of drought and diseases. The dusty water indicates conflicts and unrest.

In brief, the seed of enlightenment is obtained by taking drop of this Bumchu water thereby all the distress, evil spirits and untoward happenings are removed. And prosperity and fulfillments are rewarded in this life and one attains Buddhahood or be born in the *Riwo Potala* or *Zangdopalri* in the next life (Dokhampa, 2003).

2.8. Maghey Sankranti (*Kaok Phekwa La-gaenge*)

It is a festival for worship of Nature divinities – *Udhauli* of the Kiratas and normally falls on 13th to14th January every year. The festival is celebrated at the confluence of *Triveni*, at Teesta (Teesta and Rangit confluence) but now also celebrated at the confluence of Bara Rangit and Chota Rangit, near Jorethang, South Sikkim. The festival is also the New Year Day of the Limboo Community. The festival is celebtated – taking bath in the river in the morning and putting tika on the forehead of the fleshy root of *Ban Tarul* (*Dioscorea hemiltoni*), worshipping nature divinities and taking lots of roots and tubers such as *Ban Tarul,* Ghar Tarul (yams), and a varieties of greater yams, sweet potato, roots of Iskus, Simal Tarul (cassava), colocasia etc. In earlier days, the young Limboo boys and girls used to assemble here two to three days ahead of the festival and used to perform paddy dance (*Yialakma*) for the entire week or so, and provided a forum for love making and elopement or selection of their life partners. Now, exhibitions of all Government Departments are organized at Jorethang and the gathering people enjoy the exhibitions side by side. The Sikkim Government organizes cultural programmes for entertainment for the people who come for taking *Makar* bath at Jorethang. DGH, Darjeeling also organizes Cultural Programmes at the confluence at Teesta and Rangit at Teesta by DGH, Darjeeling (Subba, 1999).

2.9. Sawaney Sankranti (Sisekpa La-gaenge)

The festival is an auspicious day for the Limboo community of Sikkim and falls in the month of July. The Limboos celebrate the day as the end of hardship and famine. They decorate the doors and windows and hung freshly harvested cucumbers, pumpkins, ginger, fruits, maize cobs, flowers and climbers of cucurbits etc. with a sling string at the main door. At the evening at about they beat the winnowing basket (*Phoyet*) and dance running around inside the house and finally around the house shouting "*Aayen ang tho sak yen pay ro, Mangwa cha-thi chase-nudhi tya ro*". They worship *Yuma Sam* and pray for Her visit. The Limboos believe that the Almighty *God Tagera Ningwaphuma,* the earthly form or divinity form known as *Yuma Sam* visits every house on that day and provides ample food materials for them (Subba, 1999).

2.10. Teyongshi Sirijunga Sawan Tongnam:

The day falls on the full moon day of *Mangsir* (December) and is the birth anniversary of Teyongshi Sirijungha Singthebe (1704-1741 AD). The day has been declared a state holiday by the SDF Government in 1997. The Birth anniversary is celebrated annually with befitting manner at Martam Yuma Mangkhim, West Sikkim. The high officials of the government of Sikkim also participate in the celebration. Teyongshi Sirijunga was a great social awakener for the Limboos. He revived the reading and writing system of the Limboo language. He disseminated the teachings of Yumaism (Yuma Samyo) amongst the Limboos. He was born at Sinam Yangwarok, Nepal and came to Sikkim in 1734 at Martam. The *Ta-Tshang* Lamas assassinated him in 1741 at the confluence of Reshi and Kalej Khola. On his honour the state Government has named the Bermiok to Legship road as Sirijunga road. A Mangkhim has also been constructed at Martam on his honour. The birth anniversary is celebrated with prayer at Mankhim and lighting butter lamp on the photo/statue of Mahatma Sirijunga and the Mangkhim. The Limboo priests *Phedangmas* bless the visitors of their long life and prosperity (Subba, 2004).

2.11. Rakhi Poornima (*Kwanti Purnima*):

The *Kokkti-Purney* or *Kwanti Purnima* and the *Rakhi Purnima* is one of the important festivals of the Newar Community of Sikkim. On the day of *Rakhi-Purnima*, Newars prepare a special soup of newly germinated pulses known as *Kwathi* or *Kokti*. It is prepared out of nine types of pulses such as a mixture of beans (*Ghew simi, Singtamey simi, Mantulall simi, Rajmah*), Mung (*Kalodal, Panhelidal*), Field Peas (*Matar/Kerau*), Horse gram (*Gahat*), Ricebean (*Masyam*), Soybean (*Bhatmash*), Cowpea (*Tuneybori),* Gram (*Chana dal*) and lentil *(Musuridal*). The mixture is soaked in water overnight and then spread on a mat (*nanglo*) and allowed for germination for three or five days. This is the sowing season of most of the pulses, and thus germinates easily. The mixture is then cleaned of rotten seeds; then a soup is prepared with spices and taken very hot. It is full of protein and vitamins and is supposed to drive away all cold that has accumulated in the body during the rainy season. They invite family members and friends on that day to their house. The Newar community thus protects the agro-biodiversity of pulses grown in the Himalayas, and thus is one of the best examples of managing cultural agro biodiversity (Nepali, 1965).

2.12. Sakewa:

Sakewa is the festival of Khambu-Rais and falls on the full moon day - *Chandi Purnima* of *Baisakh* (May-June). The festival is also known as *Ubhauli* or *Bungbanwa* or *Dongwnga* or *Bhumi Puja* or *Chandi Puja* or *Baali Puja* or land worshiping ceremony. It is an agriculturist festival where the deities of land and crops are worshiped every year for good crop in the following season to come. The Khambu-Rais along with their shamans – priest gather in a place and form a huge circle to perform various dances lead by the *Sili Mangpa* and *Sili Mangma* such as "*Chasum Sili*" (dance depicting paddy harvesting, threshing, husking, cooking and finally eating the cooked rice); "*Paklewa Sili*" (depict the activities of animals and birds of nature); "*Narowa Sili*" (depicting lifestyle of the crane –*Karang-Kurung*, the migratory bird while returning to northern hemisphere indicates right sowing season of cucumber, pumpkin and other Kharif crops). The Government has declared state holiday since 1997. Since than, the festival has become a community event. The details of this festival have been described under the Ethnology of Khamu-Rais (Rai, 2005).

2.13. Barahimijong:

The festival of Mangar community falls on the full moon day of Baisakh. In Mangar language *Barahi* means the God, *minat* or mi means worship and *jong* means fort. Thus, the meaning of the festival is the worship of God for protection of the Magar people. During this festival the priest *Bhusal* performs worship of all the household divinities, nature divinities and others offering various types of root and tuber crops, cereals, pulses, oilseeds, fruits and vegetables. The Mangars express their thankfulness for the good harvest and also pray for good cropping season in the coming year. The SDF Government has declared state holiday since 2007 now (Ale, 2003).

2.14. Tamu Lohochar:

The New Year festival of Gurungs falls on the month of *Powsa* (December-January), and celebrated with great pomp and show. Earlier it was just a household festival but with the declaration of state holiday by the SDF Government since 1997, the festival has become a community event now. This is the time the winter ends and the days lengthen (Gurung & Lama, 2004).

2.15. Sagadawa:

This is the "triple blessed festival" and is considered as the holiest of the Holy Buddhist festival. On this day in different years of Buddha's life, he took birth, achieved enlightenment and passed away attaining *nirvana*. These three important events are celebrated in the festival of *Sagadawa*. Lord Buddha was born in Lumbini in Nepal Terai from the parents of King Sudho Dhan and Queen Maha Maya of the Sakya clan around 566 B.C. He was named Siddhartha and his parents took all the pains to make his life comfortable and keep him ensconced miseries of the world. At the age of 29 years he renounced the world and after wandering for years in search of the truth reached Buddhagaya, Bihar, where he meditated under the boodhi tree and attained enlightenment at the age of thirty-five. Buddha, the enlightent one, left for his heavenly abode at the age of eighty-one at Kush Nagar, India on attaining Nirvana or deliverance into bliss.

During this festival, processions carrying the holy books of the teachings of Buddha from Tsuklakhang and other monasteries of Sikkim are taken out around the town areas. The devotees conduct prayers in the monasteries. This festival is held on the full moon day of 4th month of the Buddhist calendar around the end of May-June (Bhutia, 2007).

2.16. Drukpa-Tsezhi:

This festival is celebrated for Buddha's first preaching of the Four Noble Truth to his first five disciples in a deer park at Saranath. The first truth is the noble truth of **Suffering.** The second is the noble truth of the origin of suffering **Karma** and **Delusion** and their causes. The third noble truth is the **Cessation** of suffering or the attainment of **Nirvana.** The fourth noble truth is the truth of the **Eight-Fold Path** leading to Nirvana. The day falls on the fourth day (*Tse-zhi*) of the sixth Tibetan month (*Drukpa*) and is held on the 4th day of the 6th month of the Buddhist calendar around August. The Buddhist devotees and Lamas assemble in the monastery and pray and preach the Buddhist teachings on the festival (Bhutia, 2007).

2.17. Lha-Bap-Dhuechen:

This festival symbolizes the descent of Buddha from the ancestor's world (may be heaven) of the 33 (thirty-three) gods and goddesses after visiting his mother. "Dhue-chen" means festival, "Lha" means ancestor's world (may be heaven) or god, and "Bap" means descent. Legend says that queen Maha Maya, the mother of Lord Buddha, did not live long after the Buddha's birth and took rebirth in *Trayastrimsa* or the ancestor's world (may be heaven) of the thirty gods and goddesses. After attaining enlightenment, Lord Buddha through spiritual powers came to know about the whereabouts of his mother and at the age of forty-one ascended to the ancestor's world (may be haven) for three months during which he delivered sermons to his mother and other celestial beings. Lord Buddha had left behind on earth of his disciples, Mougalyana as his representatives. These disciples and other devotees of the Lord Buddha could not bear the long separation and longed to hear his preaching.

Maugalyana, who possessed miraculous power, was exhorted to go upto the ancestor's world to request the Lord to return back to the earth. The gods were not willing to let Lord Buddha return back to earth but Maugalyana suggested that as the earthly beings did not have the powers to visit the Ancestor's world. On the other hand, the celestial beings could come down to the earth to attend his preachings.

Lord Buddha finally relented and descended to the earth at a place, the god of machines. The Lamas and devotees assemble in all the monasteries and offer prayer to the Lord Buddha and gods and goddesses. The High priests – Rimphuchis preach the teachings of Lord Buddha to the devotee in their turn (Bhutia, 2007) (Note: All the religions who believe in Karma philosophy do not believe in the concept of heaven and hell. Thus in this case, the word heaven has been replaced by the Ancestor's world. If somebody believes that the Ancestor's world is the heaven, Yes, it is heaven for him but not all. The concept of heaven and hell exists only in that religion where they believe only in a single life following the Greek philosophers as in the case of Christianity and Islam).

2.18. Losoong:

Losoong marks the end of the harvest season and also the end of the tenth month of the Tibetan year. As it falls in the eleventh month of the lunar calendar it is not the real New Year in the sense of the word. It is known as Sonam Losar. It is in fact an agricultural New Year, when rice and other grain-crops like millets are plentiful and the weather is moderate in sharp contrast to the actual New Year Losar, which falls in a lean season and when it is extremely cold. During the festival of Sonam Losoong or Farmer's New Year, Bhutias enjoy rich feast, wear new cloths and share love, marry-making within their own people and also share their happiness with other communities. They go from house to house for celebration and share brewed millet, liquor (*Chyang* and *Aarag*), various items, cooked meat, *Khbzey, Zhero, Biyaso, Chamdo, Changkho*, or whatever the visitors are willing to have, should be provided by the house owners (Bhutia, 2007).

3. Pilgrimage:

Many Sikkimese people especially older ones of all faiths go on pilgrimage every year. Some go to visit the birthplaces of their religious Mahatmas, Gumpas, Mangkhims, Temples, Dhams, sites along the Gangas, Hindu Temples and holy places for mental and spiritual satisfaction. Others set out to earn merit, fulfill a vow, or seek a boon from a deity. A pilgrimage may be as simple as an extended trip to a nearby shrine, or as complex as a journey that traverses much of the sacred spaces in the State or the country. Pilgrimage lifts the pilgrim from everyday life as the individual travels to a sacred crossing. This period of prolonged contact with the religious teachers (*Rimpoche, Lama, Pujari, Phedangma, Bungthing, Jhankri, Mangpa* etc.) as pilgrims halt at shrines, such as Gumpas, Mangkhims, temples, churches, Masjits, and hear teachings by religious teachers, blends seamlessly with tourism. The pilgrimage also provides a forum for interaction with diverse group of people.

4. Secular Leisure Time:

All classes of Sikkimese people enjoy many activities that are popular in other parts of India and the West: the movies, television viewing, trekking and white river rafting, going to the higher mountains, river sites and lake-sites, viewing a historical temple or archaeological site etc. Sikkim is blessed with numerous such places and sites. The third highest mountain of the world – Kanchenjunga and a range of mountain peaks are seen from any higher hills of Sikkim. The panoramic view of snow clad mountains, terrace paddy cultivation, holy Gumpas, Mangkhim, Temple, Institute of Tibetology, visit to Tsangmo lake, Nathula pass, Pelling, Rumtek Monastry, Ganesh Tok, Lachung, Lachen, Gurudogma, etc. are of immense opportunity for leisure-trip. Sports mainly football, cricket, table tennis are popular pastimes of boys and young men. Video parlors, Cinemas etc. have also gained the attention of youth.

10
Art and Culture

Art and culture provides satisfaction, aesthetic response and emotional engagement to the people and evokes culturally meaningful themes – characteristics that it shares with other art forms and with literature. Aesthetics evokes an emotional response and coincides with ancient aesthetic theory of the State or a country. Arts often reflect its influence. In many cases, styles reflect political or cultural initiatives. The audiences often find meaning in ancient art and literature. Many ancient works resonate with today's concerns. New influences and inspiration stem from global culture. The art face the impact of global culture. Shifts in consumer tastes promote artist's incorporation of global styles or their efforts to distinguish themselves from this, by developing purer, more authentic styles. Thus, art and culture changes with time and space.

Ancient art scholars synthesized art theory in the third and fourth century *Natya Shastra*. This stated that art's purpose is to provide aesthetic feelings and sentiments. There are nine basic sentiments (*i*) erotic; (*ii*) odious; (*iii*) wondrous; (*iv*) comic; (*v*) pathetic; (*vi*) furious; (*vii*) heroic; (*viii*) terrible; and (*ix*) quiescent (Henderson, 2002:59-74). Artists combine these sentiments to achieve a distinct mood.

Artists often emphasize eyes, such as the almond-eyed beauties, miniature paintings, or a deity's huge saucer-shaped eyes. The finishing touch on an image destined for sacred use is that its eyes are opened to waken the deity. Symbols of royalty include the lion, elephant, horse, bull, and fly whisk. Fertility and good luck symbols include the woman and tree motif, an embracing man and women. Buddhists regard the Banyan tree as a symbol of enlightenment, the wheel as a representation of law. Indo-Islamic traditions elaborate geometric, floral, and calligraphic motifs.

Sikkim has a very rich tradition in handloom and handicrafts, carpet weaving, Sikkimese traditional crafts, *Thanka* paintings, woodcarvings, wooden masks, cane and bamboo crafts, handmade paper, soft toy making, blanket weaving, and traditional jewellery etc. The Sikkim people take to art easily. Mother Nature, its scenic beauty and bounty encourage them. It's small size, area and altitude is also an incentive for Sikkimese to take to vocations like weaving, painting, smithy, metal works, hand made paper making, dyes making from natural resources, and carpet weaving. The household industry is practiced and taught at the Government Handloom and Handicraft training centres scattered in the State. The Sikkim Handloom and Handcrafts Development Corporation is entrusted with the task of marketing the produce of the local artisans, craftsmen and cooperatives. It's emporium at Gangtok, the capital of Sikkim is a popular tourist destination. It has also another emporium at Sikkim House in New Delhi.

1. Art and Culture of antiquity (Before 1642):

The ancient art and culture of antiquity of Sikkim comprises of simple household item of the ancient people of that time - the Lepchas, the Limboos and the Bhutias of that period. The "Nah-angs" of Lunghem near Dallam of West Sikkim, who built the staircase to heaven with earthen pots, could be one of the greatest art and culture of antiquity. The extraction of nettle bark for fiber and weaving the clothes, making mats (*Pira, Gundri, Gajra*) out of paddy straw, dry maize *Khosela*, etc. by the primitive people of that time are the art and culture, and that could be some examples of early arts of Sikkim. The primitive people's clothes, dress, cap, bags, purses etc. were the only art and culture of those days.

1.1. The Lepcha Art and Culture:

The Lepchas were basically hunters and shifting cultivators during antiquity and they use to make a number of artistic tools, implements and handcrafts for their daily use. Some of the examples of such tools, implements and other handcrafts used could be listed as "*Vir Tangsit*" (basket-traps made out of cane or bamboo splits with net in the mouth for fish trapping), *Srigli* (net) for fish catching, *chompo* (basket), *tung zyang* (basket), "*Slu* and *Chong hup*" (bow and arrow made of bamboo, string and iron), spears, *Ban* and knife for hunting, *fitok* (earthen vessels for cooking), *Tali* (wooden plates), *Zaru* (bamboo spoon), *padam* (long bamboo can to bring water), *pathyoth* (bamboo can for millet beer), *pohip* (bamboo straw pipe for millet beer), *injidut* (milk can) etc. The Lepchas are very good weavers and used to make their own clothing which are *ko-chyop* (waist belt), *thyak juk* (cap), *dam, ta gaap* (female dress), *titli* (waist coat), *dom pra* (male dress) etc. The Lepchas made ornaments such as *kow, kheri* (necklace), *charm* (ear-top), colourful bead necklaces (*alvak*), earrings (*nay-kong*) and bangles (*akager*) for women, and fingerings and earrings for men etc. (Banerjee and Das, 1962: 22-25).

1.2 . The Limboo Art and Culture:

Similarly, the Limboo's art and culture of antiquity comprised of handcrafts, tools and implements, household and kitchen articles, musical instruments, hunting weapons, etc. which has been listed by Subba (1999) in his book are as under:

(*a*) Agriculture implements: *Kekchu* (plough), *Nising* (Juwa), *Ungsing/Pensing* (Harish), *Hemek* (Dandhey), *Phehikli* (Phyauri), *Chugeng (*Phali*), Phengkhen (*Karuwa*), Kang* (spead), *Tingkang* (Kanta), *Lepkang* (Kodali), *Lungthokwa* (Hammar), *Rambho,Toondhi* (Axe), *Chendiri Chenya* (Saw), *Lokphey/Thupa* (Spear), *Thowa* (Kunjo), *Penya* (Randa), *Waphey* (Hainsiya), *Phokpheyma* (Khurpa), *Khurmi, Pokphey* (Bamphok), *Michak* (Chakmak), *Bashila, Pheja* (Khukuri), *Huk Chendiri* (Aari), *Hattaso, Bhakari, Chitra, Chandey, Yakphang* (Bhakari), *Lo* (Mandro), *Chyaphla, Phayet* (Nanglo), *Sappo/Thingey* (Doko), *Lumbhu* (Thunchey), *Khuruk/Wanglep* (Ghum), *Mangdang* (Deli), *Noyee/Pokwa* (Dalo), *Sachep* (Perongo), *Chep* (Pecha), *Phurlung, Mohola, Yangdang* (Kokro), *Sorma (*Chhapani), *Phuney, Khannam* (Namlo), *Thakpa* (Damlo), *Phethokwa/Thokwa* (Dhiri), *Kandya* (Dhungro), *Chongey, Pipsing/Tom/Pitching* (Pipsing), *Chillingey* (Chalni), etc.

(*b*) Household and Kitchen articles: *Khemba* (Ghempa), *Pong* (Theki), *Thompakwa* (Jarru), *Khookchung* (Sano Okhli), *Sumdang* (Okhli), *Kyat* (Mushli), *Thookwa/Singang* (Dhiki), *Lumsum* (Jahato), *Hato* (Temji), *Mani, Phungsari* (Kalash), *Pherik* (Mandhani), *Pokwa/ Kandya* (Dundero), *Mana, Pathi, Lophit* (Chimita), *Singkamtoongba* (Wooden beer container), *Phatoongba* (Bambo beer container), *Sapthok* (short beer container), *Phonsi* (pot used for distillation), *Yagangma* (Main part of distillation), *Nani* (Wine collection pot), *Pata* (Top part of distillation), *Yukten* (Pira), *Lombhey* (Gundri), *Changden* (Wooden table), *Yukten* (Baithak), *Rari, Burkasan, Sukwa* (Bag), etc.

(*c*) Weapons used for hunting*: Pheja* (Khukuri), *Pokphey* (Bamphok), *Mudenphey* (Sword), *Lee* (Bow), *Toong* (Arrow), *Purtha* (Guleli), *Kolya* (Matengra), *Timmok* (Gun), *Toati* (Banchoro), *Kuthupma/ Tu* (spear), *Khoo* (Dhal), etc.

(*d*) Musical Instruments: *Simikla Kom* (Binayo), *Phenjey Kom* (Muchunga), *Ke/Chyabrung* (Long Log Drum), *Nagara, Mephra (*Bansuri), *Udhungba* (Sarangi), *Yalamber muksam* (Yalamber Baja), *Tungna*, etc.

(*e*) Jewellery: The Limboo female jewellery were *Nessey* (golden *cheptey* sun), *Terengna* (silver ornament for ear), *Laskari* (gold ear-ring), *Kanthungri* (gold ear-ring), *Thungri* (nose *dhungri*), *Mundri* (gold *bulaki*), *Hebo-samyang/uppa* (*dant ko sun/chandi*), *Samyangphung* (gold *sirbondi*), *Hasuli* (gold/silver necklace), *Namloyee* (silver *Chandrahara*), *Yangyichhi* (silver coin *Raizee*), *Pongwari/Kanthi* (*Pongwaloo*), *Simikla*

Hari (bamboo bead *mala*), *Tilhari/Kantha* (gold *tilhari), Sikri* (gold chain), *Ponayee* (*Pottey mala*), *Hukpangi* (silver *chura), Banhi (banhi*), *Swagek* (gold/silver/brass finger-ring), *Mundro* (Aluminium finger-ring), and *Langpangi* (Silver *Kalli*). The Limboo man jewellary were earrings, fingerings, and *Gokul* (ibid, 1999: 653-669).

1.3. The Bhutia Art and Culture:

After 13th century blood brotherhood treaty of Khe-Bumsa and Thekong-Tek, the Tibetans also slowly migrated to the present areas of Sikkim. They also brought their Tibetan art and culture, which was slowly introduced in Sikkim. The various Tibetan art and culture brought by the migrants were carpet weaving, multi-crafts making such as *Bakhus, Dochas*, Tibetan hats, and other dresses, *Thanka* paintings, Wood carvings, Wood masks, Clay masks, Cane and Bamboo crafts, Hand-made Paper making, Soft toy making, Blanket weaving and Jewellery making etc. which will be described in detail later on.

2. Emergence and Development of Buddhist Art and Culture (1642 to 1774):

This period is extremely important for emergence, development and consolidation of Tibetan art and culture in Sikkim. The Tibetans who started migration to Sikkim since 13th century accelerated mainly during the 17th century brought the art and culture of Tibet. After the consecration of the first Chogyal Phuntso Namgyal, the three Lamas introduced not only reading and writing system in Tibetan script but also constructed a number of Buddhist monasteries since 1697 onwards scattered through out Sikkim and thus started emergence, development and consolidation of Buddhist art and culture. They spread through these Buddhist monasteries their art and culture. They taught and propagated carpet weaving, multi-crafts making such as making eight lucky signs, making warm clothes, Lepcha hand-loom making, *Thanka* painting, wood carvings and masks making, *Chokchi* making, *Bakchuk* making, furniture making, making cane items, hand paper making, toy or doll making etc..

These traditional items comprised of *Thanka* paintings of *Budha, Dolma,* Wheel of life, *Mandala*, etc.; the mount painting of eight Buddhist traditional lucky signs, dragon, tribal face, yak etc.; wooden paintings of wooden dragon, eight lucky signs; masks making both wooden and clay; woolen carpets with dragon design; bamboo paintings of eight lucky signs, dragon; wooden or silver or copper *Mani,* copper or silver *Chham lohota, Dhapang etc.;* Statues of Buddha, *Dolma* and *Tara*; copper and gold *Gyalling,* Copper and gold *Raddong,* gold and artificial stone pendants, *gao* ornament, gold bangles with dragon ends; etc.

3. Emergence and Spread of Nepali Art and Culture (1774 to 1817):

This period is marked for emergence and spread of Nepali art and culture. Weaving of different types of fabrics for Nepali clothes, jewellery designs, hand tools and implements, curios, Hindu temples, etc. are the contributions of the Nepalese after 1774 onwards. The tradition of weaving *Rardi, Burkasan* made of raw sheep wool has been the Gurung's culture of Sikkim was introduced during this period. Weaving of *Dhaka topi, Dhaka Mujetro, Dhaka Fariya-Choli*, and making of *Kothimora Khukuri*, and many such art and culture were introduced in Sikkim. The Jewellery consists of *Kantha* (Gold), *Naugedi* (gold), *Tikmala* (gold), *Tilhari* (gold), *Marwari* (gold), *Cheptey Sun* (gold), *Karnaphul* (gold), *Kopi Patta* (gold), *Sirbandi* (gold), etc. Other ornaments introduced are gold chain, gold ring, gold locket, gold pendant, gold top, gold fingerings, Silver *Kalli, Rezi, Bulaki, Dhungri, Kanphul, Sikri, Pote mala, Pawalo, Chura*, etc. They also introduced statues of *Durga, Ganesh, Shiva, Swarasati,* consists of silver and other metals. They introduced silver and copper trident, butter lamp, silver cups, silver spoon, etc. They also introduced bamboo crafts such as lamp shades, pen stand, ash tray, fruit basket, *Gajra, Gundri, Pira*, nylon baskets, *Mura* or *Baithak* made of deer skin or bear skin or bamboo work. They also introduce *Ganesh, Luxmi,* and *Durga Thankas* paintings, tea garden paintings, etc. They also introduce Tamang's ornaments such as *Chyaldang, Chyaldo, Nachyap* on nose, *Yachyap* on hand, *Chyap* on fingers, *Nhali, Aalong, Chyoldo* on the ear, "*gao*" (star-aped bracelet), bangles. Similarly, the traditional dresses, jewellery, arts and culture of other Nepali communities such as Gurung, Sunuwar, Sherpa, Thami, Khambu-Rai, Yakha, Bhujel, Majhi, Jogi, Sanyasi, Newar, etc. described in their respective ethnographical description were introduced in Sikkim.

4. Modernization of Art and Culture (1817 to 1975):

After the Titalia treaty of 1817, Sikkim came under British protectorate. Political Officers of the British Government were posted to assist the Chogyal in his administration. They started the modern education through establishment of schools spread through out Sikkim. They constructed Christian Churches and Missionary Dispensaries at various places. They introduced allopathic medicine, the Christian art and culture in Sikkim through conversion of a large number of people into Christianity especially the Lepchas. A threat of insecurity was looming large of existing traditional art and culture of the ancient people of Sikkim, mainly the Bhutia and the Lepcha culture was growing in the minds of the ruling classes of Sikkim. The Five Year Plan was also started since

1954 onwards. The Institute of Tibetology was started at Chorten, Deorali Sikkim in 1957. Taking the advantage of the Plan Economic Development, the Government of Sikkim, both for preservation and development of the traditional arts and crafts of Sikkim, has established a Centre of Cottage Industry at Gangtok in March 1957. This Institute has been imparting training to the school dropout local young boys and girls in the traditional arts and crafts of Sikkim, and its products are now popular both in domestic and export markets. The woolen carpet is one that is symbolic of the cultural expression of Sikkim. The institute imparts training to the people about seven sections of art and culture viz: a) Carpet weaving, b) Multi-craft making, c) Handloom weaving, d) Art and craft making, e) Cane and crafts making, f) Hand-made Paper making, and g) Soft Toy making.

4.01. Carpet Weaving:

Like other oriental carpets Sikkimese carpets are also hand knotted and woven in fixed vertical looms which are kept standing with the support of a wall. This art requires a high degree of concentration and is taken up mainly by women in Sikkim. Carpet designs are normally of mythical birds, flowers like the lotus, snow lions, eight Buddhist lucky signs etc. Carpets are marketed through the Sikkim Handloom and Handcrafts Development Corporation (HHDC). The time taken in making these carpets varies according to the size of the carpets, designs and the ability of the weaver. Sikkimese carpets are woven using wool in piles of knots. They are woven in beautiful traditional Sikkimese designs. Their workmanship, attractive colours, and durability, are all worlds renowned, and are much in demand abroad. The local vegetable dyes, prepared by the institute itself, are used to produce a variety of matching colours, and in order to cater for all tastes; the Institute makes carpets of different sizes and designs. For motifs and designs the Institute do not seek inspiration from other cultures, for Sikkim is resplendent with ideas and designs from her age-old culture, and the carpets produced are a standing proof of this. It produces woollen carpets of 18″ × 18″, 2′ × 2′, and 2 × 2′ × 2′ & 2′ × 5′ sizes required for Chair Cushion, Sofa Sets and Bed carpet size. The private carpet weavers also make bigger size carpets for room flooring on request. The materials used are sheep wool, cotton thread and vegetable dyes. Now, even the chemical dyes are used due to scarcity of vegetable dyes. The vegetable dyes are extracted from *Majito* (*Rubia cordafolia*), *Okhar (Juglans regia*), *Halhaley* (*Rumax nepalensis*) etc. These beautiful carpets often have the dominating figures of the Dragon, flowers etc. The common colours used are red, yellow, maroon, green, brown, orange and blue. The carpets are popular both in the domestic and export market (photo enclosed).

4.02. Lepcha Handloom and Handicrafts:

In ancient Sikkim, the Lepchas were said to have woven yarn spun out of nettle (*sisnu*) plant. Today cotton and woollen yarn is used together with vegetable dyes and synthetic colours. Lepcha weavers or "*thara*" and the Nepali weave "*Dhaka*" as it is called, is woven in loin looms with a back strap. Such looms are of small width. Traditional designs with different colours are used to make *tharas* which are in turn used to make a variety of products like bedspreads, bags, belts, curtains, cushion covers, table mats, tray cloths etc. Lepcha (aborigine) clothe woven in traditional designs and rich colours is ideally suited for curtains, bags, table-mats, belts, shawls, bed-covers, cushions, jackets, tray-cloths, etc. It is manufactured in cotton, staple, silk, and woollen yarn. These handloom designs demonstrate the very sensitive and distinctive marks of Sikkimese culture, mood and mind, representing the creative and artistic mind of the Sikkimese people. The materials used are 2/20 cotton yarns. The six traditional Lepcha colours are White, black, green, orange, maroon, and blue. The Lepcha designs are *Damaru, Teer, Tarang* (water weave) and flowers. The various articles prepared out of the Lepcha clothes are tablemat, napkins, various types, shape and size Lepcha bags, Lepcha *dari*, scarf, shawls, cushion covers, Two inch belt, curtain, screen, lepcha hat, various types of sling bags and kit bags, geometry boxes, mobile cases, various types of brocade purses, and dace purses, strap belts, news paper or magazine baskets, Tamang caps, etc. (photo enclosed).

4.3. Multi-Crafts Making:

Multi-crafts includes products like dresses such as *Bakhus*, half jackets with traditional motifs, typical lepcha caps, ladies purses, bags, dolls depicting yaks and horses, file covers, embroidery on lampshades etc. The multi-crafts embody various aspects of Sikkimese culture and crafts. Beautiful jackets, leather emblazoned with some of the emblems of longevity, hand-bags of exquisite design and workmanship, belts, cushion covers, "*Bakhus*" (the Sikkimese traditional dress), and other charming articles are produced. Other articles produced comprises of hold decorations, purses, mufflers, sweaters, eight lucky signs, flowers, dragon etc. Both woollen and cotton clothes with silk thread for embroidery, rexin, hairs etc. are used. All types of colours are used for production of articles

4.4. Thanka Painting:

Thankas are religious scrolls found hanging in monasteries and in Sikkimese homes. They are considered auspicious and is supposed to drive away evil spirits. They normally depict life sketches of gods and goddesses in different forms. They may depict the life of Lord Buddha, goddess Drolma (Tara), a Buddhist wheel of life or any other deity. The central figure in a *thanka* is always a Buddha or any other deity or Bodhisattva of Mahayana Buddhism. Other figures depicted around the main deity have their mystical significance. *Thankas* in Sikkim have a religious and spiritual significance and is regarded as a sacred object. They occupy a predominant place in monasteries and homes and are painted by artists known as "*Lharipas*". *Thankas* are not merely a piece of art but signifies a religious devotion and journey made with reference to religious texts and acting as an aid to meditation. The materials used are stone colours and vegetable dyes together with gold dust and gold thread used for the tapestry. The paintings are bordered with rich silk and brocade with heavily engraved silver knobs at either ends at the lower half of the *thanka*.

Thankas (i.e. religious scroll paintings), which depict Buddhist scenes or motif, are not only very beautiful but are rich in colour and entirely traditional in composition. They are bordered with rich Benaresi silk, with heavily engraved silver knobs at either end, which enhance the exquisite beauty of the *Thankas*. Usually, the other figures in the *Thankas* are Guru Padmasambhava, Chenrese, Mahakala or Vajrayana, Green Tara (Dolma), Tshering Thuk, *Singkhorlo* (Wheel of life), Millarapa, Karmapa, eight lucky signs etc. One of the main aims in the Government Institute of Cottage Industry is to encourage and give impetus to these paintings that so truly represent Sikkimese Art and Culture. The materials used for *Thankas* are silk, poplin clothes, Chinese brocket, wood and pure gold. The *Thankas* are lined with zinc oxide and *surs* (liquid leather), and then smoothen with water. The natural colours of mud and stone are used. Chemical dyes are used only during training of the students. Vegetable dyes are not used in *Thankas*. Red, blue, orange and green are the most common colours of *Thankas* but red and yellow are the traditional colours used in *Thankas* (photos encloed).

4.5. Wood Carvings

Woodcarving is an ancient art form of the Sikkimese. Wood carving is done on a range of products from *'chokchi'*(carved table), *'bakchọk'* (square table), wooden masks, decorative screens, luckey signs, altars, lamp shades, table-trays, beautiful Sikkimese design wall plaques and other decorative items in typical traditional designs like the dragon, birds, phoenix etc. The main material used in this craft is wood. Three types of wood are normally used such as 'Tooni' (*Toona celiata*), Rani Chaap

(*Macalia exelsa*) and Okhar (*Juglans regia*). First of all a piece of wood is cut into desired shape. After seasoning and papering it smooth, very fine chisels and tools are used to carve out the designs. The carved pieces are then assembled together and are ready for a coat or colourful paint or polish. Sikkimese woodcarving, again a traditional craft, has been brought to a high level of artistic efficiency.

4.6. Wooden and Clay Masks

Mask making is another ancient craft in Sikkim. In this craft, face masks in wood of different gods and goddesses and animals are made and worn by people during festivals, religious ceremonies and dances. Wooden masks depict serene, partly angry or animal expressions. Nowadays they are also used as wall hangings. Wooden masks are carved out of tough light wood known as "Zarushing" or "bahuni" (*Marsdenia tenacissima*), which is mostly found in high altitude areas of Sikkim. First of all a piece of wood is cut according to the size of the mask to be made. Thereafter, a curved knife is used to shape the hollows and bumps. Many chisels and tools are used to finish a mask. The surface of the mask is then prepared. Painting follows thereafter. Some mask also has a third eye symbolizing foreknowledge. A variety of masks, for example, Mahakala (red coloured), Guru Dakmar (red coloured), Lhamo Mak Zorma (maharani-blue coloured), Bull (black coloured), Tiger (brown coloured), Lion (white coloured), Garuda (green coloured), Monkey (ruddy brown coloured), Stag (fawn coloured), Yak (black coloured), Graveyard ghost (yellowish coloured), A-tsa-ra (of ordinary human size-white coloured) are made. The Mask section produce two types of masks one with clay for decoration purpose while the other wooden for Lama dance and decoration. All type of colours is used in Masks (photo enclosed).

4.7. Cane and Bamboo Crafts:

Bamboo grows in abundance all over the state but cane is found only in the limited area. Cane is obtained from neighbouring Siliguri and other parts of the North-East as well. Cane and bamboo pieces are split by using simple tools like Khukuri or knife and made thin strips. The strips are thereafter sized as per requirement and are intricately woven and modified as per the design. The cane and bamboo articles are all redolent of Sikkimese ways and habits and are finely fashioned by competent and fine artisans. The materials used are bamboos, cane, mica, wooden ply, and poster color or favicol. Colours used are red, blue, green etc. The articles produced are *Mura* (*Baithak)*, trays of various shapes and sizes, Pen stand, Ash-tray, dry flowers, fruit baskets, star baskets, Lepcha hats, fish stand for decoration, Lamp stand, hair clip, *Chapaney*, bamboo dragon, flower vase, containers, beer mugs etc (photo enclosed).

4.8. Hand-made Paper Making:

Various types of paper are manufactured, and there is a growing demand for the paper, which is prepared from bark of *Argelie* (*Egeworthia gardreiu*), a locally available bush. However, very often recycling of office waste papers, paper treaming of Government printing press, Hosiery cuttings (rags), rayon or synthetic silk, etc. are also used for paper making. Chemical dyes – direct dyes of various colours such as blue, green, rodamine etc are used as colour. Popular items, which are made of hand-made paper, are the boards, file covers, note-sheets, writing-pads, envelopes, albums, greeting cards, drawing papers, hard fancy papers, decorative papers etc.

4.9. Soft Toy making:

The section manufactures dolls and toys. This is recently modernized with latest machinery (2005). It utilizes synthetic fur (varieties of Nynex of various length), Polyboy of various length, Polyester fiber, eyes and nose plastics etc. The various items manufactured are dolls or toys of rabbit, yak, dog, cow, monkey, duck, dog, donkey, frog, and all types of animals. The dolls and toys manufactured goes for domestic as well as export market via Kolkata.

4.10. Blanket Weaving:

In the higher altitude areas of Sikkim such as Lachung, Lachen, Chungthang, Pelling, Burikhop etc., training in traditional blanket weaving is also imparted. But the demand for these have dwindled in the face of machine made superior quality blankets. DHHC is therefore upgrading the quality of this craft to sustain the market forces. These blankets are woven out of locally available raw wool in looms. It has attractive designs and is only suitable for intense winters of high altitude areas.

4.11. Jewellery Making:

Sikkimese jewellery depicts the different tastes of the three ethnic groups of Sikkim, Viz: Lepcha, Bhutia and Nepali. The "Dragon" jewellery made in private jewellery makers in Gangtok, is famous and is made in cuff-links, rings, ear-rings, necklaces, etc. The gold, silver and bead jewellery of the Nepalese is also very popular. Articles, such as ash-trays, nut bowls, spoons, and religious artifacts in Bhutia pattern are much sought after and prized (photos enclosed) (Sikkim Handicrafts, Browser 1987; *Sarkari Gharelu Udhyog Sangthan*, 1987).

5. Secularization of Sikkimese Art and Culture After 1975 onwards:

This period marks the introduction of various Indian art and culture through migration of a large number of people from the vast country to

Sikkim. However, the visionary Chogyal Sir Tashi Namgyal who started the Government Cottage Industry at Gangtok, laid a foundation to overcome the problems and has helped in preservation and development of traditional art and culture of Sikkim. Nowadays, the cosmopolitan market of Gangtok and other markets of Sikkim are flooded with a variety of art and crafts both domestic and abroad especially from Kathmandu, Kalimpong, Korea, Thailand, Tibet and China.

6. Postscript:

The Government Institute of Cottage Industry is a centre of Sikkimese culture, established mainly for preservation and development of Bhutia and Lepcha art and culture. However, there is no effort from the State Government to preserve, protect, develop and popularize the Art and Culture of the entire Nepali Ethnic Community of Sikkim (Limboo, Newar, Tamang, Sherpa, Khambu-Rai, Yakha, Sunuwar, Majhi, Bhujel, Thami, Khasas – Thakuri, Bahun, Chetri, Kami, Damai, and Sarki). Hence, it is likely to disappear the valuable art and culture of this ethnic group of Sikkimese people. Many such valuable art and crafts has already disappeared and many more are also slowly disappearing day by day. It is very high time to think over it by the State Government as well as the entrepreneurs and initiate establishment of an institute for preservation, development and marketing to popularize the Art and Culture of this ethnic group on the line already demonstrated by the Government Institute of Cottage Industry, Gangtok since 1957 in Sikkim.

11
Health and Culture

Providing basic health services are essential for better health care of the people in Sikkim. The network of allopathic hospitals, district hospitals, primary health centres and sub-centres, a medical college, Ayurvedic medical centres, Tibetan Herbal medical centres, and Homopathic medical centres under both public and private sectors scattered through out the state of Sikkim cater the need of health care of the people. Folk medicines practiced by the community health healers also exist side by side for the health care of the people. The health care systems existing in the state are described in brief in this chapter.

1. Folk Medicine:

Folk medicine has existed for as long as human beings have existed. In an effort to cope with an environment that was often dangerous, humans, and their ancestors, began to develop ways of lessening pain and treating physical and medical problems undoubtedly came through trial and error, using various plants and other methods derived from observation of how animals reacted to and treated illnesses and injuries. Over time, individuals within family and tribal groups became more skilled at helping the sick and injured, and some of these became responsible for carrying out healing ceremonies, religious rituals, and other rites designated to ensure the safety and health of their communities.

Folk medicine is an unofficial health-related practice that has traditionally existed, and is learned informally by word of mouth, and through observation and demonstration. Long before the discovery and development of modern scientific medicine such as the use of pharmaceutical drugs and doctor's surgery, traditional healing methods had been in used, and are still being used today in every culture. Various types of traditional medicine such as herbs, tree or plant roots, fruits, insects and food items are used for treatments of any illness ranging from AIDs, cancer, malaria, warts, sore throats to arthritis, impotence, high blood pressure and infected wounds.

Many of the methods for treating injuries and diseases have been passed down through families for generations, and some of these have been adopted for use by the medical profession. Those treatments not commonly believed to fit within the framework of modern medical practice are commonly identified as folk medicine. Illnesses whose etiologies are not recognized by Western medical practice are known as folk illnesses. The cultural and ethnic groups from which they emerge shape folk illnesses. They are specific to the cosmology of the cultural and ethnic group to which they belong and they have specific causative, diagnostic, preventive, and healing/curing practices that may vary significantly from how they may be viewed by modern medical practitioners.

In Sikkim a number of religious priests or shamans or herbalists or community healers of different communities inhabiting in the state, are in practice of folk medicines. They are known by different names in different tribes/castes as follows:

S.No.	*Communities/Tribes*	*Name of the Folk medicine man/women*
1.	Khasas	Dhami, Jhankri
2.	Limboo	Sada Samba
3.	Khambu-Rai	Mangba (Bijuwa), Nakchong, Mabini, Kubimi, Dowang
4.	Sunuwar	Poibo, Natso, Ngyami
5.	Sunuwar	Bhusal, Dhami, Jhakri
6.	Thami	Dhami, Jhakri
7.	Gurung	Lama, Pachyu, Ghyabring
8.	Lepcha	Bongthing, Mun
9.	Sherpa, Tamang, Bhutia	Lama
10.	Newar	Bajracharya, lama

These folk medicine men and women of different communities exist side by side with modern medical practices especially in the rural areas of Sikkim, and often at odds with it. This is primarily because it very often does not confirm with what is scientifically known about the causes of illness and disease and what are thought to be the most effective medical treatments. These medicine personals have acquired their knowledge from generations of others that have used the treatments. The materials used for treatment includes, herbs and plants for which Sikkim Himalaya is very rich, minerals, animal products and religious Mantras/ Mundhums of the communities. These folk remedies are often learned and passed down from parent to child, and the explanations for illness causation and treatment go hand in hand with this learning process. Without much understanding these folk medicine practitioners have said to have covered the four major categories of cause of illness and their treatment, for which the Western practitioners have some limitations, Viz:

***(i)* The Patient World**: is concerned with illnesses caused by factors that the patient has some control over, such as diet, smoking, drinking, and other lifestyle behaviors.

***(ii)* The Natural World:** includes problems related to animate and inanimate factors, including those caused by microorganisms and viruses, animal bites, and environmental factors such as pollution, pollens, poisons, and natural disasters.

***(iii)* The Social World:** covers interpersonal conflicts, including conditions caused by physical injury inflicted by one person on another, the stresses of daily living, and witchcrafts and sorcery.

***(iv)* The Supernatural world:** includes illness caused by spirits, ancestors, or gods who have offended through sinful behavior, the breaking of taboos, or other breaches of proper behavior.

Folk medicine practitioners use a variety of methods to treat illnesses caused by the above four major category world. These practitioners go by many names, including shaman, spirit medium, herbalist, native healer, medicine man, and other related terms. Each has specific treatment approaches, which may include prayer, dancing, medicinal herbs, massage, sweat baths, coining, cupping, hot and cold foods, and other practices not normally considered in modern biomedicine. Often their religious priests or shamans are the first to be consulted when a family member becomes ill. They are easy to access, tend to share the same illness causality beliefs, will come to the home day or night, and are much less expensive then a clinic, hospital, or doctor's office visit. Folk medicine practitioners are also often consulted when home remedies fail. If the practitioner also fails, then consultation with the biomedical community may occur.

Folk medicine exists side by side with modern medical practices in Sikkim. Herbal practitioners, prayer, magic, diet, exercise, and proper social relations are all viable tools in the effort to maintain health. For public health practitioners, an awareness of the diversity of health beliefs and practices that may be encountered among those who use more traditional folk medicine approaches, and the ability to suspend judgment about those who use them, is an important step in learning to work more effectively with the diverse folk medicine traditions they encounter in their practice (Helman, 1994; Bergner and Hufford, 1998).

2. Ayurveda:

Estimates of the origins of Ayurvedic medicine range as far back as 5,000 years. Texts believed to be more than 12 centuries old are still available today to document the sophisticated knowledge of human anatomy, physiology, health and disease handed down through the millennia to modern times. Ayurvedic medicine may well have been the first complete system of medicine. It is thought to have been the original medical discipline whose traditions were sought out by and disseminated among healers in Asia, Africa and Europe centuries ago when medical knowledge was minimal or absent in other cultures.

The principle philosophy of Ayurveda is based on the theory of *Panchmohabhuta* (five primary elements) of which all living and non-living bodies are composed of. According to Indian philosophy, there is a complete similarity between the universe and human body. This fact has been also pointed out in the Vedic literature as "*yeatha pinda tatha Brahmanda*" meaning whatever is found in *pinda* (*purusa*) the same thing is noticed in *Bramhanda* (universe or cosmos). In other words, it can be said that there is a direct relationship with individual and the universe around him. In the universe, air (*Vayu*), Sun (*Surya*) and Moon (*Chandra*) are the fundamental things, which control the physical affair likewise *Vata, Pitta* and *Kapha* are found in the body etc. for the biological control. Acharyas may substitute *Vata, Pitta* and *Kapha* as functional unit because *Tridisa* are responsible for all biophysical, biochemical and all transformation in the body. Even though *Tridosa* are composed of *panchamohabhutas*, anatomical structure of *Tridosa* cannot be found in the body. The morphological descriptions of *Tridisa* also are not found in entire Ayurvedic literature, while their qualities, character and function has been described. *Sapta dhatu* (seven primary tissues) are the structural unit of the body, as they are the constituents of various organs in body. By the interaction between *dhatus* and *dosa, Malas* are generated as the by products in the body.

Mala (impurities) should be extracted from body, as they are liable to be re-absorbed in the channel and they may abstract the path. Generally the body cannot utilize *Malas*. If any condition *Malas* is re-absorbed or obstruct the path then disease occurs. Therefore, *dosas, dhatus* and *malas* are three components of living body, which maintain the life, and health of an individual. Ayurveda considers the human being as a combination of the three *dosas, panchamohabhutas* (five elements), seven body tissues (*saptadhatu*), five senses (*panch indryas*), *Mindm* (*manas*), Intellect (*budhi*) and Soul (*atma*). The doctrine of Ayurveda aims to keep these structural and functional entities in a functional state of equilibrium, which signifies good health. Any imbalance due to internal or external factors results in disease and restoring the equilibrium, through various techniques, procedures, regimen, diet and medicine is the treatment. All the medicinal plant's action is also designed as per the *dosa*. *Rasayana* drugs have the property to clear the channels by which it acts as immulomodulators, adaptogenic etc. and delay the aging process.

Ayurveda was first introduced in Sikkim on 9th June 1997 as the Regional Research Institute of Ayurveda, at Gangtok with the following three basic objectives:

1. To undertake clinical trials for studying the efficacy of Ayurvedic drugs.
2. To survey and find out the new drug resources available in the state.
3. To cater out services in Out Patient Door (OPD), In Patient Door (IPD), Mobile Clinical Research Unit (MCRU), and Child Health Check Up (CHCP).

The Survey of Medicinal Plant Unit (SMPU) and OPD were started since the inception of the centre, the MCRU and CHCP became functional in March 1981 where as IPD and Pathology were started in March 1984. But unfortunately some unavoidable circumstances forced to close down IPD section. Beside above mentioned activities, data regarding nature, extent incidence of different diseases accruing in these areas, and also of food habits, health related customs and belief of the people were collected for providing further strengthen the research work. During the past 26 years, this centre has consolidated the liaison in all its units viz: IPD, OPD, MCRU, CHCP, and SMPU. But IPD, MCRU, CHCP and SMPU are not functioning now.

Ayurveda uses as ingredients for Ayurvedic medicines of more than 400 medicinal plants, 120 animal products and 100 minerals. As this region comes under the main Himalayan terrain, the medinical plant available here has immense value.

The general health cases being treated from this centre in chronology are gastritis, gastric ulcer, acidity, skin disorder, cold and cough, fever, influenza, piles, constipation, running nose, anemia, sinusitis, menstruation and infertility problem, throat problem, neurological problem, and highest numbers of arthritis.

The research conducted by this centre includes allergic rhinitis, Diarrhea, Skin disorder, goiter, malaria, lady's white discharge, irritable bowl syndrome, etc.

Ayurveda emphasizes on diet, life style and medicine. The Ayurvedic treatment includes *Purgation* (vomiting, massages etc), Sadhana (purificatory therapy e.g. *Panchkarma*) and Samana or palliatives therapy (Panda, 2004; text provided by and personal interview with Dr. Panda on 18th December.2006).

3. Tibetan Herbal Medicine:

Tibetan medicine has a rich heritage and is currently practiced not only in Tibet, but also in the adjacent Chinese provinces of Qinghai, Gansu, Sichuan, and Yunnan, and in the neighbouring kingdoms of Bhutan, Nepal, Ladakh, and Sikkim, where communities of Tibetan people have long been established. Many non-Tibetans also seek out treatment by this traditional system because of its good reputation. Tibetan medicine originated with the local folk tradition (known as Bon) that dates back to about 300 B.C. and was formally recorded by Xiepu Chixi, the physician to the Tibetan King Niechi Zanpu, in 126 B.C. Aspects of both the traditional Chinese and Indian (Ayurvedic) medical systems were added later; Ayurveda has had the most profound influence on Tibetan medicine. The medicine of India was introduced to Tibet as early as 254 A.D., with the visit of two Indian physicians. During the following century several physicians from India reinforced the teachings. The greatest influence from India came about when Buddhism was adopted in Tibet as the state religion.

The legend of how Tibetan medicine was introduced to Tibet is relayed in the story "The Life of the Great Physician Yuthog Yonten Gonpo" (708-833 A.D.), which has been translated and presented in the book "Tibetan Medicine" by Rechung Rinpoche. Yuthog studied medicine since an early age and was exposed to Buddhism during his teen years. He made three trips to India and studied with the great masters of Buddhist and Ayurvedic medicine there, and he eventually wrote 30 classic medical works integrating the local, Indian and Chinese medical traditions. The involvement of Chinese medicine came about in 641 A.D. when a Tang Dynasty princess, Wen Cheng, was married to the Tibetan leader Songzan Ganbu. Wen Cheng brought with her many Chinese books, including the medical books, as well as herbal formulas and medical instruments. Seventy years later, during Yuthog's life, another Chinese princess, Jin Cheng, brought additional medical books, as well as several Chinese physicians, to Tibet. Yuthog is viewed as the father of Tibetan medicine.

The general methods of diagnosis and therapeutics used by Tibetan doctors follow the Indian ***tridosa*** system; that is, being based on three humors – ***rLung*** (Vayu or wing) with basic concept of movement, breath, cold; ***mKrhispa*** (pitta or bile) with basic concept of metabolism, digestion, fire; and ***Badkan*** (kapha or phlegm) with basic concept of restraint, lubrication, moistness etc.

The imbalances in an individual are revealed by a combination of reported symptoms, pulse diagnosis, tongue diagnosis, and urine analysis.

The overall physical appearance of the person and information about their daily habits, and consideration of seasonal influences also contribute to the analysis. The Tibetan pulse diagnosis appears to be derived from the Chinese system, and is taken at the same artery of each wrist, but the method of feeling the pulse and the interpretations differ. Tongue diagnosis is simplified compared to the Chinese system (long disorders are characterized by red and dry tongue; *chiba* disorders by a yellowish tongue coating; and *peigen* disorders by a grayish and sticky coating with a smooth and moist texture). Urine analysis is unique to the Tibetan system and may have been introduced from Persia. Physicians inspect the color, amount of vapor, sediment, smell, and characteristics of the foam generated upon stirring, relying on the first urine excreted in the morning.

Traditional Tibetan medicine formulas are described mainly in terms of the diseases and symptoms that they treat, rather than their properties and influences on the humors. Many of the formulas that are still in use were established many centuries ago. The principles of herbal combining to yield a traditional formula are not clearly defined in the Tibetan system. There are complex methods of analyzing the qualities of medicinal materials: 6 tastes, 8 properties, and 17 effects, but the precise organizational principles for compounding numerous ingredients into the formulas are lost to history.

Tibetan medicine, like other traditional medical systems, is highly complex, and represents a comprehensive effort at dealing with health and disease (Dharmananda, 2006).

In Sikkim, the Tibetan medicine came with the migration of Tibetans who started migration to the present Sikkim area mainly after the blood brotherhood treaty of Khe-Bumsa and The-Kong Tek during 13th century. In my personal interview with Dr. Tashi Namgyal Surkhang, a Tibetan Herbal Medicine Specialist, Nam Nang Road, Gangtok on 20th December 2006, it was revealed that his father started practicing Tibetan medicine in 1958. After his father's demise, he is practicing it at Gangtok for the last 20 years now. In the early days he used to collect medical ingredients from Gangtok itself. Since, the Sikkim Government has banned collection of medicinal herbs from 2002, he is collecting his requirements from Amritsar, Delhi and Siliguri. Most of his clients are Tibetans but people from other communities also use Tibetan medicines. Most of his clients come for treatment of gastritis, gastric ulcer, gout, Neurological disorders, arthritis, diabetics etc. He keeps his medicines in powder form. Earlier he used to treat 50-60 patients per day but now he treats only 8-10 persons a day. He uses about 50-60 medical ingredients for treatment. He collects and prepares medicines himself (Personal interview with Dr. Tashi Namgyal Surkhang on 20th December 2006).

Classification of Herbal Properties in Tibetan Medicine:

Grouping	*Characteristics*		*Effects*
Six Tastes	Sweet	e.g., bamboo, grapes, saffron;	pacifies *long* and *chiba*; increases *peigen;*
	Sour	e.g., pomegranate, hippophae, crataegus;	pacifies lungs and *chiba;*
	Salty	e.g., salt and several minerals;	pacifies *long* and *peigen* increases *chiba*
	Bitter	e.g., gentiana, aconite, berberis;	pacifies *chiba,* increases lungs and *peigen*
	Acrid	e.g., pipper, ginger, garlic;	pacifies lungs and *peigen,* increases *chiba*
	Astringent	e.g., sandalwood, terminalia, aquilegia;	pacifies peigen, increases lung and *peigen*
Eight properties	Heavy, Smooth	To increase *chiba,* worm, sharp, and smooth medicines are used	These two treat combat long These two combat *chiba*
	Cool, soft	To increase *peigen,* heavy, smooth, cool, and soft medicines are used	These four combat *peigen*
	Light, Rough, Acrid, and Sharp	To increase *long,* rough and cool medicines are used *Long disorders tend to be*	Disease is treated by the
Seventeen	Cold, hot, warm, cool, thick, thin, moist, rough, light, heavy, steady, motive, blunt, sharp, tender, dry, and soft.	dry, light, cool, mobile, subtle, and hard; *Chiba* disorders tend to be oily, sharp, malodorous, purging, hot, flowing, and light; *Peigen* disorders tend to be cold, heavy, blunt, smooth, oily, stable and sticky.	opposite effects; a hot disease by a cold effect; stagnant diseases by a motive effect; an accumulation by a sharp effect; a moist condition by a dry effect, etc.

A Tibetan Herbal Dispensary has also been started in STNM Hospital, Gangtok Sikkim in September 1978 with a qualified practitioner and a nurse. The medicinal requirements of this dispensary are obtained from Tibetan Medical Centre, Dharmasala, Himachal Pradesh. Thus, the health care of most of those who depend on Tibetan medical system are looked after both by the public and private sector practitioners in Sikkim.

Darmasala Tibetan Centre started a Tibetan Herbal Medical Dispensary at Tibetan Centre, Nam Nang in 1987 with a practitioner. All the medical requirements of this centre are obtained from Dharmasala Tibetal Centre. The dispensary uses both powder and pallet form of medicines.

4. Homeopathy:

Dr. Samuel Hahnemann, a German physician founded Homopathic medicine, in the early 1800s (200 years ago). Hahnemann first coined the word 'Homopathy' ('homoios' in Greek means similar, 'pathos' means suffering) to refer to Homopathy's first pharmacological principle – "Simila Similibus Curentu" or "The Law of Similars". This means that a remedy that produces symptoms in a healthy person will cure those same symptoms when manifested by a person in a diseased state. Hahnemann theorized that disease is a disruption in the body's life force, that symptoms of disease are not disease itself, and that the body could be stimulated into healing itself. To prove his theory, he developed the "Law of Similars", a principle that uses substances that can create symptoms of disease to fight disease when given in minute doses.

Today Homopathy is widely prescribed by physicians all over the world and has been practiced in many countries. It can effectively treat many of the chronic ailments and conditions that so many of us suffer today, including allergies, asthma, learning disorders, emotional disorders, arthritis, and the problematic symptoms of menopause. Homopathy Clinical Research Unit was established at Gangtok in 1984. A Private Homopathic clinical centre has also been started at Gangtok after wards.

5. Allopathic or Western Medical Health Care:

***(a)* The Early Years (1880-1915):** McKay (2005) comprehensively reviewed the introduction of Western Medical Health Care in Sikkim in his article published in the Bulletin of Tibetology which is reproduced as it is for the benefit in general in this chapter.

By the late 19th century, it was established practice in the British Empire for Medical Officers (generally from the Indian Medical Service), to accompany Political Officers touring or stationed in remote areas. Originally this had been to ensure the diplomats' good health, but it had become apparent to the imperial policy-makers that the physicians could make a substantial contribution to the diplomatic success of the indigenous peoples, both elites and non-elites. The good-will gained from this was seen as an important part of the political project of obtaining indigenous consent to British rule, and this "political" role became the primary reason for the presence of Medical Officers in states such as Sikkim.

When J. C. White first took up his post as Assistant Political Officer, the military medical staff that had served on the 1888-89 Sikkim campaign remained there under the command of Dr. J.K.Close of Indian Medical Service (IMS). After his departure, a Surgeon-Captain, Dr. D.G.

Marshall, was posted to Gangtok in 1891 to act as White's Medical Officer, and Surgeon Captain Dr. A.W.T. Buist-Sparks replaced him the following year. In 1893, Surgeon Captain Dr. G.F.W. Ewens replaced him and remained there at Gangtok until 1895 (McKay, 2004: 26).

These officers were the first biomedical physicians to reside in Sikkim, and given that three of them later reached the rank of lieutenant colonel, and that Marshall had topped the examinations in his intake, they must have been among the better than average physicians in the imperial service. But Western medicine in such outputs did not then represent the scientific advances of the late 19th century as it would a decade later, and there is little evidence of their making any great impact on the medical world of Sikkim. Indeed their services may have been given only to White and his immediate circle; certainly in the absence of the banished Chogyal it was impossible to implement the usual imperial medical strategy of first impressing the ruling elites (Mitra, 1969: 6).

These early physicians do not appear to have had a proper dispensary, and even the conditions in which they lived were primitive. Describing the later development of Gangtok, White refers to an unnamed Medical Officer and his wife in this early period "who lived in a two-roomed hut built of wattle and dab", where their wooden furniture was liable to sprout in the rainy season (White, 1992: 36). A Government medical dispensary was finally opened in Gangtok in the 1896-97 housed in small shed with a very basic facility. The medicine racks and table for despensing occupied half of the space. The compounder as his residence was utilizing the remaining half portion of the shed with a partition wall. There is no record of any European physician having replaced Ewens, and it seems likely that an Indian-trained Sikkimese medical assistant then served in the Gangtok dispensary. Certainly by 1905 the dispensary was under the control of Civil Hospital Assistant H.N. Mitra, who remained there for some years. The first brief statistical report on Sikkim state provide the daily average number of patients at Gangtok dispensary between 1896-97 to 1901-02 year-wise was 6.5, 7.4, 7.4, 5.9, 5.3 and 12.8 respectively. In June 1902 another state dispensary was opened in Chidam, and around this time a third dispensary opened at Rongpo. The latter was under the charge of the Public Works Department. With the establishment of these institutions, a structural basis for future medical developments had been made (Mitra, 1969: 6).

From 1902-03, Sikkim became an important staging post for what is popularly known as the "Younghusband mission". White requested the appointment of "a man experience and tact" to administer both civil and military medical matters in Sikkim, and it was eventually agreed to establish a new IMS position of Assistant Civil Surgeon at Gangtok to supervise all medical matters in Sikkim state, including the state and missionary dispensaries, jails, schools, and personal attendance on the Chogyal and his family. The first Civil Surgeon appointed to Gangtok was Assistant Surgeon 2nd Class John Nelson Turner, born in 1871, a member of the Indian Subordinate Medical Service, and not a qualified doctor and took up his post in August 1909. He remained in Sikkim until early in 1920. When Turner arrived in Gangtok, the three government dispensaries at Gangtok, Chidam and Rongpo, had, in the previous year 1908-09 treated around 14,000 patients. In addition, three Church of Scotland Mission dispensaries in the State, to which the Government contributed an annual sum of Rs.250 had treated more than 9,000 patients (McKay, 2004: 29).

After annexation of Darjeeling area of Sikkim in 1935, and Kalimpong area from Bhutan in 1966, the Christian missionaries were already working in Kalimpong-Darjeeling by 1880 and the expansion of their activity to Sikkim was a logical consequence. In spite of the Chogyal' resistance, the Scottish missionaries were successful in opening a dispensary at Chidam staffed by a compounder, Elatji Matiyas, a Lepcha convert to Christianity in 1897. By 1906 further dispensaries staffed by local Christian Coumpounders had been opened at Rhenock, Seriyong, and Dentam. In 1906 they dealt with 5,734 cases, and by 1910 three more dispensaries had been opened. Additional dispensaries followed, and by 1923-24 there were a total of 11 mission dispensaries in Sikkim, including one opened at Lachung in North Sikkim by the Scandinavian Alliance Mission, which established a base there with two female missionaries in 1894. Compounders trained by the missionaries in Kalimpong staffed both government and missionary dispensaries, and their standards, facilities and resources must have been similar. While eventually overtaken by State initiatives, the missionaries continued to be important agents for the spread of medicine, particularly in remote areas, down to the 1930s and 1940s (McKay, 2004: 31).

(*b*) Medical Development Between 1915 to 1940: By 1915 considerable progress had been made towards the indigenisation of western medicine in Sikkim. While the colonial state did, in many senses, use medicine as a tool of empire, it was also part of the ideological justification for empire; providing humanitarian provision to the citizens of the colonial state in return for their assent to colonial rule. It was also a tool that the imperial Government wished to give up. The provision of medical services was expensive, and it became more so as Western medicine developed new therapies and technologies. The indigenisation of medicine was thus both an economic necessity, and (at least from the British perspective) a humanitarian service (McKay, 2004:33).

Tibet and Bhutan did not develop any significant indigenous Western medical tradition during the British period. But in Sikkim the indigenisation of medicine proceeded steadily. While Sikkim state's closer treaty links to British India and the political alliance that developed between the British and the Sikkimese aristocracy fostered this process, the key factor appears to have been the number of Sikkimese who had received a Western education. The Government and mission schools in Darjeeling and Kalimpong, and in Sikkim itself from 1880s, provided a small but regular supply of youths, either from the Sikkimese aristocracy or the Lepcha and Nepali Christian communities, who were educated in the Western system. Such an education was an essential precursor to the biomedical training process, imparting the modern scientific worldview necessary for the understanding of medicine. Western medicine in Sikkim thus developed local social characteristics with the Buddhist aristocracy occupying the higher positions in the developing medical structures, while the native Christians from traditionally lower status social groups, filled the lower ranks of compounders, dressers, and nurses (McKay, 2004:34).

During White's residency, no Sikkimese appear to have progressed beyond compounder qualifications, but his successor Charles Bell sent the first three students from Sikkim to Temple Medical College in Patna, two were immediately posted to a Political Department dispensary in Tibet when they graduated. These men were Tonyot Tsering and Bo Tsering, both Kalimpong educated Sikkimese, who graduated as Sub-Assistant Surgeons in 1913 and 1914 respectively. Their contemporary, Bhowani Das Prasad Pradhan, was placed in charge of the Chidam dispensary in 1913. Thus, as the structures of a state medical system began to be developed in Sikkim, the emerging Sikkimese medical graduates filled vacancies. Their training was financed from the Sikkim state revenues. Thus, in 1924-25, Lobzang Mingyur, who was sent to Campbell Medical School Calcatta was posted at the Gangtok hospital as an extra compounder after his training. During 1920s, registration of births and deaths was made compulsary, while a Civil Veterinary Department was established with a hospital and dispensary at Gangtok under a Babu Bannerjee, and dog licenses were introduced, with orders given to destroy dogs without the appropriate discs. In addition, sanitary measures were introduced in the Gangtok Bazar (McKay, 2004:33).

The 9th Chogyal Sir Thutob Namgyal, Sidkeon Tulku and Tashi Nangyal were very supportive of modernization. On 24th September 1917, Sir Tashi Namgyal officially opened the Sir Thutob Namgyal Memorial Hospital. Situated on a ridge overlooking Gangtok, it began with beds for 10 in-patients, and charge of it was given to a state Medical Officer of Sikkimese nationality. The hospital became the centre of medicine in

Sikkim, although it was initially poorly equipped until 1923-24 for example, did it have a microscope. But additional specialist wards were added; a tuberculosis ward in the late 1920s and a maternity ward in the late 1930s, after a trained midwife was posted to the hospital in 1929-30. In 1923-24, just about 8,000 patients attended the hospital, which increased to 16,000 by 1933-34. On the 1st November 1922, Dr. John Turner was replaced as Gangtok Surgeon by an Anglo-Indian, Dr. John Charles Dyer, and he was replaced by Dr. Kenneth Percival Elloy in 1928. Dr Kenneth was replaced by Dr.W.St.A. Hendricks in 1932. In the early years several individuals who had trained as compounders in Kalimpong and worked in dispensaries in the region began private biomedical practice in Sikkim, although it was not until the 1970s that fully-qualified doctors set up private practice there. Until then, any Sikkimese qualifying as a doctor would be observed into government service (McKay, 2004:33).

(c) The Modern Era (Post- 1940): The departure of the British had little medical impact in Sikkim. The last of the imperial Civil Surgeons, Dr. G.F. Humphreys IMS, was an experienced doctor who had served as the Medical Officer in Gyantse from October 1940 to May 1944, and had visited Lhasa in 1942-43 as accompanying physician to two American emissaries. As an Anglo-Indian, he stayed on in Gangtok until the mid-1950s, providing continuity throughout the transitional post-colonial period. The Sikkimese Sub-Assistant Surgeons who had served in the imperial dispensaries in Tibet withdrew back to Sikkim during 1950s as the Chinese take-over of Tibet intensified, thus increasing the pool of experienced medical practitioners available to the Sikkim state. Patient numbers continued to increase to 115,060 in 1954 to 188,526 in 1963. But throughout the 1950s and 1960s, the limited state revenues available restricted medical development in Sikkim. At the time of the Indian take-over in 1975, there were just four district hospitals in addition to the STNM Hospital in Gangtok, and the bulk of medical consultation took place in rural dispensaries and primary health care centres staffed by compounders, who thus remained the principal interface between allopathic medicine and the local patients (Mitra, 1969: 5).

During this period, the Sikkimese health services were heavily reliant on the variable commitment of Indian specialists employed on short-term contracts. But an indigenous class of medical specialists capable of administering and operating Sikkim's medical services was developing. Rather ironically, more indigenous Sikkimese occupy the higher ranks of the public health service today than was the case in independent Sikkim before 1975. The first generation of Sikkimese practitioners of allopathic medicine was not fully qualified doctors. Men like Bo and Tonyot Tsering were Licensed Medical Fellows. But by the 1940s, a new generation of qualified doctors began to emerge, largely from the small group of Western educated Sikkimese who formed a bureaucratic class serving the Chogyal and colonial governments. Among the new generation of medical practitioners Rai Bahadur Tonyot Tsering, Dr. Pemba, T. Tonyot, Dr. Tsering Tendup Kazi (first Sikkimese MD), Dr. Tsewang Palzor (first Sikkimese Surgeon), Dr T.R.Gyatso, and Dr Mrs Leki Dadul (first Sikkimese lady doctor).

Along with the doctors and licensed practitioners, the profession of nursing also developed in Sikkim, albeit that the profession is still not of particularly high status. In 1954, Mrs Sonam Eden (Phigoo) and Mrs Prabitra Pradhan, were sent for nurse training to Scottish Missionary under Dr. Albert Craig After completion of the study Phigoo was posted to the STNM Hospital where she remained until retiring in 1995 after 40 years of service (McKay, 2004:33).

(*d*) Postscript: Sikkim today, the STNM Hospital straddles a main Gangtok intersection. As of 2006, it was a 300 bed hospital, with 78 doctors including 36 specialists of staff under the chrge of Director-cum-Medical Superintendent Dr. H. Pradhan. In 1999, 351 major and 984 minor surgical operations were carried out there. The number of patients treated during 1999 reaching 140,000. For medical purpose the state is divided into four districts, each under a Chief Medical Officer who is also head of the central hospital in that district. A network of primary health care centres and sub-centres exists in each district, and medical services remain largely free of cost. A subjective judgement considering patient-doctpor relations, service morale, non-elite class access, and not least financial probity, as well as numerous statistical indicators, would suggest Sikkimese tody enjoy among the better biomedical services in India (McKay, 2004:33).

With the beginning of the 21st century, a new medical college-Manipal Referral Hospital was started at Tadong, East Sikkim in 2002 for medical education of the people. The State desires to foster a better health care umbrella with a good network of hospitals, district hospitals, primary health centres and sub-centres for allopathic treatment; Ayurvedic medical centres, Tibetan Herbal Medical Centres, and Homopathic medical centres scattered throughout the state for treatment of all types of the patients.

12

The Lepchas (Rongs, Mon-Pas)

Socio-Status: Scheduled Tribes

Origin and History:

The Lepchas (Rongs or Mon-pas) are a mongoloid people living in the Himalayas on the southern and eastern slopes of Mount Kanchenjunga. It seems certain that they were one of the aboriginal inhabitants of this large tract of mountainous land namely, the present areas. of Sikkim, Ilam area of present Nepal, Chumbi valley of Tibet autonomous region of China, Har Chu valley and Ammo Chu valley of present Bhutan. The anthropologists, those who believe on the theory of migration, suggested that the Lepchas migrated in antiquity from the various parts of Tibet and Mongolia, and a certain similarity has apparently been found between the Lepcha language and some dialect spoken in Indo-China. However, the Lepchas claim that Sikkim is the origin and home of their ancestors (Gorer, 1938: 35; Hermanns, 1954: 107). They refer to their homeland as "*ne mayel lyang*" (hidden paradise) or "*ne mayel maluk lyang*" (land of eternal purity). The Lepcha call themselves "*mutunci rongkup rumkup*" which means "children of the Rong and of God" or simply "*rongkup*" "children of the Rong". They also call themselves "*rong ?agit*" "the Rong tribe". The Lepcha word for language is *?aring*, and the Lepcha call their own language as "*rongring*" (Plaisier, 2005: 7).

The name "Lepcha" has been derived from a Nepali word Lapche, meaning "vile speakers". They call themselves Rong; the Tibetans call them Mon, and the Bhutanese, Meri. Their own tradition, however, states that their original home was in the neighborhood of the great mountain, *Kang-chen-mdzod-lnga* the third highest mountain in the world. That is the Tibetan name and means the "Great Glacier of the Five Store-rooms". The Lepcha name for the mountain is, "*King-tzum-song-bu*". *King-tzum* means "Highest part of the forehead," *song-bu* means "the highest". Literally it means, "the highest over our head." The Tibetans reproduce this Lepcha name phonetically as "*Kang-chen-mdzod-lnga*," which has quite a different meaning. The ancient tradition of the Lepcha says that the progenitor Lepchas "Fodong-Theeng" and "Na-Jong-Nyu" were created by their God *Rum* out of the snows of the untrodden peak of the *King-tzum-Song-bu* mountain. This snow-covered mountain has an important part to play as the habitat of the spirits. *King-tzum-rum* is the god of happiness; *Rum-king-tzum* is the god of fate. From it the Lepchas derive the name Rong, by which they are known. Rong means "peak" or "mountain peak" and has the same significance as the word *Arong* (Hermanns, 1954: 107; Plaisier, 2005: 7-19).

According to one opinion the Lepchas are supposed to have come from Tibet, but from the east of the mountains from Assam and Upper Burma (White,1909: 7).

The Lepchas call themselves "*Rong-Kup*" or "*Mutanchi Riongkup*". "*Rong*" means both "to wait" and "Peak", "*Mutanchi Rongkup*" means mother's loved ones.; mother here standing for Mother as creator whom Lepchas call *Itbumo*. The Tibetans know Lepchas as "*Mon-pa*", the term meaning the Kirate tribe of the low land (Singh, 1993: 89-103).

Another tradition has it that the place of the Lepcha origin is on the holy mountain *Kailasa* (*Ti se*) way up in Tibet. On the mountain is the stone Ne-long that bears the footprints of Buddha and of animals. The god, *Pum-rum*, protector of the hunters, live there. *Pum-rum* is also another name for the Supreme God of the Lepchas (Hermanns, 1954:107).

The Lepchas call Sikkim *Ney-Meyel-Renjyong-Lyang*, i.e., the sacred place inhabited by honest and peace loving people. The Tsongs or Limboos call it Yioksom (one of the fortified place) and later Sukhim i.e. the new palace/home. The Bhutias call it Denjong, i.e. the land of paddy. The Lepchas or Rongs claim that they are the indigenous people of the sacred hidden land, which was also called *Lep* in ancient time. The Lepchas love to call themselves *Rong-Kup-Pum-Kum,* i.e., the beloved children of Mother Nature and god (Subba, 1999; Gurung & Lama, 2004:107; Plaisier, 2005: 7-19).

The chronology and history of the Lepchas are obscure and it is said that they had no written document as they were not having their own script and writing system developed or the records and manuscripts were destroyed during the Tibetan invasion (Foning, 1987). It is said that the Lepcha King (petty tribal king of Sikkim region) Tarvey Panu ruled the land around 1420 A.D. Out of the ten Panus the name of Thekung Tek comes up prominently as the leader of the Lepchas, but he was a spiritual leader rather than a political one (Gurung & Lama, 2004: 108). The date mentioned for the Blood Brotherhood agreement of Kabi Lungchok between Thikung Tek and Khe-Bumsa, is often recorded as 13th century (1275 AD). Phuntsho Namgyal, the first Chogyal of Sikkim (1642) was the sixth generation of Khye-Bumsa. In the absence of any historical evidence regarding the Blood Brotherhood Treaty of Kabi Lungchok and the Lepcha Panus (Kings), it is very difficult to ascertain the date of the event and the reign of the Lepcha Panus (Mullard, 2005).

According to Halfdan Sieger (1967) the Lepcha chieftainship of Mayel Lyang (present Sikkim) were ten in numbers, namely, Thekong Adek (7-8th Century), Thup Athak (9-10th Century), Thekong Tek (13th Century), Rujo Panu/Athing (1353 – 1410 AD), Tarvey Panu (1425-1454 AD), Tarsong Panu (1454-1481 AD), Tar-eng Panu (1481-1520 AD), Tarjyi Panu (1520-1564 AD), Tar-eak Panu (1564-1595 AD), and Thekong Mun Solong Panu (the last Panu who witness the consecration of the First Chogyal of Namgyal Dynasty 1595-1642 AD).

According to Thotup Namgyal and Yeshe Dolma (translated by Dawa Samdup in 1908: 19-29), "The three communities the Lhorees (Bhutias), the Monrees (Lepchas) and the Tsongrees (Limboos) are the oldest inhabitants of Sikkim. Among these the origin and history of the Lepcha race as far as can be ascertained runs thus":

"The foremost tribe of Lepchas who are known to have existed in Sikkim, was called "***nah-angs***" who were a race of barbarians who dwelt in a place called Lunghem near Dallam, but this tribe soon died out and there are none of them now in Sikkim. There appear to be in reality about 12 different clans among Lepchas. They are: (1) The Sengdeng-mo, (2) Lingsim-mo, (3) Hee-mo, (4) Karthok-mo, (5) and the descendants of Thekong Salung. The rest are named after the places they inhabit, e. g. (6) Tug-nyee-mo: living towards Chumthang, (7) Sampa-putso-mo, living towards Namthen and Tsidam, (8) Targok-mo: living towards Rinchenpong, etc. There are 36 such different clans mentioned in the list of the Maharaja. Each family has been called by the name of the place where they lived. .... Further each clan of Lepchas again ascribes their own origin". The Maharaja has mentioned in details of the origin of each of these clans, mode of worship, life rituals etc. in his unpublished book (ibid).

Contrary to the Maharaja's "nah-angs" above and that of "nah-angs" mentioned in Encyclopedaea Britanica, A.R.Foning states that the word "***Na-ong***" in Lepcha language means "dumb" or "Simpleton" which is a "Tung-bor" or "innuendo" commonly referred to the ones who erected the Tower of Babel at Daramdin, West Sikkim. It refers to the Lepcha tribes only (Foning, 1987: 170-171).

Population and Settlement:

According to 1891 census, the total population of Lepchas in Sikkim was 5,762 persons (2,362 males, 2,399 females and 1,001 children) i.e.

18.92% of the total population and the highest amongst the communities of Sikkim. In 1931, the Lepcha population was 13,060 that was 11.89% of the total population. According to the voter list of 2004, the Lepcha population of Sikkim was 48,811 persons that was 8.46% of the total population of Sikkim. There are only about 29,854 Lepcha mother tongue speakers in the country (Census of India, 1991).

Geographical Distribution:

The areas with higher concentration of Lepcha population are: Dzongu, Mangan, and Kabi-Tingda in the North district; Ragdong-Tintek, Rumtek, Ranka, and Assam Linjey in the East district; Wok and Rateypani. in the South district; and Rinchenpong, Daramdin, Dentam, and Tashiding in the West district of Sikkim. They live in extreme cold climate with high rainfall and medium snowfall. They do not stay in snowbound places but live in lower altitudes in contrast to the Bhutias. The Dzongu area, which consists of 13 Revenue blocks, out of the 45 Revenue Blocks in the North District, has been treated as a Lepcha reserve for quite some time and lies in the lower ranges of Kanchenjunga where the main river Teesta flows. Outsiders are not allowed to settle in this Lepcha reserve area (Singh, 1993:89-103). .

Bio-anthropological Information:

Except serology and genetical information other bio-anthropological information is not available. So far as serological data are concerned, only three samples are available for the Lepcha population. These data were collected mainly from Sikkim and the Darjeeling district of West Bengal. The gene frequency ranges from 22-23% for p, 16-19% for q and 59-61% for r. The gene p^2 is found to be absent whenever sub-grouping has been conducted. Data on Rh and Mn systems are also available for this population. Besides serological data, data on the secretor facrtor, taste ability (PTC) and colour-blindness are also available for the Sikkimese Lepchas (Morpurgo et al. 1983).

Food Habits:

The Lepchas are non-vegetarians. They eat beef, pork, mutton, but beef is their favorite dish followed by pork and mutton. Their staple food is maize, wheat, rice, millet and buckwheat. The root and tuber crops, fern shoots, bamboo shoots, several types of fungi and innumerable kinds of wild plants are their favorite dish. Their favorite fermented foods are *Gnuchi, Shakampo, Kargyong, and Kheuri*; alcoholic beverages are *Chee, Bhatijaanr, Makai ko jaanr, Gahoon ko jaanr, Simal tarul ko jaanr, Jao ko jaanr, Phapar ko jaanr,* and *Arak*; traditional non-fermented foods are *Kalungey chew, Kanney chew, Nakima, Thukpa, Gyathuk, Nya phachung,*

Moongarbuk, Kasalok, Sorongbee tuluk, Cho-nyok, Po Nguzom, Khu zom, etc. (For details please see Food culture). The Lepchas use a lot of fermented drinks and their life is very much associated with *Chee* (fermented liquor) and *Arak* (local distilled alcohol). They need it in every phase of their life, even in sacramental rites and rituals. Their cultural as well as natural surroundings provide them an ample opportunities to common alcohol, which keeps them warm and provides them energy to maintain social relation and their cultural heritage (Tamang, 2005).

Family Pattern:

The Lepchas have no caste distinctions but they are divided into groups by birth and marriage. The Lepcha family is patrilocal or exogamous *putse/ptso*, which is believed to have originated from some supernatural or legendary ancestor. The descent is reckoned through the male. Some of the *putse* are *sangdenmoo, lingsingmoo, karyokmoo, heemoo, karyakmoo, thyungmen-solongmoo* etc. The chief function of the *putse* now consists in regulation of marriage and prevention of incestuous relationships. In earlier days the *putse* represented a geographical unit. Each *putse* is under the guardianship of a certain supernatural being whom all the male members of the putse worship. The exact number of clan/*putse* in the tribe is not known. Some of them use clan names as surnames. The father is economically head of the family (Gurung & Lama, 2004: 128-131; Singh, 1983: 90).

Family Property:

After the father's death, the living sons equally divide the landed properties of their father, while the mother's ornaments is generally provided to the daughters. The eldest son succeeds after his father's death. Since the widow and daughters do not receive any share of the land, and as they usually live with the eldest son of the deceased person, he gets an extra share of the property for their maintenance (Singh, 1983: 90).

Gender Issues:

Women have no right of inheritance. They have a great role however in the agricultural operation from sowing to harvesting. They feed and nurture the animals, but women must never on any account kill an animal. They collect fuel and fodder for the family, and portable water from the spring. Women can spin and men weave. Women have a role in other economic activities and social functions too. Women prepare the meal and distribute it in the family. They have a role in religious and ritual spheres too. The Lepcha women can become a *Mun* (Singh, 1983: 90).

Kinship and Social Organization:

The Modern Lepcha divide themselves into four main groups according to region they inhabit. The Lepcha from Kalimpong, Kurseong,

Mirik and Darjeeling are known as "*tamsangmu*", the Lepcha from Sikkim are called "*renjongmu*". The smaller group of Lepcha living in the Ilam district of eastern Nepal are known as "*?ilammu*" and the Lepcha who live in prolyang "Bhutan" are referred to as "*prõmu*". A special area in North Sikkim holds the Dzongu Lepcha reserve, a Lepcha conservation area where but few outsiders have been allowed to settle. The type of the Lepcha family is nuclear and vertically extended. There is a tendency now towards the nuclear family and a steady decline of the joint and extended family systems. The Lepchas are divided into various clans or families known as '*putsho*' and each clan has its own '*da*' "lake" and "cu" "mountain peak". The '*cu*' are regularly honoured in '*cu rumfaat*' 'mountain worship' ceremonies. In the Kalimpong area, the origin of the clan names is traditionally explained as follows: when the evil king *hlaso mung* 'Lhasa Devil' was killed by Tamsang Thing 'Lord Tamsang", then the Lord Tansang expressed his gratitude to 108 men by bestowing upon each of them an honorary title, as well as placing each of them under the protection of a specific lake and mountain peak. Thus, honorary titles developed into clan names, such as Luksommu, Simikmu, Sadamu etc. Although most Lepcha know to which putsho they belong, they do not always know the corresponding '***da***' and '***cu***'. Today the full clan name may be shortened, e.g. Simik from Simikmu, Foning from Fonyung rumsongmu etc. (Gurung & Lama, 2004: 124).

Avoidance relationships exist between mother-in-law and son-in-law, daughter-in-law and father-in-law, sister-in-law and (y) BW and elder brother-in-law H(e) B etc. A free relationship exists between sister-in-law (e) BW and brother-in-law H (y) B, with sister-in-law W(e) S and W(y) S and brother-in-law W(e) B and W(y)B and grand-parents and grandchildren. Whenever required one family helps to other especially at the time of house-building, marriage, death and on other occasions whenever help is sought.

Economic Activity:

Land and forest are the main sources of their economy. While individual proprietors control the land, the Government controls the forest area. Traditionally they had been hunters and food-gatherers and preferred animal husbandry before they became cultivators. Now they cultivate rice, maize, millets, barley, ginger, potatoes, all kinds of vegetables, oranges, peach, plum, pear, guava, banana and large cardamom. As a subsidiary occupation they go for business, government services and self-employment. Urban Lepchas are mostly service holders.

Dresses:

The Lepchas can be identified by its typical dress. With the advent of the western way of living the Lepchas living in the towns and nearby towns have adopted the western style in their dress. In the far flung areas of the villages one could still come across people wearing their tribal dresses. The Lepcha women still weave the clothes of cotton fibres in their handlooms of different designs or pattern for their daily use. The Lepcha men wear:

Dum-Praa: It is also called *Gada* and is woven for men. It has two uses as a dressing garment during the day and as blanket during the night. These dresses have the following design and patterns: (*a*) *Tagaap*: The oldest design; (*b*) *Khemchu*: It has scissors like pattern; and (*c*) *Tamblyoak*: it has a butterfly like design.

Koojoo Vaadoah: This oldest dress is made of Koojo a kind of nettle plant. It has a natural colour of darkish green.

Thakroah: It is made of soft fibers and does not have any embroidery. It is multi-coloured with typical Lepcha patterns.

Menchhyo: It has beautiful embroidery at the top and the end of the dress.

Tago: A loose shirt with stiff high neck. It is worn during hunting and fishing expeditions.

Tomoo: Lepcha trousers reaching up to the calf. These are worn while working in the fields. They are whitish in colour and are made of thick cotton fibers.

Tanggyip : It is also called *Tokvyoal* and is a typical Lepcha bag and is hung on the shoulders.

Thyaak Tak: It is known as *Shymboo*. It is a round Lepcha hat made of fur or black velvet. The hat is decorated with bird feathers and generally worn during ceremonies and social functions.

Papri: A hat made of cane or bamboos and is worn during fishing or hunting expeditions.

Samoak: It is artistically made with fine and small cane splits. The hat is fine specimen of Lepcha art and craft. In the olden days a male Lapcha Mu wore it. This was also the headgear of the Sikkim guards during the Chogyal regime. The hat now costs about Rs. 5,000.

Yaanglo: It is a shawl generally worn by rich Lepcha gentleman. It has no pattern and is maroon and white in colour.

The Lepcha women wear *Dum Bun, Jyoordong Tago, Tago* and *Taroa.*

Dum Bun: The other name is *Dum Den* or *Dumdyan*. It is a Lepcha ladies dress and is made from the silk.

Jyoordong Tago: A long sleeved flowing gown over *Dam Bun* and is worn by the married Lepcha ladies. Rich ladies wear gown of Chinese velvet silk.

Tago: A loose blouse worn with *Dum Bun* but it has no pattern and is reddish in colour.

Taroo: A scarf of white colour worn by women around their heads.

Usually, the men's upper garment is called the *gada* and the lower garment is the *tamoo*. Men wear half *pyjamas* (*Tomoo*) down to the knees, and a robe, upon a white cotton cloth crossed over the chest and shoulders and descending till the calves leaving the arms bare. A loose jacket is worn over the robe and is bound round the waist by a girdle called the *khingjiya*. They also wear strings of coloured beads round the neck, earrings (silver, coral, gold etc.) and a long knife called the *banfok*, or *payak*, constantly worn by male members of all ages and ranks. Women wear the *dumdyan or Dum Bun*. They wear a full sleeve blouse (*Tago*), and the *Boku* (*itisko*). As headgear they wear a striped scarf in a different style. Women also wear colourful bead necklaces (*alvak*), earrings (*nay-kong*) and bangles (*akager*) (Gurung & Lama, 2004: 128-131; Singh, 1983: 90).

Folk Musical Instruments:

The following are the main folk instruments of the Lepcha:

Palitkeng : Flute with four holes;

Pentong : Flute;

Pentong Palit : Bigger Flute with Four Holes;

Nibryok Palit : double barrel flute;

Satsang : Sarangi;

Tanbuk : A kind of Sarangi or Vina;

Tang Dar : A small round drum;

Chakpurjang : Longish drum;

Bom Pochuat : A kind of whistle;

Tangue : a small musical instrument made of bamboo and played by tongue;

Sahnai : A kind of Sahnai (Gurung & Lama, 2004:128).

Folk Songs:

The folk songs of the Lepchas are broadly divided into the following categories:

1. *Lenchyovom*: Love songs;
2. *Thanung Savom*: Songs of humour;
3. *Asyot Vom*: Ceremonial songs;
4. *Rum Kat Vom*: Songs relating to agriculture;
5. *Bivom*: Songs sung during marriages;
6. *Lyang-Niro-Chyko-Vom*: Patriotic songs;
7. *Apart-Apok-Vom*: Songs of planting season; and
8. *Aprya-Vom*: is a prayer to god.

There are nine *Saat* or Ragas in Lepcha songs. Some of these are: *Tashekyonto Saat, Apik Saat, Pildon Saat, Heet Saat, Tang Sang Saat,* and *Palik Saat.* These have been evolved and classified according to the sounds produced by the humble bee, humming bird, hedge sparrow and other natural sounds. The Lepchas believe that the ragas have come out from the mouth of the holy ***Mun*** (Gurung & Lama, 2004: 124).

Folk Dances:

The Lok or the folk dances of the Lepchas are broadly classified as follows:

1. Nature Dance;
2. *Zomal-lok*: Dance relating to agriculture;
3. *Fen-lok*: War dance;
4. *Pasyalyon* or *Guru-lok*-Historical dance;
5. *Yaba-lok*: Mystic dance; and
6. Dance relating to Mythology.

The nature dance tries to catch the spirit of its different subjects in various forms. This dance imitates the different movement of different creatures. *Zoma*l dance exhibit five distinct agricultural activities viz:, ploughing, sowing, weeding, harvesting, and thrashing. The dancers wear maroon colour head band and crown on their head. They wrap colourful home woven cotton clothes around their bodies which are attached with bamboo pins. The hair of the girls are done in such a fashion that they look like the parted tail of a bird called *Chahem fo* (Gurung & Lama, 2004: 125).

Festival:

1. Naam Soong or Namboon: It is the Lepcha New Year, which falls every year in the month of Lepcha calendar (*Kurnyit Lavo*) during the last week of December to the first week of January, which is celebrated for a week in Sikkim, Kalimpong and Darjeeling. This is one of most important festivals of the Lepcha and is connected with the legend when truth triumphed over evil and brought ever-lasting peace in the land of the Kanchenjunga. Rum (God) created the earth, the hills, dales and mountains, the sun, the moon, and the stars. He also created the air and the water, the trees, vegetation, animals and many other things of the earth. God also created day and night. At last he picked up two fistful of snow in both hands from the top of the sacred Kanchanjunga, and from the right hand he created "Man" whom he called "*Fodong-Theeng*" which means most powerful and from the left hand he created "*Na-Jong-Nue*" the woman which means full of everlasting bliss. The Lepcha believe that these two were their first ancestors. Out of the progenies some became demons while others the Lepchas. The demons wanted to kill the Lepchas but the God created "*Tamsang Theng*" who killed all the demons and saved the Lepchas. To this day Lepchas celebrate a victory over the demon king "*Lasho-Mung_Panu*" every year. This is the festival of triumph of good over evil. The Lepchas go door to door singing "*Lasho*". The happy tidings are thus conveyed to every house of the Lepchas.

2. Tendong Lho Rum Faat festival: This festival is celebrated on the 8th August every year with great pomp and splender in Sikkim. The State Government has declared state holiday since 1997. This festival is connected with a legend of deluge which nearly swallowed Sikkim which was ultimately stopped by Rum (God) and saved Sikkim from drowning. (See details under Folk Culture).

3. Muk Zikding Rum Faat: This festival is connected with nature and its greenery. It is observed in the month of February every year. It is the season of sprouting of all vegetation, trees, shrubs and is also the mating season of all animals and birds. The *Boongthing* offers prayers to Rum for timely rains and sunshine, clean air and water and to save the world from the natural calamities of flood, landslide and famine in this festival. The altar is decorated with all kinds of shrubs, medicinal herbs, food crops, flowers and a stone pillar called *Lungchaok* is erected near the altar.

Language and Literature:

The Lepchas have their own language known as "*Rongring*", and their own Lepcha script "*Mutanchi Rong Aming*" with 28 consonants and eight conjoint letters. The Lepcha language has been recognized as an official language in 1977. During Namgyal Dynasty the Lepchas were not allowed to develop their language and literature and they had to study Tibetan language and literature compulsorily. Since 1977, the Textbook

Unit of Education Department, Government of Sikkim is preparing textbooks for the schools. Since 2000 AD, College level study of Lepcha, Bhutia and Limboo language has started and thus, the textbook Unit is also preparing colleges textbooks for the college level study for all these three languages also. Now, the Lepcha language is taught in schools and colleges, there is a textbook unit that develops official learning materials, there is a Lepcha edition of a government newspaper, the Sikkim Herald, and the government radio station broadcasts news bulletins and cultural programmes in the Lepcha language.

Religion and Belief System:

The central religious roles in the Lepcha community are traditionally occupied by the *bongthing* and *mun*, who both function as shamans. The *bongthing* is traditionally a male shaman who presides at recurring religious ceremonies and seasonal festivals and may heal acute illness. The *mun*, often but not necessarily a female shaman, is a healer who exorcises demons, helps to heal illness and guides souls to the afterlife. It is possible for a *bongthing* to develop into a *mun*, in Sikkim such healers are known as *Padem*. In the 18th century, the Lepcha people were converted to Buddhism, although indigenous Lepcha shamans managed to coexist with Buddhist customs and beliefs. Both Buddhist Lamas and Lepcha shamans preside at many important ceremonies in Lepcha life, each to perform their own rituals. Since the middle of the nineteenth century, a significant number of Lepcha people have converted to Christianity. Many Christian Lepchas have lost their language and have distanced themselves from the old shamanistic rituals and beliefs (Plaisier, 2005: 7-9).

The Lepchas consider themselves as the children of the Himalayas. The first man and woman were created by *Rum* (God) out of the snows of the untrodden peak of Kanchenjunga. They are nature worshippers. E.B. Tylor the anthropologist has called it Animism. Many anthropologists think this term is wrong. Animism refers to the worship of nature and natural phenomena, such as rocks, mountains, rivers, streams, thunder and lightening, to ascribing inanimate things as having a soul. The Lepcha, however, do not outright worship these phenomena. They respect their natural surroundings but do not ascribe souls to them. Rather, they think that these places are where spirits live. The spirits as such are not identified with the rocks or trees themselves, but are seen as separate from them. Religious specialists are called shamans, in the west, after a word used by the *Thungus* of Siberia to denote such a person. In the Lepcha language, however, they are called by several names, reflecting a hierarchy of the power that a certain shaman has. The highest class is called *Tung li Mun*. Lower ranks are *Yeba* and *Mun*, and *Bongthing*. The right term to refer this type of religion is Shamanism (Jeffrey, et al, 2000:35).

The Lepchas of Sikkim believe in two types of spirits, the good, which bring, good things to the people and the bad, which do harm to them. They perform religious ceremonies to ward off evil spirits from doing harm to them. They believe in the powers of *Bongthing* and the *Mun* the priest and the priestess. They perform all the ceremonies from birth to death for the Lepcha society as a whole. The term *Bongthing* comes from the two Lepcha words *Aboong* and *Athing*. *Aboong* means mouth and *Athing* means a good orator or speaker. He has powers to stop evil spirits from doing harm. He acquires these super natural powers by constant prayer and deep meditation. There are many Boongthings, but it is said that seven of them are most powerful and respected accordingly. They are: *Thikong-Tek, Thikong-Men-Slong, Tehikung-Daari, Thikong-Aatha, Thikong-Akik, Thikong-Penjo, and Thikong-Sayathon.* They do not only possess supernatural powers but are also able medicine men. They cure the patients by mantras, but also rare medicinal herbs about which they have deep knowledge (Das and Banerjee, 1962: 105-119).

The *Mun* Lepcha priestess too has an equally high place in Lepcha society. The *Muns* have similar powers. It is said that it was *Boongthing* himself who had given the power to them for the good of the society. The *Muns* too are of seven categories: They are *Aabor-Mun, Pin-Don-Mun, Anngan-Mun, Tangli-Mun, Mun-Jyom-Mun, Aur-Mur-Mun* and *Lyang-Ith-Mun*. While chanting the mantras the *Mun* imitates the melodies of different birds, insects, and the sounds coming out of the bamboos with their rubbing due to the flow of the wind. These melodies or ragas are called *Heet-Sat, Tro-Kinto-Sat, Apil-Dan-Sat and Pok-Sat.* These melodies are not loud but like the droning of the bumble bee or the humming of birds.

Various rhythmic tones are used in singing the Lepcha religious mantras. According to P.T.Simick Ngasey (Aachulay 1998), there are seven different tones and they are as follows:

1. *Pomic-Potong-Nyumjyo*: This tone is imitated from the sound of bamboos which is produced due to the blowing of wind in the morning and evening when the bamboos rub each other while swinging to and fro;
2. *Fodong-Nazoane-Nyujyo*: This tone is said to be lamentation of the first Lepcha man Fodong-Theen and the first Lepcha women Najongue. This tone is sad and melancholy.

3. *Lakok-Lanye-Nyumjyo*:
4. *Koying-Duren-Nyumjyo*;
5. *Lafo-Ladong-Nyumjyo*: The above three tones have been adopted from the chirping sounds of a male cicada.The chirping start from March and last upto November in the hills of Sikkim;
6. *Nyulik-Mundong-Nyumjyo*: It is believed that this tone is a gift of Rum (God) to the *Boongthing* and the *Mun*. This tone starts in a slow rhythm but gradually gets faster and faster until the singer starts panting due to exhaustion.
7. *Shim-Vomu-Ungtuk-Sot-Nyumjyo*: This tone flows like the babbling brook of the hills of like the rhythmic flow of a small stream (Gurung & Lama, 2004: 124).

Today, the Lepchas of Sikkim are divided into three religions, Viz., Shamanism or Animism, Buddhism and Christianity.

Rites of Passage (Life-Cycle): Birth, Marriage and Death are the major events of life.

(*a*) Prenatal care: The Lepchas believe that a child's life starts from the baby's movement in the mother's womb. About a month before delivery some especially strong *chee* (Millet beer) is prepared for consumption on the *Thung-Chee* fat, the third day after delivery. After a month again a stronger *chee* is given to the mother. The mother gives birth to the baby in a convenient place. A Mun has to be called in to give his services to help in a difficult delivery or warding off the evil spirits. For the first three days of life, the baby is considered to be still in the womb and all the pre-natal precautions have to be observed. For those three days the mother is forbidden to touch the ground.

(*b*) Birth: On the third day of the birth of the child, a feast on the *Thungbong fat* is performed. The *Mun* performs the birth ceremony of a newly born baby by chanting a prayer for long and peaceful life; protect the child from all ills and the evil spirits, accidents, injuries and all kind of diseases. In the early days for a male child an ox, a pig or a goat was killed for the feast while for a girl child no animal was killed. Now the people cannot afford to do this. During the feast every guest is given three pots of special *chee* and a sufficient quantity of cooked rice. The child's horoscope is prepared at an early date by a Lama. This horoscope contains the sacred name of the child. Finally the child is given a temporary name in keeping with the name of the day on which the child is born. The baby is given a tiny ball of pounded rice mixed with butter, and thereafter a small bit of this mixture is given three times a day. The mother is then only be allowed to go outside, for by then she feels that she is strong enough to perform the household chores.

(*c*) **Marriage:** The marriage is called *Bri* in Lepcha. It actually means the joining of two different parts into one. The Lepchas believe that the union of two people is also the union of two clans, two families and also of two villages of the bride and the bridegroom forever. For the Lepcha marriage is a sacred union and the parents, uncles or aunties generally arrange it.

The Lepchas first send a reliable person or persons to the house of the girl to know the wish of the parents and the girl. It is called *Niyom-Veyet*. According to Maharaja's book (1908: 25), the person had to present a body of the cock, some rice and wine, before the question of proposal for the hand of the maiden is opened. The uncle thereupon after due consultation with the parents of the girl, conveys the acceptance through a *Barmi* (goer between). If the proposal is acceptable, then the *Barmi* is deputed to go to the parents of the girl with a *pathi* of millet beer, and Re.1/= in cash, which is called the *Kha-chang* (wine for the opening of the proposal) called in Lepcha *Abnong-og*. The maternal uncle is presented with Rs.5/-, paternal uncle Rs.5/-, these presents are called *Zhe-go* (*Khelat-a* feast) another Rs.5/- to the brothers and sisters. Next comes the formal naggchang the formal ritual consists of a whole pig, one *Saptu* (basket) of millet beer, one *pathi* of rice, with Rs.5/- in cash, which being duly accepted, a supplementary request with a fee of Re.1/- is offered requesting permission for the intended bridegroom to come into the family, and asking them to fix a date, and to make festive preparations for the occasion.

On the appointed day, the paternal and the maternal uncles of the boy escort him to the house of his intended wife. They are met on the way by the maternal and the paternal uncles of the girl with the body of a fat chicken and wine. The aunts of the bride, both the paternal and maternal uncles' wives do the same also; and this reception they call in Lepcha *Lam-log-tsog*. The Lepchas also have the custom of the elderly females of the bride's side, treating the intended son-in-law and his party to a thrashing with thorns, which also can be averted by the present of Re.1/- to the matrons from the bridegroom. As soon as the latter enters the house and has to be seated, there is a Lepcha custom of placing before him a winnowing vessel of cane work *pikkyab* in Bhutia the bodies of two fat Chicken covered with rice, and any other delicacy. On the whole this is meant to be as nice a treat as the means of the party will admit. Then the Lepcha head or *Bongthing* or *Mun* asks the bridegroom formally where he is going, where he lives, and what he has come for etc. Having answered these questions in the most approved metaphorical style, he then pays the price of the bull for the feast and the milch cow for the price of the girl, the bull is sacrificed and the family gods worshipped. Then the bridegroom presents his bride with a Re.1/- in cash and a pair of silver bangles. Then the bride's parents give some return present to the bridegroom. The price of the girl generally is a milch cow, valued at Rs.15/-, a copper vessel valued at Rs.15/- to Rs.12/-, and cash present of Rs.15/-. Then the mother gets Rs.5/- as *amo-kamchong* and a piece of cloth called *Amo-dum-dem* (mother's raiment), and a *kumberband*. These must be given as they are the customery presents.

Then after 4 days the son-in-law once goes back. Three years after this the final marriage ceremony must be held, to do which, the *Bam* must be sent and permission obtained, which when granted (by the bride's parents), the bride is allowed to leave her parent's house, and go to that of her husband's. She goes escorted by her uncles both paternal and maternal, and her bride-maids, and she has to take with her a present of whole pig, one load of millet beer and Re.1/-, also one pathi of rice. This present is called *Nyom-tsoom*. As soon as she arrives, she is treated to a dish of a whole quarter of a pig fried, which is called *Nyom-zo-olsod*, which means that it is meant to wipe away the perspiration of the bride.

Then the guardians of the bride, that is, her paternal and maternal uncles, as well as one of the elders of the village who might have escorted the bride, fix upon the price of the bull to be sacrificed for the feast, and arrange also the final payment of the price of the girl. As soon as the bull is sacrificed they take the head and the right leg and worship their family gods and deities with it. After this is over, the feasting and drinking begins and is kept up for two or three days, during which both the uncles of the bride are made much of and another fee of Rs.5/- each is presented to each of them. As soon as the feasting is over, the bride is once allowed to visit her parents. She has to take as present her parents Rs.15/- in cash, one load of millet beer, a body of pig. These have to be provided by her husband. After a year, the son-in-law goes to worship the family gods of his wife at her parent's house which ceremony is called *Rum-Faat*. That means another bull, one load of millet beer, one pathi rice, with another cash of Rs.10/- or Rs.5/-, when the family gods are worshipped. This is the final ceremony, after which the husband and wife are sent back together. Then according to the means of the girl's parents the dowry or portion is given, which consists of ornaments, clothings, ponies, or cattle, fowls and pigs, and over and above these the customary portions of one milch cow and calf, Rs.15/- in cash, one bronze vessel, one plate, one *lota*. Only after this has taken place is the ceremony considered to be complete. After this the girl goes to live with her husband permanently as his wife. These customs were so from a very long time (Namgyal and Dolma, 1908:25-27).

But these customs have changed with the passage of time. Now, this old tradition has more or less disappeared and the marriage ceremony is performed combining all the rituals into one. The *Bongthing* performs the marriage ceremony. The bride and the bridegroom are seated on a high pedestal representing the two mountain peaks of the Himalayas. The *Bongthing* then begins to chant the religious prayers on the occasion holding a wooden cup in his right hand filled with rice and millet beer and a small quantity of butter. He then begins to address the gathering saying that they have all gathered on this solemn occasion to marry these two young couple. This is the wish of the almighty God. The first couple to be married was their ancestors *Tar-Bongboo and Narip-Nom.*

He blesses the bride and the bridegroom by saying that their lives be steady and peaceful like the two sacred peaks of the Himalayas. Let them be no harm to them from any where. Let their married life be filled with everlasting peace. Let them bear children to increase the Lepcha race and let them be strong and healthy. The Boongthing then sprinkles the millet Chee towards the sky also on the bride and bridegroom. He then hands over the cup to the bride from which she sips the Chee thrice. The bridegroom also does the same followed by the relatives of the bridegroom. It is a sacred drink for the sacred occasion, which binds one another into a holy union. After completing the ritual the cup is again handed over the Boongthing. The cup is filled up again as before. The Boongthing then announces the names of the bride and the bridegroom, and declares that they are now husband and wife from this day. He hands over the cup to the bridegroom who takes out some butter from the cup in his fingers and put some on the parting of the hair of the bride and also puts on the bangles on her wrists. That is the end of the final ceremony, which ends with the gifts handed over to the couple by their relatives and other people (Gurung & Lama, 2004:131-132; Das and Banerjee, 1962: 71-104).

Buddhism subjected the Lepcha community of Sikkim after thirteenth century as well as by Christianity after 1817 when Sikkim came under the influence of the British India. Since then, a great chunk of the Lepchas adopted Buddhism as well as Christianity leaving aside their original faith of Animism. This is reflected in their belief system and also on the passage of rites right from conception to birth, marriage to death. Very few people really believe and perform their original ancient pre-natal, birth, marriage and death rituals now in Sikkim.

***(d)* Death:** In the early days, when a person dies, they sacrificed a bull or cow, a fowl or a pig, and believe that this is the present of the deceased for the spirits of the ancestors. The *Bongthing* or *Mun* goes on reciting some prayers or incantation for three days and nights. The Sengdenmo Lepchas believed that the spirit of their dead go to the Kinchenjunga local deities, through the gate of *Un-Boo-lep* (a horse's mouth shaped cave in Monphu) right through a subterranean passage to the palace of the local deity of Kanchen. The Hee-mo Lepchas believed that their spirits are conveyed through another subterranean passage beginning at a fall called *Phim-leb*, at the rock of Sing-dang in Samdong to the same destination as mentioned above. The Ligsomo Lepchas again believed that their spirits enter the subterranean passage, at a cave, having the shape of a gorilla's mouth called *Dret-gang* just below the Mendong of Gye-Zhing below Rabdentse. The Namphakmo Lepchas believed that as they were descended from the local deities of the sacred Mennam peak, their spirits go to the Mennam hill through a cave called Phim-leb in Lepcha situated below the Mangsher mendong of Lingmo. They call the Mennam peak *Mennam-chung* in Lepcha language (Namgyal and Dolma, 1908:28).

In other words, the Lepchas were created by the God on the hill-tops or mountain tops and their soul has to be accompanied by the Lepcha shamans and reached to the mountain peaks, and handed over to their ancestors as in the case of the Limboos in Yumaism.

Traditionally the Lepchas are buried. The dead body is put is a box and carried to the burial ground away from the village. The place of burial is known as *Chyok-Brang* or *Chyok-Bram* or *Da-Taath.* The corpse is taken out from the other open place or from the main door of the house making a bamboo-split door over it, which depends on the Lama's advice. The corpse is seated in a sitting position, the face facing the Himalayas and with hands folded in a praying position. A *Mun* or a *Bongthing* accompanies the funeral procession. Reaching the burial ground the priest announces the name of the deceased three times and tells him or her not to return to the world again. Some eatable things or drinks are also placed in the coffin box. After the burial a big stone is kept on the grave and is fenced. Each night after the burial a red hot stone is thrown outside the house taking the name of the deceased telling him not to come back to harm the dear and near ones (Das and Banerjee, 1962: 71-104).

Pits are dug of different shapes and sizes, according to the custom prevalent in different clans. Some corpses are buried in sitting position, some in sleeping position and some are buried in a half sitting position with the feet spread. Different kinds of graves are known as *Chyok-bom, Chyok-Bli* and *Chyok-Dey*. In the grave of small children a big stone is kept on the grave, which is encircled by three small stones. They are buried in a sleeping position. Before the burial the palms of the baby is rubbed with his or her mother's milk. Toys are also placed in the coffin box.

The death rites vary according to their adoption of different religions by the Lepchas these days. The system of cremating the dead must be the influence of Hinduism. The Christians are not cremated but buried according to the Christian rites.

With the passage of time the customs has changed now. The purification ceremony is performed three days after death. It is called *Sangl Yon*. On that day the *Mun* announces the name of the deceased person. They believe that the soul of a dead person remains loitering in the air above. On the chanting of the mantras by the *Mun* the dead person enters her body and starts speaking through her. She promises the dead one that she would take her or him straight to the village of ancestors (may be heaven). So she starts praying to open the door of the ancestor's village for the deceased. The Lepchas like any other believers on Karma philosophy do not have the concept of heaven and hell. The concept of heaven and hell is only for the Christians and Islam who believe only in one life. (Note: the concept of heaven and hell, and born only once in life, seem to be the influence of Christianity and not that of the Lepcha concept). The next morning the *Mun* takes all the family members to nearby pond or stream and sprinkles water on them to purify their body and soul. *Songl Yon* ceremony is always performed outside the house (Gurung & Lama, 2004:131-132).

Most of the Lepchas has abandoned Shamanism or Animism (*Bongthism* or *Munism*) now and have adopted Christianity and Buddhism. Thus, their Rites of Passage differ depending on their adoption of the different religion now.

13

The Bhutias (Lhorees or Lhopos)

Social Status: Scheduled Tribes

Origin and History:

The name Bhutia sometimes spelt and pronounced as Bhotia is derived from their original habitat "Bhot" (Tibet). The Bhutias although originally migrated from Tibet had been known in Sikkim since 13th century onwards as a "Lhopo" or "Lhopas" which means "the dwellers of the southward" and one of the earliest inhabitants of "The Greater Sikkim". They professed Tibetan Mahayana Buddhism but they have their own entity in cultural aspects such as folk songs called "*Beyul Nyekyi*" which has a starting lyric as "*Ney La Kyipa Nye La Kyipa Beyul Demozong*". This song gives about the topographical description, flora and fauna, bravery of its' peoples and extra ordinary blessings of Maha Guru Padmasambhava who made Sikkim as a Sacred Place (may be heaven) on the Earth (Bhutia, 2007; Subba, 1999).

The Bhutias are known by their place of habitations such as the Drukpas are people from Drukul of Bhutan; the Chumbipas, people from the Chumbi valley (now eastern Tibet); the Dhopthapas, inhabitants of Dhoptha, a place in south Tibet; the Tromopas or Do-mu-pas, inhabitants of Do-mu; the Lachungpas, inhabitants of Lachung Valley migrated from Hah Valley; Lachenpas, inhabitants of Lachen Valley migrated from Hah Valley and Tibet under the leadership of Lempen; are all Bhutias. Many of the above mentioned areas such as Chumbi valley, Har Chu valley, Amo Chu valley of Tibet and Bhutan were the part and parcel of "The Greater Sikkim" (Namgyal & Dolma, 1908; Singh, 1993; Subba, 1999: 140-142).

According to Namgyal & Dolma (1908), the unpublished manuscript (English version) that the Bhutias, are said to have descended from the 8 (eight) clans known as *Beb-Tsan-Gyat* of the great ancestor of Khe-Bumsa, a prince or chief from Dome in the Kham province of Tibet, while others say that it was from Khe-Bumsa's three sons that they have descended and multiplied. According to the later tradition, it is said that the Beb-Tsan-gyal (eight clans of settlers), and the *Tong-du-ruzhis* (the four regiments of 1,000 in each), were descendants from *Trag-tsan-dar* sons of Khe-Bumsa. Of these two, the four tribes or regiments of *Tongdus* are named as follows: (*i*) Shandarpa, (*ii*) Tse-chu-dar, (*iii*) Guru Tashi, and (*iv*) Nyimagyalpo. Then there is the Lingserpa, the descendants of these who gradually got separated afar were said to have been called the *Beb-Tsan-Gyat* (8 clans), and are Viz: (*i*) Bonpas, (*ii*) Gonsarpas or Gantagputsas, (*iii*) Namtsangkors, (*iv*) Tagchungdars, (*v*) Karsorpas, (*vi*) Gyonto-pas, (*vii*) Tsungyapas, and (*viii*) Topas or Dokhangpas. These 12 Clans (4 + 8) are said to be the pure 12 Bhutias or Lhorees and eligible for entrance into the Pemayongtse monastery as priests. The 12 tribes are known as *Nyorpog-phutsos*.

Again the Bonpas are sub-divided into five classes. They are called (*i*) Bonpo-Nagding, (*ii*) Lhasung, (*iii*) Wo-cha-Bonpos, and (*iv*) Nabons. Gonsarpas again descended to Bonchungs. These constituted the original Bhutia clans who settled in Sikkim prior to the time of Raja Phuntsog Namgyal in 1642.

After Sikkim came to be under a Raja and Ministers, had a settled form of Government. Other Bhutia tribes and settlers from Paro and Hah in Bhutan came from time to time and settled in various parts of Sikkim, who becoming naturalized came to be ranked amongst the Bhutia tribes of Sikkim, though considered to be inferior to the former ones.

Other tribes and sub-tribes of Sikkim: were called (*i*) Butsawopa, (*ii*) Lagdingpas and Gorongpas, (*iii*) Botpas, (*iv*) Gyengap, (*v*) Gorongpas, (*vi*) Topas, (*vii*) Sharpas, (*viii*) Barphung-putsos, and (*ix*) Adenputsos. These again include the Topas or Tromowas, who are subdivided into the following clans (*i*) To-Lhagopa, (*ii*) To-Jamyangpa, (*iii*) To-Chu-Khapas, and (*iv*) Chumbipas.

Topas of Tromo: They again are subdivided into (*i*) Lhambodar, (*ii*) Genynputso, (*iii*) Agon, (*iv*) Athub-putsos, (*v*) Dozho-pa and (*vi*) Khyim-pharpa.

The Lachung and Lachen people: Originally they came from Tibet to Hah Chu valley of Bhutan and then to Sikkim and call themselves of the Lapon Lhundrub tribes.

The Lower or Minor Tribes: They are (*i*) Assampa from Assam in the Mochu Valley (*ii*) Mang-baypas (*iii*) Nam-mangpas, (*iv*) Shagtsangpas, (*v*) Dorobpas (*vi*) Gang-gyabpas (*vii*) Ahpas,(*viii*) Mang-tsangpas, (*ix*) Pathingpas, (*x*) Boripa, (xi) Kargyalpas, and (*xii*) Dotrapas.

According to Chie Nakane (1966/1979), Bhutia migration seems to have started in the sixteenth century. According to Namgyal and Dolma (1908), the migration took place continuously in many ways and through different routes, from the northern and western passes of Sikkim after the blood brotherhood treaty of Khe-Bumsa and Thekong- Tek which took place in 13th century AD.

Population and Settlement:

According to 1891 population census, the total population of Bhutias in Sikkim was 4,894 (1,966 males, 1960 females and 968 children), and 16.07% of the total population amongst the communities of Sikkim. As per the voter list of 2004 published by the election commissioner of Sikkim, the Bhutia population was 74,164 (12.39%) of the total population of Sikkim. The Bhutia language speakers were 12.71% in 1891 and 16.00% in 1991 in Sikkim. In 1891 the Bhutia population was the second highest only next to the Lepchas, while in 2004, it has been reduced to third highest population amongst the communities of Sikkim, the first and second being Khambu Rais and Chettris respectively. The Lepcha population was the highest with 18.92% of the total population in1891 which has been reduced to the sixth position with only 8.16% in 2004 . The Limboo population was fourth in 1891 (11.02%) is still maintaining at the fourth highest position in 2004 also, but with only 9.15% of the total population of Sikkim. The Bhutias live in hilly terrain, of high altitude and cold climate, where there is high rainfall with medium snowfall and high humidity with dense forests.

Geographical Distribution

The highest concentration of Bhutia population is in the Lachen Mangshila and Kabi Tingda constituencies of North District; Gangtok, Ranka, Assam Lingjey, Rumtek, Sang Martam, Ragdong Tintek, Pathing, Rigu, Khamdong in East District; Ralang, Wok, Temi-Tarku, Damthang in South District; and Yoksam, Tashiding, Gyalshing, and Rinchenpong in West District of Sikkim. The Sangha constituency is represented by 100% Bhutias (Voter list of 2004).

Bio-anthropological Information

No bio-anthropological information is available on them except serology and genetic. Both the data on ABO and MN are available for the Bhutias of Sikkim (Morpurgo et al. 1983). The gene frequencies are as follows:

P = 23%, q = 21 to 56%, m = 67% and n = 33%.

The data on other genetic markers, mainly red-cell enzymes like glyoxalose (glo), Adenosine Aminose (Adi), Acid phosphates (ACP), Phosphoglu commutase 1 (PGM 1), Phosphexose Isomerseo (PHI) and 6 Phosphoglucomutase De-hydrogenase (PGD) are also available for the Bhutias of Sikkim (Morpurgo et al., 1983).

Food Habits

The Bhutias are non-vegetarian but prefer beef and pork to mutton. Their staple diet is rice (*tho*) with meat (*shy*). They take seasonal fruits and vegetables. For mid-day refreshments, they take a dumpling meat ball (*momo*), fried maize, flat rice and maize, *murai* and vegetable dumplings (*zino yenten*), *gyathuk* (noodles in soup), the *phakthuk* which is good for winter, the *Khudi* made out of buckwheat powder, prepared like *dhosa* and *khuon* bread. In villages the medium of cooking is animal fat and butter, whereas in towns it is mustard oil. The Bhutias drink milk and tea. A local drink (*Chhang*) and wine (*arak*) prepared by them from millet, rice, fruits, etc. are taken by both adults and children.

Cuisine

The popular Bhutia cuisines are *Bom, Dhem, Chongbu, Phiyam, Lhakha, Kosa, Riku, Pako, Thokeu, Lobeykeu, Keuka, Keuma, Phicham, Riee, Senzam, Chhenyog, Khoo, Shyogkhoo, Khoodi, Genton, Phiboou, Thuko, Lepchong, Fito, Saiyon, Chhadungbiyasu, Chhadongbiyasu, Khayerbiyasu, Biyabiyasu, Them, Zero, konchong, Soltrumsya, Gyari, Naihu, Gyuma, Kargyang, Nangthu, Phochung, Klagyang, Nangcha, Chinpo, Bangroi, Kokyou, Dhong, Socha, Pacha, Shyamo, Kichhoe, Gonag, Yangyed, Gadu, Biyacham, Monchya, Champo, Monchya Knoo, Nacham, Champo and Shyambim* (Bhutia, 2007).

Family Pattern:

The father is the head of the family followed by the mother and the eldest son. Daughters are not given that much priority in decision-making process in the family. All the important decisions of the family are taken by father or jointly by the father-mother. In their absence, the eldest son of the family takes the decision. In the case of death of the father of the family, the mother takes the responsibility of the family until the eldest son gets married.

Family Property:

The property of the family remains under the full control of the father until his sons and daughters get married. Thereafter, the property is divided equally amongst all the sons. A small portion of land is reserved in the father's control as *Pazhik* (*Zyuni*). This *Zyuni* will be passed on to those sons or daughters who serve their father and mother in their last breath or moment. In some places willingly their father and brother donate a small portion of the land as a gift to the daughters by taking the permission of the family members.

Gender Issues:

Girls from urban areas mostly go to schools and colleges to educate themselves. At the economic, social, ritual, religious and political levels, they have equal rights with the men. They manage the family affairs. Now women are also found in services in a large number, especially in government service.

Kinship and Social Organization:

The marriage is endogamous at the community level and exogamous at the 4 *ru* and 8 *ru* level in the early days but now this is not strictly followed. Sororate junior and levirate junior are also in practice. Modes of acquiring mates were by service in the early days but negotiation has been a common practice now. Now monogamy is the general practice, except in the North district, where fraternal polyandry is noticed. Till very recently there was polyandry on a wide scale in Lachung and Lachen but now the occurrence has declined. The married Bhutia women wear a striped apron called the *pangden* as a sign of the married state.

Now, most of the families are nuclear and vertically extended, though some carry remnants of the joint family also. Avoidance relationship exists between mother-in-law and son-in-law, daughter-in-law and father-in-law, sister-in-law (BW) and elder brother-in-law (H (e)B), etc. Joking relationship exists between sister-in-law (e) BW and brother-in-law H(e)B, with sister-in-law W(e)S and W(y)S with brother-in-law W(e)B and W(y)B, grand-parents with grand-children, etc.

Economic Activity

The Bhutias depend on agriculture, dairy farming and pastoralism. In summer months, people of Lachen and Lachung go to a higher altitude, to graze their animals. They stay there in the summer months when the land is covered with grass. When winter starts, they come down to the lower altitude with their animals and practice cultivation, mainly for potato, wheat, barley, large cardamom, etc. While some of them are in service, land remains the major source of income.

Dresses and Costumes

The identifying mark of the Bhutias is the *Kho*, a long-sleeved coat with a belt or *kera*, locally called the *Bokhu* and worn by the males whereas women wear the sleeveless *kho* with the *honju*, a blouse with long sleeves.

The male Bhutias wear the *tson-ta-ti,* a shirt underneath the *Bokhu.* The traditional dresses of Bhutia man are: *Bheshya* - Woolen cap or *Hashya* - Fox-skin cap or *Thorizyamo* - embroiled male cap; and *Kyamthue* - ribbon (Lacha) on the head. They wear *Kho - Bakho*; *Hontas* -shirt with thuklung button; *Denzi* -half *Bakhu* worn by *Gomdens*; *Jya-jya* - male Jackets; *Khama* - ceremonial red shawl; and *Kera* cloth belt for *Bokhu* on the main body. At the lower par of the body they wear *Gyador* - pant; *Megyok, Somkham* - boot (shoes) or *Lham* -shoes; *Kaugshop* -shocks and *Zhampo* -woolen boots, The male ornaments are *Zuku* - finger ring and *Along* -earring.

The females wear *Tahering Keugap* -female embroiled cap or *Syambo* -hat/cap and *Gopu* -scarf to cover head; *Kyamthue* - hair ribbon on head; *Khatti* -muffler for ladies on the neck; *Gho* or *Bakhu*; *Honzyo* - ladies shirt to wear with *Gho*; *Kushen* - ladies jacket; *Phangden* - front cover on top of *Gho;* and *Thorm* - trousers on the upper and lower body. The ornaments of the female comprise of *Thrachung* - necklace (stone), *Gacchung* - golden ornament (emulate), *Dopchem* - golden ornament embroiled with precious stones, and *Zhizing* - precious stones (Bhutia, 2007).

Folk Musical Instruments:

The Bhutia folk musical instruments are *Sangnga, Yingting, Radong, Gyaling, Suna, Khar-ngan, Dhung, Ngaa, Rolmo, Suneg, Kangling, Lingbu, Kongtang, NGachung and Drilbu* (Bhutia, 2007).

Folk Songs:

There are two types of folk songs in Bhutia community;

(*a*) *Zhung-Lhu* folk song: It is a group folk song sung during *Zhung-Shey* folk dance making a circular ring during wedding ceremony; house warming ceremony and Losoong festivals.

(*b*) *Tey-Lhu* folk song: It is a folk song sung by one or more persons in line up manner during *Tey-Zhey* folk dance.

Folk Dances:

The Bhutia folk dances can be basically divided into two types:

***(a) Zhung-Shey* Dance**: is a group dance in circular manner with the tune of the country songs called "*Zhung-Lhu*". These dances are performed during the main ceremony of *Ngen-Chhan Thung* (wedding ceremony), *Kyimsa Tashi* (house warming ceremony), and in *Losoong* (New Year of the Bhutia's calendar).

***(b) Tey-Zhey* Dance:** is performed by either one or more persons in lined up manner or sometimes moving forward and backward with the tune of folk songs called "*Tey-Lhu*". The lyric of the song normally praises the honour like *Kowali* of Hindi or *Dohori* of Nepali. There are many types of songs and dances that can be performed with these two types of dance forms in all the occasions.

Festivals

There are many festivals of Bhutia communities such as *Losoong, Pang-Lhasol, Kagyed Dance, Sagadawa, Drukpa-Tsezhi, Lha-Bap-*

Dhuechen, Guru Rimpoche's Thrungkar Tsechu, Bumchu etc. All these festivals have been described under festival chapter in detail. Besides, the Bhutias participate in other festivals of other communities like *Dasai, Tihar*, and other secular festivals.

Language and Literature

The Bhutias speak in their own language among themselves. It is one of the oldest languages spoken in the ancient times by "*Bhompu*" or the "*Bon*" people. Although its use was not there in the written form during the British advent in the Indian Sub-continent, the language was one of the *lingua franca* in the Himalayan region. This language is different from the official Tibetan (*Thomi Sambhota*) and is simpler. Have there been efforts to invent a script of this language, it would have develop into an advanced language by now.

Sikkimese Bhutia language had so far been a spoken dialect only and for all literary, cultural and educational pursuits, Tibetan was the official language used by the Bhutia population due to the influence of the religious priest –Lamas of the Monasteries on administration for the entire period of 333 years of Namgyal Dynasty in Sikkim. Therefore, the need to render it into a written form was being increasingly felt by the common Bhutia people of Sikkim. After the integration of Sikkim into the Indian Union, the State Assembly adopted and passed the Sikkim Language Act, 1977 recognizing the three languages – the Lepcha, the Bhutia and the Nepali as the official languages of the state. However, its development into a viable literary form capable of serving the educational and cultural needs of the people who speak it will naturally require a lot of work. The single most essential step in this direction will be to ensure a much wider use and application of the language in the relevant field. The Textbook Unit of the Department of Education, Government of Sikkim, took the task of preparing Textbooks in Sikkimese Bhutia language since 1977 onwards. Norden Tshering Bhutia and P.R. Lama are among the pioneer textbook writers whose contribution on this difficult task has been immense. There are several teachers who have contributed in the preparation of textbooks in this language. Dorjee Rinchen Lama, Senior Lama of the TNA is one among them. With his experience and vast knowledge, he had been very active in contributing articles for the preparation of the Bhutia language textbooks. His book of poetry titled "*Tsigchethi*" has been selected as a textbook and is being taught in the College level. Similarly Bhaichung Bhutia, textbook Officer, HRDD, Government of Sikkim has written many textbooks for the schools and colleges. The Bhutia organization "*Bhutia Kay-Rab-Yargay Tsogpo*" established in 1983 is also contributing a lot on conservation and development of the culture, tradition, religion, language and literature of Bhutias in Sikkim (Bhutia, 2007).

Religion and Belief System:

The Bhutias are Buddhist by religion. Their chief deity is the tutelary galaxy of Buddha and Bodhisattwas, followed by the guardian deities, including local deities, family deities, village deities and Khanchendzonga. Most of the deities are identified with mountains, lakes and forests. In the Bhutia religion, the monastery or the *Gumpa* plays a major role. Most of the villages have their own *Gumpa*. At the centre of the *Gumpa*, there is the Buddha surrounded by other images. The Lama officiates in the rituals in the *Gumpa*. The lady Lama is called Anne. *Chotimba* is the head of the *Annes*. Both Lamas and *Annes* can marry, if they like. The Bhutias offer money (*guo-ten*) and gifts to the monastery, but there is no compulsion.

Rites of Passage (Life-Cycle):

During the period of pregnancy (*Phuchain*) there is no restriction on women. According to Bhutia (2007), the rites of passage of the Bhutia community is as under:

(*a*) Birth: After the birth of a baby, both mother and child are cleaned and washed and kept in a separate room, yet no restriction as such is imposed. After the child is born, a little butter is given to the child with one or two drops of honey. From the second day, powdered rice is given to the child, with butter. As soon as the mother is able to walk and work, she goes to the kitchen. Three days after being born all the family members and relatives gather in the house of newly born baby and the Lama priest will perform purification rite for the child, the mother and the house and rejoice. This purification and name-giving ceremony is known as *Phyakey* or *phangsang* in Bhutia language. The Lama performs a short prayer followed by offering of *khada* and gift to the newborn baby by relatives.

(*a*) Marriage:

The marriage (*gnen*) procedure of Bhutias is very elaborative and expensive and could be described in various parts as follows:

(*i*) Dichang: It is the first step of marriage whereby the uncle of would be bridegroom or in his absence one capable elder person from village accompanied by a mediator (*phami*) and 2-3 persons seek the hand of the girl by visiting girl's house. With them they carry brewed millet or liquors. An astrologer follows after this procedure. The astrologer will match the *Lotak* of the boy and the girl. He will also look for the auspicious day of marriage solemnization. After going through various formalities the group come back to the boy's house. Within three days if the girl's side returns the brewed millet or liquor it ultimately means they are not interested. But if the materials are not returned within the mentioned days, they assume that they are agreeable to give away their daughter as a bride.

***(ii)* Khachang:** After making the decision of handing over their daughter, the paternal uncles and paternal aunts of would be bride gather together to rejoice in the bride's house. In this occasion brewed millet is offered to the Lama invitee and after being sip by the Lama rest of the family members take sip of it turn-wise.

***(iii)* Preparation for Khachan in Bridegroom's House:** Preparation for Khachan involves arrangement of the following items; Viz:

- *Ngo-ten Shuve* Chanzel (Gift items);
- *Chaphi* (Tea); *Champo* (Wheat flour);
- *Chang Phochi* (brewed millet);
- *Melamki Thaten Gor Zos* (rupees for good wishes); and
- *Dha Ashi Chik* (one Scarf).

After the preparation of the gift items, the two paterntal uncles visit the bride house with the above gift items with the gift carriers. In this occasion middle man (paternal uncle) brief on the intension of their visit to the bride house by offering gift items. The briefing will be on the requirement of the bride for his nephew to continue their race and look after the family members of bridegroom.

***(iv)* Nang-Chang:** During Nang-chang the middle man again visit the bride house and held discussion with maternal uncle of bride to know about the demands from would be bride as follows:

- Money as per demand;
- Whole body of Pig (killed and eviscerated);
- One bag of rice;
- Brewed millet;
- Wheat flour;
- Tea;
- Butter;
- Khada (Scarf long one).

With due preparation of the demand items of the bride house, and getting the information of an auspicious date for marriage as sought from girl's side from the astrologer, the date for marriage solemnization is fixed.

(v) Ngen-Chang Thung (Wedding ceremony): In this ceremony, Lamas are invited in the bride house and seating arrangements for bridegroom, bride middle man and other members of bridegrooms side are made in the Altar room itself. Along with all the relatives, friends, neighbours of the bride are invited on this day to rejoice. It is a moment of enjoyment for all. Everyone eat, drink, dance and offer *khada* and gifts or money as per their desire to the bride and bridegroom and make wish for a happy and prosperous married life.

(b) Death: The death and funeral ceremonies of the Bhutias are very intricate. They are believers of Mahayana Buddhism and thus they believe that death itself does not means an end but is a step for a reincarnation to another life. Rituals and prayers must perform in a manner that this transformation happens in the most favourable way. The death ceremony continues for many days and incur huge expenditures involving hiring of Buddhist monks, purchase of ritual offerings, feeding the mourners who come to pay their condolences and visit to monasteries by the bereaved. After death the body is placed in cross-legged curled pose in the coffin, which is kept inside the house. The monks perform prayers and rituals using trumpets and cymbals sitting in front of the body. Meals are served to the deceased through out the period following death until the rituals are over. The visitors pay their condolences by handing over a folded *khada* and some money to the eldest of the bereaved family. Food and refreshments are served to the visitors. The cremation takes place on the day decided by the astrologer and it could be even a week after the death has taken place. Monks blowing trumpets, conches and slamming the cymbals lead the funeral procession. When the funeral pyre is lit, the family members and well wishers throw mud or wood in the fire and wish that the deceased should has a good reincarnation. The ashes of the deceased are usually collected and dispersed in the river. The *Kutse Shegu* ceremony is held on the 49th day following the death and is aimed to purify the family and relative members as well as the atmosphere. Invitations are sent to well wishers to visit the houses of the deceased. Food and drinks are served to the visitors. Also those who could not pay their condolence earlier do so now by offering a folded *khada* and some money to the bereaved family (Bhutia, 2007).

Buddhism, like several other Indian traditions, does not see death as the cessation of consciousness. Instead, death marks the dissolution of the physical elements of the person. The mental elements generally referred to as consciousness or life-flux, persist, to once again take physical form through the process of rebirth. It is believed that there is existence of an intermediate state between the moment of death and moment of conception in the next life. The intermediate state could last as little as an instant or as long as forty-nine days. This period is known as *Bardo Thodol* in Buddhism. The deceased life-flux or consciousness passes through this process of *Bardo Thodol* as described in Buddhist philosophy (Subba, 2005: 3-5).

Dzumsa of Lachen and Lachung:

The *dzumsa* is the traditional administrative system of the villages of Lachen and Lachung, high altitude communities speaking a Tibetan dialect and settled in Sikkim's North District. This system of self-governance was initially established during the first half of the 19th century in order to provide structure and cohesion for these societies and their activities. These communities were too far removed from the central authority to follow rules applicable to other regions of Sikkim. During the rule of Namgyal Dynasty, the *dzumsa* and the *pipons* or village chiefs were recognized and used by the kings as a means of delegating his authority. After integration of Sikkim into Indian Union in 1975, the state introduced the Panchayat system of local government, but the new system was not imposed in the valley of Lachen and Lachung. Eventually, the *dzumsa* was officially recognized in 1985 and continues to function today.

The *dzumsa* or general council of Lachenpa or Lachungpa villagers are directed by a group of people, elected or designated by villagers depending on the period, to represent them and manage village affairs. This council of representatives, referred to as the *lheyna* and now better known as the panchayat, is composed of two *pipons*, six *gembos*, two *tsipos* and two *gyapons*. This council or lheyna is changed every year unless the public wishes to renew its mandate. It is responsible for the application and respect of the community's laws and regulations, and for the organization of the main village events. It schedules the meetings of the village's general council where decisions are taken and meets before each one in order to discuss the agenda and measures to be proposed. Thus, *dzumsa* functions as an effective local self-government for all purpose in the valleys (Sabatier, 2004: 93-104)

14

The Sherpas (Sharpa, Nubripa, Bhote or Lama)

Socio-Status: Scheduled Tribes

Origin and History

The Sherpas are of Tibetan origin. The name *Sherpa* means "Eastern people" in the Tibetan language. The *Sherpas* in Nepal are said to be the people who have come there from the East of Tibet. They lived originally in the frontier districts in the Tsing-hai-Sechwan provinces of China (Kham). This is in Eastern Tibet, they are called Sharpa, the Eastern people (Hermanns Fr. M., 1954:23). The Sherpas, present inhabitants of northeast part of Nepal (Solukhumbu) and all the four districts of Sikkim, were not the original inhabitants of their present homeland. This is shown by the idiographic study of Michael Oppizt (1974: 122) and nomothetic study of the present context (Kunwar, 1989: 118). In early/ first half of 18th century Phuntsog Namgyal, Chogyal of Sikkim married the grand daughter of Rabden Sherpa. Sherpa were in Sikkim long before the date given by the Western social authorities. They used to be called Sherpa, which gradually accumulated with Bhutia of Sikkim like Dopthapa, Chumbipa, Amdo, Dukpa etc. in later part of 20th century. According to Radcliffe-Brown (1952: 1), "in an ideographic inquiry the purpose is to establish as acceptable certain particular or factual propositions or statements. A nomothetic inquiry on the contrary has its purpose to arrive at acceptable". As Oppitz (1973: 233, 1974: 122) writes on the ground of historical documents that the Sherpa's original homeland was in Kham region of Eastern Tibet (China), which is almost 1300 miles from their present homeland, i.e., Solu-khumbu. Due to the politico-religious and internal religious conflict, they were bound to leave their ancestral homeland. Their first migration started in 1530 A.D. and that continued till 1850 A.D.

The other two scholars, Sange Tenzi Lama (1971: 150-160) and Downs (1980: 3) have opined that the Sherpa's migration occured due to harassment given by Mongol. Haimendorf, on the ground of the Sherpa-belief, writes "that their ancestors migrated south along the

Rongshyar Chu-west of the Rolwaling Himal- and then, turning east, settled first in Solu, where they ousted an earlier Kiranti population. From Solu they moved- according to this tradition – northwards into Khumbu (Haimendorf, 1964: 18; Jerstad, 1966: 35), but a contradictory belief is expressed in the view that their ancestors came to Khumbu straight from Tibet across the Nangpa La (19,050 ft) the main trade-route between Khumbu and Dingri region of Tibet (Sherpa: 1982). Paul (1970: 5) is of opinion that the Sherpas' ancestors might have migrated in 17th century A.D. because of not getting any document of establishment of Gompa before the mentioned date. It is not clear why they left. Harassment by marauding Mongol tribes, or religious persecution by the reformed Tibetan Buddhist sect have been suggested, although it seems equally plausible that there was some local upheaval in the feudal social structure (Ortner, 1978: 10).

According to *Mola*, (a speech-making tradition which is orally narrated sometimes like a story on the occasion of wedding in Bigu), "their original homeland was in Kham. People from other country came to attack over there and then the inhabitants of Kham ran away. Consequently they arrieved in Lhasa and from there they came to Dingri. Some of them settled in Khumbu. Even from Khumbu some people got down to Solu and settled in Gomba dzyung (present Junbesi). Later on ppulation increased and some people reached Chortung La (the ridge of Jiri) from where they took to the north-western side.There they saw some empty land like a granary in six which was present Bigu. Very few of them settled in that village". The *mola* further notices that the Sherpas had already occupied the adjoining villages like Khartal, Labtang, Khasa and Lamobagar. This oratorical tradition notices that the reason of their ancestor's migration was not due to the religious persecution but due to the political conflict. It also speaks not about Rongshyar chu but about Dingri and Nangpa La pass. It shows that they first settled in Khumbu, then only in Solu. Then gradually they immigrated to the northwestern as well as northeastern parts of the present homeland. But it does not give any idea to calculate the date of migration (Kunwar 1989: 120). From the viewpoint of settlement though they became different nationals, they could not forget Tibet and frequently visited there not only with a view to follow trade but also to have religious education. Linguistically, environmentally and religiously, it was suited for them to keep good touch with the people of Tibet. It continued till 1959 and after that when Tibet was captured by China, their visit also stopped. Now, a very few Sharpas visit China for the purpose of small trade (Kunwar, 1989: 121).

The Sherpas came into contact after the summit of Mt. Everest by Tenzing Norgey Sherpa and Edmund Hillari on the 29th May, 1953. The earliest reference to Sherpas in annals of mountaineering occurs in 1907 where it is recorded that Dr. A. M. Kellas recruited a few Sherpas from Darjeeling to accompany him to the Sikkim Himalayas as high altitude porters (Kohli and Verghese, 1962: 61). Thus, it is clear that the Sherpa immigrants of Darjeeling were the first to used the word "Sherpa". According to oral tradition, the Sherpas immigrated into Kalimpong about two centuries ago, most of them directly from Solukhumbu and some via Sikkim for the purpose of better fortune (Gupta, 1980: 95). When mountaineering and trekking was opened in Nepal Himalayas, the Sherpas of Darjeeling also went to these Himalayas being a high altitude porters and came in contact with the people of Solukhumbu. Then they also borrowed the term "Sherpa" as their surname from the Sherpas of Darjeeling. But, the landmark of using the term "Sherpa" by the people of Solukhumbu should be 1950s. Previously they were known as "Sharpa" (easterner), or "Nubripa" (westerner), Bhote or Lama. Finally, this term "Sherpa" was given separate, independent and full ethnic identity. Even though, they use two terms while giving their identity with insiders and outsiders, which is used here by, auto-name i.e. "Serwa" and exo-name i.e. "Sherpa". One would say *nga Serwa hin*, meaning, "I am Serwa". But for outsiders, he would prefer to say "I am Sherpa". Since 1953, after the summit of Mt. Everest, people came to know them as highianders of the Nepalese Himalayas as well as prominent climbers. With the introduction of the Panchayat System in Nepal in 1959-60, the Sherpas are recognized as one of the *Janajati* (Sheduled tribes not caste) (not as *jat* or caste) of Nepal (Kunwar, 1989: 122).

Population and Settlement:

According to 1971 census, the total population of Bhote Sherpas in Nepal was 79,218 (Pokharel, 1979: 85), which is less than 1% of the total population of the country. The Indian census of 1961 has shown 6,173 Sherpas living in India (Gordon, 1969: 2). On the basis of voter's list of 2004, the population of Sikkim is about 25,808 persons which constitutes about 4.31% of the total population of Sikkim.

Geographical Distribution:

The areas with higher concentration of Sherpa population are: Ribdi, Bharang, Okharey, Upper Thambong, higher elevation areas of Tashiding constituency, Begha, Upper Bermiok, Siribadam, Singling, and Buriakhop, of West District; Ralang, Nayabasty, Wok, Damthang, of South District; Regu, Pathing, and Khamdong of East District; and Kabi Tingda area of North District of Sikkim.

Food Habits:

The Sherpas are non-vegetarians. The Sherpa's staple food is potato and wheat from which they prepare varieties of items for their consumption. A staple diet of potato, rice and buckwheat, provides ample calories but obesity is uncommon. Green vegetables and fruits are available during monsoon; milk and cheese are also plentiful. Beef is more commonly taken than expensive mutton or chicken or eggs. Rice is the highest status food eaten by the Sherpas who can afford it, while potato is the main food for the poor families. The Sherpas have to live in a very cold place, so they require energetic food to undertake hard work and remain warm. Their food varieties are: boiled potato (*Khaponi sawo*), roasted barley flour (*tsampa*), potato bread (*riki kur*), boiled flour or local pudding (*syan* or *gonde*), mashed potato mixed with wheat flour (*rildok*), food, made from wheat and bread (*pakril*), a kind of sweet-meat, a steamed food or vegetable or meat or chicken (*momo*), fried bread (*khapse*), noodle (*thukpa*), etc. are prepared for occasional consumption. Roasted barley or wheat flour (*pak* or *tsampa* or *chyamdur*) and tea are taken for breakfast, boiled potato, *riki* and hot spices or *stan* or *gonde* are taken for lunch, thukpa or yeri or shyakpa taken as dinner, but there are no hard and fast rule. The other food varieties like food made from tuber crop (*thow* or *twa),* lambursyak (a kind of soup), raw corn flex cooked with rice (*Kaksyer*), dried green corn mixed with *shyakpa (falgi*), *sharkam* (fermented dried vegetables) etc are occasionally and seasonally consumed. They take sugar tea (*ngar chya*), butter-tea (*suchya*) and alcoholic beverages like *chhyang* and *arak*. They take fruits and plenty of vegetables. The Sherpas use a lot of fermented drinks and their life is very much associated with chhyang. They need it in every phase of their life, even in secramental rites and rituals. Their cultural as well as natural surroundings provide them an ample opportunities to common alcohol, which keeps them warm and provides them energy to maintain social relation and their cultural heritage.

Family Pattern

The Sherpa family is patrilocal and descent is reckoned through the male. The father is economically head of the family. The types of families amongst the Sherpas are Nuclear, Stem, Nascent and Broken family. The nuclear family is common. The Sherpa society is basically patricentric, monogamous, residence is normally patrilocal and inheritance is normally patrilineal.

Family Property

After the father's death, the living sons equally divide the landed properties of their father, while the mother's ornaments is generally provided to the daughters. The eldest son succeeds after his father's death.

Gender Issues

The Sherpa family is almost female feaded. The Sherpa female are more enterprising and have control in family and household. Normally, property is not given to women. But according to a Sherpa custom called the *laru*, the father gives a portion of his land (when there is enough) or utensils, or gold ornaments to his daughter after she has given birth to a child, as the father considers it the point when a tie is forged between his daughter and her husband with the birth of the child. The women play an active role in agriculture, animal rearing, collection of fuel, and in rituals, and social functions; They earn money and carry out household obligations (Singh, 1993: 156).

Kinship and Social Organization:

The Sherpas of Sikkim use both honorific and non-honorific kinship terms. They prefer to speak almost Nepali terminology like *mama, phupu, kaka, baje* and so on. In many areas where the Sherpa population is concentrated they use their own kinship terms such as *chuchu* (brother), *achyu* (brother on known basis), *pappa* (father), *Gaga* (grandmother) and *Pagawa* (grandfather), *pin* (own brother), etc.

In the Sherpa community the clan is known as *ru* which is a basic element of their social structure. *Ru* refers either to bone or descent from recognized ancestors or community known as clan (Levine, 1981: 55-56). Haimendorf (1964: 19) has listed 21 clans of Solukhumbu Sherpas. Oppiiz (1968: 101) listed some more clans. The Sherpas of Sikkim may be divided into two endogamous groups, viz. (*i*) the Sherpas and (*ii*) the Yukpas, the former enjoying a higher status than the later. They are divided into a number of exogamous divisions known as *ru*, viz. Shalakha, Phinasha, Lama Sherpa, Chayaba, Goperma etc. Some of the divisions in their turn has a number of sub-divisions known as *pin*, viz. Khambase, Paldorje, Pankarma, Shalakha of Goperma; Thakto, Gwali, Gorza of Rinasha; and Lama-Gombu and Lama Sherpa of Lama Sherpa. Marriage is prohibited within the sub-division (*pin*) of the same division *ru* (Singh, 1993: 155).

There is a respectful relationship between mother-in-law and son-in-law, and a free relationship exists between brother-in-law H(yB) and sister-in-law (eBW). Inter-family linkages are maintained through invitations, clan members helping during festivals, rituals or in any other need.

Economic Activity:

Their traditional economy of animal husbandry and grazing has a limited scope in Sikkim. Land is their main resource, and it is controlled individually. They are primarily dependent on terrace cultivation. They are specialized on production of seed potato, off-season vegetable such as cabbage, peas, radish, etc., as they inhabit above 2,700 m. from the sea level. Subsidiary sources of income include livestock rearing (stall-fed cattle rearing), labour, service, acting as helper, or guide on mountain expeditions. They depend on market both for sale of their produce and purchase of food and other household items.

Dresses:

The Sherpa dress has become important cultural trait from which one can easily recognize the secular or lay people and sacred or religious people. They broadly use the two terms, which are known as *mikya* or *jiktemba* and *chhops* or *geddhyunwa*. The first one refers to white dressed (secular) man and the latter refers to the yellow dressed (religious) man. The Sherpas are certainly not white dressed, but they prefer to wear either black or brown or any in colour. Mostly the religious groups wear yellow dress named *thache*.

The traditional laity people's dress seems to be quite thick which also suits the local climate. The dress also distinguishes the sexes. For the sacred dress, they call *chhowi manja, khyokpi manja* for male and *phumpeji manja* for female. The traditional dresses are in black colour. The name of the male dresses are: *chhyuwa* or *chhyubi* (a long gown made of Tibetan wool), *tyetung* (the inner shirt), gown (5-6 ft. long), Nambu, hat, *kara* (a belt made of cloth), pant and *kacha* (Tibetan shoe). The traditional dresses of women are: *angi* or *angdung* (a long gown), *syamjar* (a thin blouse), *kenam* (garb), *kara* (broad silk cummerbund), *kacha* (the Tibetan shoe), *dongtil* (black dress) and *matril* (the multi-colored apron-front dress).

The Sherpa Dresses are of Four Types which are Used on Different Occasions

(*i*) Ritual wedding dress for groom: *chhyube* and *pagari* in some places or *syamu chyanpda* and *hochhen chhyuwa* in others;

(*ii*) Ritual wedding dress for bride: *angdung* or *tangja, cholo, gaa, genjin* and *syamu* in some places; or *syamu paksa* and *sikok* (like angi) in others.

(*iii*) Thache: is worn only by the lama, monks and nuns – consists of *syando ringa* or *ringok, syan* or *yoljen*.

(*iv*) *Wongje* – esotericism and symbolism dresses worn by lama and monks during big festivals and sacred performances. These dresses are *chuktor, ringa* (symbol of pancha dhyani Buddhas), *urgen* and *tingap dokang* are also attached with each other. *Sewak* (cap), *dokang ngachhya* (like *chhuwa*), *gyaptar* (black dress) and kacha are worn during esoteric dances at monasteries during *dumje* and *manirimdu* festivals.

Folk Musical Instruments:

Ghoori Ghanta – made of iron or brass; tied on the neck of horses or mules when grazing in the forests;

Ghyabuk – cymbal made of brass; used by religious priests in the monasteries and worship ceremonies.

Chaunri Ghanta – brass bell tied on the neck of cows and yaks.

Chyoder – just like *Damaru*, made of *Khaya*r wood and deer skin; ritha seed tied on the tip of the string; used by the religious priest.

Tungna – made of rhododendron wood with four wires; used by shepherds.

Dongmen – bigger than *tungna* 3. to 5 ft. long with 6-8 wires; used during *Sebru* and *Selo* dance in Nepal.

Dhwanipatra – made of brass, rolled with a small wooden stick; helpful during meditation.

Piwang – made of horse tail, two wires and pine wood; used at high altitudes.

Lawa – made of copper, 5 pieces of hollow, joined while using, 12-15 ft. long; used in monasteries and worship ceremonies.

Sherpa Ghyaling – made of Khayer wood; used in monasteries and worships.

Hyanzing – just like *tungna* with 8 wires; used in different social functions.

Sangdung – the large flute-type wind instrument.

Ghetamta bukshel – conch used for death.

Hya – a round-shaped drum made of skin.

Folk Songs

They sing *Sebu, Selo, tashi-sol-che, yongdoshiba* etc.

Folk Dances

They perform folk dances such as *Tashi-sol-che, yongdoshiba,* Lama dance, etc.

Religion and Belief System

The Sherpas follow Buddhism. They worship the Buddha, and Guru Rimpuchey as the family deity, and visit monastery (*Gumpa*) as the sacred centre. The priest (Tulku or Lama) has a significant role in performing rituals, worshipping and healing diseases. He belongs to the same community.

Festival

The Sherpas celebrate *Guru Rimpochey's Trungkar Tshechu, Saga Dawa, Dukpa Tsheshi, Lhabab-Duechen, Pang Lhabsol, Loosung* and several other festivals of their own, and celebrate the Tibetan New Year Day.

Rites of Passage (Life-Cycle): Birth, Marriage and Death are the major events of life.

(*a*) Conception and Pre-Natal: A married Sherpa couple possesses complete knowledge about the biological consequences of mating. If pregnancy does not occur in time the couple visit the sacred lakes, places, incarnate priests asking for baby. The conception leads stopping of menstruation, vomiting tendency, loss of appetite, liking to have hot spices, diary products, sour food from two months onwards. This morning sickness *chhernegeu* confirms that she is on the family way. The pregnant woman is advised not to go outside the village, not to follow hard work and not to go to forest. Sexual intercourse should be stopped but many couple followed upto seven months or upto the period suits to both of them (Kunwar, 1989: 155).

(*b*) Birth: When the labour pain, *kesuk* or *chhyujak*, starts, the expected mother for her *primi-gravida*, feels much uneasiness during confinement. But from the second time onwards they do not feel much difficulty due to physiological changes. *Thoosur* or *Shang-sirkim* is the purificatory rite takes place on the third day after the birth of the child, and performed by the Lama who chants mantras, plays a particular kind of small drum (*chyoder*) in his left hand and a sacred bell (*tilu*) in the right hand and sprinkles holy water (*thoo*) all over the house. All members of the family have to sip the *thoo* to purify them. Relatives and neighbors attend the ceremony. When an illegitimate baby is born to an unmarried girl, the *tipsur* is performed. Generally *ming daup* (to give the name) occurs on the same day but within eight days by the Lama or by the parents.

(*c*) Marriage: Rules of exogamy are observed at the level of exogamous divisions (ru). Arranged marriage (*lungjang giyangu*) is the norm among them, though marriage by elopement (*kabtindop*) is not unknown. In the case of elopement they have to perform *gengu kibja* at groom's house. The main wedding rite is known as *genu* among them. They prefer adult marriage, with a bride price paid in kind and cash. Monogamy is the usual norm in the society. Diverse takes place after social approval, on grounds of maladjustment and insanity. Either party can seek a divorce. No compensation is given to either party normally. Either the mother or the father takes the liability of the children. Remarriage of widow, widower, male/female divorcee, junior levirate and sororate is permitted. There is no sign of marriage borne strictly, though some would use a piece of cloth tied in front but below the waist (*pangden*). Rituals are on their way out; invitation cards have come into use, the age for marriage has been going up over the years.

The *Sodani* or *Tinchang* is the first step for a marriage, when the boy's relatives go to the bride's house with two bottles of liquor (*arak*) and ask for the consent of the bride's parents to the marriage proposal. With the acceptance of the *denchang* in which the boy's parents receive liquor made of millet (*kodo-ko-zanr*), 20 kg of *kodo* and a white scarf (*khada*), on the tenth day of the new moon (*aushiko dasami*), from the bride's parents, uncles, relatives etc., the marriage day is fixed. Sometimes, money may be given in the *denchang* in lieu of *Kodo* (millet). There is yet another custom, in which 30 kg of millet and *marcha* (yeast) are to be given by the boy's party to the bride's parents. On the day of marriage, the boy's parents have to take as many members of the marriage party (*zanti*) and as many white scarves (*khada*) as desired by the bride's parents. On the day of marriage, the groom has to wear a *bokhu* (*chuwa*) with full sleeves and a cap (*aptok*). A sleeveless *bokhu* (*chwa-angi*) and a cap (*tsering-king-gok*) and ornaments like the *kau* form part of the bridegroom's ceremonial dress.

The Lama has to carry the *Binchaj khalu* depicting *nag-nagini* as the lord of the earth and conducts the *Khalu puja* (*Khalu-serkim*). When the marriage party reaches the home of the bride, they are welcomed with an array of vessels and wooden bowls containing the *chhang* liquor (*surjyang*). The bridegroom and all members of the party put vermilion on their foreheads. Before the host is requested to bring the bride escorted by the groom's representatives to the place marked for the wedding, the *zanti* offers five *khadas* with one rupee; five *khadas*, three *khadas* and one *khada* each are given to the mother of the bride, the Lama of the bride's side, the father of the bride, and uncles and relatives of the bride respectively by the boy's party. After the arrival of the bride (*nama*) at the halting place for the *zanti* (*dera*) one of the elder members of the zanti stands up and makes an announcement about the wedding ceremony between bride and groom (*makpa*), repeating it twice; this is known as *mola*. The bridegroom hands over his *chuwa*, the marriage dress of the groom, to the bride for safe custody. The bride is taken back to her house. The *zanti* and relatives of the bride spend the night singing and dancing. Next morning, the Lama of the groom's side performs the *serkin*. The bride is again brought to the *dera* and she gives back the *Chuwa*, and the *aptok* to the bridegroom, when she is asked for them. The zanti moves with the bride to the bridegroom's house after light refreshments. During this time, one of the zanti members is held back at the bride's house for some time. This is called the *Yang-chyap* meaning holding back the good fortune of the house. He has to be served *chhang* and *khada* before departure.

At the bridegroom's house, the bride, the bridegroom, the Lama and members of the zanti go round the house three times from the right before entering it. Inside the house, the Lama chants mantras and blesses the bride and the bridegroom putting butter on their heads. The Lama asks the bridegroom to put vermilion on his own forehead and the bride's forehead. Others too bless the young couple. A feast is arranged. The elders dance, singing the Sherpa song, known as the *tashi-sol-che*, meaning the end of marriage, custom, song and dance. The bridegroom introduces the bride to the clans and relatives. On the third day after marriage, the bride has to be taken back to her home by the groom with three bottles of *arak* known as *karma loka* (Singh, 1993: 157-158).

(*d*) Death: The Lama is called to read religious scriptures (*Bardo Thodol*) when a person is about to die or dies. *Chomin* and incense sticks are burnt in the room. The Lama reads the scripture (*Chi*) to locate an auspicious date and time to take the dead body to the cremation. He plucks a few hairs from the middle of the head (*sin-pho*) of the deceased. On the way to the crematorium the dead body is kept in a sitting posture either in a vessel or in a wooden box. The funeral procession is led by a person carrying a *thanka* (*shiba khola*), depicting the three gods. This is followed by the monks carrying and blowing *sang dung*, *geyling*, *bupshyal*, and a big drum with a handle (*ya*). The Lama holds in his left hand the *khada* tied to the vessel or box containing the dead body and in his right hand the ritual bell (*tilu*). The Lama sets fire to the dead body, amidst the chanting of mantras. Butter mixed with barley and paddy is put on the pyre from time to time: this is known as *zinshak hawan*. The Lama prepares an image of the dead body by putting the clothes of the deceased on the image made with the ashes and sunburn bones, which is called the *ten*. The rite of the third day is called the *napur*. Poorer people finish the death rites on the third day itself in a ceremony called the *symbi-napur*. The final purification rite (*shibju-serku*) is held on the forty-ninth day with a feast to which relatives, neighbours, and well-wishers etc. are invited. In the evening, the *sindijougshi* or *sendi khingur* is performed to drive away the evil spirits from the house. After a year, butter is set alight in the house or the monastery (*gumpa*) (Kunwar, 1989: 195-197; Singh, 1993: 158-159).

15
The Ancient Kiratas

The word "**Kirata**" was termed for the people inhabiting the Himalayas by the Aryans after they came in contact with them. The present day Kiratas - the Limboos, Khambus (Kirawa), and the Yakhas call themselves as "Yakthungba", "Khambu" or "Kirawa" and "Yakha" respectively. There is no single word as "Kirata" in their ancient oral tradition known as "Mundhum". Opinions are divided on the origin of the people of Kiratas between theose who believe in the theory of migration of Kiratas and those who believe to be the auctothenous of the Himalayas. **A Kirata identity** empowers a community with certain claims over the geographical space that was once known as the land of Kiratas no matter how ill-specified the boundaries of such a space or identity might be.

In ancient Tibetan literature, the non-Tibetan dwellers south of the Himalayas and around the border of Tibet or people that resided (and continue to reside) were known as Mon-pas or Kirate tribes (Mullard, 2005: 39).

An Ethnographic Study Commission constituted by the Government of Sikkim headed by Dr. A.C. Sinha has extensively studied the available literature about the Kiratas, and submitted a comprehensive report to the Government is reproduced here as it is for the benefit in general as follows (Sinha, et. al., 2005):

In ancient Sanskrit literature, the Kiratas have been described as a distinct class of tribes, including the aboriginal non-Aryan mountain tribes of northern, central and eastern Himalayas, the hill tribes of the North-East, the tribes in the valley of Nepal, the tribes having settlements in the Gangetic basin, and those who were the degraded members of the Aryan stock leading the savage life of foresters (Singh, 1990: 95).

The word "Kirata" has been derived possibly from *Cirata* or *Cireta*, also known as Kirata-*tikta* or Anarya-*tikta* – a very bitter plant of the non-Aryans (Shastri, 1957: 4, 143) – grown in the lower regions of the Himalayas, one of the habitats of the Kiratas. *Cirata, Cireta* or *Cirayita* is the name of the drug which was obtained from the Kiratas by the Aryans and used for medicinal purposes. It is also possible that the Kiratas

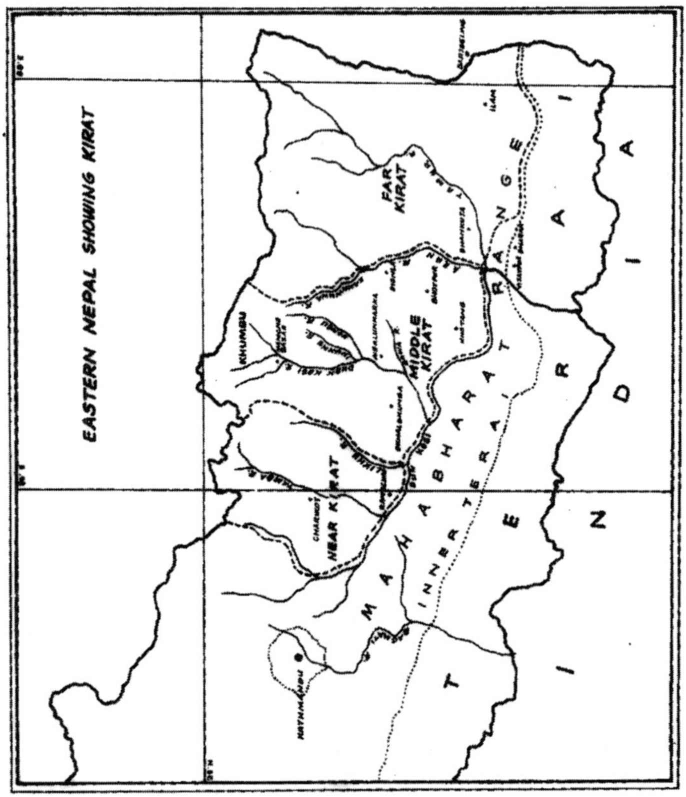

Source: Pradhan, K. (1991). The Gorkha Conquests.

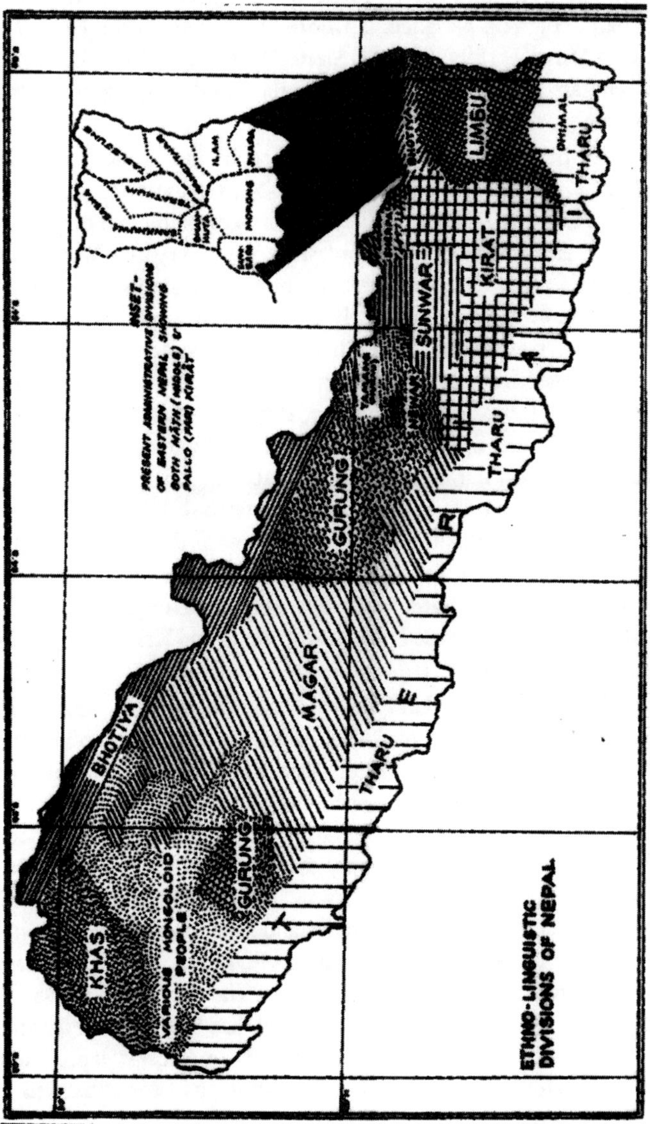

Source:
Pradhan, K.
(1991).
The Gorkha
Conquests.

themselves might have given the name to this drug (Banerjee, 1873: 187). The most popular Pali and Prakrit forms of an appellation Kirata, used in Sanskrit and common parlance, is *Cilata* (Trenckner, 1880: IV 8, 94, 327-31; Rhys Davids, 1894: 203-04; Stein, 1948: 100). Some Buddhist and Jain scholars as Calat or Kalat knew the Kiratas living along the Himalayan range.

The description of the Kiratas provided in the Vedic literature (Weber, 1852; Griffith, 1899, XXX 16: 257-58; Godbole, 1898, III, 4, 12.1; Pandit, 1895-98, X, 2, 4, 14) gives us an impression that they were basically cave and mountain dwellers. The Vedic Aryans themselves determined their place of habitation. The position assigned to them as explained in one of the texts (*Yajur Veda*) is indicative of the fact that they were the tribes of low status and living outside the Aryan fold during the Vedic age. The allusions to a separate family of the Kiratas (Kirata *Kula*) in some of the *Brahmanas* (Vagisha, 1869: 74; Shastri, et al., 1984: I, 1, 4, 14) indicate that they were the original inhabitants of India in the Vedic age. Relying on the information available in the Vedic *Samhitas* and *Brahmanas*, herein referred to, it has been stated that the name Kirata was applied to the aboriginal hill people. They were the class of people who inhabited the woods and the caves of mountains and supported themselves by hunting and gathering. They were "barbarous" non-Aryan tribes representing the "degraded" race (Macdonell and Keith, 1912: 157-58; Griffith, 1968: I: 208, II: 16).

It is not correct to state that the term Kiratas was loosely applied to any hill people (Chatterjee, 1974: 28) or used only for the primitive cave dwellers of the Himalayas, foresters and uncivilized or barbarous mountain tribes (Macdonell and Keith, 1912: 157-58). It is also not a correct explanation that in Sanskrit literature the term seems to have been used indiscriminately to designate only the border tribe of the northern and eastern frontier (Walker, 1961: 156-58, 162). Nor is it proper to call the Kiratas mere Himalayan mountaineers and to identify them only with the Kirantis who once reigned over a large portion of eastern Nepal (Gait, 1926: 12) which was known as *Kiratadesha* (land of the Kiratas) in ancient times. In fact, the entire Himalayan belt has been regarded as the land of the Kiratas. It seems probable that the Kiratas were once specifically the Himalayan people but that term was later expanded to embrace any hill tribe.

In the Mahabharata, the Kiratas have been described as dwellers of the Himalayan region, particularly the eastern Himalayas (Satavalekar and Sharma, 1969: 64, 21; 1972: 10, 49-55; 1973: 73, 19-20; 1975: 4, 7).

Their seven principalities situated in the eastern Himalayan region on the north of Videha have been distinctly referred to. We are told that their seven kings (Chiefs) were living close to Indrakeel mountains (Sikkim) and ruling over a vast dominion (Sabha Parva, 1982: 27, 13). It has been rightly observed that "The Great epic-Mahabharata – mentions several principalities all along the borderland of the Himalayas ruled by the Kirata kings…." (Nath, 1948: 13-15). The territories of seven Kirata kings are said to have been located between the seven Gandakis and seven Koshis which roughly corresponds with the ancient Kiratadesha in the eastern Himalayas comprising the greater part of the mountain regions of present Nepal (Agrawala, 1977: 156; Regmi, 1969: 22; Hodson, 1847: 1235ff). It can be added here that the seven tributaries of the river Gandak – Bhagirathi, Narayani, Shveta Gandaki, Matsyandhri, Trisul, Dharmadi and Gandi (all originating from the mountain ranges of Dhvalagiri and Gosainthan) – combined together is called Sapta-Gandaki and is in central Nepal. Likewise the seven tributaries of the river Koshi – Arun, Dudhkoshi, Tamrakoshi, Likhu, Tambor, Sunkoshi and Milanchi or Indrani combined together called Sapta-Kaushaki is in eastern Nepal. "The region lying between the two rivers – Arun and Dudhkoshi is still known as Kiratadesha" (Atkinson, 1883: 14). It has been stated that "the Alpine basin of the Sapta-Kaushaki or the country of the seven Koshis was the original homeland or the seat of the Kiratas of Nepal who were once very powerful and dominant race though they have long since succumbed to the political supremacy of other races" (Atkinson, 1973: 365).

According to tradition of the Kiratas mentioned in the great epic noted above, Belkakoth in the hilly region of Morung to the west of Sikkim and situated between Nepal and Bhutan was the site of the capital of their kingdom in ancient times, as recorded by B.H. Hodgson (1847: 12). Belkakoth (near Koshi) was located in a convenient location for both the dominions of the Kiratas in the hills and for those in the lower region. In the Kiratadesha of Morung, several old princes and chiefs are recorded to have maintained their principalities (Martin, 1831/1976: 38-40).

The tradition of calling the Kirata chiefs "Subba" and "Rai" in Nepal virtually commenced in the early medieval period. The Kirata chiefs represented by Rai are still found in the hilly areas of present Nepal, West Bengal and Sikkim. They still have an age-old seven clans among themselves. Some of them represent the posterity of the seven Kirata chiefs of the epic age (Singh, 1990: 354).

The Kiratas on the other half of the Himalayas and in the mountains of the east (sun-rise mountain) clad in Sikhs, living on fruits and roots and using deadly weapons are also described in one of the *Parvas* of the *Mahabharata* (Sabha Prava, 52, 8-10).The Kiratas living on the mountain slopes have been depicted in the *Puranas* as *Parvatasrayins*. Their settlements near the slopes of the Himalayas, northern and eastern, have also been mentioned therein (Vayu, 1987: I, 45, 136; Matsya, 1985: I, 13, 56; Brahma, 1976: 53, 15; Brahmanda, 1913: V, 1, 5, 16, 68; Markandeya, 1983: 57; Vaman, 1968: 13, 58; Padma, 1893-94: 2, 13, 8; 6, 46, 52). Some of the Puranas have placed them on the border of eastern India (Markandeya, 1976: 57, 8; Vayu, 1987: 45, 82; Matsya, 1985: 113, 11; Brahma, 1976: 17, 8; Vishnu, 1984: II, 3, 8). It is noteworthy that the Aryans as a group of tribes whose original home was in the Himalayan slopes knew the Kiratas. Their original settlements near Mt. Kailasha and in the territory around Manasarovara (Tibet) in the northern Himalayas and that they were worshippers of Lord Shiva – their supreme God – can irrefutably be proved on the combined testimony of the Mahabharata, (Aranyaka Prava, 1969: II, 13, 17-18, 20-21, 25-26, 30-47; Vana Prava, 1973: XXXIX: 186-89) Kalidasa (Kale, 1972: IV, 76-77, 95-96) and Bharavi (Sen, 1940: XIV, 33: 60-61; Ray and Ray, 1938, XII, 39: 61). Their descendants are found also in Sikkim. The migration of the Kirata tribes from Tibet (ancient Indian name Tribistapa and Chinese Tu-fan, called Bhotadesh for the first time in the 7th century A.D) to Nepal and Sikkim in successive waves took place in both pre- and post- seventh century A.D.

The classical accounts of the Kiratas on the confines of India on the east also deserve our notice. Among the early writers, Megasthenes, the Greek historian of the fourth century B.C, was the first to speak of them. His Scyritaes or Skiratais (identical with Kiratas) were one of the fabulous races and nomadic tribes of India (McCrindle, 1877: 80, 173-74). Pliny, the Roman geographer and historian of the first century A.D., also calls them Scyrites (Risley, 1962, VII: 2, 14-22). J.W. McCrincle, an authority on classical writings on ancient India, describes them as a "barbarous people" who inhabited the mountains and lived by hunting, and were of diminutive stature. He further says that the distinctive features of that race are indicative of their "Mongolian origin" (McCrindle, 1877: 74-75).

The Sesatai, Besatae or Cirrhadae mentioned by a Greek merchant and traveler (Annonymous) of the first century A.D. in his *Periplus Maris Erythraei* (McCrincle, 1879: 145, 148; Schoff, 1912: 47-48) has also been identified with the Kirata, a "Tibeto- Burman tribe" (Schoff, 1912: 47-48). Lassen, a German Indologist, categorically and unequivocally states that the Kiratas were a tribe of Sikkim (Lassen, 1847-62, 3:38). We are informed by the author of the *Periplus* that the Cirrhadae, a savage tribe of short figure with their broad face and flat noses but mild in disposition (Majumdar, 1981: 307, McCrindle, 1879: 145-48; Schoff, 1912: 47-48; McCrindle, 1901: 199) used to come to the border of Thinai or This (China) for their trade in Malabathrum (*Cinnamomum albiflorum*) with the Chinese (McCrindle, 1879: 148; Schoff, 1912: 48). W.H. Schoff opines that the author of *Periplus* locates them on the borders of *This* indicating that Tibet was then subject to China. On the authorities of Freshfield ("The Roads to Tibet", Geographical Journal, London, XXIII, Jan-March, 1904; "The Highest Mountains in the World", Ibid, XXI, March 1903), O' Connor (Routes in Sikkim) and Louis (Gates of Tibet) he asserts that the location of their annual fair (for trade) must have been near the modern Gangtok (27^{0}20'N; 88^{0}38'E) above which the Cho-La or the Jelap-La pass leads to Chumbi on the Tibetan side of the frontier from where the overland route was there. Other passes from Nepal, particularly by the Arun river, seem possible but the route through Sikkim involves the least deviation (Schoff, 1912: 278-79). He notes that the Cirrhadae mentioned in the *Periplus* was a Bhota tribe whose descendants are still known as Kirata living in Morung (Nepal), west of Sikkim, with marked Mongoloid features, formerly independent and powerful, having provided a dynasty of considerable duration in Nepal. Their location in the valleys of the Himalayas is beyond dispute (idid: 253). Lassen also calls them the Bhota race, which name survives in modern Bhutan. They were allied to the Tibetans. According to him, the Kiratas were one of the ten different tribes with several branches. The native capital of one branch of them was at Makwanpur in eastern Nepal. "They were a warlike, uncultivated, polygamous race whose native animism yielded imperfectly to Brahman or Buddhist teaching, and whose neglect of religious rites caused the Brahman Hindus to reduce them to the rank of Sudras" (Lassen, 1847: 441-50).

The Airrhadoi or Kirrhadia of Ptolemy, the Greek geographer of the second century A.D., is identical with the Kirata (McCrindle, 1885: 191-92, 219) which, according to G.E. Gerini, who carried out an extensive research on Ptolemy's Geography, is a generic term for the mountain tribes with Mongoloid features. They inhabited the hill and mountain tracts. He has placed them in the hills of North-East India, Burma (ancient Brahmadesh, now Myanmar), up to borders of Tibet, and in Assam, Bengal and Orissa (Gerini, 1909: 28f, 829-30).

Lassen says that the Kiratas belonged to the Bhota (bhotadesh or Tibet) and are still found in Nepal and Sikkim. He places one branch of them on the south bank of the Koshi in Nepal. They, according to him, were a widely diffused tribe. They had spread themselves in different directions in earlier times. They had wandered from north to the eastern Himalayas and into the other regions long before the time in which Ptolemy lived (Lassen, 1862, II: 235-37). A French scholar, St. Martin, deriving his authority from the ancient Indian, Greek and Roman writers on the subject writes that the Kiratas or Kirrhadias are one of the branches of the aboriginal race, the widest spread and most anciently known. In different passages of the epics and of the Puranas, their name is applied in a general manner to the "barbarous tribes" of the eastern frontiers of Aryavarta, notably in the eastern districts of Nepal (Martin, 1858: 340-44).

The Kiratis or Kiratis living between the Sapta-Kaushaki and Sapta-Gandaki (representing ancient Nepal) have been correctly identified by Hodgson with classical "Cirrhadae"or (Kiratas) (Atkinson, 1973: 365). He adds that in the generic term also, the Kiratas include the Limboos, Rais, Yakhas and others and that in appearance and habits they are all very much akin to each other. With regard to the affinity of the tribes, thus conjoined, he observes that they are closely allied or cognate race having essential commonality of customs, traditions and manners and they all intermarry. They are sub-divided into various tribes. Some sections of them are believed to have come from the province of Chung in Tibet. A vast majority of the Rai-Limboos now found in Sikkim. Nepal and Darjeeling still call themselves Kiratas (Singh, 1990: 116). The ancient name Kirata still survives as the designation of a sub-Himalayan tract extending from Dudh Koshi to Arun river in east Nepal. This region, which has been known as Kiratadesha from very ancient times, was the habitat of the tribes collectively known as the Kiratis or Kirantis (Levi, 1905-08: 72-78; Mishra, 1904: 7; Atkinson, 1883: 14). The most powerful section of the said tribes who settled down in the valley of Nepal in ancient times, probably in the pre-Christian era, and are identified with the present day Rais, specially Kulung, Thulung and Yellung (Regmi, 1969: 55-56; Thapa, 1981: 8-9).

It has been rightly pointed out that there was a "Cirata's country" (Kiratadesha) to the east of Nepal (i.e., Sikkim) (Tucci, 1979, II: 253). Ancient Nepal and Sikkim were the two famous Kirata territories.

B. H. Hodgson, while dealing with the aborigines of the sub-Himalayas and of the eastern frontier in the late 1840s tried to establish that the ancient Kirata tribes of North-East India and Nepal were all of Tibeto-Chinese or Mongoloid origin (Hodgson, 1847: 1235-44, 1849: 967-75). Sylvain Levi was another scholar to propose (in 1905) the racial affinities of the Kiratas of the sub-Himalayan and Himalayan regions of India with the Mongoloid people (1908, II: 75f). Ever since then it became almost a convention to connect the Kiratas in all parts of the Himalayas with the Mongoloids merely on the basis of their physical characteristics – yellowish complexion, dwarfish stature, round face, projecting chin, broad head, flat nose, oblique eyes, etc. whose descendants are believed to be mountaineers and foresters.

Rahul Sankrityayana opines that the Kiratas dwelling in the valleys of the Himalayas were the oldest tribes. In spite of belonging to the Mongoloid race they were not closely allied with the races of Chinese origin. The several branches of the Kiratas – Khambu (Rai), Limbu, Yakkha and Lepcha –living in the mountain regions of Nepal and Sikkim were the speakers of their own languages (1973: 295; 1958: 97).

The statement of Suniti Kumar Chatterji, a philologist of international repute and one of the authorities on the Kiratas, that "the Kirata, Indo-Aryan word, is Sanskritisation of some Sino-Tibetan tribal name" (1974: 28) is no longer tenable in historical perspective. According to him, "the Sanskrit term Kirata indicated Himalayas and in the North-Eastern areas of India, who were Mongoloid in origin. These Kiratas were connected with the *Cinas* or the Chinese, the Bhotas or the Tibetans and other Mongoloid peoples" (*Ibid*: 26). He further states that the original home of the Kiratas – the Sino-Tibetan speaking Mongoloid tribes – was western or north-western China. They spead from the upper reaches of the Yang-tse-Kiang and the Hwang-Ho rivers in different directions. They entered India partly from Tibet down the valley of Brahmaputra and partly from China through Burma before 1000 B.C. Their movements, according to him, began at large scale in the early part of the first millennium B.C. Their migration, as stated by him, covers the period extending from the pre-historic age down to the beginning of the Christian era. The said Mongoloid tribes gradually spread into different parts of North-East India and northern and eastern Himalayas. The Tibeto-Burman groups of Sino-Tibetan speaking tribes penetrated the frontiers of India and established themselves in the sub-Himalayan and Himalayan tracts. By way of Tibet and further crossing the Himalayan barrier, they moved to Garhwal-Kumaon, Nepal and Sikkim. Most of the Kirata tribes of Nepal and Sikkim, notably Mangar, Gurung, Sunwar, Limbu, Yakha and Rai are speakers of languages belonging to the Tibeto-Burman group or branch of Sino-Tibetan family (Ibid: 5, 15-16, 18-19, 21-23, 26, 36-38, 41, 44, 58; 1965: 143-45, 169-70, 169-70; 1978: 659-61; 1936: 43-49).

It is worthy of remark that neither all Kiratas were Mongoloids nor all Mongoloids Kiratas. Kasten Ronnow, a pioneer in the field of study of the Kiratas, remarked that "Sunita Kumar Chetterji's extension of the term Kirata to be an equivalent for Indo-Mongoloids was unfortunate" (Ronnow, 1936: 97f). He divides the Kiratas into two sections –those who have affinities with Mongoloids and those who are of mixed origin. Most of the ancient Kirata tribes of Northern and Eastern India, according to him, were of Indian origin (*Ibid*: 93, 100, 115, 123, 138, 145, 153). Robert Shafer, a noted ethnographer, also quated the view of Ronnow but did not support it. He has categorixed the Kiratas under Mongoloid race on the basis of their golden complexion. It is on linguistic basis that he has included the Kiratas of the eastern Himalayan section among the Sino-Tibetans. He considers them Mongoloid by race and Tibeto-Burmans by speach (Shafer, 1954: 124-25).

Migration is professedly a law of civilization. It is true that successive hords of immigrants from the great hive of the Mongoloid race in Western China had poured into the valleys and hills of north-eastern India and many of them have now formed a significant section of the tribal population there, but they are not all Kiratas (Sinha, et al 2005: Ethnographic Report, Government of Sikkim p-14). Some authorities have admitted the migration of Mongoloid tribes of China on the history of China (Nourse, 1938: 141f). It has also been very clearly pointed out that the southern group of Mongoloid tribes inhabited north-east Tibet and the slopes of the Himalayas. Their incursions took place in the "early middle age" (Bouquet, 1932-35: 118, 175-76). One of the authorities on the ancient history of China in particular has categorically stated "It was in the early centuries of the Christian era that racial movements started from China" (Hirth, n.d.: 6f). Those who migrated from Tibet towards eastern frontiers, sub-Himalayan tract of Nepal or eastern Himalayan state – Sikkim, before the seventh century were of Tibetan origin. The Mongoloid tribes of China migrated from the seventh century onwards (Sinha, et al., 2005: 15).

Depending fully on a racial classification by an anthropologist, (Guha, 1944: 8, 16-17; Majumdar, 1958: 30-32) an attempt has been made by historians to prove the Kiratas, as depicted in ancient Indian literature, the 'proto-Mongoloids" or "Palaeo-Mongoloids" (Brachycephals or long-headed and the broad-headed types) who formed a dominant element in the tribal population of North-East India and sub-Himalayan region (Chattopadhyaya, 1973: 2, 10, 72-73). Attempts have been made by a number of scholars to connect the Kiratas of northern and eastern Himalayas, including Assam, Bengal, Nepal and Sikkim, linguistically with the Tibeto-Burmans or Sino-Tibetans and ethnographically with the tribes of Mongolian origin (Choudhury, 1855: 170; Bettany, VIII: 110-12; Crooke, 1973: 31-32; Bhattacharya, 1964: 60-61; Pargitaer, 1897: 85, 105, 108-10). Historians, Indologists, philologists and anthropologists generally call the Tibeto-Barman groups of the entire eastern Himalayas - Kirata. The eastern Himalayan tracts including Sikkim, Bhutan and adjacent tracts were the lands of the Kiratas (Sinha, et al 2005: Ethnographic Report, Government of Sikkim p-15). The present day Kirata tribes are the Limboos, the Khambus and the Yakhas. The other analogous Kirata tribes are the Sunuwars, Mangars, Gurungs, Thamis etc.

KIRATA COMMUNITIES

I. The Limboos (Limbus, Yakthumbas, Tsongs)

Social Status : Scheduled Tribe

Origin and History:

The **Limboos** or **Limbus** or **Yakthumgbas** or **Tsong** or **Tshong** or **Chang** or **Chung** are the descendents of ancient Kiratas from the pre-historically occupied areas of "Limbuwan" (the land of the Limboos) prior to Prithivi Narayan Shah's Gorkha invasion of 1774 (Stiller, 1968: 109-110). According to Dr.R. K. Sprigg a renowned linguist of the world "The Limbus (the Limbu word was used for the first time by the Gorkha rulers only in 1774) were living in Sikkim before there was a Sikkim for them to live in! ...that Limbus have inhabited the area in which they now predominate (or in which predominated until recently) from time immemorial; but Sikkim has been in existence only since 1642, a Water Horse Year, and the year in which Phuntsho Namgyal ascended the throne as First Chogyal at Yoksom Norbugang in what is now Western Sikkim (Subba, 1999: v).

In his book "Kirat-jana-kriti" (1974) S. K. Chatterji has to say that "From the 'Yajurveda' onwards, the mountain regions of North and North-Eastern India – The Himalayas particularly, are well attested as the abode of the Kiratas. In the 'Mahabharata' (p. 30), the Kiratas are dwellers in the Himalayan regions, particularly in the Eastern Himalayas"; " ..and the Limbus are well known to be one of the principal Kirati (or Kirata) tribes, together with Rai (or Khambu) tribes, such as Bantawa, Chamling, and Khaling, and the Sunuwar tribe. Indeed, one might say – paradoxically again – that the Limbus inhabited Limbuwan and parts of Sikkim even before they were known as Limbus. This is because the original name of the Limbus, the name that they prefer to use for themselves, is not Limbu but Yakthungbas or Yakthumbas. The Gorkhas named them Limbus for the first time after 1774 A.D." (Subba, 1999: v).

Sprigg pointed out that an early reference to the Limbus as "Tsong" or "Tshong", comes in Hooker's "Himalayan Journals" (1854/1905); next to the Lepchas, the most numerous tribe in Sikkim is that of the Limbus (called "Chung" or "Chang" by the Lepchas); they abound also in East Nepal, which they once ruled (Hooker 1854: 194). Mainwaring's Lepcha-English dictionary gives "Tsong", also "Tshong" as borrowed words from Tibetan; they mean; "the Limbu-tribe according to Hooker I: 137 from Tibetan Tsang (sic, gtsang) province of Tsan; according to Mainwaring Waddel the "merchant-people" (Waddel, 1979: 313). "The Gazetteer of Sikkim" cites Waddel as explaining, "the Lepchas and Bhutias call them "Tsong" (which in the vernacular means "a merchant", and the Limbus were the chief cattle-merchants and butchers in Sukhim)" (Risley, 1894: 37).

Sprigg pointed out that the word "Tshong" or "Tsong", is important because it occurs in the Tripartite Treaty of "*LHO-MON-TSONG-SUM*", the treaty through which the existence of "The Greater Sikkim" occurred, and which also identifies the Tibetans, Lepchas, and Limbus as the Original Races of the Kingdom of Sikkim in the time of the First Chogyal (1642-70); "Lho" "South" refers to the southern Tibetans who settled in Sikkim and Bhutan; "Mon" "Foothills" refers to the Lepchas as inhabiting the lower slopes of the Eastern Himalayas; and "Tsong" refers to the Limbus, either on the supposition that they originally came from Tsang, one of the two Central Provinces of Tibet, though for this view there is no historical support, or, more probably, because they engaged in commerce (Subba, 1999: vi).

He further say that it must be remembered that Sikkim was much larger in the time of the first Chogyal than it is these days. The Maharajah of Sikkim's "History" (1908) gives the frontiers of his ancestor's new Kingdom – "**THE GREATER SIKKIM**" as "Dibdala in the north, Shingsa Dag-pay, Walung, Yangmag Khangchen, Yarlung and Tamar Chorten in the west, down along the Arun and Dudh Kosi rivers, down to the Maha Nodi, Nuxulbari and Titalia in the south, on the east Tagong La, and Tang La on the north". These frontiers would include in the greater Sikkim of those days the whole of Limbuan, now in the eastern most part of Nepal, southern Tibet from the Nathu La and the Jelep La to the Thang La, beyond Phari Jong, western Bhutan up to the watershed range between the Ammo Chu valley and the Har Chu valley, and the northern plains of Bengal as far south as Titalia (Subba, 1999: vi).

The most significant event in the history of Sikkim is the signing of Tripartite Treaty "***LHO-MON-TSONG-SUM***" i.e., between Bhutia, Lepcha and Limboo in Tibetan language in the "Water Horse Year" at

Denzong Phuntsong Khangsar between the Ministers of Chogyal Chempo, on one side and leaders of Lepchas and Tsongs, on the other side. They pledged and put their seals to the agreement that the "People of *Lho-Mon-Tsong Sum*" will here after not have separate self government but abide by one order only the commands of the King, his sons and Gurus. We hereby pledge that we will have one destiny and one government. This agreement might have been reached between Chogyal Phuntsog Namgyal or his representative on one side and Chiefs of the Lepchas and Tsongs, already inhabiting the land, as well as on other side as a consequence of a "Monpa" war mentioned in the agreement. It also stipulated the punishment of breach of Pledge payment of three ounces of gold and he made that physical punishment to the extent of death (as translated by Prof Ringu Tulku in 1984) (Subba, 1999: 125-128).

The various migration theories of Kiratas put forward by the various anthropologists inclusive of the Ethnographic Report prepared under the Chairmanship - Dr. A.C. Sinha, are based on historical assumptions and not on evidences. The migration theories may hold true for many but not to the Limboos, Rais, Yakhas and Sunuwars (Kiratas). The volumes of centuries old Mundhums (oral traditions) of the Limboo community (*sruti-parampara*), and Yakha community recorded from the life-performances of various rituals from Sikkim and Nepal, compiled and written as *Yakthung Re Tendham Mekkhim Mundhum* (1989), pertains to marriage myths and rituals; *Yakthung Re Phungsok Timma Mundhum* (1998), pertains to the myths and rituals of offering the newly harvested crops and flowers to the god and goddess; *Sumsemba Tongsing Took Mundhum* (2001) pertains to the myths of protection of clan and family from evil spirits; *Mujoklung Khajoklung Mundhum* (2003), pertains to the mythology of creation of the Universe, plannets, non-living and living beings inclusive of human beings; *Simering Mundhum* (2004), myths and rituals of death; point out repeatedly that the *Yakthumbas* (Limboos) have been originated at the base of *Phuktanglungma Pembenlungma* – Kumbhakarna (Jannu) mountains of the Himalayas. They always point out North as China and Tibet (*Sinyuk-Muden*), south as plains of India (*Teymen worong*), East as rising sun (*Namgen* – as direction and sign of progress of the community) and West as sunset (*Namdha-* as direction and sign of deterioration of the community). In the Mundhum repeatedly mentions *Thosu Saju-chua* (hot spring of the Northern higher Himalayas) and *Yosu Challen chua* (down river Ganga water) as the secret water required for offering to their deities. The Mundhum describes all the rivers right from the Brahmaputra river (*Yoom Yonghong*) in the east to Arun river in the West. Keeping in all those view of the Mundhums the Limboo community believe that they believe on the myths of their origin in the Himalayan Region only and are the aboriginal tribes of the Himalayas. They do not believe on migration theory put forward by so many anthropologists without any historical evidences. They neither believe on **migration theory** nor on **theory of abiogenesis**. They firmly believe on **biogenesis theory** of origin of life and also believe that the Yakthumbas are the aboriginal tribes (*Khambongba-Lungbongbas*) of the Himalayas. The Philosophy and Concepts of Yuma Samyo Tradition and Concept of life after life and funeral practices in Yuma Samyo Tradition has summeriesed the belief systems of the Limboo Community (Subba, 2005).

On the basis of the above facts the Yakthumbas as they call themselves from the time immemorial, are one of the ancient people inhabiting both Nepal and Sikkim. They are the ancient aboriginal tribes of Sikkim who contributed in the formation of "*The Greater Sikkim*" through '*Lho-Mon-Tsong-Sum*" tripartite agreement along with the Bhutia and Lepcha tribes of those days in 1642. The Bhutia tribes knew them as "*Tsongs*" or "*Tshong*" and the Lepcha tribes as "*Chung*" or "*Chang*" during those days. However, the earliest written record is available only in the Tripartite Treaty of "*Lho-Mon-Tsong Sum*" (1642), "Hooker's "Himalayan Journal" (1854). While the earliest written record of the word "Limbus" is available from the Gorkha rulers of Nepal in 1774 (1831 B.S.) as the Gorkhas called them the Yakthumbas as "Limbus".

Tradition has it that, after the Lepchas, the Limboos are the oldest inhabitants of Sikkim having setteled there before the Tibetans and the Nepalese came to settle in the land (Hermanns 1954:109).

Population and Settlement:

Based on the 2004 voters' list of Sikkim, the projected population of the Limboos constitutes 54,750 persons (number of voters x 2.14), about 9.15% of the total population (4th highest community) in 2004. During 1891 census the population of Limboo was 3,356 persons, (4th highest community) with 11.02% of the total population next to the Lepchas, Bhutias, and Khambu-Rais in the State.The Khambu-Rai population was 3,983 persons, the third highest community during 1891 census. There is a decrease in percentage of Limboo population by 1.87% in 113 years (Subba, 1999: 119-121).

Geographical Distribution:

The Limboo population is mostly concentrated at Daramdin, Soreng, Hee, Dentam Lingchum, Khaniserbong, Samdong, Yuksam and Darap in the west district; Rabitar and Namphok in South District; Assam Linzey, Aho and Pakyong in East district and Mangshila in the North District (Subba, 1999: 153-156).

Food Habits:

The Limboos are non-vegetarians; pork is their preferred meat, and many eat beef and buffalo also. Depending on their *thars* prohibitions (tabos) of eating chicken or mutton or buffalo etc. are there in different *thars*. For example, *Khewa thars* do not eat chicken, *Nembang thars* do not eat mutton, *Mangyung* thars do not eat buffalo. The *thars* included in *Lahsa-keyubas* (close neighbours of Tibetans) eat beef. Similarly many *thars* included *Kanshi-kethangbas* (close neighbour of Khasas) do not eat beef. Rice is their staple food. They produce finger millet for preparing and offering fermented beer to their deities. They produce various kinds of pulses (*dal*), soybean etc. both for consumption and offering to their deities. They use mustard oil and pig fats as cooking medium. They consume and offer various kinds of roots and tubers such as sweet potato, cassava, greater yam, colocasia etc.; various kinds of seasonal fruits and vegetables. They drink alcohol, both homemade and purchased from the market. They take milk, milk products and potato and other vegetables. They smoke cigarettes and loose tobacco.

Limboo Cuisines:

According to a self-study book on food and drinks published by Kirat Yakthung Chumlung, Nepal (2002), and Subba (1999), the food and drinks of the Limboos are:

(*i*) Food items: *Chyakhla ko bhat* (food cooked out of crushed maize-grains), *Dhinro* (food cooked out of maize or finger millet flour), *Poponda* (bread of finger millet, maize or wheat flour cooked under burning fire), *Lungdhakcha* (food prepared from freshly harvested maize flour wrapped in maize husk), *Sigolya* or *Penagolya* (food prepared out of barley or finger millet flour made into lumps and cooked), *Kangba* (Wheat, barley lumps put into rice and cooked), *Pena Manda* (food prepared like soup out of finger millet flour), *Khareng* (*roti* out of finger millet or barley or maize flour prepared on *tawa* or *bhumbro).*

(*ii*) Curry items: *Chembigik* or *Kinama* (fermented soybean), *Kinima Sumbak* (fermented soybean curry), *Yangben* (curry prepared out of Lichen collected from the trees), *Yangben-sumbak* (food prepared out of lichen and pork meat and pork blood), Sargyangma or Karjyang (Pork souses), *Sagi Sumbak* (Nettle curry), *Nakthuk Sumbak* (mushroom curry), *Kattakwa nook sumbak* (fern curry), *Phanook sumbak* (Bamboo shoot), *Kasakpa* (meat of pork fats), Yanglukma Chaa, Sirukma chaa, Khiringtukma chaa, Khekrokma chaa, Sura sumbak, Surakeek Sumbak etc.

(*iii*) Achar items: *Philingey Machhi* (Achhar of Philingey), *Nambong Machhi* (achar of perila seed), *Phando Machhi* (achar of soybean), *Yakkhosi Machhi* (achhar of pumpkin seed), *Mesu* (fermented Bamboo shoot), Sura muchhi, Surakeek muchhi.

***(iv)* Drinking items:** These items are *Marcha* (yeast cake) used for fermentation purpose, *Mangdok thi* (fermented finger millet), *Thi toongba* (finger millet or any foodgrain fermented and put in a bamboo or wooden can), *Sejongwa or Raksi* (home-made wine), *Thiseep* (fermented and sieved beer), , *Phatti thi, Pirisey Sejongwa, Phungkhey Sejongwa*, etc.

Family Pattern:

The Yuma religion has a tremendous influence on the youth-life, marriage, social structure and social activities of the Limboos. The family is the most fundamental, vital and the smallest social unit of the Limboos. Nuclear family is most prevalent, but stem- families are also commonly present. A few horizontally extended families are also to be found. Bonds of love and affection tie all the family members together. There has been a rise of nuclear families and decline of extended families. It is expected that all the families would help each other at times of need and distress.

Family Property:

Sons inherit father's property equally divided among the sons. The eldest son succeeds the father. Daughters, if unmarried, also receive a share of the father's property. This is the main point of family conflict.

Gender Issues:

Woman cannot inherit father's property, though she performs different roles in agriculture and animal husbandry operations. Daughters receive a share of father's property only if she is unmarried. Limboo women are hard working and they work in agricultural fields as daily labourers, collection of firewood and fodder, and contribute to the family income. The mother plays a key role in keeping the family united. Women also participate in the social, ritual and religious spheres and some of them are incarnate *Phedangmas* (*Yemanis*). The Limboos pray the Almighty God in the form of female Goddess –*Tagera Ningwaphuma* and thus they do not discriminate women in religious hierarchy or on religious rituals. However, they do not have decision-making powers and thus have a low status.

Kinship and Social Organization:

The Limboos are divided into a number of exogamous patrilineal *thars* (clans) and Sub-*thars* (Sub-clans). There is no caste system in Limboo community. Other castes or tribes adopted by the Limboo families as well as married by the Limboo individuals are also inducted in the community by the *Thumyanghangs* (Limboos community leaders) after a ritual of touching *Shamyok* (*Dubgrass*) and stone with promise

(*Lakubey-Namkubey Sakey-yekma*). Pedigrees of various groups of Limboos are maintained. Khagendra Singh Angbohang (1978) has listed 218 *thars* and sub-*thars* under 16 major *thars*, the *thar* Mabohang listed 26 sub-*thars*, Thegim 11 sub-*thars*, Shreng 10 sub-*thars*, Phago 20 sub-*thars*, Sanwa 19 sub-*thars*, Bokhim 5 sub-*thars*, Khoyohang 17 sub-*thars*, Nembang 14 sub-*thars*, Hukpahang 17 sub-*thars* and Khewa 22 sub-*thars*. However, it is very difficult to distinguish between *Thars* and Sub-*thars* of Limboos unless the *Bangsawali* is known for all the major *Thars* of Limboos for a layman. Subba (1999: 87-89) has listed about 300 *thars* and sub-*thars* of Limboos in his book. Regulation of marriage alliances and indication of descent are the main functions of the *Thars* and Sub-*thars*.

The kinship system of the Limboos may be termed, as "Classificatory" as the fundamental feature of this system is the application of the same terms for a number of persons, belonging to both lineal as also collateral relationship. Besides the classificatory form, a few denotative terms are also used. Subba (1999: 163-168) has listed 113 kinship terminologies of the limboos in his book.

Family Inter-personal Relationship:

Interpersonal relations are maintained through avoidance relationships between mother-in-law and son-in-law, daughter-in-law and father-in-law, sister-in-law (y)B and elder brother-in-law H(e)B. A free relationship exists between sister-in-law W (e)S and W(y)S, brother-in-law W(e)B and W(y)B, grandparents and grandchildren.

Intra-Family Relationship:

The lower Khasa the Damais serve them as tailors and as musicians and dancers in their festive occasions like marriage and other marry making festivals with their *Panchai Baja* and *Naumati Baja*. The Kamis serve them as blacksmith, goldsmith, silversmith and manufacturers of agricultural implements. The Sarkis acts as cobblers for making shoes, cover of *Khukuri, Laphija* etc. The Limboos can formally marry only with the Rais, Yakhas, Sunuwars, and Lepchas outside their own community. These four communities are believed to have descended from the common Kirata stock and are called *rit-bhatey.*

Intra-Family relationships are maintained through a number of customs and tradition practiced by the Limboo communities such as (*i*) *Chokphung Thim* (adopting a member of any tribe or nationality as a consanguineous relative of that family and clan); (*ii*) *Samyoklung Thim* (solemn promise and confession by touching *Samyok –dubgrass* and stone); (*iii*) *Soobu/Soona* (bond friendship with members of other community); (*iv*) *Phudong* and *Henamepma* (extending hospitality); and (*v*) Cooperation in need; etc. (Subba, 1999: 185-196; Subba,1995).

Economic Activity:

The Limboos are agriculturist and mainly depend on their land and landbased activities. The land is owned by individual proprietors and are mainly a land-owing community. With the increase of population, now, most of the households are small and marginal farmers. Their main source of income is from terrace cultivation of agricultural and horticultural crops, and livestock rearing. Some of them are engaged in various white collar jobs like teaching at schools and government and private services. They are dependent on the market for their cash crops like large cardamom, ginger, orange, off-season vegetables, livestock products and for their daily needs (Subba, 1999: 171-180).

Dresses:

The Limboo male wear *Paga* as head gear, also adopted *Takkhok/ Muyesup/Tapri* as hear gear; *Paothang* (Bridegroom shawl); *Ningkheng* (Maflar); *Sardokpa* (upper body dress); *Sunghreba* (Coat type upper body dress); *Alphi* (shirt); *Ascoat* (west coat); *Suthekwa* (coat); *Lappeta* (upper body dress); *Pagappa* (upper body dress); *Hangchang* (upper body dress for royal family); *Paohao* (main body dress); *Laoghek* (*Daura* type main body dress); *Phaoee* (*Patuka*/waist belt); *Yuppen* (belt); *Jangsumba* (*Suruwal* type lower body dress); *Sumba (Suruwal* type lower body dress); *Hangpen* (Lower body dress for royal family); *Langsuppa* (stocking); *Huksuppa* (hand gloves); *Ladhop* (Shoes); .

The Limboo female *wear Sunghamba* (blouse), *Mekhlee* (upper body bridal dress), *Hembaree* (breast shawl), *Phaoee* (Patuka), *Paothang* (bridegroom shawl), *Thakumey* (common shawl), *Sungnam* (bra), *Nukheng* (bra), *Chunglokek* (*cholo*), *Chaubandi* (*cholo*), *Sim* (*gunue*), *Langsuppa* (stockings*)*, *Huksuppa* (hand gloves), *Ladhop* (shoes), and *Lachha* (*Lachha*) (Subba 1999: 664-665).

Ornaments:

The Limboo male wear *Gokul* (gold or silver ear-ring), *Hebo-Samyang* (*Dant ko sun/chandi*), *Namloyee* (*Chandrahar* made of silver), *Sikri* (gold or silver chain), *Hukpangi* (*chura*), and *Swakep* (finger-ring made of gold, silver or brass).

The Limboo female wear *Nessey* (golden *cheptey* sun), *Tereng* (gold or silver ornament for ear), *Loskari* (gold ear-ring), *Kanthungri* (gold ear-ring), *Thungri* (nose *dhungri*), *Mundri* (gold *bulaki*), *Hebo-samyang/uppa* (*dant ko sun/chandi*), *Samyangphung* (gold *sirbondi*), *Hasuli* (gold/silver necklace), *Namloyee* (Silver *Chandrahara*), *Yangyichhi* (silver coin

Raizee), *Pongwari/Kanthi* (*Pongwaloo*), *Simikla Hari* (bamboo bead *mala*), *Tilhari/Kantha* (gold *tilhari*), *Sikri* (gold chain), *Ponayee* (*Pottey mala*), *Hukpangi* (silver *chura*), *Banhi* (*banhi*), *Swagek* (gold/silver/brass finger-ring), *Mundro* (Aluminium finger-ring), and *Langpangi* (Silver *Kalli*) (Subba, 1999: 667-668).

Folk Musical Instruments:

The Limboo musical instruments comprises of *Niyara Hongsing Ke* or *Ke* or *Chyabrung* (a cylindrical hollow log-drum), *Miklakom* (Bamboo harp of *Simikla* bamboo/*Binayo*), *Chethya/Yethala* (brass plate), *Ta* or *Soyeng* (brass cymbal), *Tungeba* (Ektar), *Ungdung* (tungna/Sarangi), *Yalamber Baja* (Acoustics), *Tetlafekwa* (tender leaves of monocot plants), *Mephrama* (flute/*Bansuri*), *Negra* (a pair of kettle drum), *Yea Pongey, Khiring Pongey, Yehang Pongey, Sirpong* (all different types of brass or metal bells), *Puttungey* (*Damaru* type musical instrument), *Phakwa* (split bamboo instrument), *Phamuk* (bamboo instrument), *Phenjekom* (Iron or metal harp/*Muchunga*), *Megphama* (bamboo instrument made of *Nigalo*) (Kandel, 2004: 23; Subba, 1999: 203-208).

Folk Songs:

The Limboos are fond of singing songs. They are of various types such as (*i*) *Khyali* (dialog songs of the youth), (*ii*) Duet love songs which are mainly of three types depending on tune and dance Viz: (*a*) *Shorakpa Palam Samlo*, (*b*) *Palam Samlo*, and (*c*) *Tamkey Ookma Palam Samlo* (maize interculture working songs); (*iii*) *Hakpare Samlo* (Gentle men or women duet Songs) (*iv*) *Nisammang Sewa Samlo* (Ritual or Ceremonial songs sang by *Phedangmas* for the deities and divinities), *Ke Samlo* (Songs of *Ke lang* dance) (Subba, 1999: 208-213).

Folk Dances:

Limboo dances are slower as they continue to dance from few hours to several days and are divisible into the followings types:

(*a*) Dances of nature – comprises of Ke-land in which mimicking of various birds, insects and animals takes place accompanied by *ke* or *Chyabrung* through their foot steps. Both men and women take part in this dance;

(*b*) Agricultural dance – comprises of *Tamkey Ookma, Yialakma* etc. These dances are life performances while working in maize first interculture and paddy threshing operations, which could be seen in west Sikkim even today. The dances are slow but continuously sing duet love songs by both men and women whole day while working. Such dances are performed on the stages also.

***(c)* War dances** – comprises of *Nahangma* dance of *Phedangma* during *Nahangma* ritual for "head lifting" and protecting the head of the family. d) Mysticism and Mythological dance performed by the Shamans/ *Phedangmas* at *Yagrangsing* or *Tongsing* altar (For detail see Subba, 1999:213-222).

Religion and belief system:

The Limboos have their own distinct religion known as "Yuma Religion" or "Yuma Samyo" or "Yumaism" which believes on Supreme Almighty Goddess "*Tagera Ningwaphuma*", and She is Omniscient (all knowing), Omnipresent (present in all places at all times), Omnipotent (all powerful), Infinite (without beginning or end), and Eternal (force, light or power of existence) (Subba, 2005: 1-39). They believe on female form of God, and have their own concept of God, biogenesis theory of creation of life, concept of creation of the universe –division of the atmosphere and inner earth into 18 layers (*tal-atal/Dens*) (Subba, 2005: 40-110), concept of life and destiny (Subba, 2005: 163-183), concept of multiple souls (*Yetchham*) (Subba, 2005: 22-32), concept of afterlife (Subba, 2005: 1-54), recognize 18 number of life stages (Subba, 2005: 8-10), and the purpose and meaning of life. The Limboo Community believes that their life is guided by the Philosophy of "Yuma religion", and is intimately linked to the Almighty Goddess *Tagera Ningwaphuma*. They believe that the Creator god *Sigera Yabhundinmang Porokmi Wambhamimang* could create mortal human progenitors only from easily degradable materials (ashes of *Simikla* a kind of a Himalayan bamboo, fowl excreta, water collected on rocks and wooden logs and various plants and herbs); and put life only with the blessing of the Almighty Goddess. Thus, they believe that the purpose of human existence in this world in a physical form is to earn positive "*Karma*" and develop a close relation with the Almighty Goddess so that they can go to live with their ancestors at *Sangram Pedang Den* as long as their "Karma" account allows them to stay where the Almighty Goddess also lives. One cannot obtain this purpose of life with positive "*Karma*" alone as in the case of Buddhism, but also have to develop a closer relationship with the Almighty Goddess through daily prayers and devotion to her. The negative "*Karma*" and negative relation with the Goddess leads one's soul to "*Khema Yongsong Den*". Since the souls either at *Sangram Pedang Den* or at *Khema Yongsong Den* have no physical body, have no opportunity to earn "*Karma*". The human beings must try to develop a closer and closer relationship with the Goddess along with positive "Karma" in this world (Subba, 2005).

They also pray and worship a number of other gods and goddesses which are distinguished into three categories, Viz., The *Mangs* (Deities or messenger gods and goddesses of the Almighty Goddess *Tagera Ningwaphuma* requircd for creation and sustainance of the universe), *Sammangs* (Divinities- Sam/Soul/Spirit/incarnates of Goddess, Deities/ messenger gods and goddesses) and *Sammangchyangs* (minor divinities – retinue of divinity gods and goddesses). *Mangs* or Deities comprises of the Almighty Goddess *Tagera Ningwaphuma*, creator god *Sigera Yabhundinmang Porokmi Wambhamimang* and a large number of *Sijoingmisa* (messenger gods and goddesses). The second category *Sammang* or Divinities comprises of all incarnations of *Mangs*/Deities (soul/spirit/San forms) inclusive of *Yuma Sam Sammang* (Soul/Spirit/Sam form of *Tagera Ningwaphuma),* and a host of divinity forms of the Almighty Goddess and gods and goddesses of nature. *Sammangs* are again divided into divinity forms of the Almighty Goddess, *Him Sammangs* (household divinities), *Tap Sammang* (nature divinities), *Thokley Sammangs* (clan-specific divinities) and *Sam Sire* (incarnations of Limboo Shamans – *Phedangmas*). The *Sammangchyangs* are the retinues of Sammangs forming a coterie of attendants around each of the *Sammangs*. Most of them are known as malicious, obnoxious, detrimental and wicked. They have to be propitiated before initiating the invocation rite of the main divinities so that they may not cause disturbances beforehand. e.g. cosmic retinues of *Nahen* (god of envy and jealousy) (Subba, 1999:284-337; Subba, 2005: 22-39).

They have their own shaman priest collectively known as *Phedangma*. They are classified into nine types namely *Muhikkum Ongshi, Phejiri Phedangma, Samboko Samba, Yaboko Yeba, Yaboko Yema, Yuma Sam, Sammundhums, Yepmundhums, and Dida-Sambas*. The former five are the incarnate priests while the remaining four are not incarnate. They have their own function in their priesthood in the society. Yuma Samyo has its own philosophy and teachings (for details see Subba, 1999: 339-390; Subba, 2005:12-21)

Festival:

The Limboo festivals comprises of the followings:

(i) Chasok-Thisok Tongnam: harvest festival, celebrated during low season – *Udhauli* (November-December) when newly harvested finger millet beer, rice, flowers etc. are offered to the *Him sammangs – Yumasam Sammang, Mudenhang, Thungdangmang, Theba or Kappoba Sammang,* and others. The fermented beer (*Thisok*) is also offered to the *Phedangma* family priests for further offering to their "*Sam Sire*" incarnate deity and the ancestors of the family.

(ii) Phungsok Thim: This is the festival when the *Phedangmas* offer newly harvested foodgrains, fermented beer, and flowers to their "*Sam Sire*" incarnate deity during the full moon day of *Mangsir* (December). The *Phedangmas* dance for about three day and night propitiating various *Mangs, Sammangs,* and *Sammangchyangs*. In the last day the *Phedangma* offer feast to his clients and neighbors.

(iii) Yokwa or Yumang: It is the festival of worshipping nature divinities before starting agricultural activities in the season indicated by the first blooming of *Phangrek* (peach) - *Ubhauli*. The entire village assemble on the top of the hillock, contribute rice and fermented beer for offering to the nature divinities of rain for favourable season of the crops as well as avoidance of accidents, wounds and bruises while working, and floods, epidemic diseases and other natural calamities. They propitiate with offering of fermented beer and rice to *Yumasammang, Thebasammang, Khamjiri Khambongba Lungjiri Lungbongba* (lord of the land), *Magui Thallunghang* (primeval ancestor who initiated agriculture), *Yabhungen Yabhungrekma* (female divinity of seeds), *Madenhang Lungumhang* (primeval ancestors who taught to remove weeds), *Nugohang* (primeval ancestor who taught better technique of working, storage etc.), *Hayuhang* (ancestor who saves farmers from accidents, natural calamities and help for good harvest).At the end they celebrate marry-making whole day.

The I imboos also celebrate auspicious Days as follows:

(i) Kak Phekwa La-Gaenge/Maghey Sankrant/ **the Limboo's New Year Day**: The day falls on 15th of January or *Maghey Sankranti*. The people assemble at the confluence of Teesta and Rangit –*Tribeni*; worship the nature divinities (*Tap Sammangs*) and take plenty of roots and tubers, greater yams, wild lesser yams *(bontarul* which ıs a must), sweet potato, cassava, colocasia etc. and enjoy dancing *Yialang* with *Pallam* (duet love songs) by the youths.

(ii) Sisekpa-La Gaenge (Sawaney Sankranti): The day normally falls in the month of July and is observed as an auspicious day. They celebrate the day as the end of hard, difficult and famine. They believe that the goddess of harvest brings them plenty of cucumber, pumpkins, ginger, fruits, maize cobs, flowers and climber twigs etc. and hence decorate their house doors and windows with these fresh food items. In the evening, they beat winnowing basket (*Phoet*) and dance running around inside and outside the house and shouting that the period of famine is over and the goddess has brought plenty of harvest.

(iii) Balihang Tongnam: This falls on the new moon day of *Kartik* (October-November). Incidentally it is also celebrated as *Tihar* a Nepali festival. The festival is celebrated with lighting of *La-semi-Nam-semi* (light) at the doors and corridors and dramatizing *Laringgekpa-Namlinggekpa* (*Dewsey-Bhailey*) as the anniversary occasion of the King Balihang who got his new life after his entire subjects prayed for his long life. (For details see festival chapter)

(iv) Teyongshi Sirijonga Sawan Tongnam: This day is the birth anniversary of Mahatma Sirijonga Teyongshi (1704-1741), the great literary and religious figure of the Limboo Language and Yuma religion. It falls on the full moon day of Mangsir (December). The Limboos assemble at every Mangkhim mainly at Martam where he taught to read and write limboo language in Limboo script and also taught the teachings of Yuma religion. The State Government has declared a Government holiday. They celebrate remembering his contributions and praying to *Tagera Ningwaphuma* at the *Yuma Mangkhim*. He was assassinated in 1741 at the confluence of Reshi and Kalej Khola (Subba 1999:197-199; Subba 2004).

Language, Literature and Script:

The Limboo language belongs to the Bodic –Himali-Kiranti section of the Tibeto-Burman language group and shares affinity with other Kiranti languages. The Limboo language has been broadly divided into *Chathare, Tammerkhole, Phedappe and Panchthare* but *Panchthare* has been recognized as standard language of the community both in Nepal and Sikkim. Writing, publication, reading, media, non-formal and formal education in the schools and colleges, and all Limboo language and literature development activities are being done in this language.

The Limboo language is written in Limboo script or Sirijonga Script or Kirant Limboo Script. According to Hamilton, F.B. (1819), at about 4,000 B.C. the Saumer Kiratas used to have a kind of script. According to Vansittart, E (1896), during the ninth century, the famous Sirijonga Hang (882-925 A.D.), the deified hero of the Limboos became the King who found out the Limboo script from the cave of mountains and taught the Limboos the art of writing by further development with a kind of character (p. 135).

Although, there is no evidence to prove but the Limboos believe that the Saumer Kirata script of 4,000 B.C. was revived and improved by Maw Rang Raja of seventh century for "*Rong Chhyo*" of the Lepchas; and also rediscovered the Limboo Script from the cave of *Kumbhakarna* mountain (*Phoktanglungma Pembemlungma*) by Sirijonga Hang, and further improved, taught and thus revived the art of writing system to the Limboos during the ninth century. After about 800 years of King

Sirijonga, his incarnate Teyongshi Sirijonga Singthebe (1704-1741) along with his eight disciples came to Hee-Martam, West Sikkim in 1734 and started Limboo language and Yuma religion teaching for which he was assassinated in 1741. Now, the Limboo language has been recognized as an Official language of Sikkim State since 1981. The Limboo script in known as Sirijunga script in honour of the King Sirijunga who further developed and revived the script. Now the Limboo language is being taught in Government Schools and Colleges as a regular subject and thus, the language has attended as high as 4b GIDS rating in Sikkim (Subba, 1999: 227-276; Subba, 2002).

Rites of Passage (Life-Cycle): Birth, Marriage and Death are the major events of life.

(A) Pre-Natal Worship:

The Limboo recognizes 18 stages of human life, right from the day of conception to the death. Hence, there is pre-natal ceremony called the *Sappok-Chomen* at least two months before childbirth. During this ceremony the *Phedangma* worship *Mujina Kheyongnama, Kudap Sammangs* (nature divinities), *Him Sammangs* (household divinities), *Apchara Pakchana, Wagongma, Mangenna* etc. for the protection of the developing child of the womb and the mother (Subba, 1999: 400-407; Kaila, 1991; Subba, 2005: 10)

(B) Birth:

The Limboo observe birth pollution for four days in the case of male child and three days for a female child. After the pollution period is over "*Yangdang Phongma*" or birth purification ceremony and name-giving ceremony takes place accordingly. This is to be conducted early in the morning before the sun rises. The mother and the child is given bath and house is cleaned with mud-water. Then, the Phedangma or the Tumyanghang (Elderly people) sprinkles the holi-water (*Wadumbokwa* - rain-water collected from rocks and tree logs or water collected from eight springs from eight different directions or water collected from Himalayas hotsprings - *Saju-chuwat* mixed with water from Ganga river - *Challan-Chuwat*) for purification in all the places inside the house, newly born child and mother, then the family members of the house. Now, the father takes the child at the main door and holding the child on his hands, and he gets out and in four times in the case of male child and three times in the case of female child singing a song of birth ceremony which addresses the child as "you have to go out of this house time and again for work, but you have to return quickly and so and so on..." This is to initiate the newly born child's *Ni-sam* (soul of sight) by exposing the child to the day light or sun for the first time. Similarly, by addressing the child means initiation of the child's *Khem-sam* (soul of hearing). It is believed that from this day onwards through this action of exposing to the light and addressing the child initiates the development of the souls of perception (animal souls) *Ni-sam* and *Khem-sam* in the newly born child.

Then, the *Phedangma* performs "*Mangenna*" (lifting of head) for both the child and mother, protecting from evil spirits etc.and touch the forehead of the child with one rupee silver coin known as "*Mangenna Yang*". Now, the father or elderly family name the child who is known as "*Mangenna Ming*". The *Phedangma* sprinkles "*Wadumbokwa*" (water collected from eight springs or collected from rocks and wood logs) to the mother, child, and the entire house for purification. The Child is given "*Phoondak*" (Cradle). The naval residue of the child gets dry and falls called "*Peychalam*" which is kept safely. A snail shell is hang at the edge of the cradle. *Chamuksam Chama* (*Bhat Khuwai*) at 3-6 months, and *Muyesup Khemsang* (clothing ceremony of the girl child) at 3 years age, and *Chanwaphungwa Leksingma* (clothing ceremony of boys) at 12 years age are also observed but not very common (Subba, 1999: 399-410; Subba, 2005 : 9-11).

(C) Marriage:

In the early Limboo social laws, the tribe recognizes 15 types of marriages. They are namely, *Na-aksingma Mekhim* (arrange marriage), *Nanupna Khepma Mekhim* (loved and elopement marriage, Marriage after having children, *Jari* Marriage (elopement of other's wife), *Namna Mekhim* (love marriage), Marriage with in-laws, *Khupna Mekhim* (elopement marriage), Marriage with agreement, Polygamy Marriage, Marriage with *Papchokma* (divorce marriage), Widow Marriage, Widow Widower Marriage, Dependent relative's Marriage, Orphan's Marriage, and *Yok's* Marriage (servants' marriage (Yakthung, 1992; Subba, 1999: 417-418). However, arranged and elopement marriages are common forms of marriages in the society today. Out of all above marriages, *Na-aksingma Mekhim* (*Mangni biya*) is considered to be the best marriage. In this type of marriage, the Limboo marriage rites of "*Limellung*" or "*Char Kalam Dos Rite*" are performed completely. However, the expenses involved in such marriages are very high. Now-a-days people cannot afford to do such marriages, resulting rare occurance of such a marriage.

The various social formalities involved in such type of marriages are:

(a) **Naksingma** – is obtaining consent of the girl's parents for marriage. This is the **First Kalam** out of the four Kalams, which involves offering presents of local wine (*Sechongwa*) to break the ice. If agreed by the parents, handing over of *Thupparung* (*baina*) to the girl by the boy personally; and presentation of two bottles of *Sechongwa* (wine) and *Thokkeywa* or *Sewa Yang* (money) for the girl's parents and close relatives takes place through *Ingmeba* (matchmaker and spokesman from the boy's side). The *ingmeba* of the girl's parent side counts the *Sewa Yang* and *sechongwa* and hand over to the girl's parents. Then, the date for marriage, numbers of *metkesama* etc. are fixed.

***(b)* Bringing of the Bride:** The marriage ceremony known as *Metkam* takes place at the groom's residence. This is the **Second Kalam** of the Marriage. The bridegroom now, known as *Nalisang* has to go to the bride's house now known as *Sisamey*, along with some relatives, a *Sangopla* (*lokandey*) and the same *ingmeba* who was present during *Naksingma* to bring the bride to the bridegroom's house. Usually they stay there overnight and bring the bride the next day. The bride party consists of some friends of the *Sisamey*, a *Sisagoplama* (*lokandi*), a *niya* (father's sister), and an *ingmeba* from the *Sisamey* side also. The guests are welcomed by the bridegroom's house with *Lamdhan, Ke-lang*, flowers, local beer etc. before they reach home. Usually the guests take rest on a temporary accommodation built for the purpose that night near the main house.

***(c)* Singgok Kakma:** If anyone of the groom's elder brother or uncle is unmarried, the *Nalisang* places a rupee coin and do *sewa* in the presence of *Tumyanghang* and asks forgiveness for getting married before his turn.

***(d)* Welcoming the *Sisamey* in the house:** This is the **Third Kalam** of the marriage. The next day, *Nalisang* wears the bridegroom dress comprises of *Thoksup-Langsup, Phoyee, Laphija* sewn in the *Phoyee, Paga, Namloyee* and *Shyaphung* on the forehead. The *Sisamey* is taken out of the temporary residence and asked to wear bridal dress comprises of *Simna, Sangchin, Thakumey, Phoyee, Hembari,* and ornaments. *Nalisang* and *Sisamey* are collected and asked to approach the main door of the house. The people assembled welcome them with Ke-lang, flowers and acheta (rice grains). The parents of Nalisang welcome at the main door from inside with Shyaphung and lead to the house. The guests take some rest and than taken out to a place at the higher side of the house for the people assembled there for *darshan*. Now, the relatives and villagers are served with food and drinks. They also contribute *Chumyang* (cash) and millet beer or wine for the feast.

***(e)* Metkam Thim:** At evening the *Metkam* celebration is solemnized by the *Phedangma* in the presence of *Tumyanghangs*. This is also the continuation of the **Third Kalam** of the marriage. The *Phedangma* performs *Mangenna* (lifting of head) for both *Nalisang* and *Sisamey* with a pair of chicken sacrifice. In many cases the ceremony is also hinduized by putting Vermillion (*Sindur*) on the Sisamey's forehead and *Potey Mala* necklace, which has practically no significance in the Limboo tradition. A pair of *Negra* and half a dozen *Chabrung* are beaten, gun fired, if Damais are called *naumati baja* is beaten (not essential) and the people cry saying "*Metkam Pokhe roo*" or "*Lagan Bhayo hai*".

After *Mangenna* is over, the *Sisamey, Nalisang* and *Ke-lang* party circle around the main pillar of the house, singing and dancing *Ke-lang*. *Tumyanghangs* perform the ritual of "*Sakey Ayekma*" (promise of *Nalisang* and *Sisamey,* and then *Nalisang's* mother not to give any trouble to the newly wed *Sisamey* and stay in close harmony in the family) with *Miphonglung* (*Dalsingdhunga*) and *Michak* (*Chakmak*). The *Phedangma* invokes the *Aakwanama* –the divinity of the main pillar, performs "*Yehang Sema*", "*li-toong seekma*", "*Sayiet Naakma*", and "*Phungwa Changma*" rituals. Now, the *tumyanghangs* sing the songs of *Phungwana Samlo, Hakpare Samloo*, while the young boys and girls sing *Palam* and dance *Yialang, Ke-lang* whole the night. Now onwards they are called *Ymeba-Meyt*. The next day the *Sisamey's* party with *ingmeba* of *Sisamey's* side returns and report to the bride's house about the marriage. The *Sisamey,* now, leaves with her husband at the *Nalisang's* house.

***(f)* Limellung (Char Kalam Dos Rite):** This is the **Fourth Kalam** of marriage. Sometimes after the marriage *Limellung* has to be prepared and submitted to the *Sisamey's* house. It involves submission of presents to the parents, relatives and village heads comprising of *Thibong* (Ten) rites and it completes "*Char Kalam Dos Rite*" as follows:

1. ***Yangthokma*** (permission to stay a night at the bride's house): comprises of one rupee, one *Chep* pork decorated with flowers, one bottle *Sechongwa* or one *Saptu* Thi;
2. ***Man Takma*** (accept the presents): comprises of one rupee coin, one basket pork, decorated with flowers, one bottle *Sechongwa* for all well wishers of bride;
3. ***Sepma Tooma*** (meat for evidance of marriage): one rupee, right front leg of sacrificed animal decorated with flowers.
4. ***Sadakoppa*** (full body pig for the *Lokangi*): One full *Hoktang* decorated with flowers for feast and five rupees for *lokondies*.
5. ***Thisap Temma***: one rupee and one *Saptu Thi* for acceptance of presents.

6. ***Yargsingma Yang***: one rupee, one *Chep* pork decorated meat and one bottle wine for Ingmeba;
7. ***Phungdongyangma***: five rupees, one *Chep* meat decorated with flowers for *Kutuni* or *niya* (aunt) who accompanied her during *Mekhim.*
8. ***Turayepma:*** Five rupees for village headman who writes the agreement of marriage.
9. ***Metkesamas Yang:*** Two rupee fifty paise, one *Lingdok thi*, one *Chep* meat with flowers for *Metkesamas.*
10. ***Pan Chupma*** : Five rupees for the *Tumyanghangs* who witness the *Dasturis.*

Thus, 10 (ten) items of presents is submitted through the *ingmeba* (spokesman as well as matchmaker) of groom's party, which is received by *ingmeba* of Bride's party and hand over the presents. The party stays that night singing *Hakpare* and *Yialang* and return the next day (for details see Subba, 1999: 411-453)

Residence after marriage is patrilocal. Both husband and wife can divorce each other with social approval, the reasons generally adultery, barrenness, maladjustments, impotency, chronic sickness, cruelty, insanity, practice of witchcraft and sorcery. If the wife runs away with another person, her husband is entitled to receive compensation (*jarikal* or *jaridanda*) from the paramour. If the wife does not remarry after divorce, she receives alimony from the husband. Children are the liability of the father in case of divorce. Remarriage of widow and widower is permissible.

(D) Death

Limboos believe that the Creator God *Sigera Yabhundinmang Porokmi Wambhamimang* tried to create immortal human beings with abiotic materials such as gold, silver, bronze and other such materials (*tattwa*) but failed. Finally, He took the advice of the Almighty Goddess *Tagera Ningwaphuma*, and on Her advice He succeeded with the biotic materials such as *Simikla Khappu* (Himalayan bamboo/ *Deoningalo Arundinaria recemose*), *Wahichelleckna* (fowl's excreta), *Wadumpakwa* (rainwater collected on rocks and tree trunks), various plant-parts/gums and *Pongen Surit* (atmospheric air). He made two idols with these materials and put atmospheric air on them. The female idol came alive on the eighth day and the male idol alive on the ninth day. The messenger God wanted to create immortal human beings and thus was not happy with the human being made of such easily degradable biotic materials. In disgust He cursed the idols with mortality.

Based on this Mundhum of Yuma religion the Limboos who are the followers of Yuma religion thus believe on biotic theory of origin of life and mortality of the human beings. Thus, death is inevitable so long as we exist with our physical body in this world but our destiny is only with the Almighty Goddess who created us. This is the reason why the human beings should develop a closer relationship with the Almighty Goddess for better afterlife. Yuma religion also believes that the quantum and qualitative attachment of the worldly pleasure and pain on our soul complex (*Yetchham*) depends on the life-stages of the individual. It also believes that the last thought at the moment of death have a tremendous effect on the deceased soul complex (Subba, 1999: 453; Subba, 2005:57-61).

Depending on these factors Viz., (*a*) deceased's relationship with the Almighty Goddess *Tagera Ningwaphuma*; (*b*) deceased's Life-stage at the time of death; and (*c*) the last thought process of the deceased, Yuma religion recognizes mainly seven types of death as under:

1. *Lamdoba* or *Sasik:* death of a child just after birth;
2. *Susuna:* death of a child before appearance of milk teeth (8-10 months);
3. *Tanglinghangsa's* death: death of a child after appearance but before shedding of milk teeth (15-24 months);
4. *Kuso?lamba* or *Kudopma Lam*: a natural death of an individual after shedding milk teeth;
5. *Sogha*: A death due to suicide;
6. *Sokup* or *Sugut*: a death caused by violent accident or child- birth; and
7. *Nahang*: individuals killed in a war.

In the first three types of death the deceased soul-complex has no or not much experience of the worldly pleasure and pain and has no attachment to this world. In view of this, no death ritual performance to guide the deceased's soul-complex is required. The soul complex is left to lead its own destiny. Simple burial of the body takes place and the *Phedangma* instructs the soul-complex not to harm the living by pegging down the *Muktus* (*Ghungring*) and tying the top with raw cotton thread with Mundhum (Subba, 2005: 62-64).

In the cases of *Sogha* or *Katchingba, Sokup* or *Sugut* and *Nahang*, the burial methods differ depending on sex and type of death. Yuma religion believes that such type of death occurs only with the influence of the evil spirits. The Almighty Goddess *Tagera Ningwaphuma* sent the *Phedangmas* for protecting the people from such evil spirits. But they failed to avail the opportunity due to their negligence of their own life. Thus, they deserve punishment due to their own fault and are not entitle to get the normal death rituals. Further, their soul-complex has been drastically affected due to their last thought process and hence cannot be tamed and reached to the ancestors. The deceased soul complex in these cases needs to be separated from the evil spirit first and then reached by the *Yeba* to the *Khema Yongsong Den* for punishment and torture so that they may not turn into evil spirits and affect other livings in their turn. At last they may also get a chance to take birth and thus repeat their Karmic cycle. However, if the deceased after violent incidence regained consciousness and remained alive for four days for male and three days for female, and the learned persons or *Phedangmas* guided his or her mind for normal death in peace, the death may be treated as normal death (Subba, 2005: 65-69).

In the case of *Kuso Lamba* or *Kudopma Lam* (norma death) the various death rituals and funerary practices are very elaborate. The dead body is buried in the *Yeebungden* (graveyard). The corpse is covered with a sheet of white cloth and is carried to the burial ground in a *Chydhap* made of bamboo. The corpse is placed lying on its back with the head to the west. The various steps followed are (*a*) preparation of corpse for *Cheydhap*, (*b*) preparation of *Cheydhap*, (*c*) the last journey to burial place, (*d*) burial of the corpse purchasing grave yard from the *Khambongba Lungbongba Mangs*, (*e*) *Sam-Sama* Ritual – reaching the soul to the ancestor's village and handing over to the *Hangsam*, (*f*) death pollution –observation of pollution, not taking salt and spicy foods, meat etc. for 8 days in the case of female and 9 days in the case of male (*g*) *Yum Tel Naakma* – opening the restricted foods by the *Phedangma,* (*h*) final death ritual – final good by of the deceased soul-complex (*i*) handing over the oracular divinities to the nature divinities, (*j*) construction of *Yeebungden-Kapur* – offering final feast to graveyard soul, (*k*) construction of *Falaincha* – offering final feast to the *Pungsam* soul, (*l*) the *Phojee* or *Tachina* – final feast to the relatives, villagers and *mallamis* , (*m*) *Sam Chaomma* ritual - collecting the soul-complex of the dead and again reaching to the ancestors, (*n*) *Khauma* ritual – final good by from the living world, (*o*) *Sitongsing Khema* and *Yagrangsing Aangma*-accompanying of the deceased soul to the Village of ancestors by the *Phedangmas*, (p) *Nahen* sacrifice – worship of god of envy and jealousy, (*q*) *Sitongsing Khema* separating the deceased soul from the living souls, (*r*) *Mikwanangwa sangma* wiping of death pollution tears of family and close relatives, (*s*) *Phungwa Changma* – lifting the head of the family and relative members, (*t*) *Him Warumma* – purification of house from death pollution, (*u*) *Miphoongma* purification of the fireplace, extinguishing the polluted fire and recreating the fire for livelihood, and finally (*v*) *Silam Sakma-* blocking the path of death for the family etc. There is no scope of dealing these steps in detail here (Subba, 1999:453-508; Subba, 2005: 55-137).

Statutory Panchayats:

Social control is maintained both through the traditional council known as *Tumyanghang* and formal statutory Gram Panchayats. The traditional council consists of ten elders from different clans and is called the *Thibong-Yakthung*. Maintenance of social boundaries in respect of connubial norms and setting of intra-ethnic disputes are its main functions. The council with the help of a similar counterpart sometimes solves even inter-ethnic disputes. Adultery, elopement and disrespect of traditional norms are the common offences for which social boycott and excommunication are imposed as punishment. . The Gram Panchayats look after the general development activities of the village as a whole.

II. THE KHAMBUS -RAIS (JIMIDARS):

Socio-economic Status : Most Backward Class (MBC)

Origin and History:

Khambus, Jimidars or Rais are the descendents of ancient Kiratas from the pre-historically occupied areas of "Khambuwan" prior to Prithivi Narayan Shah's Gorkha invasion of 1772-73 (Stiller, 1968: 109-110). The Kiratas are the oldest inhabitants of Nepal and are known as Kiranti or Kichak. They came from the north and first settled there in the 15000th year of the Dwapar Ingar and ruled the land for ten thousand years (Hermanns, 1954:7-10). Prior to the Nepal unification started by Gorkha King, Prithivi Narayan Shah in 1744 A.D. Nepal was divided into a number of princely States ruled by the Chiefs. The Kirata country (Kiratadesha) was divided from West to East into (*i*) Wallo Kirant or Hither Kirant - from Sunkoshi river to Likhu river; (*ii*) Majh or Middle Kirant – from Likhu river to Arun river; and (*iii*) Pallo or Farther Kirant – from Arun river to Teesta river. Wallo Kirantand Middle Kirant were mostly inhabited by the Khambu-Rais and Pallo Kirant (Limbuwan/ Limbudesha) was inhabited by the Limboos (Charles Macdougal, 1979: 2-3; Pradhan, 1991).

The "Rai" is a title given by the King Prithivi Narayan Shah to those who were chiefs ruling small estates until the political unification of Nepal in 1769 (Hermanns, 1954: 7). Hence, all the Khambus are not Rais while all Rais are the Khambus. The Gorkha king conquered both the Wallo Kirat and Middle Kirat of the Khambu-Rais by 1772-73, and Pallo Kirat in 1774. The title "Rai" was either applicable not only to Khambus but also to other chiefs conquered by him before 1772-73. This was substantiated by Kumar Pradhan, a historian of repute, writes that the title "Rai" is said to have been conferred on the Khambu chiefs by Prithivi Narayan Shah after the Gorkha conquest of Khambuwan; but even prior to that the Sen poten(t)ates of Eastern Nepal had referred to them similarly. However, the title which was spelt as Raya was changed to Rai by the Gokhalis" (1991: 52). He further writes "In 1880 Hastabir inquiry was conducted. The Kipatiyas (landlords) who could offer a land producing 60 muri paddy and Rs.30/= cash were conferred a title of "Subba" while those who could offer land producing 30 muri paddy and Rs.15/= cash were conferred a title of "Rai". The process of conferring title of "Subba" and "Rai" continued during Rana regime and anybody who could offer land and cash to the Gorkha Government could obtain the rank of "Subba' or "Rai"" (Shrestha, 1995). Hence, the use of these titles as surname is not correct, as it does not necessarily indicate a particular community of Limboos or Khambus, e.g. Subba Ganga Nanda Acharya of Gorkha community was conferred a "Subba" title. Hence it was appropriately advised to the Limboos to write "Limboo" and not "Subba" or their "Thar" (Clan) only but thar may be written in after surname as Limboo (thar) (Subba, 1999: 87). The same may be applicable to the Khamus also. They call themselves "Kirawa", whereas others generally prefer to call them as Khambus, Jimidars, and Rais (Vansittart, 1890: Reprint 1993:124; Sinha et al., 2005).

The Khambus or Rais are one of the few communities with antiquity of settlement in the eastern Himalayas, and have close affinity with the Limboos of Sikkim. More than that of the Limboos they are the Gorkha victims of Nepal unification – (*i*) Militarily, (*ii*) Politically, (*iii*) Legal and Judicially, (*iv*) Administratively, and (*v*) Culturally and Religiously, and thus loosing almost all Khambu-ethnographic characters. Although, the Gorkha Military invasion which was started during 1744-45, continued upto 1809, extending the Gorkha Kingdom from east of Kashmir (1809) to Teesta River (1774 and again 1789), the above other processes of Nepal Unification – one Hindu Nation, Hindu culture and tradition (*Char Jar Chattis Varna*) remained continuously active in the society. The Western part of "The Greater Sikkim" from the West of Teesta River to the East of Arun River remained under the control of Gorkha/Nepal Kingdom for many (25/34) years (Subba, 1999: 13-20). Thus on the basis of the historical evolution and developments during different period of "The Greater Sikkim" (after Lho-Mon-Tsong-Sum Treaty of 1642 to 1774) (Subba, 1999: 126-128) and "The Greater Nepal" (from 1774 to 1815) (Stiller, 1968:110, 186-209), there was no watertight compartment either on geographical area or on the people of these two countries of the Himalayan region. The political boundaries of Sikkim and Nepal had not been the same throughout the period of historical evolution in the past. Parts of Nepal had been under Sikkim's jurisdiction at one time and parts of Sikkim in a similar manner were under Nepal. Darjeeling district of West Bengal was an integral part of Sikkim and it was ceded to British India in 1935. Thus, it was quite natural that the various communities living in Sikkim, Nepal and India moved freely and settled wherever they wished. Thus, one can come to the conclusion that the Khambus, (Jimidars or Rais) like any other hill-tribes of the Himalayan region have been living with other tribes or migrated during the historical evolution in the geographical areas of present Nepal, Bhutan, Sikkim, Northern areas of West Bengal, Assam and other Himalayan areas of India since ancient times with harmony but maintaining their distinct ethnographic characters as far as possible.

Population and Settlement:

The Khambus are scattered throughout the state except North District of Sikkim. They are predominantly found in areas like Chakung, Jorethang, and Damthang, although in smaller numbers they are found all over the state except the North district. They also predominate in the State of Sikkim, Darjeeling district of West Bengal (inclusive of Kalimpong, Kurseong, Mirik and Dooars). A large number of Kirat Khambus are also living in other North Eastern States and Eastern Nepal (Rai, 2005:14-15). They were 3,983 persons constituting 13.08% of the total population during 1894 in Sikkim (Risley, 1894: 27). Based on the 2004 voters' list, the Khambu-Rais were 75,708 persons, constituting about 13.54% of the total population in 2004 in Sikkim. The percentage of Khambu-Rai population in Sikkim has increased by 94.74% in 110 years on 2004. In Nepal, the Khambus (Jimdars or Rais) are 6,35,151 persons conprising about 2.79% of the total population.

Bio-anthropological:

The anthropometric survey indicated that the Khambus are relatively short and the mean stature varies within a small range of 1571 mm to 1605 mm. The cephalic index of the Khambus can be distinguished from other groups in having the highest mean cephalic index (82.61) which comes under the brachycephalic class. The total facial index of the Khambus is on the border-line between the euryprosopic and mesoprosopic categories. (Bhasin et al., 1986).

Food Habits:

The Khambus are generally non-vegetarians but many of them who adopted Hinduism are vegetarians. The Pranami, Joshmani and Kabir Panthi religious groups are purely vegetarians and do not take alcohol and meat. Maize and millet have been their traditional staple food. They take popcorn, soybean, root and tubers (colocasia, greater yam, roots of iskus, sweetpotato, cassava, potato), and fermented millet beer (*Jaarn/ Umma/Hengma/Arakha*) in the morning. At the daytime, they take *Bhat* (*Dhero/Jaulo/Yuwa*) and *kalodal /Panhelodal/Gahat* etc.(pulses), and *Sisnu* (stinging neetle) along with few pegs of *Arakha* (home made wine) or millet beer. At dinner, they love to eat pork (*Baksha*), and chicken (Beef or *Pisha* is taken by those who have adopted Christianity) with corn millet *dhero* or *roti*. But they do not eat mutton. They take all kinds of vegetables. They are very fond of fermented-soybean (*Kinama/ Goyong*). Home made wine or corn-millet beer and is a must before they take rest in bed. *Wachippa* made of chicken is a delicacy of the *Khambus*. For non-vegetarians, the outer feathers of the fowl is plucked, the inner down feathers is burnt and collected in a dish. This *titey* (bitter) black powder along with the cut wing-pieces of the chicken and rice is cooked as *Khichary*. This makes the *Wachippa*, a delicacy of the *Khambus*, which must be eaten by all family members and guests during Mang (*pitripuja*), ancestor worship and other special occasions. The vegetarian *titey* (*Damleppa/Nakhilbung)* is prepared with *Hallalumbey* flower/bitter flower collected, powdered, mixed with rice, and cooked and served to the family members and guests (Rai, 2005: 27-29). Hot tea with or without sugar and milk is widely taken as a non-alcoholic drink. Now, association with various hill tribes, they take all kinds of food such as *momo*, *thukpa, sale roti, gundruk*, etc. They also take tubers and root crops, seasonal fruits like guava, *suntala, naspati* etc.

Family Pattern:

Nuclear family is common but generally extended families are also present.

Family Property:

Sons inherit father's property and succession goes only to the eldest son. This is the main point of family conflict.

Gender Issues:

Woman cannot inherit father's property, though she performs different roles in agriculture and animal husbandry operations. They do not have decision making powers and thus have a low status.

Community Relationships:

The *Khambus* or Rais have different clans (*thars*) like Bantawa, Chamling, Thulung, Kulung, Lohorung, Baying, Dungmali, Nechereng, Khaling, Chaurasaya, Rungchengbung, Dumi, Chinthang, Athpahare, Sangpang, Lambichong, Sotang, Thilung, Yaku, Mewahang, Puma, Waling etc. The above 22 *thars* are the main sub-groups/*thars* but at present there are more than 50 such *thars*, speaking different dialects (Gaenszle Martain, 1991: 3). Again they have different *pachhas* or *sub-thars*. Marriage is allowed within the same *thar* but the *pachha* of the boy and girl must be different. These *thars* and *pachhas* are used for regulating marriage alliances since they indicate descent. For marriage, there are Rais who consider *thars* for seven generations, counting descent from the father's side so that marriage can take place between the same *thars* or *pachhas*. Similarly marriage can take place between Rais of the same *thars* and *pachhas* tracing the mother's lineage to beyond five generations. They cannot marry a father's sister or a brother's child or mother's sister's/brother's child. On occasions of marriage, *nauran*, or death, all relatives, neighbouring families, and friends' families are expected to help one another. A rise in the number of nuclear families and a decline of the extended family system are noticeable changes.

Family Inter-personal Relationship:

Interpersonal relations are maintained through avoidance relationships between mother-in-law and son-in-law, daughter-in-law and father-in-law, sister-in-law (y)B and elder brother-in-law H(e)B. But joking relationship between sister-in-law W(e)S and W(y)S, brother-in-law W(e)B and W(y)B, grandparents and grandchildren.

Socio-Economic Activity:

Although, Khambus-Rais are mostly small and marginal farmers in Sikkim, the land is their major resource, owned and controlled individually, which are mainly the agricultural community. Now, their primary occupation is terrace cultivation of agricultural and horticultural crops, livestock rearing, and miscellaneous services etc. The farmers are mixed farmers engaged in agriculture, horticulture and livestock rearing. They are also employed in service in different white-collar jobs in government service, as schoolteachers, bank employees, scholars, teachers, engineers, and members in defense services etc. They have a direct link with the markets and depend on them for their daily needs.

Characteristics of Khambus:

The Khambus have short robust body, broad chests, flat nose, thin, pointed whiskers (*Baagjunge*). Their eye slit is narrow, skin is lighter in colour, and hair is black and usually stiff. They have dark eyes; scanty beard and the muscles of their legs are well developed, being mountainous people (Sueyoshi Toba, 1992: 8-9).

Dresses:

The Khambus male wear head gear (*Pagari/Sayabung*), *Daura* (*Lockchham* - a kind of upper garment), Sleeveless coat, *Surwal* (trouser), *Patuka* or *Chakchhinma* (waist band) and *Khukri* (dagger, *Dabhay/ Betho*). Footwear was not worn in the rural areas but now is a common. The Khambu female wear Shawl (*Mujetro/Burkey/ Tangdoma*) on the head, blouse (*Cholo/Yamlung*), sari (*Guniu/Tamphey*), waist band shawl (*Hembari*), waist Sash (*Patuka/Chhakchhima*). They also keep *Khurmi* (a small curved knife), pig hair round brush (*Kuchi*), Musical instrument (*Binayo/Dong*), hair band (*Lachha/Tangkhi*), (Rai, 2005: 26).

Ornaments:

The Khambu male ornaments are earrings *(Kundal/Phingrang)*, and finger ring *(Aunguthi)*.

The Khambu females wear gold necklace (*kantha/Lolopot*), Gold necklace (*Nawgerdi/Bhitat*), Nose stud and nose ring (*Dhungri-Bulaki/ Nathen Nabit*), *Chura* (*Chhuklung*), *Rejee* (*Yangchang*), *Hansuli* (*Phetlung*), Flat gold earring (*Chheptesun/Nadup*), Earring (*Kandhungri*) (Rai, 2005: 26).

Folk Musical Instruments:

Gojey Murali – (Flute made of Nigalo bamboo) -used by cowboys at Khotang and Okhaldhunga area of Nepal and Sikkim.

Tungma – made of bans; used by Khaling Rais of Khambu areas of Eastern Nepal.

Dhool – made of hollow wood and skin with both ends equal size, is a famous Rai baja, one side beaten with stick and other side with hand.

Thanowro – tongue-like baja, made of iron, is a Khambu Kirant's tongue-like baja; used during Sili dance of Sakewa festival.

Pung – made of bull-horn with a hole at the tip; used by Kirati Rais of Solu area to please ancestors while offering prasad etc.

Bans Tumba – made of two and half feet long hollow brass; used in Bhojpur area of Nepal.

Binayo – made of three years old red or strong *nigalo*-bamboo; keep tying on their *tuna* and used by Kiranti women

		while taking rest after collection of fuelwood and fodder.
Bimbili	–	like that of flute, made of nigalo bamboo; used by Kiratas during *maruni* dance in eastern hills of Nepal.
Mathuuri	–	made of nigalo or bamboo; used by Rais of Bhojpur areas of Nepal.
Yalamber	–	made of Bhalu bans with two wires; used by Kiratas and named after the Kirati king Yalamber.
Sapoksa	–	cymbal made of brass; used by Rais during Sili dance in Sakewa festival or during Ubhuli and Udhauli festivals; and
Siling	–	made of iron with serrated ends both side and iron rings all around; used by Rais during their Sili dance of Sakewa festival (Kandel, 204: 24).

Folk songs:

The Rais has a rich oral tradition. Both men and women sing folk songs. The songs are usually accompanied on a kind of drum called *Dhol*. They have an elaborate folklore and a rich stock of folk tales.

Folk Dances:

They use *Dhol, Siling, Thanowro, Gojey Murali,* cymbals etc. as accompaniment to dance. Both men and women participate in the dance. *Sakkewa* or *Chandi Natch* is most important folk dance of this community. There are three major patterns of folk dances in *Sakkewa* dance: first mimicking agricultural operations like sowing of seeds, weeding, and harvesting; second mimicking craftwork like basket making for men and weaving for women; and third mimicking the habits of animals and birds. The *Mangpa* the Rai priest must guide the dance group to sacrifice goat to the deity (Subba, 1999: 119-110).

Religion and belief system:

The Rais do not follow any religion in the strict sense of term. The oldest religion of the Rais is shamanism. Many denote this set of beliefs and practices "**animism**" and nature worshipers, but this term is wrong. Animism refers to the worship of nature and natural phenomena, such as rocks, mountains, rivers, streams, thunder and lightening, to ascribing inanimate things as having a soul. The Rais, however, do not outright worship these phenomena; they respect their natural surroundings but do not ascribe souls to them. Rather, they think that these places are where spirits live. The spirits as such are not identified with the rocks or trees themselves, but are seen as separate from them. The religious specialists are called shamans, after a word used by the Tungus of Siberia to denote such a person (Jeffrey et al., 2000). In the case of Rais these shamans are:

(i) *Mangpa* or *Bijuwa* - who is the main priest; conducts *Samkhalung* ritual- household deity, performs *Thomwa/Chinta* etc.

(ii) *Nakchhong* - who conducts the Sakewa (Worship of nature); *Dongwangna*, god of cultivation of crops; *Donglasha* god of harvesting crops.

(iii) *Mabimi* – who conducts the last rite of the deceased. *Mabimi* allows the souls of natural death to live in the *Samkhalung* (hearth), as a venerable ancestor; the souls of unmarried men/ women are allowed to live in *Rongeli* (the atmosphere of outside the main door of the house); the souls of immature married or adopted persons are allowed to live in *Namelung* (ever sunny stone on the lap of highest mountain); the souls of persons who dies due to accident or suicide and other unnatural death are allowed to live in *Hillaten* (blood shaded rocky places); and souls of women dies during delivery are allowed to dwell in *Mannangten* (gloomy and steep rocks).

(iv) *Kubimi* – conducts the last rites in absence of *Mabimi*.

(v) *Dowang* – performs only the miner religious rites and to cure the sick. He chants the spell to ward off the affcted evel spirits. He also used herbal medicines. Some senior *Raopas* may also conduct some minor religious rites in absence of Mangpas. The collective term used for all above Khambu-shamans is *Bijuwa*.

The most venerated deities are *Sumnima* (Parvati) and *Paruhang* (Shiva) who are regarded as the creaters of the Kirat Khamu Rai people. Then come the ancestors of the sacred kitchen with three-stones/fire place – the main shrine of Khambus called *Samkhalung*. Only clan members are allowed to go to *Samkhalung*. They believe that all the souls of the dead Raipas and Raimas dwell here. The Rais believe in various deities of nature such as *Aitabarey, Sikary, Aathaney, Naya, Buddheni* and *Yowa* and worship them from time to time. The Khambus are ancestor worshippers and have no concept of God and do not believe in heaven or hell (Rai, 2005: 40-44).

In recent years many Khambu families have adopted *Parnami, Joshmani* and *Kabir Panthi* sects of Hinduism, and follow the practices of Hindu religion. A number of their families especially after the late nineties of twentieth century, have adopted Christianity in large scale in

Sikkim, and hence follow the practice of Christianity even in the rural areas now.

Festival:

The main festivals of Khambus are *Sakewa* and *Sakela. Sakewa (Ubhauli /Bungbanwa/ Dongwnga)* –is an agriculturist festival where the deities of land and crops are worshiped every year for good crop in the following season to come. The festival is also known as *Bhumi Puja* or *Chandi Puja* or *Baali Puja* or land worshiping ceremony by others, and celebrated on full moon day of *Baisakh* (May-June). The Rais along with their shamans – priest gather in a place and form a huge circle to perform various dances lead by the *Sili Mangpa* and *Sili Mangma* such as "*Chasum Sili*" (dance depicting paddy harvesting, threshing, husking, cooking and finally eating the cooked rice); "*Paklewa Sili*" (depict the activities of animals and birds of nature); "*Narowa Sili*" (depicting lifestyle of the crane –*Karang-Kurung*, the migratory bird while returning to northern hemisphere indicates right sowing season of cucumber, pumpkin and other Kharif crops).

Now, the *Nakchung* priest perform *Akta Swang Sengma* (water spout/ *Dhara* ceremony) on the altar consists of Phallic Stone and trident (*Linga/ Narilung/Pao*) on hill-top as the Rais believe that they are descendants of *Paruhang* (Shiva) and *Sumnima* (Parvati) of the Himalayas. They offer rice and wine in *wabuk* (*cindo*/dried lauki). They may also sacrifice chicken or pig or both and other produce of their field for good harvest of the crop. Now, the *Nakchung* fixes a bamboo pole on the ground in front of a house. He now, performs *Khutlung Khutma* (fire place worship) for the ancestors of the house at *Sankhalung/Situlung/Sutulung* (hearth of the house) offering ginger and blood of Chicken (*Mang Hulu*) on the fire-stones. Finally the villagers enter the house, dance around the fireplace, wine dine and proceed to the next house. (Rai, 2005: 45-47).

Sakela (*Udhauli/Dongdawa/Donglasa*) is celebrated on full moon day of *Mangshir* (Nov-Dec.) for thank giving for the good harvest of the season and peaceful climate. They worship Mother Nature offering grains and sacrifices for the good rain, good sunshine and harvest. Besides, they also celebrate *Dasai, Tihar, Chaite Dasai*, *Maghe sankrati*, etc. along with other communities of the state.

Language, Literature & Script:

The Khambus have no common language other than Nepali; but they speak a large number of dilects which appear to differ greatly from place to place. All, however, belong to the eastern sub-group of complex pronominalized languages, and are inclined in the Tibeto-Burman family

(Morris, 1933: 102-03). The dialectical variation among Rais is, however, not based on ecological variations of their habitat but on clans although Bantawa dialect is considered by all Rais to be the most widely spoken and understood in both Nepal and Sikkim. However, the *Khambus* of Sikkim have resolved to use the Bantawa dialect as Rai language, which belongs to the Tibeto-Burman family of languages on 15th June 1996. And on 23rd May 1998, they adopted the scipt developed by Kripasalyan Rai of Daramdin in West Sikkim as the Rai script with some modifications to make the letters compatible with computer system (Rai, 2005: 48-55). The clan-based dialects are basically so because different clans occupied different territories making it possible for clan dialects to sustain themselves. Since there is no ecological support-base for clan-dialects in Sikkim the other clan dialects are likely toturn into territorial dialects, as single clan Rais are nowhere found in this state. The Rai language was recognized as one of the official languages of Sikkim on 21st March 1995. Now, the Kirat Khambu Rai language is being taught in the various schools run by the Rai associations all over Sikkim (Rai, 2005: 48-55). However, *Khas Kura* or Nepali or *Gorkhali*, written in *Devnagari* script; is the *lingua franca* in Sikkim.

The Relationship between the Land and the People:

The various tribes of Sikkim such as the Kirata Communities (Limboo, Rai, and Yakkha), Communities analogous to Kiratas (Sunuwar, Mangar, Gurung, Tamang, Newar, and Bhujel, Thami,), other communities such as Sherpa, Bhutia, Lepcha, Jogi/Sanyasi, etc. having their own language, culture, religion etc. have been clubbed as a single community –called "Nepali", while maintaining the Lepcha and Bhutia community distinctively separate. However, all these communities are living in perfect harmony and peacefully, as they are intimately inter-dependent as stated under the *Khasas* of Sikkim.

Rites of Passage (Life-Cycle): Birth, Marriage and Death are the major events of life.

(*a*) Birth: The birth of a child generally takes place in the husband's house and at times in the house of the wife's parents also. Some women seek the help of experienced women. The husband assists in making a cradle for the newborn. Now-a-days, the nurses in the village in Sikkim attend most of the delivery cases. Birth pollution (*sutak*) period observed for 3 days for girls and 4 days for boys. On the expiry of birth pollution, the *Mangpa* performs purification as well as name-giving ceremony. The house is washed with mud-water; purification bath is given to the mother and the child. The *Mangpa* performs the rites of "*Sayachongma*" (lifting the head) for both mother and child. This is to exorcise any evil spirit, which may have been present at the time of birth. The relatives and neighbour may bring chicken and millet beer for the mother. Later, a feast is given and all the people present at the rite participate for the feast. *Bhatkhowai* or *annaprashan* – first rice-eating ceremony is performed when the girl child is at the age of five months and six months for the boys. The Athpaharia and Bantawa clans celebrate rice-giving ceremony while Khaling, Kulung and Mewang do not celebrate. Hair cutting ceremony (*Chhewer)* also performed for the sons when they are at the age of three years by some clans while other do not (Sueyoshi Toba, 1992: 17-22). The birth rites of *Khambus* tribes vary from clan to clan and also on the religion they have adopted (*Paranami, Jashmani, Christianity* etc.) The birth rites of passage are considerably Hinduized today (Sinha et al., 2005: 25-27).

(*b*) Marriage: The *Khambu* tribes follow endogamy at the community level and *thars* and *pachas* exogamy for marriage. They consider *thars* or *pachas* for seven generations, counting descent from the father's side, and five generations from mother's side so that marriage can take place between the same *thars* and *pachas*. Junior sororate is allowed. Adult marriage is in vogue now. Mates are acquired through negotiation (*mangni biha*), elopement (*chori biha*), and mutual consent. Monogamy and rarely polygyny are the marriage forms.

In the case of *mangni biya*, the initial marriage ceremony (*Sagun/ Niwa*) is performed in various stages such as "*Sodhana*" (boy's parents request to the girl's parents through *Kongpi/Bongpa*), '*Multheki*" (presentation of liquor and payment to the girl's parents), and "*Bhakha*" (date fixing of marriage ceremony). The Groom party go to the bride's house to perform "*Sainu phernu*" (rites of changing relationships), and "*Makamundri*" (presenting dresses and ornaments to the bride) and the bride is brought to the Groom's house. On arrival of the Groom's house "*Daplo Kuin*" rite is performed when the millet beer or wine brought from the house of bride is poured on each of the three sacred hearth stones, walking around in a clockwise direction and finally on the altar (*Than/ Damphe*). The guests are served with food and drinks. The elderly people gathered here sing the songs of "*Sakumbo Kura*" (blessing songs for the bride-groom).

The final marriage rite can take place only if the wife's family agrees, for which the husband of the couple goes and approach the wife's family members for final "*Wak Datta*". This may take ten or more years after the initial marriage and the couple living together. The bridegroom party along with two *Kongpies* or *Bongpas* go to bride's house with one ceremonial gourd and one large earthen pot, both full of millet beer, two large wooden vessels filled with liquor (*Arakha/Hengma*), a leg or head of pig, twelve seers of grain along with the "*Lastur*" (consisting of a set of eight copper vessels). Outside the house, they are met by the Bongpas/ Kongpies of the wife's side and the two parties ceremoniously greet each other and offer liquor to each other. *Daplo Kuin* is performed and then food and beer is served. Later in the evening, the husband side presents the "*Lastur*" to his wife's family and request for "*Wak Datta*". The bride family agrees and gives "*Wak Datta*" by final declaration that the family has given his daughter to the bridegroom in presence of witnesses. In the case of elopement the unmarried girl is abducted willingly or unwillingly. The abductors inform the girls' parents within three days and pay fine to her family as damages done for having flouted their authority over her marital destiny. After that the other marriage formalities are carried out. Elopement with another's wife (*jari*) is also practiced but such persons should face the *Pancha* (comprising five elderly *Khambus*) who generally impose fine (*jarikal*) on the person to pay the former husband (Allen, LXXXIII: 100-101: 15-33; McDougal, 1979: 103-121; Rai, 2005:60-63).

The marriage rites of Khambus tribes also vary from clan to clan and also on the religion they have adopted (*Paranami, Jashmani, Christianity* etc.). For the families who have adopted Hinduism, the marriage symbols for women consist in putting of vermilion (*sindur*) in the parting of the hair and wearing a green bead necklace (*poty*). The marriage ceremony is solemnized through *Kanyadan*. The families who have adopted Christianity follow the rites of that religion and the wedding is solemnized in the church.

Residence after marriage is patrilocal. Both husband and wife can divorce each other with social approval, the reasons generally adultery, barrenness, maladjustments, impotency, chronic sickness, cruelty, insanity, practice of witchcraft and sorcery. If the wife runs away with another person, her husband is entitled to receive compensation (*jarikal* or *jaridanda*) from the paramour. If the wife does not remarry after divorce, she receives alimony from the husband. Children are the liability of the father in case of divorce. Remarriage of widow and widower is permissible.

(c) Death: The Khambu tribes adhere strictly to their tribal death rites, and look for the most competent priest possible for this rite, especially if the death has taken place unnaturally. The dead body is buried, rarely cremated. The funeral rites of Rais are divided into two parts: (*a*) "*Mishia*" is performed soon after death, when the deceased is buried in a field near the house; and (*b*) "*Shilum Kattu*", is performed on the third day in case of women, and fifth day in the case of men (McDougal, 1979: 124-127). Mourning is observed by the nearest kinsfolk of the deceased who abstain from eating salt, oil, meat and milk during pollution period. The body is generally laid flat on a mat but in Kulunge Rai the body is flexed, with the arms crossed on the chest and knees drawn up and tucked into the body, as in the fetal positions. The corpse is wrapped in a white cloth and this is secured by tying it with cord. It is then placed on a tilted platform prepared from bamboo, and at the head and at the foot of the platform is placed a basket containing buckwheat. A bamboo vessel containing beer also is put beside the corpse. The corpse has to be placed on the west side of the house with the head pointing north. In case of man, a set of bow and arrow, and a Khukuri is placed to the left side of the corpse to protect it from evil spirits. In case of woman, a khurmi is kept. One brass plate is kept facing down on the head and one on the feet – "*dabuko ghoptyo*". A copper oil lamp is kept burning at the head end of the corpse.

The first part of funeral rites of Khambu tribes is known as "*Mishia*". It is performed soon after death, when the deceased is buried in a field near the house. It is not mandatory to call a Rai-priest (*Mangpa, Nokchho or Nakchung*) in Mishia, but one is usually summoned. One unit of grain is collected from every household in the village, if they attend the funeral they must bring liquor also. Clansmen of the deceased bring an offering of buckwheat in a basket; in addition they bring a small offering of liquor and an offering of beer. The priest or an elderly Raipa addresses the deceased, explains to him that he is being put to rest, and ritually feeds some buckwheat and beer to drink. One of the priest's assistant kneeling at the foot of the corpse choops downwards through the air repeatedly with a *Khukuri* chanting *whi, whi,* while another assistant kneeling by the head, and holding a bow and arrow, alternately chants *hai, hai.* Meanwhile, some persons prepare the "*Sibalo*" commemorating flags to be set by the grave. When the burial place is reached one of the parties shoots an arrow on the ground and the grave is dug. The burial ground is purchased with one rupee coin even if it is the owner's land. The grave should be six feet deep and should be located at the lower side of the house and to the south or towards the stream. One cock (if the deceased is male) or a hen (if female) is killed and a leg is put inside the grave and the remainder is thrown away. The deceased is carried around the fire hearth in a counter clock-wise direction, taken out from the back door to the grave, circumambulate in a counter clock-wise direction, setting the body down and putting on the grave. The family members, clan members and others present, throws a handful of earth on top of the grave. The women then file back into the house, being purified with water mixed with *marcha* (fermenting agent of millet beer). The men construct a roof over the grave consisting of matting on top of a bamboo frame. A basket with a bamboo container of millet beer is placed on top of the roof as an offering to the deceased. The eight *sibalo* (dead flags) are then placed along the sides of the grave, four on each sides. The entire party then goes to the stream, where they wash to purify themselves. Meal and millet bear are served at the house of the deceased.(Rai, 2005: 64-65).

The last rite called *Shilum Kattu* is performed on the third day (for females) and fifth day for males. It vary from clan to clan and in *Kulunge* Rais a minimum of one month should transpire before the *Shilum Kattu* rite is performed. The rite cannot be performed unless there is some beef on hand (as token amount) – some dried beef is kept for such occasions. All households contribute cooked grain, fermented beer etc. It is mandatory to summon a priest (*Mabimi*) on the occasion of "*Shilum Kattu*". The participants gather in the house of the deceased. The participants consisting of men, women and children leave the house to visit the grave, offer final offerings of food, beer, others (tobacco, sugarcane, taro, potato etc.) and cut the "*sibalo*"(dead flags) and placed under the roof covering the grave. Now, the priest perform "*Daplo Kuim*" ritual of pouring a libation of beer over the hearth stones, moving in a counter clock-wise direction. The beef for the deceased is roasted and beer poured on it. *Mabimi* facing the fire hearth, holding a long bamboo bow and arrow, with the pointed wrapped in his left hand, and holding a sickle on his right hand starts chanting "*Sakumbu kura*". The priest instructs the deceased regarding the road to the land of the dead called "*Pomlalubum*" and enjoins him to begin the journey. Time to time the priest simulates firing the arrow from the bow, shouting at the same time. This is to exhort the deceased soul to depart. During the night *Chinta* or *Tomwa* is performed by the *Mabimi* to persuade the soul of the deceased to go and reside in the *Samkhalung*. He chants the Mundhum and performs the last rite. Such a rite normally involves the sacrifice of fowls or a pig and offering of food, drinks and other food items for the deceased soul (Hodgson, 1858: 450-451; Rai, 2005: 64-66).

The death ritual is certainly not so simple today, as they have been heavily influenced by the various religion they have adopted (*Paranami, Jashmani, Christianity* etc.) in recent years (Sinha et al., 2005: 25-27).

Statutory Panchayats:

Social control is maintained through community organizations as well as formal statutory Gram Panchayats, which are responsible for the maintenance of peace in the villages and settlement of petty disputes of theft, assault, adultery and any small offences. They also oversee various social functions and also look after the development programmes. They are responsible for overall village plans, programme implementation and development of the villages.

III. THE YAKKHAS (DEWANS)

Socio-economic Status: Most Backward Class (MBC)

Origin and History:

The ***Yakhas*** or ***Dewan*** or ***Jimi*** are the descendants of ancient Kiratas from the prehistoric times inhabiting both in "Khambuwan" (land of the Khambus) and "Limbuwan" (land of the Limboos) historical areas from the prehistoric times in the Himalayan region. The Yakhas generally use "Dewan", (a title given to the Yakhas by the Gorkha Kings in Nepal) as their surname (Subba, 1993:198). The Yakhas are in negligible demographic size in Sikkim as well as in Nepal. There are also some clans with similar name as that of clans of the Rai community and some clans as in the clans of the Limboo Community. They also lack a clear identity, and are often counted as they are among the Rais and sometimes even among Limboos. It is obvious that while the Yakhas share certain cultural traits with Limboos and Rais they are also distinct in several respects. It is further obvious that being a very small and highly dispersed community they have not been able to withstand the influences of other neighbouring communities in terms of language and culture. There is a prima facie reason to believe that they are an autonomous community, although under severe stress for assimilation either with Limboos or with Rais (Sinha et al., 2005: 36-43).

As a small tribal group, the history of the Yakha (sic) has tended to be subsumed under the history of other ethnic groups, first Kiranti, then in some quarters (after the "unification" of Nepal in the late 18th century) Rai (Russel, 1992: 97). They are more inclined to Rais than to Limboos (Morris, 1974: 216; Vansittart, 1993: 126). On the contrary Subba (1999) opined that the Yakhas are perhaps of Rai origin but considerably Limbuised, as their habitat fell under Limbuan and the Yakha men married Limboo women more frequently than Rai women. The Limboo women usually spoke in their own language, making it difficult for their children to learn the Yakha language.

The Western part of "The Greater Sikkim" from the West of Teesta River to the East of Arun River remained under the control of Gorkha/ Nepal Kingdom for many years (Subba, 1999: 13-20). Thus, on the basis of the historical evolution and developments during different period of "The Greater Sikkim" (after Lho-Mon-Tsong-Sum Treaty of 1642 to 1774 and 1789) (Subba, 1999: 126-128) and "The Greater Nepal" (from 1774-1915) (Stiller, 1968:110, 186-209), there was no watertight compartment either on geographical area or on the people of these two countries of the Himalayan region. The political boundaries of Sikkim and Nepal had not been the same throughout the period of historical evolution in the past. Parts of Nepal had been under Sikkim's jurisdiction at one time and parts of Sikkim in a similar manner were under Nepal. Darjeeling district of West Bengal was an integral part of Sikkim and it was ceded to British India in 1935. Thus, it was quite natural that the various communities living in Sikkim, Nepal and India moved freely and settled wherever they wished. Thus, one can come to the conclusion that the Yakhas or Dewans or Jimis like any other hill-tribes of the Himalayan region have been living with other tribes or migrated during the historical evolution in the geographical areas of present Nepal, Sikkim, Northern areas of West Bengal, Assam and other Himalayan areas of India since ancient times with harmony but maintaining their distinct ethnographic characters asfar as possible.

Population and Settlement:

The Yakha population is not recorded separately in the censuses of Nepal or Sikkim not because their number is negligible but because they are counted among the Rais due to lack of clear ethnic identity. Although they share many cultural and linguistic properties this in itself does not make them one community. One of the most important points to be noted in ethnic identification is self-identification, i.e., how a community wants to identify itself. Justification for a separate identity on the basis of objective criteria is neither always easy for a community nor easily accepted by other communities. Oftentimes there are indeed no clear boundary lines between communities claiming to be different from each other, but no one perhaps has the right to deny any such claim. According to a self-report prepared by the Akhil Kirat Dewan (Yakha) Sangh of Sikkim they are a separate community with close affinity with Raia and Limboos, and their total population in Sikkim is about 600 in 2005 (Sinha et al., 2005).

Geographical Distribution:

Ghum Yakha Village (7 households), South Sikkim,

Tadong (3 households), East Sikkim..

Food Habits:

The *Yakhas* are generally non-vegetarians but most of them would not eat beef and buffalo. Those who adopted the Vaishnavite sect of Hinduism like the Kabirpanthi, Raidas or Pranami Dharma, do not take any meat at all; some of them would not take even garlic and onion. Their staple food is rice, though they eat almost every cereal, pulse or root available. They take vegetables and fruits. Alcoholism is by and large common. In general the food habits of Yakhas are similar to the Rais or the Limboos.

Family Pattern:

Nuclear family is common but joint and extended families are rarely present.

Family Property:

Sons inherit father's property and succession goes only to the eldest son. This is the main point of family conflict.

Gender Issues:

Woman cannot inherit father's property, though she performs different roles in agriculture and animal husbandry operations. They do not have decision-making powers and thus have a low status.

Kinship and Social Organization:

The Yakhas, like the Limboos, emphasize on clans (*thars*, and sub-*thars*). There are a large number of clans and sub-clans. The most distinctive aspect of Yakha kinship system is perhaps the institution called *Samaiti*. This is a little known institution and scholars on Rais like Barnouw (1955), Allen (1987) and Toba (1992) have paid little or no attention to it. This institution is apparently related to ancestor-ancestress worship, but in their case ancestor-ancestress are not husband and wife but brother and sister. There are a number of brother-sister ancestor-ancestress *Samaits* to which different clans belong either singly or in groups. It is important to know which *Samait* one belongs to particularly at the time of marriage and death, for if two persons belong to the same *Samait* they cannot marry even if they now belong to two different clans.

Family Inter-personal Relationship:

Interpersonal relations are maintained through avoidance relationships between mother-in-law and son-in-law, daughter-in-law and father-in-law, sister-in-law (y)B and elder brother-in-law H(e)B. But joking relationship between sister-in-law W (e)S and W(y)S, brother-in-law W(e)B and W(y)B, grandparents and grandchildren.

Economic Activity:

Like Rais and Limboos, the Yakhas are mostly small and marginal farmers in Sikkim, the land is their major resource, owned and controlled individually, which are mainly the agricultural community. Now, their primary occupation is terrace cultivation of agricultural and horticultural crops, livestock rearing, and miscellaneous services etc. They are mixed farmers engaged in agriculture, horticulture and livestock rearing. They are expert bamboo craftsmen, but they have never gone for commercial crafts. Some Yakhas are also employed in service in different white-collar jobs in government service, as schoolteachers, bank employees, scholars, teachers, engineers, and members in defense services etc. They have a direct link with the markets and depend on them for their daily needs.

Dresses:

The Yakha male wear *Dhaka topi* as head gear, *Daura* (a kind of upper garment), Sleeveless coat, *Surwal* (trouser), *Patuka* (waist band) and *Khukri* (dagger). Footwear was not worn in the rural areas but now is a common. The Yakha female wear Shawl (*Mujetro*) on the head, blouse (*Cholo*), sari (*Guniu*), Farreya (skirt), waist band shawl (*Hembari*), waist Sash (*Patuka*) (AKDS, 2005: 7).

Ornaments:

The Yakha male ornaments are earrings *(Kundal)*, and finger ring *(Aunguthi)*.

The Yakha females wear gold necklace (*Kantha*), Gold necklace (*Nawgerdi*), *Bulaki* (nose-ring), *Dhungri* (nose-flower), *Chura* (wriest ring), *Rejee* (*Yangchang*), Flat gold earring (*Chheptesun*), Earring (Kandhungri) (AKDS, 2005: 7).

Folk Musical Instruments:

Phu-lulu-wa -a three holes flute;

Aang-gum -a type of instrument made of *Negalo* (Bamboo) like *Binayo*.

Folk Songs:

The Yakha has a rich oral tradition. Both men and women sing folk songs while dancing folk dances such as *Dookhanilak*, *Pasekapma* and *Tenthambana*. Musical instruments mentioned above usually accompany the songs. They have an elaborate folklore and a rich stock of folk tales.

Folk Dances:

Dookanilak : In this dance there are two female dancers one of which plays the role of the goddess of wealth and hides in a wicker basket and the other, who is actually the goddess of nature, disguises herself as a man. During the dance the one who has disguised herself as a man goes around in undulating movements protecting the goddess of wealth and does not allow to touch her (AKDS, 2005).

The other folk tradition is a game called *Pasekapma*. This basically signifies archery competition among the Yakha youths and handing over the crown made of cloth and peacock feather to the best archer and consecration of the person as headman of the village, whose duty will thence be to protect the village from enemies (AKDS, 2005).

The other folk tradition may be mentioned here is a dance called *Tenthambana*, which symbolises a ritual performed between 2 and 10 years for protection of the village from natural calamities and diseases. In this dance a group of men are divided into four teams: the first team goes to collect water, the second goes for preparation of the ritual, the third team prepares the food, and the fourth team protects the village. They dance half-naked with their face and upper body painted white with mica-rich clay and dance in circular movements (AKDS, 2005).

Religion and Belief System:

According to a self-report prepared by the Yakhas of Sikkim they mainly worship *Tagera Ningwaphuma* – the almighty Goddess of Yumaism of the Limboos. They also worship *Sangdangma* – the goddess of nature, and *Rajerangma* – the goddess of wealth, *Marangma* – goddess of food –grains, *Pandurangma* – goddess of forest, *Samserangma* – goddess of plants and herbs, beside worshipping the land, the sky, the river, etc.

On their religion, Russel writes: "Although there appeared to be no word for "religion" per se, the word *muntum* represented the oral tradition on which Yakha indigenous religious practice was based (1992: 163). Comparison of the literature on other *Kiranti* groups suggested that this concept was shared, viz., *Muddum* in Mewahang Rai, *Mundhum* in *Yumaism* of the Limboos, *Mukdum* in Sunuwar, *Dum-la* in Chamling (Gaenszle, 1989 cited in Russel, 1992: 163). Russel further remarks "In the opinion of most Yakha religious practitioners to whom we spoke, for example, the Yakha and Limbu versions of the *Muntum* were essentially the same, while the Rais were different" (1992: 165). On the sacred specialists, Russel writes that "The *muntum* was regarded as the domain of the ritual specialists, and while some people knew smatterings of the myths and stories contained in the *muntum*, very often these versions did not tie up with or were contradicted by what we subsequently heard from a specialist" (1992: 166). The main deities among the Yakhas in Madi Mulkharka, Sankhuwasabha district of Nepal are *Pangchyang* or the household god, *Yasokeni Boju* or the goddess of Yasok (a place near Fedim), and *Dhankute Devta*, which is called *Thungdangba* by the Limboos. Besides they have a host of affinal deities called *Minumachyang* or cat god, *Puchakchyang* or snake god, *Pubangechyang* or monkey god, *Kumma Sammang* or ancestor god, *Maumachyang* or forest god, *Mangmechyang* or eagle god and so on (Subba, 1999: 99). In *Yumaism*, the God and Goddesses are divided into "*Mang*", "*Sammang*" and "*Sammangchyang*". All the above-mentioned gods and goddesses are nothing but Yakha version of Mangs, Sammangs and Sammangchyangs of Yumaism and worshipped both by the Limboos and the Yakhas. It is thus, appears that the religion of the Yakhas is essentially the "*Yumaism*" being "*Tagera Ningwaphuma*" as their Supreme Almighty Goddess.

In recent years many Yakha families have adopted *Parnami, Joshmani* and *Kabir Panthi* sects of Hinduism, and follow the practices of Hindu religion. A number of their families especially after the late nineties of twentieth century, have adopted Christianity in large scale in Sikkim, and hence follow the practice of Christianity even in the rural areas of Sikkim now.

Festival:

The Yakhas celebrate the various Hindu festivals like *Dashain* and *Tihar*, but *Chasuwa* (*Ubhawali*), which falls on Mangshir Purnima, is claimed to be their main festival. This takes place in November-December every year after the harvest is over, as a gesture of thanks giving to their Supreme Goddess – *Tagera Ningwaphuma*. They also celebrate *Maghey Sankranti*, *You-chang* (*Udhawali*), *Sawaney Sankrinti* etc.(AKDS, 2005: 3-5).

Language, Literature & Script:

The Yakha language belongs to the *bodic* section of the Tibeto-Burman language group and shares affinity with Limboo and a few Rai dialects like Bantawa, Athpahariya, Lohorung, Mewahangand, Yamphu (Russel, 1992: 113). Not many speak in Yakha language properly. They often restrict their conversation in their language to their kinship terminologies and a few words related to domestic space. They mainly speak Nepali.

Rites of Passage (Life-Cycle):

Birth, Marriage and Death are the major events of life.

(*a*) Birth: The Yakha rites of passage have a lot of commonality with those of Limboos and Rais. Birth pollution (*Sutak*) is observed for 3 days for daughters and 4 days for sons is born, after which *nuaran* and name-giving ceremony is observed. Rice-feeding ceremony takes place after 3 months for girls and 4 months for boys. Tonsuring of the head in case of male child is not normally done, but piercing of the ears, as the Limboos do, is still practiced. The Yakhas invite their shaman who performs the rites of "*Sayachongma*" or "*Mangenna*" (lifting the head) for both mother and child. This is to exorcise any evil spirit, which may have been present at the time of birth. The relatives and neighbour may bring chicken and millet beer for the mother. In many cases they have adopted either Hindu way or Christian way of purification depending on their adoption of the religion. The birth rites of Yakha tribes vary from place to place and family to family due to the religion they have adopted (*Paranami, Jashmani, Christianity* etc.) The birth rites of passage are considerably Hinduized today (Sinha et al., 2005: 25-27).

(*b*) Marriage: Once a boy grows into adulthood and agrees to marry, someone from his clan or village, "who knows to speak", goes to the house of the girl who is identified as her potential bride. He takes two bottles of liquor along with him and proposes a marriage of the girl with the boy who accompanies such a negotiator. If the girl and parents agree they accept the bottles of liquor, which is immediately served to the visiting guests and a date is fixed sooner or later for the final marriage, which basically involves feasting and receiving blessings from senior relatives from the clan and community. However, it is important that a Yakha shaman or an elderly Yakha is invited on the occasion in which he announces the marriage between the boy and the girl, and their clans, villages, and most importantly their *Sammelung*. If their *Sammelung* is same the marriage cannot take place (AKDS, 2005).

The marriage rites of Yakha tribes also vary from the religion they have adopted (*Paranami, Jashmani, Christianity* etc.). For the families who have adopted Hinduism, the marriage symbols for women consist in putting of vermilion (*sindur*) in the parting of the hair and wearing a green bead necklace (*poty*). The marriage ceremony is solemnized through *Kanyadan*. The families who have adopted Christianity follow the rites of that religion and the wedding is solemnized in the church.

Residence after marriage is patrilocal. Both husband and wife can divorce each other with social approval, the reasons generally adultery, barrenness, maladjustments, impotency, chronic sickness, cruelty, insanity, practice of witchcraft and sorcery. If the wife runs away with another person, her husband is entitled to receive compensation (*jarikal* or *jaridanda*) from the paramour. If the wife does not remarry after divorce, she receives alimony from the husband. Children are the liability of the father in case of divorce. Remarriage of widow and widower is permissible.

(*c*) Death: The Yakhas perform the death rituals on the fourth day in case of a male and third day in case of a female by a shaman, who may well be a Yakha or Limboo or Rai but has to be export in recalling the soul of the dead person and guide the soul all the way, through deep forest, rivers and high mountains to where the souls of all the deceased persons are supposed to go. If such a shaman is not "good" at his work, the soul is believed to wonder around and not only suffer itself, but also make the living members of the family suffer in different ways. If such a situation arises, a "bigger" shaman is identified and called in to perform the funerary rites of Yakhas. Until the death ritual is over the family members of the deceased abstain from eating meat, salt, chilly etc. Within one year, the final rite is performed after which no death rite is performed.

The death ritual is certainly not so simple today, as they have been heavily influenced by the various religions they have adopted (*Paranami, Jashmani, Christianity* etc.) in recent years (Sinha et al., 2005: 25-27).

16

The Communities Analogous to Kiratas

I. THE SUNUWARS (MUKHIAS, KOINCHS)

Socio-economic Status: Most Backward Class (MBC)

Origin and History:

The Sunuwars or Mukhia or Koinch are the aboriginal tribes inhabiting on both banks of the Sun Kosi river, but more especially to the west and north, and they might roughly be described as inhabiting that portion of Nepal which lies to the north of Nepal Valley, between the Gurungs on the west and the Rais on the east, with Tibet (China) as the northern boundary (Vansittart, 1896: 177). The Sunuwar have settled in the northeast, from the district of the Rai to that of the Newar. Kisi and Busi, two places rather centrally situated, are said to be the most important settlements. Djoi and Kimb were near the Tibetan frontier. Tradition relates that the Sunuwar came to Nepal from the very distant land of Churdji Langchi after the Newar but before the Brahmins (Hermanns, 1954: 20). The Gorkhas knew them as "***Sunuwar***" derived from the Sun Kosi river area of their habitation. Contrary to the migration theory put forward by numerous anthropologist and historians (Vansittart, 1896:177; Chemjong, 1967:86-87; and others), and following this view the self-study report prepared by the Sikkim Sunuwar (Mukhia) Koinch (2005), their Mukudum (oral tradition) has no mention of any such migration but describes the places, rivers, and mountains of the Himalayan region, which gives us the evidence that they are as old as the rivers and mountains of the Himalayas. The word "***Mukhia***" is known to be a title given by the Gorkha conquerors. They call themselves "***Koinch***", because they believe to have originated in a cliff called Kuin (Pradhan, 1999: 161). The Sunuwars of Sikkim are not only much less known but perhaps much less developed community than others.

The political boundaries of Sikkim and Nepal had not been the same throughout the period of historical evolution in the past. Parts of Nepal had been under Sikkim's jurisdiction at one time and parts of Sikkim in a similar manner were under Nepal. Darjeeling district of West Bengal was an integral part of Sikkim and it was ceded to British India in 1935. Thus, as in the case of Sunuwars also, it was quite natural that the various communities living in Sikkim, Nepal and India moved freely and settled wherever they wished. Thus, one can come to the conclusion that the *Sunuwars* like any other hill-tribes of the Himalayan region have been living with other tribes or migrated during the historical evolution in the geographical areas of present Nepal, Sikkim, Northern areas of West Bengal, Assam and other Himalayan areas of India since ancient times with harmony but maintaining their distinct ethnographic characters as far as possible (Subba, 1999: 13-20; 126-128; Stiller, 1968:110, 186-209).

Despite of all odds to the Sunuwars, they have been able to retain a clear identity. The Sunuwars of today are partly influenced by Aryan culture, are Mongoloid in looks, have their own language and script, pay little heed to the principles of purity and pollution, and are not really an organic part of the Hindu caste system (Sinha et al., 2005: 49).

Population and Settlement:

Sunuwars are a small community numbering only 2091 in the whole of Sikkim, according to the voter's list of the State for 1999 (Sinha et al., 2005: 45).

Geographical Distribution:

Sunuwars are settled in Mendo Goan, Chyakhung, Chumbung, Ongchum, Gyalshing, Rinchenpong, and Khecheperi in the West; Rameng, Nij, Rameng, Tingmo, Kitam, and Pokhlok in South; Tarjin, Nazitam, Tirkutam, Chandmari, Rongyek, Bagey Khola and Bhusuk in the East; and Rangrang in the North (Sinha et al., 2005: 45).

Food Habits:

The Sunuwars are non-vegetarians, and eat buffalo, pork, fish, mutton, chicken and eggs. They abstain from beef. Though rice is their staple food, the poorer section consumes maize, wheat, millet and other rough grains. They take different varieties of pulses, vegetables, local fruits, root and tuber crops etc. Alcoholism is by and large common. They take tea very often with milk and sugar.

Family Pattern:

Nuclear family is common but joint and extended families are rarely present.

Family Property:

Sons inherit father's property and succession goes to the eldest son or person of the family or wife. This is the main point of family conflict.

Gender Issues:

Woman cannot inherit father's property, though she performs different roles in agriculture and animal husbandry operations. They do not have decision-making powers and thus have a low status.

Kinship and Social Organization:

Traditionally the Sunuwars are divided, like Gurungs, into two hierarchical classes of clans called *Bara Thar* or "twelve clans" and *Das Thar* or "ten clans", the former occupying a higher social status than that of the latter, although intermarriage between the two classes were permissible. It appears that the social classification of higher and lower status seem to be the prolong influence of Hinduism. The Sunuwars of Sikkim and Darjeeling do not maintain any hierarchy between the groups of 12 and 10 clans today (Sinha et al, 2005: 47).

Family Inter-personal Relationship:

Interpersonal relations are maintained through avoidance relationships between mother-in-law and son-in-law, daughter-in-law and father-in-law, sister-in-law (y)B and elder brother-in-law H(e)B. But joking relationship between sister-in-law W (e)S and W(y)S, brother-in-law W(e)B and W(y)B, grandparents and grandchildren (Singh, 1983).

Economic Activity:

Traditionally Sunuwars were hunters and now they are agriculturist and majority are mixed farmers – cultivating regional comparative agricultural and horticultural crops; and livestock rearing. They are known to have a very good bamboo craftsmanship qualities and a number of them are engaged in commercial weaving of winnowing *(Nanglo)* and various types of baskets (*Daloo*) and thus supplement their income. They are also known for their hunting skills in Sikkim. Some of them are in government service, as schoolteachers, bank employees, scholars, teachers, and members in defense services etc. They have a direct link with the markets and depend on them for their daily needs.

Dresses:

The Sunuwar's main dress resembles the dresses of other Nepali community in Sikkim, over and above which they wear their own special apparels. Men wear a colourful scarf, *Kamar Bandhi* and *Namja* (purse slung over shoulder and hangs over the waist on one side). These are hand netted and decorated with shining glass beads and tiny mirrors. Women wear similar colourful headgear, which is also hand-knitted out of thread prepared from *Bhangre Sishnu* (stinging nettles), which is no more in vogue these days (SSK, 2003: 8).

Folk Musical Instruments:

Kaptera – a bamboo *malingo*'s green sticks made as tongue used as musical instrument during death rituals in Okhaldhunga area of Nepal;

Galambey – a brass-bell tied on the neck of the dogs while going for hunting.

Tohung – made of a hollow wood with wire-string in the middle used in Okhaldhunga and Ramechhap areas of Nepal;

Pudipu – made of round earthen hollow pot with holes on the top and sides.

Phatphatey – made of two and half feet long dry bamboo split into two or hree times; used in *Majhrirat* area of Nepal;

Sunuwar Dhol – most important musical instrument of Sunuwars used in Nepal and Sikkim.

Symbals – made of brass used along with other instruments (Khandel, 2004:29).

Folk Songs:

Both men and women take part in folk songs. They have their own folklore and folk tales and sing these as songs. They sing with dance and musical instruments.

Folk Dances:

The Sunuwars have four important folk dances namely: (*i*) Main *Shandar Sheel* (*ii*) *Bhor Puincha Sheel*, (*iii*) *Buoor Sheel*, and (*iv*) *Nougee Sheel*. Main *Shandar Sheel* has fifteen different types of dances in which movements of birds, animals and insects are imitated. It is characterised by dances of various kinds, sacrifices and merrymaking. The shamans play an important role in this festival, as in the case of *Sakkewa* of Rais, which falls same day, is mainly observed to please the goddess called *Shandar*. Usually in *Shandar Sheel* eight different *Natso* dance with eight different drums. The Sunuwars have started participation in various festivals in Sikkim only very recently (SSK, 2003: 4).

Religion and Belief System:

The Sunuwars are animists or shamanisms and they believe to have been blessed by the Goddess *Shandar* for their protection and food, and were granted the mantras of *Mukudum* that are pronounced by the *Poibo*, *Natso* and *Ngyami* of the Sunuwar shamans to this day on all rituals and ceremonies. They observe and perform various ceremonies and *pujas* on different occasions by these shamans as under:

1. *Sagoon*: This is a minor worship done twice a year by *Natso* with *Syanboo*, incense, *bospati* (*Oroxylum indicum*) to propitiate their gods and souls of the deceased ancestors.

2. *Chhengoo*: This is ancestor worship performed by *Poibos*. The shaman invokes Sunuwar deities and the souls of deceased ancestors throughout the night twice a year for peace and prosperity of all (Pradhan, 1999: 181). Thus altars are prepared, drums are beaten by the *Natso* and rice cones are made as offerings to the souls. They also prepare bow and arrow and a bird called Chirinamdi and places it on the largest rice cone. As the ritual begins the Sunuwar shaman guides the resting souls through the hunting grounds to the distant abode of ancestors (SSK, 2003: 6).

3. *Geel*: One of the best-known and most expensive folk traditions is the celebration of *Geel*, which is a community festival. In this festival they sacrifice 360 birds and animals. The members of this community pool their resources and celebrate this festival to fulfill their various wishes (Sinha et al., 2005: 48; SSK, 2003: 6).

4. *Kash* and ***Shandar*** are also performed by the Sunuwar-shamans.

According to Dor Bahadur Bista (1980: 71), one of the best-known anthropologists from Nepal, one class of Sunuwars had followers of Hinduism and the other class, had follower of Lamaistic Buddhism. In actual practice, however, they are known to be paying their tribute to both Hindu and Buddhist deities.

Festival:

The Sunuwars celebrate the various Hindu and Buddhist festivals along with their own such as *Shandar, Geel, Sagoon, Chhengoo,* and *Kash. Dashain, Tihar, Maghe Sankranti, Panglapsol* etc. are also celebrated in Sikkim (SSK, 2003 :6-7).

Language & Literature:

The Sunuwars speak *Koinchlo*, which belongs to the Tibeto-Burman family of languages. Their script is believed to be of ancient origin and has 6 vowels and 16 consonants (SSK, 2003). Due perhaps to their extremely small size and wide distribution it has not been possible for them to use their language for interaction, although some old Sunuwars might be using their language for communicating between the family or clan members (Sinha et al., 2005: 47). The influence of "Unification" of Gorkha/Nepal with promotion and development of only *Khas Kura* (now Nepali/Gorkhali language), only Hindu religion, and only *Khas* culture prohibited use of all other languages upto 1930 in Nepal. The cultural identity of any community was taken as a threat to the national unification by ruling elites until the recent years. The use of other languages was banned and the possession of hill tribal writings out of law since later half of eighteenth century (Davids & Driem, 1985). There was no specific law about it, but Security Act was enforced for such cases under the strong directives of Kathmandu. Such attitude of the state mechanism, left the entire 59 Hill Tribes of Nepal far behind in social awakening, cultural development and economic progress. Similarly, in Sikkim also the rulers of Namgyal dynasty banned not only reading and writing of Limboo language and literature but also maintaining any identity of other communities of Nepali origin since 1741 after Teyongshi Sirijonga was assassinated at Hee-Martam (Subba, 1999: 246).

Rites of Passage (Life-Cycle):

Birth, Marriage and Death are the major events of life. Sunuwars are considerably Hinduized like some other communities of Nepal and Sikkim but have, despite their small size, been able to maintain their pre-Hindu characteristics to a large extent. They still indulge in sacrifice of animals and birds in the name of deities through their own ritual specialists, who get into a trance when in communion with the spirits, who they are expected to propitiate, use for knowing the future, or drive them away if they are causing any harm to the human beings. They have bamboo altars called *Laga* in northern and southern corners of every house. Such altars have several chambers for various deities, mostly ancestors, to be worshipped on new moon and full moon nights by the eldest member of the family. Any ritual that involves invoking the deities is normally performed by their shaman, who often advises sacrifice of animals and birds, which are subsequently eaten by the members of the family or those who have assembled to witness the ritual (SSK, 2003: 3).

***(a)* Birth:** The Sunuwar birth ritual *Baslasyo* is a name giving ceremony that takes place on the third day after the birth of a child. In the case of male child the rite takes place in front of the house and in the case of a female one in the back of the house. The eldest male member of the family performs it. The next birth rite is called *Khome Umcha,* which is a rice-feeding ceremony that takes place five months after a daughter is born and six months after a son. The child's mother or grandmother has to walk some distance announcing loudly that the rite is over. Finally, six months later, there is a head-shaving ceremony in which the child's maternal uncle plays a very important role like in most other communities. Eating and drinking mark the ends of these above rites (Sinha et al., 2005: 46).

***(b)* Marriage:** The next important rite is when they attain the age of marriage. The types of marriage are same as seen about other communities described here except that they have a tradition of junior levirate as well as junior sororate marriage. While their marriage rituals were earlier conducted by their own shamans they are today conducted sometimes by a Hindu priest, which indicates Hindu influence on their marriage rituals. There is however a sense of revivalism among them today and a keenness to go back to their pre-Hindu rites (SSK, 2003: 5).

(*c*) Death: As regards their death rite, the dead body is covered with a shawl as soon as possible and an oil lamp is lit and kept on a brass plate with rice. Some rice is also wrapped in a piece of cloth and kept on the chest of the dead body. The death rites are usually quite elaborate and they indicate that they might have come under Buddhist influence earlier to their coming under Hindu influence. The influence of Hinduism on their death ritual is however limited to the practice of cremation and remaining in abstention for 13 days. Otherwise their *Poibos* take care of guiding the soul of the dead person to wherever they believe it should finally go (SSK, 2003: 5-6).

Statutory Panchayats:

Social control is maintained through formal statutory Gram Panchayats, which are responsible for the maintenance of peace in the villages and settlement of petty disputes of theft, assault, adultery and any small offences. They also oversee various social functions and also look after the development programmes. The Sunuwars participate in the Gram Sabha and take responsibility for over development of the villages.

II. THE MAGARS (MANGARS, MANGS, MONGPAS)

Socio-economic Status: Most Backward Class (MBC)

Origin and History:

The **Magars** or **Mangars** or **Mang** or **Mongpa** are the autochthonous tribes of the central and lower parts of the mountains between the Jingruk (Rapti of Gorkhpur) and Marsiangdi rivers. They came into prominence as a great power in about 1100 A.D., when Mukunda Sen, the Magar King of Palpa and Botwal, invaded and conquered the Nepal Valley, and committed terrible atrocities during the reign of Hari Deva, King of Nepal (Vansittart, 1896: 103). Their tradition relates that they came from Bokim, a land behind Nepal somewhere in Tibet. Larger colonies of the Manger live in Kangpachen in the northeast near the Tibetan frontier (Hermanns, 1954: 13). Hamilton says that the Magars, who resided to the west of the Gandak river, seem to have received the Rajput princes with much cordiality (1819: 103). The chiefs of Rising, Ghiring and Gajarkot were related to the Palpa family by birth, and from which it seems very probable that the rulers of Palpa and all other Chaubisia chiefs were really Magars. The Magars are described by Hamilton (1819) as a Himalayan tribe "wallowing in all the ancient abominations of the mountaineers", and found anywhere in the Himalayan region (Vansittart, 1896: 104).

The Mangars inhabited and ruled at least some parts of Sikkim before establishment of "**The Greater Sikkim**" through "***Lho-Mon-Tsong Sum***" Tripartite Treaty. The land resources of the Lhorees (Bhutias), Monrees (Lepchas) and Tsongrees (Limboos) were integrated and thus extending the area of "The Greater Sikkim" from Chumbi Valley in the north (now Tibet-China), Har Chu Valley and Am Mochu Valley in the east (now Bhutan), to the east of Arun River in the West (now Nepal), signing the agreement by the leaders of the three communities at Denzong Phuntso Khangsar in 1642, a Water Horse Year, and the year in which Phuntsho Namgyal ascended the throne as First Chogyal at Yoksom Norbugang in what is now Western Sikkim.

In the Tripartite Treaty, translated in English by Prof. Ringu Tulku, there is a mention that:

> "During the last **Mongpa war** some people's action were noted and let them be beware of now from this year of Water Horse Year onwards we will abide by the commands of the King, his Guru and his sons and will never let arise a bad thought against Sikkim".

From this paragraph of the Treaty, it reveals that the Mangar chiefs opposed the supremacy of the Bhutia rulers and formation of "The Greater Sikkim", which was crushed by force and the chief, disappeared from the area of The Greater Sikkim or killed. However, it is not clear whether the Mangpa war mentioned was of the war which took place between Manger Chiefs and the Bhutias at "Khagpachen valley and Tamber valley" of Limbuwan or Mangarjong area of Mangsari, West Sikkim of "the Greater Sikkim" mentioned by Vansittart (1896: 103-107) (Subba, 1999: v-vi, 125-128).

As usual, most of the anthropologists and historians believe on migration theory of the Hill tribes of the Himalayan region and Magar is no acceptation. Fr. Hermanns writes, "they came from "Bokim", a land behind Nepal somewhere in Tibet" (1954: 13). Chemjong opined that the Mangars came to Sikkim from "Shin" and settled in Sikkim, built Jongs or Forts or castles, whenever they settled and they called the place Mangar Jongs. In the East of Nepal and Sikkim, the Mangars are known as "Mang" or "Mong" or Mongol people. The Chinese and Burmese people called them "Mang" or "Mong" for Mongolians, and "ar" or "arwn" means children (1967: 70-73).

Risley opined that their original homeland was in western Nepal from where they migrated to eastern Nepal and finally came to Sikkim (1891: 74). But Hooker viewed them as aborigines of Sikkim who were driven westwards by the Lepchas (1848: 139). From the Maharaja's History of Sikkim, it reveals that they were in Sikkim prior to 1642 as evident from the account of a travel of the first Chogyal Phuntsho Namgyal of Sikkim, who was consecrated in 1642, across the kingdom. The travel account describes the evidence of their presence as under:

> "The next day they (Phuntsho Namgyal and his followers/officers) crossed over the Rag-dong Bridge, and proceed (sic) through Yangang. While passing through Yangang, where were Lepchas and Mangars, as the party happened to be riding on ponies and some of the retainers had matchlock guns, which they went firing along the road, the simple natives who have never seen ponies nor firearms, said to others, the entire party rode on huge hogs, and some of them bore sticks which when pointed towards you produced great sounds" (Namgyal and Dolma, 1908: 19).

An autochthonous community of Nepal and Sikkim and that has keenly guarded its traditional customs and practices despite centuries of strong Hindu influence on them, Mangars represent the typical experience of communities at the crossroads. While the temptation to go back to what they consider as truly Mangar traditions, including their own language and script, is strong and is growing stronger in the recent past shedding what they have adopted in the past several centuries has not been easy for them. This is an issue of cultural identity of the community and is better left to them (Sinha et al, 2005: 52).

During 1600 A.D. or so the chief Santisati (Santu Pati) Sen had established a Magarjong at Mangsari, West Sikkim, and ruled surrounding areas many years (period not known). The ruins of the Magarjong at Mangsari, West Sikkim is still there. Similarly, ruins of many Magarjongs such as one at 15 Km away from Sukiya Pokhari of Darjeeling; Mansong Magarjong of above Rangpo, Magarjong of suldung, Kamrang Magarjong, Famtham Magarjong, Sudunglakha Magarjong, Kitam Magarjong, Magardalam, Magarthang, Barthang-Barfok Magarjong, Rateypani Kateng Magarjong and many such Magarjongs of West and South Sikkim have been stated to have existed before the formation of "The Greater Sikkim" in 1642 (Ale, 2003:3-69; Sinha et al, 2005: 52). But it is very difficult to believe that the Magars were in so much population during that time of 1642 in Sikkim. Since, Jongs or forts were common for all the rulers of the Greater Sikkim that time, all the Jongs mentioned by Alle (2003) in his book above may not be necessarily the Jongs of Mangars.

The Ethnophraphic team led by Dr. Sinha visited Suldung village of West Sikkim under Chakung Constituency and confirmed that the Magar settlement of the village is since antiquity. There is a Magar fort or castle at the top of the village. The village seems to be in existence when the Gorkha occupied West Sikkim and ruled during 1780/1788 to 1814 (34/26 years). There is also a Kali temple at the bottom of the hill that has a copper plate showing 1856 as the date of its establishment (Sinha et al, 2005: 52).

Population and Settlement:

The Mangars were 901 in Sikkim during 1891 (Risley 1894: 27). Their population increased to 13,373 by 2004 (93% increase in 113 years as per the voter' list of 2004 of Sikkim). The self-study census of the Mangar organization conducted in 2003 has reported a population of 25,003 persons (14,300 males and 10,703 females) (Sinha et al, 2005: 52). The huge difference in the population figures for Mangars of Sikkim is inexplicable (ASMA, 2005).

The Magar population of Nepal is 16,22,421 in 2001, constituting 7.14%, the third highest community of the total population of the country. Out of the total population of Nepal 3.39% speak Mangar language, and thus about 47.48% Mangars have retained their own language (Census 2001 Nepal).

Geographical Distribution:

The most important Mangar concentrations are in Chakung, Kamling, Suldung, Tinzerbong, Takuthang, Mabong, Khanisirbong, Budang, Ribdi, Barthang, Berfok, Chingthang, Bermiok, Dhuppidanra, Karzi, and Mangnam in the West; Assangthang, Ahlley, Mamley, Kamrang, Wok, Dhar Goan, Salghari, Ramabong, Rong, Kitam, Mungram, Kateng Mangarjong, Chiya Dara, Maniram Bhanzyang, and Namthang in the South; Kadamtam, Pacheykhani, Subaney Danra, Rongli, Sudunglakha, Rhenock, West Pandam, Rumtek 9th Mile, Pakyong, Dochhum, Gangtok, Duga, Sirwani, and Khamdong in the East Sikkim (ASMA, 2005).

Food Habits:

The Magars are non-vegetarians, and eat fish, pork, mutton, chicken and eggs but do not take beef. Though rice is their staple food, the poorer section consumes maize, wheat, millet and other rough grains. They take different varieties of pulses, vegetables, local fruits, root and tuber crops etc. Mustard oil is used for cooking. Alcoholism is by and large common. They take tea very often with milk and sugar. They smoke cigarettes and take *khaini*. Their food habits are quite different from other *matwali* or drinking communities of Sikkim due to their early contact with the Aryans and the continued sanskritisation process under the influence of the Vaisnavite sects like Josmani and Kabi Panthi. They are often teetotalers and avoid meat or any other non-vegetarian food. They prepare *Han* by fermenting millet, maize, wheat, or rice. Further distillation of this is also done to prepare a highly alcoholic drink (ASMA, 2005: 26).

Family Pattern:

Nuclear family is common but vertically extended families are also found.

Family Property:

Sons inherit father's property and succession goes only to the eldest son. This is the main point of family conflict.

Gender Issues:

Woman cannot inherit father's property, though she performs different roles in agriculture and animal husbandry operations. They do not have decision-making powers and thus have a low status.

Kinship and Social Organization:

The community is divided into a number of exogamous and patrilineal *thars*, namely, Pulami, Ale, Kepchake, Guranga, Darlami, Pun, Lungalim, Lamichani, Khapangi, Sibakota, Purbachane, Rana, Mangratey, Lumrey, Gholey, Maske, Balangpak, Molalay and Sitong, all having equal status. A clan and a lineage is never a permanent one, and clans constantly break into lineages and lineages evolve into clans. To regulate marriage alliances is the main function of the *thar*. Each of these *thars* has one or more *gotras*. Marriage alliances are made on the basis of these patrilineal, ancestral gotras (Singh, 1993:118-119). They had a distinct practice of cross-cousin marriage of both maternal and paternal kind, which is quite rare among the various communities in the eastern Himalayas (Subba, 1989:41). The earlier practice of marrying one's maternal uncle's daughter and punishment in case one failed to do so is also mentioned elsewhere (ASMA, 2005: 20).

An important aspect of Magar social organization, also shared by Limboo, Rai, and Yakha communities, is ritual adoption of a person from outside the community. Such person, usually a woman who has eloped with a Magar, has to cook rice and black mung and offer the same to 12 Magars. One of the Magars present at the time of adoption ritual has to give bride his clan and symbolically agree to "become" her father or brother before she is accepted into the family. She also has to offer some meat and one coin to each of the 12 Mangars (ASMA, 2005: 20-21).

Economic Activity:

The traditional economy of Magars used to be hunting, dry farming, livestock rearing, collection of tubers, honey from the forest, and weaving of bamboo baskets. The women weaved blankets out of the wool of the sheep they reared. They constituted a prominent part of the fighting force of the Gorkhas in the second half of the 18th century and were keenly sought in the British army since the Treaty of Sugauli signed in 1815 (Sinha et al, 2005: 55). However, they are mainly engaged in cultivation of agricultural and horticultural crops, and livestock rearing. Some of them are engaged in Government service as teacher and other white color jobs, business etc. for their livelihood.

Dresses:

Traditional Magar clothes were made of animal skin, wool and the bark of nettle-grass. As a matter of fact, nettle-grass was a major source of fibres for weaving clothes for many other communities in the past. They had no footwear. But subsequently they adopted the *Khas*-Nepali dress as their national dress. The mans traditionally wear *Bhoto, langoti, ascoat,* and *topi*/cap; while the female wear *chaubandi choli, gunue, lorphu/mujetro, hembari/hapa, pacheuri/barak, patuki, tikki and ghalek* (Alle, 2003:106).

Folk Musical Instruments:

Alanka	–	made of cherry sticks and orchid blades used as musical instrument during *Sarungya* dance by the youths holding on one hand accompanying *Madeley* dance with 32 *tals* at Sisney and Jaljal area of Nepal;
Kutkutey	–	made of copper and skin; tied on waist and used during *Tappa* songs - beating with two wooden sticks at Srkhet, Salyan and Ruku region of Nepal.
Kaura Khainjadi	–	used in as *Khainjadi*
Jharra	–	made of hollow iron with outer-side open and with iron balls inside; wear like *Kalli* by the unmarried girls while dancing *Kaduwa* dance in Tnahu, east Palpa and Sanjya regions of Nepal.
Dauri	–	it is a small instrument like a Dholak, used in happy occasions, as well as worship ceremonies at Ralpa-Rukum region of Nepal..
Neywer	–	made of hollow iron with iron balls inside, wear as *Kalli* while dancing singaru, paisari and

		Tappa dances in Rapti and Bheri Anchal of Nepal.
Paluwa-		tender leaves of plants, used by cowboys.
Piwnra-		made of tender plant-bark, used by cowboys.
Pothi Muchunga	–	It is a small *Muchunga* made of iron and gives sweet but strong sound and could be used only by experts as it often stick to the teeth.
Macheta	–	brass cymbal used in Tappa songs and dances, mostly used in Rukum, Rolpa, Salyan areas of Nepal in all happy occasions of all Nepali tribes now.
Madal	–	originally the musical instrument of Magar tribes, but now the most popular musical instrument of the entire Nepali world It is made of wood and skin; with *Khari* in the middle of both end – one bigger known as *bhalle* while other side smaller known as *Pothi*. It is the most extensively used musical instrument for all types of Nepali folk songs.
Rani Madal	–	It is a bigger Madal used by the Magars of Pachim Anchal – west of Palpa, mainly used while singing Sunimaya, Yanimaya etc. It's sound is very sweet.
Salaijyo Damphu	–	a trangular Damphu made of wood and skin (Khandel, 2004:23; Alle, 2003: 110-118).

However, only a few above musical instruments such as *Madal, Ranimadal, Salaijyo Damphu,Pothi Muchunga,*and *Paluwa,* are used in Sikkim.

Folk Songs:

Both men and women take part in folk songs. They have their own folklore and folk tales and sing these as songs. They sing with dance and musical instruments. The important folk songs are *Sarungya, Tappa, Lahare Tappa, Garra, Khamta, Chokra, Samala, Khali, Bibhas, Sohrathi, Asis, Sunimaya, Yanimaya*, and *Maruni* songs (Alle, 2003: 118-128; Khandel, 2004: 23).

Folk Dances:

The Mangar dances comprise of *Sarungya* dance, *Tappa* dance, *Kaduwa* dance of unmarried girls, *Singaru* dance, *Paisari* dance and *Maruni* dance. One of the most well-known Magar folk-dances is the

Maruni dance during *Tihar* festival. In this dance the main dancer wears a women's dress, has someone to mimic her dance and one person to beat a *Madal* or *Rani Madal*. This dance is believed to be of divine origin and is directly linked with mythology. The role of the person beating the *Madel* is considered to be the most important, and even the one who mimics the main dancer is actually considered to be the protector of the dancer. He wears a mask, entertains the crowd by his own gestures, etc. The wearing of the dress by the dancer is given a ritualistic position, as the dancer's dress, are elaborately laid along with flowers, rice etc. on a brass plate or a winnower. The dance begins with worship of *Madal*, the dress, and other ornaments to be used by the dancer, followed by obeisance to all gods and goddesses like *Saraswati*, Rama, Sita, and innumerable gods of the forest and environment. The dance ends with blessings to the family that has offered alms to the dancing group and brings the dance to an end ritualistically (Alle, 2003: 110-118; Khandel, 2004: 23).

Religion and Belief System:

The Mangar Hill tribes are the first in Nepal to receive the influence of Hinduism, as their habitat was the first to be touched by the Hindu emigrants taking refuge there during the rise of Muslim power in India. They are but known to have their own priest called "*Bhusal*" (Sharma, 1982: 270).

Mangars are essentially Animists in the sense that they, in spite of strong Hindu influence on them; worship a host of spirits through their own shamans. Worship of ancestors is another critical religious element among them. They sacrifice animals for their gods and goddesses (Alle, 2003: 91-92).

Festival:

The various Hindu festivals like *Dashain, Tihar*, and *Maghey Sankranti, Chaitey Dasain, Sawaney Sankranti*, are celebrated by most Magars, but ancestor-worship, which is practiced by both shamanistic and Vaisnavite Magars. The shamanistic Magars offer sacrifices of goats, sheep, pigs and chicken whereas the Vaisnavite Magars make do with flowers, water, and burning of incenses. The festival is known as *Barajimijong*, which is dedicated to the worship of ancestors. They consider their ancestors as god or "*Barahi*" in their language and their worship takes place on the 5th day of the full moon in Mangsir (November-December). This is a thanks-giving festival to the ancestors for showering successful harvest, which is offered to them with the help of a Shaman called *Dhami* or *Jhankri*. To honour the Magar festival of

"*Barahimjong*" the State Government of Sikkim has declared an annual State Holiday by vide Notification No.94/Home/2006 dated 02/12/2006 (Alle, 2003: 93-96; ASMA, 2005: 27-29).

Language and Literature:

The Magars have their own language and script. Their language has been recognized as the official language in Sikkim in 27th March 1996. The Mangar language is a Tibeto-Burman language. The Mangar language is being taught in the schools of Sikkim up to Class IV (Alle, 2003: 170-183; ASMA, 2005: 26).

Rites of Passage (Life-Cycle): Birth, Marriage and Death are the major events of life.

(*a*) Pre-Natal: Before the child is born there are restrictions on both husband and wife. The husband should not touch the dead body lest the child is wrapped with hair at the time of delivery, and the wife should not eat leopard's flesh, least she should snarl like a leopard.

(*b*) Birth: At the time of birth, the whole household becomes polluted the moment a child is born till the naming ceremony is held on the 3rd, 5th, 7th, 9th or 11th day of his/her birth. On that day, sprinkling cow's urine did purification of the house earlier but the same ritual is performed with gold-dipped water also. The followers of various Va snavite sects among them purify themselves by putting holy ash on thei forehead by a *Sadhu* or an ascetic (Alle, 2003: 70-73).

Rice-feeding ceremony for the child is done between the 5th and 8th months, depending on whether the child is a male or female and also at times which clan the child belongs to. The first feeding is done with a silver spoon. Head shaving ceremony for a boy is held on the 3rd, 5th or 7th year after consulting an astrologer for an auspicious day. His maternal uncle does this (*ibid*: 72).

(*c*) Marriage: Community endogamy and *thar* and *gotra* exogamy are in practice among the Magars who accept cross-cousin marriage. Junior sororate is allowed. The marriage signs for women are vermilion and the green bead necklace. Bride price amounts to one to three rupees in cash, liquor, rice, pork and goat in kind. Marriage are basically of three types – negotiated marriage, love marriage and marriage by eloping with someone's wife/husband. There are usual formalities of a negotiated marriage and the risks to life in the third type of marriage, which is actually not a marriage because it is never solemnized. Widow re-marriage is permitted but is concluded without any fanfare. On the other hand, a widower remarriage is often accompanied by a lot of fanfare, especially if the widower is rich enough to offer food and drinks to the guests (ibid: 73-84).

(*d*) Death: When a person dies, he or she is kept on the ground and a brass plate with rice and an oil lamp on it is kept near the head of the dead person. The dead body is constantly guarded so that cat or god does not touch it. Before it is taken out for burial it is covered with white cloth and pinned at nine places with tiny dry sticks. Due to the influence of Hinduism some Magars have started the practice of cremation. When the funeral procession returns after burial or cremation they all have to cross the road in the middle of which they keep some thorny plants with a stone on them to stop the spirit of the dead person from returning to the house. The sons of the dead person earlier remained in abstention for 13 days like the *Khasas*, but of late certain changes are noticed regarding the number of days in abstention when they cook the food by themselves and perform certain rituals every day. They also have their heads shaven clean before they start their abstention. As for the ritual specialists, they all invited Brahman priests earlier for conducting the funerary rites, but now they use their own shamans or *sadhus* to perform such rituals. This shows a slow distancing of themselves from Hindu identity due to growing ethnic consciousness as "Magar" since the last decade of the previous century (ibid: 85-89).

III. THE GURUNGS (TAMUS)

Socio-economic Status: Most Backward Class (MBC)

Bio-Anthropological Information:

Serology and genetical information are available. The gene frequencies are p=26%, q=13%, r=61%, m=61% and n=39%. data on red cell enzymes like Glyxolose (Glo), Adenosine Aminase (ADA), Acid phosphatase (ACHP), Phosphoghicomutase I (PGMT, phosphohexose isomerase (PhI) and 6 phosphoglucomutase Dehydregenase (6 PGD) are also available for Gurungs of Sikkim (Morpurgo et al, 1983).

Origin and History:

The Gurungs or Tamus are the autochthonous tribes of the Himalayas of Western Nepal. The Gurung tradition relates that they claim to have come from Po hiung, a land that lies beyond Nepal somewhere in Tibet (Hermanns, 1954: 1954:14). According to Vansitttart (1896) "a chief, who was Raja of Kaski, settled in Gundrung, where the Gurungs were most predominant. These people were strongly attached to his descendants, by whom they were not disturbed in their religious opinions or customs, and in their own homes they practically still continue to follow the doctrines of Sakia as explained to them by Lamas of their own tribe" (p 96). Pignede (1966) specified the Gurung country, which extends from 82^0 30" and 84^0 degrees longitude East, and 28^0 to 28^0 30" latitude North, an extremely mountainous territory of Nepal (p 23). Geographically, the Gurung country lies between the Himalayan region and inner *terai* region at an altitude of about 4,000 to 9,000 feet above sea level. The Annapurna mountain Chain and Himal Chuli in the central region of high hills surround its north. To the south it is limited by a series of flat valleys like that of Pokhra. Kali Gandaki from that of the Modi river constitutes the western frontier and Buri Gandaki forms the eastern frontier. Thus, the Gurung territory extends east to west about 140 kms long and from north to south 35 to 45 kms. A series of rivers flow from north to south intersecting this area into small parts. The main settlements of Gurungs in Nepal are in Lamjung, Kaski, Syanja, Manang, Tanahu, Gorkha, and Parbat districts of Gandaki Zone (Regmi, 1990: 65).

Chemjong a historian who believes on theory of migration for all the Himalayan tribes including his own, traces the Gurungs' origin as "The Gyarung (sic) tribes were one of the seven tribes of North Tibet who had migrated from there to Kham province of Eastern Tibet and from there to Unan province of Southern China where they mixed up with Tai Shan tribes and spread towards south and western directions under their leaders Sai-ik Shan and Segop Shan... So after the demise of Segop Shan nine officers of the Gyarung regiment made a league and settled separately in Bhindi, Tenahang, Ghandrung, Siklis, Kaski, Milung, Pokhra and Parvat in West Nepal and ruled their villages independently. They called the federal state by the name of Gu-rong or nine chiefs which later on became the Gurung tribe..." (1967: 58-59).

Messerschmidt (1954), the best-known scholars on Gurungs, writes that they are "a people of Mongoloid physical stock who migrated to the southern slopes of the Himalaya in central Nepal many centuries ago" (p-1).

Mary Des Chene (1996), who uses the word "*Tamu*" for Gurung, takes a more cautious view of their origin and history and considers the subject to be rather complex and needing a lot more historical research than is available so far (pp- 117-118). The word "*Tamu*" (*ta* means thunder and *mu*, sky) metaphorically means brave or fearless people, and is a recent adoption, albeit for reasons difficult to understand, as the new name is in no way more empowering than the earlier one.

According to a self-study report prepared by All Sikkim Gurung (*Tamu*) Buddhist Association of Sikkim (2005) there is suggestion that Gurungs are descendants of Gandharvas mentioned in the Vedas (p-2), but there is indeed no evidence of that. It is also indeed difficult to prove their prehistoric existence in Sikkim whose history begins as late as in

1642. They started to settle in the old Sikkim soon after they began to be recruited following the Anglo-Nepal war of 1814-15, as Magars and Gurungs of western Nepal were the first to be recruited by the British. The Gurung families at Dentam were settled about 8 generations ago, who must be some of the earliest Gurungs to settle in Sikkim. It was further revealed that some Gurung families were copper miners and coin minters besides some of them like Dhanu Thikadar and Param Thikadar, who had leased in land from the Estate Department of the Namgyal rulers (Sinha et al, 2005: 63).

As in the case of Khasas, Sunuwars, and many other hill tribes, the political boundaries of Sikkim and Nepal had not been the same throughout the period of historical evolution in the past. Parts of Nepal had been under Sikkim's jurisdiction at one time (upto east of Arun river between 1642 to Gurmed Namgyal's Time of 1734) and parts of Sikkim in a similar manner were under Nepal (upto western border of Teesta river in 1774 and again West Sikkim between /1789 to 1817 Titaliya treaty). Darjeeling district of West Bengal was an integral part of Sikkim and it was ceded to British India in 1935. Thus, it was quite natural that the various communities living in Sikkim, Nepal and India moved freely and settled wherever they wished. Thus, one can come to the conclusion that the Gurungs like any other hill-tribes of the Himalayan region have been living with other tribes or migrated during the historical evolution in any other geographical areas of present Nepal, Sikkim, Northern areas of West Bengal, Assam and other Himalayan areas of India since ancient times with harmony but maintaining their distinct ethnographic characters as far as possible (Subba, 1999: 13-20; 126-128; Stiller, 1968:110, 186-209; Chemjong, 1967: 221-230).

Population and Settlement:

The Gurungs were 2,921 in 1891 in Sikkim during 1891 (Risley, 1894: 27) making them the fifth largest community at that point of time. The voters' list of Sikkim shows that their population increased to 39,042 by 2004 (93% increase in 113 years) as per the voter' list of 2004 of Sikkim).

In Nepal, the population of Gurung is 5,43,571 persons, the eleventh highest population with 2.39% of total population of the country (Census 2001). Out of the total population 1.49% speak Gurung language, which means 38% of mother tongue retention. In other words 62% Gurungs do not speak their own dialect in Nepal.

Geographical Distribution:

The most important Gurung concentrations are in Dodak, Buriyakhop, Chakung, Rinchenpong, Dentam, and Sardong in the west district; Temi-Tarku, Chubba, Nagi, Borong, and Pathing in the south district; and Regu in east district of Sikkim.

Food Habits:

The Gurungs are non-vegetarians, and eat fish, mutton, chicken and eggs but do not take beef and buffalo. Though rice is their staple food, the poorer section consumes maize, wheat, millet and other rough grains. They take different varieties of pulses, vegetables, local fruits, root and tuber crops etc. Mustard oil is used for cooking. Alcoholism is by and large common. They take tea very often with milk and sugar. They smoke cigarettes and take *khaini*. They prepare millet beer by fermenting millet, maize, wheat, or rice. Further distillation of this is also done to prepare a highly alcoholic drink (ASMA, 2005: 26).

Family Pattern:

Nuclear family is common but vertically extended families are also found.

Family Property:

Sons inherit father's property and succession goes only to the eldest son. This is the main point of family conflict.

Gender Issues:

Woman cannot inherit father's property, though she performs different roles in agriculture and animal husbandry operations. They do not have decision-making powers and thus have a low status.

Kinship and Social Organization:

The Gurungs have two social divisions, "four-Clans" or Hinduized word "*Char-jaat*" are the Ghale, Ghonde, Lama and Lamichane. The "Sixteen-clans" or Hinduized word "*Sola-jaat*", although initially sixteen, contain more than sixteen clans now, viz. the Ghyabre, Kyabchne, Kurumchhe, Jangre, Thorje, Dorjali, Rilami, Poju, Chormi, Pom, Thin, Migi, Khatra, Yog, Paingi, Kholali, Sogun and Thorjami. The Char-jaat enjoys a higher status than the Sola-jaat. Traditionally, these two groups are distinctly two endogamous units. The Ghales are the aristocrats among the Gurungs. They and the Ghyabres observe many ritual taboos and do not eat meat or chicken, as the other Gurungs do. Some of the clans are again divided into *pads* (sub-clans). The Gurungs are the tribes not castes like Hindus but due to their early contact with them many recognize themselves under Hindu *varna* system as *Vaishya*, which is not correct.

Avoidance relationships exist between mother-in-law and son-in-law, between daughter-in-law and father-in-law, and sister-in-law (Y) BW and elder brother-in-law H (e)B. Joking relationships exists between sister-in-law (e) BW and brother-in-law H(y)B, with sister-in-law W(e) B and B and W (y) B and grandparents with grandchildren.

According to *Ngolo-Ngolsyo* tradition, the parents of the bride and the bridegroom do not meet and interact with each other until they are formally introduced with exchange of gifts in the form of alcohol and a coin. The relationship between them is extremely formal even after that and is marked by exchange of gifts and extension of utmost hospitality to each other whenever there are occasions for them to meet. *Aashyong Pratha* is also a unique folk-tradition of Gurungs in which the place of the maternal uncle is seen to be so important that until he performs this ritual no other ritual performed earlier is considered to be complete (ASGBA, 2005: 10).

Economic Activity:

Waddell (1979) has described "*Gooroongs*" as "a nomad pastoral tribe of the uplands" (p-307), which gives us some idea about what their traditional economy was. He further notes, while describing his travel in early 20th century along the southern ridges of Mount Kanchanjunga (in Sikkim) thus: "On the way we met a few of that nomad tribe of Nepalese herdsmen, the Gooroongs, a shifting people, here to-day and away to-morrow, who live in rude bowers of leafy branches" (ibid: 368). According to Messerschmidt (1976), the early economy of Gurungs was "herding, hunting, and swidden (slash and burn) agriculture adapted to the rugged highlands and high forests. Gurungs also have an early tradition of trans-Himalayan trading (p-2).

The self-study report prepared by them described that the Gurungs' main occupation in the past were sheep husbandry and agriculture. They are also described as transhumance people who moved along with their flock of sheep. The women had developed excellent skills in yarning and weaving blankets and other materials out of the raw sheep wool (Gurung et al, 2005: 6).

Traditionally, Gurungs took their herds of sheep to lower altitudes in cold months and higher altitudes in warm months. When the sheep were brought down they were kept on agricultural fields, which thus got automatically fertilized with the dung and urine of those animals. In summer, they went up to 13,000' or above to graze their sheep on thick and fresh grass coming out of the melted snow. They constructed little huts on their way up and down to protect themselves from inclement weather (Gurung et al, 2005: 8).

Now, the Government of Sikkim has banned grazing in the forest and thus the Gurungs' economy is totally dependent on settle agriculture.

Many have ventured out for white color jobs like teachers, and other official works in the public and private sectors.

Dresses and Ornaments:

The traditional dresses of Gurung male folks are *Bhangra* which is worn cross-wise on the upper part of the body, *Kachhar* worn on the lower part of the body, *Kuley* (cap) on the head, *Jogi* (cloth belt or *patuki*), *Daura* worn on the upper part of the body and *Lukuni* (a coat made of raw wool of sheep). The females wear *Doye* (*Lungi*) on the lower part of the body, *Galek* (*Shawl*) worn one side, *Tikis* worn on the backside, *Jogi* (cloth belt or *Patuki*), *Choli* (*Chaubandi*) on the upper part of the body, and *Kamo* or *Sirbandi* on the head. The women wear ornaments known as *Regi* (silver coin garment), *Jantar* (a square garment) made of gold, and *Ashey Mala* (*Kaju* and *Phiru*). The female also wear fingerings. The male wear fingerings and sometimes earrings.

Folk Musical Instruments:

Ekpatey Nho – made of wood and one side leather; used as musical instrument by *Ghyapring* Gurung priest during religious ceremony in western Nepal.

Ghoral Singi – made of a horn of *Ghoral*, the tip with a small hole; used by Gurung priest for driving away of evil spirits to protect man and his domestic animals.

Nya – it is a *Dhangro,* made of wood and skin on one side; used by Gurung priests during their ancestor's worship.

Chhangla – brass cymbal; used by *Pachyu* and *Ghyapring* priests in all birth to death rituals. It is also used in *Lochhar* and other religious ceremonies.

Twahutu – *dhol*-like musical instrument; used by *Pachyu* priest during ancestor worship of *Ghewa*

Dhanu-Sarangii – it is a bow-shaped *Sarangi* with 3 to 4 wires used by shepherds of Dudhpokhari, Lamjung area of Nepal.

Mirdunga – almost like a Madel, made of hollow *Dar*-wood with leather both sides, one side thin *khari* and other side with thick *khari*; used by Gurungs of northern Tanahu area in their *Rodhi* house and other musical occasions (Khandel, 2004:29).

However, only a few above musical instruments such as *Nya, Chhangla,* and *Twahutu*, are being used in Sikkim.

Folk Songs:

Gurungs are distinct from many other mountain communities because they have an institution called *Rodi* (also spelt as *Rodhi* and *Rodhin*) or youth dormitory, where young women used to weave and sleep. They also sang and dance there and the young Gurung men joined them with musical instruments. This institution is perhaps unique particularly in the sense that the young women can assemble at any house where a widow or an elderly couple is staying without children. The girls assembled there, weaved, sang, dance and slept there and hence provided social security to people in old age as they learnt the songs, dances, and crafts from them while the men folk were away with sheep herds in the grazing forest, thus establishing a fictive parent-children relationship. This institution is still exists in remote villages but slowly disappearing with the decrease of sheep population and ban of grazing in the forest in Sikkim (Chene, 1996; ASGBA, 2005: 7).

Folk Dances:

They have various kinds of folk-dances of which *Chyaantu* may be mentioned here as a special dance. Unlike most other dances, which took place in *Rodhi*, this dance is performed in the house of the deceased, depicting the life after death for consolation of the bereaved members of the family. They also have a dance drama called *Sorathi* in which the story of a king and his 16 concubines is enacted by the dancers (ASGBA, 20005: 24).

(a) *Ghanto Dance Drama*: *Ghanto* and *Sorath*i are essential Gurung folk dances. *Ghanto* is a socio-religious event of great importance, the central feature being a legend reminiscent of the Ramayana epic (Messerschmidt, 1976: 73).

(b) *Sirathi*: The dance continues for sixteen day related to sixteen stories of an actor king, astrologer or saint. A *Sorathi* girl narrates the infidelity of Brahman priest Jaya Singe.

(c) *Chalitra Dance*: This is based on a Sanskrit epic. It is performed by chorus of men and boys who beat drums, clang cymbals, sing and dance. Chickens are sacrificed for goddess *Saraswati* and the members organize a feast. However, such dances are rarely seen in Sikkim.

Religion and Belief System:

Like most mountain communities, Gurungs apparently followed Bonism, a mixture of Animism and Lamaism. It was characterised by animal sacrifice and *tantrism*, but Buddhism as well as Hinduism later considerably influenced them, next perhaps in extent only to Magars.

Messerschmidt (1976) writes, "Early Gurung religion was animistic and shamanic, akin to the pre-Buddhist Bon religion of Tibet" (p-2). The Gurung religion is characterised by worship of nature, ancestors, clan deities, etc. For instance, they celebrate *Khema Sildo Naldo*, which is the worship of sky, land, mountain, hill, river, etc., which takes place at the boundary of the village once in a year for better harvest, non-occurrence of natural calamities, better health, etc. *Khema Lhutan* is worship of the ancestors, (*Khe* = male ancestors; *Ma* = female ancestress). This is performed every fortnight on full moon night by offering water and lighting butter lamps. They remember *Khema* before they start anything important. They also celebrate *Paytan Lhutan*, which is an utmost secrecy. In this ritual the clan deity is offered the blood of animals. They keep yeast, wild tuber, black mung etc. in a small room where incense is burnt and butter lamps are lighted every full moon and new moons (ASGBA, 2005: 9-10).

The holy book of Gurungs is càlled *Kharlo*, which combines Bonism and Buddhism (ASGBA, 2005: 11). Their priests are called, *Lama, Pachyu* and *Ghyabring*. A Gurung shaman wears a white frock covering the whole body and hangs all kinds of things like horns, bones and teeth of wild animals, feathers of birds, porcupine quills, and different kinds of grass and organic beads and stones around his neck. He is also seen with a drum and a stick to beat the same (Gurung, 2005: 12-14).

Festival:

The various Hindu festivals like *Dashain, Tihar*, and *Maghey Sankranti, Chaitey Dasain, Sawaney Sankranti*, are celebrated by most Gurungs, but *Lochhar*, which is celebrated in great pump and show in Sikkim.

Language & Literature:

Gurungs have their own language and script, which they have now named *Tamu Kye* and *Khema Prhi* respectively. It has been recognized as one of the official languages of Sikkim and textbooks, magazines and dictionaries have just begun to be published in their own language and script. The 59 Hill tribe people of Nepal suffered from two dark periods: seventy-eight years of educational neglect (1768-1846), and one hundred and four years (1846-1950) of opposition to education (Uprety, 1962: 18-19). Ultimately the total dark period consists of one hundred eighty-two years. This is near about two centuries when Nepal kept itself aloof and isolated from the world (Regmi,1990: 66). Similarly, the 15 tribal communities of Sikkim also suffered culturally as well as educationally for a period of 333 years (1642-1975) and itself kept aloof and isolated from the world (Subba, 1999: 227-248; Subba, 2002: 1-21).

Rites of Passage (Life-Cycle): Birth, Marriage and Death are the major events of life.

***(b)* Birth:** Singing and dancing in the courtyard of the house where the birth has taken place marked the birth of a son. The naming ceremony takes place on the 9th day in the case of a male child and 7th day in the case of a female child. The name is given by a *Khegi*, which is a general referent to a priest, who ties a sacred thread with well-specified number of knots around the neck of the child. The next ceremony is rice-giving called *Kain Kowah*. This ceremony takes place when a girl is 5 months and a boy is 6 months old. *Khema* is worshipped to seek blessings for the child. The maternal uncle, called *Aashyon*, feeds the child with a silver coin and offers gifts. This is followed by hair-cutting rite called *Kolo Krafawa* for the boys. The boy's maternal uncle does this. For this rite they have to avoid the *Loh*, or the 12-year cycle, of both the parents, which is not difficult to identify because each *Loh* has a name after a bird or an animal, which is typical of all Buddhist communities in the entire Himalayas. The boy whose head is to be served is taken to the cowshed and symbolically tied to a post and the shaving on any odd day, month and year (ASGBA, 2005: 12).

***(c)* Marriage:** Traditionally, cross-cousin marriage between brother's son and sister's daughter was practiced, leading to addressing the father-in-law as *Aashyon* and mother-in-law as *Phane*. This is not prohibited now but clearly discouraged, and parallel cousin marriages are not allowed at all. A marriage is not deemed concluded until the father of the bride utters *wakdutta* in which he declares before all those present and their ancestors that his daughter is now married to so and so person and he is no more responsible for her welfare (ASGBA, 2005: 14).

***(d)* Death:** Finally, about death rites, which are called *Cra Tohwa*. They cremate the dead, although the dead bodies of children are always buried. They abstain from eating meat, drinking liquor, etc. during the mourning period that lasts for 7 to 14 days. The Buddhist Gurungs mourn the death for 49 days during which there will be constant supply of food and drink to the officiating monks from nearby monastery. The relatives of the deceased help in both cash and kind; and see that the family of the deceased does not suffer on account of material help (Gurung et al., 2005: 18).

Statutory Panchayats:

Social control is maintained through community organizations and formal statutory Gram Panchayats, which are responsible for the maintenance of peace in the villages and settlement of petty disputes of theft, assault, adultery and any small offences. They also oversee various social functions and also look after the development programmes. The Gurungs participate in the Gram *Sabha* and take responsibility for over development of the villages.

IV. THE TAMANGS
(LAMAS, MURMIS, NISHUNGS, ISHANGS, SAINGS)

Socio-Status: Most Backward Class (MBC)

Origin and History:

According to their tradition, the Tamangs came from a place, which was about a fifteen days journey inside Tibet. This homeland of theirs is called "Chivali". Another report says that they came from "Mudimirge" in Gipod (Hermanns, 1954: 21). Ancient history point out that the Tamangs are the original inhabitants of Nepal. Hamilton (1819) writes "The Murmis or Lamas are by many considered a branch of Bhutias. The Gurkhali by way of ridicule call the Murmis "Siyena Bhutias", or "Bhutias who eat carrion". On the contrary Vansittart opined "The Murmis show in a marked manner that they come of Mongolian stock. In fact they probably are nothing more or less than a Thibetan tribe whose ancestors wandered into Nepal. Ancient history would seem to point out that they were the original inhabitants of the Nepal Valley, but that after a certain lapse of time they were conquered by some other races who subjected them to many indignities, and made practically slaves of them, forcing them do all the hard labour, such as tilling fields, carrying loads, hewing wood, etc. To escape this, numbers wandered away into Eastern Nepal, and settled there. Intermarriage or anyhow connection with other races for ages, has had the natural effect of giving to what was probably a pure Thibetan tribe, a certain foreign strain which can be traced in the appearance of almost every Murmi nowadays" (Vansittart, 1896: 183). To escape this hardship, some of them might have settled in "The Greater Sikkim" and then to the present Sikkim.

The Tamangs are a Mongolian or semi-Mongolian tribe and are probably descended from a Tibetan stock modified by intermixture with Nepal races (Darjeeling District Gazetteer, 1947: 73-74). Dor Bahadur Bista (1967: 48) opined that the Tamangs form one of the major Tibeto-Burman speaking communities who were originally called "Bhote", meaning Tibetan, and that later on the term "Tamang" was attached to them because they were horse traders. "*Ta*" in Tibetan means "horse", "*mang*" means "trader". The term Tamang has remained ever since as the term "Bhote" was felt to be highly derogatory and objectionable to most of Nepalese. The term "Bhote" or "Bhutia" refers to the nomadic tribes living in the high hills bordering the Himalayas. Tamangs in particular and allied tribes like Sherpas, Drukpas, Kagatays or Yolmos in general are called "Bhote" throughout Nepal from where all these tribes migrated to India. Tamangs having acquired much of the cultural traits of Hinduized Nepali who were in majority considered themselves more as Nepali avoiding the "Bhote" or "Bhutia" epithet.

Prof. Samten Norboo (The Tibet Journal, 1981: 6:1:39) states in his article entitled "Migration of Tamang tribe from Tibet" that amongst the tribal groups originating from Tibet are the Tamangs, Yolmos and Sherpas as well as the Ladhakis, Sikkimese Bhutias and the Drukpas along with some other tribes in the Indo-Tibet frontiers. He has cited several historical evidences inferring that Tamangs are originally from Tibet and that they are a distinct tribal people. However, it is very difficult to accept his view, as he has not been able to cite any evidence to indicate either their existence in Tibet or the period of their migration to Nepal or Sikkim.

On the basis of the information obtained from His Holiness the Dalai Lama, the self-study report of the Sikkim Tamang Buddhist Sangh (2000: 1), claim that the "Tamangs" were originally a group of Tibetan cavalry. They made an expedition to famous Magadha city in order to obtain relics for the famous Samye cathedral during the reign of Tibetan King Khri-stron Deutsen in the 8th century A. D. without having to wage a war the disciplined cavalrymen returned back successfully through Nepal. Yet a group of them settled on the border region of Tibet and Nepal, from whom are popularly believed to have descended the Tamang tribe. This fact is supported by the similarities of language, religious customs and others between the Tamangs and the Tibetans. However, no historical evidence to support this theory of migration is available till date.

There is yet another view that the name has its origin in a place name in Nepal – Tagmaluijin. Vansittart (1896: 185) opined that "The first and original home of the Ghising is said to be Taljur, but as they increased in numbers, the Ghisings spread out and formed other homes; thus we find the Modi, Tilbung, etc. These again formed fresh homes for themselves as they increased in numbers, but they are not to be considered as sub-divisions or clans of the Ghisings, but merely "*kipats*" or places of residence". In Hemilton's, Risley's and Vansittart's account, the Tamangs are also described as Murmis, Lamas, Tamangs, *Ishangs* or *Saings*. According to J.D. Hooker, the Murmis are of Tibetan origin and are called *Nishung*, coming from the names of two districts "*Nimo*" and "Shung", both on the road between Sikkim and Lhasa. However, this community is widely known as the Tamangs in Sikkim. There are different speculations as regards to place of origin of the Tamangs. According to Tibetan folklore, the Tamangs were originally a group of Tibetan cavalry. After examining the names of the *rus* (clan) of the Tamangs, with their derivative connections with the Tibetan language, physical characteristics, and exogamous divisions, Risley suggests that they have descended from Tibetan stock modified more or less by intermixture with the Nepali races (Risley, 1894). Denying the Tibetan origin of the Tamangs, Colonel Santa Bir Lama is of the opinion that the Tamangs are natives of Nepal. He also believes that the Tamangs learnt the Tibetan language near about the seventh century A.D. when Nepal came under the Tibetan king (Singh, 1993: 172).

Population and Settlement:

The population of Tamang was 2,867 persons in Sikkim in 1891 (Census 1891). On the basis of voter's list of 2004, the population of Tamang is about 35,194 persons, constituting about 5.88% of the total population of Sikkim. There is an increase of 12.27 times the population of Tamangs within 113 years. In Nepal, Tamang population was 12,82,304 persons during 2001, constituting about 5.64% of the total population. The mother tongue retention was about 92% in Nepal.

Geographical Distribution:

The Tamangs of Sikkim are found mainly in the lower Teesta valley and Rangit valley, i.e. in the districts of East, South and West. Hill slopes, tops of the outer spur, and narrow riverine valley on the resistant rock of the Darjeeling ridge of the lower Teesta and Rangit valley are the places inhabited by the Tamangs. The Tamang concentrated areas are Soreng, Rinchenpong and Chakung in the West disrict; Jorethang, Damthang, Melli, Rateypani and Temi-Tarku in South district; Central Pandam, Assam Linzey, Ranka and Gangtok in the East district of Sikkim.

Food Habits:

The Tamangs are mostly non-vegetarian. They take all kinds of meat, fruits and vegetables. They take rice, maize, *moong*, peas, beans, *masur* and use mustard and rapeseed oil as cooking mediums. They consume roots, tubers, vegetables and fruits. They drink milk, and a few of them smoke. They are occasionally drinkers, taking home-brewed alcoholic drinks or even generally marketed stuff. *Blon thar* Tamangs do not take buffalo. *Negi* and *Lopchen thar* Tamangs do not take pork. Champa is the favourite food at higher altitudes. *Khabjey, Narama Jhiro, Chukpa, Babar; Syalroti, alum* and beef are their favorite food.

Family Pattern:

The nuclear family is more in evidence, though an extended family is not unusual.

Family Property:

Males divide their parental property equally. The eldest son succeeds his father.

Gender Issues:

Tamang women do not inherit any property. They perform household work, economic activity, rituals and religious ceremonies; but have an almost negligible role in politics and social control.

Kinship and Social Organization:

The Tamangs are an endogamous group and are divided into a number of exogamous clans (*ru*). According to Vansittart (1896) "The Murmis or Lamas are divided into two great divisions; viz. (*i*) **Barathamangs** and (*ii*) **Atharajat.** The Barathamangs are the pure Murmis and .....are considered socially superior to Atharajat....Being merely Thibetans there was no such thing as caste amongst the Murmis in olden days, and although prior to the Gurkha conquest the Murmis were divided into Barathamang and Atharajat, nevertheless there was no social difference between them. Prior to the Gurkha conquest the Barathamangs and Atharajat eat and drank together and intermarried. The term Atharajat was given in those days to the progeny of a Murmi with any foreigner, merely as a distinctive name for a mixed breed, but it in no ways caused any social superiority or inferiority. This breed, although of mixed blood, was accepted into the Murmi nationality without question and enjoyed all the privileges of any other Murmi. But with the Gurkha conquest and the consequent influences brought to bear, many changes have taken place. Originally the Barathamangs were divided into twelve clans (*ru*) only; viz: Baju, Bal, Dumjan, Ghising, Giaba, Gole, Mikchan, Mokthan, Pakrin, Siangdan, Thing, and Yonjan. Nowadays there are a very much larger number. The Atharajat were divided into three clans (*ru*); viz: (*i*) Gothar (progeny between Murmis and Khasas or Thakurs); (*ii*) Narba (progeny between Murmis and Newars); (*iii*) Sangri (progeny between Murmis and Magar, Gurung, Limboo, Rai ,or Sunuwar). The Barathamangs are also known as *rui choprat*. Marriage is prohibited among the *rus* of the respective groups (Ibid-183-178).

Economic Activity:

Land is a major resource controlled individually. There are both landholders and landless people in the community. Traditionally they have been traders. Cultivation of comparative advantage agricultural and horticultural crops and livestock rearing are the main sources of livelihood. They depend on market for cash. Employment as agricultural labour, raising of commercial crops and employment in white collar jobs are some of the more recent changes(Singh, 1993: 176).

Dresses:

About 20 to 30 years ago the male Tamangs used to wear *Bankatey Bhoto, Kachar, Daura-Suruwal* (Black colour), *Ista-coat, White cap or Feta, Waist-belt* (White) and *Khukuri* in the waist-belt. While the female Tamangs used to wear *Chit Ko Fariya* (*Syahama*), Red or maroon colour *Fariya, Makhamali Cholo, Mujetro,* Hand woven *Burko* and *Bakhu* or *Syahama*. But now, they became conscious of their traditional dresses. The male Tamangs also wear their traditional dresses such as *Chuwa* (*Bukhu*), *Tunga, Bhoto, Birkey topi, Gada* (*Gya*) and *Surki* (coat). The females wear *Syahama* (*Gunyu*), *Dorma* (*Fariya*), *Cholo, Chuwa* (*Bakhu*), *Pangden* and *Docha*. The small girls wear *Dhandhar* (*Fariya*) (Tamang, 2004). The Tamang's general habitat being at higher elevations the cold climate marked by forest and occasional snowfall necessitates people the use of warm garments. The occasional dress of a Tamang differs little from that of Tibetan or a Sherpa. Both sexes wear a long gown "*Bakkhu*" that extends right upto the feet. The man headdress may be of wool or fur known as "*Tagi*" or "*Usya*" and the footwear an exceedingly warm "*Ducha*" and "*Punga*". The men of warmer places wear "*Khenjo*" or "*Khenjar*", *Surlung*, and *Surtam*. The women wear "*Guney*" or "*Shyama*" and *Pangden* on the backside. They wear "*Hangrey*", "*Kragu*" or "*Ghakel*" on the upper body and *Sirphul, Ringa* on head. The female ornaments are *Chyaldang, Chyaldo, Nachyap, Phuli* and *Mundri* on nose, *Yachyap, Bala* on hand, *Chyap, Chakka* on fingers, *Nhali, Aalong, Chyoldo, Chepto sun, Dhungri, Butil, Jyadum* on the ear, *Jantar, Red munga, Shi* as garment, and *Kalli* on legs "*Gao*" (star-shaped bracelet), and bangles. Married women wear *Potey, Potey-Tilhari*. The males wear earrings called *Biku* or *Aalong*. Male babies are also given silver bangles on the first "*bhat khwai*" (*kaan khwaba*). The urban Tamangs wear either "*Daura Suruwal*" or western coat and pant now (ATBS, 2000: 5).

Folk Musical Instruments:

Koling – like *Damphu* made of wood and skin on one side; used in Sindhupalckok areas of Nepal.

Khani – a very old instrument; made of wood and sheep or bullock skin on both sides; hung and beaten with cane or bamboo stick in monasteries.

Gonggup – just like *muchunga*; used in olden times.

Gyapung – made of brass like *jhurumma* but bigger than that.

Nha – made of *aamusing* wood; beaten with sticks in Gumpas while chanting mantras by the priests.

Jorungey – made of bamboo can with skin on one side; used in Dhating areas of Nepal.

Domba or *Damphu* – made of *aamu* wood and skin on one side fixed by 32 bamboo nails and a carving of *Danphey chari*; believed to be made by Pemdorjee for the first time; essential instrument while singing and dancing of Tamang *Sello*.

Dilbu – a typical bell made of brass or *panchdhatu* or *austadhatu*.

Tamang Ghyaling – long Sanahii type instrument having seven holes in it ; used in pair in religious, cultural occasions and death rituals.

Tamang Tungna – made of soft rhododendron wood with horse carving on the top; have four wires, used with *nigalo* stick by Tamangs of Sailung area of Nepal during *Sello* songs and *Sello* dances.

Tung – used in the Helombu area of Nepal by the Buddhist in religious rituals.

Thunder – just like small *Damaru*; used by Lamas during religious rituals in Gumpa or *Ghyang* worship.

Pihung – made of copper, hollow inside with holes in it; used at Sindupalchok area of Nepal.

Puli – flute-like instrument made of nigalo bamboo, used in *sello* songs in different ceremony and occasions.

Bupsale – big brass cymbal; used in Buddhist Gumpas.

Bhante Madel – made of bamboo; used in Sindupalchok area of Nepal.

Sindung – made of wood and skin; used in different occasions.

Silongyan – small cymbal made of brass; used in different occasions along with other instruments (Kandel, 2004: 24).

Folk Songs:

The folk songs are about the naiveté of their life and culture, varied in content and meaning, composed in Tamang dialect and Tamang "*whai*" reflect the philosophy and ethos of civilization. They sing the songs in all festive occasions along with *Damphu* dance. These song are *Domphu* songs, duet songs, religious songs of Lamas or *Bakpa*, Tamang *Sello*, etc.

Folk Dances:

Damphu Sello dance, Lama or *Bakpa* dance of the monastery. The popular folk dance of Tamangs are *Damphu nach, Chomlu nach, Mhendomaya nach, Lama Bakcham nach, Manichhepa, Tormamharso nach,* and *Jungwa nach.*

Religion and Belief System:

The Tamangs were "Bonist" (animist) in the beginning but now have adopted Mahayana sect of Buddhism. However, they have retained many "Bonist" practices such as *Khepa-Soom* (a practice of paying homage to the ancestors with blood sacrifices), *Bonbo Sherab* (an act of giving affectionate farewell of the departed soul "*Thunda Sorshi*" with offerings), etc.

Festival:

The Tamangs observe festival of their own such as *Lotshar* which take place on December-January, along with many Buddhist festivals such as Guru Rimpochey's *Trungkar Tshechu, Saga Dawa, Dukpa Tsheshi, Lhabab-Duechen, Pang Lhabsol, Loosung,* and join the Hindu festivities of *Dasai, Tihar*, etc.

Language and Literature:

Tamangs have their own script and language. The Tamang language shares several words in common with the Tibetan language. The State government of Sikkim has recognized the Tamang language as one of the State languages of Sikkim. Now, the Tamang Language is being taught in the schools upto the primary level of education.

Rites of Passage (Life-Cycle): Birth, Marriage and Death are the major events of life.

(*a*) Birth: The Lama conducts the worship of the Buddha and the *Phola* or the family deity and the ceremony at the time of birth, held as a purificatory rite. The purification ceremony and the worship are performed on the fifth day after birth for a boy and on the third day for a girl. The naming *(thapsang*) of the child is done on the same occasion. Utensils used by the mother and child is kept separate till the ceremony of *thapsang* is over. The Lama gives the name and what the name would be depends on the time of birth. The Lama also makes predictions about the future of the child. For the assumption of priesthood there is no prescribed age, though it is normally gone through between eight and ten years – in a ceremony called the *tachet*, performed by the senior most Lama (*Loben*) and the younger Lamas. The head of the person intending to become a Lama is shaved completely (Singh, 1993: 174-175).

(b) Marriage: Endogamy is the norm among the Tamangs, though the cases on community exogamy have been increasing these days. A marriage through negotiation (*magne*) is the common practice, though elopement (*yhuram*) is becoming popular to avoid heavy expenses on marriages. The Lamas are allowed to marry, except those who want to become *Galong*. Monogamy, junior levirate and junior sororate are the general forms of marriage. Residence is patrilocal. Divorce and separation on grounds of maladjustment with social approval are allowed. A widow or a widower, a male or female divorcee can marry. "Jarikal" is also in practice.

An interesting feature of a Tamang matrimony is the "*REM*" (*RIT*) system in which the bridegroom on his party will have to submit twelve different varieties of articles to the bride's parents. This payment is not to be considered as a compensation for the bride but it is a token of gratitude and respect to the bride's parents for having agreed to offer their daughter. The *Rem* is a social custom which also serves to highlight and solemnize the occasion. The articles may include perishable items like oil-cooked rice breads, home made liquor, raw meat etc. and non-perishable items like money, rice, living fowl, etc. The articles are decorated with ***kokomhendo*** (*totola ko phul*). The marriage rituals are performed in a number of stages that include: (*i*) selection of partner and consent to the marriage by the girl's parents; (*ii*) Submission of presents to the bride's parents; (*iii*) invitation to the guests; (*iv*) recitation of mantras by the Lama in the groom's house; the dressing of the groom, the elders' blessing to the groom; (*v*) the wedding procession with the groom arriving at the bride's house with dancing parties of "*Damphu Whai*" songs and *Damphu* dance/ *Sello* dance; (*vi*) welcome by the elders and the dance party of the bride side; (*vii*) a function called the "*Phydan*" held to introduce the bride to the groom and groom's relatives; (*viii*) the marriage solemnization; (*ix*) a welcome given on the return of the bridal party to the groom's house; (x) introduction of bride and the serving of food at the groom's house; (*xi*) the return of the couple to the girl's house after three days and presentation of alcohol to the girls parents in *duran* ceremony (Singh, 1993: 175; ATBS, 2000: 7).

No Tamang marriage can be deemed to be complete without the due observance of "*Chardam Saimundri*" a common practice in many hill tribes, which forms a very important and unavoidable part of the ceremony. In this, the elderly family members inclusive of parents of bride and elderly villagers of both sides, witness and formally pronounce or declare the fact of the marriage between the bride and the groom and this will be patiently heard by all present. This also involves the taking of oath verbally by both the bride and the groom that they shall never separate from each other and shall always live as true husband and wife. As per tradition, the bridegroom will submit certain prescribed eatables, a hen and a cock as well as a sum of twelve rupees for this ceremony. The fowl curry along with the liquor and all as a mark of the ceremony having been accomplished then eat other items. The marriage is now, deemed to be officially solemnized and confirmed (STBS, 2000: 7).

Nowadays, in many cases the groom putting the vermilion mark at the parting of the bride's hairs; and *potey* put around the neck of the bride at the auspicious time of marriage is also in practised before the sacrificial fire due to the influence of Hinduism, while the Lama chants mantras (Singh, 1993: 175).

(c) Death: After a death, funeral rites are performed under the direction of the Lama. A sacred lamp (*chimi*), a dagger (*goja*) and a looking glass are placed near the dead body. The Lama indicates the time and the direction in which the dead body would be taken out. Sacred flags (*lungdras*) flown on the occasion come to 108 or fewer. The dead body is cremated. Mounning (*somra*) continues for three days, with the ancestors being worshipped. Use of salt and oil items is prohibited during this time. A piece of deceased's bone is sometimes kept in the monastery (*gumpa ghonba*). The purificatory rite begins after an interval of seven days, and the final rite takes place on the forty-ninth day after the death and is known as the ceremony on the forty-ninth day (*dungu*). Considerations of expenses are now coming in the way of the elaborate ceremonial, and the ritual are now being curtailed (Singh, 1993: 175-176).

V. THE BHUJELS (KHAWAS/ GHARTIS)

Socio-Status: Most Backward Class (MBC).

Origin and History:

The origin and migration of the ***Bhujels or Khawas*** or ***Ghartis*** are not clearly known, except that they came from Nepal sometimes in the past. They have been slaves of the royal family and the nobles, as palanquin carriers and beaten rice makers. The women were engaged in fetching water. But at a later date, a king of Nepal freed them all from their masters, by paying cash from the royal treasury (Singh, 1993: 34).

The word "Bhujel" is derived from Bhujikot, a river valley in the southern slope of Mt. Dhaulagiri in Nepal (ABS, 2005: 2). It is further claimed that their own kingdom comprising of 1700 villages had 22 kings (?) who ruled between AD 885 and 1315. The Mallas defeated them, who after defeating the Bhujels, ordered that all Bhujel males above 12 years be slaughtered. Some manage to escape to safer places in Nepal, Sikkim, Darjeeling etc. (ABS, 2005: 5). In the absence of any historical source cited by the self-study report it is not possible to accept it, although such a claim does not appear weired at all in the pre-1769 history of Nepal (Sinha et al, 2005: 71).

Bhujels are also known as Ghartis, although the common surname they use is Khawas. They are believed to have been slaves once and were considered low in ritual status. They were traditionally palanquin bearers.

The Bhujel and the Gharti are both traditionally occupational clans of Magars, who for reasons not yet fully clear, emerged as an autonomous community with its own identity. The names of Bhujel clans and lineages provided in the self-study report of the Bhujels (2005: 4) also clearly indicate that they might have once been a part of Magar Community. Some of the Magars having been converted assumed the sacred thread, whilst others did not; hence we find Ghartis, Ranas, and Thapas, who appear as tribes belonging both to the Magars and to the Khas (Vansittart, 1896: 104). Hamilton (1819) writes, "The Ghartis are of two kinds, Khas and Bhujial. The former are admitted to the military dignity, but the later wallow in all the abominations of the impure Gurungs, and do not speak the Khas language" "The Ghartis as they seem to be far more mixed than any of the other five Mangar tribes. The Bhujial Ghartis live in the valley and high mountains to the north of Gulmi, above the Puns, but immediately below the Karantis. This tract of country runs along both sides of the Bhuji Khola (river), from which they probably derive their name" (Vansittart, 1896: 108).

Population and Settlement:

The total population of Bhujels, on the basis of 2004 voter's list of Sikkim, is 5061, constituting 0.84% of the total population of Sikkim.

Geographical Distribution:

The main area of their habitation are Daramdin, Salangdang, and Soreng in the West district; Gomkitam, Turuk, and Tokal Bermiok in the South district; Jitlang, Pakyong, Rhenock, and Tadong in the East district of Sikkim.

Food Habits:

The Bhujels are non-vegetarian, taking fish, mutton, chicken, pork and eggs, but not beef. For their staple food they have rice, maize, millet and wheat in cereals; all kinds of dal in pulses; and used mustard oil as a cooking medium. They take all types of vegetables and fruits..

Family Pattern:

The Bhujel family is of a vertically extended type, linked by the father-child relationship; with a more and more predominant tendency towards the "nuclear type" family.

Family Property:

After a person's death, his sons inherit his property equally. Succession goes to the eldest son.

Gender Issues:

The daughters do not get the landed property. Even if some property is inherited, it is movable which goes directly to the in-law families and not to the daughters. Only some jewellery is given to the daughters. Thus they have lower social status.

Kinship and Social Organization:

Like Magars, they are divided into a number of clans, which are exogamous groups. The various clans are all equal, although some of them are dominant in some villages on account of their number.

Economic Activity:

The traditional occupation was palanquin bearers, but this job must have been seasonal and done mostly by young men only. The women also made beater rice. The economic activity of early Bhujial Ghartis is generally a shepherd. He used to live principally on the milk of sheep, and is almost invariably a man of very good physique and heavy limbs (Vansittart, 1896:108). The Bhujels in Sikkim are agriculturist, livestock rearers, and a number of them are in government jobs as schoolteacher and other white color jobs.

Dresses: Same as that of Magars.

Folk Musical Instruments: Same as that of Magars

Folk Songs: Same as that of Magars.

Folk Dances: Same as that of Magars

Religion and Belief System:

Like Magars, they are evidently all animists to begin with but have all been considerably Hinduized. However, they still worship ancestors, various gods and goddesses of forest, mountains, rivers, animals, birds etc. They also continue the practice of sacrificing of animals and offering of millet-beer and alcohol to various deities and spirits to make them happy. They also worship *Dhorbarahi* as a community deity with the help of a shaman and with animal sacrifices.

Festival: Same as that of Magars.

Language and Literature:

Nothing is known about their language besides the claim that it is very similar with that of Magars.

Rites of Passage (Life-Cycle): Birth, Marriage and Death are the major events of life.

***(a)* Birth:** As soon as the child is born they perform ancestor-worship through a very simple ritual following which the umbilical cord is cut and placed on a silver coin before the midwife finally buries it in a clean place, a little away from home. On the sixth day, they do a ritual again to propitiate the ancestors, as they believe that the child's fate is written on that day. Traditionally the naming ceremony took place on the 11th day, although it can also take place on the 3rd, 5th, 7th or 9th day, just as the Magars do. Similar to Magars again, on this day the whole house is daubed with clay mixed with cowdung and cow's urine or gold-dipped water is sprinkled all over the house to "purify" it. But unlike Magars, Bhujels tie the child's hands, legs, waist and neck with thread dipped in turmeric paste and take him/her out of the house to show the world outside for the first time. The head of the family on the basis of the child's horoscope does the naming usually or simply after the name of the day he/she is born. This is followed by feasting and drinking (ABS, 2005: 8).

The next important rite is rice-feeding ceremony, which takes place on the 5th month in case of a girl and 6th month in case of a boy. This ceremony begins with obeisance to ancestors and ends with drink and feast again. The rice mixed with curd is first fed to the child by a vergin boy or girl depending on the sex of the child, and in case of a girl her maternal uncle has to present her a silver bangle on the occasion.

Magars pierce the nose and ears of a girl and ears only of a boy anytime after the rice-feeding ceremony but before the next ceremony for a son in which his head is tonsured. The tonsuring is done by his maternal uncle at the age of 3, 5, 7, or 9 years.The hair removed from his head is collected in a clean piece of cloth and stuffed in the hole of a tree (ABS, 2006: 9).

***(b)* Marriage:** The next important rite of passage for Bhujels is marriage and interestingly, like Magars, they practised maternal cross-cousin marriage. Although there is no particular age for marriage, a girl who has attained puberty is considered to be ready for marriage. Divorcees and widows can remarry (ABS, 2005: 10).

***(c)* Death:** Finally, a little about their death rites; as soon as a person dies, the dead body is taken out of the house and kept in the roofed porch in the facade of the house and cremated on the same day or the day after. Cremation of the dead and throwing the half-burnt body into a river is also seen as an influence of Hinduism, as the traditional practice of the disposal of the dead has been known to be burial. Non-Bhujels are not allowed to touch the dead body until a ritual called *dagbatti* is performed. Like Magars again, the period of abstention for Bhujels is 10 days and they perform the final funerary rites on the 10th day. Bhujels also believe in communication between the spirit of the dead person and their shaman and the dead person expresses his/her wishes through the shaman. Such wishes are carefully fulfilled exactly 6 months after the death of the person by offering the articles wished by the spirit on a makeshift altar. A hen in case of a man and a cock in case of a woman may also be sacrificed if the spirit is not satisfied with the initial offerings (ABS, 2006: 11).

The overall economic condition of Bhujels is deplorable and school drop-outs are a major problem. Very few are educated up to Class XII and even fewer employed as government servants.

VI. THE THAMIS (THINGMIS , THANMIS)

Socio-Status: Most Backward Class (MBC)

Origin and History:

The Thamis or Thangmi or Thanmi are the autochthonous Hill tribes, of Dolakha, Sindhupalchok, and Rameychap districts of Janakpur Anchal of Nepal; inhabiting these areas from the time immemorial. Now, a considerable population of Thamis is found even in areas of Jhapa, Morong, Ilam, Udayapur, and other districts of Purbanchal areas of Nepal (Nepal Thami Samaj, NTS, 1999: 3). They are a very little known community and there is a great deal of confusion about their origin and identity in both Nepal and Sikkim. One of the reasons why their identity is often misconstrued by them as well as by other neighbouring communities is their demographic size, which is indeed negligible, which in turn may of course be due to lack of a clear identity, counted as they often are among the *Khasas* and sometimes even among Rais or Tamangs (ASTA, 2005: 1).

The historians, anthropologists and other writers were often confused and the Thamis were included with other communities of the Himalayan region. For instance, Vansittart (1896) has included the "*Thamis*" of Nepal as one of the Sub-clans of "*Adhikari*" under the "*Khasas*" (pp-66-70). He has also recognized the "Thami" as one of the sub-clan of Burathoki Magar (p-87); and again they were included as an unclassified clan or sub-clan of "Rais" (p- 134-135). Dor Bahadur Bista (1972) say that they are economically and religiously quite close to the Tamangs while J.L.

Sharma (1982) claims that linguistically their affinity with the Rais is quite obvious and even considers them as one of the Rai groups. Their physical features, however, suggest that they are closer to the Tamangs and Gurungs than to the Rais. They normally have a dark complexion, while most Rais are yellowish (Singh, 1983: 184). Now, they inhabit in the various parts of Nepal and Sikkim. Due to their closer affinity to Kiratas, the Thamis are categorized under the Communities analogous to the Kitatas.

According to the self-study report of Thami community, they might have migrated from Asia Minor and settled down in "Simroungad" (the capital of Tirhutdoya in 1097-1326 AD), bordering present India and Nepal in Western Indian frontiers and some people were traveled through the Himalayan region on Tibetan side and entered East India via Burma and further towards the West of Brahmaputra Valley and might be settled in India and Nepal. They also claim that they are indigenous habitants of North-East region of India, inhabiting the remote areas of Sikkim, Darjeeling and Jalpaiguri (Doors) long before establishment of the Namgyal Dynasty in Sikkim in 1642 (ASTA, 2005: 1). In the absence of any historical source cited in the report it is not possible to accept such a claim. However, the Thamis were subjects of the kings of Nepal as well as Sikkim in different point of time during the historical evolution in the past. Thus, there is every reason to believe that they might have been migrated and settled in Sikkim also during this period of historical evolution as in the case of other communities like Gurung, Sunuwars etc.

Population and Settlement:

As per the survey conducted by the "All Sikkim Thami Association" the total number of Thamis in Sikkim are around 600 to 700 people (ASTA, 2005: 10). The Thamis were 22,999 during 2001 in Nepal (Census 2001).

Geographical Distribution:

The Thami concentrated villages are Rhenock, Rongli, Sang Martam, and around Gangtok.

Food Habits:

The Thamis are all non-vegetarians and eat almost any kind of meat. There are a few who do not eat beef, but they are mainly those who have closely intermixed with other Hindu communities. Their staple food consists of rice, wheat, barley, maize and millet in cereals, all type of pulses, vegetables, root and tubers, and fruits. Mustard oil is used as cooking medium. Alcoholism is quite common among the male members except children.

Family Pattern:

The nuclear family is predominant. Joint or extended families are noticed only temporarily and occasionally.

Family Property:

It is only the sons who can inherit the land, though the daughters generally inherit the gold and silver ornaments belong to the mother after marriage. The succession takes place along the male line, and according to seniority of age in the family.

Gender Issues:

The contribution of women to the family labour and income is significant, but due to meagre inheritance of parents' property women have lower status. From the "*Devikot* and Thami *Nari Puja*", it reveals that the women take active part and leading role in this religious ceremony. There is no discrimination in their religious functions. The mother is often given more respect and love than the father.

Kinship and Social Organization:

The Thamis are divided into clans and sub-clans, and the major clans are: Rishmi, Anglami, Dolakhe, Dugpali, Ishirishmi, Dangurishmi, and Shirishmi. Each of the clans is believed to have originated from a common ancestor. The father never jokes with his daughter-in-law and the elder brother with the younger brother's wife. The younger brother, however, can always joke with his elder brother's wife (Singh,1993: 184-188).

Festival:

They celebrate *Dasai, Tihar, Sawane Sankranti, Maghey Sankranti* etc. along with the above mentioned religious festivals. On *Mahge Sankranti* the Thami offer worship to Siva with *belpatra*, and then eat lot of wild tubers.

Economic Activity:

The chief economic resource of the Thami people is land, which is controlled by the head of the family. They are mainly landless and cultivate land on a *kut* or sharecropping basis, which demands that the tenant pay a stipulated amount of grain every year to his landlord. They are primarily mixed farmers cultivating agricultural, horticultural crops and rearing livestock. A few work as teachers and other white color jobs in the government.

Dresses:

Their traditional dress was *"Labaeda"* for male and *Gunew* for female made of nettle fibres, but now the male wear *daura suruwal, patuka, lukuni,* and cap while female wear *phariya, cholo, patuka* and *lukuni.* Ornaments worn by the female are *Chaptae soon* and *bulaki* (ASTA, 2005:8-9).

Folk Musical Instruments:

They extensively use *Jhyali* and *Madel* while dancing.

Folk Songs:

Folk songs of Nepali.

Folk Dances:

In Maghe Sankranti they go dancing to the Siva temple carrying *bel* and water. They participate in all Nepali dances during different festivals.

Religion and Belief System:

The Thamis are Animist but also influenced extensively both by Hinduism and Buddhism. They worship *Dolakha Bhimsen,* their main deity along with a number of other deities such as *Bhumya, Nagey, Bisakarma, Gosai, Chirkun, Nepalya Deva, Chan Deva, Lakhin, Gatyako Deva, Shyakri Deva* and *Bahara Deva*.

Bhumya is a god of agricultural crops and provides food to the people with good harvest. It is worshipped twice a year once before starting cultivation *Ubhauli* (February – March) for good cropping season; and other after the crop is harvested *Udhauli* (December) for thanks giving and offering newly harvested crops. *Nagey* is the god of nature and worshipped for protection of houses, agricultural farms and land from natural calamities. *Bisakarma* is a god worshipped for protection of the family from diseases, sickness and happiness. *Gosai* god is worshipped for protection of buffalo. Livestock rearing is an important activity of Thamis. *Chirkun* is another god worshipped for protection of other domestic animals such as cows, chicken, duck etc. They also worship *Narayaini* (Vayu devta), *Budaeni, Khola Ko Mai, Kalingchoke Mai, Gamalae devta, Shikari,* etc. They offer small copper trisul to Shiva temple as a token of their worship and devotion

Language & Literature:

They speak Thami dialect known as *Thami Kham* or *Thami Wakhe,* which is a Tibeto-Burman language, but use Devnagari script.

Rites of Passage (Life-Cycle): Birth, Marriage and Death are the major events of life.

(*a*) Birth: When the baby born, the mother should be purified on the 7th day for a male child and on the 5th day for a female. The child is named on the same day. The "*Khami*" performs an important puja called "*Shang*" on the very day of purification and naming ceremony for the protection of mother and her child. This is the naming ceremony and on this day also the floors are cleaned with the same cow dong and water mixture and the *"Khami"* purifies the household in the same way with cow's urine, "*Khurank, lekhu* and water. Then, the child's wrists, waist and ankles are tied with threads wet with turmeric and made yellow. The threads must go three to five or seven rounds being tied at the places. The maternal uncles are invited to witness the ceremony. Food is served and dispersed (ASTA, 2005: 6-7; NTS, 1999:62-68).

***(b)* Marriage:** The Thami marriages are of three types viz. *Mangni biya*, elopement or marriage after the birth of the children. The marriage of Thami is performed with a specific sort of tradition among the various prevalent social initiations. Thami do not follow the cross cousin system of marriage. One should not be one's own consanguine relative. On the maternal side, one can marry after the third generation. If one performs elopement marriage, then unless and until the full rituals are not completed as in a regular marriage, this marital union is not socially accepted. The *Lhangmi* or *Lhami* (negotiator) conducts the process of negotiation. The *Lhami* negotiates for the girl presenting 3 numbers of bread and full pot of wine to the girl's parents. If the girl's parents agree, the marriage dates etc. are fixed. Another batch of present for the girl's parents has to be offered that consists of 18 number of breads, five full bottle wine, a solid live cock, a he goat on hoof, and 10 pathi grain.

The day before the marriage *Jhankri* priest erects on ancestral symbol of deity on the banana leaf in the kitchen room of the boy's house. The ancestral deity is made of flour of rice, lead powder (*sindur*), stamen (a yellow powder *kesari*) and traditionally decorated with a full plate of raw rice, 12 numbers of eggs, one solid live cock, 12 *manas* of rice or grain, flower of *totola* (*Apoxylum indicum*), green grass leaf (*Dubgrass*), a dreadful leaf (*bhimsenpati*), a worm wood on bitter leaf (*titepati*), *dhupi* (*Cryptomaria sp.*), couple of bamboo sticks etc.

Thereafter, the *Jhankri* priest usually appeals to the different ancestral deity of Rivers and its shore chanting mantras and beating drums, bells by offering the flesh of solid cock for blessing for the long life of the couple. A garland of three numbers of Camalia's bud, flower, handful of *dubgrass*, 14 numbers of *totola* flowers hang over the hearth. The *Jhankri* dances around the ancestral deity's altar erected on the banana leaf with all the requisites kept on the tray of bamboo, chanting mantras, beating drums, ringing bells, and then drops a few grains of rice into the cup of water kept over the heap of millet. Then, he picks up a few grains floating rice from the water and gives it to the bridegroom.

Then, the cock is killed and offered to the ancestral deity. Thereafter, the priest picks up the garland hanged over the hearth and ties around the neck of the bridegroom. Then the bridegroom wears new dress and ornaments, obtains blessing from the parents and elders, then leaves the house for the bride's house along with other members of the wedding party consisting of *Lhangmi* and unmarried teenage girls. Before leaving the house the bridegroom not only obtains blessing from her mother but he has to suck his mother's breast atleast three times (ASTA, 2005: 5-6; NTS, 1999:69-84).

Marriage takes place in the bride parent's house. The marriage symbols are vermilion and poteymala but the married women rarely use vermilion. Marriage is not so ritualized today as it used to be earlier. After the marriage the bride lives with her husband (Singh, 1993: 185).

(*d*) Death: The Thami death rites differ depending on the age at the time of death as in the case of the Limboo community. If the child dies before sucking the breast-milk of the mother, the dead body is placed or put in the cave without cover. It should not be covered, as the Thamis believe that the cover blocks the womb for coming issues of the mother. No death pollution or funeral rites are performed in this case. If the child dies between the ages of 1 to 8 years, the dead body is buried. In this case, the deceased is entitled to get death pollution and funeral rites. If a person dies above the age of 9 years, the dead body is cremated unless the deceased was infected by dangerous disease in which case it is buried in the deep.

Like that of the Limboos, the Thamis have cremation ground on the higher hills divided according to their clans. The deceased is cremated as per their specific clans cremation area. If a deceased has died in other's house the dead body will be taken out from window and not from the main door. The corpse is wrapped with white cloth and put on green bamboo poles. If the deceased is female, a sickle and a spade and in the case of male a *Khururi* and a axe are placed at the head and foot side of the corpse. The *Jhankri* priest ties a raw white cotton thread on the toes of the right foot on one end and on the head of the eldest son and drop it three times one by one. The family serves rice to the dead and the sons take out the corpse from the main door. Now, the face of the corpse is washed, ash *tika* is put on the forehead, and the sons take it to the cremation hill-lock leading the leg-side towards it. The Jhankri, who hold Khukuri on one hand and fried paddy on the other, leads the corpse. The others who hold wood, fire with three wood-sticks etc follow the corpse. The eldest son from head-side and the youngest son from leg-side put the fire on the funeral pyre.

The deceased's sons from the day of the death observe death pollution. They abstain eating meat, curd if the deceased is father, and milk in the case of mother. They take salt only once a day. Two days after, all the brothers and the *Khami* or *Jhankri* priest assemble and decide on constructing a *chautari, pati, kuwa* etc. for the deceased. On the 3rd day the sons and brothers of the deceased go to the site of the *chautara* and shave their heads living no top knot and perform the *kalo ghyava*. A fowl is slaughtered and placed on a *tapari* (leaf plate) but upside down with some uncooked rice grains also. This ritual ends after three days, thus ending the death pollution also. The ones observing pollution come out and wear a white cloth (on their heads) called *jhopa*. *Thulo Ghyava* is done in *poush*, and it is after this that all rituals are considered over and all bans are lifted. The custom of constructing *chautari, pati, kuwa, sanghu, pauva* etc. are works done after the *thulo ghyava* is over. Then when everything is over an oil-lamp is burnt at the shrine of Mahadev and then only they commence eating stinging nettles which is otherwise banned (ASTA, 2005: 9:; 85-92).

17
The Khasas

Ancient literature of India such as *Puranas* and *Mahabharata* contains frequent references to a tribe whose name is usually spelt as *Khasa, Khasha* or *Khasiya* (Grierson, 1916: 2). They were a group of tribes and were in the extreme north-west of India more particularly on the Hindu-Kush and in the Western Punjab. They once occupied an important position in Central Asia, and the *Kashgar* of *Chitral*, and were named after them. Before the sixth century they had apparently penetrated along the southern slope of the Himalayas as far east as Nepal, and in the 12th century they certainly occupied considerable areas in the hills of south, southwest and south-east of Kashmir. At present their descendants, and the tribes who claim descent from them, occupy a much wider area. Their language was more or less like Sanskrit. They were considered to have lost their claim to consideration as Aryans, and to have become "*Mechchhas*" or "barbarious", owing to their non-observance of the rules for eating and drinking observed by the Sanskritic peoples of India. These *Khasas* were a warlike tribe, and were well known to classical writers (Grierson, 1909: 7-8).

Looking at the *Khasas* from the Brahmanical point of view, that the *Khasas* are the offsprings of outcaste *Kshatriyas*, and also among the tribes, the *Khasas* are those who become outcaste through having neglected their religious duties (Grierson, 1916: 5). Atkinson is of the opinion that the *Khasas* are looked on more as heretical members of the great Aryan family than as outcaste aborigines, and from a very early period they have been recognized as an important tribe in upper India. They have for centuries been under the influence of the Brahmanical priesthood of the plains of India. As a result, they must have adopted a number of Hindu practices. But the great mass of the population of the eastern Himalayas professes a belief little differing from the orthodox Hinduism of the plain (Atkinson, 1874: 269-283).

Eden Vansittart (1896) states that in ancient Hindu writings, the country between the Nepal Valley and Kashmir was called *Khas*, and its inhabitants were called *Khasiyas*. He also finds that in about 1000 A.D. a race of Hindus called the *Khas*, were residing about Palpa and the southern portion of Nepal, in the '*Khas* nation' in the region of Narendra Deva of Nepal. This means that the *Khas* existed as a nation at some period prior to 1100 A.D. This gives us the *Khas* a far more ancient origin than is usually accepted. Hindus were known historically to have existed within Nepalese territories for centuries before the birth of Christ. It is stated in ancient history that during the reign of Stunko, the fourteenth king of the Kiranti dynasty, Ashoka, the Raja of Pataliputra (Patna), having heard of the fame of Nepal as a sacred place, came on a pilgrimage to Nepal (about 230-250 B.C.). He gave his daughter Charumati in marriage to a descendant of a Chhetri, named Devapala. The original seat of the *Khas* is ordinarily said to be *Gorkha*. The polished Hindus migrated from the plains no doubt found the women of the various hill races only too willing to welcome them to their arms, but their progeny were called *Khas*, perhaps, as a term of reproach, from the word "*Khasnu*" – "to fall". In time, however, the number of *Khas* must have become so great as to form a nation, and to the nation struck the name of *Khas*. It will thus be seen that the *Khas* are derived from three sources:

1. Progeny of Brahman and *Chatris* with women of the hill tribes.
2. Converted barbarians, and
3. *Ektharians* (the descendants, more or less pure, not of the Brahamins by a *Khas* female, but of Rajputs and other *Khastriyas* of the plains who either sought refuse in Nepal from the Musalmans, or voluntarily sought military service as adventures).

From the advent of these thousands of foreigners and their numerous progeny sprang a new race, called *Khas*, and with this new race also came a new language, which was called the *Khas-Kura* (now known as Nepali/ Gorkhali), which is nowadays the *lingua franca* of the Himalayan Region including Nepal, Sikkim, Darjeeling, Assam and many parts of other Himalayan States of India (Vansittart, 1896 : 82-102).

According to Oldfield "The progress of Mahomedanism in Hindustan daily drove fresh refugees to the Nepalese mountains. The "*Khas* tribes" availed themselves of the superior knowledge of the strangers to subdue the neighbouring aboriginal tribes. They were uniformly successful; and in such a career, continued for ages, they gradually merged the greater part of their own ideas, habits and language (but not physiognomy) in those of the Hindus. The *Khas* language became, and still is, a corrupt dialect of Hindi, retaining not many traces of primitive barbarism."(*ibid* pp-88).

Today, the *Khasas* universally define themselves as Hindus with distinct caste system of higher Bahuns, then Chhetris at high *Khasas* and lower *Khasas* caste Kamis, Damais, and Sarkis who are in same respects culturally distinct from others of their religion and tribes (not castes). The two ancestral stocks are generally believed to have contributed the present *Khasa* population: High castes *Khasa* comprise – Bahuns, and Chhetris; and lower caste *Khasas* are Kamis, Damais and Sarkis.

Characteristics of *Khasas*:

The *Khasas* have narrow face, long and permanent nose and deep-set eyes. They have dark eyes and skin varies from place to place. Some are black and some have fair skin. The muscles of their legs are well developed owing to the inhabitants of mountainous region. They have family deity – *Masto*, which is worshiped by sacrificing animals like goat and ship.

Dresses:

The *Khasas* male wear *daura* (a kind of upper garment), *Surwal* (trouser), *Patuka* (waist belt) and *Dhaka topi* (cap). Waist coat known as *Istakot* is also commonly used by male members. The male dress is considered incomplete unless he keeps a *Khukri* (Nepali dagger) inside *Patuka*. Female members usually wear *Guniyue cholo* (upper and lower garment). However, on different occasions they wear *Phariya* (sari) and *Hembari* (shawl) with *Chaubandi cholo* (blouse). Female also use *Patuka*. The *Khas* women use various kinds of ornaments such as *Sirbandi* for heads, *karnaphul* for upper ear, *dhungri* to the left-side and *bulaki* in the middle nose, *rezi, tilhari, sikri, pote,* and *pawalo* necklaces, ear ring, *chura* (bangles) made of precious metals such as gold and silver.

Religion and Belief System:

They are Hindus; worship various Hindu gods and goddesses, e. g. Pashupatinath Shiva, Kali, Durga, Vishnu, Ganesh, Lakshmi, Saraswati, etc. They have their own priest known as Pandit or Bahun who perform all life rituals–birth, marriage and death of the community. *Satyanarayana* is worshipped as the family deity. *"Kul"* is another household deity. For pilgrimage, they visit sacred Hindu shrines and centres like Kathmandu, Puri, Kashi etc. Brahmans act as the sacred mentors. They also worship nature divinities "*Mastha*" (Nature God), and *Kul deota* through their own oracular shaman *Dhami* and *Jhankri*.

Festival: *Dasai, Tihar, Tij, Sansari mai ko puja, Dewali, Chaite Dasai, Maghe sankrati, Masto* worship, *Vaisakhi,* etc.

Language, Literature & Script:

Khus-Kura or Nepali or Gorkhali is the language spoken by this group of people. The language is written in *Devnagari* script. The language and literature is well developed; is the *lingua franca* of Sikkim, Nepal, Bhutan and many Himalayan states of India.

The Relationship between the Land and the People:

The relationship between the people and their land is fundamental to an understanding of the history. At every turn of events the land exerts its influence, sometimes broad and obvious, at other times subtle. But this influence is always there. The unification of Greater Nepal, which was started by Prithivi Narayan Saha, a petty *Khasa Gorkha* Kingdom in 1744 A. D. exerted a tremendous influence on the land and the people in the Himalayan region.

The various degrees of union in terms of the type of unification has been described by Ludwig F. Stiller (1968: 66-67) in five stages such as: (*i*) Military Unification, (*ii*) Political Unification, (*iii*) Legal and judicial Unification, (*iv*) Administrative Unification, and (*v*) Cultural and religious Unification. By 1774 Nepal had gained the whole of the eastern Hills, including all the territory west of Singalila watershed. In the Tarai the *Gorkhalis* controlled the entire territory as far east as the Teesta River. The military unification process was continued by the successors of Prithivi Narayan Shah, namely Pratap Singh Shah, Rajendra Laxmi (queen), and Ran Bahadur Shah till the Kingdom was extended from Kangra of Himachal Pradesh (1809) to Teesta River (1774).

Although the military unification ended after the Treaty of Sugauli in 1815, and the area between the Mechi River and the Teesta River was returned to Sikkim through the Treaty of Titaliya in 1817, the other four unifications mentioned above by Stiller (1968) are continuously exerting its influence both in Nepal and Sikkim as of now. The recent unrest of Nepal is the result of this unification process as all other 59 Hill and Terai tribes of Nepal were left behind in all aspects of development inclusive of their ethnic, linguistic, cultural and religion. Sikkim was also not spared as the Nepal ruled parts of Sikkim upto west of Teesta River from Singalila range and plain areas since 1774/1789 to 1914 for 40/25 years, and also occupied West Sikkim 1789 to 1814 for 25 years. The unification exerted negative impact on a number of tribes in Sikkim (15 tribes) also and were left behind in all aspects of development inclusive of their ethnicity, linguistic, cultural and religious developments. The unification influence has done away the special status of the Limboos of Sikkim in the May 8th Agreement as well as influenced the Article 371F of the Indian Constitution 1975. The various tribes of Sikkim such as the Kirata Communities (Limboo, Khambu-Rai, and Yakkha), Communities analogous to Kiratas (Sunuwar, Mangar, Gurung, Tamang, Thami and Bhujel), other communities such as Sherpa, Bhutia, Lepcha, Newar, etc.

having their own language, culture, religion etc. has been clubbed as a single community –called "Nepali ethnic group" along with the Khasas (Bhahun, Chettri, Kami, Damai and Sarki) and the Communities analogous to Khasas (Thakuris, Jogi-Sanyasi and Majhis) inspite of the Limboos/Tsongs having their separate identity in Sikkim, while maintaining the Lepcha and Bhutia community distinctly separate. The unification of Nepal tremendously brought about the development of the *Khas Kura* now known as Nepali/Gorkgali language and literature, culture and customs, tradition and religion of the *Khasas*. Simultaneously, it exerted a negative impact on the development of the language and literature, custom and culture, tradition and religion, of all other tribes of Nepal (59 tribes) and Sikkim (15 tribes). This resulted extinction or almost extinction or remained under developed of many Hill and Terai tribes of Nepal and Sikkim. Now, the *Khus Kura* primarily the language of *Khasas* has been the *lingua franca* of not only in Nepal and Sikkim but also in Northern districts of West Bengal, some parts of other seven North Eastern States, Uttaranchal, and Himachal Pradesh.

The positive impact of this unification process of the visionary Gorkha King Prithivi Narayan Shah is that it has provided a strong social fabric to bind the entire hill castes and tribes in a single bundle of "Nepali" or "Gorkhali" known to this world today. This is the strength of this Himalayan community for development and is required for sustainence in this ever changing society as a complex of "unity in diversity" provided the ethnic diversity is allowed to florish.

In recent years many amateur writers often refer to the *Encyclopaedia Britanica*, Vol. 21 and try to prove that the Lepchas and the Limboos, the aboriginal tribes of the Greater Nepal (present Kangra district of Himachal Pradesh to Teesta River) and the Greater Sikkim (the Chumbi Valley of Tibet-China, the Harchu and Amochu Valleys of present Bhutan to Arun River of present Nepal) are also the later migrants like others. It is to be understood that the information on prehistoric period of Nepal and Sikkim are very sketchy. Over depending on information access to the British writers on the prehistoric period yields wrong conception in many aspects. The wrong information mentioned on the text needs to be corrected as follows:

(*i*) The word "*Na-ong*" in Lepcha language means "dumb" or "Simpleton" which is a "*Tung-bor*" or "innuendo" commonly referred to the ones who erected the Tower of Babel at Daramdin, West Sikkim. It refers to the Lepcha tribes only (Foning, 1987:170-171).

(*ii*) The word "*Chang*" is nothing but referred to the "Chong" or "Tsong" or "Tshong" tribe means the tribes believed to be the Limboos the migrants of Chang or Tsong province of Tibet (China). The Bhutia communities of Sikkim believe that the Limboo community of Sikkim were migrated from Chang or Tsang Province of Tibet (China) and hence call them the "Chang" or "Chong" or "Tsong" or "Tshong" Community (Rishley, 1894: 36-37).

(*iii*) The word "*Mon*" basically means the Lepcha tribe. In the early history of Sikkim the Lepchas were known as "Monrees" or "Monpas" or "Mon"; the Bhutias as "Lhoress" or "Lho" and Limboos as "Tsongrees", Tsongs or Chongs etc. (Namgyal & Dolma, 1980).

On the basis of the available information of historical evolution and developments during different period of "the Greater Nepal" (from 1774 to 1815), "the Greater Sikkim" (from 1642 to 1817) and Bhutan (1700-1708) there was no watertight compartment between the three countries either on geographical area or on the people of this part of the Himalayan region. The same was true between Nepal, Sikkim, Bhutan and India as there was no pasport system. Thus, one can come to the conclusion that the *Khasas* like any other hill-tribes of the Himalayan region have been living with other tribes of Himalayan regions of present Nepal, Bhutan, Sikkim, Northern areas of North Bengal, Assam and other Himalayan States of India since ancient times with harmony maintaining their distinct identity. They cannot be identified as, or compared or equated with the orthodox Rajputs and Brahmins of the plain areas of India.

Population:

The *Khasas* are now, dominating tribes of Nepal as well as in Sikkim not only in the demography but in respect of language and literature, customs and culture, tradition and religion. The *Khas* population of Nepal is 35.56% (Chettri 15.80%, Bahun 12.74%, Kami 3.94%, Damai 1.72%, and Sarki 1.40%); 80.51% are Hindus and 48.61% *Khas Kura* (Nepali/ Gorkhali) speakers out of the total population (Census 2001).

In Sikkim, Higher Khasas were 2,243 persons (1,414 Bahuns and 829 Chhetris) and Lower Khasas were 1,957 persons (1,670 Kamis and 287 Damais) making a total of 4,200 (13.79%), fourth highest (next only to Lepchas, Bhutias, Khambu-Rais) of the total population of Sikkim in 1891. Now, the state has a total population of 5,40,851 persons (Census 2001). As per voter list of 2004, the *Khas* electorate of Sikkim was 26.87% (Chettri 12.65%, Bahun 8.42%, Scheduled castes such as Kami,

Damai, Sarki and Majhi 5.80%) constituting estimated population of 162,984 persons (126,116 Higher Khasas and 36,868 Lower Khasas). *Khas-Kura* (Nepali/Gorkhali) is the *lingua franca* of the State. The *Khasas* have dominated all other hill tribes of Nepal and Sikkim in respect of language and literature, customs and culture, tradition and religion in Sikkim as well as in Nepal.

Although the identity of the *Khasas* have been rigorously subjected by social intercourse, economic interdependence and cultural reciprocity between the various autochthonous hill tribes of Nepal and Sikkim, they have been successful in retaining and developing their distinct *Khas* character, culture and social customs, language and literature, tradition and religion.

Family Pattern :

Nuclear family is common but vertically extended families are also present. A few are horizontally extended.

Family Property :

Sons inherit father's property and succession goes only to the eldest son. This is the main point of family conflict.

Gender Issues :

Woman cannot inherit father's property, though she performs different roles in agriculture and animal husbandry operations. They do not have decision making powers and thus have a low status.

Family Inter-personal Relationship :

The relationship between parents and children is one of love, affection and reverence. Avoidance terms exist between mother-in-law and son-in-law, daughter-in-law and father-in-law, sister-in-law (y)B and elder brother-in-law H(e)B. But joking relationship between sister-in-law W (e)S and W(y)S, brother-in-law W(e)B and W(y)B, grandparents and grandchildren.

Inter-*Khasa* and Intra Hill-tribal Community linkages:

Inter-family linkages are maintained through cooperation on socio-religious occasions, share joys and sorrows with neighbors and help one another at times of festivals, rituals or at times of need. Traditionally, the linkage between the high *Khasas* the Chhetris and the Bahuns is very close. The Bahun priest presides over all their rituals and religious functions and accepts water and food from the Chhetris. Intermarriage between the Chhetris and the Bahuns are permitted and the girl is socially accepted into the Chhetri community without much fuss and also vice versa. The high *Khasas* accept water from all other hill communities, except from the scheduled castes, like Kamis, Damais, Sarkis, Majhis, etc. They take and eat *roti* and fried vegetables from other hill tribes but do not take and eat *bhat* (boiled rice) and *dal* (pulses) from them. If a person establishes a relationship of *miteri saino* or *maha-miteri saino* or ceremonial friendship with another person within his own community or usually into a different community, their off-springs should not enter into a matrimonial relations.

The lower *Khasas* – the Kamis serve them as blacksmiths, goldsmiths, silversmiths, and manufacture all types of male and female ornaments; agricultural and household implements including the *Khukuri* (Gorkha dagger) for both Khasas and other tribes in the Himalayan region. The Damais serve all the *Khasas* and other tribes of the Himalayan region as tailors, musicians (*Panchi baja, Nauwmati baja* etc), and dancers (*Maruni Nach, Madaley nach*, or other Nepali folk dances). The Sarkis act as cobblers "shoe makers", "cover of *Khukuri, Tarwar* etc.makers" for all the communities. The Majhis serve as boatman as well as fisherman for all the communities.

They share common properties like *Khasmahals, Gawcharan*, shrines and temples, spring water for drinking, water for irrigation, reciprocal relationship of mutually exchanged labour called *parma* for agriculture, livestock and house building activities, schools and colleges for their children's education, interact with other communities in Gram Panchayats, development activities etc. By virtue of their numerical strength, the *Khasas* play a dominant and significant role in the political activities of the state. They play a leading role in various socio-political movements in Sikkim, like the demand of citizenship rights, land reforms, landlord-tenant and cultivator-labour relationships etc. Thus, there is a close linkage at the personal level of all ages of the different *Khasa* communities as well as between all ages of the existing hill communities of the Himalayan region.

I. THE HIGH CASTE KHASAS - BAHUNS

Social Status : Other Backward Class.

Distribution:

Scattered throughout Sikkim, having greater concentration in the East District of Sikkim.

Bio-anthropological:

Bahuns are high castes *Khasas*. The anthropometric survey indicated that the Bahuns are the second tallest community only next to Bhutia measuring 1631 mm and tend to be short to below medium in stature.

The mean value of the nasal index is comparatively lower; total facial index is predominantly mesoprosopic or medium-faced (Singh, 1983).

Food Habits:

Bahuns are generally vegetarians. The Upadhyaya Bahuns do not take onion and garlic. They take all types of seasonal vegetables; staple food – rice, maize, wheat, millet, dal moong, masur, gram, kalodal, pahenlidal, peas, soybean, mustard oil, root & tubers, locally grown fruits *naspati, suntala* etc. Hot tea with sugar and milk is widely taken as a non-alcoholic drink. Now, association with various hill tribes, they take all kinds of food such as momo, thukpa, saleroti, gundruk, etc. They take food thrice a day – morning, during day and evening. Saleroti is mainly prepared during festivals of *Tihar*. They are very fond of milk and milk products. Now a day, most of them drink alcohol both home-made and purchased from the market. They also smoke bidi, bungali, and khaini.

Community Relationships:

The Bahuns have two endogamous divisions, viz. the Upadhyaya and Jaishee, the former higher in status than the latter. Within the division, however, there are several exogamous *gotras* like Bashishtha, Kashyap, Attreyi, Parashar, Valmiki, Batsya, Bharadwaj etc. The Upadhyaya is mainly responsible for conducting rites of worship. Those who are well conversant with the *Puranas*, are known as *Pandits*. The Bahuns have a feeling of superiority over all *Khasa* communities.

Socio-Economic Activity:

Although, Bahuns are mostly small and marginal farmers in Sikkim, the land is their major resource, owned and controlled individually by the communities, who are mainly the agricultural community. Traditionally, Bahuns are entrusted with priesthood. Now, their primary occupation is terrace cultivation of agricultural and horticultural crops, livestock rearing, and miscellaneous services etc. They are employed in service in different white-collar jobs in government service, as schoolteachers, bank employees etc. They have a direct link with the markets and depend on them for their daily needs. The Bahuns have entrepreneurs, scholars, teachers, engineers, and members in defense services etc.

Folk Musical Instruments :

Kasta Kartal, Gawri shankha, Gaw Ghanta, Jhamtar, Jhal, Jhyali Damphu, Dubdub, Dolle Shankha, Dhonde Kartal, Nirgun Khaijardi, nuwakot Khainchardi, paira, Balan Khainchardi, Balan tal, Moti Shankha, and Roiula Khainchardi (Kandel, 2004: 31).

FolkSongs :

Both male and female take part in marriage songs, shilok, Baramasay (seasonal songs), Juwari or Dohori (duet songs), Sangini, Khainjari, Bhajan, Balan, Maruni etc.

Folk Dances :

Madale Nanch, maruni nanch, Sangini Nanch, Khainjhardi Nanch, Bhajan Nanch, and other varieties of Nepali folk dances (Gurung & Lama, 2004)

Education :

The standard of literacy is poor among the older generations, but young boys and girls attend schools. Literacy is growing among them. Both boys and girls study upto the secondary level and drop out mainly under economic pressure. Girls mainly drop out after secondary level due to marriage.

Major Life-Cycle rituals:

Birth, Marriage and Death.

(a) Birth: Expectant mother abstain from performing any *puja*, since it does not yield any result; avoid killing of animals and long distance traveling. Birth pollution (*sutak*) period observed for 5, 7 or 9 days in case of a boy and 3, 5,or 7 days in case of a girl. The name-giving ceremony (*nauran*) is performed by a Brahaman after the *sutak* period is over. The purification by bath, *gount* (calf-urine) sprinkled on the mother and the baby, and the baby is given name after consulting the *cheena*. *Bhatkhowai* or *annaprashan* – first rice-eating ceremony is performed by the maternal uncle after six months. At the age of three or five years the male child has its hair cut for the first time (*chewar*) by the mother's brother. The sacred thread (*janai*) is given to the male children at an age between seven to twelve years. The Brahman through an elaborate ritual known as *bratamantra* gives the janai. On that occasion, the hair of the boy has to be shaven clean. As a customary law, the wearing of the sacred thread is compulsory for the boy before marriage. If a married male has never had a *janai*, the old people will not accept pulse (*dal*) from him. The girls have their hair shaved if required, in a ceremony known as the *chhewar*. On attaining puberty – girls are isolated for a period of five days, followed by a purification bath (Singh, 1983).

(b) Marriage: They follow endogamy at the community level and *gotra* exogamy by Bahuns. Junior sororate is allowed. Adult marriage is in vogue now. Mates are acquired through negotiation (*mangni biha*), elopement (*chori biha*) and mutual consent. Monogamy and rarely polygyny are the marriage forms. Marriage symbols for women consist in putting of vermilion (*sindur*) in the parting of the hair and wearing a green bead necklace (*poty*) and marriage ceremony solemnized through *Kanyadan*. Rites include gift or presentation of ornaments, garments etc. made to the bride by the groom's family. Residence after marriage is patrilocal. Both husband and wife can divorce each other with social approval, the reasons generally adultery, barrenness, maladjustments, impotency, chronic sickness, cruelty, insanity, practice of witchcraft and sorcery. If the wife runs away with another person, her husband is entitled to receive compensation (*jarikal* or *jaridanda*) from the paramour. If the wife does not remarry after divorce, she receives alimony from the husband. Children are the liability of the father in case of divorce. Remarriage of widow and widower is permissible. Marriage rites are performed at bride's residence.

The Brahman fixes the match as well as the date of marriage after consulting the horoscopes *(cheena)* of both bride and groom. Later the groom visits the bride's house accompanied by two friends. They carry with them one sacred thread (*janai*) and a few betel nuts (*suparis*). These are presented to the bride's father, confirming that the marriage is fixed. On the wedding day, the marriage party (*janti*) consisting of the bridegroom, his friends and relatives, start for the bride's house. They are received with honour and jokes are exchanged. Sweet balls made out of beaten rice and *gur* (*kasar*) are served to them and *acheta*, a mixture of rice and flower petals, is showered over the party. Shilok songs are sung. The bride changes into a new dress, and is brought in by the groom. The bride and groom sit together at the mandup and a Brahman performs the sacred fire (*yogya*) ceremony to the chant of mantras. Then they exchange garlands and rings, in the ceremony called *swayambar*. Later in *gora-dhunu*, the feet of the bride and groom are washed and the parents or even all the elderly close relatives of the bride make the gesture of drinking that water. In the ritual of sindur-potey the groom puts vermilion (*sindur*) on the bride's forehead and ties a green bead necklace (*potey*) around her neck. Their clothes are tied together and they go around the holy fire three or seven times (*teen* or *saat phera*). They also eat each other's half-eaten food.

Next day, the bride is taken to her husband's residence where consummation of the marriage takes place. A feast is given in honour of the bride. Three days after the wedding, spent in *shilpa-puja*, the bride cooks with her own hands and serves it to the family members, in a ceremony known as *bahu-bhat-yar*, after which she gets access to the family hearth. When *bhat-ghat* is observed within 16 days after the wedding, the couple pays a return visit to the bride's parents with sat roti, dahi, khowa etc.(Singh, 1983).

(*c*) Death: The dead body is cremated at cremation ground by the side of a *khola* (river). The children are generally buried. The corpse is dressed in new clothes and is carried to the cremation ground on a frame made of green bamboos, which is eventually placed on a pyre and the eldest son lights the fire. Then they bathe and shave their heads, eyebrows and faces. The dead pollution (*marao*) is observed for thirteen days. During this period, the sons eat self-cooked food consisting of boiled rice and unsalted butter only. Eating of meat, fish, mustard oil and salt are prohibited during this period. The Brahman performs the death ritual (*kriya*), at the end of the thirteenth day. Only sons cut their hair on the head and eyebrows saved off clean. Purification is through *shraddha* ceremony, featuring ancestor worship, urine is sprinkled all around, salt and oil are distributed among members of the family by the community priest, offering gifts to the priest, feast for relatives, neighbors and friends. Bones collected after the cremation and brought at home are taken to the Ganga for immersion. The Brahman receives a cow as a gift from the sons of the deceased person. The Jogi receives back clothes, food grains, oil, butter etc. as gifts; this is called *Jogidan*. The Pinda-sradh is observed, one year after the death. The sons of the deceased however would not take milk for one year in the case of the mother's death and take no curd in the case of the father's death (Singh, 1983).

II. THE HIGH CASTE KHASAS - CHHETRIS

Social Status : Other Backward Class.

Distribution:

Scattered throughout Sikkim, having greater concentration in the East District of Sikkim.

Bio-anthropological:

They are high castes *Khasas*. The anthropometric survey reveals that the Chhetris are relatively short stature and varies within a small range of 1571 mm to 1605 mm. The Chhetris have a relatively lower mean value of the nasal index in comparison to other groups (Singh, 1983).

Food Habits:

Both Vegetarians and Non-vegetarians. The non-vegetarians, eat mutton, fish, rarely chicken, and egg but do not take pork and beef. They take all types of seasonal vegetables; staple food – rice, maize, wheat, millet, dal moong, masur, gram, kalodal, pahenlidal, peas, soybean, mustard oil, root & tubers, locally grown fruits *naspati, suntala* etc. Hot tea with sugar and milk is widely taken as a non-alcoholic drink. Now, association with various hill tribes, they take all kinds of food such as momo, thukpa, sale roti, gundruk, etc.They take food thrice a day – morning, during day and evening. Sale roti is mainly prepared during festivals of Tihar etc. Mutton is taken regularly and specially prepared during dasai festival. They are very fond of milk and milk products. Now-a-day, most of them drink alcohol both home-made and purchased from the market. They also smoke bidi, bungali, and khaini.

Community Relationships:

The Chhetris are divided into a number of patrilineal thars, e.g. Bista, Subedi, Basnet, Adhikari, Nirula, Bhardari etc. having equal status. The *thars* are also used as surnames. Each of the thars has a specific corresponding exogamous ancestral patrilineal gotra. For example, Bista – Kashyap, Katwal – Mandaw, Subedi – Vatsya, Basnet – Kaushila etc. To regulate marriage alliances and indicate descent are the main function of *gotra*. The Chhetris are placed only next down to the Bahuns in the social hierarchy of *Khasas.*

Socio-Economic Activity:

Although, Chhtris are mostly small and marginal farmers in Sikkim, the land is their major resource, owned and controlled individually by both the communities, who are mainly the agricultural community. The Chhetris are traditionally cultivators and are engaged in terrace cultivation of agricultural, horticultural crops and livestock rearing. They are construction labourers; employed in service in different white-collar jobs in government service, as schoolteachers, bank employees etc. They have a direct link with the markets and depend on them for their daily needs. They have entrepreneurs, scholars, teachers, engineers, and members in defense services etc.

Folk Musical Instruments:

Same as Bahuns.

Folk songs : Same as Bahuns.

Folk Dances : Same as Bahuns..

Financing : Usually depend on village moneylenders and shopkeepers in rural areas but banking facilities have become familiar in urban areas now.

Major Life-Cycle rituals :

Birth, Marriage and Death.

(*a*) Birth: Expectant mother abstain from performing any *puja*. Birth pollution (*sutak*) period observed for 11 days in case of a boy and 7 days in case of a girl. The name-giving ceremony (*nauran*) is performed by a Brahaman after the *sutak* period is over. The rituals of purification, *Bhatkhowai* or *annaprashan, chewar*, *bratamantra* etc. are same as that of Bahuns

(*b*) Marriage: Follow endogamy at the community level and *gotra* exogamy by Chhetris. Junior sororate is allowed. Adult marriage is in vogue. Mates are acquired through negotiation (*mangni biha*), elopement (*chori biha*) and mutual consent. Monogamy and rarely polygyny are the marriage forms. Marriage symbols for women consist in putting of vermilion (*sindur*) in the parting of the hair and wearing a green bead necklace (*poty*) and marriage ceremony solemnized through *Kanyadan*. All other marriage rituals are same as that of Bahuns.

(*c*) Death: The dead body is cremated at cremation ground by the side of a *khola* (river). The children are generally buried. The corpse is dressed in new clothes and is carried to the cremation ground on a frame made of green bamboos, which is eventually placed on a pyre and the eldest son lights the fire. Then they bathe and shave their heads, eyebrows and faces. The dead pollution (*marao*) is observed for thirteen days. All other death rituals are same as that of Bahuns (Singh, 1983).

III. LOWER CASTE KHASAS – KAMIS (VISWAKARMAS, LOHARS, SUNARS)

Social Status : Scheduled Caste .

Distribution: South, East and West districts of Sikkim.

Food Habits:

Non-vegetarians, eat pork, mutton, chicken, beef, egg, vegetables; staple food – rice, maize, wheat, millet, dal moong, masur, gram, kalodal, pahenlidal, peas, mustard oil, root & tubers, locally grown fruits naspati, suntala etc. Take alcohol (rakshi), jarn, smoke bidi, cigarettes.

Community Relationships:

They are endogamous and except exogamous clans or *thars* viz: Dural, Darnal, Scintury, Rasaily, Gadaily, Baraily, Lakri, Dhanukey, Dhomala, Ghimirey, Tiruwa, Lohar, Khati, Seti-Sural, Lami Chhaney, Sapkota, Langadey, Gahatraj, Ruchal. They have two *gotras*, namely Bishnusakha and Kaushilasakha. They consider themselves superior to the Sarkis and Damai. Use thar names as Surnames.

Socio-Economic Activity:

Traditionally make articles of iron, agriculture implements, gold and silver smithy and selling serve as their major source of income. But now their main economic activity is agriculture and livestock rearing in rural areas. A small numbers have begun involving themselves in administration, teaching, service, business, and politics.

Folk musical instruments	: Naumati baja.
Folk songs	: Both male and female take part in *Juari,* marriage songs, *shilok* etc.
Folk Dances	: *Madale Nanch, Maruni Nanch*
Education	: Literacy is growing among them. Both boys and girls study upto the secondary level and drop out mainly under economic pressure. Girls mainly drop out after secondary level due to marriage.

Life-Cycle rituals Observed : Birth, Marriage and Death.

(*a*) Birth: Expectant mother takes country liquor (*rakshi* and *jaarn*), forbidden to move in jungle. Birth pollution observed for 7 days in the case of a boy and 5 days in the case of a girl, purification by bath, *gount* (calf-urine) sprinkled on the mother and the baby, followed by name-giving ceremony (*pachani* or *nauran*) by the community priest. *Bhatkhowai* – first rice-eating ceremony arranged after sixth month after birth. At the age of five or six, the male child has its hair cut for the first time by the mother's brother. The girls have their hair shaved if required, in a ceremony known as the *chhewar.* On attaining puberty – girls are isolated for a period of five days, followed by a purification bath.

(*b*) Marriage: Follow endogamy at the community level and exogamy at the clan (*thar*) level. Life partner chosen generally through negotiations but courtship and elopement are not uncommon. The boy's parents go to girl's parents to take their consent carrying with them fruits, flowers and milk (*sogun*), which are presented to them. On the second visit the boy's parents present *Chabapatra* to the girl's parents before wedding. Monogamy is the usual practice; few cases of polygamy also exist. Sororate and levirate are in practice. Signs of married women are vermilion mark, and green beads necklace (*poteymala*). The marriage party goes to bride's home with Damais for *Baja-gaja.* Marriage ritual is generally *Kanyadan* gifted to the bridegroom before a sacrificial fire at the moment of *lagan*. Rules of residence is both neolocal and patrilocal. Divorce is permissible with social sanction, reasons generally adultery, barrenness, maladjustments, impotency, chronic sickness, cruelty, insanity, practice of witchcraft and sorcery. Aggrieved party is compensated grant. Children are the liability of the father in case of divorce. Remarriage of widow and widower is permissible. Marriage rites are performed at bride's residence. The groom with the bride returns to his home a day after. At groom's residence, feast is arranged and bride lives in her husband's house. On the fourth day, the bride groom return to the bride's home known as *duran pharakauna*. On the fifth day the bridegroom return to the groom's home and live in her husband's house.

(c) Death: Dead body is cremated at cremation ground by the side of a khola (river). The children are sometimes buried. Pollution for children lasts for 3 or 7 days and 7 or 9 or 13 days for elders. Till the purification they abstain from eating of fish, meat, salt, and oil and whatever food is taken, has to be prepared by the side of a stream, and prepared by the sons of the deceased, after they have offered prayers for the deceased. The sons offer food to the deceased and then take food. Other family members take food at home. Only sons cut their hair on the head and eyebrows saved off clean. Purification is through *shraddha* ceremony, featuring ancestor worship, urine is sprinkled all around, salt and oil are distributed among members of the family by the Kami priest, offering gifts to the priest, feast for relatives, neighbors and friends. The sons of the deceased however would not take milk for one year in the case of the mother's death and take no curd in the case of the father's death (Singh, 1983).

IV. LOWER CASTE KHASAS – DAMAIS (DARJIS, MASTERS)

Social Statu : Scheduled Caste.

Distribution : Scattered throughout Sikkim, having greater concentration nearer the market spots.

Food Habits:

Non-vegetarians, eat pork, mutton, chicken, beef, egg, vegetables; staple food – rice, maize, wheat, millet, dal moong, masur, gram, kalodal, pahenlidal, peas, soybean, mustard oil, root & tubers, locally grown fruits *naspati, suntala* etc. Hot tea with salt or sugar and milk is widely taken as a non-alcoholic drink. Take alcohol (*rakshi, jaarn*), smoke bidi, cigarettes.

Community Relationships:

They are endogamous and except exogamous clans or *thars* vig: Pariyar, Sundas, Bagdas, Mothey, Dass, Ranapaheli, Darnal, Karkidodli, Maley, Bhitrikoti,, Bardewa, Sewa, Labar, Suji, Hingmang etc. These *thars* regulate marriage alliances and indicate descent. They consider themselves superior to the Sarkis. Use *thar* names as Surnames.

Socio-Economic Activity:

Damais are professionally engaged in tailoring as their major source of income. They are also involved in agriculture and livestock rearing in rural areas to supplement their income. A small numbers have begun involving themselves in administration, teaching, service, business and in politics. Damais are very good folk musicians and serve as folk musicians for all the hill tribes of Sikkim and Nepal. Some have a part-time profession of playing nine types of musical instruments (*naumati baja*) during marriages, a traditional profession inherited from their ancestors.

Folk Musical Instruments:

Damais are rich in folk musical instruments. They are: *Aawj, Karnal (Annapurna), Karnali baja, Kalash karnal, Kahal (Kahal), Chhatish nagara, Jhurumma or Jhiyali (Jhurma), Tipsahaney, Tyakko, Tyamko or Tinamko, Dhonre Sahanai, Dholaki, Turahi, Damaha, Daeenu Damaou, Dibya (Dum) Nagara, Nagara, Nagara nisan, Narsinga, Baeenu Damaou, Banu, Bijulibana, Bheri, Rasa, Sikhar, Sahana, Hurko. Naumati baja, Madal*. *Panchai Baja* consists of *Teep Sahanai, Jhurumma, Dholaki,, Damaha,* and *Tyamko. Nawmati Baja* consists of nine musical instruments. In addition to the above five of *Panchai Baja*, *Nawmati Baja* includes *Karnal*, *Narsingha, Dhodre Sahanai,* and *Bikul*. Some more musical instruments may also be added to this such as Tyakko, Turahi, Dahinu Damau, Bheyri, Rasa etc.(Gurung & Lama, 2004; Kandel, 2004: 31).

Folk songs: Both male and female take part in marriage songs, *shilok, Baramasay* seasonal songs), *Juwari* or *Dohori* (duet songs) etc.

Folk Dances : *Madale Nanch*, *Maruni Nanch*, Variety of Nepali folk dances.

Education:

Literacy is growing among them. Both boys and girls study upto the secondary level and drop out mainly under economic pressure. Girls mainly drop out after secondary level due to marriage.

Major Life-Cycle rituals : Birth, Marriage and Death.

(*a*) Birth: Expectant mother takes country liquor (*rakshi* and *jaarn*), forbidden to move in jungle. Birth pollution observed for 11 days. Purification by bath, *gount* (calf-urine) sprinkled on the mother and the baby, followed by name- giving ceremony (*nauran*) by the community priest (the *Sarma*) who chooses a suitable name for the child. *Bhatkhowai* – first rice-eating ceremony arranged six month after birth. At the age of five or six, the male child has its hair cut for the first time by the mother's brother. The girls have their hair shaved if required, in a ceremony known as the *chhewar*. On attaining puberty – girls are isolated for a period of five days, followed by a purification bath.

(*b*) Marriage: Follow endogamy at the community level and exogamy at the clan (*thar*) level. Life partner chosen generally through negotiations but courtship and elopement are not uncommon. The boy's parents go to girl's parents to take their consent carrying with them fruits, flowers and milk (*sogun*), which are presented to them. On the second visit the boy's parents present *Chabapatra* to the girl's parents before wedding. Monogamy is the usual practice; few cases of polygamy also exist. Sororate and levirate are in practice. Signs of married women are vermilion mark, and green beads necklace (*poteymala*). The marriage party go to bride's home with *naumati baja*. Marriage ritual is generally *Kanyadan* gifted to the bride before a sacrificial fire at the moment of *lagan*. Rules of residence is both neolocal and patrilocal. Divorce is permissible with social sanction, reasons generally adultery, barrenness, maladjustments, impotency, chronic sickness, cruelty, insanity, practice of witchcraft and sorcery. Aggrieved party is compensated grant. Children are the liability of the father in case of divorce. Remarriage of widow and widower is permissible. Marriage rites are performed at bride's residence. The groom with the bride returns to his home a day after. At groom's residence, feast is arranged and bride lives in her husband's house.

(c) Death: Dead body is cremated at cremation ground by the side of a khola (river). The children are sometimes buried. Pollution for children lasts for 7 days and 11 days for adults. Till the purification they abstain from eating of fish, meat, salt, and oil and whatever food is taken, has to be prepared by the side of a stream, and prepared by the sons of the deceased, after they have offered prayers for the deceased. The sons offer food to the deceased and then take food. Other family members take food at home. Only sons cut their hair on the head and eyebrows saved off clean. Purification is through *shraddha* ceremony, featuring ancestor worship, urine is sprinkled all around, salt and oil are distributed among members of the family by the community priest, offering gifts to the priest, feast for relatives, neighbors and friends. The sons of the deceased however would not take milk for one year in the case of the mother's death and take no curd in the case of the father's death (Singh, 1983).

V. LOWER CASTE KHASAS – SARKIS (MISTRIS)

Social Status : Scheduled Caste .

Distribution : East, South and West District of Sikkim.

Food Habits:

Non-vegetarians, eat pork, even beef, egg, Vegetables; staple food – rice, maize, millet, dal - moong, masur, gram, *kalodal, pahenlidal*, mustard oil, root & tubers, locally grown fruits – *naspati, suntala* etc. Take alcohol (*rakshi*), *jaarn*, smoke bidi, cigarettes.

Community Relationships:

Except exogamous clans or *thars* vig: Dudroka, Mungrati, Purkuti, Khilinge, Bogoti, Achani, Tolangi. Use *thar* names as Surnames. Claim a position above that of the Damais.

Economic Activity:

Traditionally shoemakers but their main economic activity is agriculture and livestock rearing.

Folk songs dance: Both male and female take part.

Education:

Both boys and girls study upto the secondary level and drop out mainly under economic pressure. Girls mainly drop out after secondary level due to marriage.

Life-Cycle Rituals Observed : Birth, Marriage and Death.

(*a*) Birth: Expectant mother takes country liquor (*rakshi* and *jaarn*), forbidden to move in jungle. Birth pollution observed for 11 days, purification by bath, followed by name- giving ceremony (*nauran*) by the community priest. *Bhatkhowai* – first rice-eating ceremony arranged after six month after birth. On attaining puberty – girls are isolated for a period of five days, followed by a pacificator bath.

(*b*) Marriage: Follow endogamy at the community level and exogamy at the clan level. Life partner chosen generally through negotiations but courtship and elopement are not uncommon. Monogamy is the usual practice, few cases of polygamy also exist. Soragate and levirate are in practice. Signs of married women are vermilion mark, and green beads necklace (*poteymala*). Marriage ritual is generally *Kanyadan* gifted to the bridegroom before a sacrificial fire. Rules of residence is both neolocal and patrilocal. Divorce is permissible with social sanction, reasons generally adultery, barrenness, maladjustments, impotency, chronic sickness, cruelty, insanity, practice of witchcraft and sorcery. Aggrieved party is compensated grant. Children are the liability of the father in case of divorce. Remarriage of widow and widower is permissible. Marriage rites are performed at bride's residence. The groom with the bride returns to his home a day after. At groom's residence, feast is arranged and bride lives in her husband's house.

(*c*) Death: Dead body is cremated at cremation ground by the side of a *khola* (river). The children are sometimes buried. Pollution for children lasts for 7 days and 11 days for elders. Purification is through *shraddha* ceremony, featuring ancestor worship, offering gifts to Brahmans, feast for relatives, neighbors and friends (Singh, 1983).

18

Communities Analogous to Khasas

I. THE HIGH CASTE—THAKURIS (THAKURS)

Social Status : Other Backward Class.

Origin and History:

The Thakuris are known to be of Rajput ancestry, and the local people often call them "Chhetri-Thakuris". The Thakuris are Hindus, bearing caucasoid physical features and Aryan cultural characteristics.

Distribution:

Gangtok, Rhenock, Ranipool, East District, and Namchi, South District, Sikkim.

Population :

Thakuris claim descent from the ruling family of Nepal. They are very few in number, not exceeding a few thousands or so in the whole of Sikkim.

Food habits:

Thakuris are generally pure vegetarians, but most of them allow fish and egg to be cooked at home. Many younger generation Thakuris eat mutton, egg, fish etc. They take all types of seasonal vegetables; staple food – rice, maize, wheat, millet, moong, masur, gram, *kalodal, pahenlidal*, peas, soybean, mustard oil, roct & tubers, locally grown fruits *naspati, suntala* etc. Hot tea with sugar and milk is widely taken as a non-alcoholic drink. They take food thrice a day – morning, during day and evening. *Saleroti* is mainly prepared during festivals of *Tihar*, etc. They are very fond of milk and milk products. Now a day, most of them drink alcohol both homemade and purchased from the market.

The Thakuris have Nuclear family but vertically extended families are also present. The sons inherit father's property and succession goes only to the eldest son. This is the main point of family conflict. The woman cannot inherit father's property, though she performs different roles in agriculture and animal husbandry operations. They do not have decision-making powers and thus have a low status. In respect of language and literature, religion and belief system, intra and inter personal and family relationship, festivals, dress and ornaments, the Thakuris are same as that of the Chhetris. The Thakuris have no family deities. They worship *Goraknath* as clan-deity.

Community Relationships:

The Thakuris clans claim to be equal. Traditionally, the three clans – Shah or Saha, Khan, and Sen – married only among themselves and not with the remaining clans, from the belief that these three clans had a discernible royal ancestry while the others could not claim such a distinction. The various clans of Thakuris are Shah, Khan, Sen, Ram, Bansi, Chand, Hamal, Kalyan, Man, Nawakotya, Pokhrali, Raika, Ruchal. Sahi, Singh, Surybansi, and Uchai. They have no sub-clans and the clan names are also used as surname. The Thakuris maintain a strict clan exogamy. But ritually they follow the practice of marrying maternal cross-cousins.

Socio-Economic Activity:

The Thakuris are agriculturist; depend on cultivation of various agricultural crops, horticultural crops and livestock rearing. They are employed in service in different white-collar jobs in government service as school teachers, bank employees etc.

Major Life-Cycle Rituals:

Birth, Marriage and Death are the major life-rituals. These rituals are observed same as that of the Chhetris. In respect of folk musical instruments, folk songs, folk dances etc. are also same as that of the Chhetris. The standard of literacy is poor among the older generations, but young boys and girls attend schools. Literacy is growing among them. They avail of the facilities of modern healthcare and are favourably disposed towards family planning. Use both modern and indigenous medicine. Mainly use fuelwood, Kerosene, rarely LPG and electricity for cooking. They depend on Fair Price Shop in the rural and grocery shops in urban. For financing, they usually depend on village moneylenders and shopkeepers in rural areas but banking facilities have become familiar in urban areas now. Their attitude towards savings is discouraging (Singh, 1983).

II. THE LOW CASTE—JOGI (SANYASIS)

Social Status: Other Backward Class (OBC)

Origin and History:

Jogis (Sanyasis) are occupational caste people who, according to Dor Bahadur Bista (1980: 6), are offspring of Bahuns and Chhetris or the high caste *Khasas* bearing caucasoid physical features, Hindu religious, and Aryan cultural characteristics.

Population and Settlement:

Sanyasis are same as Jogis and the total population of this caste is 2367 persons, slightly larger than the Sunuwars of Sikkim as per the voters' list of the state for 1999. They are highly dispersed, which might be due to their main profession of guarding the villages from the ill-designs of various ghosts and spirits. They live in small huts and interact very little with members of other communities and between themselves as well. They do not seem to have any association to look after their common grievances or to represent themselves before a committee duly constituted by the government.

Distribution:

Upper Bermiok, Dorong in Kamling block, Hathidunga, Rinchenpong, Lingchom, Soreng and Tatopani of Reshi Block in West District; and Ralang in South District block, Sikkim.

Rites of Passage: Same as those of Bahuns and Chhetris.

Kinship and Social Organization:

Jogis belong to specific *gotras*, which are believed to be as many as 108 named after famous ascetics of the pre-historic period like Kaushalya, Kashyap, and Shandilya. They mostly intermarry with the members of Mangar and Sunuwar communities.

Traditional Economy:

They are traditional occupational caste people and go around the villages at night blowing the ***baranth*** horn to drive away ghosts and evil spirits. They collect alms the next day from the houses they visited at night. The alms include black urd, rice, turmeric powder, red chilly, black pepper, salt, mustard oil, coins, black cloth pieces etc. They are also agriculturist and grow crops as well as rear livestock for their livelihood.

Language & Literature: Same as those of Bahuns and Chhetris.

Material Culture:

Being ascetics and mendicants they had very few things in terms of their material belongings. But not all adult Jogis, and no women among them, practiced this occupation. They are engaged in agriculture and animal husbandry, which made their houses and other domestic and agricultural implements no different from those of other peasant castes/ tribes and communities living in relatively lower altitudes.

Folk-Traditions:

Adult Jogis are trained in the art of communicating with the world of spirits and ghosts. They visit villages at night blowing "Baranth Horn" or conch shells or shin bones of human beings and driving away ghosts and evil spirits. They go around every house three times blowing the instrument and chanting mantras. The next morning they collect the alms, which the householder display on a winnower and offer them. They come with a bundle of black and white cloth-bags for collecting alms that identify them to be Jogis and saying "*Jai Gorakhnath*" but they do not speak with the people.

Religion:

They are an ascetic people who are followers of the Hindu sect called "*Gorakhnath*" to which the Shah kings of Nepal belonged. Thus, Jogis or Sanyasis also claim to be royal priests, but unlike the Bahun priests they do not officiate on any ritual in any house. They worship *Kali* and *Bhairav*.

They are economically as well as educationally very backward, but the scant information available on them is not enough to justify any claim that they might like to make as an autonomous community (Sinha, et. al., 2005).

III. THE LOW CASTE MAJHI (JALHARI, BOATMAN)

Social Status: Scheduled Caste

Origin and History:

Majhis are often categorized under Lower caste of Khasas. They are an occupational caste people who are bearing caucasoid physical features, Hindu religious and Aryan cultural characteristics.

Distribution:

Majhigoan (near Jorethang) south District and Majhitar (near Rangpo) East District, Sikkim.

Food Habits:

Non-vegetarians, eat mutton, chicken, beef, egg, but no pork or beef, vegetables; staple food – rice, maize, wheat, millet, dal moong, masur, gram, kalodal, pahenlidal, peas, soybean, mustard oil, root & tubers, locally grown fruits *naspati, suntala* etc. Hot tea with salt or sugar and milk is widely taken as a non-alcoholic drink. Take alcohol (*rakshi,* jarn), smoke bidi, cigarettes.

Community Relationships:

They are endogamous and except exogamous divisions known as *ghats* vig: Varleni, Chusunka, Parbeli, Maikule. These *thars* regulate marriage alliances and indicate descent. Majhis belong to the Kashyap gotra which is used in maintaining rituals. They consider themselves superior to the Sarkis, Damais and Kamis. *Use ghat* names as surnames.

Socio-Economic Activity:

Traditionally they have been boat drivers and fishermen, now business and building and supplies contracts are their major source of income. While many of them own and control land individually; there are several who make a living as agricultural labourers, terrace cultivators, wood workers, milk sellers, and labourers. They depend on the market for the sale of whatever meagre products they produce. Inclination towards business is a change becoming visible among them. In respect of language and literature, religion and belief system and others they are same as that of Lower *Khasas*.

Folk Musical Instruments:

They have their musical instruments namely *Ghanta Ghanro,Jhuli* and *Bhati.*

Folk Songs:

Both male and female take part in marriage songs, *shilok, Baramasay* (seasonal songs), *Juwari* or *Dohori* (duet songs) etc.

Folk Dances: *Madale Nanch, Maruni Nanch*, Variety of Nepali folk dances.

Education:

Literacy is growing among them. Both boys and girls study upto the secondary level and drop out mainly under economic pressure. Girls mainly drop out after secondary level due to marriage.

Financing:

Usually depend on village moneylenders and shopkeepers in rural areas but banking facilities have become familiar in urban areas now.

Major Life-Cycle rituals : Birth, Marriage and Death.

(*a*) Birth: Birth pollution observed for 7 days in the case of a boy and for 5 day in the case of a girl. On purification day both mother and child are given bath and name-giving ceremony is held. The baby is taken outside, and shown the sun. Threads (*dori*) are tied about the hands and legs of the baby, and then the father names the child. No priest is invited. First rice giving ceremony *Jawlikhowaiki* is observed in seventh month in case of a boy and in the fifth month in case of a girl. The meal served on the occasion includes fish, curd, ghee, meat, egg, rice, and is served with a silver coin (*mohar*). The father serves the first and then the mother. When the child is three years old his head is shaved completely, and the child wears new clothes for the occasion, known as *Chari katiko riase*. No priest are involved in the ceremony.

(*b*) Marriage: Follow endogamy at the community level and exogamy at the *ghat* level. Life partner chosen generally through negotiations (*mangni biha*) but courtship and elopement (*chori biha*) are not uncommon. The boy's parents go to girl's parents along with the boy to take their consent carrying with them two bottles of country liquor (*rakshi*), which are presented to them. After the formal consent is given, another date is fixed for the engagement when items like gold or silver, money, millet, mutton etc are presented to the girl's parents. They pay bride price in cash and kind to the bride's parents. Monogamy is the usual practice; few cases of polygamy also exist. Sororate and levirate are in practice. Signs of married women are vermilion mark, and green beads necklace (*poteymala*). The marriage party goes to bride's home with *naumati baja*. Rules of residence is both neolocal and patrilocal. Divorce is permissible with social sanction, reasons generally adultery, barrenness, maladjustments, impotency, chronic sickness, cruelty, insanity, practice of witchcraft and sorcery. Aggrieved party is compensated grant. Children are the liability of the father in case of divorce. Remarriage of widow and widower is permissible. Marriage rites are performed at bride's residence. The bridegroom with the bride returns to his home a day after. At bridegroom's residence, the bride enters the house, passing through a winnowing fan (*suksa*) set by the mother-in-law. Paddy put in a measuring copper pot (*pathi*) is set by her on the winnowing fan inside the house with a one rupee coin, hidden in by the mother-in-law, is drawn out by the bride. It is done thrice. This is a ceremony known as *sangin*. A feast is arranged and bride lives in her husband's house for three days. On fouth day the couple return to the bride's house, where they stay for about six days, a period known as *duran*. The boy is required to bring eighteen loaves of bread, country loquor and a leg of mutton to in-law's home. In case of chori biha too, the formal selection would be examined; if by any chance, they have the same *ghat*, marriage would not be allowed.. Marriage with other scheduled castes (Kamis, Damais, Sarkis) is not yet permitted.

(c) Death: No priest is called for the rites for the dead. It is only the elders with knowledge of custom and belief (*ajay*) who are called for the occasion. Dead body is put in a box. The first son usually makes three rounds of the dead body, with water and an earthen pot. A daughter makes the rounds in case of no male issue. The dead body is buried. The sons shave their heads. The death pollution is observed for 6 days. Till the purification they abstain from eating of fish, meat, salt, and oil. The eldest son stays inside a room *(kunri)* and sit on a mat. On the sixth day, all the sons and daughters go to the nearest stream. The sons make offerings (parno) to the deceased on a banana leaf. Cow's urine, sesamum (*til*), barley, grassdub and mustard oil are mixed and thrown in as a mark of the remembrance of the bereaved family and then death pollution is dispelled. In the fifth month, the final purification rites are observed on a full moon day (Singh, 1983).

19
The Newars (Pradhans)

Social Status: Other Backward Class (OBC)

Origin and History:

The Newars are the original inhabitants of the Kathmandu Valley in Nepal. The word *Newar* is derived from the name of the country Nepal itself. The Nepal name has derived from the famous ascetic and patron saint of Nepal "*Ne Muni*" who installed the son of a pious cowherd as king, and thus started the cowherd (*Gopala*) dynasty. Despite the 1769 Gorkha conquest of the Nepal Valley and their subjugation by the state administration through "Nepal Unification", the Newars managed to maintain their distinct arts, crafts, culture and traditions. Their culture has remained highly influential throughout the history of Nepal (Vansittart, 1896; Stiller, 1968; Toffin, 1984 and 1993; Levy, 1992; Gellner, 1996). The Newars are also considered to be a skilled and successful trading community, and their involvement in trans-Himalayan trade was already well established many centuries ago. They have succeeded in maintaining this image in Sikkim also (Subba, 1989: 134; Sinha, 1981: 192). As an educated community, the Newars also occupy many important administrative posts in both Nepal and Sikkim (Shrestha, 2005: 25).

The Newars of Nepal have been widely studied (Nepali, 1965; Toffin, 1984; 1993; Levy, 1992; Geller, 1996; Shrestha, 2002). Ample literature exists on the Nepali diaspora both in India and Bhutan (Subba & Datta, 1991; Timsina, 1992; Hutt, 1994, 1997) and on Sikkim as state (Temple, 1977; Nakane, 1979; Jha and Mishra, 1984; Bhasin, 1989; Subba & Datta, 1991; Dhamala, 1991; Lama, 2001 and Sharma and Sharma, 1997). Shrestha (2005) has studied the Newar diaspora in Sikkim.

The Newars of Sikkim are numerically very few, but they have played an important role in ethnic politics and are active in trying to promote their language, culture, rituals, traditions and religions across Sikkim. In 1998, the State Government of Sikkim introduced several laws and sanctioned state budget lines to facilitate the promotion of the languages and cultures of the Newars and other groups (Pradhan and Josee, 1998). The school curriculum now includes the Newar language, and language interpreters are employed in the state Legislature to translate speeches delivered in Newar into other languages. In 2003, the State Government of Sikkim also recognized the Newars as the Other Backward Class (OBC), for whom a percentage of jobs and higher studies are now reserved (Shrestha, 2005).

"The Newars totally deny their origin from Simraun, and allege that they are the original inhabitants of the Nepal Valley. Their houses have a great resemblance to those of the Bhutias, while in many points their customs resemble those of the other tribes of Mongolian descent. This would seem to conclusively prove the Newars to be of Thibetan extraction originally, whatever admixtures of blood may have been introduced in after-times. Until the Gorkha conquest there was probably little intermixture, except in the descendants of the governing family. The present race of the Newars is a mixed one, derived from Indian and Thibetan stocks, and their religion naturally presents a corresponding mixture of the Indian and Thibetan creeds. The predominance of the Thibetan over the Indian stock in the composition of their blood is as evident in the religion of the Newars as it is in their language, their characters, and their physical appearance. The Nepal Valley is undoubtedly the real home of the Newars. There is every reason to believe that the Newars are the earliest or aboriginal inhabitants of the valley of Nepal" (Vansittart, 1896: 119-122). The Newars are of a middle size, with broad shoulders and chest, very stout limbs, round and rather flat faces, small eyes, low and somewhat spreading noses.

In the absence of any historical evidence, the theory of Tibet (Chin) origin of Newars is difficult to believe. The Nepal Valley was the center of civilization of the entire Himalayan region in ancient times. It is known to all that the Buddhist religion and Buddhist architecture spread from the Nepal Valley and not from Tibet. According to Stiller (1968), the people of Tibet were not having their own currency and were using currencies manufactured in Nepal Valley when the Gorkha invasion was started in 1744-45.

According to a Tibetan belief, Nepal was occupied by Tibet in 640 AD. Tibetan chronicles even talk about the marriage of the powerful Tibetan king, Srong-btsan Gampo, with Amsuvarma's daughter, Bhrikuti of Belsa who along with her Chinese co-wife is given the credit for introducing Buddhism in Tibet (Shakabpa, 1967: 25). But this is vehemently disputed by Nepali scholars (Regmi, 1960: 155-157).

Although the question of early migration to Sikkim is still to be addressed by historians, it is believed among Newars of Darjeeling and

Sikkim that some of their ancestors began migrating to the region soon after the Gorkha conquest of Nepal in 1769. The Gorkha administration occupied "The Greater Sikkim" west of Teesta River and Singalila range on the top and Terai area of Sikkim after 1774 A.D. (Stiller, 1968:110). They also occupied West Sikkim upto Teesta river from 1789 to 1814 A.D. (25 years) (Hamilton, 1819: 120). Bhutan also invaded and occupied the entire Sikkim in 1700 A.D. and ruled for a period of 8 years (1700-1708), and annexed Kalimpong area, Har Chu Valley and Amo Chu Valley permanently (Risley, 1894: 14). Thus, the people were some times the subjects of Bhutan while the same people were subject of Nepal or Sikkim on the other. There was no watertight compartment between the areas of Bhutan, Nepal and Sikkim. They freely moved and settled wherever they liked. The boundary of Nepal and Sikkim were finally settled only after Titalia Treaty in 1817 (Hamilton, 120; Chemjong, 1948/67: 224-226; Namgyal & Dolma, 1908: 76-79; Risley, 1894; Subba, 1999). Many have suggested that with the arrival of the legendry Laksmidas Pradhan (Kasaju), a Newar from Bhaktapur, in Sikkim, many other Newars migrated to Sikkim. There are a number of stories in circulation about how and when Laksmidas left Nepal. While some suggest that he escaped from the Nepal Valley to save his life right after the Kot massacre of 1846, others believe that he left Nepal long before this incident. Daya Prasad Pradhan writes that Laksmidas and his brother Chandravir arrived in Sumbuk abound 1850 (1997: 2). Similarly, Pranab Kumar Jha states: "Laksmidas with his uncle Keshav Narayan came to Darjeeling in 1853 from Nepal and probably no other Newar had come to Darjeeling before them (1985: 130). He further suggests that they settled in Sikkim in 1867 in order to work in a copper mine in Tukkhani in South Sikkim and went on to work in a number of other copper mines later. Some have suggested that the then king invited Laksmidas to Sikkim to act as the collector of land revenues, as Laksmidas had become famous in Darjeeling as a successful businessman (Shrestha, 2005: 26-27).

However, I do not personally believe on one point that the Newar, a veteran business community could follow only one family for migration and settle down to the Greater Sikkim areas after one century after migration of other Nepali communities. In my opinion, it is not correct to say that the Newars were migrated to Sikkim only following a single-family Laksmidas Pradhan as mentioned above. Since the present west district of Sikkim was under Gorkha rule for about 25 years, many Newars might have migrated to this Gorkha occupied areas along with other castes and tribes after 1789 onwards and settled there. The Laksmidas Pradhan might be a prominent man in the eyes of the

Maharaja. The rulers may not know many common Newars that time who migrated to other areas of Sikkim and settled. Sikkim citizenship identity was maintained only after the promulgation of Sikkim Subject in 1961/62. Hence, to say that the Newars were migrated to Sikkim only after 1867 may not be correct.

After the 1861 Tumlong treaty was signed between British government and Sikkim authorities, the British began to encourage Nepalese settlers in Sikkim. On 1st February, 1835, the East India Company took over Darjeeling a part of "The Greater Sikkim", ending Sikkim's control of the area. While in 1839 Darjeeling was a home to about 100 people. In 1901, the Newar population of Darjeeling was 5,880; 2.36% of the total population of 249,117 (O'Malley, 1907).

Population and Settlement:

The Newar population in Sikkim was 727 in 1891 (Census 1891). Based on the voter's list of 2004, the population of Newars was 26,082 persons, which have increased to about 36 times in 113 years, constituting 4.36% of the total population of Sikkim. The Newars' population of Nepal was 12,45,232 persons in 2001 constituting 5.48% of the total population. The mother tongue retention of Newars was 66.24% in Nepal (Nepal Census 2001).

Geographical Distribution:

In Sikkim, the Newar populated areas are Melli, Rateypani, Jorthang, Damthang, and Temi Tarku in South District; Rigu, Rhenock, Central Pandam, Gangtok, Ranka, Rumtek, Sang-Martam, and Khamdong in East District; Soreng, Daramdin, Dentam and Gyalshing in the West District.

Food Habits:

Though the Newars are non-vegetarians, eating of pork, wild boars, pigs, beef, and yak are prohibited. Buffalo meat, which is taboo for most of the hill communities, is a favorite delicacy for the Newars. Rice is their staple food but wheat and maize are eaten when rice is scarce. They take pulses like *moong, masur*, gram, beans, peas and prepare these like curry. Preparation of *Kwati* or *Kokkti* (germinating pulses as curry) during their Rakhi festival is a must in the community. They use mustard and rapeseed oil as cooking medium. They consume locally available roots and tubers; and all kinds of vegetables and fruits. They consume a variety of drinks, viz. wine, millet beer, rice beer, and alcoholic drinks. Newars take two principal meals and two refreshments, viz. breakfast and afternoon refreshment. They take tea and flattened rice with *puri*, meat and vegetables. They also take *Sinki, Gungruk*, and bamboo shoots.

Cuisine:

Masaurya, Gundruk, Sinki, Khalpi, Selroti, Dahi, Chew, Mahi, Chhurpi, Sukako Masu especially of *Bhainsi ko, Kodoko Jaanr, Bhati jaanr, Raksi, Dheroh, Phulaurah, Khalo dal, Pahenli dal, Kwathi (kokti), Kodoko roti, Mithe Phapar ko roti, Chambrey, Royo sag, Ban jarul, Shimrayo, Patley sisno, Niguro, Tama, Chew, Chhwelaa, Lhaka :nari, Dalle Khorsani, Chimping, Nakima, Kabra, Silam, Bhatamash ko achar,* and *Philinge.* Some of the special meat dishes of the Newars include *Syapati kimila, gorma, chula, chhakula, chhoila, chhyala, taha-kha, Naga, pupala, bulla, lago-lao, lapi, lakula, sanya-khunya, sa-pu, hicha,* and *haiyla.* Of these, *chula, chhoiyla* and *tah-kha* are the most popular dishes (Nepali, 1965; Tamang, 2005).

Family Pattern:

The traditional Newar family is a patrilineal joint household, consisting of the descendants of several generations and with common arrangements for cooking, and joint ownership of property under a single head. However, the present trend is towards smaller households – nuclear families.

Family Property:

The property is equally divided among all the sons but succession is the right of the eldest son. Conflicts arise over property.

Gender Issues:

In the matter of inheritance the wife is always dependent on her husband. Generally unmarried daughters can inherit her father's property along with her brothers, though on her death such a share of property would revert to her brothers. A wife from a lower sub-caste cannot perform rituals through her social position otherwise remains the same. She is also not allowed to enter the kitchen in the case of a joint kitchen or worship her husband's family deities. Women have their roles in trading, agricultural activities, animal husbandry, collection of fuel, bringing water; and in the social, religious and political spheres. They contribute to the family income, control the family expenditure and are ranked equally with men. However, the wife is always regarded as subordinate to her husband (Singh, 1983).

Castes, Kinship and Social Organization:

Traditional Newar society in Nepal is a complicated structure with caste divisions and internal hierarchies. The nineteenth century chronicle, the Bhasavamsavali, credits the fourteenth century king Jayasthiti Malla with introducing the occupational caste system to Newars of Nepal Valley (Lamsal, 1966: 37-50). Jayasthitimalla fully relied on the Hindu lawbook and organized the caste system with the help of five Brahmans, Kirtinath Upadhyaya Kanyakubja, Raghunath Jha Maithili, Srinath Bhatta, Mainath Bhata, and Ramnath Jha from India (Daniel Wright, 1877:182). The Newar society was divided into four varnas and sixty-four castes on the basis of the hereditary occupations and genealogies (Nepali, 1965: 146). The Brahmans were further divided into three groups, Panch Gauda, Pancha Dravida and Jaisi. The Thakurs like the royal Mallas were regarded as Kshatriyas. The Josi and Achars, though allowed to wear sacred thread, were enjoined to marry Shresthas. Thus, they were given the status of the Vaishya with the part privilege of the Brahman. Between the Shresthas and Jyapus were a number of artisan groups. Placed lower than the Jyapus were the unclean and untouchable castes respectively (Nepali, 1965: 167). Buddhist Newars were also segmented into different castes. Thus, the entire Newar community in Nepal is internally divided into castes on the basis of heredity, tradition and occupation (Rosser, 1966 :74). In Nepal, caste discrimination is still felt in all traditional Newar settlements and Newars still use their caste or occupational names. The Newar tribe has a number of castes; and each caste has a number of clans/ *thars*, and has become difficult to distinguish these days. The following scheme of caste hierarchy is generally accepted in the Kathmandu valley (Nepali, 1965: 150):

Note: Castes on the same horizontal plane are regarded as of equal social status.

Bhaichand Pradhan (1997: 20-36) has described some of the castes of Newars in his book as follows:

(1) Vajracharya and Sakya:

They are Vajrayana or Mahayana Buddhist and prefer to known them as Sakyabhikchu or Sakyabangs. Their priests are known as Bajracharya. The Bjracharyas perform all kinds of priesthood for the Newar community, and known as "Gubhaju" or "Gurujyu". The Sakyas are occupationally experts in making ornaments of gold, silver, precious stones and also known as "Banras".

(2) Udas:

They are also Vajrayana or Mahayana Buddhist and also known as "Uras". They are the village artisans or the business community of the Newars. Some of the clans/thars of Udas are Tuladhar, Sthapit (wood-workers), Sikrikar, Kanskar (Brass-workers), Tamrakar/Tamot/Tamwa (workers of copper and brass), Awa, Rajkarnikar, Silakar (stone workers), Kasaju etc.

(3) Rajoppadhyaya:

It is believed that some Bhatta Brahmans of ancient *Panch-Drabirh* came to Nepal and settled there adopting the culture and traditions of the area. They also served as priest of the Malla Kings, and known as "Rajoppadhyaya". They are also known as *Dhyabhaju, Dhyabrahmyu* and *Juju.*

(4) Shrestha:

They are known as *Sasya* in Newar language. They are usually Hindus by religion but some are Buddhist also. It is believed that they are *Chatriyas* but later on mixed with Rajputs and Khasas. Some of the Clans/thars are Bharo, Malla, Karmacharya/Aachaju, Pradhan/Pama, Rajbhandari/Bhalin, Joshi/Daiwagya, Gurucharya, Maskey/Mayakey, Raya, Khayarguli, Mathema, Aamatya, Pradhananga, etc.

(5) Jyapu:

They are believed to be the most ancient races of Nepal. They fall under Gopal Bangsa, and are rich in culture especially on folk music, folk dance and folk songs. They are agriculturist in occupation and are divided into 32 clans/thars. Some of the common clans/thars are Maharjan, Suwal/Suwa, Dangol/Dangu, Munikar/Mu, Singh, Prajapati/ Kuma, Sapu, Jyapu, Pachai, etc.

(6) Nau:

They are Buddhist and also known as *Naw* or *Hajam* and use Vajracharya as their priest. They serve the community as barbers and is a must in religious occasions.

(7) Khus:

They are Buddhist and also agriculturist by occupation and are expert in rice, bitten rice preparation and sale. They also play on "ka" (Yamturya) a musical instrument required during dead procession. They are also known as Tandukar or Khusab or Khuswa.

(8) Kau:

They are Buddhist, ironsmith by occupation and make agricultural implements. They are also known as Lohakar or Nakami or Nakarmi.

(9) Saymi:

They are oil expellers by occupation. They also prepare local alcoholic drinks. They are good businessman of food items specially of bitten rice. They are Buddhist and also known as Saymi/Salmi, Tusiya/ Tusya, Manendhar, and Dhajadhar.

(10) Malakar:

They are Buddhist, occupationally florist and cultivate flowers and also collect flowers for market. They are known as Gathu and Mali.

VI Untouchable Castes: Pore – Kullu

↓

Chyame

NEWAR CASTE-HIERARCHY

	Hindu Newars	Buddhist Newars
I. Priestly Castes:	Deva Brahmin	Gubhaju or Bajracharya
	↓	↓
		Varna or Bare
		↓
II. High Castes:	Chhatharia Shrestha Panchtharia Shrestha	Udas

↓

III. Upper Lower Castes: Pahari-Jyapoo — Hale or Guala

↓

IV. Lower Castes: Gathu-Nau-Khoosa-Chitraka-Chheepa-Manandhar-Kow (Mali), Pu (n), Ranjikar, Salmi

↓

V. Unclean Castes: Du(n)yeeya(n)-Balami-Sanga or Sangat

↓

Bha

↓

Kasai

↓

Kusule (or Jogi)

↓

Hara Huru

Note: Castes on the same horizontal plane are regarded as of equal social status.

(11) Pun:

They are artists and draw arts of God and Goddesses. They are Mahayana Buddhist and also known as Punyakar or Chitrakar.

(12) Chipa:

They are Buddhist and print clothes and also known as Ranjitkar.

(13) Duyi:

They are occupationally salers of flower, apple, fuel-wood. They organize kumari-jatra, bhairav-jatra, sav-jatra, bhaku-jatra etc. They are known as Rajbahar, Narkoti, Putuwa and Dali.

(14) Kulu or Charmakar:

They are occupationally cobblers and makers of musical instruments, teach to use musical instruments, repair the instrument and make leather handbags.

(15) Naya:

They are occupationally livestock rearers, and rear buffaloes, milk salers, meat salers, etc. They also serve as Dholakias of the Government. They are believed to have migrated from Nayar Pradesh of South India. They are known as Kharkey/Khargi, Kasai, Meyepu and Sahi.

(16) Dhabya:

They are Hindus and occupationally Dhobis. They wash cloths. They are known as Rajak, Sanghat, Dhobi, Madhyiya and Kanaujiya.

(17) Jogi:

Their occupation is to clean the temples, play musical instruments, play Panchey Baja on religious, marriage occasions etc. They practice bagging, and are also cultivators. They are known as Darsandhari, Kapali, Kusuley, Byapali, and Denya.

(18) Dyala:

They are occupationally sweepers, chawkidars, and do bagging at the time of solar and lunar eclipse. They also do fisheries. They are known as Pwadar, Porey, Po, Chyamkhol, Chamey, Halahulu, and Poicha.

The differentiations amongst the above castes are at the social, religious and occupational levels. The functions of the social sub-divisions are to regulate marriage alliances and to indicate social status besides descent. The Rajupadhyaya occupies the highest rank in the Newar social hierarchy. They serve as priests to those Newars only whose household religious ceremonies are not like those of the Nepali Brahamans. Those Rajupadhyaya work as farmers like other non-Brahamans and do not follow the profession of learning as such like other Brahamans. They have now been mostly replaced by Nepali Brahamans whom the Newars call Prabatiya Brahamans.

There are three criteria regulating food restrictions from the ritual point of view: (*i*) the larger group who can share smoking (*hooka*); (*ii*) the inner group who can share a feast where *thalthale*, a special kind of meat, dish, is served; and (*iii*) the smallest sub-caste who can only eat boiled rice touched by each other and can also enter each other's kitchen. Only near relatives are considered as within this group.

Thus, the process of acculturation had continued for centuries and the Newars were probly the first group of Tibeto-Burman speakers in the Himalayan region to undergo a socio-cultural metamorthosis under the caste domination from outside. The process started in the fifth century AD, only to be intensified with passage of time. Indeed the Newar society was a miniature nation in itself till they were concured by the Gorkhas (Pradhan, 1991: 31).

Against the background of Nepal described above, the disappearance of caste hierarchies among Sikkim's Newars is remarkable and may be the single most salient feature of the diaspora population. But these traditions described above are extinct in the diaspora Newar society now living in Sikkim under the impact of a process of modernization. The community has surnames like Joshi, Pradhan, Shrestha etc. and they wrongly recognize the *varna* system of Hinduism and locate themselves below the Brahamans and Chhettris (Shrestha, 2005).

With a few exceptions, all Newars in Sikkim are now called "Pradhan". The term "*Pradhan*", the family name of one caste of Nepal's Newars, has come to stand for all Newars in Sikkim and Darjeeling (Shrestha, 2005: 35). At certain period, this was not without controversy. During a dispute between two rival groups in Darjeeling, each claiming higher status over the other, the Nepalese authorities wrote a letter stating, "Pradhan is among the highest classes of the Newars" (Singh, 1991: 102). According to Bhuvan Prasad Pradhan (1883: 13), the British Government in India awarded the title of "Pradhan" to Laksmidas for his excellent service in 1913. Laksmidas later asked for all Sikkimese Newars to be permitted to use this title as their family name to prevent caste divisions within their community. A different interpretation is advanced by Khagendra Pradhan, who believes that Laksmidas ordered all Sikkimese Newars who had escaped Nepal to exclusively use Pradhan as a surname to protect their lives after the 1846 Kot massacre, thereby helping them hide their actual identity (1998: 57). Changing all Newar surnames to Pradhan helped to eliminate caste hierarchies among the Newars of Sikkim. Many do not know as they had lost contact with their relatives in Nepal, while other who continue to have regular contact with their relatives in Nepal were aware of having caste names other than Pradhan. Recently, a few families in Sikkim have begun tracing their former caste names, and have started to use their family names. It does not seem likely this will revive the caste hierarchies, which were so effectively eliminated among the Newars in Sikkim (Shrestha, 2005: 36).

There is an avoidance relationship between mother-in-law and son-in-law, younger sister-in-law and daughter-in-law and father-in-law and elder-brother-in-law etc. A free relationship exists between the elder sister-in-law and younger brother-in-law, grandparents and grandchildren etc.

Economic Activity:

The primary occupation of the diaspora Newar community in Sikkim is trade, which is largely confined to the upper strata of the society. Government services follow in importance. The lower strata diaspora Newar community depends on agriculture, horticulture, animal husbandry, etc in rural areas of Sikkim. The subsidiary occupations are weaving, carpentry, and casual labour. Handicrafts constitute the main occupations, and include metalworking especially in urban areas of the State. The diaspora Newar community of Sikkim does not follow the occupational economic activities specified for different castes of Nepal and this may be one of the main reasons to shade away the evil occupational caste system in Sikkim (Shrestha, 2005).

Dresses:

The men wear *La (n)* or *Labeda* (upper garment which covers upto knees) and *Suruwa* (lower garment). Over the upper garment the *Patuka* (cloth belt) is worn. The male head-dress is *tapali* (*topi* in Nepali). The female wear *Parsi* (sari), *Misa-la(n)* (long sleeved blouse reaching upto the waist), *Ga* (shawl) and *Jani* (*Patuka*) which is wider and longer than the one used by the male. The girl children wear *Janghwal-Suruwa* and *La(n)*. The male children wear *Suruwa* and the *La(n)* with *Jani.* They wear *Tapali* as head-dress. At the time of Sraddha or funeral procession, the Deo-Bhaju, the Vanra and the Shrestha Newars have to wear *dhoti* instead of the traditional *Suruwa*. Whenever an aged male relative is to be honoured, he has to be presented with turban, *Pheta.* The traditional foot-wear of the Newar used to be made of cloth with a thick cloth or rope-sole but now replaced by the modern shoes (Nepali, 1965).

The head ornaments of Newar women are *Sinduri, Sir-bandi, Lu(n)-we-Swa(n), Kata* and *Jyapoo-Sikha.* Of these, *Sir-bandi* and *jyapoo-Sikha* are ritually important at the time of *Yihee, Bara* and marriage. The ear-ornaments are *tusi, mundari, palawari-tuci*, and *maka-phosi.* The neck ornaments is *Wo-Sikha* and is ceremonially important as a symbolic of *Suhag* or being married. The waist ornaments are *Luchuri, Bahi* or *Baju* and *panch-ratna-churi*. Rings on fingers are used and *Kalli* (now *Powjeb*) are used on ankles (Nepali, 1965).

Folk Musical Instruments:

The Newars of Nepal are the richest in folk musical instruments among all the hill tribes of the Himalayas. They are:

Kanyapi, kanshi baja, kanta dabdab, kai fu, korbing, kwata, khandali, khicha khon gon, khwalimali, gopal dandi, ghari ghanta, ghor bansuri, jor nagara, jhwa khin, jyayo gano, jhautal, taktukley, tinglicha, tip bansuri, dabdab, tanmokcha, thah, tainam, tatali, tanimuni, danga khni, damo khni, dakchin baja khni, durga damaru, dibya damaru, dibya ghanta, dyo khni, neku, pakhawaj, pachima, pasta khni, ponga, paita khni, phyai ghno, babhu, bosah, bhatayoh, mangaley angaley ghno, mang khni, mak kathi, majhwan bansuri, mridanga, yak khni, laghu khah, lakhey peti, latha khni, lal khni, sipibharuwa bansuri, sipibharuwa murali, swakunla, hwan (dhwti), hitimnga, alopo dhimey, kakuwaya, koncha khni, dhaw, dah, piwancha, bayocha, bhusyaha, majhula dah, ma dhimey, and *yakucha wabhu* (68 Nos.) (Kandel, 2004). Out of these musical instruments only a few are being used by the diaspora Newar community of Sikkim.

Folk Songs:

The Newars are lovers of music. The educated modern Newars are lovers of modern and classical music. Each and every house of a Newar family has either a sitar or a harmonium. Many Newars have gained name and fame in this sphere but the rich and ancient cultural traditions of the Newars have been enriched by their ancient folk songs and dances which still exist to some extent in the far away villages untouched by the modern ways of life. The followings are some of the folk songs of Newars: (*i*) *Sinhajaya* (a song sung while transplanting paddy); *Yatra* festival; (*ii*) Love song – sung by the youth; (*iii*) *Fagu* song – emotional songs; etc. A special kind of song is sung by the women folk in the evening outside the dark room where a young girl is confined for twelve days and nights to lift her spirit. *Khiyali* songs are sung during the *Yatra* festivals (Nepali, 1965).

Folk Dances:

The ancient puppet dance called the *Daya Laximi* has more or less disappeared now. A dance called *Lakhay* still exists in some remote villages, and in festive occasions on the stages. The dance is accompanied with beating of a drum and *Sahanai* like musical instrument. This dance depicts the love story of a young Newari girl who is compelled to kill her lover the demon by a weapon. The dance is very popular in Sikkim (detail in folk dances chapter).

Religion and Belief System:

Though there are a few Newar Christians and Muslims, Newar society in Nepal can as a whole be considered a Hindu-Buddhist mix. In Sikkim, however, there are a fair number of Christian Newars alongside

(1965) and Shrestha (2005), the passage of rites of the Newar community has been described as under:

(*a*) Pre-natal Care: During eclipse the pregnant women is advised not to touch her abdomen with her fingers. She is forbidden to see or touch the pictures or idols of fierce deities, such as *Bhairava, Narsingha avtar* and *Bajra*. Just a few weeks before the delivery, the representatives of the woman's natal home pay her a visit. This custom is known as *Dhau Bajee Nake Wanegu* or going to feed the woman with flattered rice (*Bajee*) and curd (*Dhau*). After feeding the woman to her heart's content, the visiting members go away.

(*b*) Birth: A woman is never allowed to give birth to her child in her parents' house. At the time of delivery, and also afterwards, the woman is given a small quantity of mustard oil to drink. The purification ceremony known as *Macha-Bu Benke-gu*, is done after six days on the birth of the first child and after four days for subsequent children. Some of the *Sivmargi* Shresthas perform this ceremony on the tenth day, after the fashion of the Gorkhas. On the purification day all the members of the family and other agnates of the child are required to undergo the purification ceremony of *Nisi-Yae-gu* and include, besides bath, the rituals of *Lusi-Thikegu* and *ala-taye-gu*. The barber performs the functions involved in the last two named rituals. The ritual act of cutting the nails (*Lusi-Thi-kegu*), and dying the toes and fingers (*Ala-taye-gu*) as part of the purificatory rites, is peculiar to the Newars. Besmearing with cow dung solution and sprinkling cow's milk known as *Sa-Duru-Ha-Ha Yae-gu* purifies the house. The father gives the child two names, one horoscope name by Joshi on purification day, and the common name before 2 years of age (Pradhan, 1997; Shrestha, 2005).

However, a leaflet compiled by Bharatia Newar Sangathan (BNSD), Darjeeling, (2002:7-10) states that "*Jayavili*" (*Sutak*) is observed from the time of cutting of umbilical cord of the child and the naming of the child is done by *Thakali* (elder women of the family) on the 5th day for the girls and 6th day for the boys.

The rice-feeding ceremony known as *Macha Junko* of a boy is held after the sixth or eighth months, even months, while of a girl is held on fifth or seventh months, always insisting on odd months (Pradhan, 1997; Shrestha, 2005). Here also BNSD states that the rice feeding ceremony is observed after 5 months for girls and 6 months for the boys. The first hair cutting of the boy is called *Churnakarma* (*Buskha*) and is observed after 3 years of age of the boys; while *Bratabandha* (*Kayatapuja*) of the boys also carried out together with *Churnakarma* (BNSD) or when he is seven or eight years of age. The initiation ceremony of a boy into adulthood is called *Kaita-puja*, which is celebrated at the age of 14 years and signifies the admission of the boy into full-fledged adult.

(c) Marriage: Endogamy at the community levels determines the rules of marriage. The exogamy is based upon consideration of blood, taking seven generations into consideration both on the father's and mother's sides. But now people have started marrying women from the third or the fourth generation. Both cross-cousin and parallel cousin marriages are taboo. Marriage modes are negotiation, elopement, and also courtship.

Traditionally, the Newar girls are married three times. Firstly, marriage will be with a "*Bail*" (wood apple fruit); Secondly marriage with "the Sun"; and finally marriage with a man. Among the Newars the system of "*Ehi*" is very important, which means marriage. The traditions have been described by Pradhan (1997) as under:

(i) The Marriage of a Girl to a Wood Apple (*bel-biya* or *Iihi sanskar*):

It is a marriage of the girl with God Shiva (symbolically with a wood apple), and is done before attaining puberty is very significant among the Newar community. It is performed just like any marriage ceremony. Generally it is organized collectively in a house gathering all the girls for the purpose. The girls wear all the clothes and ornaments of a bride. There is chanting of the mantras of a marriage ceremony by the priest (or *Thakali*)). The *Nawmati Baja* of the Damais is also played on this auspicious occasion. Vermilion is put on the parting of the hair of the girl. The wood apple is then kept inside a box after the completion of the ceremony. A married girl of Newar family never becomes a widow after the death of her husband once this marriage has held. She is free to marry again.

(ii) The *Barhang Taygu* or *Gupha Rakhney* ceremony:

It is the next ceremony after the wood apple marriage ceremony of a Newar girl. This is to be performed at the age of 9, 11 or 13 years before the girl attains puberty. (In earlier days this was done only after the first menstruation). The girl is asked to take bath, wear new clothes, fed with curd and is kept confined to a dark room for twelve days. No male member is allowed to go near the room as the girl confined to such a room is not supposed to see the face of any male. The girl remains inside along but outside singing goes on suitable for such occasions. On the eleventh day, the face of the girl is washed with a mixture of rice-flour, mustard oil and water, which is known as "*Kwna chink sakyegu*". The day of performing this differs from clan to clan and the puberty pollution also differs accordingly. On the completion of the twelfth day the priest performs the puberty ritual and then the girl is taken out of the room at sunrise when she sees the first ray of the sun. Then, the girl is asked to see *"jwala nhyank"* (a kind of looking glass) and with *Chammer* the priest performs worship of *Ganesh.* It is a kind of marriage with the Sun. This kind of tradition is to keep the purity and sanctity of a virgin girl.

(*iii*) The Marriage with a man or *Ihipa*:

A *Lami* (middle man or woman) goes to the house of the girl to have preliminary talks with the parents of the girl. If the talks are favourable, the boy's parents send 10 pieces of whole beetle nut, a brass cup, one rupee coin and fruits to the girl's parents through *Lami*. This custom is known as *Gway Bigu* (*Supari Dinu*). The bride remains at home while her elders and friends go to fetch the groom. On the marriage day there is a grand feast in the bride's family. At the bride's place *Ganesha* is worshipped at first followed by several other deities like *Bhairava, Bhagavati, Ashta-Matrika,* and the *Kul* deity of the bride's parents. After the gods have been worshipped, there follows the *sambaja-anke-gu,* a communal feast, which in its turn is followed by the *sagal*, when gifts brought by the relatives are offered to the bride, who then, in a ceremony called the *gue kaiye gu*, offers to her kinfolk betel nuts provided by the bride-groom's party. In the ritual called *tuti-bagi-naye-ke-gu*, just before the bride joins the bridegroom's party, the eldest male member of the bridegroom's party touches the feet of the bride and ties the *bagi* (a foot ornament *kalli* or *powjeb*) on to her feet.

The first ceremony that takes place in the bridegroom's house is known as *honke gu*, the worship of the bride by the kinsfolk of the bridegroom. This is followed by the *thai bhu*, designed to give social recognition to the marital bond. As part of the ceremony, the bridegroom and the bride have to share food from the same plate. The eating together ceremony is followed by, the ritual of *klampoo*, to ward off the influence of evil spirits. After the visit to the presiding deity of the locality, there is the *sincho-faye-gu* ceremony, when vermilion is put on the bride's forehead. Now the bride and the bridegroom are regarded as husband and wife on all scores and are allowed to share the same bed.

(*d*) Death: The Hindu theory of the transmigration of scul and the law of Karma form the pivot of Newar philosophy, which governs their death rituals. Therefore, beliefs regarding death are akin to those of the other Hindus. The soul of a person, after death, is believed finally to go to the abode of *Yama.* A person is rewarded or punished according to the virtues practised or sins committed by him on the earth.

In Newar society, rituals are as important for those who have died as for those who are alive. In Sikkim, even after death, the Newars employ Parbate Brahmin priests. The Newars cremate their dead. Funerals may take place on the day of death, but in most cases occur the following day. The Newars do offering of *pindas* to the soul of the deceased before cremation unique rituals of the Newars. As far as possible, sons of the deceased must bear the dead body to the cremation ground, but relatives and neighbours may also help to carry the body. At the cremation ground, the chief mourner lights the body and it burns down to ashes. The chief mourner and any other sons then shave their heads and bathe in the river.

The pollution period lasts for thirteen days. Married daughters are unclean only for four days. During the pollution period pulses, soybean, arecanuts, curd and milk are prohibited. On returning home, sons of the deceased keep their distance from others for ten days during which time no one can touch them. They also cook their own food. Every day for ten days, they may perform *sraddha* at a nearby river. On the tenth day, a purification rite is performed and close relatives may also shave their head. On the eleventh day, 365 floating bowls made of leaves (*khochi bagaune*) are prepared. On the twelfth day, *pinda* are offered to the deceased. On the thirteenth day, a *sraddha* is performed, and beds, sheets, dresses and utensils (*sarya dana*) are given to the priest in the name of the deceased. Those who joined the family in the funeral procession and extended their condolences must be invited for a feast meal on this day. All of these visitors give the family an amount of money as a gesture of their support. Such a feast may not contain meat. Nowadays, many stop wearing the mourning dress on the thirteenth day, but some continues to wear mourning clothes until they perform a *sraddha* on the 45th day. Monthly *sraddha* is no longer common, but most Newars in Sikkim do perform a *sraddha* at sixth months and a year after the death. Wearing white for the whole year has now become a rare practice. Such rituals performed after death in Sikkim, as expected, do not match to the rituals performed by Newars in Nepal. The rites of passages of the diaspora Newars of Sikkim do not follow many birth, marriage and death rituals mentioned in "*Janma Dekhi Sijyasammako Sanskar Padhati*" by Bharatuya Newar Sanghathan, Darjeeling, may be due to absence of the required priests of their own..

The diaspora Newars of Sikkim perform their death rituals as in the case of other Buddhist Bhutia and Lepchas employing Bhutia Lama priests, as they do not have their own priests. Some times they obtain their priests from Nepal or Kalimpong to perform their rites of passages.

(*e*) Jya Junkwa (Bura-Buri Junkwa): The Newars observe days of honoring their elders; Parents and grandparents. The celebration is known as *Jya Junkwa* which has been divided into five stages as follows:

(*i*) The first *Junkwa* is known as "*Bhimratharohan*" and is observed when a person attains the age of 66 years, 6 months and 6 days old;

(*ii*) The second *Junkwa* is known as "*Chandraratharohan*" and is observed when a person attains the age of 83 years, 4 months and 4 days old;

(*iii*) The third *Junkwa* is known as "*Dev Ratharohan*" and is observed when a person attains an age of 88 years, 8 months and 8 days old;

(*iv*) The fourth *Junkwa* is known as "*Dibyaratharohan*" and observed when a person attains an age of 99 years, 9 months and 9 days old; and

(*v*) The fifth *Junkwa* is observed when a person attains an age of 108 years, 8 months and 8 days old.

The occasion is celebrated with the worship by conducting *Yagya* and *naugraha astachiranjivi puja* and providing *daan* to the priests etc. The female person is given gold *tika* while the male is given *Betali* (*Pheta*).

Glossary

Bahpa, Zolung and Tshong-skyed	Forms of Taxes introduced by Rabden Sherpa Gyalpo in Sikkim during 1734-40s
Bakchok	Carved square table of Lhopos of Sikkim
Barahimjong	Magar's worship festival
Bardo Thodol	Buddhist's intermediate state between the moment of death and moment of conception in the next life
Beb-tsan-ruzhis	The eight great ancestors of Khe-Bumsa
Beyul Nyekyi	Bhutia folk song
Bhuiphutta tribes	Aboriginal Limboo inhabitants of Limbuwan
Bijuwa, Mangpa, Nekchhong, Mabimi, Kubimi and Dowang	Khambu-Rai's shamans
Boongthing	Lepcha Shaman
Changzot (d)	Prime Minister post of Namgyal Dynasty
Chokchi	Carved rectangular small table of Lhopos of Sikkim
Chotimba	Head of Annes in Buddhism
Chotlung	Fortified place in Yumaism
Chupon	Havildar during Namgyal Dynasty
Demazong	The valley of rice - the name of Sikkim in Lhopos
Ding-pon	Chief Officer during Namgyal Dynasty
Dokpas	Migratory Yak and sheep Grazers of higher altitudes
Donyer	Dewan during Namgyal Dynasty
Dukenculee	Lepcha's dwelling house
Dzongs	Districts during Namgyal Dynasty/fort of Petty Kings of Sikkim
Dzumsa	Traditional administrative Institution of Lachung and Lachen people
Heybum Panu or Dungpemsar	Petty Lepcha king of Chumbi valley
Him Sammang	Household divinities in Yumaism
Itbu-moo	Almighty God in Lepchas
Jongpens	District Administrative Officer during Namgyal Dynasty

Jya Junkwa	Newar's way of honouring their elders
Kabtindop	Sherpa's marriage by elopment
Kahlons	Ministers during Namgyal Dynasty
Khainjari and Balun	Form of Dances of the Khasas
Khambongba-Lungbongba	Aboriginal tribes in Limboos
Khema Yongsong Den	Human Soul's punishment place/world/ hell
Khutlung Khutma	Khambu-Rai's fireplace worship ceremony
Kinema	A kind of soybean fermented food
Koshang	Council during Namgyal Dynasty
Kutse Shegu	Buddhist's 49th day death purification ceremony
Kwati or Kokkti	Newar's germinating pulses curry
Kyimsa Tashi	Bhutia's house warming ceremony
Lapon Lhundrup tribes	Refers to Lachung-Lachen tribes
Lho-Mon-Tsong-Sum	Tripartite Treaty of Bhutias, Lepchas and Tsongs
Lungjang giyangu	Sherpa's arranged marriage
Lakhey	Newar's Demon dance
Macha-Bu-Benke-gu	Birth purification ceremony of Newars
Mahisasur and Raktabij	Hindu Demons
Malsiri	Sanskrit text - read during Durga Puja
Mangdhan	Limboo community's household worship place
Mangkhim	Limboo's community worship place
Mangenna	Lifting of head worship of the Limboos
Mangs	Deities in Yumaism
Manusmriti	Hindu Law book
Mishia and Shilum pattu	Khambu-Rai's death rites
Miteri or Maha Miteri Saino	Ceremonial friendship between the persons of two or more different communities
Mola	Sherpa's oral tradition during wedding
Mon-Loong-Kha-bzi	Area of greater Sikkim from the present Kalimpong District to Tegongla area of the present Bhutan
Monpas	Refers to non-Tibetan dwellers south of the Himalayas and around the border of Tibet or people that resides (and continue to reside) in the Greater Sikkim prior to migration of the Tibetans, namely Lepchas, Limboos and Magars

Mundhum	Oral myth of the Limboos in Yumaism
ne mayel lyang	Hidden paradise in Lepcha
ne mayel maluk lyang	Land of eternal purity in Lepcha
Ngen-chham Thung	Bhutia's wedding ceremony
Niyara Hongsing Ke	Chyabrung, Limboo musical instrument
Nyer-Chen	Counciller during Namgyal Dynasty
Nyorpog-phutsos	Refers to 12 Bhutias or Lhopo Tribes eligible for entrence into the Pamayongtse monastery as priests
Panchai Baja and Nawmati Baja	Damai's musical instruments
Panchamahabhuta	Five primary elements in Hinduism
Pawo and nejum	Bhutia shamans
Phoktanglungma Pembenlungma	Kumbhakarna, Jannu mountain in Limboos
Phyakey or phangsang	Bhutia's birth purification and name giving ceremony
Poibos, Natsos, Ngyami	Sunuwar shamans
Rongpas	Dwellers of steep country, the Lepchas
Rong-Chham	Buddhist's religious dance
Sammangs	Divinities in Yumaism
Sammang Chyangs	Retinue of Divinities in Yumaism
Sam Sire	Deity of Avtars or Incarnations in Yumaism
Samyukna Den	The world of the souls in Yumaism
Sangram Pedang Den	Almighty Goddess's world, Ancestor's village
Sawa Yethangs	The eight mythical ancestors of the Limboos
Sey-Sey Lungma	Kanchenjunga mountain in Limboo
Shangrila	Hidden Paradise on Earth in Bhutia
Singkhorlo	Wheel of life in Buddhism
Sodhung Lepmuhang	Demi-God, the mythical father of Sawa Yethangs of Limboos
Song-du-ruzhis	The four closer decendants of Khe-Bumsa
Susuwa Lilim Yakthumba	The brave fighter-forefathers of mythical eight brother Limboo descendants
Tagera Ningwaphuma	Almighty Goddess in Yumaism
Takpoo	Warlike demons in Buddhism
Tap Sammangs	Nature Divinities in Yumaism
Ters	Hidden Religious Texts in Buddhism

Tertons	Discoverers of Ters in Buddhism
Thankas	Religious scroll paintings in Buddhism
Thibong Yioks	Ten Regions of Limbuwan
Thokley Sammangs	Clan Divinities in Yumaism
Thums	Sub-divisions in Limbuwan
Tumyanghangs	Limboo Community leaders
Tungli-Mun	Lepcha shaman
Trung-yig	Secretary post in Namgyal Dynasty
Wadumbokwa	Rain-water collected on rocks and tree trunks, which is a Holy water in Yumaism
Yakthumba	The great Limboo fighters of Limbuwan regions
Yetchham Thim	Eight soul Limboo Tradition
Yiok	Regions of Limbuwan
Zhung-Lhu and Tey-Lhu	Bhutia folk songs

Selected References

Acharya, Baburam (1968). Sri Panch Bara Maharajdhiraj Prithivi Narayan Shah Ko Sanchipta Jiwan. Kathmandu, Nepal.

Agrawal, A. P. (2006-07). Sikkim - Bhutan. Pub. by Nest & Wings.

Agrawala, V.S. (1977). Bharata Savitri. Delhi: Indological Publication.

Akhil Bhujel Sangha (ABS). (2005). Ethnography of the Bhujel Tribe. A Self Study Report submitted to Ethnographic Committee.

Akhil Kirat Dewan (Yakha) Sangh (AKDS). (2005). A Self Study Report of Yakhas Submitted to Ethnographic Study Committee.

All Sikkim Gurung (Tamu) Buddhist Association (ASGBA). (2005). The Gurungs of Sikkim: A short Report on the Historical Backgrounds, Traditions, Culture and Religion. Gangtok: ASGBA.

All Sikkim Mangar Association (ASMA) (2005). Historical Background of Mangars of Sikkim. Self study report submitted to the ethnographic committee.

Allen, N.J. (1976). Studies in the Myths and Oral Traditions of the Thulung Rai of East Nepal. Ph.D.Thesis, Oxford Univ.

Allen, N.J. (1987). Thulung Weddings: The Hinduisation of a ritual cycle in East Nepal. L'Ethnographie, LXXXIII, 100-101: 15-33.

Alle, Rashmi Prasad (1963). Nepali Sahitya Sammelan, Darjeeling, Vol. 4 (16).

Alle, Santosh (2003). Magar Jatiko Itihas ani Sanskriti – Sikkim ko Sandarvama. Gangtok, Sikkim.

Angbohang, K.S. (1978). Gaunjee Thar. Hangpang, Taplejung: Nepal.

Ashley, Eden (1863-64). The Bootan: 55-113

Atkinson, E.T. (1883). Notes on the History of the Himalaya of the N.W.Province, India. Calcutta.

Atkinson, E. T. (1974). Religion in the Himalayas. New Delhi Cosmos Pub.

Atkinson, E.T. (1973). The Himalayan Gazetteer. Delhi: Cosmo.

Bandyopadhyay, S. and Singh, T.P. (1998). Climatology with reference to Sikkim. pp. 49-58. In. Sikkim: Perspective for Planning and Dev.

Banerjee, S. (1873). Journal of the Asiatic Society of Bengal.

Banerjee, S. K. & Das, A.K. (1962). The Lepchas of Darjeeling District. Special Series No. 2. Bul. of the Cultural Research Institute.

Barnouw, Victor (1955). Eastern Nepalese marriage customs and kinship organisation. Southeastern Journal of Anthropology 11: 15-30.

Basnet, L.B. (1973). Sikkim: A short History. New Delhi: S. Chand and Co.

Benny, M. and Antony, B. (2006). Blood Groups and Food Habits. Spice India, 19(10).

Bergner, P., and Hufford, D. (1998). Folk Remedies: Healing Wisdom. Lincolnwood, IL: Pub. International, Ltd.

Bhadra, Madhumita (1992). Sikkim – Democracy and Social Change. Minerva: India.

Bhasin, Veena (1989). Ecology, Culture and Change: Tribals of Sikkim Himalayas. New Delhi: Inter-India Publications.

Bhattacharya, P.C. (1964). A few elements of the Indo-Mongoloid Bodo Culture. J. of Assam Research Society, 16.

Bhutia Bhaichung (2007). Unpublished Manuscript on Cultural aspects of the Sikkimese Bhutia or Lhopo.

Bista, Dor Bahadur (1972/1980). The People of Nepal. Kathmandu: Ratna Pustak Bhandar.

Bouquet, A.C. (1932-35). Comparative Religion. Cambridge Univ. Press.

Brahmanada Purana (1913). Bombay: Venkateswara Press.

Buffetrille, Katia (2004). Pilgrimage and incest: The case of Chorten Nyima (Mchod rten nyima) on the Tibeto-Sikkimese border. Pub. by Namgyal Institute of Tibetology, Gangtok, Sikkim Vol. 40(1).

Chakravarty, K.R. (1988). Verdict in Sikkim – 1979-85: A Sikkim Express Study, May.

Chanda, R.P. (1916/1978). The Indo-Aryan Races. Delhi: Cosmo.

Charles, Mc Dougal (1979). The Kulunge Rai.

Chatterji, S.K. (1936). Non-Aryan Elements in Indo-Aryan. J. of the Greater India Society, 2(1).

Chatterji, S.K. (1965). Race Movements and Prehistoric Culture. In: R.C. Majumdar, ed. The Vedic Age. Bombay: Bharatiya Vidya Bhawan.

Chatterji, S.K. (1974). Kirata-Jana-Kriti: the Indo-Mongoloids, their contribution to the History and Culture of India. Calcutta: The Asiatic Society.

Chhattopadhya, S. (1973). Racial Affinities of Early North-Indian Tribes. Delhi: Munsiram Manoharlal.

Chand, Raghubir (2007). Forest dwellers of North-Eastern Himalayas: A case study of Monpas of Bhutan; Seminar on SARD-NE held on 5th to 7th March 2007 at Gangtok, Sikkim

Chaudhuri, S.B. (1955). Ethnic Settlements in Ancient India. Calcutta.

Chemjong, I.S.(1948). *Kirant Itihas*. Pub. by *Akhil Kirant Chumlung*, Darjeeling

Chemjong, I.S. (1967). History and Culture of the Kirat People. Kathmandu: Tumeng Hang.

Chene, Mary Des (1996). Ethnography in the Janajati-yug: Lessons from Reading Rodhi and ther Tamu Writings. Studies in Nepali History and Society, 1(1): 97-161.

Chichidarpo, Bhaichung (1998). Lhokey Bhasa Ko Sandarbhama. Pub. in Lipi Sangalo: Gangtok, Sikkim.

Chopra, P.N. (1979). Sikkim. New Delhi: S. Chand and Co. Ltd.

Choudhury, M. (1998). An outline of the Physical geography of Sikkim. pp. 17-23. In: Perspective for Planning and Dev.

CI (2005) *Global Hotspots Map*. Washington DC: Conservation International. http: www.biodiversityhotspots.org/xp/Hotspots Crooke, W. (1973). Races of North India. Delhi:n.p.

Dahal, D.D. (1984). Sikkim Ko Rajnaitik Itihas. Subba Prakashan. Gangtok.

Das, B.S. (1982). Sikkim Saga. New Delhi: Vikas

Das, A.K. and Banerjee, S.K. (1962). The Lepchas of Darjeeling District. Special Series No.2. a Bulletin of the cultural research institute.

Deepak, Subhas (2004). Sikkim Study Series: Vol. V. Language and Literature: Pub. by Inf. & Pub. Relation Department, Govt. of Sikkim.

Dhamala, R. R. (1991). A Socio-Economic Study of the Pemayongtse Monastery of Sikkim. In

Dharmananda, Subhuti (2006): Tibetan Herbal Medicine – with examples of treating Lung diseases using rhodiola and hippophae.

Dokhampa, R.N. (2003). Origin of the Bumchu (bum chu) of Drakar Tashiding (brag dkar bkra shis sdings). 39(1): Bulletin of Tibetology: Namgyal Institute of Tibetology, Gangtok Sikkim.

Downs, H.R. (1980). Rythms of a Himalayan Village. Sanfrancisco: Harper and Row Pub.

Draft application (2007). For The Globally-Important Ingenious Agricultural Heritage Systems (GIAHS) Programme.

Foning, A.R. (1987). Lepcha my Vanishing Tribe. Chyu-Pandi Farm: Kalimpong.

Gait, E. (1926/1964). A History of Assam. Calcutta.

Gaunley, Gopal (2002). History of Democratic Movement. Pub. Information & Public Relations Deptt. Govt. of Sikkim.

Gellner, David N. (1992/1996). Monk, Householder, and Tantric Priest. Newar Buddhism and its Hierarchy of Ritual. New Delhi. Cambridge Univ. Press.

Gerini, G.E. (1909/1974). Researches on Ptolemy's Geography of Eastern Asia. Delhi: Oriental Books.

Godabole, N. (1898). Taittiriya Brahman of the Krishna Yajurveda. Poona: Anandashram Sanskrit Series Pub.

Gorer, G. (1967). Himalayan Village, An account of the Lepchas of Sikkim. London: Thomas Nelson and Sons.

Grierson, G.A. (1016). Linguistic Survey of India. Pub. Motilal Banarasidas.

Griffith, R.T.H. (1899). The Texts of the White Yajurveda. Varanasi Chaukhamba.

Griffith, R.H.T. (1968). (The Hymns of the Atharvaveda. 2 vols. Varanasi Chaukhama Press.

Guha, B.S. (1944). Racial Elements in Indian Population. Oxford Pamphlets on Indian Affairs, 22.

Gupta, R. (1980). The Sherpa of Upper Khumbu and Their Migrant Counterpart in Kalimpong. In: I.P.Sing & S.C. Tiwari's (eds), Man and his Environment. New Delhi: Concept Pub. Co. pp. 93-110.

Gurung M.B. et.al. (2005). Gurung Tamu: The Tribal Ethnography. A Self study report submitted to the Ethnographic Committee.

Gurung, Meghraj (Tamu) (1998). Khema Lipiko Parichaya. Pub. in Lipi Sangalo. Gangtok, Sikkim.

Gurung, M.M. and Lama, R.P. (2004). Sikkim Study Series – Culture Vol. III. Pub. by Information and Public Relations Department, Govt. of Sikkim.

Hamilton, Fransis (1819/1971). An account of the Kingdom of Nepal. Edinburgh. Reprinted in 1971.

Hanpon, Gerd. (1991). The Rais of Eastern Nepal: Ethnic and Linguistic Grouping. Kathmandu: Linguistic survey of Nepal and Centre for Nepal and Asian Studies.

Hasrat, B.J. (1971). History of Nepal as told by its own and contemporary chroniclers. Hoshiyarpur: local stockist: V.V. Research Institute Book Agency.

Helman, C.G (1994). Culture, Health and Illness: An introduction for Health Professionals, Bristol, UK: Butterworth-Heinmann.

Henderson, C.E. (2002). Culture and Customs of India. Greenwood Press. London

Her Majesty's Stationery Office (HMSO) (1965). Nepal and the Gurkhas. London: HMSO.

Hermanns, Matthias (1954). The Indo-Tibetans: The Indo-Tibetan and Mongoloid problem in the Southern Himalayas and North Northeast India. Bombay.

Hiltz, Jackie (2003). Constructing Sikkimese national identity in the 1960s and 1970s. Bulletin of Tibetology: 39(2): Pub. Namgyal Institute of Tibetology, Gangtok Sikkim.

Hodgson, B.H. (1874). On the Aborigines of the Sub Himalayas. J.of the Asiatic Society of Bengal, 16.

Hodgson, B.H. (1849). On the Aborigins of the Eastern Frontier. J.of the Asiatic Society of Bengal, 28, Pt.II.

Hodgson, B.H. (1858). On the Kiranti tribe of the Central Himalaya. J. of the Asiatic Society, 27, 5(5).

Hooker, J.D. (1848). Himalayan Journals. London: Wardlock Bowden.

Hutt, Michael (1997). Being Nepali without Nepal: Reflections on South Asia Diaspora:

Hutt, Michael (ed) (1994). Bhutan: perspectives on Conflict and Dissent. Scotland: Kiscadele Asian Research Series No. 4.

Indian Newar Organization, Central Committee Darjeeling (2003). "*Janma dekhi Sijyasammako Samskar Paddhati*"

Jeffrey, S., Tuinstra, S. and Vaidya, J.P. (2000). The Lepcha of Nepal. Udaya Books, Kathmandu, Nepal.

Jerstad, L.G (1966). Mani – Rimbu. Un-published Ph.D. Thesis, Univ. of Oregan.

Jha, A. and Avasthe R. (1999). Nature folktales from Sikkim and Arunachal Pradesh. Pub. by WWF for Nature; India

Jha, P.K. (1985). History of Sikkim (1817-1904). OPS Pub. Pritate Ltd. Calcutta.

Jha, S.K. and Mishra, S.N. (1984). Sikkim Government & Politics. ESS Pub. New Delhi.

Jha, T. (1976). Brahma Purana. Pryag: Hindi Sahitya Sabha.

Kale, M.R. (ed.) with Trans. (1972). Raghuvansha of Kalidas. Delhi: Motilal Banarasidas.

Kazi, Jigme N. (1994). Against the Tide: Inside Sikkim. Gangtok: Hill Mrdia Pub.

Kandel, Ram Prasad (2004). Nepali Lokbaja (Folk Musical Instruments of Nepal). Pub: Nepali Lokbaja Songrahalaya, Kathmandu.

Keshi, Surendra (2002). Nepal Ko Jatiya Prashna: Awastha Ra Dristhikon. Pub. by Kathmandu Chumlung Smarika Sambat 2060-62: 21-24.

Khambu, C.M. (2005). Rai Ko Hun? Namchi, Sikkim.

Khamthak, Harka (2007). (Ed) Emeytnasung. Vol. 28; Pub. Darap-Yuksam, Sikkim.

Kharel, M.P. (2002). Socio-economic condition of Sikkim under colonial domination (1889-1947): An Authenticity Discourse. Thesis submitted to Uni. of NB.

Kohli, M.S. and Vergese, B.G. (1962). The Sherpas. In: M.S.Koli (ed.) Himalayan Endeavour. Bombay: A Time of India Pub.

Kotturen, G. (1983). The Himalayan Gateway: History and Culture of Sikkim. New Delhi: Sterling.

Kumar, R.R. (1989). Fire of Himal. An Anthropological Study of the Sherpas of Nepal Himalayan Region. New Delhi: Nirala Pub.

Lall, K. (1966). The Thami, in the Rising Nepal. Kathmandu.

Lama, M.P. (2001). Sikkim Human Development Report. Social Sc. Press. New Delhi.

Lama, S.T. (1971). Sherpa Book. Solukhumbu: Serlo Monastery.

Lamsal, D.P. (1966). Bhasa Vamsavali. Kathmandu Nepal.

Lassen, C.H.R. (1847-52). Indische Alterthumskunde, 4 Vols. Leipzig:n.p.

Levi, S. (1905-08). Le Nepal, 3 Vols. Paris:n.p.

Levy, Robert (1992). Mesocosm. Hinduism and the Organization of a Traditional Newar City of Nepal. Delhi: Motilal Banarsidass.

Macdonell, A.A. and Keith, A.B. (1912/1967). Vedic Index of Names and Subjects. Delhi: Motilal Banarasidas.

Majumdar, D.N. (1958). Races and Cultures of India. Delhi:n.p.

Majumdar, R.C. (1981). The Classical Accounts of India. Calcutta: Firma KLM.

Mainwaring, Col. GB. (1876). A Grammar of Rong (Lepcha) Language, Calcutta.

Martin, Gaenszle (1991). Origins & Migrations of Mewahang Rai.

Martin, M. (1831/1976). The History, Antiquities, Topography, and Statistics of Eastern India. Studies in Indian History, 4(14).

Martien, St. (1858). Etude Sur La Geographic Crecque et Latin de L'Inde. Paris: n.p.

Mathur, M.V. (1976). Extending Educational Opportunity in Sikkim. (Foreword). A report on the Staste's School System with Special Reference to its Adm. by Veda Prakash.

Matsya Purana (1958). Gorakhpur: Gita Press.

McCrindle, J.W. (1877). Ancient India as described by Megasthenes and Arrian. London: Turbner & Co.

McCrindle, J.W. (1879). The Commerce and Nevigation of the Erythraean Sea. London: Turbner & Co.

McCrindle, J.W. (1885). Ancient India as described by Ptolemy. London: Trubner & Co.

McCrindle, J.W. (1901/1984). Ancient India as described in Classical Literature. Delhi: Today & Tomorrow.

McDougal, Charles (1979). The Kulunge Rai: A Study in Kinship and Marriage Exchange. Kathmandu: Ratna Pustak Bhandar.

Mckay, Alex (2004) The indigenisation of Western Medicine in Sikkim. Bulletin of Tibetology: Vol. 40(2), Namgyal Institute of Tibetology, Gangtok, Sikkim.

Messerschmidt, D.A. (1976). The Gurungs of Nepal, New Delhi: Oxford & IBH Pub. Co.

Ministry of Environment & Forests, GOI: Carrying Capacity study of Teesta Basin in Sikkim;

Mishra, B.P. (1904). Nepal ka Itihas. Bombay: Venkateshwara Press.

Mishra, S.N. and Jha, S.K. (1984). Sikkim–Government & Politics. New Delhi.

Mitra, S.K. (1969). Present Day Health Organization in Sikkim. Indian Journal of Public Health: XIII(I).

Morris, C.J. (1938). Living with the Lepchas: A Book about the Sikkim Himalayans. London: William Heinemann.

Morris, Col. J. (1933/1985). The Gorkhas: An Ethnology. Delhi: B.R.Pub.

Mukhia, R.B. (1998). Aouta Ganthan. Pub. Lipi Sangalo, Gangtok, Sikkim.

Muktan, Harish (1999) (ed). Hyulba. Pub. by Akhil Bharatiya Tamang Budha Sangh. Gangtok, Sikkim.

Mullard, Saul (2005). A history from hidden land: Some preliminary remarks on a seventh century Sikkimese chronicle.

Munshi, S. and Lama, U. (1978). The Tamangs of Darjeeling. A Study of a Group Identity, in Journal of the Indian Anthropological Society. 13(2).

Nakane, C. (1966/1979). A Plural society in Sikkim: a Study of the interrelations of Lepchas, Bhutias and Nepalis, New Delhi.

Namgyal, Thotup and Dolma Yeshe (1908). History of Sikkim. Translated by Lama Dawa Kazi Samdup, MS. (unpublished).

Nath, R.M. (1948). The Background of Assamese Culture. Shillong:n.p.

NBSAP (2002) Sikkim State Biodiversity Strategy and Action Plan. Prepared under National Biodiversity strategy & Action Plan India 2002, Government of India.

Nepali, G.S. (1965). The Newars: an ethno-sociological study of a Himalayan Community. Bombay United Asia.

Northey, W.B. and Col.J.Morris (1974). The Gorkhas: Their Manners, Customs and Country. Delhi:Cosmo Pub.

Nourse, A. (1938). A Short History of the Chinese. London:n.p.

Nunes, Antonio B. (1996). Statistics On Religion, Internet.

Other Backword Class (OBC) Report of Commission 1998, Government of Sikkim.

Oertel, H. Trans. (n.d.). Jaiminiya Brahmana. Joun. of the American Oriental Society, 16. OIOC, V/10/1977. Administrative report of the Sikkim State for 1914-1915.

Oldfield, H.A. (1880). Sketches from Nepal. London.

O'Malley, L.S.S. (1907). Darjeeling District Gazetteer. Gyan Pub. House, New Delhi.

Oppitz, M. (1974). Myths and Facts: Reconsidering some data concerning the clan history of the Sherpa. Kailash. Kathmandu: Vol.II No.I and II.

Ortner, S.B. (1978a). The Sherpas through their rituals. Cambridge Univ. Press.

Padma Purana (1893-94). Poona: Sanskrit Series Pub.

Panda, A.K. (2004): Principle of Ayurvedic Medicine.

Pani, Jiwan (2000). Indian Folk Dances. Ministry of Information and Broadcasting, Government of India.

Pargiter, F.E. (1897). Ancient Countries in Eastern India. J. of the Asiatic Society of Bengal, 66, Pt.I

.Patiram, and Subba, J.R. (2002). Indigenous Farming Systems of Sikkim Hills and Perspective Planning. ICAR. Bulletin.

Paul, R.A. (1970). Sherpas and their Religion. Unpublished Ph.D. Thesis. Univ. of Chicago, Illinois.

Pemble, J. (1971). The Invasion of Nepal. Johan Company at War, Oxford

Phenomenal Twelve Years (1979-1992) Pub. by Inf. and Public Relations Department

Plaisier, Heleen (2005). A brief introduction to Lepcha orthography and literature. Bulletin of Tibetology: 41(1). Namgyal Institute of Tibetology, Gangtok Sikkim.

Planning Commission (2002) *India Economic Road Map: The Next Five Years 2002-2007*. The Essence. Planning Commission Government of India, New Delhi.

Population Census of Nepal 2001, Government of Nepal.

Population Census of India 2001, Government of India.

Pradhan, Bhaichandra (1997). Newar Jati.Mani Printing Press, Kalimpong.

Pradhan, Bhuvan Pd. (1883). Sikkimka Sva Laksmidas Pradhanko Yogdan, Gangtok, Sikkim.

Pradhan, Budhiman (1999). Kirantbangshi Sunuwar (Mukhia) Koinch. Gangtok, Sikkim.

Pradhan, Daya Pd. (1997). Pakimaka Taksari Chandravir Pradhan (Maske) ko Jivani. Pradhan, Khagendra (1998). Baburam Pradhanko Vamsa ra Jivan. Smarika Darjeeling Newar Samgathan, 55-57 pp.

Pradhan, Kumar (1991). The Gorkha Conquests: Calcutta: Oxford Univ. Press.

Pradhan, P.R and Josse, M.R. (1998). Sikkim still Backward after nearly 24 Years of Integration: Pawan Chamling, People's Review Dec. 24-31.

Pradhan, N. K. (1998). Ak Dui Kura – Aphnai Bhasa Barema. Pub. in Lipi Sangalo, Gangtok, Sikkim.

Pradhan S.K. (1985/1995). Limbuwan Ko Itihasik Adhyan. Nepal.

Prakash, Veda (1976). Existing Educational Opportunities in Sikkim. National Staff College for Education Planners and Adm. New Delhi.

Ramanujan, A.K. (1991). Folktales from India. Pub. Penguin Books.

Ranaldshay, Lord (1923/2005). Lands of the Thunderbolt Sikkim Chumbi and Bhutan. Pilgrims Publishing, Varanasi.

Rai, Krishna Das (1998). Dui Sabda. Pub. in Lipi Sangalo: Gangtok, Sikkim.

Rai, S.C., Sharma P. (2004) Carbon flux and land use/cover change in a Himalayan Watershed. *Current Science.* 86 (12) 1594-1596.

Rai, S.K. (2005). Kirat Khambu Rais of Sikkim and Eastern Himalayas. Shivika Enterprise, Deorali Gangtok.

Rao, P.R. (1972). Sikkim: The Story of its Integration with India. New Delhi: Cosmos.

Ray, S. and Ray, K. (1938). Kiratarjuniyam of Bhairavi. Canto XII. Calcutta: Punthi Pustak.

Redcliffe-Brown, A.R. (!952). Structure and function in Primitive Societies. The English Language Book Society and Cohen and West Ltd.

Regmi, M.C. (1999). Imperial Gorkha: an account of Gorkhali Rule in Kumaun (1791-1815). Delhi: Adroit Publication.

Regmi, D.R. (1960). Ancient Nepal. Calcutta:n.p.

Regmi, M.P. (1990). The Gurungs- Thunder of Himal. A cross Cultural Study of a Nepalese Ethnic Group. New Delhi: Nirala Pub.

Rhys Davis, T.W. (1894). The Questions of King Milinda. Vol.36, Pt.II. Oxford Univ. Press.

Risley, B.Trans. (1962). Naturalis Historia of Pliny. London: Loeb Classical Library Edition.

Risley, H.H. (1891/1981) reprinted. Tribes and Castes of Bengal: Ethnographic Glossary, Vol 2. Calcutta.

Risley. H.H. (1891). Tribes and Castes of Bengal. London

Risley, H.H. (1894). Gazetteer of Sikkim. New Delhi. B.R. Pub.

Ronnow, K. (1936). Kirata: A Study on some Ancient Indian Tribe. Le Monde Oriental, 30.

Rosser, Social mobility in the Newar caste system, p 74.

Russell, Andrew (1992). The Yakha: Culture, Environment and Development in East Nepal. Ph. D. thesis, Oxford Univ.

Rustomji, Nari (1987). Sikkim, A Himalayan Tragedy. Delhi: Allied Pub.

Sabatier, Sophie Bourdet (2004). The Dzumsa of Lachen: an example od a Sikkimese political institution. Vol. 40 (1): 93-104.

Sankritayan, Rahul (1958). Purattva Nibandhavali. Allahabad: n.p.

Sankritayan, Rahul (1973). Pali Sahitya ka Itihas. Lucknow: Hindi Samiti.

Sarkari Gharelu Udhyog Sangthan (1987). Bulletin published by the Government of Sikkim.

Satavalekar, D. and Sharma, S. (ed.) (1969, 1972, 1973, 1975, 1982). Mahabharata. Paradi: Sanskrit Pub.

Schoff, W.H. (1912). The Periplus of the Erythraean Sea. London: Longmans, Green & Co.

Sen, S.N. (Ed.) & Trans. (1940). Kiratarjuniyam of Bhairavi. Canto XIV. Calcutta: Punthi Pustak.

Shafet, R. (1954). Enthography of Ancient India. Wiesbaden: n.p.

Sharma, E., Sharma, R., Singh, K.K., Sharma, G. (2000) A Boon for Mountain Populations. Large Cardamom Farming in the Sikkim Himalaya. *Mountain Research and Development* 20(2): 108-111.

Sharma, G., Liang, L. (2006) The Role of Traditional Ecological Knowledge Systems in Conservation of Agrobiodiversity: A Case Study in the Eastern Himalayas. Proceedings of International Policy Consultation for Learning from Grassroots Initiatives and Institutional Interventions, 27-29 May 2006. Indian Institute of Management, Ahmedabad, India.

Sharma, Ghanashyam, Liang, L., Koji Tanaka (2006) On-farm Agrobiodiversity Management in Mountain Márginal Farms in the Sikkim Himalaya. Proceedings of the International Workshop on Shifting Agriculture, Environment Conservation and Sustainable Livelihood of Marginal Mountain Societies, Guwahati, 23-25 September 2006.

Sharma, G., Sharma, E., Sharma, R. Singh, K. K. (2002) Performance of an age series of *Alnus*- cardamom plantations in the Sikkim Himalaya. Biomass, Productivity and Energetics. *Annals of Botany* 89: 261-272.

Sharma, G., Sharma, R., Sharma, E., Singh, K. K. (2002) Performance of an age series of *Alnus*-cardamom plantations in the Sikkim Himalaya. Nutrient Dynamics. *Annals of Botany* 89, 273-282.

Sharma, J.L (1982). Hamro Samaj: Ek Adhyayan, Kathmandu: Sajha Prakashan.

Sharma, R. C. (2002). Studies on ethnobotany of Hee Berniok (West Sikkim) with special reference to Limboo Community. M Sc. Thesis

Sharma, R., Sharma, E., Purohit, A. N. (1997) Cardamom, mandarin and nitrogen-fixing trees in agroforestry systems in India's Himalayan region. II. Soil nutrient dynamics. *Agroforestry Systems* 35, 235-253.

Sharma, S.K. and Sharma, U. (eds.) (1997). Encyclopaedia of Sikkim and Bhutan. New Delhi: Anmol (3 Volumes).

Shastri, A.C., Shastri, P. and Dikshit, R.N. (1984). Shatapatha Brahmana. Varanasi: Chaukhamba.

Shastri, D.N. (1983). Markandeya Purana. Meerut: Sanskrit Series Pub.

Shastri, H. Ed. & Trans. (1957). Amarakosha of Amarsingh. Varanasi: Chaukhamba Pub.

Shastri, R.P. Tripathi, Ed. with Hindi Trans (1987). Vayu Purana. Prayag: Hindi Sahitya Sabha.

Sherpa, Dawa Gyatso (1998). Sambhoti Lipi ani Serpa Jati. Pub. Lipi Sangalo: Gangtok, Sikkim.

Sherpa, M.N. (1982). Sherpa Culture Sagarmatha National Park.

Shrestha, B.G. (2002). The ritual composition of Sankhu. The socio-religious Anthropology of a Newar Town in Nepal. Ph.D. thesis, Univ. of Leiden.

Shrestha, B.G. (2005). Ritual and identity in the diaspora: the Newars in Sikkim. Bulletin of Tibetology: 41(1): Namgyal Institute of Tibetology, Gangtok, Sikkim.

Sikkim Handicrafts, Browser (1987). Leaflet Published by the Government of Sikkim.

Sikkim Livestock Census 1977, 1988, 1997, 2003.

Sikkim Sunuwar (Mukhia) Koinchbu (2003). A self Study Report Submitted to Ethnographic Committee.

Sikkim Coronation 1965, Sikkim Livestock Resources Estimates (2004).

Singh, G.P. (1980). Kiratas in Ancient India. New Delhi: Gian Pub. House.

Sieger, Halfdan (1967). The Lepcha Culture and Religion of the Himalayan people. Part – I: Copenhagan pp: 29.

Singh K.S. (1993). People of India – Sikkim. Anthropological Survey of India. Cal.

Singh, N.M. (1991). Nepal in Transition. Kathmandu: S. Printers.

Sinha, A.C. (1981). Resource Distribution and Multiple ethnic identity in Sikkim. New Delhi. In: C. von Furer Haimendorf (ed.) Asian Highland Societies in Anthropological Perspective pp. 183-202.

Sinha, A.C. (1975) Politics of Sikkim: A sociological study. Faridabad: Thomson Press.

Sinha, et al (2005). Ethnographic Report on Selected Communities of Sikkim. Submitted to the Govt. Of Sikkim.

Sprigg, R.K. (2005). Shedding some light on the History, Language and Literature of the Lepchas. Mani Printing Press, Kalimpong.

Stiller, Ludwig F. (1968). Reprint (1995). The Rise of the House of Gorkha. Kathmandu.

Stein, O. (1948). The Jinist Studies. Ahmedabad: Jain Sahitya Sanshodhak Pratisthan.

Sukkla, S.R. (1976). Sikkimn, the Story of Integration. New Delhi: S. Chand and Co.

Subba, C. (1995). The Culture and Religion of Limbu. Kathmandu, Nepal.

Subba, Tanka B. & Karubaki Datta (1991). Religion and Societies in the Himalayans. New Delhi: Gain Pub. House.

Subba, J.R. (1984). Agriculture in the Hills of Sikkim, Gangtok, Sikkim.

Subba, J.R. (1997). Vegetable Crops of the Himalayan Region. Gangtok, Sikkim.

Subba, J.R. (1999). The Limboos of the Eastern Himalayas with special reference to Sikkim. Pub. by SYMS, Gangtok, Sikkim.: 283-583 pp.

Subba, J.R. (2002). Biodiversity of the Sikkim Himalayas. SYMS, Gangtok, Sikkim.

Subba, J.R. (2002). History and Development of Limboo Language. SYMS, Gangtok.

Subba, J.R. (2004). Mahatma Sirijunga Singthebe – The Great Social Awakener. SYMS, Sikkim.

Subba, J.R. (2005). The Philosophy and Concepts of Yuma Samyo Tradition. SYMS, Gangtok, Sikkim.

Subba, J.R. (2005). Life After Life and Funerary Practices in Yuma Samyo Tradition. SYMS, Gangtok, Sikkim.

Subba, J. R. (2006). SARD-M: Horticulture is an Economically viable and environmentally sustainable Driver of Socio-Economic Development in Mountainous Sikkim,FAO/ICIMOD Project.

Subba, T.B. (1998). Dynamics of a hill society. The Nepalis in Darjeeling and Sikkim Himalayas. Delhi: Mittal Pub.

Subba, T.B. (1999). Politics of Culture: A study of three communities in the Eastern Himalaya. Hyderabad: Orient Longmand Ltd.

Subba, T, B, and Datta, K. (eds.) (1999) Religion and Society in the Himalayas. New Delhi: Gyan Pub. House, 58-76.

Sueyoshi, Toba (1992). Rites of Passage – An aspect of Rai culture.

Tamang, J.P. (2005). Sikkim Study Series: Vol. IV. Food Culture of Sikkim: Pub. by Inf. & Pub. Relations Department, Govt. of Sikkim.

Tamang, J.P. and Nikkuni, S. (1996). Selection of starter culture for production of kinema, a fermented soybean food of the Himalaya. World Journal of Microbiology and Biotechnology 12: 629-635.

Tamang, K.M. (1998). Tamoyeg Tamang Lipi, Bhasa ra Sanskriti. Pub. Lipi Sangalo: Gangtok, Sikkim.

Tamsang, K.P. (1983). The Unknown and Untold Reality about The Lepchas. Kalimpong, Mani Press.

Tamang, Rudrasingh (2004). Tamang Rite and Culture. Katyhmandu, Nepal.

Temple, J.G (1977). Travels in Nepal and Sikkim. Kathmandu: Ratna Pustak Bhandar.

Thami, T.B. (1999). Thami Samudaya Ko Aitiasik Chinari ra Sanskar Sanskriti. Nepal Thami Samaj.

Thapa, N.B. (1981). A Short History of Nepoal, Kathmandu: n.p.

Thapa, Y.B. (1998). Kehi Sabdaharu. Pub. in Lipi Sangalo: Gangtok Sikkim.

Timsina, S.R. (1992). Napali Community in India. Delhi: Manak Pub.

Toba, Sueyoshi (1992). Rites of Passage: An Aspect of Rai Culture. Kathmandu: Royal Nepal Academy.

Toffin, G (1984). Societe et Religion chez les Newar du Nepal. Paris:

Toffin, G (1993). Le Palais et le Temple. Paris: CNRS.

Trenckner, V. (1880). Milinda Panha. London: Pali Text Society.

Tucci, G. (1962). Nepal, The Discovery of the Malla. London: George Allen and Unwin Ltd.

Tucci, G. (1979). An Account of the Kingdom of Nepal. Asiatic Researches, 2.

Tucker, F. I. S. (1975). Gorkha: the story of the Gorkhas of Nepal. London: Constable.

Twenty-Five Years of Statehood (2000). Pub. by Dept. of Information and Public Relations, Govt. of Sikkim.

Uprety, T.N. (1962). Financing Elementary Education in Nepal. Ph.D. Dissertation, Univ. of Oregon.

Vagisha, A.V. (1869). Pancavimsa Brahmana. Calcutta: Punthi Pustak.

Vamana, Purana (1968). Varanasi: Chaukhamba Press.

Van Driem, George (1987). A Grammar of Limbu. Ph.D. thesis, Univ. of Leiden.

Vansittart, Eden (1896). Notes on Nepal, Calcutta.

Vansittart, Eden (1915). Gurkhas. Calcutta: Supdt. of Govt. Printing.

Vishnu Purana (1984). Gorakhpur: Geeta Press.

Waddell, L.A.(1979). Rept. Among the Himalayas. New Delhi: Mittal.

Weber, A. (1852). Vajasaneyi Samhita ofthe Shukla Yajurveda. London: Cambridge Univ. Press.

Whelpton, John (2005). A History of Nepal. Cambridge Univ. Press.

White, J. Claude (1992). Sikkim and Bhutan. Pub. A. Sagar Book House, Del. India.

Wilson, H.H. Trans. (1961). Vishnu Purana. Calcutta: The Asiatic Society.

Yakthung, Rishi Kumar (1992). Yakthung Chokthim. Kiranti Prakashan, Kalimpong (W.B.).

Yakthung Kirat Chumlung (2002). Limboo Khana ra Peya Padartha Haru. Kathmandu.

Index

N

U & V